Justice

The International Library of Essays in Law and Legal Theory
Second Series
Series Editor: Tom D. Campbell

Titles in the Series:

Justice

Edited by

Wojciech Sadurski

European University Institute, Florence

Ashgate

DARTMOUTH

Aldershot • Burlington USA • Singapore • Sydney

Published by
Dartmouth Publishing Company
Ashgate Publishing Limited
Gower House
Croft Road
Aldershot
Hants GU11 3HR
England

Ashgate Publishing Company
131 Main Street
Burlington, VT 05401-5600 USA

Ashgate website: http://www.ashgate.com

British Library Cataloguing in Publication Data
Justice. – (International library of essays in law and
 legal theory. Second series)
 1. Justice
 I. Sadurski, Wojciech, 1950–
 340.1'1

Library of Congress Cataloging-in-Publication Data
Justice / edited by Wojciech Sadurski.
  p. cm. — (International library of essays in law and legal theory. Second series)
 Includes bibliographical references.
 ISBN 0-7546-2088-3
  1. Justice. 2. Social justice. I. Sadurski, Wojciech, 1950– II. Series.

 K246 .J793 2001
 303.3'72—dc21   00-036221

ISBN 0 7546 2088 3

Contents

PART IV   FEMINIST CRITIQUES OF LIBERAL JUSTICE

Acknowledgements

The editor and publishers wish to thank the following for permission to use copyright material.

Blackwell Publishers for the essays: Phillip Montague (1980), 'Comparative and Non-comparative Justice', *Philosophical Quarterly*, **30**, pp. 131–40; Julian Lamont (1995), 'Problems for Effort-Based Distribution Principles', *Journal of Applied Philosophy*, **12**, pp. 215–29. Copyright © 1995 Society for Applied Philosophy; Deborah Kearns (1983), 'A Theory of Justice – and Love; Rawls on the Family', *Politics*, **18**, pp. 36–42.

Cambridge University Press for the essays: T.D. Campbell (1974), 'Humanity before Justice', *British Journal of Political Science*, **4**, pp. 1–16; Loren E. Lomasky (1995), 'Justice to Charity', *Social Philosophy and Policy*, **12**, pp. 32–53. Copyright © 1995 Social Philosophy and Policy Foundation.

Harvard Law Review Association for the essay: Michael J. Sandel (1994), 'Political Liberalism', *Harvard Law Review*, **107**, pp. 1765–94. Copyright © 1994 Harvard Law Review Association.

The Philosophical Review for the essay: Joel Feinberg (1974), 'Noncomparative Justice', *Philosophical Review*, **83**, pp. 297–338. Copyright © 1974 Cornell University. Reprinted by permission of the publisher.

New York University Law Review for the essay: John Rawls (1989), 'The Domain of the Political and Overlapping Consensus', *New York University Law Review*, **64**, pp. 233–55.

Princeton University Press for the essays: Michael A. Slote (1973), 'Desert, Consent, and Justice', *Philosophy & Public Affairs*, **2**, pp. 323–47. Copyright © 1973 Princeton University Press; Christopher Ake (1975), 'Justice as Equality', *Philosophy & Public Affairs*, **5**, pp. 69–89. Copyright © 1975 Princeton University Press.

Sage Publications, Inc. for the essay: Robert E. Goodin (1985), 'Negating Positive Desert Claims', *Political Theory*, **13**, pp. 575–98. Copyright © 1985 Sage Publications, Inc. Reprinted by permission of Sage Publications, Inc.

University of Calgary Press for the essays: Francis Snare (1986), 'Misfortune and Injustice: On Being Disadvantaged', *Canadian Journal of Philosophy*, **16**, pp. 39–61; Alan H. Goldman (1987), 'Real People (Natural Differences and the Scope of Justice)', *Canadian Journal of Philosophy*, **17**, pp. 377–93.

Preface to the Second Series

The first series of the International Library of Essays in Law and Legal Theory has established itself as a major research resource with fifty-eight volumes of the most significant theoretical essays in contemporary legal studies. Each volume contains essays of central theoretical importance in its subject area and the series as a whole makes available an extensive range of valuable material of considerable interest to those involved in research, teaching and the study of law.

The rapid growth of theoretically interesting scholarly work in law has created a demand for a second series which includes more recent publications of note and earlier essays to which renewed attention is being given. It also affords the opportunity to extend the areas of law covered in the first series.

The new series follows the successful pattern of reproducing entire essays with the original page numbers as an aid to comprehensive research and accurate referencing. Editors have selected not only the most influential essays but also those which they consider to be of greatest continuing importance. The objective of the second series is to enlarge the scope of the library, include significant recent work and reflect a variety of editorial perspectives.

Each volume is edited by an expert in the specific area who makes the selection on the basis of the quality, influence and significance of the essays, taking care to include essays which are not readily available. Each volume contains a substantial introduction explaining the context and significance of the essays selected.

I am most grateful for the care which volume editors have taken in carrying out the complex task of selecting and presenting essays which meet the exacting criteria set for the series.

TOM CAMPBELL
Series Editor
The Faculty of Law
The Australian National University

Introduction

The Concept of Justice

By the end of his essay, 'What Is Justice?', Hans Kelsen confesses his inability to give a satisfactory answer to the question posed in the title:

> I cannot say what justice is, the absolute justice for which mankind is longing. . . . I can only say what justice is to me. Since science is my profession, and hence the most important thing in my life, justice, to me, is that social order under whose protection the search for truth can prosper. 'My' justice, then, is the justice of freedom, the justice of peace, the justice of democracy – the justice of tolerance. (Kelsen, 1971, p. 24)

As this passage indicates, justice occupies a very special and cherished place in the pantheon of liberal social, legal and political values. Justice is also, at least in some of its uses, a nebulous concept which requires a degree of fine-tuning if it is to play a distinct role in political and legal argument and if it is to be saved from collapsing into an undifferentiated, positive praise of that which is considered 'just'. Yet even the most cursory reflection on our linguistic intuitions suggests that not all that is good is so by virtue of being just. And not all just rules, characteristics of persons or states of affairs are optimal, all things considered. Thus John Rawls, the most influential contemporary philosopher of justice, emphasizes 'the limits of a theory of justice' and reminds us that, in such a theory, 'many aspects of morality [are] left aside' (Rawls, 1971, p. 512).

It is therefore important to precede more substantive reflections about the normative standards of justice with a preliminary consideration of what 'justice' is about. It has become customary in contemporary literature (and not only in literature about *justice*), to characterize these two levels of discourse as referring, respectively, to 'conceptions' and 'concepts' where a normative 'conception' is discussed within a definitional framework provided by the 'concept' of justice. As Ronald Dworkin helpfully put it many years ago, the distinction between a 'concept' and 'conception' corresponds to the distinction between posing a moral issue and trying to answer it (Dworkin, 1978, p. 135). It is the distinction between what justice *is about* and what it *requires* – between the conceptual borders of the term and the substantive content of one's ideas about what a just person, society and law would look like.

While this distinction is helpful in promoting clarity in discussions about justice, one should be aware that such clarity comes at a price. Such a distinction may encourage an illusion that the concept of justice is value-neutral, as opposed to conceptions of justice which are undoubtedly value-laden. In fact, statements about *concepts* of justice are morally meaningful, and hence controversial, though in a different way to the inevitably ideological and normative discourse about *conceptions* of justice. To identify a particular domain of moral discourse as belonging to the sphere of justice is, at the very least, tantamount to attributing to it a high moral value: judgements about justice (whatever they are) are not trivial. Most contemporary writers about justice suggest that 'justice' is principally about the way in which benefits and burdens are distributed in a society, and such a *concept* of justice presupposes that the distribution of benefits and burdens is near, or at the top of, moral concerns. But this is not a morally neutral statement, nor is it uncontroversial. Indeed, Marx's theory can be interpreted as being not based on disapproval for the *injustices* of capitalism, or on a positive proposal for a *just* society, precisely because the matters of distribution were, for Marx, of a secondary and derivative character (Brenkert, 1979; Buchanan, 1982, pp. 50–85; Wood, 1972). Under this interpretation – which is just *one* interpretation, and one not shared by all commentators on Marx (for example, Cohen, 1981; Husami, 1978; Ryan, 1980) – Marx's critique and positive visions are imbued with a strong moral content, but this content should not be characterized in terms of 'justice'.

This immediately suggests that an attempt to coin a concept of justice that is not coextensive with a conclusive positive judgement about a rule or state of affairs produces the problem of how to rank justice vis-à-vis other legal and political values. If justice is an important, but specific, value which encompasses only part of the field of social morality, it becomes inevitable that justice will sometimes be balanced against, and perhaps subordinated to, other values. This theme permeates the texts by Tom Campbell and Loren Lomasky in Part I of this collection, and their essays contain good examples of arguments by philosophers who take seriously the idea that the concept of justice must have relatively clear and distinctive limits. They demonstrate that we must carefully consider situations in which an insistence on 'doing justice', no matter what, is morally unappealing and/or fails to capture the nature of the moral and political claims at stake.

Campbell's essay (Chapter 1) does not explicitly refer to the concept/conception distinction, but he suggests right at the start that 'justice in the narrow and specific sense' is primarily concerned with distribution according to desert (or merit), thereby implying that different conceptions of justice are yielded by different understandings of the grounds for desert (or merit). There is no doubt that the idea of desert is central to many – and perhaps most, though certainly not all – theories of justice; this is a topic to which we will return below, and which is covered by a range of essays reproduced in Part II. What is particularly interesting about Campbell's essay is that, consistent with his assumption about a 'narrow and specific' concept of justice, he 'downgrades' the role of justice in many significant social contexts, and does so quite dramatically: 'Justice as one amongst other moral values may quite properly be required to give way to other considerations' (p. 6). And so it does, in Campbell's discussion. His chief concern in this essay is to delineate the distinction between the requirements of justice and those of humanity, or 'the obligation to work for the relief of suffering'.

Some might not agree with Campbell's confinement of justice considerations to those related to desert or merit. And some will probably argue that his notion of the relationship between needs and merit is in fact more far-reaching than he suggests: that the degree of needs-satisfaction required to create conditions of genuine equal opportunity, which is central to his 'meritorian' vision, would probably absorb more need-satisfaction interventions into the realm of justice than his call for a 'narrow and specific' concept of justice would allow. But these are contingent and controversial points. What is important about his essay is that it is a good illustration of a conscious attempt to articulate the concept of justice as relatively narrow and not necessarily paramount.

It will become immediately apparent to readers that Campbell and Loren Lomasky (whose essay is reproduced as Chapter 2) come from widely distant ideological perspectives. Campbell is a social democrat committed to welfare rights while Lomasky is a free-market libertarian.

But the latter, like the former, insists on the importance of keeping considerations of justice distinct and separate from other moral demands. In his complaint about the dominance of a 'jurisprudential paradigm' of morality (which he understands as a tendency to identify all morality with the language of rights and duties), he seems to be indirectly confirming Campbell's suggestion that perhaps 'justice is an inherently legalistic concept which cannot function usefully outside a legal or quasi-legal context' (Campbell, 1988, p. 5).[1] Like Campbell, Lomasky believes that we should alleviate other people's misfortune and distress, but he is not prepared to characterize our 'ought' as a matter of duty with a correlative right belonging to the person who is distressed. Indeed, the main thrust of Lomasky's essay is to oppose what he calls the 'social-justice conception' and to carve out a sphere of morality which is controlled by virtues rather than by justice. Naturally, the reason for such a claim is not terminological or conceptual, and one important factor of Lomasky's text is that he makes his reasons for such a proposal explicit; his fundamental concern is about 'the preservation of a realm of discretion in which individuals are able to pursue various ideals of moral excellence' (p. 39). Whether such a 'realm' is undermined by a 'social-justice conception' is a matter for substantive debate and some will certainly disagree with Lomasky. But what is important here is that his text illustrates both the distinctiveness of the notion of justice and the fact that such a concept must be defended on non-neutral moral reasons.

It is pertinent at this point to ask what it is that is specific about justice, which allows us to distinguish it from other important values, and which therefore informs the contours of the concept of justice. Common responses suggest that all rules of justice employ a form of the principle of equal treatment of equal cases, *or* that they are rules about the distribution of goods (or 'bads', as in the case of punishment), *or* that they are comparative in nature. Let us put to one side the first of these answers: as many writers have suggested, it is too thin a basis for identifying the concept of justice because it corresponds to a principle of conduct according to general rules and may therefore apply to the types of conduct which we do not normally associate with judgements about justice. However, the two latter answers seem to be more fruitful. Judgements about justice are often found to be fundamentally comparative, in that their application necessarily seems to involve a comparison of the treatment meted out on one person with the treatment of some other person(s) (Frankena, 1962, p. 9); and also distributive, in that they regulate the distribution of benefits and burdens. As Rawls famously stated: 'the primary subject of justice is . . . the way in which the major social institutions distribute fundamental rights and duties and determine the division of advantages from social cooperation' (Rawls, 1971, p. 7).

It is important not to conflate the theses that justice is necessarily comparative and that it is necessarily distributive. Some writers suggest that it can be the latter without being the former. Brian Barry, for example, claimed that justice belongs to a category of distributive political principles (as contrasted to aggregative ones), but that it can be either comparative or absolute (Barry, 1965, pp. 43–44). In contrast, Joel Feinberg believes that some principles of justice may be non-distributive and non-comparative. His discussion of cases of 'non-comparative justice' is included in Part I of this book, as is a thoughtful critical analysis of this discussion by Phillip Montague.

In Chapter 3 Feinberg claims that practices such as unfair punishments and rewards, 'merit grading' and derogatory judgements are examples of non-comparative injustice because, to ascertain the injustice of a practice, we do not need to compare the treatment given to one person with the treatment of other persons. It is an important, though not uncontroversial, point. Is 'merit grading' indeed as non-comparative as Feinberg suggests it is? Or does the standard against which a person is measured incorporate comparative considerations? If the latter is the case, can we still claim that it is possible to judge a person 'on her merits' regardless of how others are judged in this context? Consider, for example, the practice of grading student exams or essays. If an essay is given a particular grade, doesn't it already presuppose a particular ranking? And isn't it done against a background supposition about a predictable, typical range of quality of essays and exams? Further, not everybody will agree that some of Feinberg's examples of 'non-comparative' even belong to the realm of justice. When he suggests that broken promises are typically unfair because they are forms of 'one party taking advantage of another' (though it is important to stress that Feinberg notes that not *all* broken promises constitute instances of injustice), one wonders whether he perhaps overextends the concept of justice beyond its intuitively plausible borders. As Kurt Baier suggests in an essay reproduced in Part III of this volume:

> If I have undertaken to get you to the church on time, then that is what is due to you from me and if I get you there on time, I have given you that due. But I have not exhibited the virtue of justice, I have not been just to you or done you justice. . . . I would not have been unjust to you if I had not got you there on time either, though I would have failed in my duty, and so on. This is simply not a case in which either justice or injustice is applicable, as we commonly conceive of it. (p. 325)

Justice – Desert – Redistribution

I have referred earlier to Campbell's endorsement of a conception of justice based essentially on the notion of 'merit' or 'desert', and it is now time to consider this view more closely. Indeed, the idea that justice is fundamentally and primarily a matter of giving to each what they 'deserve' is perhaps the most traditional, strongly established view in our thinking about justice. But how much mileage can we get from the notion of 'desert' in developing a substantive 'conception' (as opposed to a 'concept') of justice? Very little, if 'desert' is considered to be a mere equivalent of an entitlement. If by 'she deserves this reward' all we mean is that she should be given a reward according to the accepted rules of distribution (whatever they are), then the relationship between justice and desert is merely tautological. We may well accept a terminological convention, whereby a desert is a proxy for an all-things-considered entitlement to a distributive share but such a notion of 'desert' merely marks the beginning of a moral argument about the real grounds for a just distribution. It does not provide a conclusion to such an argument.

The notion of desert can, however, be used in a thicker sense, in which it provides not merely a proxy for other moral arguments about just distribution but also a moral ground for such a distribution. To perform this role, 'desert' must be seen as having a more specific meaning than 'entitlement': it must be regarded as the basis for an entitlement. Elsewhere, I have suggested that such a substantive notion of desert must, at a minimum, have these three characteristics (Sadurski, 1985, pp. 116–22). First, desert considerations are related strictly to a person whose desert we consider. This is not trivial: the criteria of desert must identify and discard those putative grounds of distribution which are based on facts or characteristics over which a person has no control. It makes no moral sense to say that X deserves Y on the basis of Z, if there is nothing that *X* can do about (having or not having) *Z*. Second, desert considerations are intrinsically value-laden in the sense that a postulated basis for desert must be an object of moral admiration by the person who makes a judgement about desert. This, among other things, distinguishes judgements about desert from those based on needs (the basis of a legitimate need is, *per se*, not something that we evaluate highly) and from those based on entitlements ('entitlement' here being understood in a quasi-institutional sense, as the grounds for a distribution according to announced rules). This, incidentally, is a different approach to Robert Goodin's attempt to debunk desert-based discourse in his essay reproduced in Part II. Goodin adopts a notion of 'desert' which is indistinguishable from any entitlement based on a valid rule. Third, desert considerations are past-oriented: the basis of desert is related to something that has already happened – to past actions or characteristics. This serves to distinguish desert judgements from those based on the expected consequences of a proposed reward.

The essays by Michael Slote and Christopher Ake, reproduced in Part II of this volume (Chapters 5 and 6), are good illustrations of the use of a thick notion of desert employed in the service of a broader, egalitarian theory of justice (see also Milne, 1986; Sadurski, 1985, ch. 5). It is interesting that, for all the differences between their approaches (as indicated by Ake in his essay), they converge on a number of important points. First, they both agree that a conception of justice is but a part of a broader ideal of a good society. Second, they both believe that the notion of desert is crucial to a conception of justice (although Ake introduces the notion of desert indirectly, through the role it will inevitably play in his idea of justice as the balance of social benefits and burdens). Third, they both emphasize that the most relevant aspect of 'desert' is a socially beneficial effort undertaken by an individual, and they largely dismiss contribution-based conceptions of desert. Understood as the objective worth of the success of one's actions, 'contribution' is at best an imperfect measure of the effort actually undertaken. Fourth, both Slote and Ake factor into their notion of desert the laudable intentions of the person whose effort we choose to reward.

To recite these features of desert-based conceptions is also to immediately indicate some of the problems raised by these theories. If desert is based purely on those characteristics for which a person can claim moral credit (and this seems to be the main reason why both Slote and Ake discard 'contribution'-based desert), can we meaningfully distinguish between those elements of effort-*cum*-intentions which *are* subject to a person's conscious decisions (or, in Ake's framework, which correspond to the burdens on a person's life) and those which are fortuitous? After all, one's predisposition to undertake socially beneficial burdens may be due to factors for which a person cannot, or can only partly, take credit, such as upbringing, familial stimulation and genetic endowments. As John Rawls noted:

> The assertion that a man deserves the superior character that enables him to make the effort to cultivate his abilities is . . . problematic; for his character depends in large part upon fortunate family and social circumstances for which he can claim no credit. (Rawls, 1971, p. 104)

As a matter of fact, some would deny that the desert-for-effort theory is egalitarian at all: different people exert widely varying amounts of socially beneficial effort in society, and it may be that these differences 'depend heavily on the social–genetic lottery, in which different people receive different amounts of effort-inclining characteristics' (Zaitchik, 1977, p. 384). Should a desert-for-effort theory therefore be supplemented by the further proviso that those effortful actions which are largely determined by 'social-genetic' conditions be disqualified from affecting a just distribution?

Further, even if, in principle, we can draw a line between those putative grounds for desert which *do* correspond to effort and those which attach to an actual contribution, can we draw such a distinction in real life? Slote anticipates such an objection and suggests that the impracticality of a moral ideal is not a good argument against the moral attractiveness of the ideal, and all that the impracticality objection to his notion of desert shows is that 'it is difficult to decide what is just and to recompense people accordingly' (p. 109). This answer might be fair enough from the perspective of a philosopher but, for those who believe that the demands of moral or political philosophy should be capable of implementation, it might count as a fatal argument against that notion of desert. They are more likely to be convinced by the arguments in Julian Lamont's essay (Chapter 7), which insist that there are no clear and sharp distinctions between effort-based and productivity-based principles of just distribution, if the proponents of the former principles are committed (as they must be) to increasing the social product. Lamont also lucidly lists some of the main problems with implementing policies based on individual effort and concludes that productivity (or actual 'contribution') may be a better measure of a just distribution after all. If accepted, this conclusion naturally reduces much of the moral weight of rationales for desert-based theories of justice.

The arguments of desert theorists, as exemplified by the essays by Ake and Slote, attach great importance to the relationship between the grounds of just reward and something that can be traced to a conscious, deliberate and valuable fact about an individual, in particular, to her effortful actions. This presupposes that we can draw a line between those characteristics which are 'arbitrary from a moral point of view' and those for which we can properly claim moral credit. Socially caused inequalities (that is, those which are attributable to difference in wealth inheritance, upbringing and various other socially fortuitous circumstances) are often, and rightly, represented as belonging to a category of morally arbitrary factors. However, it is clear that many 'natural' differences which *also* affect our place in the social distribution of resources are 'undeserved' insofar as they are affected by our inherited superior natural abilities, skills or talents. If the role of justice is to be a means of redress for those characteristics that are arbitrary from a moral point of view,[2] then there seem to be no good moral reasons to treat natural and social 'fortuitous' factors differently.

This is the position of Francis Snare (Chapter 9) who considers the relationship between luck and justice. Snare believes that '[b]oth natural and social contingencies will present barriers to opportunity which provide some basis for rectification' (p. 194) because both these categories of 'contingencies' are equally arbitrary.[3] In this, Snare is a good representative of a line of thought in our thinking about justice, the *locus classicus* of which can be found in a famous and oft-quoted article by Herbert Spiegelberg. Spiegelberg's argument has a form of a syllogism: '(1) undeserved discriminations call for redress, (2) all inequalities of birth constitute undeserved discriminations. . . . (3) all inequalities of birth call for redress' (Spiegelberg, 1944, p. 113). The operative is, of course, the first premise, which is taken by Spiegelberg to be self-evident. The same conclusion is reached in Rawls's 'difference principle'[4] (with acknowledgement to Spiegelberg), which is characterized by its author as representing 'an agreement to regard the distribution of natural talents as a common asset and to share in the benefits of this distribution whatever it turns out to be' (Rawls, 1971, p. 101). Rawls clearly assigns an equal standing to natural and social contingencies. He believes, for instance, that 'when the principles of fraternity and redress are allowed their appropriate weight, the natural distribution of assets and the contingencies of social circumstances can more easily be accepted' (ibid., p. 512). The equal moral arbitrariness of the natural *and* social 'lotteries' serves as a basis for equally justified redistributive action in egalitarian conceptions of a 'common pool' of benefits deriving from natural and social assets (ibid., pp. 100–8), in Ronald Dworkin's (1981) conception of 'equality of resources' which is not 'endowment-sensitive', in Campbell's (1974–75) 'meritorian' or 'handicapped' theory of equality of opportunity and so on.

This view is not unopposed in contemporary theories of justice, and not all of its opponents necessarily reject the very idea of justice as a system of countering the adverse effects of bad luck and misfortune in general, although some certainly do: Richard Epstein's statement that '[i]n general the effort to use coercion to counter the adverse effects of luck tends only to make matters worse' (Epstein, 1988, p. 17) and Milton Friedman's laconic 'Life is not fair' (Friedman, 1980, p. 168) belong to a category which rejects wholeheartedly a societal duty to redress for inequalities which result from social and natural contingencies alike. Incidentally, it is significant that Friedman explicitly endorses the moral equivalence of natural and social contingencies by saying:

> The inheritance of property can be interfered with more readily than the inheritance of talent. But from an ethical point of view, is there any difference between the two? Yet many people resent the inheritance of property but not the inheritance of talent. (Ibid.)

In this, he seems to agree with Spiegelberg, Snare and Rawls, but he draws the opposite normative conclusions from this equivalence.

There have also been those who claim that there is *no* moral equivalence between natural and social inequalities, and that the relevant difference between these two sorts of inequality suggests that, while a just society has a duty to remove the benefits of undeserved social inequalities, no such duty applies to unequal natural talents, skills and capacities. This view is expressed and defended in an essay by Alan H. Goldman which is reproduced as Chapter 10. Goldman's central claim is that the morally relevant difference is between natural differences, which 'derive from, or rather equate with, the distinctness of physically embodied persons' and, on the other hand, social advantages which do 'not affect the basic identities of persons' (p. 208).

Goldman's main appeal is to the idea of respect for the separate identities of particular persons. The appeal is certainly very weighty. The charge that one's opponents do not respect individuals' separate identities has been used often and effectively in modern theories of justice.[5] It is, however, uncertain how useful this appeal can be in drawing the line between natural and social assets in order to perform the job it is assigned in Goldman's essay.[6] Goldman's proposition about a strong link between natural inequalities and individual identity is backed by a claim about a strong link between a person and her body. But some may believe that this is a *non sequitur* – that a right to keep the products of one's differential native skills and capacities (a right which has to be asserted in order to deny a social duty to redress for those 'contingencies') does not follow from a set of rights over one's body. As Anthony Kronman argues: 'Although a person obviously possesses his own attributes, it does not necessarily follow that he is also their owner, with the right to exploit them, within limits, for his own benefits' (Kronman, 1981, p. 65).

Even if one grants, *arguendo*, Goldman's equating of one's identity with one's body, and even with the product of one's labour, it may still seem question-begging to say that redressing for the differential *effects* of human abilities reaches the abilities (and hence, identities) themselves. In order to uphold a morally relevant distinction between natural and social contingencies, Goldman would need to show that differential rewards for higher skills, capacities and talents belong to that sphere of individual identity which must not be nullified without risking a violation of the human self. A critic might claim that this identification of the products of one's labour with one's identity assumes that which is in question: what should be subject to redistribution. Ultimately, it may collapse into a debate about the boundaries between the natural and the social – whether what is 'the fruit of one's labor' is socially constructed and affected by legal and social norms of property, taxation, inheritance and so on or whether it belongs to a pre-political, 'natural' order of things.

Political Liberalism and Justice

It is impossible to overestimate the importance of John Rawls for the theory of justice. Indeed his book under this title has rightly become a modern classic, and hardly any writer who considers the problems of justice can fail to relate, either approvingly or critically, to his work. *A Theory of Justice* has become so well known and so widely discussed since its publication 30 years ago that it would probably be redundant to include essays devoted to it in this book. However, more recently Rawls published a second book, *Political Liberalism* (preceded, as was *A Theory of Justice*, by a number of essays that foreshadowed its main themes), which has also become the subject of an important philosophical debate. Part III of this book attempts to reflect some of the most interesting features of this debate by reproducing two of Rawls's articles which came before *Political Liberalism* and three important critical commentaries about this new stage of development of Rawls's thought.

The relationship between *A Theory of Justice* and the later work by Rawls, which culminated in *Political Liberalism*, has been the object of disagreement and a cause of a degree of perplexity, among Rawls's commentators who disagreed about whether *Political Liberalism* develops and extends *A Theory of Justice*, or whether it marks a major change in Rawls's theory. However, rather than attempting to identify aspects of continuity and change in Rawls's theory, it is perhaps more useful to see *Political Liberalism* as addressing a fundamentally different set of issues to his first book.[7] While *A Theory of Justice* was concerned mainly with articulating and defending a conception of justice for an ideal society, *Political Liberalism* can be seen to identify the terms on which the proponents of such an 'ideal' conception may live together, and agree to common arrangements, with the proponents of other (including the non-liberal) theories. As John Rawls insists in *Political Liberalism*, the fundamental question which his second book addresses is: 'how is it possible for there to exist over time a just and stable society of free and equal citizens, who remain profoundly divided by reasonable religious, philosophical, and moral doctrines?' (Rawls, 1993, p. 4). So perhaps it is useful to see *Political Liberalism* as an inquiry into a second-order theory of justice – a theory about how to reconcile, in one society, on just and equal terms, proponents of different first-order theories, including the theory espoused in Rawls's first book.

'Only ideologues and visionaries fail to experience deep conflicts of political values and conflicts between these and nonpolitical values' (ibid., p. 44). Rawls is neither an 'ideologue' nor a 'visionary' in this sense that he describes, and his later work clearly points to the need for a 'political' solution to the problem of conflicts of various first-order theories of justice. Jeremy Waldron's characterization is apposite. The aim of *Political Liberalism*, Waldron says, is 'to put the "political" back into "political philosophy"' by inquiring about the role that a theory of justice 'could be expected to play in the life of a society whose members disagreed radically in their cultural, religious and philosophical beliefs' (Waldron, 1993, p. 5). Rawls himself, in the last two paragraphs of the essay reproduced as Chapter 12, 'The Idea of Public Reason Revisited', explains the 'fundamental difference' between his two books precisely along these lines: while *A Theory of Justice* is presented as a 'comprehensive liberal doctrine', *Political Liberalism* is about a vision of a society in which 'public reason is a way of reasoning about political values shared by free and equal citizens [and it] does not trespass on citizens' comprehensive doctrines so long as those doctrines are consistent with a democratic polity' (p. 293).

The idea of a theory of justice belonging to the 'political, not metaphysical' realm constitutes one of the main themes of *Political Liberalism,* and it has been expounded by Rawls in his essay 'The Domain of the Political and Overlapping Consensus' (Chapter 11). This essay also contains, as the title suggests, the idea of a stable constitutional regime resting as it is on the consensus of citizens who share an understanding of certain basic rights and liberties even though they may not agree on 'comprehensive' doctrines. This shared understanding occupies the space of 'an overlapping consensus'. In his second essay reproduced here, 'The Idea of Public Reason Revisited' (Chapter 12), Rawls discusses the other main pillar upon which the construction of *Political Liberalism* rests – namely, the idea of 'public reason' which he defined in *Political Liberalism* as 'the reason of equal citizens who, as a collective body, exercise final political and coercive power over one another in enacting laws and in amending their constitution' (Rawls, 1993, p. 214). The concept of 'public reason' plays the important role in Rawls's theory of supporting a liberal principle of legitimacy which proclaims that the exercise of political power is legitimate only when exercised in accordance with a constitution, the essentials of which all citizens may reasonably be expected to endorse in the light of ideals acceptable to them.

All three ideas (justice as 'political not metaphysical', overlapping consensus and 'public reason') have been subjected to stringent critical scrutiny from political and legal philosophers. First, there have been a number of critics who pointed to the impossibility of separating 'metaphysical' from 'political' conceptions of justice, and who discerned certain 'metaphysical' presuppositions in Rawls's work as well. William Galston's essay (Chapter 13) is a good example of this sort of inquiry. He claims that it is impossible to divorce political philosophy from all metaphysical questions and, in any event, that Rawlsian liberalism rests on an idea of the 'divided self', composed as it is of one's specific aims and attachments on the one hand, and capacity for critical reflection on such aims on the other. Accordingly, Galston is not persuaded by liberalism's claim for neutrality among opposing 'comprehensive' doctrines: some doctrines will be privileged and others disadvantaged under Rawlsian 'political liberalism'.

Second, the conception of 'overlapping consensus' has been subjected to criticism. The criticism has taken at least two forms: that 'overlapping consensus' is unattainable, and that it is unnecessary to achieve the aims assigned to it by Rawls. The first claim is implied by Galston's critique: if Rawlsian 'political liberalism' indeed rests on specific and controversial metaphysical foundations, such as certain controversial views about the self, then overlapping consensus is unlikely to be formed among the adherents to doctrines which reject those metaphysical premises. Galston's example of 'religious fundamentalists' who might find the Rawlsian conception of a self-critical personality 'a sophisticated, and therefore dangerous, brand of secular humanism' (p. 298) is a good case in point. But the 'overlapping consensus' with this degree of 'thickness', which is envisaged by Rawls, might also be *unnecessary* to provide a basis for a stable social unity. As Kurt Baier claims, in Chapter 14, all that is needed is a 'constitutional consensus', which consists of common commitment to established legal procedures 'which embody at least some (though perhaps confused or inconsistent) principles of substantive justice . . .' (p. 316).

Third, the Rawlsian conception of 'public reason' has also been criticized (for example, Scheffler, 1994, pp. 16–17), mainly on the basis that its rigorous implementation would lead to an excessive impoverishment of public discourse in a democratic state. If we were to rule out from public discourse (say, from views expressed publicly by citizens during electoral debates or from legislators' publicly stated motives for voting in favour of this or that law) all those arguments which cannot be accepted by all the adherents to divergent 'reasonable' doctrines, we would end up with an extremely bland public debate about the matters of common interest. As Waldron says, 'it is pretty clear that if people do hold their political principles for different reasons, they will naturally want to interpret them in the light of those reasons and thus disclose those reasons publicly in interpretive debate' (Waldron, 1993, p. 6), even if some of those reasons belong to more 'comprehensive' moral and religious doctrines not shared by all members of the society. This is one of the main themes of an essay by Michael Sandel reproduced here as Chapter 15. Sandel implies that the 'restrictive character of liberal public reason' would not only lead to highly counterintuitive results by ruling out much of the public discourse currently considered widely as legitimate, but it would also produce results which are not necessarily supportive of the value of toleration. This connects with other major themes of Sandel's criticism: that 'bracketing' grave moral questions is not always reasonable, and that a 'reasonable pluralism' of moral views in a democratic society applies not only to substantive moralities ('the good'), but also to conceptions of justice ('the right').

Feminist Critiques of Liberal Justice

Part IV provides a selection of critiques of liberal theories of justice and, in particular, of Rawlsian theory, which are much more fundamental than those included in Part III which could be seen as originating from the liberal 'mainstream'. In contrast, the essays included in the last Part of this volume subject liberal theories of justice to criticisms from the points of view of feminist theorists. Susan Moller Okin (Chapter 16) depicts what she considers to be ambiguity in *Political Liberalism* about the place of family with respect to political principles of justice: is family part of the 'basic structure' (and thus controlled by principles of justice), or does it belong to a 'private' realm, immune to justice-based control? She believes that Rawls's treatment of gender reveals an unstated assumption that families, in liberal–democratic societies as we know them, are just; and she also claims that the asymmetrical treatment of racial and gender inequalities, which she discovers in Rawls, is evidence of gender bias in his theory. The essays by Carole Pateman and Deborah Kearns (Chapters 17 and 18) constitute important statements of feminist disagreement with liberal justice, both in its methodological and theoretical assumptions and in its policy consequences. These three feminist writers do not necessarily speak with a single voice, and they do not claim to express a unique feminist perspective. Deborah L. Rhode, another important writer on justice and gender, has written: 'Contemporary feminist theory offers no single view of our appropriate destination, but it suggests certain preferred means of travel' (Rhode, 1989, p. 317). And as the essays in Part IV show, these 'preferred means' include a rejection of the dominant liberal vision of a just society.

Notes

1   Note that the suggestion in brackets is expressed by Campbell in a tentative rather than a conditional fashion.
2   This view is defended by Rawls (1971, pp. 100–8).
3   It should be noted that at the end of his essay Snare puts forward some reasons in favour of leaving some morally arbitrary inequalities unrectified. However, those reasons do not strictly belong to a theory of justice.
4   The difference principle proclaims that 'the higher expectations of those better situated are just if and only if they work as part of a scheme which improves the expectations of the least advantaged members of society' (Rawls, 1971, p. 75).
5   See Rawls (1971, pp. 29–30, 187–88) for a critique of utilitarianism; also Nozick (1974, p. 172) for a critique of redistribution through taxation.
6   For a more extended argument, see Sadurski (1990, pp. 157–75).
7   'It is no exaggeration to say that the two books are not about the same subject' (Estlund, 1996, p. 68).

References

Barry, B. (1965), *Political Argument*, London: Routledge & Kegan Paul.
Brenkert, G.G. (1979), 'Freedom and Private Property in Marx', *Philosophy & Public Affairs*, **8**, pp. 122–47.
Buchanan, A.E. (1982), *Marx and Justice*, London: Methuen.
Campbell, T.D. (1974–75), 'Equality of Opportunity', *Proceedings of the Aristotelian Society*, **75**, pp. 51–68.
Campbell, T.D. (1988), *Justice*, London: Macmillan.
Cohen, G.A. (1981), 'Freedom, Justice and Capitalism', *New Left Review*, **126**, pp. 3–16.
Dworkin, R. (1978), *Taking Rights Seriously*, London: Duckworth.
Dworkin, R. (1981), 'What is Equality? Part 2: Equality of Resources', *Philosophy & Public Affairs*, **10**, pp. 283–345.
Epstein, R.A. (1988), 'Luck', *Social Philosophy & Policy*, **6**, pp. 17–38.
Estlund, D. (1996), 'The Survival of Egalitarian Justice in John Rawls's *Political Liberalism*', *Journal of Political Philosophy*, **4**, pp. 68–78.
Frankena, W. (1962), 'The Concept of Social Justice', in R.B. Brandt (ed.), *Social Justice*, Englewood Cliffs, NJ: Prentice Hall.
Friedman, M. (1980), *Free to Choose*, Harmondsworth: Penguin.
Husami, Z.I. (1978), 'Marx on Distributive Justice', *Philosophy & Public Affairs*, **8**, pp. 27–64.
Kelsen, H. (1971), *What is Justice?*, Berkeley: University of California Press.
Kronman, A.T. (1981), 'Talent Pooling', in J.R. Pennock and J.W. Chapman (eds), *Human Rights*, New York: New York University Press, pp. 58–79.
Milne, H. (1986), 'Desert, Effort and Efficiency', *Journal of Applied Philosophy*, **3**, pp. 235–43.
Nozick, R. (1974), *Anarchy, State, and Utopia*, Oxford: Blackwell.

Rawls, J. (1971), *A Theory of Justice,* Oxford: Oxford University Press.

Rawls, J. (1993), *Political Liberalism*, New York: Columbia University Press.

Rhode, D.L. (1989), *Justice and Gender*, Cambridge, MA: Harvard University Press.

Ryan, C.C. (1980), 'Socialist Justice and the Right to the Labour Product', *Political Theory*, **8**, pp. 503–24.

Sadurski, W. (1985), *Giving Desert Its Due: Social Justice and Legal Theory*, Dordrecht: Reidel.

Sadurski, W. (1990), 'Natural and Social Lottery, and Concepts of the Self', *Law and Philosophy*, **9**, pp. 157–75.

Scheffler, S. (1994), 'The Appeal of Political Liberalism', *Ethics*, **105**, pp. 4–22.

Spiegelberg, H. (1944), 'A Defense of Human Equality', *Philosophical Review*, **53**, pp. 101–24.

Waldron, J. (1993), 'Justice Revisited', *Times Literary Supplement*, 18 June 1993, pp. 5–6.

Wood, A.W. (1972), 'The Marxian Critique of Justice', *Philosophy & Public Affairs*, **1**, pp. 244–82.

Zaitchik, A. (1977), 'On Deserving to Deserve', *Philosophy & Public Affairs*, **6**, pp. 370–88.

Part I
The Concept of Justice

[1]

B.J.Pol.S. 4, 1–16
Printed in Great Britain

Humanity before Justice

T. D. CAMPBELL*

Advocates of the welfare state often appeal to social justice as the moral basis of their claim that distribution of scarce resources ought to be made in proportion to the needs of potential recipients, at least to a certain minimum level of satisfaction. More generally, it is commonly assumed that need is certainly one and perhaps the main factor which ought to determine any just distribution of benefits and burdens. Thus, when the Labour Government abolished medical prescription charges under the National Health Service in 1964 the then Prime Minister, Harold Wilson, defended this step in the House of Commons by saying that it was 'unjust' to put such 'burdens on the old and sick' and he went on to cite the principle 'from each according to his means, to each according to his needs'.[1]

This use of the language of justice in the formulation of demands for, or justifications of, improvements in the welfare of disadvantaged sections of the population is not confined to the rhetoric of political debate. It can be found, for instance, in the more measured statements of such theoreticians of social reform as Richard M. Titmuss who saw 'the future development of welfare policies', especially relating to poverty amongst the old, as a matter of 'redistributive social justice'.[2] Similarly, C. A. R. Crosland, in discussing the uneven distribution of pecuniary and other benefits asserts that 'inequality in the distribution of these resources among the elderly, the sick and those with large families constitutes a definite social injustice'.[3]

Against this tendency to subsume the principle of allocation in accordance with need under the heading of justice I wish to argue that it is conceptually mistaken and tactically unwise for welfare moralists to imply that need *per se* is a criterion of a just distribution and that their case would be more clearly stated and therefore more securely based if they were to appeal to beneficence or humanity instead of to justice.

My thesis rests on the premise that there is a close logical association between the concept of justice and that of desert or merit, an association which, I will

---

* University of Stirling.

[1] House of Commons Debates, 3 November 1964, Cols. 701–77. See also Hugh Gaitskell's equation of social equality and social justice, *Socialism and Nationalisation* (London: Fabian Society, 1956), pp. 3–4.

[2] 'Limits of the Welfare State', *New Left Review*, XXVII (1964), 28–37, p. 34. See also *Essays on 'the Welfare State'*, 2nd edn. (London: George Allen and Unwin, 1963), p. 221, and Kathleen Slack, *Social Administration and the Citizen* (London: Michael Joseph, 1966), p. 68.

[3] *The Future of Socialism* (London: Jonathan Cape, 1956) p. 214; cf. *The Conservative Enemy* (London: Jonathan Cape, 1962), p. 40.

I

2   CAMPBELL

argue, rules out any simple and direct conceptual link between the principle that distribution ought to be proportional to need and the idea of justice.

It would, of course, be naive to speak of *the* idea of justice if this were thought to imply that there is and could be only one such idea. I concede, for instance, that 'justice' is sometimes interpreted so broadly as to include all morally relevant criteria of distribution and even all principles of social morality. As such it becomes almost indistinguishable from 'rightness'. Nevertheless, when we speak of justice in the narrow and specific sense in which it is equivalent to one but not to all moral principles of distribution, then it is normally in relation to a distribution which is primarily concerned with the merits and demerits of the distributees. Indeed it is arguable that justice, in its distinctive meaning, is to be *defined* as distribution in proportion to the deserts of the possible recipients. However, I shall presuppose only the weaker thesis – which is all that is required for the argument of this paper – that desert is a necessary criterion of justice in that no just distribution can properly ignore the deserts of the recipients, where desert is taken to refer to any feature of personal behaviour, character or achievement for which someone can properly be praised or blamed.

Even this may be thought to assume too much for, despite the immediate appeal and the respectable philosophical ancestry of what I shall call the meritorian analysis of justice (versions of which were held by J. S. Mill[4] and Henry Sidgwick[5]), most present day philosophers assume that desert is, at the very most, one among many possible criteria of a just distribution. The standard contemporary view is that 'the central core of the idea of justice is not the requital of desert but the exclusion of arbitrariness',[6] a formula which has no difficulty in accommodating distribution in accordance with need as a principle of justice.

While the main purpose of this paper is to indicate how, taking the meritorian analysis for granted, we should interpret and classify arguments which invoke differences in people's needs to justify differences in our treatment of them, a brief consideration of two of the arguments which lie behind the current and widespread denial that there is a logical connection between justice and desert may help to provide a preliminary exposition and defence of the meritorian position.

The first of these arguments, used to place a wedge between justice and desert, is that, while it seems clear enough that justice involves giving each person his 'due', this may be interpreted, not as treating each person according to his deserts, but as treating each in accordance with his rights. Justice, it is argued,

[4] Cf. *Utilitarianism* (London: Fontana, 1962), p. 299: 'It is universally considered that each person should obtain that (whether good or evil) which he deserves; and unjust that he should obtain a good, or be made to undergo an evil, which he does not deserve. This is, perhaps, the clearest and most emphatic form in which the idea of justice is conceived by the general mind.'

[5] Cf. *Methods of Ethics*, 7th edn. (London: Macmillan, 1963), p. 283: 'it is the Requital of Desert that constitutes the chief element of Ideal Justice, in so far as this imports something more than mere Equality and Impartiality'.

[6] M. Ginsberg, 'The Concept of Justice', *Philosophy*, XXXVIII (1963), 99–116, p. 109. For a contrary view see Roger Hancock, 'Meritorian and Equalitarian Justice', *Ethics*, LXXX (1969–70), 165–9.

has to do with rights[7] and to say, for instance, that it is unjust for person A to be deprived of benefit x is equivalent to saying that A has a right to x, but this is not the same thing as saying that A deserves x. Thus those who argue that, as a matter of justice, the poor ought to receive financial assistance from the State, are asserting that the poor have a right to such assistance without implying anything about their deserts; indeed it may be argued that the poor have welfare rights whether or not they deserve them and that this is precisely the force behind the demand that the poor be treated justly.

This argument confuses formal and material justice.[8] Formal justice, which involves the consistent application of the relevant established rule or law to all cases which are alike within the terms of that rule or law, may indeed be regarded as requiring treatment of persons in accordance with their rights irrespective of their deserts. Thus, if there is a law to the effect that whenever A needs x then A is to be provided with x by the State, then A has a right to x and formal justice requires that he be provided with x. It is therefore a matter of formal justice that underprivileged groups receive those benefits to which they are entitled by law; in a welfare state, poverty confers rights, and to be treated in a formally just way 'needy' persons must receive that to which they are entitled, whether or not they are deserving. From the point of view of formal justice, what is due to a person, what he is entitled to, depends on his rights not on his praise-worthiness. And while it may be possible to speak of such entitlements as 'legal deserts' this seems artificial and is really only a way of disguising the fact that, in the case of formal justice, desert, as it is normally understood, is not a relevant factor in determining how persons are to be treated except in so far as this may be required by the relevant law. It must therefore be granted that the meritorian analysis requires reformulation if it is to cover formal justice.

However, the arguments in which we are interested are arguments about the justification rather than the application of welfare legislation, and these concern material not formal standards; that is, they have to do with the rightness or wrongness of the rules themselves rather than with their correct or incorrect administration. Such arguments raise questions about whether or not the 'needy' ought to have rights: that is, whether or not there ought to be a welfare state. In so far as justice is relevant to justifying arguments about welfare legislation, it is to material rather than to formal justice that we must turn, and it is material and not formal justice that the meritorian analyses as treatment in accordance with desert. For while formal justice may be defined as the exclusion of arbitrariness in the sense that it requires that the treatment of persons be rule-governed, material justice is concerned with the exclusion of a particular sort of arbitrariness in the content of these rules, an arbitrariness which arises from the failure to relate treatment to desert. In the case of material justice, what is to count as a person's

[7] Cf. D. D. Raphael, *Problems of Political Philosophy* (London: Pall Mall Press, 1970), pp. 48 and 190, and G. Vlastos, 'Justice and Equality' in R. B. Brandt, ed., *Social Justice* (Englewood Cliffs, N.J.: Prentice-Hall, 1962), p. 53.

[8] For a fuller discussion of the relationship between rights and justice see T. D. Campbell, 'Rights without justice', *Mind*, (forthcoming).

4   CAMPBELL

'due' does depend on his deserts, and once the distinction between formal and material justice is made clear there is no reason to loosen the connection between material justice and desert on the grounds that this connection does not hold in the case of formal justice.

Even if the meritorian confines his analysis to material justice, this may still appear unconvincing, for surely desert is not the only criterion which is relevant to the determination of what rights a person ought to have? If a person's rights are what he is entitled to in accordance with the law or rules of his community, is it not the case that many laws and rules are morally legitimated by moral considerations other than that of desert? The meritorian has no difficulty in accepting and accommodating this point for he does not claim that justice is the only moral standard by which laws may be justified. Many laws affecting our economic rights, for instance, are based on considerations of utility, a moral norm which notoriously tends to conflict with that of justice; and, to give another example, no one would want to argue that quarantine regulations, which confer on the citizen the right to be protected from certain avoidable risks of infection, must be justified on grounds of justice. Justice is not therefore the only moral standard relevant to the moral determination of what rights people ought to enjoy and we do not therefore have to define material justice in such a way that it covers all those standards in terms of which laws may be morally justified. If evaluation of laws in terms of justice is confined to those cases in which desert is a relevant factor, then the logical association between justice and desert can still be maintained.

A second reason for denying the analytical connection between justice and desert reflects contemporary doubts about the moral significance of desert and the ideas of individual responsibility that go with it. Even amongst those who do not dismiss the view that individuals are morally accountable for their actions, there are many who admit that much poverty is not the result of the moral failure of poor persons so that the deserts of the poor appear to have less moral and political significance than they were once thought to have. To see why this evaluative downgrading of the significance of desert should affect our ideas about justice it is necessary to appreciate the extent to which justice has been regarded as the 'overriding' moral value.[9] If justice is morally overriding, then to define material justice as distribution in accordance with desert implies that desert ought always to take priority over all other moral considerations in determining the distribution of benefits and burdens, and this seems implausible.

However, the idea that justice must be overriding attaches to the rather vague use of 'justice', in which it is equivalent to rightness, rather than to its narrower and specific meaning. Justice as one amongst other moral values may quite properly be required to give way to other considerations. For instance, it is one of the purposes of this paper to demonstrate the conceptual propriety of holding the substantive moral position that what I shall call 'humanity' ought to come before justice in the determination of our social and political priorities. If this is accepted, then the second reason for diluting the traditional meritorian conception

[9] Cf. John Rawls, *A Theory of Justice* (Oxford: Clarendon Press, 1972), p. 3.

of justice is countered, since there is no longer any cause to argue that if a criterion of distribution is held to have high priority it must be classified as a criterion of justice.

Moving on to the offensive, the meritorian can argue that, while those contemporary analyses of justice which have taken justice to be overriding and have therefore played down the importance of desert may have provided lists of the most fundamental moral reasons for differential distribution, they have not set themselves the more precise task of saying what sets justice apart from other moral goals. Thus, there is an important sense in which they are not analyses of justice at all because they do not enable us to distinguish justice from other political values.[10]

It is important to see what is at stake in choosing between competing analyses of justice and the sort of political discourse which they license. To fuss about the accurate and consistent use of the language of justice is not mere academic pedantry. The connection between justice and desert is deeply embedded in the moral and political discourse of everyday life, and one consequence of this fact is that to most persons it appears that those who commend – as a requirement of *justice* – provision by the state of a minimum standard of living for all its citizens are implying that *all* poor persons *deserve* such assistance as is necessary to bring them to this level. But, unless desert is defined in unusually broad terms, such a view is implausible, and to put forward a poverty programme in the name of justice is, therefore, to invite the response that, since at least some of the poor are undeserving in that they themselves are largely to blame for their situation, universal provision for the poor is mistaken.

The welfare theorist who capitalizes on the language of justice can hardly deny the appositeness of this rejoinder and yet it is an objection which is irrelevant to the essence of his doctrine which is that need is, by itself, a sufficient reason for differential distribution. If he wishes to avoid being drawn off into what must be, for him, a pointless debate about the deserts of the poor and hopes to state his case clearly and efficaciously, then he must drop the terminology of justice and look elsewhere for his moral support.

There are many reasons why this suggestion may be resisted, reasons which do something to explain why misplaced appeals to justice are so common. For instance, the word 'justice' has strong emotive meaning such that to describe one's policies as just can be rhetorically efficacious. Also, since, as has been pointed out, it is often supposed that justice is the overriding value of social practices, it tends to be assumed that showing a course of action to be a just one is equivalent to ensuring its definitive vindication. These are not advantages to be given up lightly.

Moreover, the obvious alternative to regarding the relief of need as a requirement of justice is to classify it as an objective of charity and, since 'charity' carries with it ineradicable overtones of supererogation – being usually looked

---

[10] Cf. S. I. Benn and R. S. Peters, *Social Principles and the Democratic State* (London: George Allen and Unwin, 1959), p. 111: 'To act justly then is to treat all men alike except where there are relevant differences between them.' The same could be said of Rawls, *A Theory of Justice*.

6 CAMPBELL

upon as an optional extra of the moral life – it is felt to be an inappropriate basis for the sort of legislative action that is being demanded. The whole point of the welfare state, it can be argued, is that the needy have rights and that their assistance should not be left to the chance benefactions of wealthy individuals and voluntary organizations, and, although we have seen that rights need not be justified by appeals to justice, the absence of any obvious alternative leads people to adopt the terminology of justice in order to dissociate themselves from that of charity.

Backing up these practical points concerning the tactics of political argument – to which I shall return – those who object to my thesis could argue that distribution in accordance with need *can* often be subsumed under the principles of justice even if justice is defined in meritorian terms. Where need, for instance, is the consequence of maltreatment at the hands of another, the relief of that need by the guilty person could be regarded as a matter of remedial justice, which is a species of meritorian justice.

To meet this sort of point it will be necessary to go into some analytical detail over 'need' statements and their relationship to moral claims. This will enable us to set out the variety of ways in which need *may* relate to desert and so to justice; it will, however, at the same time make clear that the relief of need as such, where no distinction is made between the deserving and the undeserving, while it may be a moral requirement, is one which has nothing specifically to do with justice. This exploration of the complex but contingent relationships between need and justice will, I hope, help to explain why it often seems to be, but is not in fact, conceptually in order, as well as rhetorically advantageous, to regard all cases of distribution in accordance with need as applications of principles of justice.

To reveal more of our destination from the outset, the alternative principle which, I suggest, could serve as a surer basis for welfare ideology is, in traditional terms, beneficence, or, in more familiar philosophical language, utility. What I have in mind is the doctrine of negative utilitarianism,[11] which is that form of utilitarianism which gives priority to the relief of suffering over the promotion of pleasure. This I call, partly for brevity, but also so as not to be done out of my share of emotive meaning, the principle of humanity. In fact, I would argue that the duty of humanity – the obligation to work for the relief of suffering as an end-in-itself – is not only distinct from the duty to be just but may properly be regarded as at least on an equal footing with (and perhaps as overriding) justice in the determination of our moral priorities for the distribution of benefits and burdens.

I

Much of the confusion surrounding the analysis and justification of the maxim 'to each according to his needs' arises from the disparity between the wide use of 'need' as the term occurs in ordinary discourse and the narrower definition of need which those who use the maxim obviously have in mind.

[11] Cf. H. B. Acton, 'Negative Utilitarianism', *Proceedings of the Aristotelian Society*, Supplementary Volume xxxvii (1963), 83–94.

Anything can be said to be needed which is required for the attainment or completion of any purpose, state or condition whatever. Sometimes the relation between the thing needed and the relevant purpose or condition is definitional where the thing needed is required in order to license the application of a particular description, as when it is said that ice-cream needs to contain a certain percentage of milk fat without which a substance cannot properly be called ice-cream. Sometimes the relation is causal where the thing needed is a causal condition for the occurrence of the end in question but is not itself part of that end, as when it is said that a car needs petrol, meaning that petrol is a necessary condition of the car's functioning.

Thus, a human need is anything which is definitionally or causally necessary for the existence of any human condition or for the achievement of any human goal. In fact, the idea of a need is, in the abstract, almost indefinitely elastic because of the very wide range of possible human conditions and purposes. Thus, political scientists like Noel Boaden, who use the concept of need to identify one type of objective feature of a political system which, in combination with other features, determines policy outcomes, are able to regard the absence of such facilities as swimming pools and concert halls as constituting needs, and there is no reason why almost any conceivable objective of government policy should not be described as fulfilling some need or other.[12] And so, to argue that distribution ought to be in proportion to need may be to say no more than that resources ought to be allocated so as to minimize the absence of anything which is definitionally or causally necessary for the realization of some human condition or purpose.

In these general terms, distribution in accordance with need is a highly questionable moral principle. All human conditions and purposes are not of moral significance and many are morally undesirable. A man may be in need of a spanner, a cigarette or a win in a lottery, as well as in need of food, shelter and clothing, and he may need any of these things for the pursuit of evil as well as of good. For need to form the basis of a moral claim for differential distribution it is necessary to show that the thing needed is required for the achievement of some positively evaluated goal. That is, to be morally relevant a need statement must not only be descriptive, asserting that x is logically or causally necessary for the existence of some end state, but also prescriptive or normative, stating that the end in question has moral value.

This has led one philosopher to say that a statement about needs may have, in itself, no prescriptive force,[13] and another to argue that distribution in accordance with need is not in itself a justificatory principle because, in order to provide a reason for action, a 'need' statement must be used in conjunction with a principle which justifies the objective which gives rise to the need.[14]

[12] *Urban Policy Making* (Cambridge: Cambridge University Press, 1971), p. 22. Allardt and Hannu Uusitalo include the 'need for love' and the 'need for self-actualization' as representing welfare values in relation to which the performance of governments can be measured: 'Dimensions of Welfare in a Comparative Study of the Scandinavian Countries', *Scandinavian Political Studies*, VII (1972), 9–27, p. 12.

[13] Paul W. Taylor, ' "Need" Statements', *Analysis*, XIX (1959), 106–11.

[14] Brian Barry, *Political Argument* (London: Routledge and Kegan Paul, 1965), pp. 47–9.

8   CAMPBELL

Conclusions of this sort certainly follow from an inclusive analysis of the meaning of 'need' statements in the full range of their everyday uses. But in most discussion about human needs it is contextually implied that the relevant end is of a sort which cannot but be positively evaluated so that most need statements – in the informal logic of everyday discourse – are taken to be *prima facie* recommendations of the requisite remedial actions. Indeed it is sometimes the case that the evaluative use of 'need' takes over from its descriptive use so that in the context of political debate, for instance, to speak of a possible political goal as a need can be merely one way of saying that it is a desirable policy objective. The pervasiveness of this ill-defined normative use of 'need' is one of the factors which has led some sociologists who have been attempting to deploy the idea of need as a basis for devising social indicators to argue that 'it may be that the word "need" ought to be banished from discussions of public policy'.[15] This suggestion is unduly pessimistic about the prospects of theorists' being able to refine the ordinary language of politics and adapt it for use in the policy sciences; but the very fact that there is this danger of the descriptive use of 'need' being overshadowed by its evaluative use illustrates the prescriptive implications of employing this slippery and ambiguous term in certain contexts. Certainly those who advocate, in the context of discussions about the welfare state, that distribution be in proportion to need imply both that to be in need is to lack something which is necessary for the realization of a certain human condition and that there is a moral and political obligation to bring this condition about.

It is also interesting to note that it is this combination of descriptive and prescriptive meaning which makes the concept of need attractive to political scientists seeking to explain political behaviour.[16] For instance, those who use the concept of need to interpret statistical correlations between social indicators and policy decisions, and who suggest that perception of the 'need' for which the social indicator is taken to be a measure is a factor in determining policy outcomes, clearly assume that it is explanatory to speak of needs in this context

[15] A. J. Culyer, R. J. Lavers and Alan Williams, 'Health Indicators' in Andrew Shonfield and Stella Shaw, *Social Indicators and Social Policy* (London: Heinemann Educational Books, 1972), p. 114. Allardt and Uusitalo, on the other hand, are happy to proceed on the basis that 'the concepts of value and need will be treated as synonyms' ('Dimensions of Welfare', p. 11). They side-step the evaluative problems involved in deciding what is to count as a need by assuming that, because needs are 'socially defined', they can be empirically determined by recording the 'modicum of agreement over what the most important needs are' in any society.

[16] Cf. Boaden, *Urban Policy Making*, p. 22: 'the absence of such facilities [such as swimming pools, concert halls, town halls and theatres] should be seen as a need or a deficiency, and . . . such a view greatly assists understanding of local decisions about them, and about other services. Need then becomes an objective condition of a community which can be ameliorated by council action but in relation to which the provision of relevant service is either inadequate or, as in the cases just cited, non-existent'. See also p. 136. Boaden masks the evaluative arbitrariness of his selection of needs by taking it for granted that the general nature of the goals of local government activity are determined by central government. See also Erik Allardt, 'A Frame of Reference for Selecting Social Indicators', *Commentationes Scientarium Socialium*, 1 (1972), 5–16, p. 6: 'Indicators contain or produce incitements to action. Under such circumstances a systematic consideration of individual needs becomes all the more important.'

because the perception of something as needed commits the percipient to accepting that, given the resources, it ought to be provided. That is, it is assumed that a person will not perceive the absence of something as a 'need' unless his system of values leads him to judge that the absence of the thing 'needed' is regrettable and that this will prompt him to do what he can to alleviate the 'need'. This is the reason why, other things being equal, the greater the need for a social service the greater expenditure on that service will tend to be.

There is a difficulty here however. The statistical correlations which are being fitted into this explanatory scheme are formed on the basis of a purely descriptive or 'objective' sense of 'need' in which it can be equated, for instance, with certain population characteristics such as the percentage of old persons in a given local authority area.[17] But this 'objective need' does not fulfil the explanatory role which is required of it since the existence of objective need will not evoke a political response unless it is perceived as need by the relevant political agents concerned. That is, it is because of the evaluative element in the language of need that it seems explanatory to say that variations in need explain variations in social expenditure. So, while the political scientist may seek an objective description of need (i.e. one which is not relative to the values of the political agents whose behaviour he is trying to explain) which can function as an independent variable in a causal model of the policy process, this is difficult to marry with an explanatory framework which depends on using the idea of need in its everyday evaluative sense in which what counts as a need is dependent upon the values of the persons using the term. However, despite the problems involved in this enterprise, the rationale for keeping the idea of need as an organizing concept in the policy sciences is that it provides a possible basis on which not merely to describe but also to explain certain aspects of political behaviour. From this point of view it would be self-defeating for political theorists to purge the idea of need of its evaluative overtones in an effort to become more scientific.

Even if the 'need' statements with which we are concerned are interpreted in this way as having both a descriptive and a normative element, the maxim of distribution in accordance with need requires to be stated more precisely if it is to make explicit the intentions of those who put it forward, whether as a requirement of justice or of humanity. When welfare theorists speak of human need, it is to imply that there are certain persons who are 'in need' in the restricted sense that they lack those things necessary to achieve, not just any of their morally proper goals, but a certain condition of themselves defined in accordance with some norm setting out what constitutes a minimum tolerable level of material existence.

'Need' in this restricted sense does not cover 'adventitious' needs as Braybrooke calls those things which can be thought of as necessary means to any transitory goal and which therefore 'come and go with particular contingent projects'[18] (as when Mr *A* needs a bicycle to visit a friend and Mr *B* needs a car to go on holi-

[17] Cf. Boaden, *Urban Policy Making*, p. 76.
[18] David Braybrooke, 'Let Needs Diminish that Preferences may Prosper' in N. Rescher, ed., *Studies in Moral Philosophy* (Oxford: Blackwell, 1968), p. 90.

day). Nor does it include 'functional' needs as we may call those needs which arise in the course of a person's employment or social role, such as the carpenter's need for his tools or the comic's need for an audience. Rather, it has to do with 'course-of-life' needs which, in Braybrooke's words, 'people have all through their lives or at certain stages through which all must pass',[19] such as the need for food and education.

Yet even this is not specific enough to define the principle of distribution in accordance with need, for many course-of-life needs, such as the need for pleasant companions, are not of sufficient importance for the deficiency in question to count as being 'in need'. However, within the class of course-of-life needs it is common to single out certain needs as 'basic' or 'essential' on the grounds that they are necessary for all human beings to attain a certain minimal standard of health and happiness. Exactly what this standard is depends on the experience, expectations and values of the group of individuals involved, although it cannot be equated in any straightforward way with what certain persons or even all human beings want. That something is wanted does not prove that it is, in the relevant sense, needed. To speak of a need in the sense of a basic course-of-life need presupposes some generally accepted norm of what constitutes a tolerable human existence. Needs are in this sense more objective than wants. The extent and basis of this relative objectivity is, of course, open to question, for, even if rational agreement can be reached about man's basic biological needs in the sense of what is necessary for his survival and health, there are well-known difficulties in going beyond this and finding a rational basis for fixing on an agreed criterion of poverty.[20] Yet some such criterion is pre-supposed when we speak of someone

[19] Braybrooke, 'Let Needs Diminish that Preferences may Prosper', pp. 91–2.

[20] Cf. W. G. Runciman, *Relative Deprivation and Social Justice* (London: Routledge and Kegan Paul, 1966), p. 251, and Nicholas Rescher, *Welfare* (Pittsburg: The University Press, 1972), Chap. 6. One classification of needs which is sometimes used to suggest that there is an objective hierarchy of needs is that which was formulated by Abraham Maslow (cf. 'A Theory of Human Motivation', *Psychological Review*, L (1943), 370–96). This hierarchy depends on the idea that certain needs are, in the main, causally prior to others in that they require to be satisfied before these other needs manifest themselves. In Maslow's terminology, 'physiological needs', for example, are more 'prepotent' than 'safety needs' in that the need for safety tends not to affect human behaviour when physiological needs are unsatisfied. However even if such a causal hierarchy of needs could be scientifically proved, while this would have obvious practical implications for policy making, 'prepotency' cannot be equated with evaluative importance. If 'basic' is taken to mean that which is most important for living a minimally *human* existence according to some norm of a worthwhile human life, then there is no reason why needs which are less fundamental in Maslow's causal serial ordering should not be more fundamental in terms of human values. Thus, while Maslow's 'self-esteem' needs may normally be more prepotent than his 'self-development' needs, this may conflict with the ordering of these needs in our scale of values. Without, therefore, invoking the spectre of the 'naturalistic fallacy' in order to forbid the deduction of moral goals from factual statements about human nature, it is nevertheless clear that the relationship between needs and values is too complex for us to go along with Christian Bay who, in developing a theory of political legitimacy on the basis of Maslow's hierarchy of needs, assumes that 'a psychologically prior need must legitimate a politically prior right': 'Needs, Wants and Political Legitimacy', *Canadian Journal of Political Science*, I (1968), 241–60, p. 248.

as being 'in need', a phrase which is normally used, and which I shall use, to indicate that a person lacks one or more of those things which are prerequisites of a minimum acceptable level of human existence. Let us call the principle that each ought to receive what is necessary to meet his basic course-of-life needs the welfare principle and turn to a consideration of the relationship of this principle to the concept of justice.

If need is defined in the widest sense so as to cover all varieties of its everyday use, then no one, I think, would want to argue that need is always a criterion of a just distribution. Adventitious needs cover too wide a range of requirements for such a proposition to be plausible. However, it might be argued that need, in the restricted sense in which it occurs in the welfare principle, is a criterion of justice. This would be to say that it is only when the needs in question are basic course-of-life needs that it is just to distribute in accordance with need.

This seems mistaken for two reasons. The first reason is that if, as most people would hold, the relief of suffering is an ultimate moral goal in that it does not require justification by reference to any other desirable objective, then it is misleading to express this in the language of justice with its implied reference to the rights and wrongs of the human behaviour which has led to the suffering in question. We would regard it as inhuman to make relief for refugees dependent on proof of their innocence, or the assistance of wounded persons or malformed children dependent on who, if anybody, was responsible for the occurrence of the injury or malformation. The plight of refugees, the sufferings of the wounded and the handicaps of the disabled may be the result of injustice in that they are the unmerited infliction of harm by other human beings, and this may give rise to a set of obligations which have to do with the compensation of those in need and the punishment of those whose behaviour was instrumental in bringing it about, but these obligations should be distinguished from the prior and possibly more stringent obligation to minimize suffering for its own sake, whatever its origin.

A second reason for objecting to the classification of the welfare principle as an expression of justice is that, where need is relevant to justice, this can occur in the case of adventitious, functional and non-basic course-of-life needs as well as in the case of basic course-of-life ones, so that, in so far as need does relate to justice, this has nothing specifically to do with the welfare principle. For instance, the justification of the goals implied by adventitious needs may be of any moral type, including that of justice. My need for a book may give rise to a justified claim to be given a book because it is required for amusing a child (utility), or for developing my intellectual capacities (self-realization), or for rewarding a diligent pupil (justice). In fact, as will become clear in the next section, justice is often relevant to distribution in accordance with needs other than basic course-of-life ones. It cannot therefore be argued that, where distributive disputes which involve appeals to the needs of the persons involved raise issues of justice, this means that they must concern either the validity or the application of the welfare principle. It is therefore wrong to say that the maxim 'to each according to his needs', even when this is interpreted in the terms which I have outlined, can be used to distinguish those cases where need is relevant to justice from those cases where it is not.

II

A more satisfactory picture of the relationships between need and justice emerges if we consider the ways in which need and merit are characteristically associated. I suggest that need is a criterion of justice only when it is connected with merit in one or more of the following ways.

Firstly, need may arise as a result of or in the course of meritorious behaviour, as when one soldier is wounded in the act of rescuing another, or a clergyman needs a bicycle in order to visit the sick. There are really two types of case here. In the latter example what is needed is the necessary means to complete a worthwhile task, while in the former a deprivation has arisen as a by-product of a meritorious act. But in both cases it is only because the need is connected with acts which are judged to be praiseworthy (and not because the need is a basic one) that its relief is a matter of justice. Conversely where need arises as a result of morally reprehensible behaviour (the soldier is wounded whilst running away, or a burglar needs a screwdriver), justice does not require that these needs be met (although it may require that the acts which gave rise to the needs be punished).

Secondly, need may arise because of maltreatment at the hands of others, as when injury is inflicted by the intentional action or inaction or another person, or because exploitation has taken place as when one group uses its position of relative power to reap the benefits of the productive acts of another group. In the case of the deliberate infliction of injury, blame attaches to the injurer and justice requires that compensation be paid to the victim as well as that punishment be meted out to the offender. In the case of exploitation, the redistribution of scarce resources as between exploited and exploiter is appropriate, and so perhaps is punishment of the exploiters. Again this may arise in the case of adventitious and functional needs as well as of basic course-of-life needs.

For those who believe that all poverty in a prosperous industrial society is due to exploitation it is natural to regard need as a criterion of justice since *ex hypothesi* all persons in need have been deprived of the fair reward for their labour. However, even if it were true that all poverty is in fact the result of exploitation, this would be a contingent truth and would not make need as such but only need which arises from the deprivation of deserved rewards the yardstick of a just distribution.

A third way in which need relates to justice *via* the concept of merit has to do with the mechanics of calculating rewards and punishments. In making distribution of benefits and burdens in accordance with the merits and demerits of the recipients it is possible either to ignore or to take account of the benefits and burdens already experienced by the persons concerned. That is, as we divide the cake, we may or may not consider the amount of cake already possessed by those amongst whom it is to be divided.

Now, where we do take the present position of the recipients into account, it is relevant, when considering a distribution based on merit, to consider whether or not each person already enjoys the proper proportion of benefits or burdens in accordance with his merit or demerit and to calculate what if anything is required to bring about this proportion. In so far as these benefits and burdens are the result of previous distributions on the basis of desert, they should of course be ignored; but many benefits and burdens are not the result of such distributions, and it appears therefore to be fair to regard them as accidental from the point of view of justice and therefore to vary the allotted rewards and punishments accordingly. Thus, if a deserving person already has the good fortune to be relatively well off, he would have less claim in justice to a large share of scarce goods than an equally deserving person who happened to be relatively badly off and perhaps (but not necessarily) 'in need' in that he lacked some of these things normally considered requisite for an averagely happy life in his society. That is, need can be relevant to a just distribution in so far as it features in the calculation of just rewards and punishments, for existing needs, particularly course-of-life needs, have to be taken into account in order to establish an average position of well-being relative to which any advance can be regarded as a reward and any diminution a punishment. This is one reason why it is sometimes appropriate to say that blameless persons in need *deserve* assistance,[21] since other persons who are blameworthy are relatively less in need.

A fourth way in which merit makes need relevant to justice depends on regarding equality of opportunity as part of social justice. For the meritorian, who is concerned to achieve a situation in which rewards are proportional to merit, it is important that whatever method is used to determine rewards should be a reasonably accurate measure of the merits and demerits of the persons involved. However, the only tests which are objective enough to operationalize depend on the assessment of achievement rather than on the measurement of the more elusive qualities of praiseworthiness and blameworthiness. Such tests are defensible on meritorian grounds only if achievement does in fact reflect merit but this, it can be argued, is rarely so since achievement depends on natural capacities and learning opportunities as well as on the personal choices and efforts of the individual. Since nothing can be done about natural capacities *per se*, the meritorian pursues social justice by striving to create equality of opportunity, by which he means that the competitions on which differential rewards are based are fair in that achievement does as far as possible correlate with merit. Equality of opportunity is therefore required in order to achieve an approximation to meritorian justice.

Now in seeking to establish the conditions of fair competition embodied in the idea of equality of opportunity it is necessary to take account of the needs of the competitors in that the lack of basic course-of-life needs, or of the apparatus required to reach a certain level of attainment, such as the functional needs of the scholar, has a direct bearing on an individual's chances of success. This makes need relevant to social justice in a very extensive way for it amounts to saying that

[21] Cf. Joel Feinberg, *Doing and Deserving* (Princeton: Princeton University Press, 1970), p. 93.

equality of opportunity requires the satisfaction of the basic needs of all those whose achievement is to be assessed and the equal fulfilment of the functional needs which all competitors have *qua* competitors.

That this does not make need in itself a criterion of justice may be seen if we distinguish between giving assistance to a poor child (1) to decrease his misery and (2) to give him a fair chance of attaining some standard of achievement recognized as meritorious in his society. In the former case, the morality of the action depends solely on its characteristic as relieving need, that is, as an act of humanity; in the latter, need is being relieved as means to a further moral goal, social justice. The two obligations may require similar acts but they should be distinguished; the former would remain but the latter would not were it demonstrated that the person in question was a non-competitor because, for instance, he was mentally handicapped or for some other reason had no chance of reaching the standard of achievement required.

III

My thesis that need is a criterion of justice only where it happens to be associated in some way with our ideas of merit and demerit may be resisted for a variety of extraneous reasons. Consideration of these reasons takes us back to my original explanations of the tendency to extend the concept of justice so as to include all cases of distribution in accordance with need. It might, for instance, be thought that one consequence of excluding need *per se* from the list of justicizing criteria must be to downgrade our obligation to remedy deficiencies in basic course-of-life needs by making this a matter of mere beneficence which, as I pointed out, is often equated with supererogatory acts of charity.

There is a sense in which they may be true, in that we might wish to hold that, other things being equal, the deserving or maltreated poor have a greater right to relief than the evil, undeserving or self-injuring poor. But there is another sense in which it is not a necessary consequence of the conceptual scheme which I am commending. For, if we take justice in the narrow sense in which it is not thought of as a synonym for rightness, even rightness in distribution, but as having to do with a specific specialized range of right-making characteristics, then it is perfectly in order to regard humanity as, in certain cases, overriding justice. Sometimes it is more important to relieve distress than to be fair. This is so in private life and there is no reason why it should not be so in public affairs also. One child has done well and deserves the one available present, but it goes to the other undeserving child with toothache; this is not just, but it is morally defensible. Similarly, it might be that considerations of justice alone would leave untended the distresses of the undeserving, perhaps blameworthy, poor because the means necessary to relieve their distress have been deployed to reward the virtuous. If we think that this is wrong, then it is better to say that in this situation humanity ought to override justice than to incorporate such obligations in an overarching concept of justice. It is better because such conceptual extension erodes the distinctive meaning of justice as a species of rightness and so obscures the nature of this type of controversy.

A second mistaken reason for resisting the exclusion of need from the list of distributive criteria of material justice is the view that a distribution based on humanitarian considerations would not be one in which the benefits allotted were in proportion to need, for humanity as a utilitarian principle only requires the minimization of total suffering not that we should do so in an equal and therefore a morally acceptable way.[22]

There is, however, no need to accept this interpretation of the principle of humanity as an expression of the pure quantitative utilitarian maxim that we should maximize pleasure and minimize pain. Humanity does not require us simply to relieve the sum total of suffering, but to relieve the suffering of individual human beings and the obligation is greatest where the suffering is greatest, in that the person who is suffering most has first claim on the available resources. That is, beneficence as embodied in the principles of negative utilitarianism embodies the distributive principle that those in greatest need ought to receive most assistance or, more specifically, that aid should be in proportion to need. The fact that this obligation cannot be subsumed under the principles of classical utilitarianism does not entail that it must therefore be an obligation of justice. It does mean that the principle of humanity presupposes the intrinsic worth of every human being in that the relief of any person's suffering is taken to be a worthwhile end in itself. This is sometimes taken to be a principle of justice.[23] But the idea of human worth, which is manifested in the view that the interests of all human beings are of equal moral significance, is quite distinct from the idea of merit. In fact, equality of human worth is presupposed by most if not all moral principles[24] and has nothing specifically to do with justice in its distinctive sense.

However, even those who accept that there is a principle of humanity might argue that, because it is possible to apply this principle fairly or unfairly, it must therefore be regarded as, in some sense, a principle of justice. If, in the process of relieving need, the distributor has regard to considerations other than need, is this not unjust?

To meet this point we require to refer back to the distinction which I drew on p. 3 between formal and material justice: fairness in the application of rules and fairness in the content of rules. Formal injustice, the unfairness of treating similar cases differently, does arise in the administration of the principle of humanity (once this principle is adopted as an authorized norm within a given group of people), as it must do over the administration of any rule. But the fact that formal injustice occurs when there is inconsistency in the application of a rule does not make that rule a rule of justice (otherwise all positive rules would be rules of justice). In fact formal justice has no relevance to the problem with which we are concerned, the formulation and justification of a principle of humanity.

[22] R. W. Baldwin calls 'justice' in the distribution of beneficence 'quasi-justice': *Social Justice* (London: Pergamon Press, 1966), p. 115.

[23] Cf. G. Vlastos, 'Justice and Equality' in R. B. Brandt, *Social Justice*, pp. 45–53.

[24] Cf. R. S. Downie and Elizabeth Telfer, *Respect for Persons* (London: Allen and Unwin, 1969), Chap. 2.

16   CAMPBELL

Returning to the practical implications of this analysis, I would stress again the political consequences of the confusion of justice and humanity: namely that, because in most people's minds justice is closely associated with merit, to say that the obligation to help a needy person is one of justice is often taken to imply that his need is the consequence of maltreatment or exploitation. If this does not seem plausible in a particular case, then the conclusion may be drawn that there is no obligation to assist that needy person or certain classes of needy persons. That is, when our obligation to help the poor is presented as one of justice, then deserved, self-inflicted and perhaps fortuitous suffering may tend to be passed over. A sounder conceptual foundation on which to base the sort of universal obligation to those in need pre-supposed in many theories of the welfare state is to identify the obligation to relieve distress, whatever its origin, as one of humanity. This frees the apologist of the welfare principle from association with the tricky and, some would say, vanishing concept of desert and sets out in a direct and unambiguous manner the real moral basis of his political views.

Because need is, as we have seen, often a factor to be considered in the determination of the treatment appropriate to deserving and undeserving persons it is easy to see why it should be thought that there is a universal connection between justice and need. But if we distinguish the obligation to relieve need when it is associated with merit in one of the ways I have outlined from the obligation to relieve basic need as such, then we are likely to get a clearer picture of the twin sources of our obligation to relieve poverty, namely justice and humanity, and may even perhaps be led to give priority to humanity over justice in those cases where they conflict. For it is compatible with such a conceptual scheme to say that justice, as the proportional distribution of desired goods according to merit, is a moral luxury as compared with the humanitarian objectives of the welfare principle.

[2]

JUSTICE TO CHARITY

By Loren E. Lomasky

I. Introduction

Despite what one may be led to believe by breathless reports in the media, the acme of misery in America is not the woes, financial and otherwise, of Donald Trump and Michael Jackson. People lose their jobs, have their assets drained by reversals of fortune, suffer from illiteracy, malnutrition, lack of shelter, and other mishaps. The circumstances in which they find themselves are genuinely distressing. It would be an odd understanding indeed that failed to find these circumstances directly relevant to what morality asks of us. If morality is to count for anything, then surely it must take notice of exigent need. This is not merely the deliverance of a late twentieth-century Western moral consciousness massaged by the blessings of comparative affluence and graced with a new-found awareness of social justice. All traditional ethical codes of which I am aware, sacred and secular, demand that one take the distress of one's neighbor as bearing on one's own activities. "Am I my brother's keeper?" is the question; the well-nigh universal answer is "Yes." The disposition to be moved by and respond to distress is the virtue of *charity*.

It would, then, seem undeniable that among the moral duties that confront us are duties of charity. The proper recipients of such duties are those who are, either locally or globally, unfortunate[1] and for whom relief from distress is not countermanded by other moral considerations.[2] The proper bearers of the obligation are those who are situated so as to be able to respond to the misfortune and who would not be unduly burdened by doing so.[3] The precise contours will, of course, be determined

---

[1] By *global* misfortune I mean a set of circumstances that, taken together, render a person's life miserable on the whole. A *local* misfortune is one that disadvantages an individual at some particular time or with regard to some particular aspect of her doings while having little or no effect on the remainder of her affairs. So, for example, destitution is a global misfortune, while being hot, tired, eight months pregnant, and unable to find a seat on the bus is a local misfortune. What counts as appropriate charitable relief will be a function in part of whether the misfortune one aims to alleviate is global or local.

[2] E.g., it is not (under ordinary circumstances) an instance of charity to pass a hacksaw to a justly imprisoned felon.

[3] Sometimes we teach our children: "Be charitable to those less fortunate than yourself." This may pass muster as elementary moral pedagogy, but as a general prescription concerning when and toward whom to be charitable it is deficient for at least three reasons: (i) If you are *very fortunate*, then some of those less fortunate than yourself will be far removed from the domain of eligible charity recipients; multimillionaires are not obliged to bestow

32

by the circumstances in which the recipient and bearer of the duty find themselves. Much remains to be specified, but at least this much seems clear: unless morality recognizes strict duties of charity, it is insufficiently responsive to the plain fact that the woe of other persons *matters*.

In what follows I shall argue that this way of putting the matter is mistaken. One can maintain both that an adequate morality takes the misfortunes of other people to be a salient datum and that positing a duty of charity is a misconceived way to underscore that salience. That misconception is, however, deeply embedded in the strain of ethical thinking that has dominated the modern era, what I shall call the "jurisprudential paradigm." Briefly, if morality is modeled on law, such that its subject matter is taken to be individuals' rights and duties, then all moral concerns will be parsed in those terms. Morality will speak in a stentorian voice concerning what *must be done* and what *must not be done*; and with regard to that which is neither, it will adopt a discrete silence. The absence of command is *permission*, and how one chooses to behave within the zone of permissions is a matter of personal preference removed from the imperatives of morality-as-justice. If I am neither morally obligated nor forbidden to play golf, then it is simply not a matter of legitimate moral concern — not for me, not for anyone — whether or not I elect to golf. Similarly, if I am merely permitted but not obligated to relieve the distress of other persons, then whether I do so or not is beyond the purview of moral concern. Because the consequent will seem false to all but the doughtiest surviving Social Darwinists, the antecedent must be rejected. Ergo, duties of charity.

Note that the preceding argument presupposes what I have called the "jurisprudential paradigm" of morality. If, however, the language of morals is more capacious than a discourse of rights and duties, it remains an open question whether acknowledging the salience of other people's distress is best rendered by positing rights to receive charity and duties to provide it.[4] I shall, after disposing in Section II of a superficially appealing argument, contend in Sections III and IV that the jurisprudential par-

---

largesse on mere unimillionaires. (ii) If you are *very unfortunate*, then you are not generally obliged to assume further burdens in order to lighten the load of those even worse off than yourself. (iii) Because misfortunes are local as well as global, charity may call on you to respond to a (local) misfortune of someone who is (globally) more fortunate than yourself.

A complete taxonomy of the duty of charity would require additional qualifications and distinctions beyond those of this and the previous two notes. Because the aim of this essay is not to explicate but rather to cast doubt on the notion of a duty of charity, I abstain from such labors.

[4] Whether (i) each right has as its shadow a duty resting on some individual or set of individuals to satisfy that right, and (ii) all duties derive from the rights of some individual(s), are discussed in the philosophical literature under the rubric of the *correlativity of rights and duties*. Note that these are two logically independent theses; (i) may obtain even though (ii) does not. (The reverse is also logically possible, but I am unaware of its advocacy in the literature.) In Section IV, I examine the claim that duties of charity are *imperfect duties*, duties for which correlativity does not obtain.

adigm is impoverished. Rights and duties are the shell of morality, the hard and inflexible casing that safeguards the soft tissue of our vital practical concerns. Absent the protection provided by that tough exterior, we would be unable to give effect to that which matters to us as moral beings. However, the shell taken by itself is lifeless. Less metaphorically, I shall argue that morality should be understood as extending to the zone of permissions, and that this is where most questions of aid to the less well-off are located—most but not all: Section V investigates the case that can be made for welfare rights. It is acknowledged that, under a limited range of circumstances and to a limited extent, there may exist rights to receive aid and duties to provide it; but, for reasons adduced there and in Section VI, these are relatively minor adjuncts to the virtue of charity. Section VII offers brief concluding remarks.

II. Why There Can Be No Duties of Charity: A Bad Argument

Someone might try to short-circuit duties of charity in this way: To be charitable toward someone entails more than transferring needed goods. It additionally requires that one do so from the appropriate sort of motive. One must give, it is said, "from the heart." When the United Way volunteer comes round and extracts from the office curmudgeon a grudgingly tight-lipped, tight-fisted pledge, the curmudgeon gives to a charity but does not give charitably. Thus, if there is a duty to be charitable, it is at least in part a duty to act from appropriate feelings and attitudes. These, though, are not under our voluntary control. I can directly will to give ten dollars, but not to do so with an open and loving spirit. By an application of "ought implies can," it follows that there can be no general duties of charity.

There are two respects in which the argument is defective. First, and most obviously, it assumes that duties of charity are necessarily duties to be charitable. We can, however, distinguish between charitable *persons* and charitable *acts*. A charitable person is one who is disposed to be moved by the needs of others and who, in virtue of that disposition (and not some incentive external to it), regularly acts to relieve those needs. The virtue manifested is the biblical quality of *agapê/caritas*, the third term in the triad "faith, hope, and charity" (better: "love"). A charitable act, by way of contrast, intends the melioration of another person's misfortune but may or may not take that melioration to be intrinsically desirable.[5] So, for example, if the office curmudgeon makes his pledge

---

[5] Reference to intention is necessary because one who inadvertently or accidentally advantages another has not thereby performed a charitable act. If the remains of the pizza I toss into my garbage pail are subsequently scavenged by a hungry family, I have not performed the charitable act of feeding them, let alone acted charitably toward them. This is true, I believe, even if I am aware when I toss out the pizza that there is a very high likelihood that it will be discovered and eaten.

because not to do so would be to make himself an object of unfriendly gossip, he has nonetheless performed a charitable act. To borrow a locution from Aristotle, he has done what the charitable man would do, though he has not done it as the charitable man would do it. Even if it is not the duty of anyone to be charitable, one can have duties to perform charitable actions.[6]

Second, and more speculatively, it is questionable whether all "oughts" do imply "cans." If my entire fortune is nine dollars, that fact is a decisive counter to the claim that I ought to give ten dollars. It is less clear that my being of a cold and haughty temperament renders it false that I ought to give cheerfully. That I am unable through an act of will to feel charitable toward my fellows has less the character of an excuse than a moral indictment. There are not only certain things that I ought to do but also ways I ought to be. If I fall short of those ways, then I am, other things equal, morally deficient. The insertion of the *ceteris paribus* clause is to acknowledge that external happenstance can mitigate or eliminate one's responsibility for character defects. But the mere fact that I am not able to reform my character through a simple act of will is not itself an excusing condition.[7]

I may be culpable for the current deficient state of my character in virtue of antecedent voluntary actions that led to my current disability. If, for example, habitual self-indulgence has deadened me to the distress of others, then my absence of feeling is a condition for which I bear responsibility. Had I then chosen to act differently I would now be a different sort of person, one who is not only capable of performing charitable actions but also of being charitable. So construed, this is an instance of "ought implies could have done."[8] But even if no causal chain is traceable between past performances and current dispositions, it does not follow that the latter are a matter of moral indifference. It may be inappropriate for others to blame the individual whose actions are acceptable though his character is deficient, but it surely is appropriate for the agent himself to

[6] Arguing similarly, Kant declares: "[L]ove as an inclination cannot be commanded. But beneficence from duty, when no inclination impels it and even when it is opposed by a natural and unconquerable aversion, is practical love, not pathological [!] love; it resides in the will and not in the propensities of feeling, in principles of action and not in tender sympathy; and it alone can be commanded" (Immanuel Kant, *Foundations of the Metaphysics of Morals*, 400, trans. Lewis White Beck [Indianapolis: Bobbs-Merrill, 1959], p. 16).

[7] Sidgwick comments: "I agree that it cannot be a strict duty to feel an emotion so far as it is not directly within the power of the Will to produce it at any given time. Still . . . it seems to me that this emotional element is included in our common notion of Charity or Philanthropy, regarded as a Virtue: and I think it paradoxical to deny that it raises the mere beneficent disposition of the will to a higher degree of excellence, and renders its effect better" (Henry Sidgwick, *The Methods of Ethics*, 7th ed. [1907; reprint, New York: Dover, 1966], p. 239).

[8] Aristotle writes in *Nicomachean Ethics*, trans. Terence Irwin (Indianapolis: Hackett, 1985), 1114a20–23: "It was originally open to the person who is [now] unjust or intemperate not to acquire this character; hence he has it willingly, though once he has acquired it he can no longer get rid of it."

LOREN E. LOMASKY

reflect, "I should be more open in my giving; I would be a better man if I were to do so." This is to offer a straightforwardly moral assessment, but it does not invoke any precondition of causal possibility.

The upshot is that one's inability to exercise direct control over one's feelings is no logical bar to the existence of duties of charity. One may, at a minimum, be morally obligated to perform charitable actions and, maximally, to be a charitable person.

III. AN ALTERNATIVE TO CHARITY AS RIGHT OR DUTY

I noted in Section I that the jurisprudential paradigm presents a dilemma: either the misfortunes of others are not morally salient considerations or they generate duties to render aid. Why, though, should this understanding of morality be embraced?

With very few exceptions, modern moral theory has taken as its fundamental project the derivation of rationally acceptable means for the resolution of interpersonal conflicts. Individuals' interests collide; that is why morality is both possible and necessary. In the absence of some peaceable means through which differences can be brokered, the denouement is a perpetual state of war in which life is, Hobbes tells us, "solitary, poor, nasty, brutish, and short."[9] And so, from Hobbes onward, it is the quest for appropriate articles of peace to which philosophers have bent their efforts. An ethic of rights and duties is the inevitable product. If some item is contested between two parties, then a resolution of that conflict must of necessity indicate which of them has a right to that item and which a duty to withdraw. Just so long as rights and duties are acknowledged, the parties can live peaceably together. What more can be asked of a theory of ethics?

Considerably more, or so was the prevailing view of premodern moral philosophy. For the ancients, the primary practical question was not "What are my duties?" but "How may I live well?" Though answers differed in particulars, the common theme is that the good life is one informed by the *virtues*. A moral virtue is understood to be a settled disposition to feel and act in intrinsically good ways. "Why be virtuous?" is a question that admits only of the question-begging answer: "Because virtues are those good-in-themselves components of a life that is itself inherently good." Less easy to supply but more informative is a specification of which traits are virtues and how these may be inculcated, harmonized, and sustained. An examination of classical responses to these questions would be out of place here, but what is worth considering is the rationale underlying this conception of ethics.

---

[9] Thomas Hobbes, *Leviathan* [1651], ed. Michael Oakeshott (New York: Macmillan, 1962), Part 1, ch. 13.

Moral inquiry in the ancient world begins with the assumption that
each of us has as a core interest the achievement of *eudaimonia*, a flourishing life. Thus, it is of considerable urgency for an individual that she
identify and come to possess its components. Because we are social animals, it is undeniably the case that one such component of *eudaimonia* is
a facility of avoiding conflicts with others and settling those conflicts more
or less amicably when they do arise. Therefore, justice — the natural home
of rights and duties — is among the virtues. The Greek world is in many
ways distant from our own, but it was one in which there existed a well-
developed conception of the importance of law as an arbiter of the affairs
of contentious human beings. The Greeks' horror of the disorder that
would ensue in the absence of law was at least as great as our own, and
thus the conditions of justice receive considerable attention in their philosophical thought.

Nonetheless, Greek ethical inquiry extends considerably beyond the
search for an interpersonal conflict-resolution device. There is more to the
achievement of *eudaimonia* than scrupulously fulfilling one's duties to others and claiming from them one's rights. Indeed, of at least as much interest to these philosophers as *inter*personal conflict is conflict waged
*intra*personally. They observed that individuals often prize in an ineffectual sort of way goods that their conduct routinely contravenes. One who
recognizes that temperance is integral to living well may simultaneously
choose to eat and drink more than he should; a man who realizes that he
ought to confront a danger may instead flee from it. *Akrasia*, "weakness
of will," is inimical to *eudaimonia* insofar as it thwarts pursuit of one's own
good (and not, say, because it thwarts the "greatest happiness of the
greatest number"). The primary problem is not right relations with others but rather the establishment and maintenance of an appropriate balance within oneself,[10] and this problem was typically depicted through
a set piece in which different "parts of the soul" war with each other,
"appetite" confronting "reason" with directive mastery of the self at stake.

That is not to maintain that other-regarding conduct is of merely
peripheral or instrumental concern. Because the good life is a life lived
among others, right relations with them is a constituent of living well. An
individual without friends or with the wrong kind of friends, or with
inappropriate affections toward them, is handicapped; and thus Aristotle
devotes two books of the *Nicomachean Ethics* to an examination of the conditions of friendship. One who lives as a wolf among men thereby renders himself bestial, and thus a disposition to act justly toward one's
compatriots is similarly prized as a constituent of *eudaimonia*. Note,

---

[10] It is the absence of such an internal balance that we overhear the Apostle lamenting
in Romans 7:15 when he confesses: "That which I would I do not, while that which I would
not I do."

LOREN E. LOMASKY

though, that the value of duties and rights is not simply a given from which ethics commences, but instead flows from an appreciation of the personal value to an individual of leading as good a life as she can. Given this conception, it would be thoroughly misleading to say that one has a "duty to be virtuous." That would suggest that virtue is something onerous, the price of admission to civil society.[11] It would be better to say that the virtuous person is *privileged* with regard to enjoying the necessary preconditions for living a fully human life. Virtue is its own reward, not in some prissy, otherworldly sense, but insofar as it is manifested in a flourishing life in this world.

I shall not offer here an extended argument concerning the respects in which the ancient conception of ethics may be judged more satisfactory than that which infuses the modern, primarily liberal tradition, or, for that matter, those respects in which liberal thought importantly supplements its predecessor.[12] The purpose of the preceding excursus into the history of moral thinking is to remind ourselves that a framework of rights and duties is not the only structure within which we can find a place for the moral salience of the misfortunes of others. A humane individual who esteems living decently among others heeds their distress irrespective of an alleged duty to aid. He does so because he understands that he has a good, that they have a good, and that these are largely complementary rather than ingredients of a grim zero-sum game. The visage of the mean-spirited, miserly man is unlovely, and not only as viewed by others; those of us who have a tolerably adequate conception of what it is to live well would not wish to become such a person. The liability of misanthropy is not only that it showers negative externalities on others but that it precludes one from experiencing the range of goods that are enjoyed only through successful sociality.

Eudaimonia, therefore, incorporates "liberality" or "magnanimity." These virtues are not quite the same as charity; they incorporate a sense of *noblesse oblige*, the open-handedness a superior shows to an inferior. Charity, by way of contrast, is expressive of a relationship between individuals who, despite differences in fortune or rank, are seen as being in some fundamental sense equals.[13] The reflection "There but for the grace of God go I" exemplifies that disposition. This may be why classical Greece and Rome lacked a precise equivalent to the concept of *charity*; it

---

[11] The price-of-admission view is embraced with characteristic bluntness by Hobbes and, disclaimers and qualifications aside, is adopted by most of the tradition of modern moral philosophy.

[12] A more extended statement is offered in Loren Lomasky, *Persons, Rights, and the Moral Community* (New York: Oxford University Press, 1987), especially ch. 3, "Projects and the Nature of Ethics."

[13] The paradigmatic relation in which natural equals stand is, for classical philosophy, friendship, and Aristotle explicitly observes that, while friendship of a sort can obtain between persons who differ markedly in their stations and virtues, true friendship is feasible only between equals.

emerges within scriptural religion as a corollary of the doctrine that all men partake of a brotherhood within God's creation. From that viewpoint equality is basic, differences in position adventitious. Thus, the classification by the Church of charity as a *theological* virtue. But whatever the origins of the concept may have been, charity does not necessarily presuppose a theistic orientation. Other stances can offer a surrogate basis for the equality on which charity rests, e.g., Kant's insistence that persons, unlike things, are ends in themselves who equally are imbued with worth.[14] Nor is it the case that, in common usage, "charity" invariably attaches itself to a presupposition of equality: we speak nonmetaphorically about acting charitably toward children and even animals. Fine points of semantics aside, there is broad recognition within both the Greco-Roman and biblical traditions that openness to the needs of others is a virtue.

IV. Charity as an Imperfect Duty

Once the jurisprudential paradigm becomes dominant, it is not surprising that a corresponding shift in the conception of charity follows. Philosophers as distinct as Kant and J. S. Mill invoke the category of *imperfect duty* to maintain that charity is prescribed by morality yet is a matter for the free, uncompelled performance of individuals. A perfect duty is characterized as one in which the manner, object, and occasion of performance are precisely specified, while imperfect duties are "those in which, though the act is obligatory, the particular occasions of performing it are left to our choice, as in the case of charity or beneficence, which we are indeed bound to practice but not toward any definite person, nor at any prescribed time."[15] Thus, while it is a strict obligation of morality to be charitable (or: to perform charitable acts), the mode in which the obligation is discharged is to be chosen by the agent.

This attempt to combine duty and discretion is, for at least four reasons, awkward. First, there is no clean line that can be drawn between duties whose manner of performance is specifiable and those whose manner of performance is not. If Mark has borrowed five dollars from Martha, then it is a perfect duty (of justice) that he repay the sum; but, at his

---

[14] "In the realm of ends everything has either a *price* or a *dignity*. Whatever has a price can be replaced by something else as its equivalent; on the other hand, whatever is above all price, and therefore admits of no equivalent, has a dignity. . . . Thus morality and humanity, so far as it is capable of morality, alone have dignity" (Kant, *Foundations of the Metaphysics of Morals*, 434–35, p. 53). For Kant, humans are equal most fundamentally as beings who are capable of being motivated to moral action.

[15] John Stuart Mill, *Utilitarianism*, ed. Oskar Piest (Indianapolis: Bobbs-Merrill, 1957), p. 61. Mill goes on to remark: "In the more precise language of philosophic jurists, duties of perfect obligation are those duties in virtue of which a correlative *right* resides in some person or persons; duties of imperfect obligation are those moral obligations which do not give birth to any right."

option, he may repay by cash or check, a little earlier or later, with a smile on his face or a frown. The contractual arrangement between them may be specific with regard to any or all of these conditions, but that is to note that specificity is a matter of degree among perfect duties rather than a criterion distinguishing perfect from imperfect duties.

Second, to the extent that imperfect duties lack specificity, it becomes difficult or impossible to determine whether they have been fulfilled. Suppose that charity is indeed an imperfect duty; then it is unquestionably the case that someone who lives out her entire life without ever once coming to the aid of another has failed to discharge the duty. Suppose, however, that at age seventeen she had extended aid and then decided that she had had enough of that sort of thing, thereafter keeping her wallet tightly shut. (Or, alternatively, she lives an initial sixty years entirely unblemished by a single charitable act but resolves to perform a few once she is pensioned off.) Has the duty of charity been discharged? "No," one may respond, "that's too little of a good thing." But if that is too little, what, then, is enough? We might, to pick a number, hold that an individual is obligated to take advantage of no fewer than 25 percent of the opportunities for charitable action that come her way. Ignore the objection that any such ratio is thoroughly arbitrary and unmeasurable in practice; it suffices to note that the proposal seeks to eliminate the intolerable vagueness of imperfect duties by transforming them into perfect duties. A duty to be charitable 25 percent of the time is as determinate as a sharecropper's obligation to give 25 percent of his produce to the landlord. The attempt to transform imperfect duties into "real" duties is akin to the military tactic of saving the village by destroying it.

Third, it is not usually the case that any special regard or esteem is due to one when he fulfills his duties. If Mark pays Martha the five dollars he owes, perfunctory thanks would be an appropriate response. Should she fulsomely laud him for this act and praise him to others, Mark would have reason to feel miffed. Such extravagance in praise suggests that he is the sort of man who cannot be expected routinely to settle his trifling debts. If charity is a duty, then its performance is no occasion for special mention; one is simply doing what one is obliged to do anyhow. Charity, though, is meritorious. We not only approve but admire the charitable person.[16]

---

[16] It can be argued that charity becomes admirable only to the extent that it is supererogatory, above and beyond the call of duty. There is a baseline, the objection continues, below which charity is merely the fulfillment of duty and is to be approved no more than other dutiful acts. Charitable performances above the baseline are, however, meritorious.

There is, no doubt, some truth to the suggestion. We will not be inclined to esteem the person who only occasionally chooses to aid others. However, this reflection only marginally buttresses the imperfect-duty model. We lack the ability to ascertain where the hypothesized baseline lies; and if we could do so, we would then have to find some analytical category other than imperfect duty for charitable acts that fall above it. The attempt to assimilate charity within the jurisprudential understanding will have been de facto abandoned.

Fourth, and most serious, imperfect duties lack a proper beneficiary. They are not duties to anyone in particular, and thus if I fail to discharge an imperfect duty, there is no one who can justifiably complain that I have thereby wronged him. If I owe ten people one dollar each (a perfect duty), then should I fail to pay any one of them, that person has been dealt with unfairly. But if it is alleged that I have a duty (imperfect) to pay ten dollars to any one of ten people (my option which), a failure to comply is a moral wrong that wrongs no one. Had I given Anderson rather than Jones the entire sum, Jones would have had no complaint at getting nothing; but then my paying no one leaves Jones no worse off than he would have been had I discharged the duty. Symmetrical reasoning applies to each of the ten.[17] The conclusion is that these duties are imperfect in the colloquial sense, that they are *luft*-duties detached from the interests of assignable individuals. Lacking a point, their status within the overall moral economy is mysterious.

Note that charity understood as a virtue does not suffer from the liabilities itemized above. That there is no sharp line separating charitable from uncharitable individuals is not a theoretical defect; dispositional traits are naturally understood as being arrayed on a continuum rather than on/off. To be charitable is to be possessed of the appropriate beliefs and attitudes about how one ought to respond to the misfortunes of others, and to be disposed to express these through appropriate action. It would be an absurd mischaracterization to identify as charitable someone who only on rare occasions extends aid to another, or who, when he gives, does so grudgingly. It is similarly absurd to regard the charitable person simply as someone who is punctilious about the fulfillment of his duties. To be charitable is not merely to do what one (morally) must but to evince a commitment to pursue one's own good in a way that meshes with the good of others. That is why the charitable man is a proper object of esteem. Conversely, the complaint properly lodged against an individual deficient in charity is not that he has withheld items he is not at liberty to keep but rather that, by grasping too tightly onto that which is his, he thereby evinces disdain for the well-being of others. We do well to avoid forcing charity into the Procrustean bed of duty. It does not fit. The construction of ersatz imperfect duties multiplies rather than solves philosophical problems. Charity—and here is meant charity conceived as a

---

[17] It is tempting to retort: "*All* of them are wronged because what I owed to each was a 0.1 probability of receiving the entire amount." The objection misfires. Suppose that my strategy for discharging imperfect duties is always to give preference, if possible, to someone whose name begins with a vowel. Given the presence of Anderson, Jones had no chance of receiving my largesse, yet I have complied with my duty. "Jones can complain that the vowel selection-strategy itself constitutes unfair treatment of him." That is true only if what is owed Jones (and each of the other nine) is an equal chance of getting the money, as with a fairly conducted lottery. That is to say, however, that the duty owed is not an imperfect one at all, but rather a perfect duty to each that he enjoy an *ex ante* 0.1 probability of receiving the amount (coupled with the perfect duty *ex post* to pay the winner ten dollars).

42   LOREN E. LOMASKY

social virtue—is a richer notion than can be paralleled by a legal model
of rights and duties.

V. CHARITY AND WELFARE RIGHTS

Although the concept of charity cannot be amalgamated without considerable loss into the jurisprudential paradigm, it does not thereby follow that there is no place whatsoever in the moral lexicon for rights to
receive aid—welfare rights—and corresponding duties to provide it.
Charity is a virtue we have reason to prize in ourselves and others
irrespective of what we judge individuals' rights to be, but just as it is a
misapplication of Ockham's razor to attempt to reduce all morally salient
considerations to rights and duties, so is it mistaken to hold that a virtue
ethics is complete unto itself. Our view of morality will be misshapen if
we dispense with either.

The proper home of virtues is human *distinction*. To possess a particular virtue is to excel in the domain in which the virtue is operative. So
understood, virtues include but extend beyond the realm of morality. The
Greek term *aretê*, which we usually translate as "virtue," is more accurately rendered by "excellence." Thus, Aristotle can speak without any
hint of paradox of the *aretê* of a shoemaker, a horse, or even a knife, and
not simply the virtues of a human being as such.[18] Our use of the term
"virtue" has largely become confined to morality (and, under the influence of Victorian sensibilities, specifically to sexual morality), but even
contemporary usage allows us to say of Barry Bonds that he exemplifies
to a high degree the virtues of a consummate baseball player insofar as
he hits, fields, and runs with distinction.

When we attempt to improve ourselves or educate our children, we
take as a model for emulation (I do not mean simply mimicry; creative
flexibility is a component of excellence) the virtuous individual. That person is the incarnate standard of high-level achievement. To learn what it
is accurately and coolly to appraise and confront dangers, we observe the
courageous man and school ourselves to behave similarly; if we aim to
develop skills in scientific or scholarly endeavors, we take our bearings
from those who possess theoretical wisdom. No set of rules in a copy-
book can encapsulate what is required for mastery in an area of practical
endeavor. That is not to say that rules are entirely without utility, but to
note that how, when, and where one is to apply them is not something
that can be learned by rote. A kind of apprenticeship is required, and that
incorporates empathetic identification with those who have already

---

[18] Within the class of virtues that pertain to human beings as such, Aristotle recognizes
two distinct subclasses, moral virtues and intellectual virtues. Just as the man who is tem-
perate or magnanimous displays a characteristic human virtue, so too does the skilled solver
of scientific problems.

achieved excellence, coupled with a regimen of habituation designed to make their traits one's own. To some extent this can be done vicariously; history and literature contribute at least as much to moral education as do tomes of moral philosophy.

Some virtues have wide-ranging application. Regardless of what ends we seek, we will do better if we act with steadfastness, temperance, and prudence. Others are more narrow in their scope, such as the specific virtues of the baseball player. Because of differences in scope, we have reason to prize some virtues above others: compassion counts for more than baseball-hitting skill.[19] Still, to the extent that we take some trait to be a virtue, we esteem the individuals who possess it — Barry Bonds as well as Mother Theresa. Were we to do what they do, we would be pleased if we could do it as they do it.

Rights and duties operate within a different sphere. Persons' rights impose what Robert Nozick calls "side constraints" on action.[20] They do not mandate ends to be achieved, but rather limit the means that may permissibly be employed to realize whatever ends one might have. It is in that sense that "Do not violate rights!" acts as a constraint on goal-directed action. Rights generate correlative duties. Depending on the right in question, these duties can be held "against the world" or against some specifiable individual. If Martha has a right to speak her mind freely, then everyone has a duty not to prevent her from doing so. If, by way of contrast, she has a right that Mark repay the five dollars he borrowed, then Mark (and no one else) has a duty to remit that amount.

While virtues aim at distinction, rights establish a moral minimum. The *least* that is permissible in one's conduct is to respect others' rights. I may — and should — do much more than merely avoid transgressing rights, but I *must not* do less. That is why no special appreciation is due to someone merely for compliance with duties. "You've gone a whole day without stealing so much as one thing from me; thanks a lot!" is either a joke or an insult.[21] We rarely invoke the category of rights when considering relationships that by their nature presuppose considerably more than minimal decency between the parties: proper conduct of friend with friend, lover with lover, or parent with child is not adequately expressed

---

[19] If an activity is judged to be unworthy in its own right, we will not admire mastery of it. Carlos the Jackal is notably more talented as an assassin than is John W. Hinckley, Jr., but we do not hold him up as a model for emulation. But one who thinks differently about the propriety of assassination — who is, say, engaged in the business of training junior hit men — may quite reasonably within that context assign *The Life and Times of Carlos* as required reading for his students.

[20] See Robert Nozick, *Anarchy, State, and Utopia* (New York: Basic Books, 1974), pp. 28–35.

[21] If circumstances render respect for rights exceptionally difficult or are such as would lead many people to give short shrift to rights, then gratitude becomes appropriate. We praise the person who makes an effort to return the cash-filled wallet found on the sidewalk because we recognize that most other finders would have pocketed the money. Here compliance with rights merges with moral excellence, and it becomes appropriate to import responses at home with the latter into the former.

44   LOREN E. LOMASKY

in the language of rights and duties. When we do resort to that language it usually indicates that the relation has entered a pathological state. I do not mean to say that there are no rights and duties obtaining, say, between spouses, but rather that success in a marital relation entails far more than the minimal deference of respect for rights that is owed to a stranger.

Rights, then, are both maximally weighty and minimally demanding moral claims. The two aspects go together. I am obliged to respect the rights of individuals for whom I have no great sympathy, for whom I even have an active distaste. "Love your neighbor" may be a sustainable injunction when the neighbor is inherently lovable, but to love someone who is clearly odious demands a moral heroism that few of us possess. To *commend* heroism is one thing, to *insist* on it another, and a morality that aspires to be practical necessarily eschews the latter. (It is different for religions. There the telos is not harmonious relations among human beings, but an imitation of the divine perfection.) Grandiose manifestos of "basic human rights" undercut themselves by pitching the demands they would place on us at a level higher than that with which we can reasonably be asked to comply. They mistakenly conflate the language of virtue with the language of rights. Such conflation has become unfortunately frequent in recent years; it sometimes seems that no individual or group is able to formulate a moral agenda (for better working conditions; for kindness to animals; for courteous behavior toward those of a different race or those who are prone to unconventional sexual practices; for whatever) without an announcement proclaiming the discovery of a heretofore unknown "right" that is henceforth to be zealously maintained. This rights inflation is yet another unwelcome consequence of the hegemony of the jurisprudential paradigm.

Even if we set such extravagance aside, there is room for considerable controversy concerning just what rights there are, who has them, and why. As crucial as these questions are, it is beyond the capacity of this essay to develop a theoretical response.[22] I shall instead offer a few remarks to show why it is at least plausible to believe that an adequate accounting of rights and correlative duties will locate them somewhere within the territory that has been marked out by the tradition of classical liberalism. By "classical liberalism" I mean the view holding that the preponderance of basic rights[23] individuals possess are negative, man-

---

[22] I attempt to do so in *Persons, Rights, and the Moral Community*.

[23] The term "basic rights" is meant to pick out roughly the class of rights that have sometimes been denoted "moral rights" or "human rights." They are to be distinguished from (i) special rights, such as those established by a contract between two parties or that might obtain between individuals enjoying a special relationship such as parent and child; and (ii) rights created by particular enactments of a government or another collectivity capable of originating rights. I prefer the term "basic rights" because it is less question-begging than the alternatives: "moral rights" may suggest that special rights are something other than moral, while "human rights" implies that all and only human beings are the beneficiaries of rights claims while, for example, animals are not and incurably comatose people are.

dating forbearance on the part of others but not active provision of aid. "Libertarianism," as I understand the term, is the view maintaining that *all* basic rights are negative. Libertarian theories, therefore, constitute a subclass of classical liberalism but are not coextensive with it.

Why should we suppose that morality needs to recognize the existence of rights? After all, rights are awkward things, blocking the reformist agendas of those who are persuaded that they could cook some wonderful omelets if only they were permitted to break a few eggs in the process. The answer immediately suggesting itself is that rueful experience has taught us to be suspicious of the culinary credentials of these would-be chefs. Many of the greatest paroxysms of misery human beings have known, not least those that have marred the twentieth century, were brought about by reformer/revolutionaries confident in their ability to engineer Heaven on Earth. What they brought us instead were living hells. If we can maintain a rule of rights, we may be able to thwart their worst excesses.

Rights so understood are indeed plausible, but they are also superficial. They are no more than a concession to human fallibility. Were we better able dispassionately to judge the effect of our designs, so as to ensure that they actually are conducive to the greatest happiness of the greatest number, we could entirely dispense with the category of rights. Since our judgments are unreliable, especially when passions or interests are engaged, rights serve as handy "rules of thumb," generally reliable signposts by means of which we can more efficiently advance overall welfare. They are superficial because, as rules of thumb, they play second fiddle to general utility. We are to respect the rights of Jones (and Anderson, and Smith, and so on) only because we thereby do better with regard to overall welfare, not because of any special moral status enjoyed by Jones. Were we more gifted social engineers, we would be granted carte blanche to sacrifice any or all of Jones's interests whenever opportunities to enhance overall utility beckoned.

What is left out of the preceding paragraph's account is how things present themselves specifically to Jones. He might complain with no little justice against those proposing to sacrifice him to the great god Utility: "I understand that by quashing my interests you will be able to achieve benefits for others, benefits which, in terms of your impersonal standard of value, score greater than what I forfeit. But that's not good enough to satisfy me. What I have primary reason to value are those ends that are distinctively mine, those that I deeply care about. From the perspective of my *personal* standard of value, I lack sufficient reason to go along with your notions of what is socially optimal." That is to say, while annihilating Jones's interests may be justifiable according to the criteria of an abstract theory of social good, *it is not justifiable to Jones*. The result is easily generalized. Each other person has equivalent reason to object to a moral schema that would leave her own deepest concerns dispensable, that would render her a mere means to the achievement of high

overall utility totals rather than an end in herself. Correspondingly, each
has reason to value the secure enjoyment of moral space within which
she is able to act on behalf of the conception of the good that is distinctively her own.

Rights emerge as the boundary markers of moral space. They establish
a regime of mutual and reciprocal forbearance. Individuals who are
rights-holders are not obliged to be the sacrificial victims or servants of
ends distant from their own, but are instead acknowledged to possess a
moral entitlement to devote themselves to projects that individually matter to them. Rights are responsive to the urgency from the perspective of
an agent of carving out a life rendered coherent and meaningful in virtue of persistent attachment by him to his own directive ends. The rational acceptability of assuming the duties generated by the rights of others
derives from recognizing that they too have reason to demand provision
of moral space. Basic rights, then, can be characterized as "those moral
constraints that impose minimal demands on the forbearance of others
such that individuals can pursue projects amidst a world of similar
beings, each with his own life to lead, and each owing the same measure
of respect to others that they owe to him." [24]

As noted above, classical liberals have traditionally understood rights
to be predominantly negative in character. One should not suppose that
this is symptomatic of a moral myopia that blinkered an earlier, less
"socially enlightened" age. Rather, it is a strict corollary of the logic of
rights. If what people have reason to demand from others and to cede to
them in return is moral space, then the primary moral right is to be let
alone. One may do more than respect the liberty of others, but one must
not do less. This is not, as critics of liberalism have often charged, arbitrarily to place liberty above all other values. Instead, it is to recognize
that whatever it is that one may value, one needs liberty to pursue it, and
one needs it from others in the form of their noninterference. Rather than
enthroning one value above all others, liberalism decentralizes questions
of value, leaving their resolution to the private initiatives of individuals.
Freedom from interference is the freedom to direct one's affairs in accord
with one's own judgments concerning what is to be cherished and what
is to be to spurned.

A requirement of noninterference minimizes the involuntary implication of individuals in each other's designs. To require that I not violate
your liberty to pursue the ends that matter to you is less invasive than to
require me actively to further those ends. The former requirement represents the acknowledgment that pursuit of your ends is primarily your
business and not, as utilitarianism would have it, a free-floating onus
incumbent alike on all moral agents who are in a position to bring about
the ends' advancement. This can, with some qualification, be understood

---

[24] Lomasky, *Persons, Rights, and the Moral Community*, p. 83.

as a judgment about relative costs: I shall likely regard as a lesser burden an obligation not to interfere with you than a requirement to render aid. For better or worse, though, that is not a universal truth. One encounters Pecksniffians and Puritans who find it intolerable to be precluded from foisting their conceptions of the good life on everyone, and when they are too numerous or too powerful the stability of a liberal order is imperiled.[25] That is why "liberal" denotes not only a political credo but also a temperament, and why an ethic of virtues must supplement an ethic of rights and duties.

But though the logic of rights indicates that they are primarily negative, it does not entirely rule out the existence of welfare rights. What each of us needs from all others is, first and foremost, noninterference, but for those who are unlucky this may not be enough. Whenever it is feasible for individuals to act on their own behalf to secure the goods they need to live decent lives, the responsibility to provide is theirs. There is, however, no assurance that liberty will universally guarantee to all persons the requisites for living as project pursuers. For one situated on the margin of exigency, adherence to an order of mutual noninterference can be extremely costly. If the choice confronting one is either to fall below a baseline of minimally satisfactory existence or to encroach on the moral space of others, one may lack sufficient reason to acknowledge a duty of noninterference. A moral hero will, we may believe, even then respect rights, but recall that what rights entail is minimal forbearance, not heroism.[26]

If a regime of rights is to be robust, it cannot demand of individuals more than they can reasonably be expected to provide. It cannot reasonably be demanded of a man that he forbear when to do so comes at the cost of all his prospects for living as a pursuer of personally valued ends. Thus, reciprocity dictates that individuals precariously perched on the edge of exigency can be obligated to respect the liberties of others only if they are simultaneously ensured a sufficiency of material goods.[27]

So conceived, welfare rights are not at odds with the program of classical liberalism. Instead, they render it justifiable at the margin. If all are entitled to a decent minimum below which they need not fall, the ben-

---

[25] An important recent investigation of the conditions of stability for a liberal order in which people profoundly differ with regard to their basic religious and ethical conceptions is John Rawls, *Political Liberalism* (New York: Columbia University Press, 1993). Although I believe that Rawls's account is hobbled by excess attachment to the jurisprudential paradigm, I cannot pursue that argument here.

[26] Hobbes, no enthusiast for heroes, observes: "When a man is destitute of food, or other thing necessary for his life, and cannot preserve himself any other way, but by some fact against the law; as if in a great famine he take food by force, or stealth, which he cannot obtain for money nor charity; or in defence of his life, snatch away another man's sword; he is totally excused . . ." (Hobbes, *Leviathan*, Part 2, ch. 27, p. 223).

[27] Two recent arguments to essentially the same conclusion are Allen Buchanan, "Justice and Charity," *Ethics*, vol. 97 (1987), pp. 558–75; and Jeremy Waldron, "Welfare and the Images of Charity," *Philosophical Quarterly*, vol. 36 (1986), pp. 463–82.

LOREN E. LOMASKY

efits of an order of rights are withheld from no one. This conclusion is accepted by virtually all major classical-liberal theorists. Locke, for example, declares: "As justice gives every man a title to the product of his honest industry, and the fair acquisitions of his ancestors descended to him; so charity gives every man a title to so much out of another's plenty, as will keep him from extreme want, where he has no means to subsist otherwise."[28] Such contingent claims to provision by others do not undercut the primacy of negative rights. The latter are the norm; the former kick in only under exceptional conditions.[29]

I conclude that welfare rights (not properly referred to as "rights to charity") are, within strict limits, justifiable. It does not follow, of course, that these are to be identified with the grab-bag of benefactions typically put forth under the banner of "welfarism." All of the following qualify the legitimacy of welfare rights:

(1) That which individuals enjoy as a matter of right is a decent minimum. The formula is vague, but not infinitely expandable. As Locke notes, it is "extreme want" that demands melioration, not relative deprivation. Welfare rights are not a blank check that may be cashed in for whatever fosters a commodious existence.

(2) Again following Locke, it is only against "another's plenty" that individuals can press justifiable claims. Redistribution that impinges significantly on those obliged to provide is unwarranted.

(3) The claim against others to welfare goods is contingent. Those who are able to supply through their own efforts the requisites of a decent life are not to be granted a place at the public trough. Being forced to starve is tragic, but choosing to do so because one finds work unpleasant is culpable imprudence.

(4) Noninterference is the primary right, and much of the indigence we actually observe is the product of unwarranted interference. In a regime in which individuals enjoy full liberty to meet their own needs, it will not often be the case that they are unable to do so. No minimum-wage or occupational-licensure laws will restrict access to employment; zoning ordinances and housing codes will

[28] Locke, *First Treatise*, Book 1, ch. 4. Where Locke speaks of charitable relief, Hobbes explicitly turns to politically authorized welfare measures: "And whereas many men, by accident inevitable, become unable to maintain themselves by their labour; they ought not to be left to the charity of private persons; but to be provided for, as far forth as the necessities of nature require, by the laws of the commonwealth. For as it is uncharitableness in any man, to neglect the impotent; so it is in the sovereign of a commonwealth, to expose them to the hazard of such uncertain charity" (Hobbes, *Leviathan*, Part 2, ch. 30, p. 255). (I do not hereby mean to be seen as taking sides in the scholarly debate over whether Hobbes is or is not to be considered a proto-liberal.)

[29] I offer a more extended discussion of rights at the margin in "Rights without Stilts," *Harvard Journal of Law and Public Policy*, vol. 12 (Summer 1989), pp. 775–812.

not restrict access to housing; and opportunities to profit will not
be ruled out of bounds by "victimless crime" statutes. Nor will
an ethos of welfarism spawn an army of bureaucrats whose live-
lihood rests on the perpetuation of generational cycles of dependency within a welfare class.

(5) Welfare rights do not supplant private charity. Even though, in
a strict sense, there is no duty to be charitable, many individuals voluntarily elect to respond to the misfortunes of others. To
the extent that charitable provision is forthcoming, coercive redistribution is illegitimate.

Although rights to welfare are theoretically well-grounded, I am
inclined to believe that the preceding stipulations, especially the fifth, render their interest largely theoretical in a different sense. A social order
graced with individuals disposed to act compassionately toward their
unfortunate fellows will be one in which persons only infrequently need
resort to welfare rights—and one in which compassion is lacking will be
unlikely to sustain a structure of rights at all.

VI. Wide and Narrow Philanthropy

The preceding argument has identified two respects in which charitable provision is superior to reliance on welfare rights. First, while rights
are pitched only at the level of moral minima, charity as a virtue is situated within the realm of human distinction. Second, because there is a
standing presumption against coercion, voluntary subscriptions are inherently preferable to mandated transfers. To these we can add a third: charity admits of discretion and imaginative application that is both
improbable and inappropriate with regard to welfare rights.

Individuals can properly be taken to enjoy as a matter of right no more
than the basic requisites for living as independent pursuers of ends that
are their own. Mandatory transfers are, therefore, restricted to goods that
are neutral among persons' possible projects. John Rawls calls these "primary goods," characterizing them as "things that every rational man is
presumed to want," because "they normally have a use whatever a person's rational plan of life."[30] Not all primary goods are tangible; among
the primary goods that have a prominent place in Rawls's theory are
rights and liberties, powers and opportunities, and the social bases of self-
respect. Whatever their importance in that context, however, intangible
goods have limited applicability to questions of transfers and redistribution.[31] Money is the most fungible and thus the most project-neutral of

---

[30] John Rawls, *A Theory of Justice* (Cambridge, MA: Harvard University Press, 1971), p. 62.
[31] Affirmative action policies do raise such questions insofar as they aim at restructuring
the network of social opportunities.

50   LOREN E. LOMASKY

goods, and therefore justifiable redistributive measures will largely be
confined to cash transfers. Of more dubious legitimacy are in-kind transfer programs. A case can be made for public provision of housing, food,
and health services insofar as these are judged to be goods that people
need irrespective of whatever else they want. That case will, however,
rely to an uncomfortable extent on paternalistic rationales, and it is likely
to conceal hidden agendas. (The construction industry will offer abun-
dant support for public housing, agricultural interests for food stamps,
and so on.) Although there may nonetheless be some legitimate role for
in-kind provision, it is less by orders of magnitude than what is observed
in the actual functioning of welfare states.

But while state-operated redistributive programs are required to maintain neutrality among competing ends, private philanthropy operates
under no such constraint. Individuals who proffer aid are not simply
responding in mechanical fashion to the misfortunes of others. Rather,
they are giving effect to their own conceptions of how to live well among
others. In this respect charitable provision is not unlike market transactions. When buyer meets seller in the market, each brings to the trans-
action her own subjective valuations; and the bargains into which they
enter are predicated on the achievement of mutual satisfaction. Similarly,
voluntary charitable giving centrally incorporates the preferences of
donors as well as the needs of recipients. One chooses not only whether
to give but also in what amount, to which beneficiaries, in what way, and
for the sake of which ends. Private judgments concerning questions of
value are thereby given fuller expression than could ever be achieved
through mandatory, monolithic governmental programs.

This aspect of private charity is especially observable in morally contested domains. Planned Parenthood and right-to-life agencies compete
for "clients" much as do Pepsi and Coca-Cola, and the competition is
imbued with moral significance for their respective supporters. In the
United States there exist thousands of foundations, large and small, ded-
icated to advancing particular conceptions of the good. To invoke the
market metaphor again, these are key players in the marketplace of ideas.
They purvey not only cash but values. Their giving intrinsically incorporates advocacy and thus enriches public discussion.

Much philanthropic activity is, of course, distant from controversial policy matters. To the best of my knowledge, there exist no consequential
pro-cancer or anti-literacy factions.[32] Feeding the hungry, sheltering the
homeless, clothing the naked, and healing the sick are consensus values.
Still, even these charitable functions are morally rich. The choice of giving to one cause has an associated opportunity cost of alternative chari-

---

[32] Although these blights are spread in copious abundance by, respectively, tobacco
companies and the public schools, in the spirit of this essay I shall charitably assume that
furtherance of these evils is not their primary intention.

table giving (or noncharitable expenditure) forgone. A dollar donated to the Cancer Society is a dollar not given to literacy projects or to any of the myriad of other potential claimants on one's resources. Thus, to provide support even for uncontroversial causes is to make a morally significant choice in a way that writing out a check to pay one's taxes is not. That is not to make the preposterous claim that every donor does—or should—deliberate at length over each potential benefaction. Time and energy spent on deliberation also come attached to opportunity costs, and the individual who dithers endlessly before dropping a quarter into the street-corner Santa's kettle presents a ludicrous figure. Umbrella agencies such as United Way are a reasonable way to economize on scarce non-monetary resources. Still, even nondeliberated, uncontroversial acts of charity are manifestations of moral character. They are a means through which one identifies oneself with certain ends above others and expresses convictions about the sort of society in which one wishes to live and how to be a contributing member of it.

Even where ends are uncontroversial, the manner in which they are served can express a particular moral stance. Most American hospitals and private colleges were founded by religious denominations. In part, this can be explained as a service function to communicants who might otherwise have been underprovided along the relevant dimension, but it also incorporated judgments concerning what it is to live decently as a Catholic or Methodist or Jew. Institutional variety encouraged responsiveness to the diverse preferences of different clienteles. Even today, in the wake of considerable homogenization, attending Brigham Young University is noticeably different from pursuing studies at Notre Dame. Diversity would be yet greater if not for restrictive state regulation and direct service provision. The optimal extent of parochial diversity in these areas is disputable, and I do not claim that more is always better than less. Note, though, that even a determination on the part of an eleemosynary agency and its supporters to blend in rather than provide markedly distinctive services is itself a morally considerable decision.

Private charitable providers are at liberty to innovate and experiment to an extent that public bureaus are not. They do not await a legislative mandate to come into existence and are not hobbled by the terms of their enabling legislation or an encrusted civil service. Most important, they are not obligated to tender their services to all comers on an impartial basis. A public agency that withholds aid from some persons who meet formal eligibility criteria, or that provides significantly different services to different beneficiaries, thereby violates a core principle of political justice. States are required to be *neutral* among citizens, and the stipulation that they not advantage some persons or conceptions of the good above others sharply limits their discretionary authority. But that which constitutes impermissible discrimination on the part of a public agency can be entirely benign when exercised by private parties. The latter are not constrained to serve everyone alike, but may instead determine for themselves how their efforts can most effectively meet the interests of clients and supporters. If a private foundation finds that it has a comparative advantage in serving one subclass of potential beneficiaries, it is at liberty to specialize in what it does best. When old programs are seen to be of diminishing effectiveness, they can be supplanted by new ones. Experiments will be undertaken and new directions charted without fear of violating duties of neutrality.

Governmental programs are not altogether fossilized. Their administrators do not simply carry out a legislated algorithm. Programs can be modified in the light of experience, and occasionally—but only *very* occasionally—they are even allowed to die. The differences between private and public programs with regard to flexibility are matters of degree, but when these are sufficiently pronounced they amount to differences in kind. Public welfare mechanisms are simply incapable of generating knowledge to the extent that private philanthropic agencies routinely do. This is yet another reason why even the most scrupulous attention to welfare rights is incapable of substituting for the functions of private charity.

VII. Conclusion

The misfortunes of others *do* matter. Attention to this evident datum has fueled the claim that, just as we have duties not to interfere with others, so too do we have duties to provide charitable relief. The hegemony during the previous three centuries of the jurisprudential paradigm adds further impetus to this presumption and promotes the metastasis of conceptions of "social justice" that are fatal to the preservation of a realm of discretion in which individuals are able to pursue various ideals of moral excellence. But if morality is primarily a menu of rights and duties, then there is no other plausible way to recognize the salience of individuals' misfortunes than to acknowledge the legitimacy of the demands of social justice.

Against the social-justice conception I have argued that relieving distress is morally important because charity is a virtue. Individuals who are not *obligated* to aid others nonetheless *should* do so. One lives more satisfactorily among others if one is alive to their weal and woe. This is not to advance the bald claim that one should be charitable because it is in one's self-interest to be such. Rather, it is to say something substantive about how one should conceive the relation between one's own interests and the interests of others. Unless one takes the well-being of others to be complementary with one's own, charity has no application. The rich might "buy off" the poor through transfer payments, but these transactions would not amount to charity.

Welfare rights *are* a species of buying off, but that is not to impugn their moral legitimacy. The whole of rights, negative as well as positive, can be understood as an elaborate system of quids being exchanged for quos. A person has reason to forbear in her dealings with others as the price of their forbearance toward her. No antecedent affection or sympathy is presumed. What is true of rights and correlative duties, however, cannot be extrapolated to the remainder of morality.[33] The social virtues, of which charity is one, resist modeling as bloodless transactions among mutually disinterested individuals. Instead, they represent a willingness to conceive of others' fates as not entirely external to one's own. Rights and duties are morality's carapace, valuable because they protect individuals' ability to direct their affairs according to their own lights, to forge relations of intimacy and trust, and to aspire to distinction.

Charity is an excellence because it manifests care for what is worth caring about. That proposition does not presuppose some one monolithic standard of value. There are an indefinite number of ways in which one can effectively display charity because circumstances and individuals' conceptions of the good are themselves various. This multiplicity stands in contrast with the fixity that rights and duties must have if they are to be practical. Contingent rights to welfare are theoretically validated because there is a baseline below which individuals cannot be obliged to fall without thereby jeopardizing the foundations of moral reciprocity. Philanthropic activity sometimes addresses itself to lifting people above that baseline, but it also serves the interests of individuals, givers as well as receivers, along numerous other avenues. Charity's responsiveness to different varieties of the good renders it an especially apt virtue for a free society. As etymology suggests and experience confirms, liberality fits well with a liberal order. Should the ministrations of the welfare state drive out private philanthropy, we will be the poorer for it.

Philosophy, Bowling Green State University

---

[33] That is why David Gauthier's *Morals by Agreement* (Oxford: Clarendon Press, 1986) is, at the very least, mistitled.

[3]

NONCOMPARATIVE JUSTICE[1]

Joel Feinberg

S UPPOSE a cautious, empirically minded philosopher who lacks any one central insight, or any one basic analytic principle, nevertheless undertakes to write a systematic treatise on the nature of justice. Such a person would naturally wish to get a preliminary idea of the lay of the land by searching through the data from which he must eventually extract his principles. What would he find? Without doubt, an enormous diversity of things. To begin with, there is a great variety of kinds of human activity in which questions of justice can arise: distributions of goods and evils, requitals of desert, compensation for loss, appraisals of worth, judgments of criticism, administration and enforcement of rules and regulations, games of amusement, settlements of disputes (by bargaining, voting, flipping coins), contracting, buying, selling, and more.

One way of imposing unity on the data of justice is to classify these diverse activities into more general kinds. Thus, from the Scholastic period on, philosophers have spoken of allocations, punishments, and exchanges under the rubrics "distributive," "retributive," and "commutative" justice, respectively. But from the point of view of theory, this classification does not cut very deep at all, and the inference from three general kinds of human activity to three distinct and theoretically interesting forms of justice would be a *non sequitur*. At best the traditional headings constitute a useful way of ordering a survey or dividing a book into chapters. An equally useful way of classifying the data of justice and one which promises more rewarding theoretical insights is that which divides injustices[2] into those that discriminate invid-

---

[1] I have profited from positive suggestions and sharp criticisms of earlier versions of this paper from Jonathan Bennett, Bernard Gert, T. Y. Henderson, Saul Kripke, Phillip Montague, Joshua Rabinowitz, Robert Richman, Arthur Schafer, Harry Silverstein, and especially David Lyons.

[2] As many writers have observed, it is much more convenient, when doing moral philosophy, to speak of injustice than to keep to the positive term, justice. That greater convenience is an undeniable fact, but I shall not speculate here whether it has any theoretical significance.

JOEL FEINBERG

iously, those that exploit their victims, and those that wrong their victims by means of false derogatory judgments about them. This is a distinction among types of wrongs that are called injustices, and cuts across the distinctions among occasions or contexts of justice. Whatever the activity, whatever the institutional background, any injustice properly so called will be, I believe, a wrong of one of these three types.

A way of achieving still more unity is to separate the data of justice as neatly as possible into two categories. Perhaps this can be done in a variety of ways, but the one in which I am interested here sorts the various contexts, criteria, and principles of justice into those which essentially involve comparisons between various persons and those which do not. In all cases, of course, justice consists in giving a person his due, but in some cases one's due is determined independently of that of other people, while in other cases, a person's due is determinable *only* by reference to his relations to other persons. I shall refer to contexts, criteria, and principles of the former kind as *noncomparative*, and those of the latter sort as *comparative*. My aim in this paper will be to clarify the contrast between comparative and noncomparative justice, and also to investigate that which they might have in common, and in virtue of which the name of justice has come to apply to both.

I

In recent years, comparative justice has received far more attention than noncomparative justice, partly because writers have been able to agree about its general nature. Surprisingly many philosophers[3] have even gone so far as to claim that all justice *consists* (essentially) in the absence of arbitrary inequalities in the distribution of goods and evils, thus ignoring completely the many and diverse contexts for justice which are nondistributive

---

[3] E.g., Richard Brandt, *Ethical Theory* (Englewood Cliffs, N.J., 1959), p. 410; S.I. Benn and Richard Peters, *Social Principles and the Democratic State* (London, 1959), chs. 5 and 6; Chaim Perelman, *The Idea of Justice and the Problem of Argument* (New York, 1963), pp. 16 ff.; and Morris Ginsberg, *On Justice in Society* (Harmondsworth, Middlesex, 1965), p. 70 *et passim*.

NONCOMPARATIVE JUSTICE

in character. There is no denying, of course, that the problems of comparative justice are real and pressing; my concern here is only to correct the imbalance of emphasis resulting from the exclusive attention lavished upon them. Let us consider first, however, some typical occasions for comparative justice: (*i*) when competitive prizes are to be awarded, (*ii*) when burdens and benefits are to be distributed, and (*iii*) when general rules are to be made, administered, or enforced.

It is illustrative to notice how competitive prizes differ from grades and rewards. We can know that a grade or reward is improperly assigned without knowing anything about the claims or deserts of persons other than the assignee, whereas a prize, having the avowed purpose of selecting out the best in some competition (or, in the case of "booby prizes," the worst) or the exact ranking of contestants against one another, cannot be seen to be justly or unjustly awarded to one person prior to an examination of the credentials of all the others. Thus the awarding of prizes is an occasion for comparative justice, whereas the assigning of grades and rewards is typically noncomparative.

All comparative justice involves, in one way or another, equality in the treatment accorded all the members of a class; but whether that equality be absolute or "proportional," whether it be equality of share, equality of opportunity, or equality of consideration, depends on the nature of the goods and evils awarded or distributed, and the nature of the class in which the assignments and allocations take place. Comparative injustice consists in arbitrary and invidious discrimination of one kind or another: a departure from the requisite form of equal treatment without good reason. When the occasion for justice is the distribution of divisible but limited goods or the assignment of divisible but limited chores, *how much will be left for the others* is always pertinent to the question of how much it would be just for any particular individual to get. And where the occasion for justice is the application or enforcement of general rules, comparative justice requires that the judge or administrator give precisely the same treatment to each person who falls within a class specified by the rule.

These observations, of course, are by now boring and commonplace. My only purpose in making them here is to help make clear

JOEL FEINBERG

the contrast between comparative and noncomparative justice. Consider now the various noncomparative occasions for justice. When our problem is to make assignments, ascriptions, or awards in accordance with noncomparative justice, what is "due" the other person is not a share or portion of some divisible benefit or burden; hence it is not necessary for us to know what is due others in order to know what is due the person with whom we are dealing. *His* rights-or-deserts alone determine what is due him; and once we have come to a judgment of *his* due, that judgment cannot be logically affected by subsequent knowledge of the condition of other parties. We may decide, on the basis of information about other parties, to withhold from him his due; but no new data can upset our judgment of what in fact *is* his due. That judgment is based exclusively upon data about him and is incorrigible, as a judgment, by new information about others. When our task is to do noncomparative justice to each of a large number of individuals, we do not compare them with each other, but rather we compare each in turn with an objective standard and judge each (as we say) "on his merits." It follows that equality of treatment is no part of the concept of noncomparative justice, even though it is, of course, a central element in comparative justice. If we treat *everybody* unfairly, but equally and impartially so, we have done each an injustice that is, at best, only mitigated[4] by the equal injustice done all the others.

The clearest examples of noncomparative injustices are cases of unfair punishments and rewards, merit grading, and derogatory judgments. Of these three kinds of activities, the third seems the most basic from the point of view of justice, and since it has been largely neglected in recent discussions, it will be the main object of attention in the remainder of this essay. First, however, I shall briefly consider possible examples of noncomparative injustices in so-called commutative and retributive contexts. It might seem at first sight that when agreements, transactions, and transfers between free and equal bargainers are unfair, or when promises are wrongfully broken, the injustice is primarily noncomparative,

---

[4] "Mitigated" in the sense that its sting might not hurt as much in a given case, not in the sense that the degree of (noncomparative) injustice in a given case is actually reduced.

for in such cases the agreement reached or the promise breached is unjust because it denies one of the parties his due, quite apart from the way in which others are treated or have been treated by the actor in question or by other actors. A businessman to whom a commercial promise is made and then broken, for example, is treated unfairly not because of the contrast between his treatment and that of others (though, of course, when such a comparison is made it may serve to aggravate the sense of injury and show that there is a derivative injustice resting on another, comparative, ground); he is treated unfairly in any case, so it would seem, because his rights, determined independently of any such comparison, have been violated. If these cases are indeed instances of noncomparative injustice, however, they are not the clearest or purest examples. Not all cases of wrongful promise-breaking are instances of injustice of any kind (*pace* Hobbes). One can, after all, mistreat a person without being particularly unfair to him. Broken promises typically *are* unfair, however, because, like cheating and much lying, they are forms of *exploitation*, of one party taking advantage of another, or promoting his own gain wrongfully at the expense of his victim. When exploitation occurs, the balance of advantages is upset, and benefits and losses are redistributed. Injustice becomes manifest in these cases when a *comparison* is made between the resultant condition of the exploiter and that of his victim. The point applies a fortiori to bargains that are unfair in the first place.[5]

Purer cases of noncomparative injustice are encountered in retributive contexts. It should be obvious, for example, that to punish an innocent person or a lawbreaker who was not responsible for what he did is to commit an injustice to the one punished irrespective of similar treatment accorded all other offenders of his class. There is, to be sure, an element of comparative injustice in the situation where a guilty person goes free and an innocent one is punished for his crime, but punishment of the innocent person would be unjust to him even if the guilty party were also punished, or suffered a fate even worse than punishment.

The category of noncomparative justice to which I shall devote

---

[5] I discuss exploitation more fully below in Part III.

JOEL FEINBERG

major attention I propose to call *the justice of judgments*. The importance of judgment in the theory has been insufficiently acknowledged, I think, by writers who (like Plato and Aristotle) concentrate on the *virtue* of justice or (like the modern utilitarians and their enemies) on the justice and injustice of *acts* and *rules*. The idea of judgmental injustice is familiar enough. In everyday discourse statements and the opinions and judgments they express are commonly called just or unjust. Sometimes one person's opinion of another may not "do him justice"; it may not be "fair to him," as we say. When judgments (as distinct from actions) are said to be unfair to the person judged, the injustice alleged is typically the noncomparative kind. When an innocent man is pronounced guilty, the record about him is falsified to the disadvantage of his reputation and to the detriment of the cause of truth. This is an injustice to him and remains so even if his sentence is suspended and no further hardship is imposed upon him. The injustice in this case consists precisely in the falsity of the derogatory allegation. It can also consist in the falsity of what is believed about the unjustly convicted man. Beliefs and opinions are often said to be unfair to those they are about, even if they are rarely voiced or disseminated to others. Similarly, if a book reviewer writes of a witty book that it is dull, or of a thorough discussion that it is superficial, or of a valid argument that it is invalid, he has not "done justice" to the book or its author. The injustice again is noncomparative. It can be discovered by anyone who reads the book in question, and depends in no way upon the other critical judgments that have been made by this and other critics about other books by this and other authors.

A hard case for the distinction between comparative and noncomparative justice is posed by judgments which are themselves comparative in form. For example, it is unfair to say that "*A* has more merit than *B*" when in fact *B* has more merit than *A*. So far, my definitional criteria are not precise enough to classify this injustice as either comparative or noncomparative. If a comparative injustice is an injustice that can be ascertained as such only after a comparison of *some kind or other* between the person unfairly treated and others, then of course the case at hand is comparative, for to establish the facts which would show the judgment in

NONCOMPARATIVE JUSTICE

question to be true or false, *we must compare* the relevant traits of *A* with the relevant traits of *B*. On the other hand, the example differs from all the examples of comparative justice considered so far in a respect which is not without importance. All the other examples of comparative injustice require *comparisons of two kinds* —not only (*i*) comparison of the relevant characteristics, merits, or performances of the individual in question, which are the basis of his claim, with those of the relevant comparison group, but also (*ii*) comparison of consequent "treatments" (for example, prizes, grades, allocative shares, rewards, penalties, and, in this case, *judgments* about) accorded this individual claimant with the "treatments" (in this case, other judgments) made about relevant others. In all the cases of comparative justice considered thus far, a critic can find that justice was done when (as Aristotle might have said) the ratio between compared claims (in this case, merits) equals the ratio between compared treatments (in this case, judgments). But in the example at hand (the judgment "*A* has more merit than *B*") we can know that the judgment is unfair to *B* simply by learning that *it* is false—that is, by ascertaining that the relational fact it asserts does not hold in reality. We do not have to compare this judgment with *other judgments* about these or other persons, as we might in other contexts have to compare a present penalty, or prize, or allocative share with corresponding "treatments" (to use the generic term) of these or other persons. In short, the injustice is not like the comparative injustices already considered because it requires a critic to make only one, not two comparisons—a comparison of the merits of claimants but not a comparison of various treatments of (or judgments about) them.

This difference, I think, is sufficiently significant to warrant the classification of invidiously false comparative judgments as cases of noncomparative injustice. This can be done by simply appending an exceptive clause to our earlier definition, as follows. When the injustice done a person is noncomparative, no comparison of any kind is required to ascertain it *except* when the treatment in question consists of a *judgment* which is itself *comparative in form* so that a comparison of the claims (characteristics or past performances) of the person judged with those of others is required

JOEL FEINBERG

simply to confirm or disconfirm its truth. In contrast, when the treatment that is unjust to John Doe is unjust in the comparative sense, we must make two sorts of comparisons to ascertain it—namely, comparisons of Doe's claims with those of others, and comparison of this treatment of Doe with various treatments of others. When these two investigations uncover an Aristotelian "disproportion" between compared claims and treatments that is disadvantageous to Doe, then the treatment in question was unfair (in the comparative sense) to Doe.

A more thorough discussion of judgmental justice would have to distinguish between (*i*) the justice or injustice of the judgments themselves which, like their truth or falsity, are properties that belong to them quite independently of who comes to believe them (indeed, even if no one comes to believe them); (*ii*) the justice or injustice of the "mental act" of forming a judgment or of simply holding or believing the judgment; and (*iii*) the justice or injustice of expressing a judgment in language, or symbolically in one's conduct. It is admittedly very misleading to assimilate (*i*) or (*ii*) to the justice or injustice of treatments of persons, even when the word "treatment" is self-consciously draped in quotation marks. At best, only (*iii*), the actual communication of a derogatory judgment to an audience, could count as the treatment of a person in the same sense as that in which the awarding of a prize and the inflicting of a punishment clearly are treatments. This qualification, however, does not prevent me from reaching the conclusion that the justice or injustice of comparative judgments in cases (*i*) and (*ii*) as well as (*iii*), is best classified as belonging to the noncomparative category, because if there are no treatments of the usual kind in their case, then it cannot be true that treatments must be compared; and, furthermore, as we have seen, it is not necessary in their case that the judgments in question be compared with other judgments of their kind.

Still another kind of barrier in the way of a cut and dried application of the distinction between comparative and noncomparative justice is that which results from the complexity of our institutionalized practices themselves. The awarding of prizes, for example, often is a process that involves elements of grading and rewarding. Rewards, too, are often similarly complex. In the

NONCOMPARATIVE JUSTICE

simpler cases, we reward people with gifts that they will presumably value quite apart from their symbolism as rewards. We do this as a way of expressing our appreciation or admiration for some good deed, but sometimes that deed is the manifesting of merit through winning a contest of skill. In that case, the distinction between reward and prize is blurred. In other cases, prizes have no value to the winners except through their symbolism as prizes. Thus a blue ribbon won at the pie-baking contest at the State Fair is a pure prize, with no element of reward, whereas ten thousand dollars given to the winner of a professional golf tournament is both a prize and a reward. Moreover, prizes are often assigned as a consequence of a process of grading and, like grades, can often be understood as expressions of judgments. Grades, moreover, can be valued by their recipients as much as prizes or rewards, a fact that tends to blur these distinctions further.

Now suppose that Mary wins the first prize (a blue ribbon) and Jane the second prize (a red ribbon) even though Jane's pie in fact was better than Mary's. Since mere ribbons have no value in themselves, there is hardly an element of reward, in any strict sense, in this situation. The awardings of the prizes, however, are expressions of judgments, in this case false comparative judgments, about the relative merits of the two pies. As such, they are unfair to Jane. As a case of judgmental injustice, pure and simple, the unfairness is noncomparative, since only one comparison (that between the two pies) is required to establish it. Still, in classifying the ribbon as a prize, and not *merely* the expression of a comparative judgment, we are ascribing to it a value that the mere public utterance of words would not have. Other ways of expressing judgments are relatively ephemeral; the prize is a judgment in the form of an enduring trophy that can be possessed and exhibited. It is not a reward because its value is not even partially independent of the judgment it symbolizes (as the value of a money prize would be); but, on the other hand, it is more than the judgment it embodies, having the character of a permanent tangible record or proof. Thus, the awarding of a prize *is* a kind of "treatment" of a person, as the mere making of a judgment is not, and in virtue of symbolic conventions, the blue-ribbon award is a better treatment than the red. Thus, injustice in the awarding of prizes can

JOEL FEINBERG

be established (only) by comparison of treatments as well as claim bases, and thereby qualifies as comparative injustice.

Before moving to the topic of *grades* as kinds of judgments, I shall obviate one important misunderstanding of the justice of judgments: noncomparative injustice is not done to a person by the expression of a judgment that treats him *better* than he deserves. The "injustice" done by undeservedly favorable criticism, for example, is injustice of another category: either indirect comparative injustice done to all other authors, invidiously aggravating the hurt done to the poorly reviewed ones and debasing the currency in which praise is given to the favorably reviewed ones, or else noncomparative injustice of a "Platonic" or other "cosmic" kind (of which I shall speak shortly). But such treatment is hardly an injustice to the lucky recipient of the undeserved praise. He has not been wronged; he has no personal grievance, no complaint coming.

Grading, too, can be subsumed under the "justice of judgments" rubric. When the object of a grading system is simply to assess as accurately as possible the degree to which a person has some talent, knowledge, or other estimable quality, then the fairness or unfairness of a given grade assessment is of the noncomparative sort. Indeed, the grade itself can be taken to express a *judgment* (or assessment, or appraisal) of a person, and thus is fair or unfair to him in precisely the same manner as other judgments. When grades come to be used as the basis for subsequent job assignments, opportunities, competitive honors, and other benefits, then an undeservedly low grade can cause a *further* injustice of a comparative kind, or of a different noncomparative kind analogous to the punishing of the innocent, or else, again, the "Platonic" injustice of preventing the square peg from entering the square hole it fits so well.

Sometimes, a grading system is understood to have a different aim. Instead of producing accurate assessments of each individual in a class, it may aim to stimulate a competition among the members of the class for positions of high rank relative to the other members of the class, as, for example, when students are "marked on a curve" so that it is a priori impossible that they all get high grades. The aim of such grading practices is to produce an accu-

NONCOMPARATIVE JUSTICE

rate ranking of persons in respect to their possession of a given trait. The individual "curve grades," like all grades, are the expressions of judgments—in this case comparative judgments—and since the ascertainment of injustices requires only the limited single comparisons necessary for the confirmation or disconfirmation of the expressed assessments, unfair curve grades are unjust in the noncomparative sense. When, however, the avowed purpose of curve grading is to stimulate competition, and the curve restrictions are well known and consented to in advance, the graded performances resemble the elements of a rule-governed game or contest, with the higher grades taken as *prizes*. In that case, the injustices resemble those of the comparative kind since they deprive their victims of something like their "fair share" of a divisible good of limited supply—the highly prized, better grades.[6]

What I have called "Platonic justice" deserves just a word in

---

[6] The curve-grading situation, for similar reasons, has much in common with typical distributive contexts—for example, the dividing up of a pie. To give one person an undeservedly large portion is necessarily to deprive someone else of his proper share, so the just distributor will have to compare the claims of all the pie-eaters, and make the relation between his "treatments" (allocations) mirror the relation between their claims. Curve-grading is often more like prize-awarding than like pie-distributing, however, in that its treatments must mirror claims only in respect to their ranking order; the "size" of the grades cannot be modified to reflect close or wide differences between the strength of claims, whereas in principle one can make a piece of pie have any size at all short of the whole pie. In another respect, however, curve-grading is more like pie-distributing, for everybody gets assigned some "share" or other, whether it be an *A*, *B*, *C*, *D*, or *E*. To preserve a near-perfect analogy with prizes, we should have to interpret *every* grade as either a positive or negative prize, and each grade as a better prize than the one behind it and a worse prize than the one ahead of it in the ranking. At any rate, to the extent that grading is a kind of public exercise, with rule-determined risks and opportunities understood in advance by graders and those they grade alike, the curve-grading context is a comparative one, even though an individual grade as such is essentially an assessment—that is, the expression of a judgment. This is a complicated result, but I think there is no contradiction in it. We can say that in so far as *C*-minus is taken to be a judgment merely, even a comparative judgment, the injustice of its assignment when undeserved is noncomparative, and in so far as the assignment of *C*-minus to one of the better students in the class deprives him of the "prize" or "share" he deserves, and awards it (necessarily) to someone else instead, the injustice is comparative. "Double injustices," as I claim in Section II in the text, are frequent occurrences.

JOEL FEINBERG

this place. (Otherwise I shall not have "done justice" to the subject.) I have no doubt that a conception of justice much like that of Plato and the pre-Socratics survives and lives side by side in our moral consciousness with its more prominent descendants. The Platonic notion, as I shall understand it, is a noncomparative one. When "functions," whether of an internal psychological kind, or a social kind, or a more general natural kind, are not performed by the thing or person best fitted by its (his) own nature to perform them, there is injustice done, at least from the cosmic point of view, whether or not any assignable individual is denied his due. The Greeks thought of all nature (as Plato thought of the state or all society) as a kind of organic system, on the model of a machine, or a living organism, in which the macroscopic functioning of the larger system is causally dependent on the proper discharging of the functions of the component subsystems and, to some extent, vice versa. Thus when a component "organ" or "mechanism" fails to function properly, the larger system of which it is a part is thrown out of kilter. (Combine this conception with the idea, also Greek in origin, that human beings have *moral* functions upon which the normal working of cosmic processes depends, and the Shakespearean notion of a foul murder throwing the universe "out of joint" becomes almost intelligible.) There is no point in trying to make this inherently vague conception more precise. My aim here is simply to point out that there is such a notion and that it is a noncomparative one, the perceived injustice not being suffered by those whose proper role is usurped (*that* injustice is the more common comparative kind) but rather by the badly used "function," and the organic cosmos in which it plays a part. "Cosmic injustice" is conceived as injustice suffered, *inter alia*, by the cosmos itself.[7]

---

[7] A quite different conception of cosmic injustice should be distinguished from the one described above. Cosmic injustice is sometimes conceived as injustice *caused* (as opposed to suffered) by the cosmos. When the best runner in the race fails to win the prize because he pulls up lame or suffers some other bad luck, a kind of injustice is done, but the unlucky runner has no grievance in that case against the judges or against his competitors. *They* have not done him wrong, and in fact his rights have not been infringed by any assignable person. If he nevertheless rails against his undeserved fate, he may conceive of his grievance as holding against the laws of nature, the fates, the gods, or

NONCOMPARATIVE JUSTICE

The noncomparative conception of injustice is sometimes implied, I think, in our talk of *states of affairs* as "not right." It is part of the conventional wisdom in Anglo-American analytic ethics that the distinction between "right" and "good" in ordinary language consists partly in the fact that "right" applies to actions only, whereas "good" is used more generally to appraise not only actions and things but any state of affairs.[8] On the contrary, we do sometimes speak of states of affairs as right or wrong, and when we do, we do not intend to say merely that they are good or bad in different but equivalent language. We say, "It is not right that such and such should be the case," and this is a stronger and sharper complaint than simply stating that it is not a good thing that such and such is the case. Moreover, we sometimes say with confidence that things are not right even when there is no individual we know to be especially wronged, and no other individual to be blamed, and even no actions known by us to have the quality or effect of injustice. "It's just not right and fitting that the President of this great country should be such a little man," we might complain, while ignorant of the identity of some bigger man who was wronged by the voters, or even while unwilling to blame the voters for their choice. When we determine that a state of affairs as such is not right, or that the universe of which it is a part is "out of joint" in something like the Platonic fashion, without reference to the claims of wronged parties, our judgment is noncomparative.

II

Applying the distinction between comparative and noncomparative justice to the real world is not easily done. The distinction

---

whatever. The conception of "cosmic injustice" which this suggests, unlike the one described in the text, is a comparative one: the winner's ability does not stand in the same "ratio" to the unlucky loser's ability as the winner's "treatment" (awarding him first prize) stands to the unlucky loser's treatment (awarding him a lesser prize or no prize at all).

[8] See, *inter alia*, W. D. Ross, *The Right and the Good* (Oxford, 1931), pp. 2-3, and Michael Stocker, "Rightness and Goodness: Is There a Difference?," *American Philosophical Quarterly*, 10 (1973), 93 *et passim*.

JOEL FEINBERG

between concepts may be clear enough, but instances of each are rarely pure, any given example of one being likely also to have elements of the other. This contributes not only to conceptual confusion but also to moral perplexity. On many occasions for justice, both comparative and noncomparative principles apply. Comparative principles all share the form of the Aristotelian paradigm: justice requires that relevantly similar cases be treated similarly and relevantly dissimilar cases be treated dissimilarly in direct proportion to the relevant differences between them. Noncomparative principles, on the other hand, are irreducibly diverse in form as well as number. Some condemn punishment of the innocent or those who acted involuntarily; some require that reasonable expectations not be disappointed; others proscribe false derogatory judgments. When principles of both kinds apply to a particular case, often enough the duplication is benign, and what is just according to one principle is also the treatment prescribed by the other. On other occasions, the relevant comparative and noncomparative principles cut in opposite ways to the stupefaction of "the sense of justice."

To treat another person in contravention of both comparative and noncomparative principles when those principles coincide and reinforce one another is to inflict a kind of "double injustice" upon him. This is a point well appreciated by A. D. Woozley, who writes that "A man's getting less than he deserved for what he did [as remuneration for his labor] is doubly unjust if somebody else got more than he, but it would still be unjust if nobody else got more, even if nobody else was involved at all."[9] The underpayment of a worker, suggested by Woozley's example, does seem to be a double injustice to him, but it is not a clear example of the duplication of comparative and noncomparative principles. The principles of "commutative justice" which determine what is a "fair wage" might themselves be comparative principles, in which case Woozley's worker is treated unfairly on two grounds: he is paid less than his relevantly similar fellow worker at the same job, and he is paid less than a national "standard worker" at his trade, and therefore "less than he deserved." In that case, he is seen to

---

[9] A. D. Woozley, "Injustice," *American Philosophical Quarterly Monograph*, 7 (1973), 115-116.

be discriminated against when *compared* with a fellow worker in his own plant and also when *compared* with workers in relevantly similar jobs throughout the country, but no noncomparative principles seem to apply to his case at all. Perhaps, however, the commutative principles that determine a fair wage for a given job, like their counterparts in the area of retributive justice that determine a fair punishment for a given crime, are in part noncomparative. If beheading and disembowelment became the standard punishment for overtime parking, as the result of duly enacted statutes, the penalty as applied in a given case would be unjust (because too severe) even though it were applied uniformly and without discrimination to all offenders. Moreover, it would be unjust even if it were the mildest penalty in the whole system of criminal law, with more serious offenses punished with proportionately greater severity still (torture, punishment of the offender's family, and so forth). In short, it is possible for *every* punishment in a system of criminal law to be unjust because too severe, which shows that criminal desert is in part noncomparative. If the analogy between commutative and retributive justice holds in this respect, then it should be similarly conceivable that *all* of the wages in a hypothetical economy are too low, so that any given worker is getting less than he deserves, not as determined by a comparison between his wages and those of other workers, but rather as determined by the merits of his own case. The analogy seems to fail, however, in one respect. The underpaid workers are surely treated unfairly as *compared* to their employers whose *share* of the wealth produced must be disproportionately great if theirs is disproportionately small. (This is the respect in which all *exploitation* is a comparative injustice.)

There can nevertheless be an element of noncomparative injustice in Woozley's example. Suppose, for example, that the case is one of racial bias, and the underpaid worker is discriminated against because he is black, though he is told (what is not true) that he is paid less because his work is inferior. On the one hand, this is unfair discrimination against one worker (or class of workers) among many, and thus is condemned by comparative principles. On the other hand, in so far as it is given the specious justification that it is based on assessments of ability, it can be

JOEL FEINBERG

taken to be an expression of nonrecognition of ability, a *judgment* that is unfair to the excluded worker who in fact has high ability, in which case, like all judgmental injustices, it is non-comparative.

When relevantly applicable comparative and noncomparative principles yield opposite judgments, there are, of course, two possibilities: what is condoned by the comparative principle is condemned by the noncomparative one, or what is endorsed by the noncomparative principle is declared unjust by the comparative one. Pure examples of the former kind are not easy to come by. The example of a slave society in which masters uniformly and impartially deprive their subjects of their due (as determined by the merits of their own cases) comes close, but even there the disparity between the resultant conditions of the privileged and deprived would be unjust on comparative grounds. A purer example is that suggested above of a system of criminal law, effectively and impartially administered, in which all penalties are disproportionate to actual culpability, for in that case (unlike the example of slavery) the judges, jurors, and jailers would not directly profit from the unjust treatments imposed on criminals; hence punishments would be unjust on noncomparative grounds, but not on comparative ones (at any rate, not if the punished offenders are compared only with each other). Even that example, however, is not perfectly pure, since comparisons of the excessive punishments of criminals may also be made to the nonpunishments of various noncriminals.

That the existence of comparative injustice is relative to the comparison class examined is a point whose importance is vividly shown by the perplexing case of a hypothetical system of criminal law in which people are punished even for involuntary infractions of rules. Imagine a system in which penalties are all exactly proportionate to moral guilt (whatever that might mean) or, in the case of "involuntary crimes," proportionate to the guilt that would have been involved had the infraction been voluntary. The courts in this imaginary system, with consistent impartiality, hold infants and insane people liable for crimes, and punish others for unavoidable accidents and innocent mistakes. These practices are, of course, grossly unfair to those who are punished, and the

NONCOMPARATIVE JUSTICE

unfairness seems at least noncomparative. It might seem at first, however, that no element of comparative injustice need be involved at all, for none of these unfortunates would be in a position to complain of discrimination, prejudice, or favoritism in the enforcement of the law. Similar cases (involuntary wrongdoing) are rigorously treated, so it would seem, in similar ways (punished) so that the Aristotelian formula is satisfied. A quite different judgment results, however, when the comparison is made between different comparison classes. When all involuntary criminals are compared with each other in all relevant respects (their infraction of rules) and all voluntary noncriminals are compared with each other in all relevant respects (their compliance with rules), no invidious treatments can be discerned. But when all involuntary criminals are compared with all voluntary criminals of the same category, the result is quite different, for we soon discover that involuntary criminals are treated the same as voluntary ones even though they are *different in a morally relevant respect*—namely, that one group acted voluntarily and the other involuntarily. But why is voluntariness morally relevant? Simply because it is unfair to a person, any person, on noncomparative grounds, to punish him for his involuntary behavior. So this intriguing example illustrates another point of importance, that comparative and noncomparative principles can dovetail in such a way that they are conceptually linked. In the case at hand, a noncomparative principle of justice determines the criterion of relevance for the application of the otherwise formal principle of comparative justice for certain contexts.

The more common examples of genuine conflict are provided by instances of treatment condoned by noncomparative principles but condemned as unjust by comparative ones. Consider something like the Augustinian theory of salvation. No man considered entirely on his own merits, prior to or independently of Divine Grace, deserves to be saved, since all men by their very natures are totally depraved. In each case, then, noncomparative justice would be served by damnation and consignment to hell-fire. Nevertheless, God, out of His infinite mercy, exercises something like executive clemency, and allows His grace to touch the souls of an arbitrarily selected minority of men, permitting them to

313

JOEL FEINBERG

achieve their own (undeserved)[10] salvations. The others then *are* consigned to hell, but noncomparative principles, at least, allow them no just complaint, since they are sinners simply getting what they deserve according to the canons of retributive justice. Yet if they think about their equally sinful but luckier comrades, they are likely to feel at least somewhat aggrieved at what they can only take to be unjust discrimination in plain contravention of comparative principles.

The more we ponder cases of the above kind, the more confused we become; for justice and injustice seem alternately to flit in and out of focus like the pictures in an optical illusion, depending upon whether we consider comparative or noncomparative factors. And such cases are not confined to theological speculation. They arise whenever an authority makes an "example" or an "exception" of one or more out of a class of subjects whose individual deserts are alike. When all the students in a class or all the soldiers in a barracks are equally guilty and only one is punished (as a threat to the others) or only one is left unpunished (out of favoritism) then the punished ones have no grievance on noncomparative grounds, since they are guilty after all, but they can complain against discriminatory treatment.[11]

Cases of this general kind also include instances of gratuitous benefaction. No person has a right to another person's charity, and yet if a charitable benefactor distributes his largesse to nine persons in a group of ten, arbitrarily withholding it from the tenth for no good reason, his behavior seems in some important way unfair to the tenth. Still, the benefactor might reply to the charge of arbitrary exclusion with the reminder that, morally speaking, he did not *have to* contribute to any of the group, and that his aid to nine was a net gain above and beyond the call of duty. The

---

[10] One might choose to say "otherwise undeserved salvations" here to suggest that God confers on the elect not only their salvation, but also their desert of salvation. But this, I think, would render the concept of desert incoherent. Even though omnipotent, God can no more make the undeserving deserving *by fiat* than He can make $2 + 2 = 5$.

[11] Cf. A. M. Honoré: "If a rule forbids parking in a certain area, it is unfair to A who has parked in that area that he should be fined for doing so, whilst B, who has done the same thing is not punished" ("Social Justice," *McGill Law Journal*, 8 [1962], 67).

NONCOMPARATIVE JUSTICE

poor excluded beggar, his sense of justice confused, will feel aggrieved and unaggrieved in rapid alternation. There is no right to charity, or grace, or clemency, or any other form of gratuitous good treatment, and yet arbitrary inconsistency or favoritism in the distribution of these goods can seem unjust to those neglected or deprived of them.

A similar example of conflict between comparative and non-comparative principles is found in the case of the distribution of a *surplus* among a group of recipients after justice has already been done to each proper individual claim. According to Woozley: "If a father in the bequests which he makes to his sons *A* and *B* has fairly met their needs, he does no injustice to *B* if he leaves the whole of the rest of the estate to *A*—unless there is some further respect, other than need, in which the distinction between like cases is unjust."[12] Let us suppose, filling in Woozley's example, that *A* and *B* are roughly of the same age, size, health, appearance, abilities, beliefs, and ideals, that each has the same basic financial needs and that the bequests more than fulfill them in each case, but that the father leaves everything else after those basic needs have been met—say, one million unsuspected dollars—to *A*, simply because he likes *A* better (there being no other reason available).[13] We can suppose further that the existence of the "extra" one million dollars was totally unknown to the sons, so that neither of them had expectation or hope of inheriting any part of it. After individual claims based on needs, deserts, and "reasonable expectations" have been satisfied, injustice, by non-comparative standards at any rate, cannot be done. Yet comparative considerations might still properly agitate the sense of injustice (*pace* Woozley) of the "deprived" son.

The oppositions between comparative and noncomparative principles illustrated by these examples are not radical conflicts originating in the concept of justice itself of the kind that would render the very coherence of that concept suspect. I have given no examples where it is conceptually impossible to have justice

---

[12] Woozley, *op. cit.*, pp. 112-113.

[13] The import of the example would be changed, I think, if the father, preferring to have the whole (remaining) fortune in one set of hands than divided (and this for non-arbitrary reasons), selects *A* by flipping a coin.

JOEL FEINBERG

both ways, cases in which satisfaction of a noncomparative principle requires violation of a comparative one, or vice versa.[14] All that the examples show is that it is sometimes possible to satisfy a principle of the one kind while violating a principle of the other kind. Such occasional and contingent opposition is one of the weaker senses in which principles can be said to conflict. In these cases of conflict, something less than perfect justice has been achieved, but that does not show that perfect justice is an impossible ideal. It is especially awkward sometimes to satisfy comparative principles, and we are tempted to take short cuts, for example, by punishing only some but not all members of a very large class of rule violators. In that event, we may choose for good reasons to compromise comparative justice for the sake of efficiency and convenience, and when we have already given noncomparative justice its due (that is, we have punished *only* the guilty) we might take our short cut with a relatively easy conscience. Still, we can easily *conceive* of what it would be like in cases of this kind to satisfy both comparative and noncomparative justice, so that the "conflict" between the two is by no means logically unavoidable. Since both noncomparative and comparative justice make valid claims on us, and since it is in principle possible for both to be satisfied, we must conclude that *in so far as a given act or arrangement fails to satisfy one or the other of the two kinds of principles, it is not as just as it could be.*

---

[14] There are easily imagined circumstances, on the other hand, in which it is *practically* impossible to do both comparative and noncomparative justice. E.g., suppose I owe A, B, C, and D each $100, but I have only $100 all together. If I pay $25 to each, there will be no comparative injustice (discrimination), but a "commutative injustice" will be done to each. But if I pay $100 to A and nothing to the others, then both comparative and noncomparative injustice is done to the others, but no injustice by any standard to A. Whatever I do, in this example, will have the effect of injustice *somewhere*.

It should be noted that I am concerned throughout this essay with the "effect" and not the "quality" of injustice. The distinction is Aristotle's. See the *Nicomachean Ethics*, V. For a convincing argument that justice in effect (justice *to* someone or other) is a more basic notion than justice as a quality of actions reflecting the virtue of the agent, see Josef Pieper, *Justice* (London, 1957). Pieper there paraphrases Aquinas: "in the realm of justice, good and evil are judged purely on the basis of the deed itself, regardless of the inner disposition of the doer; the point is not how the deed accords with the doer, but rather, how it affects 'the other person' " (pp. 36-37).

NONCOMPARATIVE JUSTICE

Another message to be inferred, I think, from our examples is that injustice by noncomparative standards tends to be a much more serious thing than comparative injustice. The right to be given one's due, where one's due is not merely an allotment or a share, but rather is determined (say) by prior agreements or by personal desert, is a more important right than the right not to be discriminated against. If a tyrant treats all his underlings "like dogs," then the injustice done underling John Doe is far more serious than he would suffer if he were given his due but everyone else were treated "like kings." Similarly, to be punished for a crime one did not commit is a greater outrage than to be punished for a crime one did commit while others who are equally guilty are let go. (The Dreyfus case was a greater injustice by far than the Calley case.)

Indeed, the superiority of the claims of noncomparative to comparative justice in some cases is so striking that one might well raise the question whether comparative justice, in those cases, makes any claims at all. Suppose an employer pays all his employees more than the prevailing scale in his industry, indeed more than any of them deserves by any reasonable noncomparative standard, but he pays Doe, a worker of only average skills and seniority, more than he pays Roe, a worker with superior skills and high seniority. If there is any injustice at all in this situation, it must consist entirely in the discriminatory character of the treatment. But where is the wrong in discrimination as such? In this example, no man is treated badly; in fact, each is getting more than his due. How then can Roe have *any* complaint? Why not describe the situation as one in which Roe is treated fairly but Doe gets *more* than his due? But to give a man more than his due is not to wrong him, and if no one is wronged, how can there be injustice? Much the same questions can be raised about the other examples considered above where noncomparative justice is satisfied and only discrimination remains to offend the sense of justice: punishment of the guilty when others equally guilty are let go, arbitrary exceptions to gratuitous benefactions, assignments of surplus goods after individual claims have been satisfied.[15]

---

[15] Still another example is that suggested by the biblical parable of the laborers in the vineyard, Ch. XX of the Gospel According to St. Matthew.

JOEL FEINBERG

Still, there is no doubt that arbitrary discrimination as such, even in the absence of any other violated claims, strikes most of us as wrong, and not merely wrong, but unfair. The explanation of this near-universal reaction involves two elements. In the first place, as a matter of psychological fact, people are *hurt* by discriminatory treatment whether or not they are wronged according to some additional standard, and secondly, the hurt is perceived to be in some important way *"offensive to reason"*—absurd, arbitrary, disproportionate, or inconsistent. These two elements, I suspect, are sufficient to account for our use of the vocabulary of "unfairness," and the spontaneous offense to our sense of justice, in cases of the kind under consideration. That it hurts to be singled out or pointedly excluded by discriminatory treatment is a plain fact which itself calls for a full psychological explanation, but a plain fact still, however it is to be accounted for. The sting of discrimination is most painful in cases of double injustice where it adds salt to other moral wounds. When one is a member of an enslaved minority, for example, it is the enslavement that does one the greatest wrong, but the perceived contrast between one's own condition and that of others not enslaved, let us suppose only because of their race, while adding nothing to the primary wrong, tends to exacerbate its immediate effect. When nearly everyone is enslaved, and cruel rules are enforced equally across the board, then the element of having been selected out for special treatment is missing. That condition is no less unjust, but it will in most cases be less constantly before the mind, less pointed in its application, and less intensely resented. So powerful is the psychological tendency to resent discriminatory treatment that it manifests itself even in cases where the discrimination is the whole of the wrong suffered and is disadvantageous only in a relative way.

The more important part of the explanation why discrimination as such is unjust, however, consists in its absolute groundlessness,[16]

---

[16] There are contexts, of course, in which comparative justice is not only compatible with arbitrariness but actually requires it. Sometimes distributive justice calls for purely arbitrary—that is, random—procedures for allocating indivisible goods or burdens. (See David Lyons, *The Forms and Limits of Utilitarianism* [Oxford, 1965], pp. 161-177.) In these cases, however, there is an intelligible rationale for the procedure, whereas in the case of unjust discrimi-

NONCOMPARATIVE JUSTICE

or grounding on morally irrelevant criteria, and the characteristic sort of offensiveness these features engender, for the general characteristic this form of injustice shares with all the others is that, quite apart from any other harm, or hurt, or wrong it might bring to the one who suffers it, it offends against impersonal reason itself. As many writers have pointed out,[17] the principle that relevantly similar cases should be treated in similar ways, put in just that general way, is a principle of reason, in much the same way as Aristotle's principles of identity, contradiction, and excluded middle are "laws of thought." It is *absurd* to treat relevantly similar cases in dissimilar ways, to ascribe different geometrical properties to identical isosceles triangles, or to assign unequal wages to relevantly equal workers.[18] Individual triangles, however, have no feelings and no interests; they do not recognize pointedly selective treatment, or partiality, or exclusion; they cannot be hurt, or harmed, or treated in relatively disadvantageous ways. For those reasons discrimination among triangles is *merely* absurd, whereas discrimination that affects the balance of advantages among beings with interests and feelings is unfair.

The moral offensiveness of discrimination is *sui generis*. In particular, it is not wholly derived from consideration of the motives of the wrongdoer, though such consideration is capable of intensifying the irritation it produces. Often discriminatory treatment strikes its victim as having something "personal" in it, an element of malice, or unprovoked insult. In other cases, like exemplary punishment, the victim may feel badly used, a mere instrument for another's purposes. But when the personal and exploitative elements are clearly missing—as, for example, when one is deprived of a shared benefit not for a morally shady motive, but for no apparent motive at all—then invidious treatment can be even more maddening.

---

nation, there is either an irrelevant criterion employed, or else there is no "procedure" and no "rationale," but only arbitrariness through and through.

[17] E.g., Isaiah Berlin, "Equality as an Ideal," *Proceedings of the Aristotelian Society*, vol. LVI (1955-1956).

[18] It is, of course, even more absurd to assign unequal wages to relevantly unequal workers in *inverse* proportion to their relevant differences—that is, to pay more to the less deserving and less to the more deserving.

JOEL FEINBERG

III

It is natural enough to respond to hurt with anger, but when the hurt seems to have been arbitrarily inflicted in the manner characteristic of unjust discrimination, anger is transmuted into moral indignation. Because the treatment is offensive to reason as well as hurtful, responsive anger borrows some of the authority of reason; it becomes righteous and impersonal, free of self-doubt, and yet disinterested and free of mere self-preference. This moralized anger is by no means peculiar to discrimination among the various modes of injustice. It is, in fact, the common element in reactions to all injustices, whether comparative or noncomparative, whether actions, rules, or judgments. Perhaps more than anything else, it distinguishes the apprehension of injustice from awareness of other kinds of wrong or harmful conduct. John Stuart Mill was perhaps the first important writer to make much of this distinctive emotion.[19] No analysis of the concept of justice is complete, he claimed, without a supplementary analysis of what he called the "sentiment of justice." Mill's own analysis, however, failed to account for the element of righteousness I have noted. He analyzed the sentiment of justice (more accurately, the sentiment of injustice) into an impulse to retaliate for injury, which he took to be a kind of animal instinct, plus a distinctively human feeling of sympathy that enables us to identify imaginatively with other victims of wrongdoing and respond angrily on their behalf as we would to our own injuries. Perhaps such elements *are* commonly part of the sentiment of injustice, but they would also be present, I should think, when we apprehend wrongdoing of other kinds, or even when we perceive harm caused to persons in an innocent or accidental way. Those elements peculiar to the sentiment of injustice that endow it with its uniquely righteous flavor have not been mentioned in Mill's account.

The sources of the sentiment of injustice are readily found in the experiences of childhood. Moral indignation in small children (in their own behalf, of course) is largely restricted, I think, to three kinds of contexts. In the first, outraged protest is directed

---

[19] J. S. Mill, *Utilitarianism*, Ch. V, pars. 16-24.

NONCOMPARATIVE JUSTICE

at what is taken to be *favoritism*. Its characteristic formulae are: "He got more than I did," or "You punished me but not him, and he did it too," or "Why does he have a privilege or benefit and not me?" Impelled originally by jealousy, children learn both to accuse others of special treatment, and to defend themselves from such charges, to find analogies and disanalogies between cases, to invoke precedents and appeal to consistency. In these exercises are found the roots of the sense of comparative justice. Personal anger directed at favoritism comes to be anger felt on behalf of, or from the perspective of, impartiality. When the feeling occasioned by hurt expands its target to include inconsistency, disproportion, anomaly, and other elements similarly offensive to reason, it becomes full-blown moral indignation, and not mere animal anger sympathetically projected.

A second source of the sentiment of injustice does not appear until the stage of peer-group orientation and co-operative play, starting at about age six.[20] A new object of juvenile wrath at that stage is *exploitation*—taking unfair advantage of another's handicaps or placing another at a disadvantage in competitive or co-operative undertakings. In competitive games, one player can secure unfair advantage over another either by exploiting natural inequalities inconsistent with the game's purpose—for example, larger size or greater age—or else by creating inequalities through cheating, bribing, or lying. In co-operative undertakings one can exploit a partner's trust by free-loading, betraying him for personal gain, or otherwise letting him down. Before the age of five or six, the child has no firm concept of a regulated competition for fun or gain in which "players" trust each other to obey the rules that are meant to nullify inappropriate influences on the outcome; nor does he have a firm concept of a joint undertaking by co-operative partners each of whom trusts all the others to do their share of the work that is necessary to their common gain. Once the child becomes preoccupied, however, with games of skill and chance, with team sports and "team spirit," and with group chores and quotas assigned by parents or teachers, the

---

[20] See Jean Piaget, *The Moral Judgment of the Child*, trans. by Marjorie Gabain (London, 1932).

JOEL FEINBERG

streets echo with charges and rebuttals of unfairness not previously heard in the nursery.

Few six-year-olds have sufficient skill at abstract thinking to arrive at the philosophical views that will one day tempt most of them as adults: that all life is a competitive game or, alternatively, that all society is one large co-operative undertaking in which each and every partner has his assigned dues and his proper shares. The latter view is that of G. H. von Wright, who points to a respect in which *all* social wrongdoing is unjust in the manner of exploitation.[21] In von Wright's usage, escaping harm from others is the "share" which each member of a moral community has in the common good, whereas not harming others is the "price" one pays, or each member's "due share" of the price, for that good. Any time one member harms another, then, he tries to have his cake and eat it too—that is, to "have his share without paying his due," and this way of taking advantage of others, which is morally akin to cheating and free-loading, von Wright calls "the basic form of injustice."[22]

An interesting feature of von Wright's analysis in his suggestion of how exploitative injustice, too, contains an element that is offensive to reason:

One can ask questions like this: "What right have you got to put yourself in a privileged position? If you get your share without paying your due, then somebody else, who is equally anxious to get his share, will necessarily be without it. Don't you see that this is unfair?" One could almost call this appeal to a man's sense of justice an appeal to a man's sense of symmetry.[23]

The "asymmetry" referred to by von Wright is common to exploitation, distributive injustice, and discrimination. All create inequalities between relevantly equal cases, and all are offensive to reason in similar ways. Exploitation leads necessarily to unequal results that are in a way doubly unjust: the exploiter gets more

---

[21] G. H. von Wright, *The Varieties of Goodness* (London, 1963), Ch. X. Cf. also Herbert Morris, "Persons and Punishment," *The Monist*, vol. 52 (October, 1968).

[22] *Ibid.*, p. 208.

[23] *Ibid.*, p. 210.

than he deserves and his victim less. Like children on a seesaw, the one goes up by the same increment as the other goes down. The imbalance produced by exploitation rests on no correlated differences in which disinterested reason can find satisfaction. There are no relevant differences between the occupants of the up and down positions that underlie and justify the outcome. The crucial difference between them was a morally "irrelevant" one —worse, a morally inappropriate one; the gainer cheated or lied and the other did not.

Von Wright's bold claim that all social wrongdoing is essentially exploitative is an overstated insight. In the paradigm case of egregious exploitation that is apparently before his mind, *A* secures a gain for himself at the cost of a loss to *B*, and he does this by betraying *B*'s trust. This model fits far more cases than one might realize before reflecting, but it surely does not fit *all* cases of social wrongdoing. Some wrongs (for example, tax evasion) lack a determinate victim, or produce a trivial harm to "society" while producing a great gain to the wrongdoer. In other cases, *A* wrongfully harms *B* without any hope of gain for himself. In typical debauched or psychopathic crimes, nobody gains anything, and in cases of self-destructive malice, both parties lose. In still other cases, there need have been no prior trust relation between an aggressor and his victim. *A* and *B* may have been enemies constantly on the alert for the other's mischief. When their animosity erupts into combat one or the other of them is wrongfully injured. It is implausible to think of all these examples as instances of exploitation. Von Wright would probably insist, however, that in a great many cases of social wrongdoing that do not at first sight seem to involve duplicity, cheating, or free-loading, there is nevertheless an element, however attenuated, of exploitative injustice. Since the concept of injustice is somewhat diluted in this very general application, perhaps it would be wise to refer to "injustice in the weak sense." Then we can still ask how we can make out a contrast between those "unjust acts" which are also unjust in a specific stronger way and those which are not. My answer to that question is that the pointedly unjust acts (in the strong sense) are either those which are directly and obviously exploitative (for example, those involving cheating) or those which

JOEL FEINBERG

are invidiously discriminatory, or those expressive of derogatory falsehood. The "sentiment of injustice" in these cases is directed at the element of "asymmetry," "inconsistency," or "falsehood," all of which are, in a manner insufficiently appreciated by Mill, "offensive to reason."

IV

In a third kind of context for juvenile indignation, moral outrage stems neither from the awareness of exploitative "asymmetry" nor from the awareness of disadvantageous discrimination between like cases, for only one "case"—the child's own—may be involved. Rather the child reacts furiously to what he confidently believes to be a false judgment that is injurious to his esteem, or degrading to his status, or which simply misrepresents him in some respect that is important to him. Consider a typical example. An older child answers a parental question correctly. A younger sibling remarks that he too knew the answer, but that he did not have a chance to speak up in time. To this, the older child replies that the younger child did not know the answer and was silent only because of his ignorance. What a torrent of rage and frustration this will produce in the younger child if he *knows* that he knew the answer! In that case he has direct possession of the truth and cannot prove it to anyone. His rage, however, will not be merely an expression of his frustrated hope of presenting evidence. Nor will it be merely his reaction to the sting of an insult, for the imputation of specific ignorance in this context may not be very insulting, and much greater defamations (in the child's eyes) will not evoke the same response if they happen to be true. "You wet your bed last night," said accusingly by the older child, will, if true, evoke shame and humiliation. If false, it will produce the righteous anger characteristic of the outraged sense of (noncomparative) justice. What provides the special flavor in the child's response to the false allegation is the sense that not only he but *the truth itself* has been injured. His anger is righteous because it is not only in his own behalf; it is also and primarily in the name of the truth, or on behalf of *the way things really are*.

There is no doubt that an interest in the truth as such retains

NONCOMPARATIVE JUSTICE

its central place in the moral outlook of adults. However we may disagree about other duties, all of us, upon reflection, will acknowledge a kind of transcendent and impersonal duty to the truth, and will also claim a kind of corresponding right to be truly ("fairly" here is a synonym of "truly") judged in matters that are relevant to our esteem. We do not insist with equal vehemence upon a right to be truly described in respects that are indifferent to esteem or to interest—for example, in respect to the color of our eyes or the shape of our fingerprints. If you describe my brown eyes as blue you will have said something false about me but not unfair to me.

The virtue of people who honor their duties of judgmental justice and respect the rights of others to be fairly appraised is called "fair-mindedness." Whatever job our voiced and written judgments may do, whatever changes they may effect in the world, they also form part of the human record, and all persons, or at least all fair-minded persons, have a double stake in that record. Everyone will wish to make his own record as good as possible, but all fair-minded persons will also wish the record itself to be accurate and untarnished, partly as a matter of common interest, but also, as we say, as *a matter of justice*, and justice in a quite basic and underivative sense. Nothing makes the head spin more than the death and burial of a known truth. Those who have read the passages about rewriting history in Orwell's *1984* will understand the "dizziness" which another writer, Albert Camus, cites as his response to "the absolute murder of a truth."[24] Our concern for the truth is also at the root of that feeling which is sometimes called "guilt" and is prominent in the consciousness of fair-minded people who sense that their own position in life implies a judgment of their merits that is too favorable, that they are therefore posing as something that they are not in fact. The moral principle behind these phenomena is that every person has a right to be treated and judged as the kind of being he is, and since this principle derives its persuasiveness and its impersonal authority from the alliance between interest and the objective truth, it also imposes a duty to

---

[24] Albert Camus, *The Fall*, trans. by Justine O'Brien (New York, 1956), p. 90.

JOEL FEINBERG

accept no more favorable judgments from others than those that
are in truth warranted. The alliance between personal interest and
the truth may not always be present, and even where it exists, it
may be short-lived, but the truth itself is timeless, and it is the
truth's prestige that supports judgmental justice even when all
connection with personal interests is severed. James Flexner writes
that it is "unfair" to call George Washington a racist, given that
he ardently and conscientiously opposed the institution of
slavery.[25] Notice how the biographer naturally thinks of doing
justice to his subject well after the subject, having long been dead,
has any personal stake in the record.

Judgmental injustice is very commonly found to be an element
of a complex injustice that includes as another element undeservedly injurious treatment. Sometimes rather subtle analysis is
required to separate out injustice to the truth (and to the victim's
"double interest" in the truth) from undeserved damage to other
interests of the victim. Suppose, for example, that the rules of my
club "allow expulsion for cheating and I am expelled [for cheat-
ing] without having cheated."[26] Note the two distinct ways in
which the expulsion is unjust to me in these circumstances. On the
one hand, it is an unwarranted deprivation of benefits, a hurt
inflicted upon me that I have not deserved (though, of course,
that deprivation, in itself, may not hurt very much if I do not
particularly care for the club anyway); on the other hand the
expulsion upholds, endorses, and affirms an unfair judgment—
namely, the false charge that I have cheated. That affirmation
would be unjust in itself even without the infliction of any further
penalty.

Similarly, one player's cheating in a game may put his rival at
an unfair competitive disadvantage, and that, of course, is a kind
of injury to the rival's interests which may cause hurt and resentment, but the sense of injustice will be greatly magnified by the
official judgment of the referee, or even the critical judgments of
spectators and journalists, that there was no cheating in the first
place. That judgment offends not only the player's interest in

---

[25] James Flexner, "Washington and Slavery," *New York Times*, Feb. 22,
1973, p. 39.
[26] The example is from Brian Barry, *Political Argument* (London, 1965), p. 99.

NONCOMPARATIVE JUSTICE

winning his match, but also it offends against the facts and involves the impersonal authority of truth as a reinforcement to the sense of merely private injury. This sort of phenomenon, which must surely provide for the philosopher one of his basic paradigms of injustice, finds a hundred illustrations in the official verdicts and decrees of courts and public tribunals. The Kent State murders, for example, angered and saddened most of us; yet the words "cruel" and "wanton" seem to describe those terrible events more naturally than the words "unjust" or "unfair" do. There was a different quality of responsive feeling, however, to the outrageous Ohio grand jury verdicts from that of the response to the actual primary happenings. Those official judgments added a new dimension of unfairness to the events they misrepresented, and thus rasped and rankled the sense of injustice as only the awareness of violated truth can.

V

Our legal system protects persons from the harm caused by certain kinds of false judgments by permitting them to sue their defamers for damages. But defamation (the generic legal term for libel and slander), while often involving judgmental injustice, is not simply to be identified with that moral category. It is useful to chart the differences between the two if only for the sake of getting clearer about what judgmental injustice is. Moreover, as so often happens when moral notions are compared with conceptual models drawn from the law,[27] we shall find that very precise questions can be raised within the framework of the law of defamation whose counterparts in the "natural" context of judgmental justice have no clear and easy answer. Some of these questions cannot simply be dismissed. In the interest of ultimate coherence, either precise answers should be stipulated for them through a reasoned process of "moral legislation," or else reasoned explanations should be given why such questions fail to make sense outside a narrow institutional setting.

Although defamation and judgmental injustice differ in crucial respects, there are several elements common to both. In the first

---

[27] See my *Doing and Deserving* (Princeton, 1970), Chs. 2-4.

JOEL FEINBERG

place, both are propositional. Both essentially involve statements or judgments about persons of a kind that could be either true or false, but are in fact false. Prosser is especially emphatic in restricting the scope of defamation to exclude insults:

> The courts . . . have held that mere words of abuse, indicating that the defendant dislikes the plaintiff and has a low opinion of him, but without suggesting any specific charge against him, are not to be treated as defamatory. A certain amount of vulgar name-calling is tolerated on the theory that it will necessarily be understood to amount to nothing more.[28]

Thus one can defame a man by calling him a drunkard, a wife-beater, or a tax-evader, but not by calling him a rat, or a son of a bitch. There may be elements of exploitative, distributive, or even retributive injustice when a victim is made to suffer wrath or humiliation by an unwarranted insult, but judgmental injustice requires some judgment of fact, as opposed to the mere hurling of epithets.

A second element, common to defamation and judgmental injustice, is the derogatory character of the propositions affirmed by each. The propositions involved are imputations of fault, demerit, and responsibility for wrongdoing, of characteristics or actions that are somehow substandard. It is not defamatory to print in a newspaper that a man is dead,[29] although it might well seem to a living man that a widespread premature belief in his death ill serves his interests. That belief, however, makes no one think any the worse of him; a man's reputation will easily survive him, if the report of his death carries no further information to his discredit. Similarly, the premature report of a person's death may harm him (in some interest other than his interest in a good reputation), but as a proposition simply, it can hardly be unfair to him.

Defamation and judgmental injustice are also similar in that they are primarily unjust to the persons they are about,

---

[28] William L. Prosser, *Handbook of the Law of Torts*, 2nd ed. (St. Paul, 1955), p. 576.

[29] *Ibid.*, p. 574. See *Cohen* v. *New York Times Co.*, 1912, 153 App. Div. 242, 138 N.Y.S. 206, and *Lemmer* v. *The Tribune*, 1915, 50 Mont. 559, 148 P. 338.

NONCOMPARATIVE JUSTICE

not to listeners or readers who are led to have false opinions. The essence of judgmental injustice is not deception, not being lied to. Indeed, one can express an unfair judgment in all good faith with no intent to deceive. Unjust judgments are like some other unjust actions in this respect. The justice or injustice of their effect on others can be determined independently of the motive or intention with which they are made.[30] Of course, where one does deceive by lying, this may be a kind of exploitation of the listener and therefore unfair, on other grounds, to him, too.

The first of the distinguishing differences between defamation and judgmental injustice is that defamation requires communication. Indeed, defamation is a relation among at least three parties. It consists of a judgment made by one person about another person and communicated to at least one other person. A judgment, however, need not even be spoken or written to be unjust simply as a judgment. If someone comes to believe an unjust judgment, then he has an unjust belief, however blamelessly he comes to adopt it, however well supported it is by the evidence, however faithfully he keeps it entirely to himself. If John Doe has a belief that is unfair to Richard Roe and he voices it directly to Roe, then he expresses an unfair judgment, but he does not defame Roe, because he has not expressed that judgment to any third parties. Similarly, Doe may hold a belief that is unfair to himself, but even though he gives impulsive statement to that belief as he stares moodily at his image in the shaving mirror, he does not—indeed he cannot—defame himself.

A second difference has to do with the source of the injustice in the two cases. Although defamation usually (but not necessarily) commits judgmental injustice, the source of the legal wrong is not simply the unfairness of the communication but the harm it tends to cause. The harm in question must be suffered directly by the victim's reputation,[31] but a reputation itself may be valued for its

---

[30] Cf. Pieper, *op. cit.*, pp. 35-40.

[31] Prosser defines defamation as "an invasion of the interest in reputation and good name by communication to others which tends to diminish the esteem [elsewhere he writes 'respect,' 'good will,' or 'confidence'] in which the plaintiff is held, or to excite adverse feelings or opinions against him" (*op. cit.*, p. 572).

JOEL FEINBERG

own sake or for the sake of some ulterior interest, social, professional, or pecuniary, and sometimes the law requires proof of
damage to one of these ulterior interests, too, before allowing
recovery. Harms to reputation and dependent interests may vary
in a large number of respects so that legal policies need to be
formulated for grading the relative seriousness of different dimensions. So, for example, a defamatory utterance may make a
major or a minor imputation of fault; the fault can be imputed
with emphatic certainty or tentative probability; the imputation
can be widely or narrowly disseminated; it can be communicated
to an important or unimportant audience (friends or strangers,
customers or creditors), and belief in its truth can threaten pocket-
book interests or interests of another kind. "He is a butcher,"
said of a surgeon, may affect his medical practice and lower his
income, whereas "He has syphilis," said about a rich playboy,
hurts almost exclusively his interest in seducing women. A court
of law can estimate pecuniary losses with reasonable exactitude
and assign a compensatory fee to injured plaintiffs in a non-
arbitrary way. Deciding on a fee to pay the playboy in compensation for his deprivation, on the other hand, requires a judgment
of the relative seriousness of this harm compared to harms that
carry non-arbitrary price tags, a comparison that is bound to be
inexact at best.

In contrast, the source of judgmental injustice as such is not
harm, but rather simple derogatory misrepresentation, harmful
or not. Most normal persons do have an interest in not being
thought worse of by others than they deserve. If only a half-dozen
widely scattered persons falsely believe that I am a wife-beater or
a plagiarizer, my interest in reputation is just to that extent
damaged, and in a perfectly intelligible sense I am harmed, even
though no other practical interest of mine is damaged as a
consequence. In the extreme case, where the public record is
forever falsified and everyone is convinced that I am (say) a
murderer, I am harmed to an extreme extent by the opinions and
judgments that are unfair to me. But those false opinions and
judgments would be unfair to me in any case even if they did not
cause me any harm.

Suppose a speaker stands up at a Harvard philosophical collo-

NONCOMPARATIVE JUSTICE

quium and accuses Professor Willard Van Orman Quine of being "the real and original Boston Strangler." I doubt whether this false derogatory judgment would do Professor Quine's reputation any harm. Nor would it be likely to distress him any. It is too patently absurd a judgment to have much of any effect at all, except perhaps to cause general amusement. And yet considered as a judgment simply, since it misrepresents the person it judges in a way that matters, it is unfair to him. Furthermore, if anyone were to come to believe it, then he would have a belief that is unfair to the person it is about.

I come finally to the differences between defamation and judgmental injustice that generate philosophical perplexities. These have to do with the nature of the standards employed in the two areas. Even within the law, there are disagreements over "the problem of the standard." "It has been held in England," Prosser tells us, "that the communication must tend to defame the plaintiff in the eyes of the community in general, or at least of a reasonable man, rather than in the opinion of any particular group or class."[32] The standard used in American courts, on the other hand, has been more realistic, "recognizing that the plaintiff may suffer real damage if he is lowered in the esteem of any substantial and respectable group, even though it be a minority one, with ideas that are not necessarily reasonable."[33] The class of persons whose esteem is lowered may be quite small, but not "so small as to be negligible." One plaintiff recovered damages as a consequence of a defendant's false public statement that her father was a murderer though clearly not many persons, and no reasonable persons, would think less of *her*, even if they believed the allegation about her father. On the other hand, no one today, not even a debutante, could recover damages for a false public allegation that her father was a coal miner or a factory worker. Hardly any person could admit without embarrassment that he thought less of her because of *that*. When the size of the group whose esteem is at issue is "substantial and respectable," however, its standards of value need not be reasonable at all. There have been many cases, in

---

[32] Prosser, *op. cit.*, p. 577.
[33] *Loc. cit.*

JOEL FEINBERG

southern courts especially, for example, in which a white man has recovered damages for the assertion or insinuation, in print, that he is a Negro.[34] While the esteeming group need not be reasonable, however, it must be minimally "respectable." No professional criminal could sue successfully for defamation on the ground that he had been falsely described as a police informer, even though that allegation may have utterly smashed his reputation with other criminals.

Whatever the correct policy decision about the standard for determining defamation, there is no reason a priori to expect it to apply also to determinations of judgmental unfairness. Indeed, as we have seen in the example of the white man who was defamed by the insinuation that he was a Negro, a genuinely defamatory utterance need not be judgmentally unfair at all. What then is the standard for judgmental injustice as such? This is a question which we should handle gingerly, since we have no guarantee in advance that it can be answered in as clear and precise a fashion as its legal counterpart. The problem requires the choice among standards of three kinds. We can choose a *subjective standard* for judgmental injustice, an *objective standard*, or the *standard of actual truth*. And there are choices within these categories. Within the subjective category, we can allow judgmental unfairness to be determined by the evaluative standards of the person judging, the person judged about, or the audience (if any) to whom the judgment is communicated. The latter possibility, while plausible enough for the determination of defamation, will not do for judgmental injustice; since we are after a standard that will apply to any judgment, expressed or not, we could hardly settle for a standard that applies to a judgment only when it is expressed. Similarly, we can eliminate the standards of the person making the judgment, for that would leave us with an anarchically relativistic result. One and the same false proposition—say, that John Doe is a Communist—would be unfair to Doe when believed by one person—say, Richard Nixon—and not at all unfair when

---

[34] One of the more recent cases is *Natchez Times Publishing Co.* v. *Dunnigan*, Mississippi, 1954, 72 So. 2d 681. See also *Spencer* v. *Looney*, Virginia, 1914, 116 Va. 767, 82 S.E. 745, and *Jones* v. *R. L. Polk & Co.* Alabama, 1915, 190 Ala. 243, 67 So. 577.

NONCOMPARATIVE JUSTICE

believed by another—say, Angela Davis. This result cannot be
ruled out dogmatically, but it does contradict a presupposition of
our inquiry—namely, that propositions about persons can be
unfair in themselves, just as they are true or false in themselves,
quite independently of who believes, affirms, or asserts them. The
most plausible of the subjective answers to our question is that
the appropriate standard for judgmental injustice is the standard
of the subject about whom the judgment is made. I shall return
to it below.

Objective standards are not necessarily those that are actually
employed by any given subject or group of subjects. Rather they
are those that ought to be employed by any subjects, those that
would be employed by all subjects if they were reasonable. Wherever the common law uses an objective standard, it refers therefore
to the standard of "the reasonable man." If we had used an
objective standard for defamation, as the English do, then
Dunnigan should not have won his suit against the *Natchez Times*
for insinuating falsely that he was a Negro, for surely he would
not be lowered in the estimation of any reasonable man just for
being thought to be a Negro. That is just another way of saying,
of course, that racial prejudice is unreasonable. Applying objective
criteria is not always that easy, especially if we permit our
standard to be tailored somewhat to the circumstances, as indeed
we often do in other contexts, when we consider that many of the
evaluative standards of actual reasonable men do not correspond
to those we would ascribe to a hypothetical ideal person whose
values transcend the limitations of a particular culture at a particular time and place. With which human characteristics should we
endow our hypothetical reasonable man if he is not to seem
superhuman? Is he simply the normal man of average insight and
sensitivity, like most of our neighbors? That is not a terribly
attractive idea, but it may be a realistic one unless we wish to hold
most of our neighbors themselves to a standard that is beyond
their reach. Supposing we give the reasonable man standards of
judgment that are a good deal closer to an ideal of correctness
than the average, what other characteristics should we give him?
Is he a reasonable Southerner or a reasonable Northerner? Does
he know a lot of history, psychology, and economics, or is his

333

JOEL FEINBERG

knowledge defective in the manner of most of our neighbors in those respects?

When we are dealing with various purely legal matters including the question of defamation, we will often wish to soften an objective standard by bringing in certain subjective elements. So, for example, the law of negligence holds a blind man to the standard of a "reasonably careful and prudent blind man," not to the more elevated standard of a reasonable man with normal vision. Similarly in the law of criminal homicide, under some rules,[35] a defendant is entitled to the mitigating defense of "provocation" if he can show that he killed a man in circumstances that would have caused even a reasonable man to lose control of himself. Such rules attribute an emotional side to the reasonable man, and even a tendency in certain rare circumstances to very human passionate anger.[36] The introduction of softening elements into objective legal standards is a concession to common human frailties intended to prevent the unfairness of holding specific persons to standards they cannot meet. In the law of defamation the softening process increases the protection given to prospective plaintiffs, but toughens the requirements imposed on prospective defendants, for it permits some plaintiffs to collect

---

[35] E.g., Great Britain's Homicide Act (1957), Sec. 3: "Where on a charge of murder there is evidence on which the jury can find that the person charged was provoked (whether by things done or by things said or by both together) to lose his self-control, the question whether the provocation was enough to make a reasonable man do as he did shall be left to be determined by the jury."

[36] Such rules are by no means unanimously approved by legal commentators. Glanville Williams writes: "Surely the true view of provocation is that it is a concession to 'the frailty of human nature' in those exceptional cases where the legal prohibition fails of effect. It is a compromise, neither conceding the propriety of the act nor exacting the full penalty for it. This being so, how can it be admitted that that paragon of virtue, the reasonable man, gives way to provocation?" ("Provocation and the Reasonable Man," *Criminal Law Review* [1954], p. 742). The authors of the *Model Penal Code*, in their Comments on Tentative Draft No. 9 (1959), p. 47, argue that "To require, as the rule is sometimes stated, that the provocation be enough to make a reasonable man do as the defendant did is patently absurd; the reasonable man quite plainly does not kill. . . . But even the correct and the more common statement of the rule, that the provocative circumstances must be sufficient to deprive a reasonable or an ordinary man of self-control, leaves much to be desired since it totally excludes any attention to the special situation of the actor."

NONCOMPARATIVE JUSTICE

damages for false statements that would not diminish their standing in the eyes of an ideal transcultural reasonable man, but would diminish the esteem of a reasonable man of deep southern background and affiliation, say, or of Orthodox Jewish religious commitment, or whatever. But when we apply a standard of judgmental unfairness quite outside of legal contexts, there are no "plaintiffs" or "defendants" to consider, nor even subjects or objects of spoken utterances or written statements to specific audiences in concrete circumstances. Here, we deal not with persons who might later complain of harsh treatment, but with *propositions* about people, and propositions have no human frailties to consider. Here if anywhere we should expect our standards to be as free as possible of subjective elements.

The most objective standard we could possibly employ would be that of actual truth: a false statement is unfair to a person if it is *truly derogatory* of him—that is, if it would lower the esteem of a hypothetical reasonable man who employed only correct evaluative standards. If we then ascribe to our ideally reasonable man complete empirical knowledge of all matters relevant to evaluations, we would be very close to identifying the reasonable man with God. In a way this is the easiest solution to our problem, for it allows us to evade difficult questions about the evaluation of human character. Unlike its alternative solutions to the problem of the standard for judgmental unfairness, this one is not merely partially but completely formal, needing to be filled in by a thorough account of what the true standards for admiring and disrespecting *are*—in short, by a long and systematic treatise in what Kant called *Tugendlehre*, or the theory of virtue.

Nonetheless, the standard of actual truth is prima facie the most plausible one for our limited purposes here. It seems to be the standard presupposed by our intuitions in clear cases, explaining, for example, why it is unfair to Quine to judge or believe him to be the Boston Strangler, even though there are few if any actual contexts in which the assertion of that proposition would defame him. An ideally reasonable man who employed only the correct principles of character appraisal would give Quine very low points indeed if he believed him to be a strangler. There may be possible if not actual cultures or subcultures which exercise such

JOEL FEINBERG

strong influences on their members that even generally reasonable men among them would think *more* of Quine for his extracurricular violence, but whatever the opinions of "reasonable *machos*" like that, our intuitions are unwavering: the proposition in question is unfair to Quine. Similarly, it would be false but not unfair to Quine to believe him to be a Negro, whatever the reaction of some hypothetically localized and humanized "reasonable man."

It would be satisfyingly simple, and superficially plausible, to leave the matter at that, but as usual in philosophy there are troublesome counterexamples and looming complications. Suppose we assume, merely for the sake of an example, that the analytic-synthetic distinction is perfectly sensible and that the arguments so far mustered against it are muddled one and all. On that assumption, would it be unfair to Quine to believe that he is a great *defender* of the analytic-synthetic distinction? If we communicated this belief to audiences of certain kinds, Quine would probably feel defamed, but that is at least partly because he believes the analytic-synthetic distinction to be untenable. Suppose, however, that an angel of the Lord comes to Quine near the end of his days and reveals to him the truth that the analytic-synthetic distinction is quite tenable, so that Quine is forced to change his mind about it. Even then, I suspect, Quine could hardly be content with the false judgment, communicated or not, that his career had been spent defending the tenability, now vindicated, of the distinction. Indeed, I should think he might even feel *wronged* by the judgment, though neither defamed, nor otherwise harmed, nor disparaged, nor belittled by it. To be misdescribed in a way that is very basic to one's conception of oneself, one might think, is to be judged or treated unfairly, even though not in any obvious way derogated or discredited.

There are better examples, often involving less controversial assumptions, that can be drawn from history's catalogue of lost causes. Those of us who are liberals might well understand how it is unfair to Bill Buckley to judge him to be a liberal, and even a doctrinaire socialist will appreciate the judgmental injustice in the false claim that T. S. Eliot was a socialist. It is unfair to any person

NONCOMPARATIVE JUSTICE

who has conscientiously believed in a proposition, taken it to heart, advocated and campaigned for it, and in the extreme case even built his life upon it, to deny that he believed that proposition, even though in fact that proposition is false. Thus, even though God might think better of Bertrand Russell if He believed him to be a devout Christian, that belief about Russell would be unfair to him, and unfair even if atheism, his actual conviction, should be false.

The conclusion I draw from these examples is that the standard for judgmental injustice is necessarily disjunctive in form. A false judgment or belief about a person is unfair to that person if *either* it is truly derogatory of him *or else* it severely misrepresents him in a way which is fundamental to his own conception of himself. (Unfairness by the second criterion would have to be restricted to violations of self-conceptions that fall within wide limits of reasonableness. The sincere subjective standards respected by that criterion cannot be so highly eccentric as to be irrational.) A judgment or belief about a person is unfair to him according to the second criterion even though it misrepresents him in a way that would elevate his standing in the eyes of an ideally reasonable being.

The disjunctive criterion suggests that we have duties of at least two kinds in respect to our beliefs about other persons. Corresponding to the first disjunct is a duty to try to avoid believing objectively derogatory things about others in the absence of firm evidence. That is a duty to give others the benefit of one's doubts, to avoid thinking ill of them without warrant—in short, to be generous. The second duty, however, cuts the other way, for in some cases it would have us also be careful to avoid believing too well of a person in the absence of firm evidence, because of the danger that a false generous belief might misrepresent him in a respect which is crucial to his own conception of himself. To take this second duty seriously, then, would be to create a disposition that would tend to counterbalance that created by the first, at least for a certain class of cases.

The morality of belief and judgment is subtle enough to begin with, and this disjunctive criterion of judgmental injustice makes it even more difficult. That result, however, should not be

JOEL FEINBERG

alarming. Given that we run such complicated moral risks when we judge falsely about our fellows, we had better make all the more sure that our beliefs and judgments are true.

JOEL FEINBERG

The Rockefeller University

[4]

COMPARATIVE AND NON-COMPARATIVE JUSTICE

By Phillip Montague

I

Discussions of justice have traditionally focused on two very general kinds of concerns. On the one hand, justice is associated with the concepts of equality, similarity, and proportionality, and in this area questions of justice are essentially comparative: whether an individual has been treated justly depends on how his treatment compares with that received by others. On the other hand, we have the idea that justice consists in giving everyone "his due", and here the questions of justice are not comparative: whether an individual receives just treatment depends on features of *that* individual, and is independent of how others are treated.

Although most contemporary writers on the subject of justice appear to recognize these two kinds of concerns, few if any deal adequately with both. Indeed, there appear to be distinct preferences among philosophers for either a comparative or a non-comparative approach to explaining the concept of justice, and these preferences show through in the various accounts of this concept that appear in the literature. For example, Benn and Peters maintain that "To act justly . . . is to treat all men alike except where there are relevant differences between them",[1] while Hospers claims that justice consists in "treating each person in accordance with his or her deserts".[2] Some discussions of justice contain both comparative and non-comparative elements. Frankena, for example, states flatly that "justice is comparative",[3] and elaborates on this theme by claiming that

> Justice is treating persons equally, except as unequal treatment is required by just-making considerations (i.e., by principles of *justice*, not merely *moral* principles).

But then, almost in the same breath (pp. 10-11), Frankena says that:

> Justice simply is the apportionment of what is to be apportioned in accordance with the amount or degree in which the recipients possess some required features—personal ability, desert, merit, rank, or wealth.

Despite the latter remarks (which contain no suggestion that justice is comparative), Frankena clearly leans toward a comparative account of justice. Along with others who emphasize the relation between justice and

[1]S. I. Benn and R. S. Peters, *Social Principles and the Democratic State* (London, 1959), p. 111.

[2]John Hospers, "Free Enterprise as the Embodiment of Justice", in Richard T. De George and Joseph A. Picher (edd.), *Ethics, Free Enterprise and Public Policy* (New York, 1978), p. 73.

[3]William Frankena, "The Concept of Social Justice", in Richard B. Brandt (ed.), *Social Justice* (Englewood Cliffs, N.J., 1962), p. 9.

equality (similarity, proportionality, etc.), he largely ignores the wide range of cases in which it is possible to determine whether someone has been treated justly with no knowledge whatever of the treatment given to others. When, for example, individuals receive undeserved punishment, when they do not receive rewards, compensations, honours, or grades that they do deserve, or when their rights are violated, they are (*ceteris paribus*) treated unjustly; and we know that this is the case without concern about questions of equality or similarity of treatment.

As far as I know, only Joel Feinberg among contemporary philosophers has explicitly distinguished between cases in which the justice of an individual's treatment depends on how his treatment compares with that received by others, and cases in which questions of justice can be answered without such comparisons.[4] Feinberg distinguishes between "comparative" and "non-comparative" justice, which he evidently regards as irreducibly distinct concepts, the applicability of which depend upon disjoint and possibly conflicting sets of principles. Feinberg's discussion of this subject is perceptive and thorough, and it deserves close attention. But while I agree with him that there is a need to distinguish between comparative and non-comparative justice, I shall argue that his position is mistaken in some important and fundamental respects. I shall also suggest an interpretation of comparative and non-comparative justice that seems to me to avoid the difficulties with Feinberg's position.

II

According to Feinberg, the following two familiar principles express the basic requirements of comparative and non-comparative justice respectively, and underlie all other principles of comparative and non-comparative justice:[5]

(P)   Justice requires the similar treatment of relevantly similar cases and the dissimilar treatment of relevantly dissimilar cases

(P1) Justice requires that individuals be treated in accordance with their rights and deserts.

Thus any situation which contains individuals who are relevantly similar or dissimilar with respect to some treatment would constitute what Feinberg calls an "occasion" for comparative justice; and any situation which contains individuals whose rights or deserts are at stake would be an "occasion" for non-comparative justice. Feinberg further maintains that there are occasions for both comparative and non-comparative justice—that there are actions the justice or injustice of which can be accounted for adequately only by appeal to both comparative and non-comparative principles. He claims in particular that there are cases in which "double injustices" occur —i.e., cases involving actions that are unjust according to both comparative

---

[4]In "Non-comparative Justice", *The Philosophical Review*, 83 (1974), 297-338; and *Social Philosophy* (Englewood Cliffs, N.J., 1973), pp. 98 ff. But see also A. D. Woozley, "Injustice", *American Philosophical Quarterly*, supp. vol., 1973.

[5]See especially the remarks on pp. 98-99 of *Social Philosophy*.

and non-comparative principles; and that there are other cases in which comparative and non-comparative principles conflict—i.e., cases in which "what is condoned by the comparative principle is condemned by the non-comparative one, or what is endorsed by the non-comparative principle is declared unjust by the comparative one" (1974, p. 312).

Feinberg provides few *clear* examples of these, but it is possible, on the basis of his remarks, to see what such cases would be like, in broad outline. Thus, a double injustice would apparently occur if some but not all members of an appropriate group (which I shall call a "comparison class"[6]) were deprived of their due; and a conflict between comparative and non-comparative principles would occur if either everyone in a comparison class were deprived of his due (an act condoned by comparative principles and condemned by non-comparative ones), or if some members of a comparison class are the objects of "arbitrary discrimination", but no undeserved burdens are imposed and no deserved benefits are withheld (an action that accords with non-comparative principles but violates comparative ones).

There is, however, something very peculiar about the first two classes of cases—i.e., those involving double injustices, and those in which actions are required by comparative principles and prohibited by non-comparative ones. In cases of both kinds principles of comparative justice purportedly require that *every* member of a comparison class be deprived of his due if *any* member of that class is deprived of his due. And this surely cannot be right. Suppose, for example, that A, B, and C comprise a comparison class, that each deserves some benefit, and that D deprives A but not B and C of that benefit. If we accept what Feinberg says about comparative justice, D would then have a reason, *arising from a principle of justice*, for depriving B and C of their just deserts. This result strikes me as quite plainly unacceptable, and it remains unacceptable even if, as Feinberg suggests, non-comparative principles routinely override comparative ones when conflicts occur. For this sort of claim assumes that comparative principles carry some weight in the situations in question, and it is precisely this assumption that I am disputing. In the above example, D has no reason whatever—at least no reason based on a principle of justice—for depriving B and C of their due no matter how he has treated A. D is not faced with a conflict between comparative and non-comparative principles, and he does not do A a *double* injustice by depriving him of his due while granting B and C theirs.

The conclusions of the above line of argument can be generalized to all cases in which actions are prohibited by non-comparative principles. In these cases comparative principles will neither reinforce nor conflict with the non-comparative ones, and hence they are not applicable to actions that are unjust according to the latter.

[6]I shall use "comparison class" to refer to any group of individuals whose relevant similarity or dissimilarity (with regard to some treatment) is in question.

Now let us consider the other class of conflict cases, *viz.*, those in which, according to Feinberg, "what is endorsed by the non-comparative principle is declared unjust by the comparative one".

As I have described these cases, they involve "arbitrary discrimination" without the imposition of undeserved burdens or the withholding of deserved benefits. This description, which I have constructed on the basis of Feinberg's examples, is not quite the same as his own, in which he characterizes the cases in question as arising "whenever an authority makes an "example" or an "exception" of one or more out of a class of subjects whose individual deserts are alike" (1974, p. 314). The trouble with Feinberg's characterization is that it includes cases in which some but not all members of a comparison class are deprived of a deserved benefit or receive an undeserved burden—which is most certainly not endorsed by non-comparative principles. In the cases he has in mind, some but not all members of a comparison class escape a deserved burden or receive an undeserved benefit. He devotes most of his attention to the latter category, and to two kinds of cases in particular: those involving what he calls "gratuitous benefaction", and those involving "the distribution of a *surplus* among a group of recipients after justice has already been done to each proper individual claim" (p. 315). For convenience I shall refer to the former as GB cases and to the latter as SB cases, and to the actions involved in each as GB acts and SB acts respectively.

Feinberg cites acts of charity as examples of GB acts, and claims that giving charity to some but not all members of a comparison class is just according to non-comparative principles, but is unjust on comparative grounds. It seems to me quite plain, however, that in making this claim Feinberg overlooks the general distinction between acts that are required or endorsed by some principle, and acts to which the principle simply does not apply. Because acts of charity—and GB acts in general—are not called for by anyone's rights or deserts, non-comparative principles of justice do not apply to them. One is not acting in accord with non-comparative principles when one performs a GB act, and GB cases cannot involve conflicts between comparative and non-comparative principles. These same conclusions hold for SB acts, to which principles of non-comparative justice are also inapplicable. For example, Feinberg maintains that an employer who compensates his equally deserving employees unequally while at the same time paying all far more than they deserve, acts justly from a non-comparative standpoint but unjustly on comparative grounds. But here again no one's rights or deserts are at stake, and hence the case is not an occasion for non-comparative justice. If injustices do occur in GB and SB cases, they must therefore be of the comparative variety.[7]

[7]Cf. N. Gillespie, "On Treating Like Cases Differently", *Philosophical Quarterly*, 25 (1975).

III

Feinberg's claims about the occurrences of comparative injustices in GB and SB cases are actually rather tentative. He himself notes how peculiar is the notion that one acts unjustly when one denies another person some benefit to which the latter has no right and which he does not deserve; but Feinberg maintains nevertheless that (P) can be violated in such cases, and hence that comparative injustices can occur. I should like to suggest, however, that here again he is mistaken.

If (P) is violated in a GB or SB case it is presumably because relevantly similar individuals are treated dissimilarly. But while there is no question but that dissimilar treatment occurs when, e.g., some but not all members of a group are given charity, it is far from clear that the others can be regarded as *relevantly* similar with respect to that treatment.

The concept of relevant similarity is doubly relational: similarity is a relation among individuals in a comparison class, and relevance is a relation between some treatment and the features in virtue of which these individuals are similar. I do not think that it is necessary to analyse the concept of relevance in great depth in order to recognize that the relation is a normative one, and hence that "relevant similarity"—as it occurs in (P)—concerns features that require or call for treatment of a certain kind. And since we are dealing here with matters of justice, it seems reasonable to identify the features of individuals which, in the appropriate sense, call for or require some treatment, with those features in virtue of which they deserve or have a right to that treatment.

Now consider again a case in which some but not all members of a group of individuals receive charitable donations. If this kind of case involves similar treatment of *relevantly* similar individuals, then those in the group must share features which, from the standpoint of justice, require that they be given charitable donations. But, as Feinberg himself appears to suggest, there are no such features, and thus individuals cannot be *relevantly* similar with respect to receiving charitable contributions. Hence (P) does not apply to cases involving individuals receiving such treatment, and they are not occasions for comparative justice. This same result applies to all other GB cases, and also—for the same reasons—to all SB cases.

Feinberg seems at times content to count individuals as relevantly similar as long as they lack relevant dissimilarities—which immediately raises the question how to explain the concept of relevant *dis*similarity. Like many other writers on the subject of justice, however, Feinberg devotes little attention to the concept of relevant dissimilarity. He concerns himself almost exclusively with that aspect of (P) which requires the similar treatment of relevantly similar cases, and largely ignores the equally clear requirement that dissimilar cases should be treated dissimilarly. I suspect that it is this view of (P) which leads him to claim that *"arbitrary discrimination is the essence of comparative injustice"* (1973, p. 99), while ignoring com-

136   PHILLIP MONTAGUE

pletely the fact that arbitrary *non*-discrimination appears to be no less a
comparative injustice according to (P).[8] Moreover, (P) can plausibly be
taken as prohibiting arbitrary discrimination and non-discrimination only if
'arbitrary' is interpreted appropriately. Feinberg apparently thinks arbitrary
discrimination is differential treatment that is not justified by reasons of a
certain sort—presumably reasons which bear on matters of justice. I should
think, however, that one violates (P) by acting *contrary* to such reasons,
and not simply in their absence. There are situations (e.g., those involving
charitable contributions) in which one's actions are not justified by considerations of justice because questions of justice or injustice simply do not
arise. Such situations are not occasions for justice—comparative or non-
comparative; if they involve acts of arbitrary discrimination or non-discrimination, they are not of a sort that can reasonably be regarded as
prohibited by (P).

IV

It follows from the argument of the preceding section that principles of
comparative justice do not apply to actions to which non-comparative
principles are inapplicable. Yet we saw earlier in our discussion of "double
injustices", and of those actions Feinberg claims are prohibited by non-
comparative principles but required by comparative ones, that comparative
principles do not in fact apply to actions that are unjust on non-comparative
grounds. Hence the only remaining actions to which comparative principles
might apply are those which are genuinely required by non-comparative
principles. Presumably, if comparative principles do apply to the latter
cases, they might either reinforce or conflict with the relevant non-comparative principles.

But one who acts in accord with principles of non-comparative justice
will deny no one his due, and will automatically meet the requirements of
comparative justice. Thus there can be no conflicts between comparative
and non-comparative principles relative to actions required by the latter.
And because in such cases the requirements of comparative justice would
be indistinguishable from those of non-comparative justice, it is hard to see
the former as *reinforcing* the latter. One who performs an action that is
just on non-comparative grounds acts justly; I see no reasonable basis for
insisting that comparative principles also apply to such cases.

We are now in a position to conclude that comparative principles of
justice, including (P), do not apply to actions required by non-comparative
principles, nor to actions prohibited by these principles; nor to actions to

[8]There is reason to believe that (P) is often confused with the very different principle
that justice requires equal treatment of all individuals unless there is justification for
treating them unequally. See Feinberg (1973), p. 99: John Rawls, "Justice as Fairness", *The Philosophical Review*, 67 (1958), p. 166; William Frankena, "The Concept
of Social Justice", esp. pp. 8-13; Bernard Williams, "The Idea of Equality", in Joel
Feinberg (ed.), *Moral Concepts* (Oxford, 1969), p. 154.

which non-comparative principles are inapplicable. Therefore there are no actions to which comparative principles of justice apply—there are no occasions for comparative justice of the sort Feinberg seems to have in mind. But to deny that there are *actions* to which comparative principles apply is by no means to suggest that these principles are vacuous. What we must recognize is that comparative principles—and (P) in particular—embody criteria for judging the justice or injustice not of particular actions but of practices, institutions, or sets of rules of certain kinds.

This distinction between the justice of particular actions and the justice of practices, institutions, etc., is overlooked by Feinberg in his discussion of comparative and non-comparative justice, and this omission may explain certain aspects of his position. Thus, when discussing cases that he regards as involving conflicts between comparative and non-comparative principles, he sometimes focuses on the justice of *actions* (e.g., acts of gratuitous benefaction) and sometimes on the justice of institutions or sets of rules (e.g., a slave society, or a system of criminal law; cf. 1974, p. 312). Feinberg apparently assumes without question that the same general sorts of principles, including (P) and (P1), will apply in both areas. Part of what I am suggesting here is that this assumption is mistaken, and that unless it is abandoned a proper understanding of the concept of justice—in both its comparative and non-comparative manifestations—is impossible.

V

The clearest applications of the concept of comparative justice are to what I shall call "desert systems". The nature and significance of these systems is hinted at, in the following remarks, by Benn and Peters:

> 'Desert' is a normative word; its use presupposes a rule having two components: (i) a condition to be satisfied; (ii) a mode of treatment consequent upon it. . . . We cannot estimate desert, therefore, in a vacuum; we must be able to refer to some standard or rule from which 'X deserves R' follows as a conclusion (p. 137).

It seems to me that the central point of these remarks is quite correct—at least if the "modes of treatment" referred to are rather specific in nature. Thus, for example, a judgement to the effect that some individual deserves to be fired from his job must be made in the light of rules which apply to the individual in question, and which relate a set of activities that count as punishable to another set of activities that count as punishments. The set of punishable activities, the set of punishments, and the relation between members of these sets comprise what I shall call a system of punishment. A system of punishment is one kind of desert system; other such systems are systems of reward, systems of compensation, and systems of grading. All these systems are composed of three elements: a relation 'x calls for y in z' where x is an activity which (borrowing a term from Feinberg) I shall refer to as a "desert basis", y is an activity referred to here as a "treatment", and z is a desert system; a set of desert bases; and a set of treatments.

Although I am largely in agreement with the statements of Benn and Peters quoted above, there is one important respect in which I have no doubt that they are mistaken. They state that judgements about individual desert (X deserves R) follow as "conclusions" from the rules of desert systems; but this is not so—at least not without the aid of additional premises. One might engage in an activity that belongs among the desert bases of some desert system, and might as a result receive the treatment called for by that activity in the given desert system, but one will not *deserve* this treatment unless the system itself is just. And while the conditions that determine the justice or injustice of desert systems vary with the nature of these systems, certain conditions apply to a number of common and important kinds of systems.

Consider, for example, systems of punishment, reward, grading, and compensation. In all these systems it is common for the activities in the desert basis and treatment sets to be ordered relative to appropriate properties. For example, the desert bases of systems of punishment will commonly be ordered relative to their gravity, and the treatments of these systems will be ordered according to their severity; the desert bases of systems of compensation for work done will often be ordered according to the skill or responsibility involved, and the treatments, which will usually involve monetary payments, will be ordered according to the amounts of those payments.

At this point we can see the proper place to raise questions of comparative justice and the proper role of principle (P). For one mark of a just desert system of the sort being discussed here is that the orderings of the desert basis and treatment sets are preserved by the *calls for* relation: the similarities and dissimilarities that exist among the desert bases of the system are appropriately reflected in the treatments of that system. In other words, just desert systems treat relevantly similar cases similarly and relevantly dissimilar cases dissimilarly. Moreover, if relevantly similar cases are treated similarly and if relevantly dissimilar cases are treated dissimilarly in a desert system, there is no *further* application of this requirement in determining the justice or injustice of individual actions that are the treatments of that system. For example, if in a system of punishment relevantly similar cases are treated similarly and relevantly dissimilar cases are treated dissimilarly, and if the system is otherwise just, then whether an act of punishing that belongs to the system is just will depend upon whether the punishment is deserved by the individual on whom it is imposed, without any reference to how others are treated. If students *A* and *B* both engage in activities that are punishable according to regulations of their school, and if a day's suspension is called for in both cases, then these regulations constitute a *just* system of punishment only if the offences in question are specified as equally grave. But whether *A* is treated unjustly in being suspended for more than one day depends on what punishment *he* deserves; questions about the similarity or dissimilarity of *A*'s case relative to *B*'s or anyone else's simply do not arise at this level.

Thus, as was suggested above, we must distinguish between the conditions under which *acts* of punishing, compensating, etc., are just or unjust, and conditions under which *systems* of punishment, compensation, etc., are just or unjust. What I am claiming here is that (P) expresses a requirement that belongs among the latter and not the former set of conditions. The justice of particular actions—at least insofar as it involves matters of desert of the kind we have discussed here—is entirely independent of (P), and is determined non-comparatively in the light of features of the individuals whose treatment is in question. Therefore at the level of particular actions that involve specific deserved treatments there is no such thing as a comparative injustice. Although I shall not argue the point here, I am convinced that these conclusions can be extended to other desert contexts, and also to situations involving individual rights. If I am correct, then questions concerning the justice of individual actions are non-comparative, and are arrived at by appealing (ultimately) to principle (P1) and never to principle (P); while questions concerning the justice of practices, institutions, and systems of rules of various sorts are (at least in part) comparative, and are answered by appealing to principle (P).

VI

I should like to conclude by commenting on a class of cases that may seem to generate problems for the position I have put forward here. I have in mind cases in which a deserved burden is imposed on some but not all members of a group when *all* deserve the burden; and *certain* cases in which an undeserved benefit is granted to some but not all members of a group when *none* deserve that benefit. I do not include in this latter category either GB or SB cases, which I believe I have dealt with adequately above. According to the arguments I have presented here, none of the actions involved in these cases are comparatively unjust; yet injustices certainly seem to occur in at least some of them, and these injustices do not appear to arise from violations of non-comparative principles. It is evidently unjust, for example, for a judge to sentence one but not the other of two persons to life imprisonment when both deserve that punishment; or for a teacher to assign an alpha to one but not the other of two students when neither deserves that grade. Yet it is hard to see how non-comparative principles —and (P1) in particular—can be invoked to explain these injustices.

The problem arises here, I believe, from an oversimplified interpretation of principle (P1) insofar as it pertains to matters of desert. As formulated above and in most other discussions of justice, (P1) seems to imply that if someone deserves a certain treatment then everyone is obliged to treat him exactly in accordance with those deserts. While it is clear that this interpretation of (P1) will not survive even the most casual scrutiny, and is

140   PHILLIP MONTAGUE

probably accepted by no one, the most likely alternative interpretation is far less obviously problematic, and appears to be accepted by many writers. On this interpretation, (P1) allows a certain latitude in reacting to individual deserts: it is unnecessary to treat everyone *exactly* as he deserves to be treated, as long as no one is denied a deserved benefit and no one receives an undeserved burden. But this interpretation of (P1) is not quite right either, since, as we have seen, there are cases in which injustices occur even though no undeserved burdens are imposed and no deserved benefits are withheld. In the two examples cited above that satisfy the latter conditions a judge refrains from imposing on a convicted criminal the punishment he deserves (but does not, as a result, overpunish anyone else); and a teacher assigns to a student a grade much higher than he deserves (but does not, as a result, assign to others grades lower than they deserve). Other cases of the same sort are easy to construct: a University promotes an undeserving member of staff (but does not fail to promote any deserving ones); a plant manager does not dismiss an employee who deserves to be let go (but fires no one who does not deserve to be).

I think there are two lessons to be learned from these cases, and from the contrast between them and GB and SB cases in particular. The first lesson is that one can act unjustly without doing anyone an injustice. The second lesson is that deserts do not give rise to general obligations (as rights do, for example); rather, individuals, in virtue of their institutional roles, have obligations to act in various ways relative to the deserts of others. It is these obligations with which (P1) is concerned when it pertains to matters of desert; and when these obligations are not met, non-comparative injustices occur. It is not necessary, therefore, to appeal to (P) in order to account for the injustices in the cases we have been discussing in this section, and the thesis that no comparative injustices occur at the level of particular actions remains intact.

Western Washington University

Part II
Justice – Desert – Redistribution

Part II

[5]

MICHAEL A. SLOTE

Desert, Consent, and Justice

In this essay, I intend to deal with an important problem about the nature of just societies.[1] I shall not endeavor to solve the problem, but hope, rather, to indicate its centrality to the whole question of the nature of social justice and to show why it is so difficult to resolve it in any satisfactory way. The issue I wish to discuss is whether an ideally just society whose members were to some appropriate degree willing to work for the general good and not merely for their own selfish interests would reward people (workers) in accordance with their actual *success* in contributing to society or in accordance with their (conscientious) *efforts* to contribute to society.

For convenience, but also because there is more than a grain of truth to it, we can consider this to be, in effect, the question whether society is more justly organized according to a democratic capitalist scheme or according to a (utopian) socialist scheme. For although there have been many other arguments for the superiority of capitalism to socialism, and even other arguments for the superior justice of capitalism, one very important argument for capitalism over (certain forms of utopian) socialism has been that those who through ability or "luck" contribute more to society in all justice and fairness deserve more from society than those who, despite their greatest efforts, make less of a contribution to society. Similarly, though there have been many kinds of socialism and many kinds of argument for socialism,

1. I am indebted to the Editors of *Philosophy & Public Affairs* for many helpful criticisms of an earlier version of this paper.

one thing that seems often to have had great force in persuading people to be socialists is the view that it is only just to reward people for their conscientious efforts, and that it is unfair for someone to reap more of the rewards society has to distribute simply because he happens, through greater innate talents or other "lucky breaks," to (be able to) do more for society.

It may be asked at this point why I speak of socialism, rather than of Marxism or Communism. My reason is not that I conceive Marxism to be one kind of socialism and thus automatically or naturally included when I talk about socialism. It is, rather, that I think there is no good reason to think that the main issue between capitalism and Marxism is over the nature of the just society or over the justness of capitalist society, in particular. Despite long-standing misconceptions on this point, it has recently been very convincingly argued by Robert Tucker and (especially) Allen Wood that Marx had no great interest in decrying the injustice of capitalist society and, even, that Marx thought that capitalist society as he knew it was not basically unjust.[2]

The problem whether a just society rewards its members in accordance with their efforts to contribute, or in accordance with their success in contributing, is an important issue that divides capitalist theorists and socialist theorists, but does not, in general, divide capitalist theorists and orthodox Marxists. Moreover, this issue, however important it may be, does not even divide capitalist theorists from non-Marxian socialists in any clean-cut way. Many socialists have held that workers should receive the full product of their labor (which they are presumed not to receive under capitalism); and this seems to entail what I have called the democratic capitalist view that one should be rewarded according to his actual contribution to society rather than according to his conscientious efforts in behalf of society. Be this as it may, there is another view about the compensation of labor that I think is more typical of socialism. This view is often expressed in the motto or adage: "from each according to his ability, to each according to his needs." It is this view, it seems to me, that brings

2. See Robert Tucker, *The Marxian Revolutionary Idea* (New York, 1969), and Allen W. Wood, "The Marxian Critique of Justice," *Philosophy & Public Affairs* I, no. 3 (Spring 1972): 244-282.

          Desert, Consent, and Justice

out the most important differences between socialism and capitalism and that is (part of) the best expression of socialism as an "ideal type." So when I speak of the differences between socialism and capitalism, I am not talking about all socialism, but only about a certain ideal type of socialism that stands opposed to a certain ideal type of capitalism. I say "ideal type of capitalism" because it is not even clear that all capitalist theorists want, or should want, to claim that distribution according to actual (successful) contribution is ideally just. A capitalistic theorist might well want to claim that such distribution is somewhat unjust, but nonetheless socially justifiable on the grounds of its efficiency or benefits, or the unworkability of alternative distributive schemes. But as a rule one who defends capitalism will feel that rewarding according to contribution, rather than effort, is fair and just; and it is such a form of capitalistic theorizing that I mean to discuss here.

I

The kind of socialism I refer to is, I have said, exemplified by the view: "from each according to his ability, to each according to his needs." But even among people who in some sense adhere to this adage there is dispute as to how, or how strictly, it is to be interpreted. For example, are aesthetic needs to count equally with "basic" needs, and what, indeed, are to be considered (basic) human needs? If, in particular, it is necessary to reduce everyone to a bare subsistence level in order, say, to keep certain people with rare diseases alive and functioning, does the adage tell us that we must (in all fairness) do so? It appears that different socialists would respond differently to these questions.[3] What can be said, roughly, to characterize socialism generally or as an ideal type, however, is that according to its conception of social justice, goods, benefits or rewards for work should be in accordance with conscientious effort in behalf of society, assuming certain basic similarities or equalities in people's needs, and, in any case, should not

3. For discussion of questions like these, see H. Spiegelberg, "A Defense of Human Equality," *Philosophical Review* 53 (1944): 101-124; D. D. Raphael, "Justice and Liberty," *Proceedings of the Aristotelian Society* 51 (1950-51): 187f.; and J. N. Findlay, *Value and Intentions* (London, 1961), pp. 301ff.

be distributed in accordance with actual success in benefiting society. And such a view, vague though it may be, does stand in sharp contrast with what I have been claiming to be the typical capitalist conception of what is necessary to a just society.

Now Tucker has claimed that the motto "from each according to his ability . . ." (which we can henceforth, for brevity, refer to as the socialist motto) expresses a social ideal, but not an ideal of social justice.[4] And there is some support for this in the fact that Marx, who believed that capitalism was not unjust, presents himself as an adherent of the socialist motto in *A Critique of the Gotha Program*. But whatever Marx's, or Tucker's, views about justice, or about the socialist motto, it is quite clear that many writers on political theory have felt that this motto expresses an ideal, often their ideal, of social justice. The impressive list of such writers includes: Babeuf,[5] J. S. Mill,[6] O. D. Skelton,[7] F. H. Knight,[8] John Strachey,[9] C. Frankel,[10] and John Rawls.[11] Furthermore, it seems obvious to me that the socialist motto can very naturally and easily, even if mistakenly, be thought to express an ideal of social justice, and perhaps the only support this assumption requires at this point can be supplied by the reader's own intuitions on the matter. If, furthermore, Tucker thinks that the socialist motto does not express an ideal of justice, that is perhaps because it expresses an ideal of social justice that he thoroughly disagrees with; for Tucker says that the socialist motto does not express an ideal of social justice because a person's needs may be in inverse proportion to his ability and to his contribution to society. Tucker, then, seems to be espousing what I have called a capitalist conception of social justice. And there are numerous other places where one can find a capitalist conception of justice expressed.[12]

4. *Op. cit.*, p. 38.   5. *La Doctrine des Egaux*, ed. Thomas (Paris, 1906).
6. "Utilitarianism," in *The English Philosophers from Bacon to Mill*, Modern Library ed. (New York, 1939), p. 942.
7. *Socialism: A Critical Analysis* (Boston, 1911), pp. 200ff.
8. *The Ethics of Competition* (New York, 1935), p. 56.
9. *The Theory and Practice of Socialism* (New York, 1936), pp. 120f.
10. "Justice and Rationality" in S. Morgenbesser, P. Suppes, and M. White, eds., *Philosophy, Science, and Method* (New York, 1969), p. 409.
11. *A Theory of Justice* (Cambridge, Mass., 1971), pp. 304f.
12. E.g., in Mill, *loc. cit.*, Frankel, *loc. cit.*, and Rawls, *op. cit.*, pp. 304-311.

In this essay, I hope to clarify the nature and sources of the disagreement between democratic capitalists and non-Marxian socialists concerning the relative importance of effort as against successful contribution in determining an ideally just distribution of goods in society. Following J. S. Mill, in "Utilitarianism,"[13] I shall argue that this disagreement stems from a disagreement about whether effort or success (i.e., actual contribution) is more important in determining what one *deserves* to receive from society. That is because, like Mill, I think that the notion of desert is crucially involved in the notion of justice. (However, an attempt will be made here to show that Mill is significantly mistaken about the *kind* of desert that is analytically involved in the concept of justice.) I shall first attempt to show why disagreement about the relative importance of effort and success in determining what one deserves from society very naturally arises and remains impossible to resolve in a way that will satisfy everyone. Then it will be argued that an appropriate notion of desert is centrally involved in the concept of justice, despite John Rawls's notable recent attempts to discredit such an idea. If all this can be accomplished, then perhaps we will have cast some light on the sources of the disagreement between capitalists and socialists about the nature of social justice, and on the immense difficulty, if not the actual impossibility, of resolving that disagreement in any philosophically satisfying way.

II

I think it will be easier to see how the question of the importance of effort as against success in determining what one deserves from society (or what one's just reward or recompense from society is) arises so naturally and remains so difficult to resolve definitively, if we consider a parallel, but non-political question. Imagine, then, that a certain woman has lost a book and two friends of hers come by and volunteer to help her find it. The friends make equally conscientious, energetic, and intelligent efforts to find the book, and one of them succeeds in finding it and returning it to the woman who lost it. One might well wonder about such a case whether the woman who actually found the book deserves more (by way of gratitude or reward) from the friend

13. *Loc. cit.*

who lost the book than does the woman who tried equally hard but
failed to find the book. And this is a difficult question. On the one
hand, it is possible to feel that since the friends made equal efforts,
etc., in behalf of the woman who lost the book, she is equally in their
debt and should reward them equally. It may seem that neither deserves more than the other at her hands. We are, after all, imagining
that the person who does not find the book fails through no intellectual, emotional or moral defect of her own and that her failure to find
the book can be attributed to "bad luck" or "accident." And can greater
desert, or a greater debt of gratitude, arise through mere luck or
accident?

But there is another side to the question. For surely there is in
general a human tendency to be more grateful to someone who tries
to help and succeeds than to someone who tries equally hard and
fails. And one may feel that such a tendency is at least some evidence
of an ethical distinction, that it reflects our recognition that those who
(somehow) do more for us also deserve more from us, other things
being equal. Furthermore, even if the two friends who search for the
book demonstrate equally good character, or equal moral worth, by
their efforts, the notion of desert at someone's hands, or desert from
someone, is different and may not apply in the same cases. For one
thing, a given person may do things for certain people and thereby
come to deserve things from those people; and yet another person,
equally morally worthy, may never enter into any relations with those
people on the basis of which he could come to deserve gratitude or
rewards from them. Of course, it could be claimed that even if desert
at someone's hands is not equivalent to moral worth or goodness in
general, desert at a person's hands is equivalent to the moral goodness
of one's (past) behavior towards, or activity concerning, that person.
But this is by no means obviously correct, even if only because in the
above example of the lost book, it is much clearer that the two help-
ing friends are equally good from a moral point of view in their behavior towards the loser of the book than that they deserve equal gratitude or reward from her.[14]

14. However, some philosophers have not, I think, been willing to say that
success in doing good is irrelevant to moral worth or goodness. Merleau-Ponty

On the other hand, there are reasons for doubting whether our
natural inclination to feel greater gratitude towards those who succeed in benefiting us than towards those who only try (conscientiously) to benefit us really indicates that we should feel greater gratitude
towards those who benefit us, or that such people are more deserving
of our gratitude or of rewards from us. Perhaps such feelings are
irrational; perhaps they have some evolutionary survival value, but are
(in some appropriate sense) morally neutral. It is hard to know what
to say. At this point, it might, therefore, be useful to examine some
other case where problems of desert and gratitude arise, and to use
our intuitions about that case to help us decide the issue of desert in
the lost book case. Imagine, then, a circumstance in which someone
accidentally falls against my heart-lung machine and turns it on.
Imagine further that if the man in question had not turned the machine on, I would have died, since the machine had accidentally been
turned of (by someone else) without anyone's knowledge. Do I owe
the person who has accidentally turned on my heart-lung machine
any special debt of gratitude? Does he deserve anything from me that
some other man in the room does not? If I feel more gratitude to the
man who has turned my machine on, is this merely a natural human
response? Is it like the case where a person feels grateful when a tree
blocks a bullet aimed at him, but does not or should not feel that the tree
deserves anything from him? Or does desert arise from the mere fact
that the man was involved in doing or causing me some good? If the
latter is the case, then it can be argued that since the fact of causing
someone good can make a difference to what is deserved in a case, like
the heart-lung machine case, where no conscientious effort occurs,
it can make a difference to what is deserved in a situation where equal
conscientious effort takes place. One will conclude that in the lost book
case the woman who actually finds the book deserves more from her
friend who lost the book. But unfortunately, the question of desert in
the heart-lung machine case seems every bit as difficult as the question
of desert in the lost book case, so I doubt whether the former can help

---

in *Humanism and Terror* (Boston, 1969) seems to be an example. My own belief
is that such a view is mistaken.

us to decide about the latter. If anything, I think the heart-lung machine case serves further to emphasize the great difficulty of deciding whether actual (success in) doing good or making a contribution can make any difference to what one deserves.[15] What I would like now to argue is that the difficulty of deciding between capitalist and socialist views about the ideally just way for a society to distribute goods in some sense reduces to, and can be understood in terms of, the difficulty of deciding the question of desert that arises in the non-political case of the lost book (or in the non-political case of the heart-lung machine). To do this I shall first show that in the area of the distribution of goods in society, a parallel, indeed virtually the same, question about desert arises as does in the lost book case (or the heart-lung machine case). More will then be said about the assumption that the notion of desert is central to the notion of social justice, and some arguments and views—among them those of Rawls—that seem incompatible with this contention will be rebutted.

III

A just society is often thought of as being something like a large corporation that fairly recompenses those who work for it. Society is conceived as a kind of agent that people benefit or try to benefit, that people can deserve more or less from according to their contributions or efforts, and that rewards and punishes. If so, then a situation in which people are doing socially useful work together in society will be parallel to that of the lost and found book. If people are to some appropriate degree working for the good of society, attempting to do work that is socially useful, even if also very concerned about their own private interests, then the difference between those who make great contributions to society through their work and those who work just as hard but fail to make such contributions is much like the difference between the friend who tries to find the book and succeeds and the friend who tries to find the book and fails

15. A parallel and difficult question about evils is whether one *deserves* more blame or punishment for murder than for attempted murder that is accidentally foiled. I take it that this is *not* the same as the question whether legal systems should impose greater punishments in the former case.

through no fault of her own. And the question whether the friend who finds the book deserves more from the woman who lost it is like the question whether those who actually contribute a great deal to society deserve more from society than those who try and fail to do so.[16]

Now one objection to our claim of parallelism might be that in the book case differences of ability between the two friends were ruled out, or said to be irrelevant, but that this does not seem possible in talking about different people's differing contributions to society, since differences in abilities are a (the?) major cause of differing contributions to society. But as long as we assume that differences in abilities do not in and of themselves make a difference to what one deserves from society, but (at most) affect what one deserves from society only as they affect one's contribution to society, the cases are, I think, close enough for our purposes. And I think both capitalist and socialist theorists would agree with such an assumption. That socialists would agree with it is obvious enough, without argument. But even democratic capitalists do not seem to hold that those with greater ability prima facie deserve more from society, independently of their relative contributions to society. Surely, to take an extreme case, a talented social parasite is not thought by them to deserve more from society than an untalented one, even if other things are equal. But even in more usual cases it is not ability taken alone that typically is stressed by democratic capitalist theorists as a source of individual desert from society, but rather ability as a means to, and sign of, greater individual contribution to society. Such thinkers, I believe, usually stress the propriety of rewarding people according to their talents or abilities because they assume that with great talents or abilities go greater contributions to society, greater productivity and greater bene-

16. Perhaps our talk about what one deserves from society and about society's rewarding or punishing people only makes sense with respect to societies where the distribution of goods for work is highly centralized. If so, then the question we should be asking here is whether in a society with centralized mechanisms for rewarding labor, those who actually contribute a great deal to society deserve more from society than those who try and fail to do so. On the other hand, perhaps the sense that people deserve (different) things from society *justifies* the creation of a centralized mechanism for recompensing work according to desert, instead of *presupposing* such a mechanism.

fits conferred. It is greater contributions that capitalists really have in mind as the source of greater deserts. According to such theorists, if two men (say, entrepreneurs) of equal talent expend equal amounts of energy to produce something that people need or want and one of them, through "good breaks" or "luck" or what have you, is more successful in doing so, then that person deserves the greater rewards or benefits he reaps through his success. So far I see nothing to mar the parallelism I have been suggesting between the problem of the lost book and the problem whether those who do more for society deserve more from it.

Another objection to this parallelism might be that it assumes an unrealistic amount of willingness on the part of people to work in behalf of society. The two women who look for the book want to help their friend to a degree that people working in society do not in general desire to contribute to society. All this may be so, but it does not, I think, constitute a serious objection. We have raised a question about desert in a certain kind of slightly idealized (and, presumably, desirable) situation where men are willing to work together for the benefit of society. And it is at least one major issue between socialist theory and capitalist theory whether in *such* a case effort or success (actual contribution) is the source of desert, or justly derived benefits, from society. It is not entirely to the point to claim that in actual fact men are not this benevolent or unselfish, at least if one is willing to grant that such people are psychologically possible. Furthermore, if someone assumes that such devotion is beyond all human possibilities, he will, I think, still be able to acknowledge a parallelism between the case of the heart-lung machine and that of the distribution of goods in society, since in the heart-lung machine case there is only an accidental and unintentional contribution to the sick person's welfare and, presumably, everyone is willing to grant that selfish people who are not devoted to their society can and do make accidental or unintentional contributions to society.

IV

We know that people differ over whether effort or (democratically regulated) success is what a just society rewards. We can explain this

Desert, Consent, and Justice

if we assume that the notion of desert is appropriately built into the notion of justice. For then the question whether social justice entails that people be recompensed according to effort or actual contribution (success) will be tantamount to the question whether effort or actual contribution is paramount in determining what people deserve from society. And we can see why *this* question is so hard to resolve because of the parallel we have drawn between it and a non-political question whose difficulty can, I think, readily be appreciated. So the assumption that the notion of desert plays a role in the notion of justice may to some degree be justified in terms of its explanatory power. It is, of course, also not a particularly implausible idea. And it is an old idea that can be found, for example, in Mill's "Utilitarianism"[17] and Henry Sidgwick's *Methods of Ethics*.[18] Indeed, both these philosophers seem to have thought that social justice consisted simply in the distribution of goods in society according to desert. I do not doubt that some notion of desert has a role to play in the concept of justice, but in no case do I think that that notion exhausts the idea of justice. There is I believe, an important further element in the notion of justice, the notion of free consent.

One way in which we could assure ourselves of a perfectly just society (or basic social structure) would be, I believe, by creating a society where all the equalities and inequalities provided for by the society—and not, say, by chance, individual differences, or certain failures to live up to the norms and rules of the society—were deserved, by which I mean a situation where everyone received from society just what he deserved from society. But this is not, it seems to me, a *necessary* condition of ideal social justice. If certain equalities or inequalities are freely consented to,[19] then the society that creates these equalities or inequalities can be perfectly just, no matter whether those equalities or inequalities are deserved or not. To give one very simple example, if there really were differences of desert among members of society, but those who deserved more from society all agreed

17. *Loc. cit.*
18. 7th rev. ed., Jones E. Constance, ed. (Chicago, 1962), pp. 279ff.
19. I am not going to try to distinguish consent from agreement and other related notions.

to everyone's receiving equally, then the equalities that resulted would not, presumably, be deserved, but no injustice would arise from their existence either. Similarly, if everyone in society x deserves equally from x, but the members of x agree to let certain popular or well-liked people have certain privileges, and do so out of sheer affection for those people, then x may still be perfectly just.

I have spoken of *freely* consented to equalities and inequalities for a reason. It seems to me that an injustice may be done if people are, e.g., literally brainwashed into being people who will consent to certain inequalities. One might say that in such a case they are not even consenting to the inequalities, but then consent is tantamount to free consent, and it will still be the case that not everything that appears to be free consent is free consent. At worst, adding the word "free" is redundant. Conditions I have in mind as eliminating free consent include: brainwashing, inability to understand certain issues, certain sorts of ignorance, the presence of threats or dangers, economic duress, certain moods, etc. I do not think I should include freedom of the will in any traditional sense as a necessary condition of free consent. By "free consent" I mean more a politically desirable kind of consent than a metaphysically desirable kind. I am inclined to assume that there is a sense of "free" that does not entail free will. Otherwise, assuming that equalities and inequalities are unjust unless deserved or (in some sense) freely consented to, we get the undesirable result that intelligent and sensitive beings who lack metaphysical free will— and thus quite possibly we ourselves—cannot, e.g., justly (or fairly) institute a situation of non-deserved equality for all by their common consent. And this conclusion is surely counter-intuitive. Sidgwick has maintained that if there is no freedom of the will, there are no such things as deserts or justice.[20] But this simply seems wrong and wrongheaded to me; and I shall assume that political theory can be made independent of the free will question in something like the way I have been suggesting.[21]

20. *Op. cit.*, pp. 284f.
21. For a similar point about the irrelevance of metaphysical free will to the existence of moral responsibility and of certain rights, see my "Free Will, Determinism, and the Theory of Important Criteria," *Inquiry* 12 (1969): 337f.

Desert, Consent, and Justice

In addition to problems about the nature of free consent, there are also problems about whether or when one consents to certain consequences of what one directly consents to. This is where the so-called paradox of democracy arises, for example. Such problems may, indeed, arise from vagueness in the notion of consent, but even if this is so, that will not necessarily constitute a problem for attempts to define justice in terms of consent, since justice itself may have vague edges corresponding to the vagueness in the notion of consent.[22]

The concepts of desert and consent both seem to play a role in the concept of (ideal) justice. Indeed, I think we can say that it is true by definition that a society is ideally or perfectly just if and only if all the equalities and inequalities it provides for are deserved "at its hands" (i.e., from it) or freely consented to by all its members.[23] If such a definition is substantially correct, we can explain why disagreement arises between socialists and democratic capitalists over the question whether ideal justice requires distribution of the benefits or rewards of work in accordance with conscientious effort for society or in accordance with actual contribution to society. And that is because of the difficulty of deciding whether effort or success is more important in determining what one deserves from someone or something.[24]

There are, however, objections to our definition of justice that I

I am defining justice in terms of free consent (in some adumbrated appropriate sense), but someone who thought he had a clear grasp of the notion of justice might want to reverse things and use that notion to give a contextual definition of the concept of free consent that I am trying to pick out. One consents freely, in that sense, to certain undeserved equalities or inequalities if and only if one's actions give rise to a fully just situation containing such equalities or inequalities.

22. For discussion of problems about ascertaining consent, see M. Cohen's "Liberalism and Disobedience," *Philosophy & Public Affairs* 1, no. 3 (Spring 1972): 283-314; and J. P. Plamenatz, *Consent, Freedom, and Political Obligation*, 2nd ed. (Oxford, 1968), pp. 19f.

23. For reasons mentioned in footnote 16, above, this definition may need to be qualified in scope so as to apply only to societies with centralized mechanisms for the distribution of recompense for work.

24. I do not think the view that universal selfishness entails that no one deserves more than anyone else or the view that universal selfishness entails that everyone gets what he deserves (or deserves what he gets) is any threat to my position here.

would like to consider. Some of these derive from the work of John Rawls, and since Rawls's work on the subject of justice is so important, and so focal for current discussions of justice, I shall try to relate what I am doing here to Rawls's work and to the criticisms he makes of ideas similar to those I have been defending.

v

In his major work, *A Theory of Justice*,[25] Rawls criticizes the view that social justice involves goods' being distributed in proportion to moral desert, and so seems to oppose a definition of justice of the sort here proposed. But in fact what Rawls is objecting to is a view slightly different from the one I have been espousing. When Rawls speaks of moral desert, he uses that expression interchangeably with "moral worth." But earlier I distinguished between moral worth (or goodness of character) and what a man deserves from some other person or from society. It is not my view that a just society will reward people in accordance with their general moral worth or desert, but rather that it will (other things, like consent, being equal) reward them in accordance with what they deserve *from it*, and as we have seen, this is conceptually different. Thus we have left it (conceptually) open that two men should make different contributions to society and there-fore deserve different rewards from society (here talk of *morally* de-serving different rewards from society seems out of place), but still be of equal moral worth. If a certain kind of capitalist view is correct, then this often happens, and in no case, in my opinion, is such a thing ruled out by the very meaning of "desert" and "deserve." If it were, how could we explain how capitalist thinkers could so easily speak in a self-contradictory manner?

Presumably, Rawls directs his criticisms of views that equate justice with distribution according to moral worth or moral desert at such historical figures as Mill,[26] Sidgwick,[27] and Ross.[28] But like those fig-ures, he does not distinguish, or at least he does not explicitly dis-tinguish, desert as moral worth from desert as desert from a particular

25. *A Theory of Justice*, pp. 310ff.
26. *Op. cit.*, p. 931.   27. *Op. cit.*, pp. 279ff.
28. W. D. Ross, *The Right and the Good* (Oxford, 1930), p. 35.

person or society for actions involving that person or society. We have defined ideal justice in terms of this latter kind of desert, rather than moral desert or worth. But our definition might still be open to Rawlsian criticisms. At one point, for example, Rawls says that the idea of rewarding desert is impracticable.[29] Though he seems to have in mind here the rewarding of moral worth or character, Rawls might want to say the same thing about rewarding desert of the kind we have been talking about. It might be argued that it is hopelessly difficult to determine what men deserve from society, so that the idea of rewarding men in accordance with what they deserve from society is hopelessly impracticable and other means or standards of establishing how people should be recompensed for their work ought to be used. Now I am perfectly willing to admit the impracticality or difficulty of using my definition of justice in terms of desert in making social decisions about how to reward people for their labor. Indeed, in arguing that one very basic question about deserts for work seems unresolvable, I have made it plain that I can offer no practical scheme for justly distributing goods in society. But I think this simply shows that it is difficult to decide what is just and recompense people accordingly. It may, therefore, be a good idea to deemphasize justice in attempting to set up or govern a good society. The fact that it is difficult to make practical use of the notion of justice as I have defined it would count against the *accuracy* of my definition only if we had antecedent reason to think that the dictates of justice are bound to be, or likely to be, capable of practical implementation. And in fact I think we have antecedent reason to believe the contrary. In the first place, there is the very fact of the existence and seeming insolubility of the issue between capitalists and socialists as to whether it is just to reward people according to their efforts or according to their actual contributions. For if it is difficult to know what is just, it is surely difficult to implement the dictates of justice. In the second place, there are our attitudes towards divine or cosmic justice. We feel that if God or the world is just, then people are rewarded according to their merits or worth, but that a man's merit or worth is enormously dif-

29. *A Theory of Justice*, p. 312.

ficult for anyone (except perhaps God) to determine. But if it is difficult to know the dictates of cosmic or divine justice, why should this not be (at least to some degree) true of the dictates of social justice. And if it is reasonable to assume that it is difficult to know the dictates of social justice, then surely we can reasonably assume that the dictates of social justice are difficult to implement. I am inclined, therefore, to think that the lack of utility of our definition of justice for social planning does not count against, and may even count in favor of, its accuracy.

Rawls distinguishes between the concept of justice and various conceptions of justice. To state what the concept of justice is is to state an analytic definition of justice, whereas Rawls himself seeks to provide a conception of ideal justice that is not an analysis of the meaning of "just" but embodies a substantive moral theory or point of view about what justice requires.[30] For Rawls, definitions of (the concept of) justice are relatively trivial and specify what is common to different conceptions of justice. Thus to define justice as the situation that exists when no arbitrary distinctions are made between individuals in the assigning of basic rights and duties and when rules determine a proper balance between competing claims to goods is, for Rawls, to say what the concept of justice is, but it is to say nothing interesting about justice because it is to say nothing substantive about what societies are not arbitrary in assigning basic rights and duties and what societies have a proper balance between competing claims to goods.

The analysis of justice offered here is not quite so trivial as all this, however, even if only because of its emphasis on free consent. That free consent plays such a role in the notion of justice that it can render any situation just is a substantive, or at least (it seems to me) an interesting, idea that is nonetheless also analytic of the notion of justice. (It is also an idea that some will find implausible; and I shall be defending it against important criticisms, below.) If I am right about this, then an analysis of ideal justice need not be as trivial as the kind

30. *Ibid.*, p. 5.

Desert, Consent, and Justice

of analysis Rawls and others[31] have proposed. The definition of justice I have suggested seems, intuitively, to be somewhere between Rawls's definition of the concept of justice and his statement of his conception of justice in its specificity or substantiveness. I think, then, that the concept of justice can be analyzed more substantively and less trivially than Rawls and others have supposed, even though I do agree with Rawls that the concept of justice must be something common to different conceptions of justice. After all, in defining justice as I have, I have specified a concept that is neutral between what I have called capitalist and socialist conceptions of justice and that can even be made use of in explaining how capitalists and socialists can easily have such different conceptions of justice.

This latter is not the kind of thing Rawls is trying to do. He is chiefly offering his own conception of justice, not trying to explain differences among conceptions of justice. But what of Rawls's conception of justice? How does it relate to the socialist and capitalist conceptions or ideas of justice that I have been talking about? Is it not, perhaps, superior to them, and if not, what is wrong with it as a conception of justice? Does our definition of justice give us any grounds for criticizing Rawls's conception of justice, or is not the reverse, perhaps, the case?

VI

Rawls is not very sympathetic to the socialist motto. He grants to it a certain common-sense plausibility, but thinks that it is ultimately unsatisfactory as compared to (the principles embodied in) his own conception of justice.[32] That is not, however, to say that Rawls rules out socialism, if by that one means a state-planned economy;[33] it is only to say that a just state-planned economy must, for Rawls, comply with his two principles of justice; and need not (or cannot) comply with the socialist motto of the Gotha program. It seems somewhat strange to me, however, that this should be so. For Rawls places great

31. For a similar "trivial" analysis see C. Perelman, *The Idea of Justice and the Problem of Argument* (London, 1963), chaps. 1 and 2.

32. *A Theory of Justice*, pp. 305f.   33. *Ibid.*, pp. 58, 280.

emphasis on political equality in society and thinks that a situation where such equality is bargained away as a means to everyone's greater happiness will be (to some degree) unjust.[34] For Rawls, efficiency and benefits for all cannot justify removing certain political (or economic) liberties or opportunities, at least from the standpoint of justice. Rawls also thinks that the distribution of natural assets among people is arbitrary and that this arbitrariness is a reason for establishing rules of justice that mitigate the arbitrary effects of the "natural lottery."[35] But he does not advocate equality of recompense for those who cooperate equally conscientiously in society. He finds unequal recompense for work and unequal inheritance of wealth unobjectionable from the standpoint of justice so long as they satisfy his "difference principle," so that, roughly, those who are worst off benefit from those inequalities. And so if Rawls is correct, efficiency and utility have a weight in the distribution of rewards or material goods for work that they lack in the area of political liberties and political and economic opportunities. And such a view seems a bit arbitrary, at least to me, though it need not on that account be mistaken. Why should the two areas be treated so differently; if the arbitrary effects of the natural lottery must, in all justice, be mitigated to the extent of letting society be governed by the difference principle, why not go further and say that the natural lottery (and the effects of luck in determining success) must, in all justice, be mitigated by rewarding people in accordance with their conscientious efforts in behalf of society? Why treat equal liberties and opportunities as axiomatic to justice, but not equal recompense (for equal effort, let us say, to make things more plausible)? In other words, if in the sphere of liberties and opportunities one should be equal with everyone else unless one is a criminal, why should one not be equal with everyone else in the area of economic reward unless one is "criminally" or immorally lazy or unconscientious in one's work (or supererogatorily industrious or conscientious in one's work)? In effect, it seems on the face of it somewhat arbitrary or odd for someone like Rawls to insist on equal political and economic liberties and yet also deny that

34. *Ibid.*, p. 84.   35. *Ibid.*, p. 74.

justice requires the distribution of goods according to conscientious effort and reject the socialist motto.[36]

Apparently Rawls wants to argue that one would not consent to the socialist motto as a means of regulating society, if one were in his "original position," so that that motto or principle is not constitutive of (ideal) justice.[37] But this seems to beg too many questions. If we wish to know whether the original position is that in which just principles are chosen, we must see what principles would be chosen in that position and whether those principles yield decisions about particular cases that fit in well with our prior views or intuitions about those cases, as Rawls himself points out.[38] Rawls believes that his views and principles about justice coincide more with those intuitive views, better account for those views and introduce more order into them, than other views and principles about justice that have been offered. So it is really not open to Rawls to dismiss a conception of justice simply because is embodies principles that would not be arrived at in his original position. If the socialist conception of justice as embodied (approximately) in the socialist motto formulates our intuitions and common-sense views better than Rawls's principles of justice, that may (tend to) show that the original position defines not justice, but at best only some other social norm or ideal. On the other hand, if Rawls's principles approximately coincide with our common views or intuitions about justice, then so much the worse for socialism as a view of justice, since Rawls's principles pretty clearly conflict with the socialist motto in particular cases.[39]

For example, Rawls's principles of justice permit the existence of great differences of wealth and income if such differences serve to improve the lot of those who are worst off in society and even if everyone makes equally conscientious efforts in behalf of society. But such

36. Of course, many people respond to Rawls's "inconsistency" here by questioning or rejecting his insistence on equal political and economic liberties, rather than by questioning or rejecting his acceptance of inequalities in the distribution of rewards for work.

37. See *op. cit.*, pp. 312f.   38. *Ibid.*, pp. 318ff., 579f.

39. Rawls has an interesting critique of the capitalist conception of justice as we have described it, on pages 308-309 of his book. I shall not consider whether it can be rebutted.

a situation conflicts with the socialist motto and with the socialist conception of ideal justice. And since Rawls is clearly attempting to put forward a conception of ideal or perfect justice,[40] Rawls's views are in sharp conflict with those of socialist theorists.

At this juncture, Rawls might point out that in the situation just described the worst off are better off than they would be if the socialist motto were in force and, if they are rational and not envious, should prefer their situation to that which would exist if everyone were rewarded equally. In what way, Rawls might then ask, is such a situation less than just? But I am inclined to think that little is proved by such an argument. Unless one already assumes that Rawls's original position is one in which ideally just principles would be chosen, he may be inclined to say that this merely shows that people faced with (the possibility of) a hard lot in life are willing to tolerate certain injustices in order to achieve certain benefits. And if one thinks that what people deserve from society simply depends on their conscientious efforts in behalf of society, he might well think that the situation we are discussing is unjust because goods are not distributed in accordance with deserts, even though people (in the original position) might be willing to accept that situation for reasons of self-interest.

Of course, Rawls might want to deny that the notion of desert (even as something other than moral worth) plays a major role in the concept of justice in the way I have specified or in the way that some socialists assume. If this were correct, it would certainly block what seem to be the main socialist arguments for the less than ideal justice of the situation described above and, in general, for the inadequacy of Rawls's conception of ideal justice. But people do speak as if questions of desert were immediately relevant to questions of justice. And, furthermore, it is hard to believe that desert plays no large role in the notion of social justice, since it so clearly plays a large role in the notion of cosmic or divine justice.[41] Even if the notion of divine or cosmic justice is somewhat metaphorical, it would

40. See *op. cit.*, pp. 9, 78, 245f., 351, 391, 477.
41. Cf. C. Card, "On Mercy," *Philosophical Review* 81 (1972): 185.

Desert, Consent, and Justice

seem reasonable to assume that there is at least *some* major element common to both social justice and cosmic or divine justice, and is not the notion of desert the appropriate common element? (Nonetheless, there are problems here because of the ambiguities, or at least the different strands, that we have pointed out within the usage of "desert.")

On the other hand, Rawls might be willing to grant the place of the notion of desert from society in the concept of ideal social justice, but insist on the correctness of the capitalist view that actual contribution to society makes a difference to what one deserves from society. He might, perhaps, then go on to claim that any situation permitted by his principles in which there were great differences of wealth or recompense for work would be one in which people got what they deserved from society, and thus (considerations of consent aside) perfectly just. For in such a situation people who get more from society make the worst off better off than they would be if everyone received equally and so, one might think, make more of an actual contribution to society than other people do. In any case, we will have doubts about the adequacy of Rawls's conception at least to the extent that we believe that the notion of justice involves that of desert and have doubts (of a socialist kind) about the capitalist view of the relation between desert and actual contribution.

Whatever the strengths or weaknesses of Rawls's views on the relation between desert and justice, I think Rawls clearly underestimates the role actual free consent has as an element in ideal justice. Rawls seems to think that certain sorts of hypothetical free consent suffice for justice, so that if people would have consented to a certain social arrangement in an original position of equality, then such an arrangement is just even when people have not actually consented to it. But the difference between actual and hypothetical (free) consent is very important in matters of justice. To give one example of this (that Rawls would, presumably, be able to agree with, consistent with his principles), consider a situation where certain people somehow manage to call off an election whose eventual winner, the incumbent, everyone knew would win in advance, and then simply arrange for the incumbent to remain in office. Clearly an injustice has been done here by denying people their right to give or withhold their *actual* consent to the incumbent's remaining in office.

Rawls seems to think that, independently of whether goods are or are not distributed according to desert in societies governed by the difference principle (and his other principles), such societies are (ideally) just because they (or the principles that govern them) would have been chosen in the original position. And I believe that this is mistaken. Where inequalities of reward and the like are undeserved, only actual consent to their existence seems to me to be capable of rendering those inequalities, and the society in which they exist, completely just. It does not, intuitively, seem enough that people would have consented to the undeserved inequalities had they been asked. For even when one knows that this is so, one may feel resentment and feel unfairly treated because one *wasn't* asked. Rawls's emphasis on merely hypothetical consent seems to me to be out of line with our actual concept of justice.[42] And there is not enough emphasis in his work on the importance of actual consent in rendering situations just. There seem to be situations involving actual consent that contravene Rawls's difference principle and yet are perfectly fair and just. Consider, for example, the situation mentioned earlier in which everyone in society x deserves equally from x, but the members of x freely agree or consent to let certain popular or well-liked people have certain privileges, and do so out of sheer affection for those people. There would surely be nothing unjust about such a society even if the privileges of the well-liked individuals in no way improved the lot of anyone else, and so even if the society offended against Rawls's difference principle. Of course, I am relying on intuition here, and perhaps the intuitions of Rawls and others will differ with mine about the two cases we have just been describing. But if what I have said about these cases is correct, then Rawls's conception of ideal justice is inadequate. (However, for our earlier definition of justice to be correct, what I have said about the situations just described must follow from the *very notion* of justice. And I am inclined to believe that this is so.)

42. See *A Theory of Justice*, pp. 15, 29, 99, 115.

345   *Desert, Consent, and Justice*

Although Rawls attempts to correct the failures of Utilitarianism, and in large measure puts justice ahead of efficiency or utility, I think our arguments here tend to show that Rawls nonetheless over-emphasizes the role of utilitarian considerations in the notion of ideal justice, or at least allows such considerations too much of a role in his own conception of ideal justice. I do not think that Rawls has succeeded in specifying, via his principles and his general ideal contractualism, an ideal of social justice. He has instead, I think, defined or specified a social ideal that is in some sense a compromise between justice and utility (or efficiency). Those who might protest the lack of ideal justice in a society meeting Rawls's principles still cannot complain too loudly, since things are effectively run for their benefit; and those who think things are not run efficiently enough can be told that efficiency is not everything and that a society should be just at least to the extent of making the worst off better off than they otherwise would be.[43] Rawls's views may not embody an adequate conception of ideal social justice, but, in the end, they may embody something even more important, an adequate conception of the society that is best at combining and compromising justice and utility, an adequate conception of the ideal practicable society. Moreover, Rawlsian societies may deserve to count as just *simpliciter*, even if they are not (all) ideally just.[44] Perhaps what I should be thought of as doing here, then, is not criticizing Rawls's enterprise in his book, but rather criticizing his way of interpreting the force and significance of his enterprise. And perhaps we should not be too surprised if it turns out that Rawls's principles are best thought of as specifying a conception of the (an?) ideal practicable society rather than a conception of the (an?) ideally or perfectly just society. For those principles are generated with reference to Rawls's original position, and it is by no means clear that people in that position would unanimously choose an ideally just society, rather than simply an ideal or ideally good society,

43. This is reminiscent of things Rawls says in section 17 of his book.

44. For discussion of questions similar to the question whether Rawlsian societies that are less than ideally just are just *simpliciter*, see my "The Theory of Important Criteria," *Journal of Philosophy* 63 (1966): 211-224. The notion of social justice *simpliciter* may well be definable in terms of the Theory of Important Criteria.

in which justice played an important, but not necessarily an all-important, role.

It might be said, however, that even if Rawls confuses justice with certain broader or more inclusive social ideals and even if he under-estimates the importance of actual consent in rendering situations just, our definition of justice sins in the opposite direction by assuming that universal free consent can make anything just. Given that definition, for example, it is in no way unjust for all the members of a society freely to consent to an equal, but unnecessary, limitation on their freedom. But Rawls's first principle of justice says that "each person is to have an equal right to the most extensive total system of equal basic liberties compatible with a similar system of liberty for all."[45] And I assume that this is incompatible with what our definition commits us to counting as just. I think, however, that the condition of the greatest possible equal liberty is not a condition on justice, but on rational social planning.[46] Universal free consent to equal, but un-necessarily limited, freedom for all is not unfair or unjust, but irra-tional or arbitrary or bad for some other reason.[47] Rawls's first prin-ciple of justice involves an extension of the notion of justice, or a confusion of justice in the ordinary sense with other social or personal ideals; or so, at least, it seems to me.

The same sort of extension or confusion seems also to be involved in the criticism that our definition has the implausible consequence that it would be perfectly just for a man freely to consent to being stoned or shot by the other members of his society and for such ston-ing or shooting to occur. Assuming that such free consent really is possible, it will, I presume, be wrong or inhuman for the other mem-bers of the man's society to stone him; but it seems to me to involve an extension of usage (or a real confusion) to say that it is unfair or unjust for people to stone a man who freely consents to being stoned. However, it might be claimed, finally, that if a man freely consents to work for the welfare of people who do not deserve his

45. *Op. cit.*, p. 250.   46. Cf. *A Theory of Justice*, p. 229.
47. Of course, if it is impossible for there to be universal *free* consent to the limitation of certain freedoms, our definition will not be open to the criticism we are discussing.

help and who take advantage of his good nature, there will exist an unjust but freely consented-to situation. If such a situation *is* possible, our definition of social justice is inadequate, but I have myself never been able to imagine such a situation in enough detail so that it is clear that *both* free consent and injustice exist within it. In describing a situation in which a man helps undeserving people, the closer one comes to seeing an injustice in the situation, the closer one seems to come to depriving the helpful man of *free* consent by imagining him as ignorant, under duress, etc. So it is by no means clear to me that any examples from this quarter can undermine our earlier definition of ideal social justice.

If people speak and think about justice in the ways that I have suggested, then there is reason to accept the definition of ideal social justice given above and Rawls's putative conception of justice is perhaps more profitably thought of as a conception of a certain kind of ideally good society.[48] But the most important result of this paper seems to me to be the fact that our definition enables us to understand better why socialists and democratic capitalists disagree so persistently and so hopelessly about social justice. Rawls neither attempts nor, I think, is able to explain the particular nature of this disagreement within his contractarian enterprise. And, of course, this disagreement is one of enormous political and social significance in the world today. Ideally, we would like to be able to resolve the issue here between capitalism and socialism; but failing that, we have at least attempted to make the important first step of understanding how and why that issue is so difficult to resolve in any definitive and universally acceptable way.

48. I shall not deal with the difficult question whether (or how) a society that is not ideally just can be ideal, or ideally good, in any sense.

[6]

CHRISTOPHER AKE   Justice as Equality

Our typical use of the concept of justice is in the evaluation of a
society's institutions, principally its legal, political, and economic
institutions. It is these societal institutions from which we chiefly
derive, and to which we usually apply, our actual working notions of
justice. Our ideas of what a just society taken as a whole ought to be
are themselves drawn primarily from these various institutional senses
of the term. Thereby we seem to assess the entire society with standards developed for certain of its parts. Normally, however, we do not
consider this kind of assessment misguided; in making such an
assessment, we take the legal, political, and economic institutions of a
society to represent adequately enough what the society in its entirety
is.

Especially if society is thought of as constituted primarily by a
state, as containing an explicit legal and political apparatus, the legal
and political senses of justice will seem appropriate when applied to
the society as a whole. But for anyone who feels less than certain
about the adequacy of this conception of a society,[1] doubts may arise
about whether such legal or political senses of justice are fully adequate. What I will consider here is whether there is a sense of the

I am indebted to the editors of *Philosophy & Public Affairs* for their helpful
criticisms of earlier drafts of this paper.

1. Some of the reasons one might give for calling this conception of a society
into question can be found in Stanley Diamond's essay, "The Rule of Law versus
the Order of Custom," in *The Rule of Law*, ed. Robert Paul Wolff (New York,
1971), and reprinted as chap. 8 of Diamond's *In Search of the Primitive* (New
Brunswick, N.J., 1974).

concept of justice, different from all its specific institutional senses, which is uniquely appropriate for determining the justice of a society as a whole.

I

Given the inadequacy of the legal or political senses of justice, one might, of course, ask if there are any distinctively economic conceptions or senses of justice which can be used in their stead, such as one based upon the general idea of fair exchange. But if such economic conceptions should also prove insufficient for this task, one might then decide that there is no sense or concept of justice at all which does not presuppose in some way a particular conception of society, or the adoption of a particular perspective or standpoint from within society.[2]

The view I will be presenting denies this conclusion. It holds that there is a substantive, although weak, sense of the concept of justice which is correctly applicable to all societies, as totalities, at all times. That it is a weak sense, given this complete generality, should hardly be surprising. That there is such a sense at all, however, may be startling. Recent views of justice, especially that of Rawls, have made it seem that (to borrow his terminology) the *concept* of justice is nearly empty, being purely formal, and that specific content is possessed only by the various competing *conceptions* of justice, each of which can be given content in the way (and to the degree) its proponent chooses.

But while the concept of justice is, in my view, more substantive than Rawls and others think, justice as a social virtue is in some ways more limited than most current thinking would allow. In particular, justice as I shall view it has a less important position relative to other

2. To some degree, such a decision seems to characterize Marx's views on justice as Allen Wood interprets them in "The Marxian Critique of Justice," *Philosophy & Public Affairs* 1, no. 3 (Spring 1972): 244–282. Wood's interpretation has come under criticism in a number of recent discussions, e.g. Derek P. H. Allen, "Is Marxism a Philosophy?" *The Journal of Philosophy* 71, no. 17 (10 October 1974): 601–612; and William Leon McBride, "The Concept of Justice in Marx, Engels, and Others," *Ethics* 85, no. 3 (April 1975): 204–218. In the present paper I am not dealing directly with Marx's (or Engels') views on justice at all.

social virtues than it does for those (like Rawls) whose analysis yields
a less substantive and apparently more realizable concept. Justice, by
itself, is merely one limited, defeasible virtue among others. This is
my first contention about justice. While in most cases people are not
ready to trade it off entirely, they think it proper in many situations,
even those they would regard as in some way socially ideal, to balance
the claims or demands of justice against those of other social virtues,
not simply to allow its claims or demands to override them. Insisting
on complete, or total, justice has roughly the same degree of rationality as insisting on some kind of complete or absolute freedom. It is
only in certain special circumstances, for example in a criminal trial,
that what justice requires can override all other demands. In a
criminal trial, failure, for whatever reason, to conform to the demands
of procedural justice may invalidate the entire proceeding. In this
sense procedural justice does indeed represent the supreme requirement or virtue involved. But this is a highly specific case; to take it as
a reference point for the analysis of justice in all its modes would
certainly be misleading.

Instead, one must try to determine whether there is a completely
general, fundamental, or primal sense of the concept of justice
which underlies the employment of the concept in law and in judicial
institutions. This fundamental sense ought to be applicable in some
way to the totality of a society, to the totality of the life of each
member of the society, but not necessarily to a government or a
political state. It ought to be abstracted not only from legal contexts
and connotations but also from the particular economic contexts and
connotations currently involved in the concept of justice.

The result of this process of abstracting must be that a sense of
the concept emerges which is a certain kind of equality, not the
specific, concrete socioeconomic sort advocated in various egalitarian
doctrines but a far more abstract one. It can be stated most adequately
in terms of benefits and burdens. Justice in a society as a whole
ought to be understood as a complete equality of the overall level of
benefits and burdens of each member of that society. This is my
second contention about justice. No doubt it will seem oversimplified
to many people, coming too close to a view of cosmic or poetic justice.
It is proposed more tentatively than the first, and is logically inde-

pendent of it. It might well turn out to be somehow mistaken while the first is correct.

The terminology of burdens and benefits represents the most general way of stating this concept of justice. It could not be put in terms of rights, for example, because we normally think, when talking about rights, in terms of specific protections or claims people have. Of course people could disagree about what rights there are, or what rights people have or ought to have; the list of such rights could always be extended. But in any case the concept of a right is one that is imported, to some degree, from legal and political institutions.

Rights are discrete, moreover, while benefits and burdens seem capable (at least conceptually) of continuous gradation and variation. The idea of something's being a burden or benefit applies equally well to a vast range of features, situations, items, and happenings in life. It may be necessary to draw upon the notion of rights to define the justice of a government or of a political state, but this is a separate question.

There may be other senses of the concept than this; one might be that of impartiality in the administration of the law. Another might be that of correctness in balancing and weighing a large variety of distinct, conflicting social virtues and considerations, one of which would be justice in this more limited sense. But if there are such other distinct senses, they must be viewed as deriving from the total or societal one, and not vice versa. Understanding the justice of particular institutions or spheres within a society requires, first, understanding what the justice of a whole society consists of. To say that what justice consists of varies from one institution or sphere to another, so that there can be no general sense applicable to a whole society, simply begs the question.

In particular situations or in particular institutions, the way to bring about or to approximate this overall equality may be by the use of various inequalities, such as an inequality of incomes. For this reason it can be misleading to speak about justice as a kind of equality when it is not made clear that the equality in question applies to the society as a whole rather than to any particular part of it. Justice alone does not require any specific kind of equality—of income, treatment, or whatever. Such particular forms of equality could only be shown to be

73   *Justice as Equality*

desirable on the basis of a particular view of society or of human nature. Nor does justice alone set any particular demands or requirements on how much a government or state must act to bring it about.

It appears that the general, or "global" equality required in this view of justice could never be realized completely in any actual society, certainly not as a result of the workings of established and recognized state institutions, whether or not the benefits and burdens of life are indefinitely divisible. Even so, this no more constitutes a criticism of this concept than saying that people could never, in any actual situation, be completely or perfectly rational constitutes a criticism of a concept of rationality.

Another kind of criticism of this concept is inevitable. What about the case of someone who suddenly comes into good fortune, perhaps entirely by his or her own efforts? Should additional burdens, any kind of burdens so long as they really are such, be imposed on that person in order to restore the equality and safeguard justice?

Suppose someone in his spare time begins to study nutrition in order to improve his stamina, health, and vigor, and eventually finds his job and other responsibilities far less burdensome. Would justice be adequately served by forcing him to do any drudgery, however meaningless? Let us consider two different cases. It might be that this person managed to study nutrition only by previously saving his money, foregoing his usual diversions, and so on; he has already assumed certain additional burdens and possibly made great sacrifices to get to his present position. If this is the case, then certainly there need be no question of subjecting him to further burdens. But, on the other hand, let us imagine that he simply stumbled, quite by accident, on a few books containing a rich, easily accessible lode of information or that someone gave him all this information, after no particular effort on his part. In this instance it would probably seem just, particularly from anyone else's standpoint, to require him, for instance, to tell others about his discovery.

But why wouldn't it be just to impose any kind of additional burden whatsoever on him in order to restore the equality? The answer is that, strictly speaking, it would be, just as strictly speaking it might turn out that a society would be most economically efficient (in the nontechnical sense of the term) if half its population were enslaved.

Doing what is completely, or most nearly, just may be as irrational, all things considered, as insisting on the greatest efficiency or on maximizing total happiness or (for an individual) on being totally honest at all times. Social values or virtues may theoretically conflict in head-on fashion; whether they must is a further question. In the present case, considerations of justice would mean that the person may legitimately have a burden placed on him; there is nothing to prevent considerations of welfare, for instance, from determining the content or nature of that burden, e.g. asking him to enlighten others about health food, in order, ultimately, to make their work less burdensome as well.[3]

This example may have an air of unreality about it because it concerns private or personal conduct. No society will be able or inclined to try to regulate personal conduct beyond some point. This inability, or disinclination, constitutes one of the reasons why we cannot expect complete or total equality ever to be realized. People's willingness to attempt to maintain an equality in the overall level of burdens and benefits will probably also depend on how near to such an equality they think they are already. In the example just given, much of our reluctance to impose an additional burden on a newly fortunate person may depend on the belief that the previous distribution of burdens and benefits was based largely on chance, so that to impose this burden is somehow futile or simply intrusive.

In addition to the one just considered, there are a number of other significant objections one could raise to the view of justice I am

3. Considerations of this sort lend support to thinking of justice in punishment as placing a necessary condition that penalties be imposed in such a way as to equalize the benefits and burdens of punished and non-punished alike. (Assuming, as a background condition, that such equality is present in the society as a whole. If it were not present, then we might not require the practice of punishing to bring it about, but this would be because punishing is too limited an institution to do this by itself, and is in this sense inappropriate for this task.)

Honderich presents such a condition as one absolute requirement among others for the justification of a practice of punishment in a possible society. See *Punishment, the Supposed Justifications* (Middlesex, England, 1971).

Further conditions may have to be satisfied for punishment to be justified, all things considered, rather than simply just. There are significant problems involved in maintaining this view of punishment, but the present paper cannot consider them.

75   Justice as Equality

proposing. It is difficult to know what a full defense of it would be. One can, however, render this view plausible by an examination of the intuitions we have about certain representative cases. It can also be compared in a direct way with a number of other views of justice, each having some current acceptance.

In what follows, I shall focus on several well-known principles or maxims of distributive justice, among them distribution according to need, according to contribution, and according to effort, in order to indicate how a view of justice as founded on distributive maxims differs from the view I am presenting and also to consider how some combination of these maxims might approximate this kind of justice. Several of the bases of these maxims—contribution, effort, need— furnish useful examples of typical burdens of life.

First, however, I want in section II to consider very briefly how the notion of justice I am proposing and a view of justice as founded on distributive maxims compare with Rawls' conception. In section III, I shall examine two of the bases of desert, contribution, and effort, in the process discussing an argument given by Michael Slote as to which of these two is more suitable as the basis for a principle of distributive justice—an argument in which he also presents a view of justice which differs from that of Rawls. I will amend his rejection of Rawls' view, and then in section IV examine several further problems involved in taking either contribution or effort as one of life's funda- mental burdens or as a basic component of justice.

II

Each of the distributive maxims just mentioned ought to be viewed in restorative terms; each can be regarded as an attempt to restore a prior situation[4] of complete equality in the overall level of burdens and benefits which could exist until certain upsetting factors come into

4. This situation is prior logically, or conceptually, rather than historically, in the same way that a hypothetical contract usually is in contract theory. Of course it is true that most societies now in existence are nowhere near such equality, nor have they ever been. Many of the apparent counterexamples to this view of justice derive their force from focussing on isolated cases in which an equality of benefits and burdens seems unjust precisely because such equality is not already present, as a background condition, in the larger context these cases occur in, or in the society as a whole.

play. Each, obviously, attempts this restoration in a different way.
Each succeeds to some degree and, in any case, constitutes only an
approximation.

Viewing the maxims in this way may have several significant consequences. It may help to show to what degree the maintenance of
justice in a society has as a fundamental aim the unity and harmony
of the society. From this vantage point, I believe it will also be easier to
see some of the limitations of Rawls' difference principle as a principle
of distributive justice.

It may turn out that if justice is related to community in a more
intimate way than Rawls thinks, then his difference principle is inadequate because his individualist assumptions and framework make
impossible any strong connection at all between justice and community. If it were true that, because of the need for community,
harmony, and unity, any acceptable principle of justice must be in
some way a principle of equality, then a major shortcoming of Rawls'
principle would be made clear. To establish these claims about Rawls'
views would obviously be a large undertaking. Here I can do little
more than point the way.

One can, of course, view Rawls' difference principle as itself a
kind of extended principle of equality, so it must be made clear in
what sense an acceptable principle of justice is an extension or modification of a principle of equality. Here Brian Barry's criticism of
Rawls' second principle in his "Reflections on 'Justice as Fairness' "[5] is
instructive. Barry's view, briefly, is this: it is not a sufficient condition
for a system of inequalities to be just that it will, if introduced into a
society which previously has none, make those who are resultantly
worst off better off than they otherwise would have been—this condition is only sufficient to make the system *justified.* Such a system
could be justified by a variety of considerations: efficiency, welfare,
etc. For Barry, justice "consists in some appropriate relationship between what a person has done or what he is now and the benefits that
he receives or the costs that he bears."[6] As a result, the size of incentive
payments, for example, is not to be determined by the criterion of a

5. Brian Barry, "Reflections on 'Justice as Fairness,' " in *Justice and Equality,*
ed. Hugo Bedau (Englewood Cliffs, N.J., 1971).
6. Ibid., p. 110.

77   *Justice as Equality*

just distribution. Justice could conflict in a direct way with public welfare and the public interest if exorbitantly high incentive payments had to be made to secure such welfare.

Now if Rawls has indeed conflated justice and welfare, then disentangling them and holding them distinct should allow us to concentrate on justice itself and bring to the surface its actual relations with other social virtues and goods. Doing this would in turn make clearer exactly what the costs, the benefits, and the general consequences are of allowing justice to be subordinated to, or balanced by, such other considerations. It may well be that Rawls must inject considerations of efficiency and welfare into his second principle of justice because his individualist construction, which deemphasizes the relational aspect of justice, would otherwise make it impossible to get a significant principle of justice at all.

How, then, can a maxim of distributive justice be one which aims to restore a situation of complete equality to the greatest degree possible? One can find an answer to this question by considering Joel Feinberg's remarks in *Doing and Deserving*.[7] Inequality of economic income could be based on desert in such a way that, with respect to the totality of social benefits a person enjoys, all persons are (ideally) equal. Those occupations which are more burdensome—whether because of risk of a disease such as asbestosis, exposure to vinyl chloride, noise, or a heavier load of responsibility—ought to have higher income attached to them, not in order to attract people into them or into staying in them, but rather so that the totality of social benefits available to the persons in them will be equal to the totality available to other persons. Such occupations might have even further financial increments attached to them precisely to get people to take them, but such bonuses would be justified, if at all, not by considerations of justice, but by considerations of welfare, efficiency, or some other social virtue or good.

On this view, none of the distributive maxims is to be regarded as a primitive or unanalyzable component of justice, since each ought to be viewed as a mechanism that contributes to bringing about as close an approach to complete equality in the overall level of burdens and

7. Joel Feinberg, *Doing and Deserving* (Princeton, 1970), chap. 4, especially the Appendix.

benefits as possible. None of the maxims is sufficient by itself; some combination, that whose resultant most closely approximates this equality, is required to serve the purposes of justice.

To illustrate this, let us consider several cases. Suppose someone becomes afflicted with an extremely severe infection, which turns out to require extensive medical treatment and exhausts the person's life savings. If his income can no longer cover the costs, it certainly seems unjust not to make some departure from strict equality of income. Thus perfect equality of income is hardly just. One might take this as showing that the correct principle of distribution is one according to need. But suppose we consider a modification of this example in which the person involved contracted the infection through his own carelessness. Perhaps he had been warned by others not to drink some suspect water, say the tap water in New Orleans, had been urged and encouraged not to, had had the dangers explained and emphasized to him, had been given more than an adequate supply of safe water, but still insisted on deliberately, willfully, drinking whatever he liked. In this instance we would be less inclined to think that justice requires giving him all the additional income he needs. Certain humanitarian motives might move us to grant him additional income, but if so, it wouldn't be solely because justice required us to do so. If this is true, then distribution according to need is not by itself a correct principle of justice, and some other maxim, or combination of them, is required.

Again, if someone chops off his hand in front of our eyes and then demands additional income, we would at least hesitate to say that justice requires granting it. Once again this could be understood as showing that it isn't need alone but also perhaps some kind of merit or moral worth, in a very general sense, upon which a just distribution should be based. But instead, in the last two cases, one could view the deliberate disregard of considerations of personal health and well-being (insofar, at least, as they affected others) as one form of acting less responsibly than one should, as dispensing with a certain kind of burden, that of acting responsibly, which other people still must bear.

It is not necessary, in this last example, that casting off the burden involved must exactly compensate for all the inconvenience and anguish which will result from losing one's hand, that the two must somehow perfectly balance one another, so that no additional income is needed to restore the equality of everyone's overall level of burdens and benefits. Someone could lose a hand because of a sudden impulsive act, but the consequences will still spread out over that person's whole life. The claim here is only that the difference in our intuitions about what is just in the two cases, and specifically our reluctance to grant additional income in the one situation, can be accounted for by understanding justice in terms of an equality in people's overall level of burdens and benefits, rather than in terms of one specific consideration, such as need alone or the voluntariness or deliberateness of the actions involved. There are many ways a person can lose a hand, and justice might require some variation in the compensation when the circumstances vary. It is certainly a historical contingency that we have the particular limited rules of compensation that we do.

III

Suppose we now focus on the maxims of "to each according to contribution" and "to each according to effort." It might seem simply mistaken to view the first of these maxims as one which produces an approximation of equality in the overall level of burdens and benefits. It might be, for instance, that certain members of a society could make vastly greater contributions than others with much less expenditure of energy or time. If, to accord with their greater contribution, they received more in income than the others, the application of the maxim would produce greater inequality than would otherwise be the case, not less.

But for the view under consideration this is not an exceptional case after all; the maxim in question carries with it a presumption that in most cases one's contribution is at least roughly proportional to one's effort or exertion (or else to something regarded as a burden, even if it is one's "deferring of consumption"). This is not to say that all those who have advocated that maxim have supposed this presumption to be true, far less have they defended it by appealing to the presumption. Instead, my claim is that with respect to most people's intuitions, when this presumption becomes questionable, the maxim itself becomes questionable as a principle of justice. There may be certain exceptional cases where this proportionality is not required or expected to hold; perhaps someone could write a symphony or construct an all-embracing theory of matter with no apparent effort at all, and a society might feel justified in rewarding such persons highly. But if so, it would, again, be for reasons other than those of justice.

The presumption mentioned above seems to indicate that employ-ng the effort maxim, rather than the contribution maxim, plays a fundamental role in establishing and maintaining justice. Yet to some the effort maxim is no more acceptable in this role than the contribu-tion maxim. Among the more serious objections one could raise against it is this: wouldn't use of the effort maxim imply, for instance, that a tone-deaf but aspiring violinist furiously and sincerely trying to sound like Yehudi Menuhin ought to be paid just as much as the master himself, or perhaps even more?

Strictly speaking it would, although there are qualifications. It should come as no surprise that, on the view of justice I am proposing, there may be instances of direct conflict between considerations of justice and those of welfare or efficiency. Only, in fact, by acknowledg-ing such cases will we be able to see what overwhelming weight we often assign to the latter considerations. That we should reward or compensate an excruciatingly mediocre violinist just as we do Yehudi Menuhin is to many persons completely unthinkable. Yet it is not an insuperable difficulty for the conception of justice presented here that it might require this. In speaking of a person's sincere effort as the basis for a maxim of distributive justice, what must be meant is his or her sincere effort to make a contribution to the society. As more and more people point out to the tone-deaf violinist that his efforts, however sincere they were initially or have been up to the present, are making no contribution, it becomes increasingly ques-tionable how sincere such effort is, not simply because no contribution is being made but because the person making the effort is now aware that no contribution is being made. Over the course of time, then, such a person could justly receive less and less if no changes in the direction of effort are made. But what if this person persists in sincerely believing that he is making a contribution by such tor-tured playing, or possibly believes that even though no contribution

81   *Justice as Equality*

is being made at present, a breakthrough is imminent? In this case considerations of justice would, evidently, require paying such a person the same fee as is paid a virtuoso. Insofar as this represents an objection to using effort as a basis for desert, a corresponding objection can be made to the use of contribution as a basis. A person might insist that something he or she has already done resulted in a significant contribution, even though no one else is yet aware of it. In both kinds of cases, certain possibly controversial criteria of what constitutes effort or contribution must be employed, regardless of how they are chosen or adopted by the society.

In order to strengthen the case for saying that the maxim of distribution according to effort plays a more fundamental role in achieving justice than the maxim of distribution according to contribution, let us examine an article in which these two maxims are discussed directly. In a recent issue of *Philosophy & Public Affairs*, an argument has been given against Rawls' view of justice by Michael Slote, who claims that justice can be analyzed substantively, that it is fundamentally a matter of desert, and that it also includes a component determined by people's free, actual (as opposed to hypothetical) consent.[8] Slote considers the dispute between those who believe that desert should be based primarily on actual contribution to the society and those who hold that desert should be based on sincere effort on behalf of the society. He provides several examples designed to show a clear conflict between the use of these two maxims.

One such example is a case in which a person who has lost a book rewards only the friend who found it, even though another friend has also searched for it unsuccessfully, but with equal effort. Slote says our intuitions go both ways here; we are inclined to reward only the friend who found it, but we are also inclined to reward both equally.

But if reward according to actual contribution has any plausibility here, it seems to me to derive from a different kind of reward situation. Let us suppose that your young golden retriever does not come back to the house one night and you decide to put up a reward notice offering $50 to whoever finds him. In this situation it does indeed seem just to give the entire amount to whoever finds him.

8. Michael Slote, "Desert, Consent, and Justice," *Philosophy & Public Affairs* 2, no. 4 (Summer 1973): 323–347.

One could say this confirms Slote's position that whatever people freely (and actually) consent to do is just, because here those who search for the dog might be strangers who are driven by no feeling of obligation toward you (or the dog); they could be actually consenting with complete freedom to spend their time looking. Even if they all made equal efforts, we would deem it just to reward only the person who actually finds the dog. If we consider another case, say in a circus where a person pays a quarter to take a chance on winning a prize, this certainly seems correct.

But it would be more accurate to regard offering a reward to whoever finds one's dog as a kind of competition in which people are rewarded or compensated strictly in accordance with the rules of the contest. By offering the reward you institute the contest, and the particular restricted kind of justice it is based on requires only that you reward the winner. Participants are presumed to be making a sincere effort to obtain the reward money, rather than to contribute to the general welfare or to yours. In consequence, you yourself are under no special obligation to reward everyone who participates in the contest.

In any case, let us put aside the problem of contribution against effort and examine what Slote says about consent. As I mentioned earlier, Slote holds that justice is a matter of free, actual consent as well as of desert. Justice is maintained, in his view, when people receive exactly what they deserve *or* when such arrangements are altered by free consent of the persons involved or affected. (This would appear to be a secondary element of justice, desert being primary, because the genuinely free consent of all may be possible only in a situation in which they all have a genuinely equal status. Otherwise, those in an inferior position might in some way be less free than those who are better off, if, for example, because of their inferior status they have less of the means required for the genuine exercise of their freedom.)

Now if justice really can be based on consent as well as desert, this would show that the view of justice as an overall equality of burdens and benefits is incomplete, and therefore incorrect, since the members of a society could freely consent to a set of institutional changes which could result in the abandonment of such equality. Possibly

they would institute gross inequalities. Would the resulting situation
be just? This question is reminiscent of the classic question of whether
a person's freedom is such that it allows him to alienate that freedom.
If justice were thought of as equal consideration or protection of rights,
then the question might be asked whether one is always allowed to
surrender any of his rights by free, actually given consent. Would it
be just, for instance, for someone to consent to his own enslavement?

Persons starting from a position of equality in their overall level of
burdens and benefits might choose, through their free, actual consent,
to enter a state in which there is no longer such equality for a number
of reasons; raising everyone's level of benefits by instituting certain
inequalities is undoubtedly the foremost. Whether such a choice would
be made depends on the persons involved. One could, for example,
view the gains accruing to those who are the least well-off after the
institution of a system of inequalities as a kind of bribe given for the
loss of their equal status, a bribe which only certain kinds of persons
would accept.

But instead of saying that any arrangements persons freely and
actually consent to are just, one could say that once they have moved
out of a state of complete equality, their institutions and transactions
are no longer completely just, although not necessarily thoroughly
unjust. In the same way, persons in an initial situation of complete
freedom might choose to move to a situation of lesser freedom, e.g. by
putting themselves in someone's custody or by granting someone dictatorial powers. Actual freedom admits of degrees, and so does justice.
They are both approached somewhat asymptotically in real life.

Our usual reluctance to call unjust any situation to which the
people involved or affected have freely consented stems, among other
things, from the influence of the judicial or legal usage in which
treating a person justly consists in not violating his rights, among
which there is usually some kind of right to free choice. But even here
free choice is not to be completely unlimited, as the case of a person
choosing to enslave himself shows. Another reason for this reluctance
stems from the vagueness of the notion of a free choice. We tend to
think that persons could not freely consent to an unjust, or less than
fully just arrangement; that if they appear to do so, then their choice
was not really free. So unless the notion of a free choice is previously

specified, this claim, that whatever results from free and actual consent is just, may be unfalsifiable. The more intimately the idea of free consent (whether actual or hypothetical) is made part of the concept of justice, the less sense it makes to say that people freely consent to a given arrangement *because* it is a just one. Finally, our reluctance stems from a tendency to confuse the situation chosen with the situation, method, or procedure of choice, so that we think if the former is not completely just, the latter cannot have been either. This last tendency seems to apply particularly in the case of lotteries.

IV

If we dispense in this way with Slote's element of free, actual consent, we are left with justice as primarily a matter of desert. Since many who find this outcome implausible would cite the problem of how to determine with any real precision at all what a person deserves, suppose we examine this problem; first for contribution, then for effort.

Normally we think of contribution in restricted terms. Each kind of activity people engage in has certain kinds of beneficial effects or consequences normally associated with it. It is these effects or consequences that we regard as the contribution of that activity, rather than all the actual beneficial effects, results, or consequences that attend it.

But there is a kind of spectrum here. At one end are activities such as menial tasks. There is normally no question whatever about the nature or scope of the contribution of this kind of activity. At the other end are activities such as artistic endeavors and scientific research and discovery. People may spend much time and effort trying to determine the exact nature or scope of the contribution of these activities.

When we consider an example from the latter end of the spectrum, we see that the contribution of such activity can be made in a variety of ways. At one extreme, there is the mad scientist or crazed inventor, the Gyro Gearloose of comic lore, who pays no attention whatsoever to the importance or consequences of his various projects or inventions. He might stumble on a cure for cancer, but he himself couldn't care less whether this happens. Were such a person to discover a cure, it seems unlikely that many people would think he deserved a large reward for the sake of justice. To go to a different extreme, if it had turned out that, quite by accident, Nazi scientists working feverishly to perfect a variety of poison gas had instead happened upon this cure for cancer, justice seems to require no reward for them, either.

From such cases we might conclude merely that an intention to make the contribution is required for reward according to contribution to be just, in the same way that effort, to qualify for reward or compensation, must be sincere. Such intention is certainly absent in both the examples just mentioned. But we can imagine cases in which such an intention is fully present at the time the contribution is made, but in which we would be unsure that justice required compensating in proportion to the contribution. Suppose a beginning pre-medical student resolves one night to find the cancer cure, to devote her entire life to the project. The next day she attends her second chemistry class. Deciding that she can never succeed in her resolve unless she uses her time fully, she stays late, making solutions of various sorts. She leaves these solutions in a number of bottles and test tubes, one of which is picked up by accident the next day and sent to the university hospital with a batch of other solutions for analysis. Upon analysis her solution is seen to have unusual properties, and on further study and examination, its power as a cure for cancer becomes apparent. Justice does not seem to require rewarding her in proportion to her contribution because, while finding a cancer cure was her ultimate intention, her specific intention at the time of actually finding it was to improve her ability to handle solutions. Thus it is a *necessary* condition that the contribution be made via activity carried out with the specific intention to make that contribution.

But is this really a necessary condition? Consider the following case. Another woman who long ago resolved in just the same way to find a cure for cancer has spent decades in stupendous effort with no apparent effect. At the end of a long day, she cleans out a batch of flasks and tubes and pours all the remains into a stopped-up tub. The next morning the remains are still there, smoking and bubbling. She investigates, and indeed finds the sought-for cure. In this case also the actual discovery was made quite by accident, but few persons would conclude that justice requires holding back any reward. Clearly, it is the immense amount of effort which makes the difference here. Even if she had decided several days previously to abandon her search, so that at the time she actually found the cure she no longer intended to find one, no one would think that she no longer deserved a reward.

Motives or intentions enter into determining desert only to the extent that they serve to express the actual burdens (or benefits) in a person's life. There are certain motives or intentions one can have only as a result of taking upon oneself, or releasing oneself from, certain responsibilities or obligations, and in the imagery being drawn upon, these responsibilities and obligations are thought of as a kind of weight. In many cases, simply accepting a responsibility, as when one resolves to devote his or her whole life to finding a cure for cancer, constitutes some kind of added burden. But the burden involved obviously becomes greater if the resolve is maintained over the course of time—this is what differentiates the cases of the two scientists just mentioned.

Someone might suggest that the relevant difference between contribution and effort is that while a contribution can apparently be made quite unintentionally, or by accident, effort cannot be made accidentally or unintentionally. There is no such thing as proceeding along in life and then later being told, or in some way finding out, that one was making an effort, or exerting oneself, to make a particular contribution, or accomplish a particular task.

This, however, is not completely true either. We can import another spectrum of activities into the picture here. At one end are those activities in which the end or purpose of the activity is clear, the means to that end are clear or apparent (or widely taken to be), and the ways in which persons engage in such activity and accomplish the goals involved are well understood (or thought to be) and are at least roughly the same for everyone. At the other end of the spectrum are those activities where either the end or purpose is somewhat indistinct or unclear, the means appropriate are unclear, the ways in which persons engage in such activity vary widely, or some combination of these conditions holds. The former end of the spectrum, again, seems to include "menial" jobs, the latter, various kinds of creative work, and work involving a great deal of individual responsibility of one kind or another. At the former end of the spectrum it may often

be clear what constitutes effort with respect to the task at hand, but
at the latter it quite often will not be.

I might exert myself a great deal on a given day, making furious
efforts, only to realize, or admit to myself, that I wasn't really doing
research on the subject of the report I am preparing, but instead on a
closely related topic that is more interesting to me. Or in the midst of a
sincere effort to focus on the report topic I may find my interest
wandering ever so slightly, if only I stop briefly to become aware of
this. So in cases of this sort the actual effort involved is extremely
difficult to determine. One could think of controlling the direction of
one's effort, or of taking responsibility for the results of one's effort,
as itself a kind of effort, or better, as a kind of burden, at least, that
one can choose to place oneself under.

Perhaps the only reasonable approach is to use the result of such
activity as the basis of desert. In the case of drawing up a report, for
instance, it is the report itself that gives structure and content to the
effort and activity involved in preparing and creating it. Such activity
might otherwise have no perceptible structure at all. There might be
no way to determine how to appraise it apart from the report. Thus
contribution, in this case the actual report, is the most reasonable
basis for judging desert after all. Or it is at the end of the spectrum
mentioned above, at least. Perhaps there is another spectrum for
desert, with effort at one end and contribution (or at least result or
product) at the other. Then injustice would result if, as so often
happens, the attempt is made to use the basis appropriate at one end
in cases from the other end.

Suppose we were to grant that there is such a spectrum for bases of
desert. We could still ask the following question: even if contribution
(or result) is in some way the appropriate basis of desert at one end
of the spectrum, is this because rewarding each person according to
contribution is itself just, or is it because, although effort is the only
fully legitimate basis of desert, contribution is, at the one end of the
spectrum, the only, or at least the best way of determining the effort
involved? Using contribution might be the best way, for example,
because it allows the person making the contribution to operate most
freely; to choose his own pattern of effort and to regulate how intense
it will be, how extended, how structured. In other words, it could be

the best way not only because it provides the most accurate way of determining or measuring effort (accuracy alone might make it the best way), but also because of various other constraints or considerations, such as productivity. Thus complete justice could still require using effort itself as the desert basis, even though productivity is such a strong consideration here that only an approximation of complete justice is acceptable.

So if it turned out that justice requires in all cases rewarding each person according to effort, there would be a separate moral question of how justice should be balanced against the other considerations of freedom and productivity.

Even if effort, rather than contribution, constituted an appropriate basis of desert in all situations, it would have to be supplemented in some ways, especially by considering need.

Effort and need are often taken as equally plausible bases for a correct principle of distributive justice. But they are actually complementary to one another; unfulfilled needs constitute one kind of burden in life and efforts on behalf of society, in most cases, another.

How these two maxims are to be combined, and which (if any) others must also be employed, will depend on what the benefits and burdens of life are taken to be. The concept of justice by itself, while it makes essential reference to benefits and burdens, does not specify what those burdens or benefits are, or how they are to be compared, or measured.[9]

9. This analysis of what justice is is more plausible the more general one takes the concepts of benefits and burdens to be. But it is also clearly dependent on the quantitative comparability of a great diversity of these benefits and burdens. Because of this dependence, one might infer that, on a Marxian approach, this analysis could be appropriate only for (and in) a mature commodity society in which an untold variety of items are quantitatively compared to one another via their exchange value. This makes an objective and completely universal quantitative comparison of life's benefits and burdens at least *seem* possible.

But I believe the inference is unwarranted. On such an approach, distinguishing between a socialist and a communist society, or between a period of transition to socialism and full socialism itself, the maxim "to each according to his labor" is regarded as the appropriate principle of justice in the earlier phase, and "from each according to his ability, to each according to his need" as appropriate in the latter phase. In the transition phase, a money economy still exists, there are shortages and scarcities in certain goods, and persons are not fully motivated to work for the common good. Thus sincere efforts on behalf of the society

89   *Justice as Equality*

Different views of what the fundamental burdens and benefits of life
are, how they are to be weighed and which ones can be balanced or
dealt with by human social arrangements will lead in turn to different
conceptions of justice.

---

constitute the most fundamental burden in the earlier phase. For these and
other reasons, the former maxim does indeed function in the earlier phase as an
approximation to equality in the overall level of benefits and burdens. If so, then
the analysis might be adequate for this stage of society as well as the previous
capitalist phase.

It may be impossible, however, to view the latter maxim in the same way.
Although it is often understood in a quantitative way, i.e. as ranking a person's
ability and need on a numerical scale, the correct interpretation may be in
purely qualitative terms: each person is to produce for the society in accord
with his or her distinctive ensemble of potentialities and powers, and to receive
from the society what specifically conforms to his or her particular needs. If so,
this would be a maxim "beyond justice" in dispensing with any quantitative
comparability whatsoever.

Journal of Applied Philosophy, Vol.12, No. 3, 1995

Problems for Effort-Based Distribution Principles

JULIAN LAMONT

ABSTRACT *Many have argued that individuals should receive income in proportion to their contribution to society (i.e. their productivity). Others have believed that it would be fairer if people received income in proportion to the effort they expend in so contributing, since people have much greater control over their level of effort than their productivity. I argue that those who believe this are normally also committed, despite appearances, to increasing the social product — which undermines any sharp distinction between effort- and productivity-based distributive proposals. However, effort-based proposals do emphasise more the importance of people having control over factors affecting their income. The second set of problems I consider is how to implement policies which hold true to this emphasis. I show that there are major problems with the accuracy of using any objective criteria to measure the level of effort a person is expending. Moreover, once any such criteria are employed the problem of 'moral hazard' arises because people modify their behaviour in such a way as to maximise their income while minimising their effort. This violates the original motivation for using effort. Because of this and other empirical considerations, I argue that productivity may well be a better criterion on which to distribute income even if one is motivated by the same concerns which have prompted effort-based proposals.*

What is the correct basis for distributing income for productive work? One set of answers appeals to certain personal, work-related attribute(s) and it is this set which will be focused upon here [1]. For instance, many have argued that individuals should receive income in proportion to their contribution to society (i.e. their productivity). Others have believed that it would be farirer if people received income in proportion to the effort they expend in so contributing, since people have much greater control over their level of effort than their productivity (this claim is examined in Sections 1 and 2). I shall argue that those who believe this are normally also committed, despite appearances, to increasing the social product (living standards, GDP, etc.). Understanding the role of this second commitment undermines any sharp distinction between proposals to base income distribution on effort and proposals to base it on productivity. However, it is true that effort-based proposals emphasise more the importance of people having control over factors affecting their income. The second set of problems I shall consider is how to implement policies which hold true to this emphasis.

I shall show that there are major problems with the accuracy of using any objective criteria to measure the level of effort a person is expending. Moreover, as we shall see, once any such criteria are employed the problem of 'moral hazard' arises because people modify their behaviour in such a way as to maximise their income while minimising their effort. This violates the original motivation for using effort. Because of this and other empirical considerations, it will be argued that productivity may well be a better criterion on which to

216   *J. Lamont*

distribute income even if one is motivated by the same concerns which have prompted effort-based proposals.

1

Proposals to make income more proportional to the level of effort an individual expends have attracted both theorists and lay people alike. To understand where this attraction comes from it is worthwhile to look at a (very) potted history of the various proposals.

Proposals to use personal qualities/actions as a basis for distributing income have been around since at least the time of Aristotle. Aristotle proposed that income should be distributed on the basis of personal virtue — a noble system indeed: the most virtuous receive the most money, the least virtuous receive the least. Unfortunately, the practicality of the proposal was dubious even in the small well-knit communities of ancient Greece, let alone in modern nation-states. However, the main proposals which succeeded Aristotle's shared, to a certain extent, a similar motivation, but were more practical for nation-states.

The next most significant desert proposal was that of John Locke who proposed that each man should receive 'the full product of his labour'. This is often cited as the inspiration for later, more refined, productivity proposals. However, since effort in Locke's day more largely determined productivity, the proposal was not that well differentiated from effort proposals. For instance, Locke tended to illustrate and motivate his distributive claims with agricultural examples, or examples from the 'state of nature'. The difference between a distribution based on effort rather than productivity often was not substantial. Hence, it is unclear if the intuitions to which Locke appealed support distributions according to effort (or labour) or to productivity (or contribution). It is also unclear if Locke thought that the intuitions which support a right to the product of one's labour in a state of nature support such a right once the transition to civil society is made, or whether, in civil society, such intuitions only support a right to the value of the contribution, not the product itself [2]. Anyway the details of the interpretations need not concern us here. The general motivation for using a person's productivity (or contribution) became fairly clear: the belief that people ought to receive the value of their contribution to society (we shall look at these motivations in more detail in the following section). Locke clearly saw this as a moral advance over previous distributive systems. In particular, Locke used it to argue against the landed classes receiving most of their income from rent. He argued that simply owning and renting land did not constitute contributing to society and hence such large amounts of income should not be distributed in this way. Such reformist prescriptions have often continued to characterise those who have advocated productivity (and contribution) as a basis for distributing income[3].

People who have advocated effort as a superior basis for distributing income have seen their proposal as simply taking the reformist tendencies of the productivity proposal one step further. Their argument usually takes something like the following form: 'If a society uses productivity rather than say, social position (or being born into a landed family), as the basis for distributing income, this gives people greater control over their destiny (a democratic ideal). For people can control their productivity to a much greater degree than they can control their social position or whether they are born into a landed family. However, people can only control their productivity up to a certain limit. What is the *moral* difference between a person who works hard digging ditches and a person who works hard performing surgery on people? There is a difference between the two: the surgeon is likely to have a higher level of natural intelligence than the ditch-digger. However, intelligence is like social position and land inheritance — it is not something over which people have much control. If we want a fair distributive system then we should not let such uncontrollable factors play such a large role in determining a person's income. Hence, the level of effort (which we have considerably more control over than our productivity) should be used as the basis for income distribution.'

It is worth noting that viewing the move from productivity to effort in this manner is one way of understanding the further move to the distributive principle of Marx and communism: 'From each according to his ability, to each according to his needs'. One motivation for this principle which follows the above line of reasoning is that people also have little control over the effort they make. Both the ability to exert certain levels of effort, and the willingness to do so [the argument goes] are products of factors over which the individual has little control [4] — family background, social class, genetics, etc.; so 'needs' rather than 'effort' are a morally superior basis upon which to distribute income.

The details of the communist development of this line of thinking are tangential to the concerns of this paper. However, it is worth noting that the proposal to use effort as a basis for income is one that has been proposed as a distributive principle in transitional socialist societies before 'ideal' communism and this constitutes one of a group of what I have called 'effort theorists'[5]. However, it would be a mistake to think of the proposal to move towards more effort-based distributive principles as simply a feature of transitional socialist societies — they have had much broader currency, advocated, for example, by liberal egalitarians and social democrats[6].

In what follows I will use, as convenient shorthand, the expressions 'effort theorists' and 'productivity theorists' to refer, respectively, to those advocating effort- and productivity-based distributive principles or policies and practices which can reasonably be deduced from such principles. I will do so without scare quotes, but this is for ease of expression only, and hence somewhat misleading, since I do not want to suggest that the main advocates for these principles (or for systems which more closely follow these principles) are mainly political, economic and social *theorists*. Those who advocate such policies are most commonly ordinary lay people, politicians, trade unionists, business people, political activitists, etc. The concerns and policy recommendations of these people should also be engaged in any discussion such as this. Moreover, many theorists commonly invoke such arguments (which can be seen as motivated by these principles) only to argue for very particular reforms. For this reason it is worthwhile to look briefly at some of the claims and policies in Western democracies which 'effort theory' has motivated.

Before doing this we should highlight a common mistaken belief which many people have about wages, salary and income in Western democracies: that they are simply set by market forces. What is peculiar about this belief is that many people think that this is what the 'experts' tell them — experts in this case being the economists. However, very few economists with any sophistication believe that incomes are set simply by market forces. What many of them do believe is that markets set certain range constraints (but even then the constraints depend on the markets being free and open and there are always lots of markets in western democracies which are not free and open and which are not likely to be in the foreseeable future). Within these constraints there are many factors which play a role in determining wage, salary and income levels: historical precedent, taxation and administrative laws, collective bargaining (including that carried out by unions), sociological factors,

218   *J. Lamont*

various government policies, and so on. It is towards affecting many of these factors that actions and policies motivated by the concerns of effort theory are often directed. Hence, many of them are best seen as proposing constraints on the market determination of income. So what are some of these actions and policies?

Comparative wage claims mounted by unions often have, as a significant part of their motivation, the concerns of 'effort theory'. The case of San Francisco fire fighters and police officers is a good example: where one group always lodges claims to match the other's pay rise because 'it is just as much work to be a fire fighter as a police officer (or vice versa)'. Such cases are repeated across all democracies and partly explain the well-documented 'leap-frogging' effect in wage claims by different occupations. It also partly explains the relatively strong rigidity over the last hundred years in the ordinal wage ranking of many occupations — people come to view their occupation as requiring a certain amount of 'work' relative to other occupations.

The same sort of factors are at work in actions and policies to prevent or promote government interference in the income levels of certain occupations. Many proposals to make the income levels more egalitarian are motivated this way — that the work levels are not that dissimilar. But the argument is not always put to egalitarian ends. For instance, there are many actions which a western government can take which will lower the incomes of medical practitioners. One of the most common arguments used to resist such actions by governments is that medical practitioners deserve the high incomes they receive because of the long hours they work and the long years of training they must undertake — an argument motivated by effort theory.

Arguments for making the income tax system more progressive are often partly motivated by the concerns of effort theory. Progressive taxation is proposed as a way of correcting for the fact that the higher income levels are mainly due to greater social opportunities, or higher levels of natural talents, rather than harder work. Progressive taxation corrects for this[7].

Arguments for pay equity for women, and for traditionally female occupations, have also often been helped along by effort theory concerns. For instance, it has been pointed out by numerous industrial unions that females work as hard as males in the same occupation. It has also been argued successfully that the reason that traditionally female occupations have been paid at a lower rate than traditionally male occupations can often be explained by sociological factors rather than anything intrinsic in the nature of the work involved. For instance, the labour involved in nursing is similar to the labour involved in ambulance work, yet nurses (who were traditionally female) were paid considerably less than ambulance drivers (who were traditionally male). This inequity cannot be justified on effort theory [8] but has come about because of a range of sociological factors — that work performed by women has historically been undervalued; that women have had less of a range of alternative occupation choices, etc.

While there is not space here to continue exploring the many different types of arguments that have as part of their motivation the concerns of effort theory, it should be clear that they are not only found in transitional socialist societies but have been a force in calls for reform (and resistance to form) in Western democracies as well. In the next section I shall try to draw out the motivating values behind these theories.

2

As we shall see *both* effort and productivity theorists share the common value of 'raising living standards (or any preferred measure of social welfare or product)'. This may seem to be a strange claim in light of how 'effort theorists' portray their theories or particular policies. We will see, however, that effort and productivity theories place different emphasis on this value and also have different modifying values [9].

The defining value or goal for the productivity theorist is that of rewarding people in proportion to their marginal product and it has as its motivation the desire for people to receive the value society places on the goods and services they provide [10].

For effort theorists, the defining value is that of rewarding people in proportion to the *effort* they exert in contributing to the social product. Although, as we shall see, the relationship between the two values of the effort theorists is a complicated one, it is generally true that the effort theorist believes there is more value in effort being rewarded proportionately than in the extra gain in living standards people may receive under productivity-based distribution principles.

Proposals, to distribute income in proportion to effort expended, take many different forms. Let us begin with a simple form of the theory in which there is some specification of the activities outside which effort expended will not count as socially productive and hence will not count as a basis for claiming income. For instance, effort expended on hobbies may be excluded. After this specification is made, as long as people are engaged in some approved occupation or activity then the amount of effort they put into the job determines how much income they should receive.

The first practical difference between the theories which needs to be explored is that they would yield different levels of social product (barring certain implausible empirical assumptions). Why? The simplest answer is that there are differences in 'efficiency' between the theories [11]. The main reason for the differences in efficiency under policies inspired by the two theories is that the different patterns of income result in different patterns of job allocation and duration. This in turn leads to different social products. It is up to empirical economics to determine the actual size of these differences, but there is good reason to believe (and this has been the received opinion) that a system employing mainly effort-based distributive policies would yield a significantly lower total social product than would be yielded under a system employing mainly productivity-based distributive policies. Why? The main reason is that people are not perfectly inclined to the occupation which it would be socially optimal for them to hold (also, they are often not inclined to perform in it for the socially optimal duration). Now, at least to some extent, money provides an incentive for people a) to work in occupations which are more socially productive and in which they would not otherwise work, and b) to work there for longer hours. A feature then of effort theories which would cause a lower social product would be that they generally do not discriminate in terms of pay rates between occupations with different levels of social productivity, or similarly between different levels of productivity within an occupation. There would be people therefore who could be more productive, but to be so is not viewed by them as worth the loss of utility they would incur in being more productive [12]. People will normally only work if there is some gain in utility in so doing. If people choose not to work in a particular occupation which would be more socially productive, then there is good reason to believe that the combination of the work involved and the potential benefits is less than or equal to alternative combinations available to them.

The fact that a system employing mainly effort-based distribution policies yields a lower social product counts against its adoption. It is very important to understand that this is true even for effort theorists. Effort theorists, when they are arguing for a particular policy often seem to imply that they are ensuring that income is proportional to effort expended. However, this is simply not true. Effort theorists are not generally monists when it comes to value. As was indicated at the beginning, traditional effort theorists, in fact, have as their primary value the raising of living standards, or increasing the social product. It is primary in the sense that only effort directed at increasing the social product counts as a basis for a claim for economic benefits. Hence, despite the emphasis on effort they have another important value which modifies this emphasis.

This dual commitment is very important and is constantly overlooked by people advocating particular effort-based policies. In fact, under a system employing mainly effort-based distributive policies, people can exert extreme levels of effort and yet have no legitimate claim to economic benefits unless those efforts are directed at raising the social product. Of course, one could propose non-traditional effort theories with different defining values or goals. For instance, in a particularly religious society the basis for normative claims to income may be through activity directed towards raising religious consciousness. But the standard effort theorists we are interested in here have, as their primary value, the raising of the social product. For them, despite appearances, a lower social product involves a loss of something which is valuable and hence counts against any proposal which entails it.

So, effort-based distribution principles result in the loss of something valuable to effort-theorists themselves — people's living standards. There are a number of ways of modifying an effort-based principle so that the gap in living standards resulting from the adoption of it would be less dramatic. An extremely blunt modification would be to reduce the number of occupations counted as socially productive. The problem with this is that the costs to society in living standards may still be great. For instance, suppose that it was proposed that people who applied their skills to artistic painting would be paid (through a taxation system) at the same rate as tradespeople [13]. Now, this is likely to result in a great increase in artists and a reduction in tradespeople with an attendant loss of living standards for the society. To counter this loss of living standards, artistic painting could be removed from the list of remunerative occupations. While this would mean that some enthusiastic but incompetent artists would put their skills to more socially productive uses, it would also mean that society would be deprived of the works of some very talented artists. As a consequence, this type of effort-based system is becoming extinct in the world — though it is important to remember that even in very recent times some former communist countries had economies which approximated such systems.

Two more realistic alternatives are available. One is to avoid restricting the occupations further and instead specify, within each occupation, a threshold for what will count as a socially productive contribution — only if this threshold is reached will the effort count as a basis for income-claims. So, for instance, only if the effort produces competent art works will the person be able to claim income in the light of that effort. Moving a step further, socially productive grades could be specified within each occupation and associated with progressively higher rates of pay. Another alternative is to rank occupations in terms of social productivity and pay progressively higher rates for socially more productive ones. These measures could be applied separately or jointly. These measures became increasingly more common in many communist countries (and continue to do so) as the cost, in terms of living standards, of the previous effort-based systems became more apparent.

The trouble with the above modifications is that, although each has the effect of raising living standards, they do so at a price for the effort theorist. Effort theorists accept the difference in social product resulting from the application of their theory in preference to productivity theory because of their relative valuations of effort and the social product. Effort theorists' complaint with the productivity principle is that it partly bases income distribution on factors over which people do not have full voluntary control. This is what the effort theorist wants to avoid, but by introducing the measures mentioned above, the effort theorist allows a greater proportion of people's income to be determined by such factors. It is this motivation — that differences in the economic benefits should not be determined by factors over which people do not have full voluntary control — which is the defining characteristic of those I have called 'effort theorists'[14]. The arguments then, of this paper, apply not just to theorists concerned with 'deserving', *but also to those egalitarians who argue that the distribution of economic benefits must depend, as much as is practically possible, on factors over which people have such control.*

So what follows from realising that effort theorists value the social product and not just effort? The first thing that follows is that we can more clearly see that the effort theorists have always been willing to compromise their valuing of effort for at least some gains in the social product. So we can see that, despite appearances, there is no difference *in kind* between effort theories and productivity theories, only a difference in the *degree* to which income will be determined by purely voluntary factors. Under effort theories some of the differences in economic benefits people receive will be explained by factors over which they have little or no voluntary control. This comes about once it is specified that only effort directed at increasing the social product will count, and it is exacerbated when any kind of restriction of occupations is made, or *any* kind of threshold or grading is instituted. *This is true of most egalitarian theories,* despite it being commonly ignored. All these measures have the effect of giving a premium to people with certain kinds of talents and/or to people who have higher levels of talents.

What also follows from this analysis is that a clearer picture can be presented of the choice which all such theorists must face. They must decide to what extent they are willing to allow such involuntary factors to influence incomes in order to increase living standards. Now despite some grand designs of those most concerned with theory, such decisions seem impossible to make rationally in ignorance of the empirical facts. For the society to judge the desirability of a proposal to reduce the degree to which income is distributed as a result of factors over which individuals have little or no voluntary control, the society will need to have a fair idea of what effect any such proposals would have on living standards. Since all traditional effort theories place some value on the social product all such theorists (and societies) must face this compromising choice. For instance, it seems clear that intelligence currently has a marked effect on incomes which people earn in western societies. It also seems clear that one's level of intelligence is something which can only be controlled to a very limited degree. For this reason there have been many different proposals to remedy this to varying degrees — from simple progressive taxation, to differential taxation for university graduates, to differential taxation applied directly on the basis of intelligence tests [15]. Now if the only value for effort theorists was having income proportional to effort then there would be no doubt that such policies would be desirable. But as we have seen, effort theorists (and most of the rest of us) value living standards as well. Hence, to assess the desirability of such policies we will need to have some idea of the effect on living standards of such policies. This knowledge does not need to be complete always — policies can be introduced in increments and the effect of their full implementation projected. But, such effects are important to know in the decision to implement such policies — and are important even to the effort theorist.

Because of the measures noted above, no effort theory ever fully eradicates the influence of factors over which individuals lack control. A symmetrical point can be made with respect to productivity theories. All practical applications of such theories give some effective weight to the criterion of effort — it is not any great mystery that one of the ways of being more productive is to put in more effort. Productivity theories can similarly be modified to place successively greater weight on effort rather than productivity until they simply blend into the effort-based theories.

3

So effort theory is not, as it is often portrayed, a radically different kind of theory from productivity theory. The choice between them is a choice from a continuous spectrum which all, productivity and effort theorists alike, must make. There is not 'justice' on the one hand and 'the social product' on the other and you choose one or the other. As we have see, effort and productivity theorists value both to some extent and incorporate both into a broader notion of justice. The choice of a particular point on the spectrum will be partly determined by the value placed on giving people greater overall economic benefits relative to the value of giving economic benefits to people in accordance with things over which they have full voluntary control. But what about this latter value which is the driving motivation behind effort theory? What I wish to do in the rest of this paper is to argue that it would be very difficult to implement effort theory, as it has been normally understood, in a way which respects this original motivation. In fact, a productivity-based theory may implement the original motivation as well, if not better.

Although it has been recognised in the past that the dominant implementation problem for an effort principle is how to measure effort there has been little exploration by either effort theorists or their opponents into just how deep and systematic this implementation problem is [16]. There seems no obvious way of telling how much effort a person expends on productive activity each day. Of course, we have some idea of effort and can make some judgments about it. We can say of a student that she is not putting much effort into her subject, and we can usually discern when she is putting in more. Similarly, we can say of a shop attendant that she is not putting much effort into her job when she checks out our groceries at a very slow rate. But once we start pushing a little beyond this — and we need to push a long way beyond this if we are going to use effort as a basis for distribution of income — then it may be doubtful whether effort is a precise enough concept to take the strain. Some of the difficulties are similar to those that classical utilitarians faced. How do we compare the effort required when activities are so diverse? Does a person expend more effort in painting rather than doing the plumbing? Relatedly, how do we go about making interpersonal comparisons? Does an accountant expend more effort in keeping accounts than a bricklayer does in laying bricks? Utilitarians eventually decided that the concept of pleasure could not take the strain. Reducing all human activity down to pleasure units was not going to work and preference utilitarianism took over. Similarly, it may be impossible to reduce everything down to effort units and to use these in any meaningful way.

Many of the socialist systems of former communist countries can be seen as partially motivated by the concerns of effort theory. Unfortunately, those who have advocated changes to the distributive systems of democratic countries to make them more effort-based, have paid little attention to describing systematic methods for determining effort. The problem with many 'lay' proposals designed to make distributive systems fairer by making income distribution more closely based on factors over which individuals have greater control is that they often provide no way of systematically assessing their claims that their reforms will have the desired effect. For instance, suppose that a high progressive tax was proposed for high income earners on the basis of the claim that the majority of their extra earning comes from their higher level of intelligence which they had no control over acquiring. Now while this is an intuitively plausible suggestion we have no way of assessing its soundness without some way of measuring the 'effort' which people have control over. 'Lay' advocates and theorists alike have tended to avoid these difficult problems. In this respect, a recent advocate for effort theory, Wojciech Sadurski, has been relatively bold in giving some (albeit too little) indication of how a thorough-going system of measurement of effort could be implemented. He cites approvingly Jan Tinbergen's '[proposed]method for establishing the relative importance of various material and non-material elements of a job'[17]. Presumably the idea would be to use a complex series of questionnaires to yield a concrete list of the 'effort-levels' associated with particular features of jobs. This list could then be used to determine the 'effort' employed in various jobs — or there could be 'bands' of jobs within a schedule of ever increasing effort. With such a schedule it would be possible then to assess the various proposals, like progressive taxation, to see how well they accord with the original motivation of effort theory. The ideal would presumably be to use the taxation system, and various other mechanisms, to make the after-tax pay track the effort levels from one band to the next. Now there may be reasons why the ideal could not be reached — but that is no criticism of the theory, as it is probably true of all distributive theories — it is the nature of these particular beasts. But one could at least imagine, in principle, how such a system would work: each degree of responsibility is associated with some fixed level of 'effort units'; each degree of flexibility in work hours is associated with another level of 'effort units'; each degree of 'possibility for further promotion' is associated with another level; and so on. One then adds up the number of effort units associated with each job and the taxation and transfer rates are set accordingly.

A system which uses such a list could be called 'weakly objective'. It is objective in the sense that some features of jobs, which effort theorists believe are measurable, are used indirectly to determine the amount of effort expended in each job. It is only 'weakly' objective because it uses a collection of expressed preferences from the general population to formulate the cardinal measures of effort associated with each feature. The problem with any such objective criteria for assessing effort is probably best illustrated by simply using a single objective criterion — the argument can be readily extended to cover other such criteria.

Suppose we have two people each making a product or performing a manual task. How is effort to be measured in such a case? The suggestion that the number of products made in a certain period be used as a criterion for remuneration is obviously not one normally entertained by the effort theorist. The most common criterion suggested in the past, and hence the one I will use here for the purposes of illustration, is *duration* of work. But this particular indirect measure of effort has problems even in this simple case. There are two obvious explanations why one person would produce more goods than another in a given

224   *J. Lamont*

period. One, he has a greater talent for producing the good than the other person. Two, he is working harder, i.e., he is exerting a greater effort. This raises the question of whether productivity might be a better measure of effort [18].

In the simple case of manual labour described above, a number of assumptions will be required to defend the effort theorists' claim that duration, or some other set of objective criteria, is a better indirect measure of effort than productivity. First,

Assumption 1: The existence of a greater talent for producing the good, rather than differences in effort expended, better explains the differences in productivity.

If this assumption is false then a more effective way *of implementing effort theory* (not productivity theory) would be to use productivity as the indirect measure of effort. An effort theorist arguing for duration as the measure of effort may try to avoid this assumption by attempting, in each case, to determine whether someone's greater productivity in a given period is due to greater talent than that of the other workers. However, two practical problems immediately arise with such a proposal. First, it does not seem that any such attempt is feasible for a whole society. It would often be difficult even in the case of two people doing the same job. With many people doing different jobs it would seem to be impossible. Second, the cost of such a determination would be totally prohibitive. Hence, Assumption 1 seems unavoidable.

The second assumption is related to the first. Even if the above determination could be made, one is still faced with the problem that, for all practical purposes, it would be impossible to determine the source of the extra degree of talent. In particular, whether it was due to some *natural* difference between the persons or due to an *acquired* difference which was the result of some form of effort. As one adds to the simple criterion of duration to make the measure more accurate the problems become more complicated rather than less — ensuring the necessity of Assumption 1. To accommodate this, some adjustment for training would need to be made. Note that the effort theorist would also be using the same sort of objective criteria (like duration) for training and hence would need to make Assumption 1 for training as well.

There are further problems. There is personal on-the-job acquisition of skills and the possible inadequacy of Assumption 1 at the training level — the accumulated errors over people's lifetimes are likely to be large. A second assumption seems necessary,

Assumption 2: The greater talent for producing the good (or service) is the result of *natural* factors rather than factors the agent had control over, unless it is the result of training for which the agent has already been paid.

Again, if this assumption is false then productivity would be a better indirect measure.

Assumptions 1 and 2 seem most plausible in the case of purely manual work. However, almost all tasks involve some mental element. Even manual tasks which involve constant physical movement do so. Duration, or whatever set of objective criteria is chosen, must be a reasonable indirect measure of effort in tasks which involve 'mental effort'. So, Assumptions 1 and 2 will also have to be made in cases which involve mental effort [19].

Although there are going to be many individual counter examples, these assumptions, at least for the case of a particular occupation, may seem reasonable enough (though it is not clear how one would go about convincing a sceptic of this). The assumptions then that must be made by effort theorists, if they are to introduce a system of paying people by objective criteria (but not productivity), can be summarised by the assumption that 'The differences in productivity between people, both within any given occupation, and between occupations, is best explained by differences in *natural* ability between the people and/or by effort in training for which the people have been already paid.'

This should be qualified. A competing claim for what best explains differences in productivity is that it is differences in social opportunity (i.e. inequality of material resources, inequality of educational and training opportunities, inequality of access, etc.) rather than natural inequality. However, effort theorists do not have to deny this. The assumption they need then is:

Effort Theory Assumption: After adjusting for differences in social opportunity, the difference in productivity between people is best explained by differences in *natural* ability and/or by effort in training for which the people have been already paid.

Now let me reiterate, in a slightly different manner, why effort theorists need to make this assumption. To do this, it is best to contrast this assumption with a competing one,

Alternative Assumption: After adjusting for differences in social opportunity, the difference in productivity between people is best explained by differences in effort, on the job and in training.

Now these two assumptions compete for the *best* explanation of differences in productivity between people. No doubt both provide *some* explanation of the differences. The question is, which provides the *best* explanation. If one answers that differences in *natural* talents provide the best explanation then duration is likely to provide a better indirect measure of effort than productivity. If, however, one answers that differences in effort on the job and in training (apart from that effort which has already been paid for) provide the best explanation then productivity will provide a better indirect measure of effort [20].

Now while the Effort Theory Assumption may be plausible as it applies to present Western democracies, effort theorists unfortunately require something stronger. The Effort Theory Assumption is made in the context of *present* Western democracies. However, present Western democracies do not operate under an effort theory. What effort theorists require is:

Modified Effort Theory Assumption: In a society operating under an effort principle, in particular a society operating under an effort principle where the proxy for effort is some objective criterion unrelated to productivity, the Effort Theory Assumption is true [21].

This modified assumption is, of course, a much stronger assumption than the original. It requires that when a system is introduced which uses a publicly known criterion, unrelated to productivity, as its practical criterion for remuneration, people will not take advantage of this fact. Effort theorists thus face the problem that even though their distribution principle may be justified in theory, it is no longer justified *on the theory's own principles* once it is introduced. This problem is very similar to that faced when insurance schemes are introduced. In both cases, the source of the problem is that people change their behaviour in light of a scheme's introduction. Once these criteria are employed which do not directly measure effort people are presented with an opportunity to exploit the system by modifying their behaviour in such a way as to maximise their income (by maximising their scores on the employed criteria) while minimising their effort within the constraints set by the system. Following the nomenclature of the insurance problem, we may call this 'the moral hazard problem of effort theory'. Unfortunately, because this is a well-documented phenomenon in the case of insurance, one should have serious doubts whether the modified assumption — the assumption effort theorists need — is true [22].

Although I have mainly used the simple criterion of duration for the purpose of illustration, this argument can readily be extended to more complicated collections of objective criteria. The result then is that even if some set of objective criteria is the best indirect measure of effort in our society, the same criteria may not be an effective measure in a society which *uses* them for the implementation of its effort theory. In fact, productivity may be a better measure in such a society. Therefore, *under the tenets of effort theory*, it would be best to use productivity as the basis for remuneration. Of course, once this happens, productivity might be inferior to duration, etc. as an indirect measure of effort because the original assumption will be true in such a society. Effort theorists are thus caught in something of a dilemma.

The 'moral hazard problem of effort theory' also bears on the discussion in Section 1. It was noted there that the introduction of more effort-based distributive policies is likely to result in an overall drop in living standards. The implication of the above is that if some set of objective criteria, independent of productivity, is introduced as the proxy measure of effort, then a further drop in living standards is likely. Since this drop would be *in addition* to that mentioned before, it counts as a separate consideration against implementing effort theory. It is important to understand that these decreases in living standards are an *internal* problem for effort theory which compromises the justice of effort-based policies on their own criterion of justice. The first worry about living standards came from people being attracted to socially sub-optimal occupations. The additional decrease in the social product implied here comes from direct exploitation of the system. Some people not only choose to work in socially sub-optimal jobs — they also choose not to work very hard in them.

Even if people do not have a direct inclination to exploit the system, results from game theory on assurance games suggest that the same behavioural pattern (and consequent decrease in the social product) may come about even if people *collectively* would be willing to work hard. This occurs when people cannot be assured that others are not exploiting the system, i.e. they are willing to work hard as long as they can be assured that others are doing likewise — but they do not want to be taken advantage of (in game theory jargon, 'suckered'). Unfortunately, it is difficult to see any way of assuring a whole society of this.

I have been considering throughout this paper the concerns of those who have been attracted to the idea that people's income should depend, as much as is practically possible, on factors over which people have control. If the argument of this section is correct then those people may well have some reason to use productivity as their indirect measure of effort in the practical implementation of their concerns.

In summary, we have identified three problems which must be addressed by anyone arguing for more effort-based policies [23]:

1. Consideration of what is valued more. The effort theorist values the effort in producing the social product more than the marginal increase in the social product, while the productivity theorist gives more weight to rewarding people according to the value by which they have increased the marginal product. As was shown, in Section 1, sub-optimal choices of occupation mean that more effort-based policies are likely to result in a lower social product than productivity-based ones. Therefore, a choice, *from a continuous spectrum of possibilities*, needs to be made about the relative importance of these values.

2. Consideration of how practical are recommendations for more effort-based policies. It was noted that 'effort' is not a conceptually robust notion for making comparisons of effort. Nevertheless, practical proxies for effort must be found if more effort-based policies are to be implemented in a society. Having exposed the necessary empirical

Problems for Effort-Based Distribution Principles   227

assumptions; the problems with the accuracy of 'effort measurement' using indirect objective criteria unrelated to productivity; and the problem of moral hazard when such criteria are used; I have argued that productivity may well be as good a proxy for effort as duration or other objective criteria available.

3. Furthermore, the implementation of more effort-based policies is likely to result in a decrease in living standards in addition to that noted in (1). This is because of what I have called 'the moral hazard problem of effort theory'. This would come about either because of a direct desire to exploit such policies or because of the impossibility of assuring people that others were not exploiting it.

Having brought into focus these problems with implementing effort theory, it is important to emphasise, in closing, that it shares many important practical policy prescriptions with productivity theory (and many of the egalitarian goals of effort theory can be effectively argued using productivity theory). This is often overlooked in emphasising the philosophical interest in what divides these two theories. Any practical application of one of the theories yields measures that are in significant conformity with the demands of the other. For example, any practical application of the productivity principle will normally make income partly proportionate to effort expended. It will furthermore restrict income in one of the main areas where each of the theories wishes to restrict it, i.e. income that goes to people for unproductive activity. As there is good reason to believe that in all Western societies there is substantial income flowing to people for unproductive activity [24], neither productivity theory nor effort theory should be identified with the *status quo*. It is a common mistake to do so, especially by associating productivity theory with Western economies, and effort theory with some former communist economies. People who support either theory can agree on a common and immediate major policy goal of restricting income flows to unproductive activity (which is not justified on other grounds such as need) and a number of other practical measures which, on *both* of these theories would make the distribution of income more just. Since the theories also normally require as a precondition for their full implementation that equality of opportunity exists in the society, they can also agree on the pursuit of this goal. It should not be underestimated then, how similar the two theories are in many of their immediate practical recommendations. If the arguments of this paper are correct, this practical congruence is much greater than has been realised in the past [25].

Julian Lamont, Department of Philosophy, University of Queensland, QLD 4072, Australia.

NOTES

[1] These theories have normally (and correctly) been proposed as partial theories of distributive justice — as restricted principle(s) governing only the distribution of income to fully functional, employed adults in a society. As such, they often presuppose that morally prior claims, say of need and welfare, have already been met and that other background institutions are just.

[2] For a clear contemporary discussion of this distinction see GERALD G. GAUS (1990) *Value and Justification* (Cambridge, Cambridge University Press), 410–416, 485–489.

[3] See, for example, DAVID MILLER (1989) *Market, State and Community* (Oxford, Oxford University Press); JONATHAN RILEY (1989) Justice Under Capitalism in *Markets and Justice*, JOHN W. CHAPMAN (ed.) (New York, New York University Press).

[4] For a discussion of this claim see GEORGE SHER (1979) Effort, ability, and personal desert *Philosophy and Public Affairs* 8, 361–376 and GEORGE SHER (1987) *Desert* (Princeton, Princeton University Press).

[5] See, for example, KARL MARX *Critique of the Gotha Programme*, in *Selected Works* (New York, 1933), Vol. 2, p. 563; MAURICE DOBB, Socialism and the market (1965) *Monthly Review*, 17 (September): 31; BEL CSIKOS-NAGY (1968) Socialist economic theory and the New Mechanism, *The New Hungarian Quarterly*, 8 (Winter). For

228   *J. Lamont*

a general discussion see PETER CLECAK (1970) Moral versus material incentives, *Social Theory and Practice* 1, 82–98.

[6] See, for instance, WOJCIECH SADURSKI (1985) *Giving Desert Its Due* (D. Reidel, Dordrecht, Holland); HEATHER MILNE 1986 Desert, effort and equality *Journal of Applied Philosophy* 3, 235–243.

[7] For a serious proposal (and one worth considering) to tax 'talents', see M. ALLINGHAM (1975) Towards an ability tax, *Journal of Public Economics* 4, 361–376.

[8] Productivity theorists can also argue against this inequity by noting that the productivity of women is similar to that of men.

[9] This way of viewing values as determining desert-bases may seem unfamiliar. For an explanation of this view see my paper (1994) The concept of desert in distributive justice, *Philosophical Quarterly* 44, 45–64.

[10] Of course, this defining value of rewarding people in proportion to their marginal product allows there to be many different forms of productivity theory because there is a range of possible (increasing and monotonic) proportionality functions. There is also a range of views, in both groups of theories, about what constitutes the 'social product'. For the sake of simplicity and for comparison let us assume the definition of the social product is the same in the two theories (even though, in practice, effort theories often give more emphasis to non-material goods and services).

[11] A system will be said to be more efficient than another system if, with the same available resources, it can produce a higher social product.

[12] Of course, there would be some possibilities for overcoming this if 'effort' was simply redefined to mean 'disutility'. However, this is more characteristic of compensation-based theories rather than the effort-based theories being considered here. For an historically interesting example of a move from a duration-based system to a system more based on disutility see JOSIAH WARREN (1863) *True Civilisation an Immediate Necessity and the Last Ground of Hope for Mankind, Being the Results and Conclusions of Thirty-nine Years' Laborious Study and Experiments in Civilisation As It Is, and in Different Enterprises for Reconstruction* (Boston), 84 and (1869) *True Civilisation: A Subject of Vital and Serious Interest to All People; But Most Immediately to the Men and Women of Labor and Sorrow* (Clintondale, Massachusetts): 42–43. I have discussed compensation-based desert principles in my article, Incentive income, deserved income, and economic rents, *Journal of Political Philosophy* (forthcoming).

[13] The Netherlands during the 1970's and part of the 1980's pursued a policy of supporting through taxes a much greater number of artists than in other western countries and basically ended up warehousing thousands of works of dubious artistic value.

[14] For a discussion of the use of the criterion of 'voluntary control' in discussions of desert see my paper (1994) The concept of desert in distributive justice, *Philosophical Quarterly* 44, 45–64.

[15] See M. ALLINGHAM 1975 Towards an ability tax, *Journal of Public Economics* 4, 361–376.

[16] Though see PHILIPPE VAN PARIJS (1991) Why surfers should be fed: the liberal case for an unconditional basic income, *Philosophy and Public Affairs*, 20, pp. 101–131; M. H. LESSNOFF (1978) Capitalism, socialism and justice in JOHN ARTHUR and WILLIAM SHAW (eds.) *Justice and Economic Distribution* (Inglewood Cliffs, New Jersey, Prentice-Hall), pp. 139–149.

[17] WOJCIECH SADURSKI (1985), *Giving Desert Its Due* (D. Reidel, Dordrecht, Holland): 152. Tinbergen's method is described and critically assessed by J. PEN (1971) *Income and Distribution* (Allen Lane, London), 303–304. See also JAN TINBERGEN (1975), *Income Differences* (Amsterdam, North Holland Publishing Company).

[18] DAVID MILLER briefly raises a similar question in his (1989) *Market, State and Community* (Oxford, Oxford University Press), 169–170.

[19] Other assumptions will need to be made. For instance, assumptions about whether duration is an appropriate criterion for comparing effort at manual tasks with effort at mental tasks. Assumptions would need to be made about when mental effort is being expended — would being located in one's office, for instance, suffice?

[20] While effort theorists may have no objection, *in principle*, to productivity being used as the indirect measure of effort, they would, presumably, be rather surprised if it turns out that their theory and productivity theory, have the same real world instantiation, i.e. result in the same distribution when applied to a society. So, while it is not strictly true that effort theorists need their assumption to be true rather than the alternative, it is nonetheless the case that the truth of their assumption will keep the effort theory distinct from productivty theory in the real world.

[21] It should be noted that if one relinquishes this exclusion of productivity as the objective criterion then one is already allowing the effective collapse of the effort principle into the productivity principle. There will, of course, be borderline criteria like 'intensity' which will again immediately raise the problem of measurement

separate from productivity. For example, the best measure of 'intensity' of work, training, etc. may well be productivity.

[22] For an economic discussion of moral hazard theory see BENGT HOLMSTROM (1979), Moral hazard and observability, *Bell Journal of Economics* 10, 74–91; BENGT HOLMSTROM (1982), Moral hazard in teams, *Bell Journal of Economics*, 13, 324–340. For an interesting essay in ideal theory in which there is no problem of moral hazard, see JOSEPH CARENS (1981) *Equality, moral incentives and the market* (Chicago, University of Chicago Press).

[23] There will, of course, be parallel (but different) considerations, not explored here, for anyone wishing to argue for the implementation of a productivity-based system (e.g. the difficulty of finding a practical measure of marginal social product).

[24] For instance, see the interesting debates on whether profits are deserved: N. SCOTT ARNOLD (1985), Capitalists and the ethics of contribution, *Canadian Journal of Philosophy* 15, 89–105; N. SCOTT ARNOLD (1987) Why profits are deserved, *Ethics* 97, 387–402; EDWARD NELL (1987) On deserving profits, *Ethics* 97, pp. 403–410; N. SCOTT ARNOLD (1987) Reply to Professor Nell, *Ethics* 97, pp. 411–413; JOHN CHRISTMAN (1988) Entrepreneurs, profits and deserving market shares, *Social Philosophy and Policy* 6, pp. 1–16.

[25] I am grateful to Chin Liew Ten, Stephen Clark, Christi Favor, Jerry Gaus, and David Miller for their comments on earlier versions of this paper. I would also like to thank the Fulbright Foundation and the Philosophy Departments at Princeton University, City University of New York Graduate Center and the University of Queensland for providing funding and facilities for me to undertake research for this paper.

[8]

NEGATING POSITIVE DESERT CLAIMS

ROBERT E. GOODIN
University of Essex

J.L. AUSTIN'S famous paper on "Ifs and Cans" opens with the immortal question, "Are *cans* constitutionally iffy?"[1] By that, he means to query whether every statement about what someone can do must, analytically, contain implicitly within it certain "if" clauses ("if one wants to," "if one really tries," "if the gods are willing," etc.). If so, then a large part of what we really mean by saying that someone can do something lies in unpacking these suppressed "if" clauses.

Here I want to raise an analogous question about the notion of personal deserts. To embody my thesis in a similarly catchy maxim, I shall be claiming that deserts are constitutionally wouldy. Or, to unpack that phrase, when we say "x *deserves* y" we are really saying "x *would receive* y in the normal course of events." Or, to unpack it further still, "x *would receive* y, in the absence of certain *untoward* interventions z."

The message of this article is that, just as we must excavate the ifs to get at the cans, so too must we focus clearly on the "untoward" intervening factors upsetting the "normal" course of events in order to fix our notion of personal desert. The upshot of my argument will be that that notion is essentially negative in character. The core notion is not that of the "deserved" but rather that of the "undeserved," of those untoward intervening factors upsetting the "normal" course of events.[2] In Austin's phrase, "undeserved" wears the trousers.

To show that this is so, simply recall that "desert" is an inherently moralized notion: To be a notion of "desert" at all, it must imply that,

AUTHOR'S NOTE: This article was written during my tenure as Research Fellow in the Social Justice Project, RSSS, Australian National University. An earlier draft was read to the Philosophy Department there. I am indebted for comments and criticisms of my friends and colleagues, most especially Stanley Benn, Tom Campbell, John Kleinig, Julian Le Grand, John Passmore, Philip Pettit, and John Watkins.

POLITICAL THEORY, Vol. 13 No. 4, November 1985 575-598
© 1985 Sage Publications, Inc.

ceteris paribus, people ought morally to get what they deserve. The negative notion of the "undeserved" is crucially moralized in this way; the positive notion of the "deserved" is not. Either it is a residual notion lacking moral force or it is a derivative one borrowing whatever moral force it possesses from other nondesert considerations. Usually it is the former. Any notion of what is positively deserved is usually merely residual, what is normally left over after certain confounding features have been factored out. No moral force necessarily attaches to that residual: Removing all that is undeserved leaves us not with something that is necessarily deserved, but perhaps merely with something that is neither deserved nor undeserved. When, as occasionally happens, there are properly moral arguments for ascribing positive deserts (e.g., to prizes or commendations), those arguments look outside the notion of desert for their moral force. It is those nondesert considerations, rather than considerations of desert per se, which give us reasons for believing that people ought—rather than just reasonably (and, in that restricted sense, legitimately) expect—to receive what they would ordinarily receive in the normal course of events.

When talking of "positive desert claims," I mean primarily to refer to "positive assertions"—claims that something or another is deserved. My central argument is that positive claims of that sort do not constitute the core of desert claims at all; rather, the core consists of negative claims about what is not deserved.[3] I shall also be talking primarily about "positive desert claims" in the sense in which the outcomes in view are "positive" (i.e., valued from the point of view of the recipient) rather than "negative" (i.e., disvalued). The latter—deserved punishments— have provided the focus for most discussions of the concept of desert. Perhaps there it is more legitimate to make positive assertions about deserved outcomes. But if so, and if my arguments here are correct, that only goes to show that punishment is a special case, importantly different from social welfare policy, for example. It cannot, therefore, be taken to constitute the paradigm case for all applications of the concept of desert.[4]

The overall aim of this article is to deny notions of positive desert any important role in social policymaking. I shall launch three separate attacks. One is essentially conceptual: The negative notion of the undeserved, rather than the positive notion of the deserved, constitutes the moralized core of the notion of desert. Two others are largely practical. One is that we can make only limited claims, if any at all, about positive entitlements to probabilistic outcomes. Another is that there are certain circumstances in which considerations of desert should be put into abeyance. These three arguments are independent of one another, in the sense that the success of any one is nowise contingent upon the success of any other. But they all converge toward the same conclusion: that notions of positive desert ought not play any important role in social policymaking.

Knocking the props out from under the notion of positive desert doubly undercuts opponents of economic redistribution. Without some such notion they can no longer claim that the poor deserve their plight, and hence ought not to be assisted; nor can they claim that the rich deserve their wealth, and hence ought not have it taken from them by the tax collector. Both those propositions play on the positive sense of personal desert that is here called into question.[5] The negative sense that remains—the notion of the undeserved—is of course what is crucial in arguing for the sort of remedial redistributions that characterize welfare state activities.

DESERTS ARE WOULDY

Notice the language we employ in describing someone's deserts. We say that "he has it coming." Or we say that "it is due him." Those are forms of words we characteristically employ in making predictions. When we say the train "is coming" or "is due," we mean to say that it will soon arrive—or at least that it should soon arrive, absent the untoward interventions of terrorists, frozen points, failing signals, and so on.[6]

Moving beyond the form of words to the substance of our ordinary judgments about personal deserts, their wouldy nature remains. We typically say that the fastest runner or the one that has trained the hardest deserves to win the race. What more is that than the prediction that, ceteris paribus, the fastest or best trained will win the race?[7] Certainly, he or she would ordinarily be expected to do so in the normal course of events, unless he or she is tripped or tricked. Likewise, we say that the best-qualified applicant deserves the job. And what more is that than the mere prediction that, ceteris paribus, the best qualified will get the job? Certainly he or she would ordinarily be expected to do so in the normal course of events, unless the selection committee were engaging in nepotism, racial or sexual discrimination, or the like.

The same pattern reemerges with the subclass of institutionalized or rule-based desert statements.[8] We say that an elderly person deserves (is

578   POLITICAL THEORY / November 1985

entitled to) a pension, provided he or she meets all the conditions laid down in the relevant law. What more is that than merely to say that social security administrators would, in the normal course of events, follow the rules and give him or her one? We say a thief deserves (is negatively entitled to) punishment. What more is that than merely to say that courts would, in the normal course of affairs, mete out such punishments as are laid down in the law?[9]

Of course, not all predictions entail desert claims. Not all things that we would predict happening in the normal course of events to person P are things we would necessarily say P deserves to have happen to him or her. We predict that P will die if his or her lungs cease functioning, but we would hardly say that P deserves to die—unless, perhaps, his or her lung failure stems from cigarette smoking.[10] The prediction "P would normally receive q" can entail "P deserves q" only where that prediction is predicated on some facts about P's character or personal history.[11] We may want to go further, saving the term "deserves" to describe cases in which the facts in view concern actions or character traits that P has voluntarily chosen. Or we may want to go further still, saying that P deserves q only if P has voluntarily acted (or voluntarily chosen character traits that lead him or her to act) with the intention of producing q. Whichever way we choose to mark off the subset of desert predictions, it is nonetheless clear that some way is needed: Not every prediction can be an ascription of desert. The converse proposition is what interests me. Are ascriptions of desert anything more than just predictions, albeit of some special sort?

"Undeserved" Wears the Trousers

There is one ready answer to such questions that is consonant with the more standard analysis of deserts as positive claims. That is to say that what normally happens does normally happen because people deserve to have that happen. Then "normal" would become just another way of saying "deserves," and old-fashioned positive-style desert claims would be vindicated.

Certainly, it is true that the "normal" or "expected course of events," as the phrase functions in moral discourse, characteristically evokes something other than just a statistical, frequentist notion of "normality" or "expectation." When some harm has been done, either accidentally or intentionally, we ordinarily assign responsibility to those who have deviated from the "normal" course of conduct, often defined in a highly moralized way.[12] Similarly, when we are trying to decide whether some proposal constitutes a morally obnoxious threat or a morally honorable offer, we look at how it compares with what would happen in the "normal or natural or expected course of events." If A's proposed action would make B better off than B would be in the normal course of events, we would say that A has made B an offer; if worse, a threat. Here again, the "term 'expected' is meant to shift between or straddle predicted and morally required;"[13] and usually the "normal" turns out to be an amalgam of the two. Refraining from physical assaults on another's person or property is both morally required and statistically expected.

Much the same is true of those courses of events that are considered as normal for purposes of assessing personal deserts. There, too, the normal course of events is not just the most frequent or most common course that events would ordinarily take, although it is that in part. In deciding what is normal in such contexts, we need to factor out the influence of certain (possibly quite common) "untoward interventions." (That is why the analysis of deserts must be cast in the subjunctive—in terms of what would happen, had nothing untoward occurred, rather than what will happen.) And notice that the notion of the "untoward" (as a sort of inverse of Nozick's "expected") straddles "unlucky" and "improper." In this sense at least, the notion of normality that enters into judgments of personal deserts is a moralized notion.

But if that is the only sense in which it is a moralized notion, then the moralism embodied in the notion of normality would underwrite moral judgments only of a negative sort. It would allow us to say that some outcomes—those proceeding from "untoward interventions"—were morally improper. It would not allow us to make any positive moral judgments about the moral propriety of the particular outcomes that would otherwise have occurred. To say that untoward interventions are morally improper is not necessarily to say that the ordinary course of events is morally proper. That is just not the part of the notion of normality that carries any moral charge, at least according to everything that has been said so far. The distinctively moral component of the notion of normality comes in factoring out immoral untoward interventions. What is left—what would be normal in an idealized world absent such interventions—is normal just in the straight statistical sense.

A tripartite division is crucially at work here. Alongside the more familiar categories of the deserved and the undeserved is a notion of that which is neither deserved nor undeserved. Cancelling out the effects

580   POLITICAL THEORY / November 1985

of untoward interventions merely moves us from the moralized category of the undeserved to that morally neutral intermediate category. Some further argument is required to move us from there to any properly moralized notion of what is positively deserved. Clearly, everything that is not undeserved it not itself deserved.

On my analysis, then, what people deserve is what they would receive (or would have received) absent the intervention of certain untoward (statistically unusual/morally improper) circumstances. What the notion of desert essentially does, I argue, is to point the finger at illicit interventions that are undeserved and that preclude people from getting what, in the ordinary course of affairs, they would receive.

Even some ostensibly positive judgments and injunctions actually carry such a fundamentally negative message. Notice, for example, that a "good conscience" consists primarily in the absence of guilt feelings. Or, again, notice that much of what a judge is doing when instructing a jury positively to "decide the case on its merits" is to instruct the jurors to ignore certain things (such as the defendant's color, class, sex, and so on) that should not be taken into consideration in their deliberations.

Or, yet again, notice how that which is deserved is often described as that which is "appropriate," "fitting and proper," "suitable." That form of words seems to point to a positive correspondence of some sort between the characteristics of the person and the characteristics of the things he or she is said to deserve. But in social contexts, just as surely as in sartorial ones, what constitutes a good fit is enormously variable, being largely a matter of taste and style. Any number of things might correspond adequately to characteristics of the person or situation to be deemed "fitting" or "appropriate." The primary use of the notion of "appropriateness" is once again negative. When the sign on the door of a restaurant makes "appropriate attire" a condition of entry, it is not really specifying in any positive way what diners should wear. (If the owners wanted jackets and ties, they would have had to say so explicitly.) The basic function is instead to remind customers of what not to wear (standardly, in Australia, singlets and bare feet). The negative—the concept of the "inappropriate"—here again seems to form the core of the concept.[14]

Positive Deserts Are Derivative,
Not Foundational

My wouldy account of desert is basically designed to undermine the notion of positive deserts. I maintain that people are usually said to deserve things merely because that is what they would ordinarily or normally be expected to receive. There may or may not be other moral reasons for their receiving what they ordinarily would. But if there are, these are not reasons of desert per se. This, then, is my second conceptual point: Positive desert claims are parasitic upon some larger scheme, whether natural or social, that gives rise to such expectations about what the "ordinary" or "normal" outcome would be.

We say that winners deserved to win, just so long as no morally groundless intervention interfered with the ordinary scheme of things. If we insist upon running footraces, then truly the lame do not deserve to win; if we insist upon running an apartheid system, then truly blacks do not deserve the same treatment as whites. What we are really interested in, however, is the external rather than just the internal evaluation of such schemes. If the proposition that P deserves q is to have any real moral force, it must imply more than merely that under existing arrangements P would ordinarily get q. It must also imply that the existing arrangements are themselves morally justifiable. Unless some kind of independent argument can be given for the outcomes that the normal course of events would ordinarily throw up, it consitutes no kind of claim at all merely to insist that, "Well, P normally would get q."[15]

Insofar as desert claims are predicated on on the normal operations of the natural (i.e., nonsocial) world, no independent argument can be given. Saying that something would normally come your way naturally amounts to nothing more than making a straightforward statistical prediction. You do not deserve, in a positive sense that is in any way morally charged, that particular outcome.[16]

Insofar as desert claims are predicated on normal operations of the social world, there may (or may not) be moral as well as statistical reasons for things to happen as they normally would. We have reasons—moral reasons, among others—for setting up our social institutions to operate as they do. And as there might be moral rather than merely statistical grounds for expecting that P would normally receive q from some social institution S, that might seem to suggest that there may be some moral grounds for claiming that P positively deserves q. That, in turn, threatens to reduce at least this part of my analysis back to the standard one once again: People might deserve what they deserve by virtue of their merits or demerits. All I have done, on this analysis, is to add an intervening variable: People deserve what they deserve by virtue of expectations about the ordinary course of events, which, in turn, are governed by people's merits and demerits.[17]

That, however, would be a mistaken analysis. Although we certainly do have reasons (maybe even moral reasons) for setting up social institutions as we do, these are not reasons of desert or merit. Indeed, to some extent what counts as merits or demerits may depend on the sort of institution we set up. Physical prowess is a merit when we set people the task of running a race, mental agility when designing a bridge; honesty is a merit when testifying in court, cunning a merit when conducting a military campaign. Insofar as merit is institution-specific, that notion cannot provide any independent basis for choosing between alternative institutions.[18]

In any case, it is evident that the notion of "desert" itself has no place in morally underwriting the scheme of things on whose ordinary operations desert claims are grounded. We may say that the winner of a footrace deserves the medal. But we would never say that anyone deserves to have bits of precious metal allocated according to the outcomes of footraces. We might be able to give all sorts of reasons for running footraces—but desert would never be among them.

My argument, then, is that there can be positive desert claims arising under a set of social rules but not to that set of social rules. Positive desert claims cannot provide the moral foundations for the rules themselves. Those must instead be derivative from some other moral values. So, too, consequently, must any positive desert claims derivative from those rules themselves be ultimately derivative from some other moral values unconnected with personal desert.

When (as occasionally we do) we use the language of deserts in connection with claims to a set of rules, we do so in an extended sense of one sort or another. Usually positive desert claims to rules are just desert claims under metarules that are actually operative in the society. When we say that he or she deserves to have the rules pertaining to treatment of prisoners of war applied to him or her, we are merely saying that there is some metarule (the Geneva Convention) that dictates that he or she receive better treatment. Similarly, we might say that anyone who can climb that rock deserves $50.[19] That, too, is probably just a reference to the fact that we have an implicit metarule in our society: Given that we offer $50 for climbing similar rocks (or for performing feats of similar difficulty), we would ordinarily expect, under that metarule, a similar reward to be offered for this one. Insofar as arguments of consistency or comparability underlie positive desert claims, they all seem to be rule-based in similar ways. Thus, desert claims—even claims to have certain rules applied—can arise under a metarule. But that metarule itself is not grounded in consideration of desert.

There is another way in which an extended sense of desert is used to lodge claims to have different sorts of rules applied. We sometimes say "there ought to be a mechanism for rewarding behavior like this" or "there ought to be a mechanism for compensating harm like this," without invoking any analogy to how we treat other cases or in any other way invoking any implicit or explicit metarule. In such cases, we truly are saying that this should be the rule, not just that it is (in some extended sense) the rule.

What is going on here might be similar to what we are doing when invoking concepts of "natural rights." To say that P has a right to x is to say that P has that right under existing law; to say that P has a natural right to x may just mean that it is what the law should be. "Desert" might be used in both intrasystemic and extrasystemic senses, although there is no clear marker (akin to "natural" in the case of rights) to warn when we shift from one sense to another. What is crucial is that the extended, extrasystemic senses of both these notions can (and in the case of "desert" I argue does) refer to the form that the entitlements should take, rather than the grounds upon which these expansions are justified. On this interpretation, natural rights are not extralegal rights, but merely claims that should be recognized by the legal system in the form of rights. So too with extrasystemic deserts: Calling them "deserts" merely suggests that they should be recognized by the system as deserts, rather than that they actually are deserts even if the system does not recognize them as such.[20]

To summarize: positive desert claims must be justified in terms of the way the existing scheme of things ordinarily works; and the justification for that, in turn, must be sought outside the notion of desert. The effect of that argument is to put positive desert claims firmly in their place. It proves, in yet another way, that desert claims cannot trump all others. The moral force of positive desert claims derives from other sorts of moral arguments, and the selfsame arguments that justify the systems in terms of which desert claims can be lodged might also justify sacrificing claims of desert to some other sorts of claims altogether.

CHANCE UNDERCUTS DESERTS

So far I have been talking in terms of certainties, of outcomes that would without doubt have obtained in the normal course of affairs. But certainty itself is far from normal. Typically, all we can say is that it is more or less likely that some particular outcome would obtain in the absence of untoward interventions.[21]

In previous sections, we were concerned with the case in which P would get q in the normal course of events. I translated that into a desert statement by substituting "deserves" for the phrase "would (certainly) get in the normal course of events." Here we are concerned with the case in which P would probably get q in the normal course of events. But that cannot be translated into a desert statement by substituting "probably deserves" for the phrase "probably would get in the normal course of events." Surely it is wrong to say that someone who has purchased a lottery ticket probably deserves the prize; and more still that someone who has bought 10 tickets is 10 times more likely to deserve the prize than the person who has bought only 1.

When introducing probabilities into the proposition "P deserves q," the probability does not attach to "deserves." It attaches instead to q. The person who has purchased 1 lottery ticket deserves a chance (i.e., some probability) of winning the prize. The person who has bought 10 deserves 10 times as many chances, or a probability 10 times greater. But we would not (at least until after the drawing) want to say that either of them either absolutely or even probably deserves the prize.[22]

The probability of getting q, which P deserves, is to be analyzed in terms of the probability that would obtain (or would have obtained) in the absence of untoward interventions, analyzed here just as before. If P bought 1 of 1000 lottery tickets, he or she deserves a probability of P = 1/1000 of winning the prize. The reason is simply that that is the probability that would obtain absent untoward interventions, such as the organizers removing his or her ticket from the box before the drawing.[23]

The proposition that P deserves the probability p of q might be boiled down still further using the notion of a statistical expectation. That is to say, what P deserves is the product of p times q. If he or she bought 1 out of 1000 tickets for a lottery, the only prize in which is $1000, his or her statistical expection is a payoff of $1.[24] That is what he or she deserves—and that is all he or she deserves. In practice, of course, he or she will inevitably get either a little less or a lot more, either nothing or the whole $1000. And that, in turn, suggests that the outcomes of lotteries (and, indeed, of a broad class of analogous lumpy, probabilistic events) are inherently, to some greater or lesser extent, undeserved: The losers always deserve more (sometimes much more) than they get; the winners never deserve as much (sometimes not nearly as much) as they receive.

That my analysis yields this result is, I think, one of the larger points in its favor. It is in this respect clearly superior to many of the more standard analyses of personal deserts. Some analysts tend to assume that you deserve whatever you get, in the absence of contraindications (what I have called untoward interventions), just so long as there is something in your character or history to ground the desert claim. Other analysts tend to assume that you do not deserve anything, in the absence of strong evidence in your character or history that you deserve it fully.[25]

Both presumptions are untenable. The person who buys a $1 lottery ticket surely has done something to deserve the $1000 prize. But surely the little thing he or she did—buy a $1 ticket—was far too little to ground the claim that he or she deserves the full $1000 prize. Setting the presumption one way leaves him or her deserving too much. Setting it the other way, too little. What he or she really purchased, and what he or she therefore deserves, is no more and no less than a chance of 1 in 1000 of winning $1000. Or, in statistical terms, what he or she bought—and what he or she deserves—is the expected payoff of $1.

Consider, again, someone who takes risks with his or her health—driving without fastening the seat belt, for example. He or she has done something silly, and in some sense deserves to suffer the consequences of such silliness. But being thrown through the windshield is surely far more punishment than he or she could be said to deserve.[26] He or she was, after all, running only a 1 in 10,000 chance of crashing. His or her deserts, calculated as in the lottery example above, would be only $1/10,000$th of the pain he or she suffers going through the windshield.[27]

This has enormous practical implications for social policy. Where people are unlucky and risks turn into disasters, they might deserve to suffer somewhat because they have taken the risks. But they do not deserve to suffer that much. We should therefore take steps to alleviate their suffering. Maybe not all their suffering. After all, they deserve some pain; it would be wrong, therefore, to do so much for them that they are left as well off as they would have been had they not taken any risks at all.[28] But more often than not nature takes care of that for us. People will typically have suffered some losses that we can do nothing to set right, so some of their suffering (whether or not it is exactly the right quantum, morally) will remain whatever we do.

PUTTING DESERTS IN DEEP FREEZE

The bulk of this article has been devoted to asking what it means to say that someone does—or, as I have argued is more nearly the paradigm case, does not—deserve something. But what "desert" means is one thing, and how far its influence should extend over social policy is another. Even if we can say that P clearly deserves q, and even if we are using the notion of positive desert in a truly moralized sense (as my previous arguments suggest we usually are not), that would not necessarily entail that P ought morally to receive q.

One reason may be that desert is only one consideration among many others carrying at least as much of a moral charge, and in any particular case those other considerations may outweigh deserts. But another reason that is more interesting and upon which I shall therefore concentrate here is that in certain sorts of circumstances questions of personal deserts are simply out of place.

Needs Trump Deserts

Imagine an automobile accident. The drivers of both cars are brought into the hospital emergency room with identical injuries and identical prognoses. One of them was clearly to blame for the accident: His negligence caused the crash, and the policemen bringing the injured drivers in make sure that the doctors know that fact. The other driver was merely his innocent victim, and the policemen make sure the doctors know that too.

Now, the innocent victim is clearly less deserving of her fate than the reckless driver is of his. In the normal course of events—that is, absent the untoward intervention of reckless drivers—she would never have suffered these injuries. Does that, however, mean that emergency room medics should devote substantially greater efforts to treating the innocent victim than the guilty driver, even though their injuries and prognoses are identical? I think not.[29] And I would stick by that judgment even where resources are desperately scarce, and we have enough to treat only one: Flipping a coin rather than examining driving records is the right way to make that sort of tragic medical choice.

Part of the reason is no doubt that the guilty, although he may deserve some sort of punishment for his recklessness, does not deserve to suffer nearly as much pain in punishment as the accident has in fact inflicted upon him. Let us suppose he took a 1 in 10 chance of crashing: Then he deserves only one-tenth of the pain he is now experiencing; the rest we would put down to pure bad luck, which is totally undeserved.

But that cannot be the whole story. If it were, we would reckon the medics right to devote ten per cent less time and effort to treating the guilty driver than the innocent; or we would think them right in treating the innocent victim first, even though she is less severly injured, just so long as her injuries are at least 90% as bad as those of the guilty driver. Both standard intuitions and the conventions of medical ethics join in rejecting that sort of conclusion.[30]

The real reason, I suggest, is that there are circumstances in which considerations of desert are simply out of place, and this is one of them. A perfectly general characterization of such circumstances remains elusive. But what is going on in this particular case is clear enough. Needs are trumping deserts. They do so not just in the sense of overriding deserts, but of actually cancelling them.[31]

That certainly happens when life is at stake.[32] But I think it also pretty clearly happens when the stakes are substantially lower. Suppose neither of the drivers in my earlier example had sustained life-threatening injuries. I think we would still balk at saying that doctors should treat the innocent driver first, even though the guilty driver was in 9.99% more pain.[33]

Similarly, I think we can all agree that it would be wrong (except, perhaps, as a deterrent to others) for social security administrators to deny public housing or unemployment benefits to people who have recklessly vacated one apartment or job without first having arranged for another. In some sense, homelessness or unemployment is something that such people might "have coming" in the ordinary course of events and, hence, in my terms, to be "deserved" by them. That is the point that those who oppose welfare payments to the "undeserving poor" want to make. But there are various reasons to resist the policy implications of their analysis.

Some have to do with what the "undeserving" poor really deserve or do not deserve. Although the undeserving poor might not positively deserve assistance, neither do they positively deserve in any sense (moral or otherwise) their plight absent assistance. Usually their only sin is recklessness or fecklessness. The most they can be said to deserve, even in purely statistical terms, is therefore some probability of suffering a bad outcome—the statistical expectation, say, of a rather worse job or house. (They might not deserve even that, if their recklessness or fecklessness were itself covered by some further excusing condition.) Complete homelessness or complete joblessness is far worse than the merely reckless or feckless have done anything to deserve.

Another reason is this: The reckless or feckless may deserve bad outcomes in some statistical sense of that being what the consequences of their recklessness or fecklessness would ordinarily be. But such

588   POLITICAL THEORY / November 1985

statements about positive deserts are without any moral warrant. All such statements tell us is the way the world ordinarily works. Whether it should work that way is an open question. That is in itself quite enough to defeat any suggestion that bad outcomes are positively deserved in any moral sense. At the very least, we must say that those bad outcomes are neither deserved nor undeserved, morally speaking. And insofar as there is a moral case for making the world work some other way—insofar as there is a moral case for the welfare state—we can go further still. Then the (morally) normal course of affairs should and hence would be one in which welfare officers stepped in to assist the reckless and the feckless. Those people thus deserve assistance. Failure to render it to them would constitute a morally important "untoward" intervention in what is morally the normal course of affairs; any suffering that followed from that failure would itself then be seen as undeserved.

Beyond all that, however, is the further question of whether it would be right to let social unfortunates suffer, even if they deserve to suffer and even if the deserts in questions were genuinely moral deserts. The argument here has been to suggest that it is not, at least where their suffering would be great. Needs trump deserts. Those who are in what might properly be described as "desperate" circumstances should be given assistance, whether they deserve it or not.[34]

Confused Causation Yields "No Fault"

There is another class of cases in which we might be inclined to put considerations of deserts, fault, credit, and blame into abeyance. The paradigm cases, perhaps, arise within the realm of the law of accidents. There "no-fault" principles are coming to enjoy increasing prominence, first (in common law jurisdictions, anyway) with the 1897 British Workmen's Compensation Act, then with various schemes of no-fault automobile insurance, and now with the far broader New Zealand Compensation Act of 1972.[35]

No doubt the no-fault impulse is largely motivated by economic considerations quite unconnected with any notions of moral deserts.[36] And insofar as there is a moral component, it may well derive largely from considerations of proportionality: Whatever fault there may have been on whomsoever's part, the harm suffered is usually wildly out of proportion to the fault.[37] But another important source of this no-fault impulse in accident law—and one that serves to define this as a separate class of exceptions to desert/fault principles—is that there is typically just too much fault on the part of too many agents to make any nonarbitrary allocation of liability or blame. That was clearly what prompted the no-fault principle in Workmen's Compensation legislation: The injured worker was ordinarily partially at fault, but so were his coworkers, his supervisors, and his employers. Likewise in automobile accidents, fault is ordinarily shared between drivers, auto manufacturers, state highway departments, and others. So, too, New Zealanders have come to appreciate with most accidents: The background conditions that society at large has created are often inextricably intertwined with personal negligence on the part of both the injurer and the injured. As the Royal Commission giving rise to this legislation observed,

> People have begun to recognize that the accidents regularly befalling large numbers of their fellow citizens are due not so much to human error as to the complicated and uneasy environment which everybody tolerates for apparent advantages. The risks are the risks of social progress, and if there are instinctive feelings at work today in this general area they are not concerned with the greater or lesser faults of individuals, but with the wider responsibility of the whole community. It is for these reasons that compulsory insurance for highway and industrial accidents is generally acceptable.

> Since we all persist in following community activities, which year by year exact a predictable and inevitable price in bodily injury, so should we all share in sustaining those who become the random but statistically necessary victims. The inherent cost of these community purposes should be borne on the basis of equality by the community [as a whole, through general taxation].[38]

The basic principle seems to be this: Notions of personal fault are appropriate only where there is a small set of actors making discrete (separate or easily separable) and readily identifiable causal contributions to the outcome. Where many causal factors are deeply intertwined, any apportionment of fault between them would be arbitrary; and principles of blame, fault, or desert should therefore not apply.[39]

Because the paradigm cases all come from accident law, the discussion here is invariably cast in terms of fault and liability for disagreeable outcomes. But the same sort of principle can surely apply, *mutatis mutandis*, to questions of how to apportion credit for agreeable outcomes.[40] There, too, desert statements only make sense where there are only a few actors who make discrete and readily identifiable causal contributions to the outcome. Where many causal factors are deeply intertwined, any apportionment of credit between them would be arbitrary; and principles of positive entitlement (the converse of fault) should therefore not apply.[41]

This, again, obviously has enormous implications for social policy. Cluttered causal histories characterize almost all outcomes of consequence in complex modern societies. There are very few things indeed that people can, therefore, be said unequivocally to deserve or not to deserve. There are many possible responses to such a finding, perhaps the most common being to introduce a presumption that will do all the work that proper analysis cannot. But the only legitimate response, I would argue, is to put notions of desert (credit, blame, fault, etc.) into abeyance in such situations. When considering whether or not to provide social assistance to some social unfortunate, in circumstances of radically confused causal relations, the appropriate question is not "do they deserve to suffer" or "do they deserve assistance" but merely "is some social interest served by assisting them?" Similarly, when considering whether or not to tax away some of rich people's fortunes, in circumstances of radical confusion about the causal relations that led to their being rich, the appropriate question is not "do they deserve their riches" or "do they deserve to have them taken away" but merely "is some social interest served by reallocating these resources?"

CONCLUSION

The practical question addressed by this article concerns the proper role of considerations of personal desert in social policymaking. Here I have offered three independent reasons for supposing that they should have only a very limited role, if any at all. The first has to do with the concept itself: Usually desert considerations will provide at most a negative moral warrant for remedying the effects of wrongful interventions in the normal course of events; they will only rarely, and even then only derivatively, provide any positive moral warrant for producing one particular outcome rather than another. The second reason has to do with the relationship between probabilities and deserts: Luck largely mitigates deserts. The third has to do with the context in which desert judgments are employed: Where causal relationships are complex or considerations of needs are in play, considerations of deserts are simply out of place.

NOTES

1. J. L. Austin, "Ifs and Cans," *Proceedings of the British Academy* 42 (1956): 109-32.

2. Joel Feinberg, "Noncomparative Justice," *Philosophical Review* 83 (July 1974): 297-338, 297 notes similarly that "it is much more convenient, when doing moral philosophy, to speak of injustice than to keep to the positive term, justice. That greater convenience is an undeniable fact," Feinberg concedes. Like so many others, however, Feinberg simply lets the point drop, saying "I shall not speculate here whether it has any theoretical significance."

3. The distinction between positive and negative desert claims cannot be made merely on the basis of their logical form: A negatively phrased predicate can always be substituted for an extensionally equivalent positively phrased one. In this respect, the distinction is similar to that between "acts" and "omissions." But here as there, contextual factors—and most especially background expectations about the ordinary course of events—will allow us to pick out negative and positive desert claims effectively enough.

4. Cf. Robert L. Simon, "An Indirect Defense of the Merit Principle," *Philosophical Forum* 10 (Winter-Summer 1978-79): 224-41. Even where punishment is concerned, "desert" is still a "wouldy" notion in some important respect. Manser, in a penetrating analysis, argues that "the phrase 'It serves you right'. . . may be taken as a typical way of referring to ill-desert," that is, deserved ill-treatment. This phrase, he observes, "seems to be used in three different contexts, first in the case of punishment inflicted by human agency, second where the 'punishment' follows the breach of some rule by natural law, and third in non-moral cases of disregard of natural laws." In the first case the punishment meted out by a judge to a convicted criminal is said to be deserved—to "serve him right"—in the sense that, given existing social rules and practices, that is the treatment such offenders should expect they ordinarily would receive. For an example of Manser's second case, imagine "a child being told not to slide on the ice, doing so, and falling down and hurting himself as a result. This would 'serve him right'. The third type of case is that where someone 'ought to have known better,' where he suffers either some physical harm or material loss as a result of ignoring a law of nature, e.g., striking a match to see if the petrol tank is full. The resulting conflagration 'serves him right.'" In all these cases, to say that the outcome "serves him right" is essentially to say "he had it coming," and that in the sense that the outcome is what would ordinarily be expected to result from such actions. See A. R. Manser, "It Serves You Right," *Philosophy* 37 (October 1962): 293-306.

5. There are, of course, various other ways of attacking such conclusions. Some might try to turn the argument on its head, asserting that the poor, the unemployed, the handicapped actually do deserve society's assistance. And even those not persuaded by these arguments might well maintain that considerations of desert are not conclusive: To say that x does not deserve welfare benefits is not to say that x deserves the ill he or she is suffering; nor is it even to say that x ought not to be aided, but only that one particular rationale (desert) for aiding x is not available although others (e.g., humanitarian ones) may be.

6. Similarly, when the analysis is cast in the past tense—"he had it coming" or "it was due her"—the basic reference is to what we would *ex ante* have predicted.

7. Desert-based claims can be either strong or weak, either conclusive or inconclusive. To say that x deserves y in the weaker, less conclusive sense is merely to say that he or she

has some desert-based claim to it. But, of course, others might have more or stronger desert-based claims to the same thing, which will therefore override x's. "X deserves y" in the stronger, more conclusive sense if and only if: (1) x has a desert-based claim to y; and (2) x's desert-based claim to y is stronger than anyone else's desert-based claim to y. Unless stated otherwise, I shall here use "deserves" in the weaker, less conclusive way.

8. The distinction between "raw" and "institutionalized" desert claims is effectively evoked by John Kleinig in "The Concept of Desert," *American Philosophical Quarterly* 8 (January 1971): 71-78, 75-76.

9. Suppose there is a rule, but that it is not ordinarily enforced by judges or administrators. Then when they actually do make an exception and enforce the rule, we would surely be inclined to describe the consequent benefit or burden not only as "unfair" or "inequitable" but also as "undeserved," in any but the narrowest legal sense.

10. What, however, of someone who jumps from a 10-story building and lives? We would say, "By rights he should be dead." It is not exactly a desert statement, agreed. But it is surely the first cousin to one.

11. Joel Feinberg, *Doing and Deserving* (Princeton, NJ: Princeton University Press, 1970), p. 58 and John Kleinig, "The Concept of Desert," pp. 73-75 both emphasize this point.

12. Suppose, for example, a speeding police cruiser runs off the road, killing several pedestrians. If the policeman were just rushing home to lunch, we would hold him responsible for the deaths, on the grounds that policemen are normally expected to obey speed restrictions just like everyone else. But if the policemam were chasing some dangerous felon, we may well decide to hold the felon rather than the policeman responsible for the deaths, on the grounds that it is he or she and not the policeman who had deviated from the normal pattern of behavior. In that pair of judgments, it is pretty clear that "normal" is being used to mean something much nearer "morally expected" than "statistically expected." See J. L. Mackie, "Responsibility and Language," *Australasian Journal of Philosophy* 33 (December 1955): 143-59; see similarly H.L.A. Hart and A. M. Honore, *Causation in the Law* (Oxford: Clarendon Press, 1959).

13. Robert Nozick, "Coercion," *Philosophy, Politics & Society,* 4th series, eds. P. Laslett and W. G. Runciman (Oxford: Blackwell, 1972), 101-35, 112.

14. Given my emphasis upon the inappropriate and the undeserved, all the interest shifts to analyzing what interferences with the normal course of affairs count as "untoward," and why. I doubt that any completely general analysis can be given. But one of the more important reasons for regarding certain interventions as "untoward" is that they are functionally unrelated (or, worse, actually dysfunctional) to the purpose, goal, or aim of the project or institution in which they intervene. The point of a footrace is, presumably, to discover the fastest runner; and tripping your opponent counts as an untoward intervention, presumably, because it interferes with that. The purpose of a history test is, presumably, to discover how much you know; and using a crib sheet counts as an untoward intervention, presumably, because it interferes with that. The purpose of a criminal trial is, presumably, to discover the guilt or innocence of the accused; and perjury or prejudice counts as an untoward intervention, presumably, because it interferes with that. Indeed, many of our arguments over "deserts"—over what count as "relevant" factors to be considered and what count as "untoward" interventions—might at root be arguments over the purpose of the institution, practice, or project at hand. Feinberg, *Doing and Deserving*, p. 80, offers the example of a disagreement over who should be Master of a Cambridge college: One candidate's backers might be looking upon the

Mastership as a "prize" to be given to the person best able to carry out the duties of the job; the other's might be looking upon it as a "reward" to be given for long and faithful service. In all five classes of desert Feinberg discusses, the standard of relevance does indeed seem to be a matter of functional fit to the aimes/purposes/goals of the institution/ practice/project; and "untoward" interventions would just be those that are nonfunctional or dysfunctional. Feinberg's list is not exhaustive, however, so whether this is true generally is an open question.

15. Richard Wasserstrom similarly observes, "For any intrasystemic claim of desert, the genuine strength of the claim depends in substantial measure upon the defensibility of the system which makes the intrasystemic claim possible. Thus, rule-based claims of desert are always incompletely defended or justified unless and until the rule which creates the claim is itself shown to be justifiable." Richard Wasserstrom, *Philosophy and Social Issues* (Notre Dame, IN: Notre Dame University Press, 1980), pp. 75-76. See similarly T. D. Campbell, "Humanity Before Justice," *British Journal of Political Science* 4 (January 1974): 1-16, 3.

16. The most that you might enter is a claim couched in terms of your reliance on reasonable expectations about the ordinary course of events: You were counting on that outcome, you incurred costs in so doing, and now that those expectations have been upset you deserve compensation for those costs. (By extension, we might compensate an infant for damages, not on the grounds of its expectations having been upset but, rather, on the grounds that ours have been upset.) But to say that you deserve compensation for reliance on reasonable expectations that y is going to happen is not to say that it is in any way morally desirable that y should happen. Suppose the manufacturers of the swine flu vaccine were compensated for reasonably relying to their detriment on the U. S. government's prediction of an epidemic. That would hardly imply that it would have been desirable, morally or otherwise, for the swine flu to have reached epidemic proportions.

17. Unlike John Rawls, *A Theory of Justice* (Cambridge: Cambridge University Press, 1971), sec. 17, I do not argue that deserts are nonsense because people do not deserve the personal attributes upon which they are predicated. Instead, I argue for that conclusion by saying that they do not "deserve," in any strict sense of the word, the social institutions that reward personal attributes. The notion of desert, I maintain, makes sense as a way of entering claims within an established system of social rules and practices, but it makes no sense (or, anyway, none if taken literally) when used to enter claims to have alternative systems of rules and practices applied.

18. This is reminiscent of J. O. Urmson's point, in his article "On Grading," *Mind* 59 (1950): 145-69, 163, that an apple that displays all the attributes of a good cabbage would be a pretty bad apple. Standards of "goodness" vary according to what we are talking about. This is not to deny that we have any independent moral notions of virtues and vices, merits and demerits. Certainly we do. I merely mean to suggest that, with the possible exception of the criminal law, our social institutions tend not to encapsulate those more basic moral notions of merit and demerit (and even the criminal law operates with a severly truncated set of such notions). Consider, for example, social security law. Whoever would say, outside the narrow confines of the law itself, that old age per se constituted a "merit" (and hence deserved to be rewarded with a pension)? Or, assuming old age is just a surrogate for poverty, whoever would describe poverty as a "merit" (and hence deserving of reward)? Whatever reasons we have for granting pensions have little to do with considerations of merit.

19. Brian Barry, *Political Argument* (London: Routledge & Kegan Paul, 1965), p. 112.

20. I am indebted to Philip Pettit for this point.

21. The familiar expression, "P deserves a break," would seem to belie this ordinary expectation analysis of desert. For a "break" is, by definition, fortuitous—a matter of chance, luck. It therefore looks like something that we are not ordinarily inclined to say with any confidence at all "would happen," however many untoward events are bracketed off. Yet we still say, occasionally, that "breaks" are deserved. This usage can be assimilated to my "wouldy" analysis of desert in either of two ways. One points to the fact that sometimes "people make their own breaks." There are various ways in which you can tempt fate or force fortune. Being in the right place at the right time might be a matter of dumb luck or of careful planning, and so on. Insofar as it is this sort of thing to which we refer when saying "P deserves a break," we are not really talking about "breaks" at all in the ordinary sense. We are instead merely saying that P has planned carefully and well, and that we would ordinarily expect such plans to bear fruit. P deserves a break in the same sense as before; that is P would ordinarily get a break in such circumstances, *ceteris paribus*. Alternatively, we might say "P deserves a break," meaning that term to be understood quite literally, when P has experienced an unprecedented run of bad luck. To say in these circumstances that "P deserves a break" is merely to express faith in the fairness of the processes that collectively travel under the name of Fortune. Someone who has rolled snake eyes five times in succession would not ordinarily roll snake eyes a sixth time. We would say he deserves a break in his luck, and mean by that that we would ordinarily not expect his luck to continue so bad for so long. Implicitly, we are threatening to start checking the dice if he doesn't get one soon. We stick to our notion of what he deserves, even in the face of mounting evidence that that is not what we should expect him to get. The reason, once again, lies with the definition of what is "normal" and of what interferences with the normal course of events count as illegitimate (e.g., loading the dice).

22. Of course, P does deserve q contingently—if the probabilities pan out, if his lottery ticket is drawn. And of course whether that contingency is realized may indeed be a matter of probabilities. So perhaps in some sense we might truly say that P probabilistically deserves q. But that is different from saying that P probably deserves q. The law has been singularly slow in coming to realize that "the chance itself is an interest worthy of redress"; see Joseph H. King, Jr., "Causation, Valuation and Chance in Personal Injury Torts Involving Preexisting Conditions and Future Consequences," *Yale Law Journal* 90 (May 1981): 1353-97, 1381.

23. Some people—John Passmore among them—reply at this point that they are so strongly opposed to talking about deserts in a probabilistic context that they would not even regard removing a person's lottery ticket from the box as violating his or her deserts. But surely this is just an overextension of the perfectly proper principle that he or she does deserve any particular outcome. Surely he or she does at least deserve a chance, once he or she bought and paid for it in the form of lottery ticket.

24. Pointing to the "statistical expectation" as the appropriate measure of deserts in such cases is essentially to invoke once again a notion of what constitutes the ordinary course of events. Calling something the "statistically expected" outcome is saying that that is what would ordinarily happen, in the sense either of it being the thing that is most likely to happen this time or of it being the thing that is most likely to happen in cases like this if they were repeated a great many times. In the ordinary course of events, this is what would happen; and that is what people therefore deserve.

25. Robert Nozick, *Anarchy, State and Utopia* (New York: Basic Books, 1974), pp. 213-27, is an example of the former; Rawls, *Theory of Justice,* pp. 73-75, of the latter. Opponents of the fault system in accident law confront the same problem in reverse: "To treat fault as a necessary condition of legal liability—'no liability without fault'—means that a person who causes loss without fault should not be required to pay for it. But it also and necessarily means that the person to whom the loss is caused will have to bear the burden. We have therefore a different rule for plaintiff and defendant; the plaintiff but not the defendant must bear the burden of loss or injury caused without his fault." Conversely, and equally unjustifiably, "fault is like a magic talisman; once it is established, all shall be given the injured party. It is generally immaterial whether the fault was gross and the consequences trivial, or whether the fault trivial and the consequences catastrophic. . . . Yet we know very well that the consequences of a negligent action are often out of all proportion to the fault that gave rise to it. A piece of momentary thoughtlessness on the road may cost someone's life with incalculable loss to his wife and children. But similar acts of thoughtlessness may be committed by scores of others every day with no such disastrous consequences. . . . Thus it seems that whether an act of negligence ends up in the accident statistics or as a near miss is almost pure chance: it has little correlation with the defendant's culpability." P. S. Atiyah, *Accidents, Compensation and the Law,* 2nd ed. (London: Weidenfeld & Nicholson, 1970), pp. 415, 417. See similarly Francis H. Bohlen, "The Rule in *Rylands v. Fletcher,"* *University of Pennsylvania Law Review* 59 (February & April 1910): 298-326, 423-53; and Guido Calabresi and John T. Hirschoff, "Toward a Test for Strict Liability in Torts," *Yale Law Journal* 81 (May 1972): 1055-85, esp. 1059, 1085.

26. If crashes were truly the "normal" outcomes of such imprudence, then within my model I would have to say that the reckless driver truly would deserve to crash. But that would be true only if the crashes were certain, or at least so common as to be the standard outcome; and in such extraordinary circumstances this conclusion might not be all that counterintuitive after all.

27. If risks are small and frequent, we may be prepared to let the wins and losses lie where they fall each time, trusting that things will all soon balance themselves out. But that rationale works only where risks are small and frequent, as pointed out by John Hicks, "The Rehabilitation of Consumers' Surplus," *Review of Economic Studies* 9 (1941): 108-16. Otherwise, people may have to bear far larger costs than they deserve for far longer than they deserve. Therein lies the fallacy of Hart and Honore's suggestion, in *Causation in the Law*, p. 243, that "the justice of holding me liable, should the harm on that occasion turn out to be extraordinarily grave, must be judged in the light of the hundred other occasions on which, without deserving such luck, I have incurred no liability."

28. For example, the British Workmen's Compensation Act originally compensated workers for only half the costs of their injuries; now it stands at seven-eights. See Atiyah, *Accidents*, chap. 14.

29. The reason has to do with the deeper duty I discuss under the heading of *Protecting the Vulnerable* (Chicago: University of Chicago Press, forthcoming). That duty admits of quasi-utilitarian, quasi-Kantian, and quasi-Rawlsian derivations, as I show in Chapter 5 of that book.

30. Officially, at least, "It makes no difference. . . . whether a disease is 'deserved' or not" in whether or how physicians should treat it. This, Vilhelm Aubert and Sheldon L. Messinger argue, is one crucial difference between "The Criminal and the Sick," *Inquiry* 1 (December 1958): 137-60.

31. If desert-based claims were not cancelled but merely outweighed by needs-based considerations, there would be some marginal cases that were so close in terms of needs that differences in deserts might decide the case. But in the hospital emergency room, surely it is never right to treat the less seriously injured before the more seriously injured, however little the difference in their injuries or however much the difference in their responsibility for the accident.

32. Once again, the notion of deserts in the context of punishment proves to be a special case. There it sometimes is said that people deserve to be put to death for some particularly heinous crime. Even if we dissent from the substance of that judgment, we are nonetheless comfortable talking there in terms of "deserts" even though life-and-death issues are at stake.

33. In practice, it is clear that physicians—especially emergency room medics—do pass "moral judgment" of a kind on their patients. That is partly a matter of blaming them for violating physicians' own norms concerning what sorts of cases should be brought to the emergency room and what sorts should be left to out-patient clinics or private physicians. But that "moral judgment" is at least in part a more general reflection on the moral character of patients and their actions. It distinguishes especially between patients who are suffering injuries that are "self-inflicted" in some sense and those who are not. On this, see David Sudnow, *Passing On* (Englewood Cliffs, NJ: Prentice-Hall, 1967), pp. 100-109; Julius A. Roth, "Some Contingencies of the Moral Evaluation and Control of the Clientele: The Case of the Hospital Emergency Service," *American Journal of Sociology* 77 (March 1972): 839-56; A. Hamid Ghodse, "The Attitudes of Casualty Staff and Ambulance Personnel Towards Patients Who Take Drug Overdoses," *Social Science and Medicine* 12 (March 1978): 341-46; Roger Jeffery, "Normal Rubbish: Deviant Patients in Casualty Departments," *Sociology of Health and Illness* 1 (June 1979): 90-107; and Robert Dingwall and Topsy Murray, "Categorization in Accident Departments: 'Good' Patients, 'Bad' Patients and 'Children,'"*Sociology of Health and Illness* 5 (July 1983): 127-48. Although it is clear from all these studies that physicians' opinions of their patients is affected by judgments of their "moral worth," it is far less clear how and to what extent these moral evaluations affect their treatment of them. Certainly, they lead to some harmful errors in classification: Someone coming into the emergency room comatose, shabbily dressed, and smelling of alcohol will often be thrown into the drunk tank without much careful investigation; and if, as may happen, his or her coma is the result of diabetes rather than drink, the consequences of this morally motivated oversight may be disastrous. Physicians' moral evaluations of patients might also affect the way in which they treat—or fail to treat—chronic conditions (such as diabetes) in which the treatment requires the active cooperation of patients. And certainly it is clear that "bad" patients get less prompt and polite treatment in emergency rooms. What is also abundantly clear from these studies, however, is that "bad patients" suffering from acute and unambiguous life-threatening conditions receive precisely the same medical treatment as "good" ones. There, at least, it seems that emergency room medics behave as this argument suggests morally they should.

34. This may well explain the common view that the welfare state is right to confine its services to those in need of a "safety net": It is right for needs to trump deserts where people's circumstances are truly desperate, but wrong to ignore deserts where they are not. What counts as "desperate" is, in turn, relative to the society in which you find yourself.

35. Such schemes often purport to be essentially insurance schemes, whether voluntary (as automobile insurance still largely is) or compulsory (as workmen's

compensation), and whether underwritten privately (as are both those schemes) or publicly (as is the New Zealand Accident Compensation scheme). But notice that when introducing the no-fault principle, we treat bad risks (faulty parties) and good risks (innocent ones) the same, which of course violates the fundamental actuarial principles that underlie any genuine insurance scheme. This is a characteristic of "social insurance" systems generally; see Richard M. Titmuss, "Models of Redistribution in Social Security and Private Insurance," *Commitment to Welfare* (London: Allen & Unwin, 1968), pp. 173-87.

36. Guido Calabresi, *The Costs of Accidents* (New Haven, CT: Yale University Press, 1970).

37. As some early critics of the fault system wrote, "The findings of the individual psychologists who have studied accident proneness show . . . that there is little correspondence between dangerous conduct and moral fault such as carelessness or recklessness. . . . They point up the emptiness of the arguments, both from morals and expediency, which are currently used to support the fault principle of liability. They represent, in short, a strong further argument for comprehensive social insurance for accidents"; Flemming James, Jr. and John J. Dickinson, "Accident Proneness and Accident Law," *Harvard Law Review* 63 (March 1950); 769-75, 794. Similar arguments against the fault system were offered by the New Zealand Royal Commission leading up to the Comprehensive Accident Compensation scheme: The fault principle "stops short of attempting to see that the damages do not become disproportionate to the conduct which is said to justify them. The extent of liability is not measured by the quality of the defendant's conduct, but by its results. Reprehensible conduct can be followed by feather blows while a moment's inadvertence could call down the heavens." *Compensation for Personal Injury in New Zealand*, Report of the Royal Commission of Inquiry chaired by A. O. Woodhouse (Wellington, N. Z.: government Printer, 1967), para. 49.

38. New Zealand Royal Commission, *Compensation*, paras. 89, 56. Compensating people for accidents but not for diseases is something of an anomaly, as Atiyah, *Accidents*, chap. 20, points out. But once we come to recognize the social sources of disease, perhaps that anomaly too will be rectified. Indeed, the New Zealand Royal Commission explicitly recognize the illogic of compensating accidents but not sickness or disease, saying in justification merely that "it might be thought unwise to attempt to one massive leap when two considered steps can be taken" and that "the proposals now put forward for injury leave the way entirely open for sickness to follow whenever the relevant decision is taken": *Compensation*, para. 17.

39. Or at least they should not apply at this level. Sometimes causation is unclear in the particular but clear enough in the aggregate. We might not be able to say whether any given worker's cancer was caused by exposure to carcinogens in the workplace, but we certainly can say that on aggregate such exposure increases the risks of such cancers by x%. In such cases it would be possible to apply the fault principle at one remove. The basic idea would be to require everyone to contribute to some common fund in proportion to their fault and draw out of it in proportion to their injuries, thus retaining the notion of fault but doing away with any notion of contributory fault for any particular accident. For discussion of such schemes, see Feinberg, *Doing and Deserving*, pp. 215-16; Calabresi, *The Costs of Accidents*, pp. 302, 306; and Jules L. Coleman, "On the Moral Argument for the Fault System," *Journal of Philosophy* 71 (August 15, 1974): 473-90.

40. The symmetry of these cases ordinarily goes unappreciated. That leads some writers on accident law to suggest, as a principle of charity, that we should compensate

598   POLITICAL THEORY / November 1985

people for undeserved losses but allow them to enjoy undeserved benefits. That makes good enough sense, perhaps, when the "undeserved benefit" in view is simply not crashing when you have been driving recklessly (although even there some would dissent—see Feinberg, *Doing and Deserving,* pp. 213-14). But when it is a vast fortune, as it may well be in the positive desert case, that principle of charity is obviously just too charitable.

41. The classic economist's reply would be that under certain conditions (e.g., continuous constant returns to scale) we can apportion responsibility for marginal products among the various factors of production. But there are powerful arguments to the effect that any such partitioning is necessarily highly arbitrary; see G. C. Harcourt, *Some Cambridge Controversies in the Theory of Capital* (Cambridge: Cambridge University Press, 1972). Furthermore, such calculations work by taking everything else as given, and computing only the difference made by factor x. Taking everything else as given is itself an arbitrary act. For one thing, status quo is as arbitrary a baseline as any other; see Douglas Rae, "The Limits of Consensual Decision," *American Political Science Review* 69 (December 1975): 1270-94. For another, there is no nonarbitrary way of specifying exactly what each agent should be able to take with him or her when withdrawing from the production process and hence for deciding how much difference his or her contribution makes to the end product. That is what most arguments over "exploitation" are really about, as shown in John Roemer, "Exploitation, Alternatives and Socialism," *Economic Journal* 92 (March 1982): 87-107. All this lends credence to my claim that there is no nonarbitrary way to apportion causal responsibility for positive outcomes, at least in ordinary economic circumstances.

Robert E. Goodin is Senior Lecturer in Government at the University of Essex (UK). He is Associate Editor of the journal Ethics *and author of* The Politics of Rational Man *(John Wiley, 1976),* Manipulatory Politics *(Yale, 1980),* Political Theory and Public Policy *(Chicago, 1982), and* Protecting the Vulnerable *(Chicago, forthcoming).*

[9]

CANADIAN JOURNAL OF PHILOSOPHY
Volume 16, Number 1, March 1986, pp. 39-61

Misfortune And Injustice:
On Being Disadvantaged

FRANCIS SNARE
Department of Traditional Modern Philosophy
The University of Sydney
Sydney, N.S.W.
Australia 2006

I The Conventional View

We can enjoy and suffer many kinds of human goods and evils. The goods (or benefits) include not only experiences and enjoyments but also the having and exercise of various talents and abilities, the receipt of recognitions and rewards, successes, employments, opportunities. The evils (or harms) include not only pains and frustrations but also defects such as ugliness, disabilities such as paralysis or retardation, lack of standard opportunities such as unemployment, financial loss, failure, disgrace. It is tempting to say that wherever a person has a good he has an advantage and when he suffers an evil he is, in that respect, disadvantaged. However this usage can make it look as if all human goods and evils

Francis Snare

are subject matter for distributive justice. In fact that is not the conventional view.

The conventional view is that some human goods (e.g., naturally acquired physical beauty) are just matters of good luck and likewise, certain evils (e.g., an early natural death) are just matters of misfortune. The conventional assumption is that there is a certain area of life where the goods and evils one bears are not matters of justice and injustice, but of happenstance. This is not to say morality does not apply at all to this area. There may, for example, be duties of charity in regard to those in need due to misfortune. But, conventionally, this is not regarded as a duty of justice. And, if a duty, it is a less stringent duty. The duty to help the unfortunate is not as strong as the duty not to deprive or disadvantage unjustly nor as strong as the duty to compensate those one has unjustly deprived or disadvantaged. Sometimes we speak of the 'disadvantaged' where we really mean the 'unfortunate.'

The assumption that the principles of distributive justice do not apply to some realm of fortune is to be found behind the usual claims made about:

   (i) Society's responsibility

  (ii) Equality of opportunity

 (iii) Distributive justice (in general)

where, of course, these may well overlap.

In making claims about (i), society's responsibility, one typically raises questions as to whether society is to be considered the cause, in the moral sense, of some harm or disadvantage. For example, some have argued that the poorer nutrition of those in the lower classes is *due to* society and social institutions. Perhaps less controversial examples would be the harms inflicted in Nazi concentration camps, or the harms and disadvantages due to the institution of apartheid. Placing responsibility on society is often a preliminary to blaming society, where the point is not simply to reproach a, possibly quite artificial, superagent, but to raise certain policy issues. For example, it might be to lay a case for changing social institutions, or for granting social compensation to those wrongfully harmed by society, or for questioning our continuing obligation to cooperate with such institutions.

Of course society is certainly not to be blamed for all the harms for which it is responsible. Some harms imposed by society are not wrongs

Misfortune and Injustice: On Being Disadvantaged

at all (e.g., justly imposed punishments). But whenever society is responsible for harm, questions of justice may be appropriately raised. This is
in contrast to the harms for which society is not responsible at all.
Sometimes it is specific individuals who are responsible for harms, e.g.,
the harms criminals do to their victims where the legal and social system
is not deficient in discouraging such acts. But also there are some harms
for which no one, not even society, seems to be responsible. These
human evils are said to be just matters of misfortune. Many natural contingencies are considered matters of luck. Even some, what one might
call 'social,' contingencies are often thought to be mere matters of luck.
Some would say that the evils of an economic depression are not
anything for which society, or anyone, is responsible. The way a lot of
individual choices works out is just unfortunate for many.

Now I mention judgments about (i), society's responsibility, so that
such judgments may not be confused with the somewhat different issues
raised by (ii) and (iii). Judgments of sort (i) are rather more likely to get
us into issues of rectificatory and retributive justice than with distributive
justice. However the issues in (ii) and (iii) are more exclusively concerned
with how social structures should be organized to accord with
distributive justice. Thus, the claims in (ii) and (iii) need not suppose that
society or social institutions are 'moral persons' which can be held morally responsible. Of course if an institution is less just than it could easily
be, then perhaps blame can be assigned somewhere for this. But that will
be a further matter, and quite possibly less important than getting down
to improving institutions. Thus, the question raised by (ii) and (iii) is not
'Who, if anyone, is responsible for this injustice?' but 'Is there a
(remediable) injustice here?'

Now admittedly one way a society might harm a person is by making
him unfit, or less fit, to qualify for some social or economic position.
Thus consideration of (i), society's responsibility for harm, can easily
lead to consideration of (ii), questions of equal opportunity. Even so,
they are not quite the same. Questions of wrongful harms to persons can
be distinguished from questions of persons' consequent loss of equal opportunity. In some cases a single harm constitutes two moral wrongs:
wrongfully harming an individual *and* thereby wrongfully denying him
of equal opportunity. In other cases a harm which does not otherwise
constitute a wrong may deny a person equal opportunity and is wrong
for that reason alone.

So let us turn to (ii), equal opportunity. *Usually* those who speak of
equal opportunity want to distinguish a realm of justice from a realm of
fortune. For example, in competitions for positions requiring high in-

Francis Snare

telligence disqualification simply on the basis of race is thought to be a denial of equal opportunity. But it is not thought to be a denial of equal opportunity that intelligence is used as a qualification and that some of the other applicants are more intelligent. And while some intellectual abilities can be acquired by hard work, a fortunate genetic endowment is a crucial factor.

There seem to be two main alternatives to the conventional view of equal opportunity: the 'handicap' view and the 'moral grit' view.[1] The former is the view that equality of opportunity requires that handicaps be applied so that the 'race' will most likely end in a dead heat. The 'moral grit' view is that the outcome of the 'race' should be determined by the moral grit, inner determination, or will power, of the 'contestant.' All other qualities of persons are to be handicapped, for a person can only take credit for his acts of will. Admittedly in practice desired positions may often have to be assigned on the basis of various other considerations such as efficiency. But one will 'deserve' his position or reward only insofar as merited by his moral grit. Natural ability and social background are 'morally fortuitous circumstances' and not a basis for desert. Also the moral grit view must hold that the grit (or determination or will) must not itself be an accident of nature and upbringing. (Some bootstrap notion of freedom of the will seems to be assumed.) Now I mention the 'handicap' and the 'moral grit' views because they both have a conception of equal opportunity which gives no place at all to fortune in the distribution of positions and rewards. I mention these two alternatives precisely because they are extreme views and not the usual view.

Considerations of (iii), basic principles of distributive justice, go beyond considerations of equal opportunity. Some views on distributive justice have hardly any place for equal opportunity. And even where equal opportunity has a place, it is only one principle or concern of distributive justice. Even if we are to agree that there must be fair, or equal, opportunity to economic and social positions, prior questions are 'What sorts of positions shall there be?', 'What shall be the socio-economic structure?', 'What rewards still attach to what positions?', and so on. Thus, distributive justice *in general* seems to be concerned with the overall arrangement of socio-economic position, offices, goods.

---

1 Cf. T.D. Campbell, 'Equality of Opportunity,' *Proceedings of the Aristotelian Society* 75 (1974-5) 51-68. Campbell rejects the 'handicap' view in favour of what appears to be a 'moral grit' view. (The invidious terms are mine, however.)

Misfortune and Injustice: On Being Disadvantaged

But of course there are other human goods besides positions, offices, and rewards. For example there are one's natural talents and abilities. Does justice have anything to do with this? Well, I think the conventional view is that it is just a matter of luck. Even if it were thought a denial of equal opportunity that some of these talents should qualify one for *additional* goods in the form of socio-economic positions and rewards, it is not thought unjust that one have the talent in the first place. One's initial abilities or disabilities are just matters of luck, even if it should be unjust for social structures to compound these initial goods or evils with further social rewards or penalties.

The conventional view, then, is that some sort of boundary is to be drawn between the realm of justice and the realm of fortune. However within the conventional view there is significant disagreement. Those on the political right tend to increase the realm of fortune at the expense of the realm of justice. For example, some on the right treat the market, in many respects, as a natural mechanism. The fact that the market favours some with certain attributes (however acquired) is ultimately a matter of luck, not justice.[2] The moralistic view that the market metes out rewards to the industrious and punishments to the lazy must at a certain point be abandoned in favour of the view that some things are matters of luck. By contrast, those on the left tend to put rather more into the sphere of distributive justice and less into the sphere of misfortune. For example, the malnutrition and consequent disabilities associated with being born into certain economic classes is more likely to be classified by the leftist as a matter of injustice than misfortune. He is more likely to speak of 'deprivation' as if society, or someone, were doing the depriving.

We might caricature the rightist as one who would turn just about every form of social injustice and exploitation either into deserved punishment for lack of industry and enterprise or else into just plain bad luck. What could be otherwise, he sees as the working out of the natural order. On the other hand, we might caricature the leftist as one who, in effect, rails at the universe, someone who tries to pin responsibility on society for every human misfortune. He sees conspiracy in what is in fact tragedy. Of course this is a caricature of the leftist because he needn't get into issues of agent responsibility. He need only argue that more human goods and evils are matters of distributive justice than the rightist allows.

---

2 Cf. F.A. Hayek, *The Constitution of Liberty* (London: Routledge & Kegan Paul 1960), 166; also cf.70.

Francis Snare

Still, we might wonder whether the leftist isn't on a slippery slope here. Will ceding some of fortune's ground to justice lead, as a matter of consistency, to ceding more and more so that in the end nothing can be reckoned a matter of luck? In sections II and III I will illustrate this tendency firstly in regard to (ii), equal opportunity, and secondly in regard to (iii), distributive justice (in general).

II   Equal or Fair Opportunity

Suppose we had already determined that a certain socio-economic structure (involving certain positions and their attendant rewards) accorded with justice. There would remain the question of how to assign particular positions and rewards to specific individuals. If 'foreman' is to be a position, who exactly will get the position and on what basis? Now principles of equal opportunity are supposed to bear on this issue. But we might first consider some of the other principles which are sometimes thought to bear as well on the assigning of positions. For example, (1a), efficiency, will normally be better secured by assigning positions in certain ways. The exact principle of efficiency will, of course, depend on the ends presupposed. It could be maximising social utility, maximising the total social product, or, perhaps, raising the level of the worst off economic position (as in Rawls' Difference Principle). Certainly the qualifications of persons occupying positions will make a difference to the degree to which the given end can be achieved. Separate, but often allied to efficiency, are (1b), incentive considerations. Often we attach rewards (and positions are sometimes rewards as well) to performance in patterns calculated to increase motivation and achievement.
    Principles of desert, (2), seem to be quite different again. Of course much depends on what one means by 'desert.' Sometimes principles of desert really come down something like (2a), the principle that reasonable expectations not be frustrated. Where a set of rules for distributing rewards is justified on other grounds (perhaps in terms of efficiency or incentives) and is, furthermore, generally accepted so that persons make choices they would not otherwise make on the reasonable expectation that the rules will be complied with, it is unjust to change the rules on them afterwards. At least it requires a very good reason. On the other hand a principle of merit, (2b), is quite a different thing again from (2a) the principle of not frustrating reasonable expectations. The winner of a lottery deserves the prize, but does not merit it. Principles of merit

44

Misfortune and Injustice: On Being Disadvantaged

require distribution of rewards and positions on the basis of qualities said to merit these human goods. Qualities such as intelligence, skill, industry, enterprise, virtue, or a morally good will might be thought to merit rewards. Notice that principles of merit are not to be confused with efficiency or incentive considerations. A person might be said to merit a desired position for which he is most qualified. But he might be more usefully employed in some less desirable position which few others can handle adequately. And the second most qualified person for the more desired position might do well enough in that position. Efficiency is a function of the overall pattern of job allocation. It will not necessarily be maximised by giving the job, in each case, to the best applicant.

Now a principle of fair or equal opportunity looks like it should be an additional principle bearing on the distribution of positions and rewards to specific individuals. Such a principle holds (3) that the socio-economic institutions which distribute positions and rewards ought to be organised in such a way as to make opportunity equal (i.e., to avoid unequal opportunity). Of course a principle like (3) may have to be balanced against other moral concerns such as (1a), (1b), (2a), (2b) so that some unequal opportunity may, on balance, be justified.

What exactly a principle like (3) amounts to will depend on what account is given of 'equal opportunity.' A rather minimal account would say that opportunity is equal as long as qualificational barriers to positions include no characteristics other than those which are morally relevant, i.e.:

D1. Opportunity is equal *iff*:

   (a)   The criterion of job allocations involves comparison of, and only of, those characteristics of applicants, which are morally relevant as qualifications.

Thus, if race, religion, or class is employed as a criterion (where of course such things have nothing to do with one's qualifications for the job), then opportunity is unequal. Of course the question of what characteristics of persons are to be the 'morally relevant' ones in the allocation of desired positions has to be supplied by some prior, distinct principle of distributive justice such as (1a), (2a), and/or (2b). The above account, (D1), of equal opportunity makes (3), the principle of equal opportunity, fairly empty. It requires prior principles and even when they are supplied adds only a very little to them.

If we went no further than this we would have the notion of 'careers

45

Francis Snare

open to actual, however acquired, talents.' However many of those who are concerned with equality of opportunity are typically concerned that some persons with natural potentials may not have had the same opportunity to develop their potentials into actual qualifications simply because of the way society is organised (e.g., because of class 'barriers' or because of educational or economic 'disadvantages'). Those with equal potential talent may not have had an equal opportunity to turn them into the actual talents which are qualifications for desired positions. This suggests a widening of the principle of equal opportunity accomplished by widening the account of equal opportunity:

D2. Opportunity is equal *iff*:

    (a)   (as in D1)

  & (b)   No one has a lesser opportunity to develop his natural potentials into actual qualifications (of the sort specified in [a]) because of his initial place in the social system.

This would make equal opportunity not just a matter of careers open to *actual* talent but also a matter of careers open to *natural* potentials to acquire the talents (given the willingness to develop them). As Rawls puts it,

> assuming that there is a distribution of natural assets, those who are at the same level of talent and ability, and have the same willingness to use them, should have the same prospects of success regardless of their initial place in the social system, that is, irrespective of the income class into which they are born.[3]

Notice that this, in effect, is to say that one's fortuitous initial position in society is *not* to be accepted as a mere matter of luck, it is a matter for justice to rectify.

    Thus (D2) really does give us a conception which makes the principle of equal opportunity a significant addition to the other principles we have discussed. But while it may have this advantage, it may also involve a certain disadvantage. It is not easy to stop with just (D2). Any

---

3 John Rawls, *A Theory of Justice* (Cambridge, MA: Harvard University Press 1971), 73

genuinely distinct principle of equal opportunity will encroach more and
more on fortune. As Rawls says,

> For once we are troubled by the influence of either social contingencies or
> natural chance on the determination of distributive shares, we are bound, on
> reflection, to be bothered by the influence of the other. From a moral stand-
> point the two seem equally arbitrary.[4]

If there is no reason to acquiesce in 'social contingencies' there also seems
to be no obvious reason to accept 'natural chance.' If one's initial place in
the social system is a morally arbitrary barrier to opportunity, why is
not also one's initial distribution of natural talents?

    If both social and natural contingencies make for unequal opportuni-
ty, this might seem to lead to the view that the principle of equal opportunity requires that positions and rewards be based on something like
'willingness' or 'effort' or 'character' where natural and social contingencies are to be equalised (perhaps through suitable handicaps). This suggests a 'moral grit' view. However the 'moral grit' view has special difficulties. As Rawls points out, even a person's 'character depends in large
part upon fortunate family and social circumstances for which he can
claim no credit.'[5] Even the acquiring of moral grit is to some extent a matter of arbitrary fortune (whether social or natural). Indeed such an argument applies against any merit principle, (2b), which is taken as ultimate
or underived from other considerations. Either such a principle must
hold that every characteristic one has which merits a reward is, in turn, a
characteristic one merits having or else the principle must hold that at
some point one's having such a characteristic is just a matter of fortune.
So principles of merit either entangle us in an implausible bootstrap
regress or else stop at some point with a characteristic the having of
which is a matter of fortune, not justice. If beauty, or culture, or
character merit a reward, the acquiring of these characteristics is, all the
more, not to be left to social or even natural contingencies.

    However this takes us back to the view that natural contingencies, as
well as social ones, count among the barriers to equal opportunity. As a
base minimum this view should have as a consequence this further
widening:

---

4 Rawls, 74-5

5 Rawls, 104

Francis Snare

> D3. Oppportunity is equal *iff*:
>
>   (a)   (as in D1)
>
> & (b)   (as in D2)
>
> & (c)   Those with inferior natural potentials are provided with remedial training and aids so that they have no lesser opportunity to acquire the actual qualifications (of the sort specified in [a]).

But even this does not seem to be enough. Some disparities in natural abilities are so great that no amount of remedial training will ever allow the worse off to equal the better off in actual acquired abilities. And even where remedial training can be given, this involves a cost to the trainee in terms of time and effort which the 'more advantaged,' as we say, do not have to bear. Indeed they will be able to use that time to develop their other abilities. There seems no way of getting around the basic unfairness of nature. Unless, perhaps, we go all the way:

> D4. Opportunity is equal *iff*:
>
>   i)   Any person born into society has at that time exactly the same prospect (given his peculiar natural potentials and his position in the social structure) of getting any position or reward as any other person in that society, where,
>   ii)   (i) is achieved, whenever possible, by means of systems of allocation which comply with (a), (b), and (c) in (D3) and,
>   iii)   where (i) cannot be achieved in manner (ii), it is then achieved by some other method of allocation (e.g., a lottery, or by 'handicaps').

Thus, when even remedial or differential training and therapy would not make for equal qualifications, perhaps something like a lottery or a handicap is required. But now we seem to have slid all the way down the slope. To many this will look like a reductio ad absurdum of the concern for equal opportunity.

But we should consider the nature of the supposed absurdity here. It seems absurd because, for example, we would have to give a retarded person the same mathematical chance at the position of, say, bridge

Misfortune and Injustice: On Being Disadvantaged

engineer as any intelligent and suitably trained applicant. But of course such a mode of assignment would be absurd precisely because it would be inefficient if not disastrous. Nor does it matter much what kind of efficiency one has in mind. For example, if the goal is to raise the economic level of the worst off socio-economic position, such an inefficient allocation of persons to positions would make the level of the worst off position very much lower than it would otherwise be.

So perhaps it is really some other principle (e.g., efficiency or incentive considerations) which keeps us from going all the way down the slippery slope. This is not to say the principle of equal opportunity is absurd, or of *no* weight. It is only to say that the concern for equal opportunity must be weighed against other concerns, e.g., efficiency. Indeed we might note that the conception in (D4) is hardly unique in that regard. Under any conception efficiency weighs somewhat against equal opportunity (not always sufficiently to outweigh it, however). Thus, in regard to conception (D3) we might note that remedial training for natural disabilities has social and economic costs. While equal opportunity might weigh in favour of such a system of training, considerations of efficiency weigh against it (e.g., the Rawlsian worst off economic level might not be as high as it otherwise could be). Again, even under conception (D2) a society which offers opportunities for acquiring abilities to those in social classes which would otherwise lack this opportunity may find, as a consequence, that it cannot achieve as much as it would in other regards. For example, it may not be able to raise the worst off position higher. Finally, efficiency can even weigh against the quite minimal notion of equal opportunity in (D1). It is empirically possible that a society which didn't bother to test for the relevant actual talents of individuals but used only rough, morally irrelevant correlates such as social class (or even race!) might on balance be better off economically. The economic loss due to the failure to take advantage of the actual talents of those discriminated against, could be less than the cost of testing individuals for their actual talents. (A discriminatory society might actually be able to raise its worst off position higher than a nondiscriminatory one!) Of course this efficiency consideration needs also to be weighed against non-efficiency considerations such as equal opportunity.

Thus, the fact that efficiency, and other considerations can weigh against equal opportunity as defined in (D4) is not significantly different from what happens when that notion is defined in one of the other ways. It is always true that equal opportunity must weigh against whatever other considerations there are (e.g., efficiency). And at some point these

Francis Snare

other moral concerns will outweigh equality of opportunity. That this is
so gives us no reason to suppose that there is some basic distinction between justice and fortune. Both natural and social contingencies will present barriers to opportunity which provide some basis for rectification.
No opportunity barrier is just a matter of bad luck. If we sometimes
allow such barriers to stand unrectified, it is not because we consider
them matters of bad luck outside the sphere of justice. Rather it is
because other considerations, such as efficiency, sufficiently outweigh
the case for rectification.

III Distributive Justice in General

A radical view about equality of opportunity rejects the conventional
view that some barriers are just matters of bad luck. However the practical consequences seem more in accord with conventional thought once
we allow that the principle of equality of opportunity is only one of
several principles bearing on the assignment of positions and rewards. It
needs to be weighed against other concerns. Thus the consequences are
not as extreme as might first appear.

But the consequences of letting justice engulf fortune seem more extreme when we turn to distributive justice in general. So far, in regard to
natural talents we have only been considering whether an unequal
natural distribution of natural talents makes for unequal access to positions and rewards. It is the justice of acquiring these further goods which
was in question, not the justice of having the natural talents in the first
place. But a more fundamental question is whether the intrinsic good of
having a talent or the intrinsic evil of having a disability is a matter of
luck or a matter of distributive justice. Most philosophers tend to reject
the view that every human good and evil (including natural abilities and
disabilities) is subject matter for distributive justice.[6] By contrast the
'radical' view is that anything alterable by individual or social 'choice' is a
matter for distributive justice.

Possibly there are some absolutely unalterable natural (and even
social) facts, e.g., that I shall die sooner or later. However that I shall die

---

6 However see Herbert Spiegelberg, 'A Defense of Human Equality,' *The
Philosophical Review* **53** (1944) 101-24.

Misfortune and Injustice: On Being Disadvantaged

at any particular time is usually not unalterable. It depends on all sorts of alterable human institutions, conventions, and choices (e.g., how food, medical care, health risks, debilitating employments, organs for transplant, etc. are distributed). Furthermore, what cannot in itself be altered may be compensated for in other ways. I might be unalterably crippled, but not, therefore, unalterably immobile. The latter will depend on what resources are at my command, and even if nothing could give me the good of mobility, there might be other human goods which could, to some degree, compensate for this evil. Of course many of the natural characteristics a person has may not be transferable. I cannot take over your natural good looks (although I might get your kidney in a transplant operation). But even where transfer is not possible what is still alterable is the particular social system we have which *protects* in various ways the natural characteristics a person has against the invasion and use by others. Your good looks can be used and exploited by others.

But if natural fortune and misfortune can be altered, or compensated for, or not necessarily protected, does this not make it fall within the sphere of distributive justice? The 'natural lottery' as Rawls calls it is not natural in the sense of unalterable. It is simply not true that we can do nothing but allow nature's distribution of human goods and ills to lie where they fall. Furthermore, if someone were to say we *ought* to let nature's distribution lie and became indignant at attempts to redistribute, he would seem to be proposing a particular principle of distributive justice for that sphere of life. Of course nature's initial distribution is just a brute fact. But the claim that we ought to let that distribution lie (and in indeed protect it!) is a claim in distributive justice. It amounts to a 'social choice' if only by default. Rawls says something like this:

> The natural distribution is neither just nor unjust; nor is it unjust that men are born into society at some particular position. These are simply natural facts. What is just or unjust is the way institutions deal with these facts.[7]

The radical view, as I understand it, involves two claims:

1. It is a confusion (and if not a confusion, morally arbitrary) to delineate off a certain area of life as the sphere of fortune claiming that principles of distributive justice do not apply to that sphere. What such a person is really doing is (paradoxically)

---

7 Rawls, 102

Francis Snare

applying a very special principle of distributive justice within
that sphere, i.e., the principle that we ought to take the
'natural lottery' as our principle of distribution within that
area.

Indeed, there seems to be no reason *at first glance* to accept any such
special principle of distribution within some area of life (as long as
human goods and ills are alterable or compensatable or open to invasion
by others). As a first principle of distributive justice it looks quite arbitrary. Even less does it seem plausible to say 'Justice does not apply to
that area' (as if it involved some sort of conceptual absurdity or category
mistake to try to do so). Least plausible of all is the view that we ought to
accept the outcomes of the natural lottery because it is more 'natural'
than any other mode of distribution. Accepting (and protecting!) the
natural lottery is as much a social mode of distribution as any other.

However the radical view also claims:

2. There are no *other reasons* for accepting fortune's distribution
    as our principle of distribution within any area of life. Even if
    in particular cases fortune's distribution happens to be the just
    one, there is no reason to suppose this is generally so.

I find myself convinced by (1). At least, when one begins to examine
the issue critically and reflectively, it becomes difficult simply to accept,
without further reason, the conventional view that there is an area of fortune to which distributional principles do not apply. On the other hand,
I cannot automatically accept (2). Perhaps some reasons can still be
found for leaving some things to fortune.

IV Whether Society Deprives when it Fails to Compensate for Misfortune

It might seem tempting to express the radical view in terms of social
deprivation: If society fails to intervene and rectify fortune's distribution
(and, indeed, protects and enforces that distribution), that is tantamount
to imposing that distribution. Thus, other things being equal, there will be
no moral difference between a world where nature's distribution of x to A
and of y to B is allowed to stand (and enforced) and a world where
nature's distribution of x to B is redistributed to A and of y to A is
redistributed to B. Again there is no difference, in itself, between a socie-

52

Misfortune and Injustice: On Being Disadvantaged

ty which cripples an individual and a society which fails to cure a naturally crippled person (where this is possible). Failing to rectify misfortune is the moral equivalent of depriving, other things being equal.

Now from a formal standpoint, this view has some appeal. When all other things are equal, how can any moral import rest on the mere order of natural events (unless, perhaps, one quite literally takes natural events to be 'acts of God'). But on the other hand we do at the level of individual choice make moral distinctions which seem to rest on some such arbitrary distinction. There is some case for saying that we do not always regard failing to save as the moral equivalent of harming (other things being equal). It often looks as if we do take something as arbitrary as the natural order of events to be morally relevant. Daniel Dinello gives this example:

> Jones and Smith are in a hospital. Jones cannot live longer than two hours unless he gets a heart transplant. Smith, who had had one kidney removed, is dying of an infection of the other kidney. If he does not get a transplant, he will die in about four hours. When Jones dies, his one good kidney can be transplanted to Smith, or Smith could be killed and his heart transplanted to Jones ... But it seems clear that it would, in fact, be wrong to kill Smith and save Jones, rather than letting Jones die and saving Smith.[8]

And, because, we assume all other things are equal in this example, it would appear that the difference between the two cases rests on the mere fact that in one case one would be killing while in the other case one would be letting die or, more generally, that in the one case one would be acting but in the other case merely omitting. And this, of course, amounts to saying that it is morally preferable to let nature's lottery stand rather than to try to interfere in the causal order.[9]

Of course such examples do not prove this beyond all doubt. Possibly the distinctions we ordinarily make really rest on other considerations. At the very least it should be pointed out that it would be unjust to change the rules at the last moment on Smith who, according to our previously accepted conventions, would be the 'winner.' The real alternative would be to have a totally different set of conventions of which Smith and Jones and everyone else was aware from the beginning and upon which they built their reasonable expectations and choices.

---

8 Daniel Dinello, 'On Killing and Letting Die,'*Analysis* 31 (1971) 85-6

9 Cf. Richard O'Neil, 'Killing, Letting Die, and Justice,' *Analysis* 38 (1978) 124-5.

Francis Snare

There are two ways to resist the view that the distinction between acts and omissions (or perhaps, causing harm and saving from harm) is *in itself* morally relevant. First, one can allow that some such view is behind our moral thinking but that this only shows that our ordinary moral thinking is based on an outrageous and arbitrary legalism which cannot withstand reflection. This requires us to change our thinking about a lot of particular cases, such as Dinello's example.[10] However most philosophers who deny the moral relevance of the act/omission distinction want to deny that, in examples such as Dinello's, other things really are equal. In certain cases acting may not be the moral equivalent of omitting, not because the one is acting and the other omitting, but because of other morally relevant features. Perhaps one should look more closely at these features because they might well explain why, in some cases, it is better to let nature's distribution stand rather than to act to interfere.

Acts frequently, but not invariably, differ from omissions in the following, morally relevant respects:[11]

(a) *Intentionality*: Acts are more often intentional. Many omissions are not intentional

(b) *Belief-states*: Persons are more likely to know the 'upshots' of their acts than of many of their omissions.

(c) *Inevitability*: the 'upshot' is more probable or inevitable in the case of many acts. For example, someone else may yet save the person I fail to save.

---

10 John Harris, 'The Survival Lottery,' *Philosophy* 50 (1975) 81-7 and his 'The Marxist Conception of Violence,' *Philosophy and Public Affairs* 3 (1974) 192-220. For general discussions of killing and letting die, see: Jonathan Glover, *Causing Death and Saving Lives* (Harmondsworth: Penguin 1977) Ch. 7 and Ted Honderich, *Violence for Equality* (Harmondsworth: Penguin 1980) Ch.2.

11 Cf. Jonathan Bennett, 'Whatever the Consequences,' *Analysis* 25 (1965) 83-102. P.J. Fitzgerald, 'Acting and Refraining,' *Analysis* 27 (1967) 133-9. Ted Honderich, *Violence for Equality*, Bruce Russell, 'On the Relative Strictness of Negative and Positive Duties,' *American Philosophical Quarterly* 14 (August 1977) 87-97. Michael Tooley, 'Abortion and Infanticide,' *Philosophy and Public Affairs* 2 (1972-73) 37-65. Richard L. Trammell, 'Saving Life and Taking Life,' *Journal of Philosophy* 72 (1975) 131-7.

Misfortune and Injustice: On Being Disadvantaged

This last example, raises a different consideration:

> (d) *Optionality*: The 'upshot' in many cases of omissions is more likely to involve 'shared responsibility.' For example, it is often not merely my failure to save, but the concerted failures of many others which required for the 'upshot' to occur.

And that raises a further point:

> (e) *Distribution*: Omissions more frequently raise distributional questions. E.g., 'Why must *I* be the person to do the saving if there are others who could do it as well?'

> (f) *Side effects*: Acts sometimes differ in side effects from omissions which are, otherwise, similar in their 'upshot.' For example, harming a person may do more damage to my character than failing to save a person I never see or think about.

> (g) *Effort and Sacrifice*: It often takes more effort to interfere with nature than to leave things as they are.

> (h) *Dischargeability*: If a kind of omission is made wrong, the burden of the duty that it imposes may be quite endless. But the burden of making the corresponding act wrong may be much more manageable. For example, to make *omitting to save from harm* wrong requires me to save everyone who needs saving) an endless duty given all the starving of the world). The wrongness of *causing harm*, by contrast, imposes a more manageable duty on me.

Now considerations such as these may, or may not, explain why we treat some omissions *of individuals* as very different from the acts *of individuals* which are otherwise similar to them. But in this discussion we want to examine whether any of these considerations might provide a reason for allowing certain distributive questions to be decided by the 'natural lottery.' I'm afraid I don't think they do. For one thing, the basic questions of distributive justice are not all that analogous to questions of individual choice. Simply because in the area of individual choice we sometimes think there are reasons to treat interfering differently from allowing to happen, it does not follow that these same reasons will bear on the basic questions of distributive justice.

Francis Snare

Now the analogy would be closer if we imagined that the basic questions of distributive justice were questions about the choice some moral agent called 'society' among different modes of distribution. And indeed this is sometimes a convenient metaphor. But I have tried, in section I, to distinguish the basic questions of distributive justice from the somewhat different questions about attributing blame and responsibility to social institutions. Notice that some of the considerations in the list (a) through (h) are mostly relevant in regard to questions of blame and responsibility. For example, if we are concerned to attribute blame or responsibility to some social institution, then considerations of the (a) intentions or the (b) beliefs of that institution will be terribly relevant. But I think such things are not relevant if we only want to ask what would be a just arrangement for society, or what are the basic principles of justice.

Even if we were to consider society as some sort of agent making choices, I think it would be wrong to suppose a 'social choice' is all that like individual choice. Consider, for example, (d) optionality. Who, or what, are the other agents who might still intervene to alter the 'upshot' of society's omission? If it is other societies, then the scope for such interference will be quite different from the scope for interference after an individual's omission. If it is some individual or group *within* the society who might yet interfere, this is possible because the society is structured in a way which allows this. But insofar as the structure is alterable, that structure is itself the result of a 'social choice.' So if further individuals or groups may yet interfere, it is only because society allows them to. Nothing like this is normally the case in individual choice.

Or consider (e) Distribution. An individual may reasonably ask 'Why should all the burden fall on *me*?' But what would it mean for society to ask that question? Who are the others who should be bearing some of the burden instead? This illustrates how it can be misleading to pose questions of distributive justice in terms of the choice of some super-person called 'society.' It makes it appear as if the basic problem is reduplicated, for now we want to know how burdens and benefits are to be distributed among all individuals *plus* this new person. But of course the point of talking of social choice at all is not to create a new claimant but to decide on the justice of various methods of distributing benefits and burdens on individuals. If we keep this in mind we shall not be tempted to imagine 'society' complaining 'But why should all the burden fall on *me*?'

I shall devote no more space to these considerations. In general, I want to say that, whatever case there is in the area of individual choice for treating certain possible acts as morally worse than the corresponding possible omissions, the case does not obviously carry over to a case for

Misfortune and Injustice: On Being Disadvantaged

distinguishing fortune from justice. Indeed, it is misleading to put the radical's view in terms of society's *failure* to intervene being morally equivalent to society's *imposing* that same distribution. That makes it sound as if it is about the acts and omissions of some superagent (which might be regarded as analogous to the acts and omissions of individuals). The radical view can be better put as the view that it is no less a principle of distribution to recognize, protect and enforce fortune's distribution of natural talents and abilities. (Indeed even a policy which did not enforce but only failed to alter nature's distribution would be a distributive policy.) Furthermore, the radical holds, there are in fact no good moral reasons to support such distributive principles and policies.

V Reasons for Leaving Some Things to Fortune

I'd like to sketch, in a rough fashion, two of the considerations which may weigh in favour of leaving some things to fortune. This is, of course, only a beginning. It will not take us nearly as far as we would want. Still, it may indicate that there is some reason for thinking the radical view is mistaken:

1 The Vices of Social Mechanisms

To leave any distribution to fortune's lottery is arbitrary, it may be said. But this arbitrariness may be preferable, in some cases, to leaving certain questions of distribution to overt mechanisms of social choice. (I say 'overt,' because of course leaving a distribution to fortune is, if only by default, also a mechanism of social choice requiring enforcement and protection.) Let us take, for example, the question of distribution of vital organs. As it is, nature favours some over others in giving them healthier hearts, kidneys and such. By contrast, we might imagine an 'overt' social system of distribution such as that described by John Harris in his article 'The Survival Lottery' (footnote 10). In the survival lottery transplantable human organs are considered social property and are redistributed (i.e. transplanted) so as to maximize the life expectancy of everyone. This will sometimes involve, in cases rather like Dinello's example, killing some in order to have organs to save many others.

Now, possibly, if the survival lottery were administered by God, or some incorruptable and efficient machine, it might not be objectionable.

57

Francis Snare

In fact, it would in many respects then be like fortune, except perhaps more benevolent (and more just) than nature (or rather our enforcement of nature) actually is. However if we imagine that the redistribution is to be decided by and administered by actual human institutions, we may as well have qualms. For one thing, I suspect that it will be the rich and the powerful (and *any* society has its powerful) who will gain. Certainly they will be strongly tempted (when their lives are at stake) to corrupt the system. And while most doctors, judges, bureaucrats, etc. are reasonably honest, there are always some who will be corrupted. My own suspicion is that almost any 'overt' system of distribution of such things will only serve to increase the advantage of the powerful in yet another respect. I, for one, would rather take my chances with (the social enforcement of) the 'natural lottery.'

Of course, much depends on the exact mode of 'overt' social choice being contemplated. Let us consider just a few possibilities.[12] First, there are various political mechanisms of social choice. But inevitably there are always some with a great deal more political influence and power than others. Furthermore, we cannot pretend the principles of justice are either agreed upon or terribly clear, even to the thoughtful. Nor can we rely greatly on disinterested, moral motivations in those who make political decisions. This means the political debates will involve trying to apply somewhat obscure principles to issues where there are strong competing individual interests. In many areas of life the vices of political decision making cannot be avoided (and are preferable to the alternatives). But in many areas the moral arbitrariness the social enforcement of the 'natural lottery' may well be the lesser evil.

Secondly, we might consider judicial or quasi-judicial mechanisms, perhaps buttressed with certain traditions of integrity and fair mindedness. But even here we cannot pretend that the relevant principles of distribution can be made clear enough to make for good law and manageable interpretation. By contrast, leaving things to fortune makes for a relatively clear principle in regard to enforcement and protection. Nor can we overlook the fact that the rich and the powerful will not lack in legal expertise and social influence. They will probably be first in the queue for such things as vital organs. Of course, these are the vices of

---

12 For a discussion of other possible social mechanisms for deciding such issues see G. Calabresi and P. Bobbit, *Tragic Choices* (New York: Norton 1978).

Misfortune and Injustice: On Being Disadvantaged

legal institutions which we are prepared to live with in other areas of life. But with respect to some areas of life the arbitrariness of enforcing fortune may well be preferable to such vices.

Thirdly, we might leave distribution, in part, to the market. This, in fact, occurs in some third world countries where persons sell their organs (e.g., one of their kidneys). Now, while such a system in part employs the natural lottery (for a person has to sell organs he has by birth) it also in part employs an 'overt' method of social choice. The market simply does *not* let fortune's lottery lie. It allows fortune's distribution to be redistributed by the social mechanism of contract. While the overt mechanisms of contract involves a fairly clear and manageable principle, it is also one which is likely to favour the powerful. The powerless are more open to exploitation by the powerful because they often have fewer acceptable alternatives to reaching an agreement. Thus the market system combines the arbitrariness of nature's distribution with a tendency to favour those already favoured in other regards.

This this brief discussion of 'overt' mechanisms of social choice I have been supposing a moderately pessimistic view of human institutions. Thus I part company with those on the left who take wildly optimistic views as to the perfectability of human nature and human institutions. I think a great deal hangs on just this difference.

2 The Burden of All Mankind

It is sometimes objected against proposed principles of morality or justice that they are outrageous because they place the burden of all mankind on the back of the morally conscientious individual. Principles are outrageous if they require sainthood of us. For example, it is sometimes said against utilitarianism that it requires one to consider whether each dollar one has might not be better spent on saving someone in the world from starvation (up to the point where one risks starvation oneself). This kind of objection can, perhaps, be raised with even greater force against principles of equality of well-being and, even principles of need. Even a minimal principle of justice requiring us to improve significantly the lot of those badly off or in distress may require too much of the individual. For example, a Rawls-like maximin principle requiring the maximizing of the worst off 'total situation' might easily have the consequence that all of society's resources, efforts, and technological advances are to be devoted to such things as giving a retarded paraplegic complicated

Francis Snare

devices so he can tie his shoestrings.[13] His bad luck is not his. It is ours. Natural evil strikes us all down so that no one has minimally tolerable existence.

Now I suppose some philosophers will say that this is no objection at all.[14] Perhaps our duties just are harsh. Perhaps justice requires a great sacrifice of us all (and not even a 'sacrifice' because it wasn't ours to start with). However, I, by contrast, do tend to think it is a reasonable objection to any theory of justice or morality that it presents *everyone* with only the prospect of a completely blighted life. Notice that this is not to be confused with the claim that being just has to be justified in terms of advantage or self-interest. I am not claiming, as perhaps Plato did, that the just life has to be more advantageous than any unjust life whatsoever. Nor does the just life have to be all that advantageous. But it does seem to me that the just life must at least offer the reasonable prospect of a life above a certain minimal threshhold if it is going to be reasonable to be just. If the principles of justice do not offer even this prospect for the individual, then (whether or not they can still motivate the individual) they will in any case lack rational foundation. If justice presents no real prospect of a minimally acceptable life, then one does better to seek consolation (false consolation, I fear) in religion or the stoic belief that economic and social goods are unimportant or, perhaps, in a tragic, absurd sense of life. (We can perhaps understand then why such views are not uncommon).

But let us suppose that it is reasonable to object to a proposed principle of justice on the ground that it places unacceptable burdens on the individual. We might then note that many of the principles which might otherwise be subjected to this criticism can avoid the criticism by leaving certain matters to fortune. (Thus Rawls wisely applies his Difference Principles to socio-economic 'positions' rather than to overall 'situations.') Then, if nature strikes some of us down, this is not redistributed in such a way that all are struck down.

Of course the argument from the intolerable burden does not once

---

13 The example is from John C. Harsanyi, 'Can the Maximum Principle Serve as a Basis for Morality? A Critique of John Rawls' Theory,' *The American Political Science Quarterly* 69 (1975) 596.

14 Cf. Peter Singer, 'Famine, Affluence, and Morality,' *Philosophy and Public Affairs* 1 (1971-72) 229-43 and James Rachels, 'Killing and Starving to Death' *Philosophy* 54 (1979) 159-71.

Misfortune and Injustice: On Being Disadvantaged

and for all draw a line between what is a matter of fortune and what is a matter of justice. With economic and social changes, matters formerly relegated to fortune can sometimes be considered matters for social redistribution. It will to some extent depend on whether this makes for an intolerable burden on all individuals. (It will also depend on whether the well-known vices of 'overt' mechanism of social choice are, on balance, preferable to the enforcement of the arbitrariness of fortune.) I might add that in this regard there is no important distinction to be made between 'natural contingencies' and 'social contingencies.' The latter can justifiably be considered as much as matter of fortune as the former — in the right circumstances. At one time the sudden and complete abolition of slavery might have only placed an intolerable burden on everyone. If, in those circumstances, an institution of slavery were as just as it could reasonably be expected to be, it might have to be said that being a slave was just one's bad luck.

Received April, 1984

[10]

CANADIAN JOURNAL OF PHILOSOPHY
Volume 17, Number 2, June 1987, pp. 377-394

Real People (Natural Differences and the Scope of Justice)

ALAN H. GOLDMAN
University of Miami
P.O. Box 248054
Coral Gables, FL 33124
U.S.A.

I The Distinction Between Natural and Socially Caused Differences

The idea that a just political system must ignore or nullify socially caused initial advantages in competing for positions and other social benefits is as old as political philosophy itself. Plato called for social mobility among his classes so that all could gravitate toward the classes for which their temperaments naturally suited them. The idea that the system must take positive steps to correct for these differences among individuals is likewise as old as the concept of public education, the supposed great equalizer. But the claim that society must correct also for natural differences among individuals — differences in intelligence, talents, beauty, and physical prowess — is far more recent, having been articulated most forcefully by Rawls.[1] The reasoning underlying this further step toward a more radical notion of equal opportunity appeals to the fact that natural differences are equally arbitrary from a moral point of view as a basis for differential rewards as are socially caused differences. A person no more deserves to be born smart than rich. Why then should the former but not the latter be allowed to influence future benefits and rewards? A negative answer, however, creates a tension within a liberal theory of justice between the demand to nullify natural differences, or to use them to the

---

1 John Rawls, *A Theory of Justice* (Cambridge: Harvard University Press 1971), Sections 3, 12, 13, 17, 77; see also Thomas Nagel, 'Equal Treatment and Compensatory Discrimination,' *Philosophy & Public Affairs* 2 (1973), 348-63.

378   *Alan H. Goldman*

benefit of those least well endowed, and the demand to respect distinct individuals that supposedly grounds such a theory.

Students often complain that Rawls's contractors are abstract and unreal, hidden behind their thick veil of ignorance. They wonder how fictitious agreements among such impossible beings could obligate real citizens. The answer to this complaint lies in pointing out that Rawls's contract, in contrast to older ones, is not intended to obligate citizens by creating promissory commitments. We are to view the original position as a dramatic device for the sole purpose of expressing our convictions regarding fairness. The fundamental problem in Rawls's system lies rather in the fact that the unreal nature of his contractors extends through their agreement into an unreal conception of persons in society. There it results in a failure to respect the integrity of real persons, in a willingness to treat them as common social assets. This willingness to view the abilities of individuals as the common property of society seems to contradict the opening lines of his book, where he tells us that 'each person possesses an inviolability founded on justice that even the welfare of society as a whole cannot override.' The tension results from the implication that we can hold persons, but not their physical and mental characteristics, inviolable.

Despite both being equally undeserved, there are initial distinctions between natural and socially caused differences that appear to be morally relevant. Natural differences derive from, or rather equate with, the distinctness of physically embodied persons, while social and economic advantages need not affect the basic identities of persons (pace Marx). If we must respect persons for what they are and what they do, and not for their external possessions, then we must recognize a distinction between attacking the two kinds of differences among individuals in the name of equal opportunity. In the view of many philosophers including myself (a view that cannot be defended here), the identities and distinctness of persons in the most basic sense require bodily criteria. (I share the view that connections among psychological states either presuppose bodily identity or remain irrelevant to the basic individuation of persons.) If we cannot conceive of genuinely distinct persons without a ground of physical differentiation, and if a fundamental, if not the fundamental, demand of justice is to respect the distinctness of persons, then attempts to equalize natural differences (that constitute or derive directly from distinct physical embodiment) would appear to be suspect.

That natural differences are undeserved means that they should not in themselves be the basis for differential rewards. We should not, for example, assign jobs or positions in schools on the basis of IQ tests (to the extent that such tests measure native intelligence). But we can maintain a distinction between basing rewards directly on inborn traits and basing them on productivity or achievement for which such traits may have been necessary conditions. It is one thing to refuse to award positions on the basis of native intelligence and quite another to refuse to award them on the basis of competence because intelligence advantages one in the quest for competence. Both rewarding native talents or intelligence in themselves and nullifying them or all their effects may be unfair in reflecting a lack of respect for distinct individuals. At least this appears to be the case if individuals are distinguished both by their distinct physical endowments, and (at the next level) by what they make of themselves through their exercise and development.

Before pressing the distinction just drawn or weighing the opposing intuition further, I want to see whether a plausible set of basic moral requirements on individuals and social institutions can be seen to follow from the fundamental demand to respect the distinctness of real, physically embodied persons. I shall argue that a genuine conception of fairness is not only compatible with this concept of a person and with this moral demand, but emergent from them. Fairness at the fundamental level is a consequence of respect for real persons and for what they make of themselves and by themselves.

II Rights of Real Persons

Respect for real, individual persons begins with respect for bodily integrity. This is why rights of individuals over their own bodies are so central, and why physical assault, forced labor, and sexual crimes are such serious wrongs. The pains or discomforts involved do not fully account for the moral seriousness of these wrongs. Causings of pain of similar intensity without invasions of the right of a person to control his own body would not be as morally grave. Recent arguments, for example, regarding women's rights to have abortions, that liken the relation of a person to her body to one of ownership, understate their case.[2] Only the identification of a person with his body explains the fundamental place of rights to control what happens to it. From the side of society, the importance of such rights explains the primacy within legal systems of criminal laws to protect people from physical harm. It also explains why the provision of a police force to control violent crime claims first priority on the use of public funds. That physical attack has always been considered a paradigm of justly illegal ac-

---

2 See, for example, Judith Thomson, 'A Defense of Abortion,' *Philosophy & Public Affairs* 1 (1971-2), 47-66.

tion is explained not only by the primitiveness of violence as a negative interpersonal exchange, but also by the fundamental place of rights of individuals as distinct physical persons.

Rights entailed by the basic demand to respect distinct persons are not exhausted by rights not to have one's body violated or used against one's will, however. This is because there is a sense in which a person is more than a physical body, though never less than a physical body. A person or self has a history and a future, is an evolving being, in a sense in which a mere physical entity is not. A person constructs herself in a continuing and cumulative way by realizing capacities and tendencies in the physical (including the mental) endowments with which she begins. The fundametal right to be respected as a person thus entails not only rights to bodily integrity, but rights to construct a reasonable set of goals or life plan and to act so as to realize one's self in accordance with these goals. The latter entail both negative rights not to have one's free actions interfered with and positive rights to basic goods and opportunities necessary for a chance at achieving reasonably set goals and life plans. These in turn equate with various demands on the social system. A just system must refrain from unjustly interfering in individuals' lives, must protect them against unwarranted interference by others, and must provide opportunities for personal development, both educational opportunities and a base of material goods that renders life plans in accord with particular individuals' capacities practicable.

Not only Rawls, but libertarians apparently at the opposite end of the political spectrum, take this right of an individual to lead (or really to construct) his own life to be central. Despite this common ground, both theories would violate this basic right in practice. Libertarians would nullify its meaning for the less fortunate by ignoring the minimal material bases and opportunities necessary for realizing it (and by exaggerating the property rights that follow from it for the more fortunate). While they emphasize the negative demands generated by this right on other individuals not to interfere with chosen courses of action, they refuse to recognize positive demands on the social system that make its exercise possible for many individuals. The radical egalitarian, on the other hand, allows the naturally more fortunate to be treated as social assets and so appears to violate the central requirement in relation to them.

It is true that there arises once more here a tension between these positive and negative demands. Individuals must sacrifice some of their freely earned income or acquired wealth in order for society to meet its obligation in this regard. But the problem from a moral point of view is not yet serious, considering how little such contribution normally interferes with reasonably chosen goals and life plans. Surely, in regard only to the right to lead one's own life or construct one's own self through one's freely chosen projects and commitments, there must be reasonable compromises between the view that no money may be demanded of anyone to satisfy this right for others and the view that we may simply use individuals, or their natural endowments, as social assets to maximize goods for others.

Perhaps slightly weaker egalitarians will want to press a distinction between nullifying the effects of natural differences on distributions of other goods, and nullifying the differences themselves (or treating them as social goods to be utilized as society sees fit). Only the latter, it might be maintained, shows disrespect for concrete persons. Some egalitarians would deny that the same disrespect is manifest in the refusal to allow the better endowed to benefit materially from their advantages (or in the demand that they benefit only to the extent that this benefits others as well). Earlier I endorsed a distinction between nullifying natural differences and their effects on the one hand, say by slanting all educational resources to the least intelligent or gifted, and refusing to base rewards directly on such traits on the other. Here the less than fanatic egalitarian notes the conjunction in my first term and distinguishes within it between nullifying natural differences, in the way just mentioned for example (if not by genetic tinkering), and nullifying their distributive effects, say by refusing to allow superior productivity or achievement dependent on native talent or intelligence to be rewarded beyond that necessary to benefit maximally the less talented and intelligent.

The problem with this modified Rawlsian position lies in a further natural extension of the right over one's own person. I have noted a first extension from more specific rights relating to physical integrity to those protecting the capacity to lead one's own life and develop oneself or one's native capacities. This enlargement of rights that derive from the fundamental demand to respect persons followed the recognition that a person is not simply a physical entity, but an evolving, self-constructing, physically embodied ego. A further extension is suggested by the fact that a person fashions her self partly by fashioning her social and material environment through her interpersonal commitments and through her labor or work. Individuals identify themselves both in terms of their relations to other real persons and in terms of their projects, goals, and accomplishments, material and otherwise. All these define roles in terms of which individuals view and define themselves and in terms of which others identify them (beyond identifying them as distinct bodies). John is not simply that person (physical body) over there; he is also the husband of Marsha, the father of Jordan, the youngest member of the philosophy department, who intends to end phenomenology forever, the author of 'Erskine's Paradox,' and so on. A person expresses himself both in his personal relations and in his work. One's works, the products of one's labor, like one's interpersonal ties, are naturally viewed, then, as an extension of one's self.

The latter point was of course central to the classic property theories of both Locke and Marx and is the source of our intuition that one has a right to keep what one makes oneself, that one deserves the fruits of one's labor. The fruits of a person's labor are his own in the deepest sense because a person realizes or objectifies himself through his labor and recognizes himself in the products of his work. This intuition underlies both free market and socialist arguments regarding economic mechanisms of fair distribution, these positions differing in part over which mechanisms provide genuinely fair returns for products and productivity.[3] If the fruits of a person's labor are rightly his own, and if this right, like the ones mentioned earlier, derives from the fundamental right to be respected as a distinct self or person, then nullifying all the effects of natural differences among individuals, in the form of differential rewards or fruits of the exercise of individual capacities, is prohibited on similar grounds to those that disallow an attack on natural differences themselves.

Here, however, the tension that threatens to divide and push us toward the poles of the political spectrum becomes more marked. The concept of fairness in distributions that has emerged so far from the basic requirement to respect real persons seeks to combine two second-level moral demands: one for the provision of a material and psychological environment sufficient for the opportunity to fashion and pursue a set of goals or life plan, in terms of which the self develops; and the second to respect the person's products and accomplishments that further embody the self in its environment. The problematic opposition in the real world between these demands, both of which derive from the more basic requirement of respect for real persons, is obvious. Given limited resources and produced wealth, it is certainly not possible for society to allow individuals to keep all the freely negotiated returns on their work and at the same time to provide a base of goods from which others, whose parents cannot or will not provide this base, can build opportunities for future self-realization.

The precise specification of the proper mixture of these two requirements is a major task for social philosophy. If persons have rights not

---

3 Another major part of the free market argument appeals to the voluntary nature of free market transactions and thus relates more directly back to the rights of persons to lead their own lives.

only to pursue reasonably set goals (reasonable in relation to both social resources and the goals of others), but also to reap the rewards
of their labor, then these full rights, at least the latter one, must be
infringed to some degree in order to universalize them in practice. If
the former is the more basic of the two, as I believe it is, then there
should be little temptation to sacrifice it entirely in relation to those
who lack the resources that make its exercise possible. We may also
question whether the fruits of one's labor can be equated with its free
market return (although a right to keep that return is supported also
by the right to enter freely into trade agreements as part of the right
against interference). Further and more specific reflections on this matter lie beyond the scope of this paper on natural differences, if not beyond the scope of justice proper. But our general sketch so far has
shown that, rather than being inimical to a correct notion of a fairness,
the full specification of the right to be respected as a concrete person,
and the notion of the self or person necessary for a proper interpretation of that fundamental right, entail more specific basic rights and an
intuitive notion of fairness in distributions of such goods as income
and wealth. Neither these rights nor the notion of fairness they
represent permit nullification of natural differences or of all their effects. (Nor do they permit distributions solely on that basis.)

It remains to explain more fully, if there is not only this compatibility, but a dependence relation between our notions of fairness and
respect for real persons, the persistent plausibility of the Rawlsian claim
that the influence of differences in natural endowments on distributions of other goods is unfair. Part of the explanation for the sympathetic appeal of Rawls's position lies in the tension between the two
requirements of fairness mentioned above, and the ease with which
we might emphasize one at the expense of the other. Another part
lies in the indisputable claims that natural and socially caused initial
differences among individuals are equally undeserved. Given that society must correct for socially relative differences if it is to honor rights
to equal opportunity, it may appear that it must correct for the equally
undeserved natural differences as well. I have argued that, despite the
truth of the two premises, the conclusion that society ought to correct
for natural differences does not follow.

The distinction between social and natural differences lies not in a
difference in desert, but in the relation of these properties to distinct
personhood. Natural differences, although undeserved, must be
respected if we are to respect distinct, real persons. Social advantages,
at least those initial social advantages with which those with rich parents are born, need not be central in defining persons to be the persons they are. That natural differences are undeserved means that they
should not in themselves be grounds for rewards; it does not mean

that we must not let them causally affect bases for differential rewards. It is not true that all causal factors that affect desert must themselves be deserved. Only that additional premise validates the Rawlsian conclusion. Given our independent reasons for respecting natural differences, the additional premise appears to lack sufficient motivation or moral force. But we have not yet exhausted the appeal of the opposing intuition. There remain two major counterarguments to consider.

III Unreal Persons at the Source of Social Theory

It might be responded first that we need not base moral demands on all features of real persons. Alternative social theories would ground such requirements in some ideal of persons in society or base them only on what they conceive to be morally significant about persons. These two alternatives might coincide in practice, if those features of real persons thought to be morally significant are all and only those possessed by persons in an ideal society. These features will be identical if what we must respect in real persons is precisely what makes them capable of moral action toward each other. The identification may seem to point precisely to those characteristics of persons emphasized by Kant and by Rawls: namely, the capacity for rationality and free choice, in the sense of the ability to achieve some distance from one's immediate desires and act in relation to demands to respect others. If these demands apply to all rational agents equally and specify all persons equally as objects of respect, then their basis lies in that degree of rationality that all persons share equally. If this characteristic alone, the capacity for free and rational choice, is morally significant in grounding the requirement for respect, then natural differences among individuals, that arise from their distinct physical embodiments, need not stand in the way of enforcing distributive rules that would be chosen by persons on the basis of their (ideally) equal rational capacities alone. Such rules, Rawls has argued, would call for nullifying effects of natural differences to the extent necessary to benefit maximally the least well endowed.

Thus there appear to be alternative groundings of moral demands on individuals and social systems in different conceptions of persons and their morally relevant properties. Since these different conceptions do not count natural differences among individuals as themselves morally significant, they do not protect them as does our derivation of rights from the requirement to respect real persons. A central question, however, is whether the alternative theories honor the distinctness of individual persons at all, whether they are capable of capturing the anti-utilitarian intuitions that both Rawls and libertarians share at the base of their social theories. It might be argued that distinctness among individuals is preserved under the ideal conception in that rational, free choosers will become committed to different projects and plans. Each will therefore have his own distinct life to lead and will recognize this fact when choosing social rules on the basis of the capacity for rational choice alone. Rawls's contractors, for example, seek to create and protect a right to pursue distinct goals and plans when they emerge from behind the veil of ignorance by choosing rules in opposition to that which calls for the maximization of aggregate utility in all circumstances.

But, aside from the question of whether rules that nullify effects of natural differences do respect the distinctness of individual persons (it might be argued that they can respect that degree of distinctness that derives from rational, free choice alone), there is a deeper question whether the appeal to different commitments of individuals is coherent in the context of a theory based on this ideal conception of persons. Different commitments of different individuals themselves derive from a more fundamental distinctness. They arise from distinct desires and emotional attachments, and from the exercise of each individual's full rational capacities, not simply from that minimal capacity for rational choice in which all persons can claim to be equal. The former once more derive from distinct physical embodiments in concrete social situations. If the ideal theory locates distinctness among individuals in different projects and commitments, and if these derive from physical differences among persons (including both differences in emotional and intellectual makeup and simple differences in location and points of view of the world), then respect for the former but not the latter seems artificial and unmotivated at best. We do not respect the capacity for making different commitments if we seek to nullify its foundation. Rational choices resulting in different life plans could not be exercised in the absence of different grounds for choosing, and these different grounds are ignored or nullified by the ideal theory under scrutiny.

Other considerations as well call into question the assumption that morally relevant features of persons, features that we must respect in others, are limited to that minimal capacity for rational choice that lies at the foundation of the moral systems of Kant and Rawls. We must respect other persons not simply for their capacity to distance themselves from immediate desires, but also precisely as desiring beings, who derive pleasure from the satisfaction of their desires and pain from their frustration. We must respect them also as emotional beings, who form emotional ties and commitments that help to define them as the distinct individuals they are. That the latter are the more basic grounds of moral demands is suggested by the fact that we are required to avoid

cruelty to all creatures capable of feeling and desire, while mere rationality (if conceivable), without desires that could be frustrated or
the capacity for painful sensations and emotions, might not give rise
to moral demands at all. It may be that rationally criticized and adjusted desires are more worthy of respect than are mere expressions of
physical instinct, but the latter cannot be ignored (especially since the
former are but modifications of them). The implicit denial of the physical source of our distinct commitments is an unhealthy heritage from
the Platonic tradition in ethics that seeks to oppose reason to physical
instinct, passion or emotion, a tradition inherited by Kant and later
Rawls.

I have been arguing that morally significant intrinsic features of persons are not limited to the capacity for rational choice, but encompass
those desires and feelings that express each individual's distinct physical embodiment. On this ground too, real persons as physically embodied, and not simply Kantian ideals of persons as purely rational
beings, must be objects of respect. As argued in the previous sections,
respect for real, physically embodied persons entails respect for those
differences that define them to be the particular persons they are. If
we shift from persons as objects of respect to individuals in their capacities for moral behavior, we find as an empirical fact that these capacities as well develop from those early emotional ties and
commitments that express our innate affective natures. It is the affective identification with the feelings and interests of certain other concrete, real persons to whom we naturally form ties that renders us
capable of later self-sacrificing moral behavior. Without such natural
identification with the interests of particular other persons, the broader requirements of more impersonal moral demands could never come
to be acknowledged or assimilated. It is therefore false that the capacity for rational choice alone renders us capable of being moral agents.
Moral agency must be developed, and its development requires as a
matter of fact early emotional ties to particular other individuals expressive and definitive of the entire personality, rather than of reason
alone.

A third party to this debate may wonder at this point where exactly
it is being joined, since both the emotional *and* the rational capacities
of humans depend on their physical makeup. My point is not to contrast the two capacities, but rather to contrast the conception of morality
that attempts to ground it in a disembodied ideal of rational agency
with one that bases moral demands on actual features of concrete persons, features that naturally differentiate individuals. We have seen
that the human capacity for choice, emphasized by the ideal theory,
is itself exercised in the choice of ends and more mature commitments
to other real persons that grow out of and express both our emotional

makeups and full, distinct rational capacities. Both persons as objects of respect and persons as moral agents therefore embody features that express our distinct physical natures, rather than some disembodied capacity for rational action. Features that we share with lower animals, as well as those emphasized by Kant that we share with angels, make us worthy of moral treatment and capable of treating others morally. Moral demands are based upon these features of real persons, not simply on the Kantian ideal of persons, as this first response to our earlier argument would have it. We cannot then avoid the demand to respect natural differences among individuals by denying the relevance of such properities at the source of moral capacities, both capacities to be moral agents and to receive moral or immoral treatment.

Thus the demand to respect in persons what is morally significant about them as objects or recipients of treatment and as agents once more leads to the conclusion that we must respect natural differences among individuals. The notion of disembodied rationality, or, less contentiously, the idea of a capacity for rationally criticizing desires and for choosing how to act in light of them, while crucial for the concept of moral agency, is not sufficient as an ideal of persons on which to base a conception of the good or the right. If we are to base such conceptions on some ideal of moral agency or personhood, we might do better to take as our model a feeling, committed person who has developed his useful natural capacities to their fullest. This ideal, rather than overriding our earlier objections to an attack on natural differences, reinforces them. While special talents may turn out to be social assets, in that they may be used for the benefit of others, treating them merely as such denies each individual's mastery over her own person that must be part of an ideal of a genuine moral agent.

We must once more admit tensions in the concept of morality and its development suggested here, oppositions that threaten to generate genuine antinomies. On the one hand, moral development, as represented above, requires emotional commitment, affective identification with the feelings and interests of particular other persons that involves elevating their concerns above those of strangers, much as one naturally elevates and acts on one's own desires and concerns. On the other hand, sophisticated moral demands may require one to place the interests of all those affected by one's actions, strangers included, on the same scale. This requires at once an artificial elevation of the interests of those with whom one is not naturally concerned and a distancing of oneself from the immediate concerns and desires both of oneself and sometimes of one's loved ones. Only reason, not natural affective identification, recognizes the interests of all to generate similar demands and constraints on one's actions. (This may be one source of the Platonic emphasis of reason in ethics.) Hume's sentiment of

388   *Alan H. Goldman*

universal sympathy, if it exists, is, as he admitted, naturally very weak. It must be developed through emotional ties to particular other individuals first, and sustained and supplemented by the rational recognition of equal moral agency in all persons. But these demands on the personality pull in opposite directions, even if the former is a precondition of the latter. There can arise conflicts between commitments to other particular individuals and the demand to treat all persons equally.

The resolution of this tension lies once more in a compromise within the recognized scope of justice and moral demands on individuals. Just as the demand for equal respect for distinct, autonomous persons required limiting the quest for equal opportunity to an attack on socially relative initial differences and their effects, rather than on natural differences among individuals, so here a compromise must be struck between the emotional commitments and emotional distancing simultaneously required of moral agents. The two balancings are closely related and arise from the same requirement of respect for real persons. Regarding the second, an individual must be permitted leeway to pursue not only his own plans and concerns, but to favor the interests of family, friends, countrymen, and so on, all of which commitments express his real nature. Yet he must also be constrained to some extent by certain interests and demands of those with whom he is not naturally concerned. The compromise cannot be struck in terms of the amount of good that could be produced by alternative activities.[4] There are always people to be saved in distant parts of the world, such that saving them would far exceed on balance what we could do for ourselves or our families and friends. But the demand to do so constantly would again treat our capacities and their fruits as worldwide social assets to be used for maximum aggregate benefit. It would swallow our personalities and freely developed commitments in exactly the same way as a more direct attack on natural differences or nullification of their differential effects.

I have defended elsewhere a more complex, if equally familiar, way of limiting the scope of moral demands on individuals. We first distinguish between rights and mere utilities, the former expressing more central interests of others and generating more direct constraints on individuals' actions. Then we distinguish negative from positive rights, the former again generating more stringent constraints, being easier to satisfy. Individuals have mostly indirect obligations to satisfy positive rights of strangers and distant peoples to goods. These take the

---

4 Contrast Samuel Scheffler, *The Rejection of Consequentialism* (Oxford: Clarendon Press 1982).

form of obligations to contribute fair shares to just social institutions. I am not concerned to specify or defend this social framework here. Its significance in this context is as one example of a way to limit the scope of just demands so as to leave individuals room in which to develop themselves and pursue their own natural concerns. Such realistic demands derive again from an appreciation of the psychological capacities and developmental requirements of real persons, not from the abstraction of a purely rational element, false as a complete ideal of moral agency.

IV Determinism and Other Problems

It was argued above that respect for distinct persons does not allow nullification of intrinsic differences among them or of effects of such differences in the form of accomplishments and products of work. At the same time, however, we are not to distribute goods solely on the basis of native characteristics themselves. While it would be unfair, for example, to ignore the naturally more intelligent in the school system until all less intelligent students caught up in achievement, it would be equally unfair to distribute positions on the basis of natural intelligence alone. Distribution on the basis of native endowments fails to respect real persons by ignoring a basic property of persons noted above—that they evolve, that individual selves are constantly in the process of being constructed through actions that build upon capacities acquired at earlier times. In recognition of this fact we must, if we are to be fair to persons, base distributions on what they make of themselves and what they make for others, rather than upon the raw materials, the native endowments most often surpassed in these activities.

Our concept of a self or person then supports this distinction between basing distributions on natural endowments and allowing such characteristics to affect distributions indirectly by affecting, as they often do, what distinct persons are able to accomplish. This concept also supports, I argued, a moral difference between natural and socially caused initial advantages, the former but not the latter being intrinsic to distinct individuals. In this final section I shall consider some further problems with these two distinctions.

A second major argument against my position derives from the fact that the difference between basing rewards on natural traits themselves and simply allowing them to influence relative achievements appears

---

5 The final part of this discussion benefitted from critical comments by Virginia Warren.

to dissolve to the extent to which we adopt a strictly deterministic view of human activity. This view, of course, contradicts the model of rational agency considered in the previous section, but it can generate a very different kind of objection. If we hold actions and accomplishments to be strictly determined by native characteristics, then there may seem to be no morally significant difference between distributing rewards or benefits on the basis of such characteristics themselves and distributing these goods on the basis of the products that flow from these characteristics. Adding environmental factors to the causal determinants does not alter the moral situation, since a person is no more responsible for such factors than for his natural endowments.

Thus a determinist premise seems to destroy a key distinction that I have been trying to maintain. It is partly because individuals seem to surpass their native tendencies in their labor and creative work that they appear to deserve the fruits of such activity. I am not certain, however, that acceptance of the premise removes the ground from the middle position at which I aim. A compatibilist might reply first that, even if all actions have sufficient causes, and even if all causal chains extend to native and environmental influences beyond agents' control, it remains the case that, between the acquisition of inborn tendencies at conception and their later realization in achievement, fall the socially productive efforts of the agents. It can be argued that such efforts merit reward even if causally determined, even if the agents could not have done other than to expend it, given the causal antecedents. The denial of such desert again seems to rest on the questionable additional premise that all causal antecedents of grounds for desert must themselves be deserved.

We need not rest the case here on a basic notion of desert. I would offer a different reply to the determinist's challenge to the distinction between rewarding inborn traits and allowing them to influence distributions by refusing to nullify them and by rewarding individual achievement. My case for respecting accomplishment or productivity was not based on the claim that an agent merits reward because of efforts that he freely chooses to put forth. Instead I argued that the products or effects of a person's activities or labor are naturally viewed as an extension of her self, so that respect for the person and the consequent right to develop her self entails the right to the fruits of her labor. The determinist thesis is irrelevant to this justification of inequalities, if there is a basic moral demand to respect persons whether or not they are ultimately responsible for what they are and what they make of themselves. If we must respect even native differences among individuals simply because this is part of what it means to respect distinct individuals, then the demand is indeed independent of the question of free will.

There remains a deeper problem. The determinist's thesis may strike at our fundamental moral premise itself, the demand that distinct real persons be respected as such. Perhaps a being not truly responsible for its self-creation does not command the same respect as that which should be accorded persons as described above. A determinist view might therefore suggest a more collectivist and hedonist moral framework, viewing persons as centers of causal forces and receptacles of pleasure and pain. Certainly Kant himself, the primary source of the alternative moral framework, thought that the thesis of free will was essential to, indeed the foundation of, his position. If free will is a fiction, if inborn traits and social contingencies not only influence, but causally determine achievement on which differential distribution is based, then perhaps a moral theory whose fundamental axiom is the inviolability of distinct persons (a premise shared by Rawls and his libertarian critics) becomes suspect. While the idea of free, rational agency may not be a sufficient ground for an individualist moral framework, it may well be necessary. How then can it be consistent to fault Rawls for a fictional view of personhood and yet admit that one's own view may rest upon a fiction? The only answer I can think of is to admit the centrality of the idea of freedom to the moral point of view, but deny that it exhausts morally relevant features of persons. The Rawlsian-Kantian conception of persons is not only a fiction, but an abstraction that ignores some of those features.

The second and perhaps more major distinction, between natural and socially relative differences themselves, will surely come under attack as well. The objections will fall into more and less interesting sets, the latter pointing out the difficulty of testing for the difference between these differences in practice, the former pointing to deeper causal interactions. There is first the notorious difficulty of separating out environmental influences in testing, for example, for native intelligence. Second, a Marxist would challenge my earlier claim that a person is not to be identified by the social class into which he is born, especially given my later admission that persons are identified partly in terms of their social roles. It must be granted that a person's identity, constituted partly by his commitments and accomplishments, may be shaped ultimately by social as well as natural influences. Finally, many disadvantages and advantages with which persons begin life represent causal mixtures of biological and socio-environmental factors. Some infants, for example, might be born physically or mentally underdeveloped because their mothers were poorly nourished, took harmful drugs, or were alcoholic during pregnancy. These harmful factors may in turn have social explanations, making the seemingly natural disadvantages socially relative. Advantages counted as natural may also appear to be socially relative on deeper reflection. What counts

as a talent, after all, depends on social demand at a time for the use
of a particular ability or characteristic. Being seven feet tall, for example, may advantage one enormously in pursuing a high income in a
society that loves to watch basketball, but disadvantage one in a society where horse racing is the only sport that people will pay to watch.

Given these difficulties in practice and theory of separating natural
and socially caused differences, can there be an intelligible position
on equal respect and equal opportunity between that of Rawls and that
of Nozick? An initial reply is to point out that vagueness at the boundaries does destroy the theoretical soundness or usefulness of a distinction. The question here is whether the distinction between natural and
socially caused differences blurs only at the boundary. It does seem
that there are at least some clear cases on either side. We can sometimes distinguish the naturally bright but poorly trained student from
the well trained one of mediocre intelligence. It is true, especially in
the case of those from deprived backgrounds, that we cannot always
discern precise causes of seeming or real differences in intelligence or
aptitude. If we are to aim at a justifiable equality of opportunity, we
therefore must make efforts across the board to devote more resources
to the developments of those from such social environments. These
efforts, if conceivably successful in removing handicaps, should also
lessen the temptation to identify persons according to their initial social classes (as opposed to later social roles).

The difficulty of maintaining the distinction in light of the relativity
of natural talents to social demand may seem more profound. Given
that relativity, it can be argued that, in refusing to correct for natural
differences, we fail to correct for socially relative differences as well.
But the distinction survives. First, since individuals normally must develop their natural abilities in relation to varied economic opportunities, we can seek to equalize the social inputs and barriers to such
development. Second, while social demand for specific talents may
vary, those natural traits that advantage individuals in their quests for
benefits are not as socially relative as the varied demand might seem
to indicate. The social value of seven foot height may vary greatly from
culture to culture; but intelligence, wit, and physical advantages such
as strength and agility are adaptable to a wide variety of social roles
and tasks. Even narrower, more specialized talents, such as musical,
artistic, or athletic inclinations, have value in many societies because
of their adaptability to specific demands.

To some egalitarians the almost universal value of certain inborn
characteristics may make distributions affected by them seem more
rather than less unfair. To others natural advantages will now seem
to reduce to those that are simply less socially variable in their usefulness. Why, if we must respect these differences, should we not also

respect initial differences in wealth, since money too is almost universally valuable? We answer both final objections in the same way, by simply reiterating the original basis for the distinction. A person's intelligence and physical traits express his unique physical embodiment that partially defines him to be the person he is. In altering these traits we directly alter the person himself. In a just social system, the money of a person's parents need not be so definitive.

These replies go some way toward answering the remaining objection to the moral relevance of our initial distinction, the claim that an individual's identity is shaped as much by social forces as by inborn capacities. If we must respect the identities of real persons, if such respect constrains our egalitarian impulses, then how can we allow correction for socially relative variances that result in deep personal differences? Does the distiction between natural and socially relative differences retain its relevance in light of this point? It does, I believe, given certain provisos. First, we concentrate on initial differences and the advantages and disadvantages these bestow. Here socially relative differences relate to the social class into which one is born, and the demand is to limit the effect of such differences on later opportunities to develop. There is a distinction between preventing initial social differences from leading to greater or lesser opportunities for development and refusing to allow expression or differential reward for personal traits that have been shaped by social forces. Second, in a just society individuals will still encounter different avenues for development and commitment depending on their places in the social structure and on the roles of those who influence them. We require only that these avenues not be broader and more rewarding for children of the upper classes and narrow and restrictive for those initially less fortunate. Surely this requirement remains relatively clear despite the complicating factors admitted above.[6]

Received September, 1985

---

6 This paper grew out of a 1983 APA symposium in which the lead paper was by Dan Brock. I thank him for that stimulating paper and discussion.

Part III
Political Liberalism and Justice

NEW YORK UNIVERSITY
LAW REVIEW

| VOLUME 64 | MAY 1989 | NUMBER 2 |

THE DOMAIN OF THE POLITICAL AND OVERLAPPING CONSENSUS

JOHN RAWLS*

In a society marked by a pluralism of comprehensive moral views, the ability of a constitutional regime to maintain widespread allegiance is due to "overlapping consensus." Those with divergent comprehensive views may nonetheless agree on a given political conception of justice. However, the idea of an overlapping consensus, as used in Professor Rawls's earlier works, has caused some misgivings. It seems to suggest that political philosophy is "political" in the wrong way. Professor Rawls answers these misgivings. A political conception of justice, such as Rawls's "justice as fairness" in A Theory of Justice, is not merely tailored by the dominant group to justify favored results. Nor does it presuppose any particular comprehensive doctrine, whether religious or philosophical. Rather, as supported by an overlapping consensus, justice as fairness falls into a special domain of the political. It gives the framework of a stable constitutional regime by resting on the consensus of citizens who share an understanding of the role of certain basic rights and liberties, even though they may not agree on comprehensive doctrines.

INTRODUCTION

In this Article, I shall examine the idea of an overlapping consensus[1] and its role in a political conception of justice for a constitutional regime. A political conception, I shall suppose, views the political as a special domain with distinctive features that call for the articulation within the conception of the characteristic values that apply to that domain. Justice as fairness, the conception presented in my book *A Theory of Justice*

---

* James B. Conant University Professor, Harvard University. A.B., 1943, Ph.D., 1950, Princeton University. An earlier version of this Article was the John Dewey Lecture in Jurisprudence, given at New York University School of Law, November 15, 1988.

[1] An overlapping consensus exists in a society when the political conception of justice that regulates its basic institutions is endorsed by each of the main religious, philosophical, and moral doctrines likely to endure in that society from one generation to the next. I have used this idea mainly in Rawls, Justice as Fairness: Political not Metaphysical, 14 Phil. & Pub. Aff. 223 (1985) [hereinafter Justice as Fairness] and Rawls, The Idea of an Overlapping Consensus, 7 Oxford J. Legal Stud. 1 (1987) [hereinafter Overlapping Consensus]. The idea is introduced in J. Rawls, A Theory of Justice 387-88 (1971) [hereinafter Theory].

[*Theory*][2] is an example of a political conception and I refer to it to fix ideas. By going over these matters I hope to allay misgivings about the idea of an overlapping consensus, especially the misgiving that it makes political philosophy political in the wrong way.[3] That is, this idea may suggest to some the view that consensus politics is to be taken as regulative and that the content of first principles of justice should be adjusted to the claims of the dominant political and social interests.

This misgiving may have resulted from my having used the idea of an overlapping consensus without distinguishing between two stages in the exposition of justice as fairness and without stressing that the idea of an overlapping consensus is used only in the second. To explain: in the first stage justice as fairness should be presented as a free-standing political conception that articulates the very great values applicable to the special domain of the political, as marked out by the basic structure of society. The second stage consists of an account of the stability of justice as fairness, that is, its capacity to generate its own support,[4] in view of the content of its principles and ideals as formulated in the first stage. In this second stage the idea of an overlapping consensus is introduced to explain how, given the plurality of conflicting comprehensive religious, philosophical, and moral doctrines always found in a democratic society—the kind of society that justice as fairness itself enjoins—free institutions may gain the allegiance needed to endure over time.

I

FOUR GENERAL FACTS

I begin with some background. Any political conception of justice presupposes a view of the political and social world, and recognizes certain general facts of political sociology and human psychology. Four general facts are especially important.

The first fact is that the diversity of comprehensive religious, philosophical, and moral doctrines found in modern democratic societies is not a mere historical condition that may soon pass away; it is a perma-

---

[2] Theory, supra note 1.

[3] For an awareness of these misgivings I am indebted to the comments of G.A. Cohen and Paul Seabright (soon after the lecture "Overlapping Consensus" was given at Oxford in May 1986), see Overlapping Consensus, supra note 1, and to discussions with Jürgen Habermas (at Harvard the following October). For a better understanding of and suggestions for how to deal with the misgivings, I am greatly indebted to Ronald Dworkin, Thomas Nagel, and T.M. Scanlon. I also have gained much from Wilfried Hinsch, to whom I owe the important idea of a reasonable comprehensive doctrine, which I have simply elaborated a bit. This idea, when joined with suitable companion ideas such as the burdens of reason, see Part II infra, and the precepts of reasonable discussion, see Part III infra, imposes an appropriate limit on the comprehensive doctrines we may reasonably expect to be included in an overlapping consensus.

[4] See Part VIII infra.

nent feature of the public culture of democracy. Under the political and social conditions that the basic rights and liberties of free institutions secure, a diversity of conflicting and irreconcilable comprehensive doctrines will emerge, if such diversity does not already exist. Moreover, it will persist and may increase. The fact about free institutions is the fact of pluralism.

A second and related general fact is that only the oppressive use of state power can maintain a continuing common affirmation of one comprehensive religious, philosophical, or moral doctrine. If we think of political society as a community when it is united in affirming one and the same comprehensive doctrine, then the oppressive use of state power is necessary to maintain a political community. In the society of the Middle Ages, more or less united in affirming the Catholic faith, the Inquisition was not an accident; preservation of a shared religious belief demanded the suppression of heresy. The same holds, I believe, for any comprehensive philosophical and moral doctrine, even for secular ones. A society united on a form of utilitarianism, or on the liberalism of Kant or Mill, would likewise require the sanctions of state power to remain so.

A third general fact is that an enduring and secure democratic regime, one not divided into contending doctrinal confessions and hostile social classes, must be willingly and freely supported by at least a substantial majority of its politically active citizens. Together with the first general fact, this means that for a conception of justice to serve as the public basis of justification for a constitutional regime, it must be one that widely different and even irreconcilable comprehensive doctrines can endorse. Otherwise the regime will not be enduring and secure. As we shall see later, this suggests the need for what I have referred to as a political conception of justice.[5]

A fourth fact is that the political culture of a reasonably stable democratic society normally contains, at least implicitly, certain fundamental intuitive ideas from which it is possible to work up a political conception of justice suitable for a constitutional regime. This fact is important when we come to specify the general features of a political conception of justice and to elaborate justice as fairness as such a view.

II

THE BURDENS OF REASON

These facts, especially the first two—namely, the fact that a diversity of comprehensive doctrines is a permanent feature of a society with free institutions, and that this diversity can be overcome only by the op-

---

[5] See Part VII infra.

pressive use of state power—call for explanation. For why should free institutions with their basic rights and liberties lead to diversity, and why should state power be required to suppress it? Why does our sincere and conscientious attempt to reason with one another fail to lead us to agreement? It seems to lead to agreement in science, or if disagreement in social theory and economics often seems intractable, at least—in the long run—in natural science.

There are, of course, several possible explanations. We might suppose that most people hold views that advance their own more narrow interests; and since their interests are different, so are their views. Or perhaps people are often irrational and not very bright, and this mixed with logical errors leads to conflicting opinions.

But such explanations are too easy, and not the kind we want. We want to know how reasonable disagreement is possible, for we always work at first within ideal theory. Thus we ask: how might reasonable disagreement come about?

One explanation is this. We say that reasonable disagreement is disagreement between reasonable persons, that is, between persons who have realized their two moral powers[6] to a degree sufficient to be free and equal citizens in a democratic regime, and who have an enduring desire to be fully cooperating members of society over a complete life. We assume such persons share a common human reason, similar powers of thought and judgment, a capacity to draw inferences and to weigh evidence and to balance competing considerations, and the like.

Now the idea of reasonable disagreement involves an account of the sources, or causes, of disagreement between reasonable persons. These sources I shall refer to as the "burdens of reason." The account of these burdens must be such that it is fully compatible with, and so does not impugn, the reasonableness of those who disagree among themselves.

What, then, goes wrong? If we say it is the presence of prejudice and bias, of self- and group-interest, of blindness and willfulness—not to mention irrationality and stupidity (often main causes of the decline and fall of nations)—we impugn the reasonableness of at least some of those who disagree. We must discover another explanation.

An explanation of the right kind is that the burdens of reason, the sources of reasonable disagreement among reasonable persons, are the many hazards involved in the correct (and conscientious) exercise of our powers of reason and judgment in the ordinary course of political life. Except for the last two sources below, the ones I mention now are not peculiar to reasoning about values; nor is the list I give complete. It

---

6 These powers are those of a capacity for a sense of justice and a capacity for a conception of the good. Theory, supra note 1, at 505; Justice as Fairness, supra note 1, at 232-34.

covers only the more obvious sources of reasonable disagreement:

(a) The evidence—empirical and scientific—bearing on the case may be conflicting and complex, and hence hard to assess and evaluate.

(b) Even where we agree fully about the kinds of considerations that are relevant, we may disagree about their weight, and so arrive at different judgments.

(c) To some extent all of our concepts, not only our moral and political concepts, are vague and subject to hard cases; this indeterminacy means that we must rely on judgment and interpretation (and on judgments about interpretations) within some range (not itself sharply specifiable) wherein reasonable persons may differ.

(d) To some unknown extent, our total experience, our whole course of life up to now, shapes the way we assess evidence and weigh moral and political values, and our total experiences surely differ. Thus, in a modern society with its numerous offices and positions, its various divisions of labor, its many social groups and often their ethnic variety, the total experiences of citizens are disparate enough for their judgments to diverge, at least to some degree, on many if not most cases of any significant complexity.

(e) Often there are different kinds of normative considerations of different force on both sides of a question and it is difficult to make an overall assessment.[7]

(f) Finally, since any system of social institutions can admit only a limited range of values, some selection must be made from the full range of moral and political values that might be realized. This is because any system of institutions has, as it were, but a limited social space. In being forced to select among cherished values, we face great difficulties in setting priorities, and other hard decisions that may seem to have no clear answer.[8]

---

[7] This source of disagreement I have expressed in a somewhat flat way. It could be put more strongly by saying, as Thomas Nagel does, that there are basic conflicts of value in which there seem to be decisive and sufficient (normative) reasons for two or more incompatible courses of action; and yet some decision must be made. See T. Nagel, Mortal Questions 128-41 (1979). Moreover, these normative reasons are not evenly balanced, and so it matters greatly what decision is made. The lack of even balance holds because in such cases the values are incomparable. They are each specified by one of the several irreducibly different perspectives within which values arise, in particular, the perspectives that specify obligations, rights, utility, perfectionist ends, and personal commitments. Put another way, these values have different bases which their different formal features reflect. These basic conflicts reveal what Nagel thinks of as the fragmentation of value. See id. I find much in Nagel's discussion very plausible, and I might endorse it were I stating my own (partially) comprehensive moral doctrine; since I am not doing that, but rather trying so far as possible to avoid controversial philosophical theses and to give an account of the difficulties of reason that rest on the plain facts open to all, I refrain from any statement stronger than (e).

[8] This point has often been stressed by Sir Isaiah Berlin, most recently in his article, On the Pursuit of the Ideal, N.Y. Rev. Books, Mar. 17, 1988, at 11.

These are some sources of the difficulties in arriving at agreement in judgment, sources that are compatible with the full reasonableness of those judging. In noting these sources—these burdens of reason—we do not, of course, deny that prejudice and bias, self- and group-interest, blindness and willfulness, play an all-too-familiar part in political life. But these sources of unreasonable disagreement stand in marked contrast to sources of disagreement compatible with everyone's being fully reasonable.

I conclude by stating a fifth general fact: we make many of our most important judgments subject to conditions which render it extremely unlikely that conscientious and fully reasonable persons, even after free discussion, can exercise their powers of reason so that all arrive at the same conclusion.

III

PRECEPTS OF REASONABLE DISCUSSION

Next I consider how, if we are reasonable, we should conduct ourselves in view of the plain facts about the burdens of reason. I suppose that, as reasonable persons, we are fully aware of these burdens, and try to take them into account. On this basis we recognize certain precepts to govern deliberation and discussion. A few of these follow.

First, the political discussion aims to reach reasonable agreement, and hence so far as possible it should be conducted to serve that aim. We should not readily accuse one another of self- or group-interest, prejudice or bias, and of such deeply entrenched errors as ideological blindness and delusion. Such accusations arouse resentment and hostility, and block the way to reasonable agreement. The disposition to make such accusations without compelling grounds is plainly unreasonable, and often a declaration of intellectual war.

Second, when we are reasonable we are prepared to find substantive and even intractable disagreements on basic questions. The first general fact means that the basic institutions and public culture of a democratic society specify a social world within which opposing general beliefs and conflicting comprehensive doctrines are likely to flourish and may increase in number. It is unreasonable, then, not to recognize the likelihood—indeed the practical certainty—of irreconcilable reasonable disagreements on matters of the first significance. Even when it seems that agreement should in principle be possible, it may be unattainable in the present case, at least in the foreseeable future.[9]

Third, when we are reasonable, we are ready to enter discussion

---

[9] For instance, consider the questions of the causes of unemployment and the more effective ways to reduce it.

crediting others with a certain good faith. We expect deep differences of opinion, and accept this diversity as the normal state of the public culture of a democratic society. To hate that fact is to hate human nature, for it is to hate the many not unreasonable expressions of human nature that develop under free institutions.[10]

I have suggested that the burdens of reason sufficiently explain the first two general facts—the facts of pluralism, given free institutions, and the necessity of the oppressive use of state power to maintain a political community (a political society united on a comprehensive doctrine)— whatever further causes those facts might have. Those facts are not, then, mere historical contingencies. Rather, they are rooted in the difficulties of exercising our reason under the normal conditions of human life.

IV

FEATURES OF A POLITICAL CONCEPTION OF JUSTICE

Recall that the third general fact was that an enduring and stable democratic regime is one that at least a substantial majority of its politically active citizens freely support. Given this fact, what are the more general features of a political doctrine underlying a regime able to gain such allegiance? Plainly, it must be a doctrine that a diversity of comprehensive religious, philosophical, and moral doctrines can endorse, each from its own point of view.[11] This follows not only from the third general fact but also from the first, the fact of pluralism: for a democratic regime will eventually, if not from the outset, lead to a pluralism of comprehensive doctrines.

Let us say that a political conception of justice (in contrast to a political regime) is stable if it meets the following condition: those who grow up in a society well-ordered by it—a society whose institutions are publicly recognized to be just, as specified by that conception itself— develop a sufficient allegiance to those institutions, that is, a sufficiently strong sense of justice guided by appropriate principles and ideals, so that they normally act as justice requires, provided they are assured that others will act likewise.[12]

Now what more general features of a political conception of justice does this definition of stability suggest? The idea of a political conception

---

[10] I have adapted this idea from Pliny the Younger's remark, "He who hates vice, hates mankind," quoted in J. Shklar, Ordinary Vices 192 (1984).

[11] Here I assume that any substantial majority will include citizens who hold conflicting comprehensive doctrines.

[12] Note that this is a definition of stability for a political conception of justice. It is not to be mistaken for a definition of stability, or of what I call the security, of a political regime (as a system of institutions).

of justice includes three such features:[13]

First, while a political conception of justice is, of course, a moral conception, it is worked out for a specific subject, namely, the basic structure of a constitutional democratic regime. This structure consists in society's main political, social, and economic institutions, and how they fit together into one unified system of social cooperation.

Second, accepting a political conception of justice does not presuppose accepting any particular comprehensive doctrine. The conception presents itself as a reasonable conception for the basic structure alone.[14]

Third, a political conception of justice is formulated so far as possible solely in terms of certain fundamental intuitive ideas viewed as implicit in the public political culture of a democratic society. Two examples are the idea of society as a fair system of social cooperation over time from one generation to the next, and the idea of citizens as free and equal persons fully capable of engaging in social cooperation over a complete life. (That there are such ideas is the fourth general fact.) Such ideas of society and citizen are normative and political ideas; they belong to a normative political conception, and not to metaphysics or psychology.[15]

Thus the distinction between political conceptions of justice and other moral conceptions is a matter of scope, that is, of the range of subjects to which a conception applies, and of the wider content which a wider range requires. A conception is said to be general when it applies to a wide range of subjects (in the limit to all subjects); it is comprehensive when it includes conceptions of what is of value in human life, ideals of personal virtue and character, and the like, that inform much of our nonpolitical conduct (in the limit, our life as a whole).

Religious and philosophical conceptions tend to be general and fully comprehensive; indeed, their being so is sometimes regarded as a philosophical ideal to be attained. A doctrine is fully comprehensive when it covers all recognized values and virtues within one rather precisely articulated scheme of thought; whereas a doctrine is partially comprehensive when it comprises certain, but not all, nonpolitical values and virtues and is rather loosely articulated. By definition, then, for a conception to be even partially comprehensive it must extend beyond the political and include nonpolitical values and virtues.

---

[13] The features of a political conception of justice are discussed in more detail in Justice as Fairness, supra note 1, at 224-34.

[14] A political conception for the basic structure must also generalize to, or else fit in with, a political conception for an international society of constitutionally democratic states; but here I put this important matter aside. See note 46 infra.

[15] See Justice as Fairness, supra note 1, at 239-40 & n.22 (discussing a "political conception of the person").

Keeping these points in mind, political liberalism tries to articulate a workable political conception of justice. The conception consists in a view of politics and of the kind of political institutions which would be most just and appropriate when we take into account the five general facts. From these facts rises the need to found social unity on a political conception that can gain the support of a diversity of comprehensive doctrines. Political liberalism is not, then, a view of the whole of life: it is not a (fully or partially) comprehensive doctrine.

Of course, as a liberalism, it has the kind of content we historically associate with liberalism. It affirms certain basic political and civil rights and liberties, assigns them a certain priority, and so on. Justice as fairness begins with the fundamental intuitive idea of a well-ordered society as a fair system of cooperation between citizens regarded as free and equal. This idea together with the five general facts shows the need for a political conception of justice, and such a conception in turn leads to the idea of "constitutional essentials," as we may refer to them.

A specification of the basic rights and liberties of citizens—rights and liberties they are to have in their status as free and equal—falls under those essentials. For such rights and liberties concern the fundamental principles that determine the structure of the political process—the powers of the legislative, executive and the judiciary, the limits and scope of majority rule, as well as the basic political and civil rights and liberties legislative majorities must respect, such as the right to vote and to participate in politics, freedom of thought and liberty of conscience, and also the protections of the rule of law.

These matters are a long story; I merely mention them here. The point is that a political understanding of the constitutional essentials is of utmost urgency in securing a workable basis of fair political and social cooperation between citizens viewed as free and equal. If a political conception of justice provides a reasonable framework of principles and values for resolving questions concerning these essentials—and this must be its minimum objective—then a diversity of comprehensive doctrines may endorse it. In this case a political conception of justice is already of great significance, even though it may have little specific to say about innumerable economic and social issues that legislative bodies must regularly consider.

V

THE SPECIAL DOMAIN OF THE POLITICAL

The three features of a political conception[16] make clear that justice

---

[16] See Part IV supra.

as fairness is not applied moral philosophy. That is, its content—its principles, standards, and values—is not presented as an application of an already elaborated moral doctrine, comprehensive in scope and general in range. Rather, it is a formulation of a family of highly significant (moral) values that properly apply to basic political institutions; it gives a specification of those values which takes account of certain special features of the political relationship, as distinct from other relationships.

The political relationship has at least two significant features:

First, it is a relationship of persons within the basic structure of society, a structure of basic institutions we enter only by birth and exit only by death (or so we may appropriately assume[17]). Political society is closed, as it were; and we do not, and indeed cannot, enter or leave it voluntarily.

Second, the political power exercised within the political relationship is always coercive power backed by the state's machinery for enforcing its laws. In a constitutional regime political power is also the power of equal citizens as a collective body. It is regularly imposed on citizens as individuals, some of whom may not accept the reasons widely thought to justify the general structure of political authority (the constitution), some of whom accept that structure, but do not regard as well grounded many of the statutes and other laws to which they are subject.

Political liberalism holds, then, that there is a special domain of the political identified by at least these features. So understood, the political is distinct from the associational, which is voluntary in ways that the political is not; it is also distinct from the personal and the familial, which are affectional domains, again in ways the political is not.[18]

Taking the political as a special domain, let us say that a political conception formulating its basic values is a "free-standing" view. It is a view for the basic structure that formulates its values independent of non-political values and of any specific relationship to them. Thus a political conception does not deny that there are other values that apply to the associational, the personal, and the familial; nor does it say that the political is entirely separate from those values. But our aim is to specify the special domain of the political in such a way that its main institutions can gain the support of an overlapping consensus.

As a form of political liberalism, then, justice as fairness holds that,

---

[17] The appropriateness of this assumption rests in part on a point I shall only mention here, namely, that the right of emigration does not make the acceptance of political authority voluntary in the way that freedom of thought and liberty of conscience make the acceptance of ecclesiastical authority voluntary. This brings out a further feature of the domain of the political, one that distinguishes it from the associational.

[18] The associational, the personal, and the familial are only three examples of the non-political; there are others.

with regard to the constitutional essentials, and given the existence of a reasonably well-ordered constitutional regime, the family of very great political values expressed by its principles and ideals normally will have sufficient weight to override all other values that may come into conflict with them. Justice as fairness also holds, again with respect to constitutional essentials, that so far as possible, questions about those essentials should be settled by appeal to those political values alone. For it is on those questions that agreement among citizens who affirm opposing comprehensive doctrines is most urgent.

Now, in holding these convictions we clearly imply some relation between political and non-political values. Thus, if it is said that outside the church there is no salvation,[19] and that hence a constitutional regime, with its guarantees of freedom of religion, cannot be accepted unless it is unavoidable, we must make some reply. From the point of view of political liberalism, the appropriate reply is to say that the conclusion is unreasonable:[20] it proposes to use the public's political power—a power in which citizens have an equal share—to enforce a view affecting constitutional essentials about which citizens as reasonable persons, given the burdens of reason, are bound to differ uncompromisingly in judgment.

It is important to stress that this reply does not say that a doctrine *Extra ecclesiam nulla salus* is not true. Rather, it says that it is unreasonable to use the public's political power to enforce it. A reply from within an alternative comprehensive view—the kind of reply we should like to avoid in political discussion—would say that the doctrine in question is incorrect and rests on a misapprehension of the divine nature. If we do reject the enforcement by the state of a doctrine as unreasonable we may of course also regard that doctrine itself as untrue. And there may be no way entirely to avoid implying its lack of truth, even when considering constitutional essentials.[21]

Note, however, that in saying it is unreasonable to enforce a doctrine, we do not necessarily reject it as incorrect, though we may do so. Indeed, it is vital to the idea of political liberalism that we may with perfect consistency hold that it would be unreasonable to use political power to enforce our own comprehensive religious, philosophical or moral views—views which we must, of course, affirm as true or reasonable (or at least as not unreasonable).

---

[19] The common medieval maxim *Extra ecclesiam nulla salus* ("Outside the church there is no salvation") was used, for example, in the famous bull "Unam sanctam" of Nov. 18, 1302, by Pope Boniface VIII, reprinted in Enchiridion symbolorum definitionum et declarationum de rebus fidei et morum 870 at 279 (33d ed. H. Denzinger & A. Schönmetzer eds. 1965).

[20] For clarity on this point I owe thanks to Wilfried Hinsch and Peter de Marneffe.

[21] See Rawls, Overlapping Consensus, supra note 1, at 14.

VI

How is Political Liberalism Possible?

The question now arises, how, as I have characterized it, is political liberalism possible? That is, how can the values of the special domain of the political—the values of a sub-domain of the realm of all values— normally outweigh any values that may conflict with them? Or put another way: how can we affirm our comprehensive doctrines as true or reasonable and yet hold that it would not be reasonable to use the state's power to gain the allegiance of others to them?[22]

The answer to this question has two complementary parts. The first part says that values of the political are very great values indeed and hence not easily overridden. These values govern the basic framework of social life, "the very groundwork of our existence,"[23] and specify the fundamental terms of political and social cooperation. In justice as fairness some of these great values are expressed by the principles of justice for the basic structure: the values of equal political and civil liberty, of fair equality of opportunity, of economic reciprocity, the social bases of mutual respect among citizens, and so on.

Other great values fall under the idea of free public reason, and are expressed in the guidelines for public inquiry and in the steps taken to secure that such inquiry is free and public, as well as informed and reasonable. These values include not only the appropriate use of the fundamental concepts of judgment, inference, and evidence, but also the virtues of reasonableness and fair-mindedness as shown in the adherence to the criteria and procedures of common sense knowledge, and to the methods and conclusion of science when not controversial, as well as respect for the precepts governing reasonable political discussion.[24]

Together these values give expression to the liberal political ideal that since political power is the coercive power of free and equal citizens as a corporate body, this power should be exercised, when constitutional essentials are at stake, only in ways that all citizens can reasonably be expected to endorse publicly in the light of their own common, human reason.[25]

---

[22] Recall here the formulation of political liberalism a few lines back, namely, given the existence of a well-ordered constitutional democratic regime, the family of great values expressed by its principles and ideals, and realized in its basic institutions, normally has sufficient weight to override whatever other values may come into conflict with them. See Part IV supra.

[23] J.S. Mill, Utilitarianism, ch.5, ¶ 25 (3rd ed. 1867), reprinted in John Stuart Mill: A Selection of His Works 216 (J. Robson ed. 1982).

[24] See Part III supra.

[25] On this point see the instructive discussion by Jeremy Waldron, Theoretical Foundations of Liberalism, 37 Phil. Q. 127 (1987).

So far as possible, political liberalism tries to present a free-standing account of these values as those of a special domain—the political. It is left to citizens individually, as part of their liberty of conscience, to settle how they think the great values of the political domain relate to other values within their comprehensive doctrine. We hope that by doing this we can, in working political practice, firmly ground the constitutional essentials in those political values alone, and that these values will provide a satisfactory shared basis of public justification.

The second part of the answer as to how political liberalism is possible complements the first. This part says that the history of religion and philosophy shows that there are many reasonable ways in which the wider realm of values can be understood so as to be either congruent with, or supportive of, or else not in conflict with, the values appropriate to the special domain of the political as specified by a political conception of justice for a democratic regime. History tells of a plurality of not unreasonable comprehensive doctrines. That these comprehensive doctrines are divergent makes an overlapping consensus necessary. That they are not unreasonable makes it possible. A model case of an overlapping consensus of the kind I have considered elsewhere shows how this is so.[26] Many other such cases could make the same point.

VII

THE QUESTION OF STABILITY

Justice as fairness, as I have said, is best presented in two stages.[27] In the first stage it is worked out as a free-standing political (but of course moral) conception for the basic structure of society. Only when

---

[26] See Justice as Fairness, supra note 1, at 250. The model case of an overlapping consensus is one in which the political conception is endorsed by three comprehensive doctrines: the first endorses justice as fairness, say, because its religious beliefs and understanding of faith lead to the principle of toleration and support the basic equal liberties; the second doctrine affirms justice as fairness as a consequence of a comprehensive liberal conception such as that of Kant or Mill; while the third affirms justice as fairness as a political conception, that is, not as a consequence of a wider doctrine but as in itself sufficient to express very great values that normally outweigh whatever other values might oppose them, at least under reasonably favorable conditions. Id. See also Overlapping Consensus, supra note 1, § III, at 9-12 (more fully discussing this model case).

[27] These two stages correspond to the two parts of the argument from the original position for the two principles of justice contained in Theory, supra note 1. In the first part the parties select principles without taking the effects of the special psychologies into account. Id. at 118-93. In the second part they ask whether a society well-ordered by the principles selected in the first part would be stable, that is, would generate in its members a sufficiently strong sense of justice to counteract tendencies to injustice. Id. at 395-587. The argument for the principles of justice is not complete until the principles selected in the first part are shown in the second part to be sufficiently stable. So in *Theory* the argument is not complete until the next to last section, section 86. Id. at 567-77. For these two parts, see id. at 144, 530-31.

this is done and its content—its principles of justice and ideals—is provisionally on hand do we take up, in the second stage, the problem of stability and introduce the idea of an overlapping consensus: a consensus in which a diversity of conflicting comprehensive doctrines endorse the same political conception, in this case, justice as fairness.

In describing the second stage, let us agree that a political conception must be practicable, that is, must fall under the art of the possible. This contrasts with a moral conception that is not political; a moral conception may condemn the world and human nature as too corrupt to be moved by its precepts and ideals.

There are, however, two ways in which a political conception may be concerned with stability.[28] In one way, we suppose that stability is a purely practical matter: if a conception fails to be stable, it is futile to try to base a political structure upon it. Perhaps we think there are two separate tasks: one is to work out a political conception that seems sound, or reasonable, at least to us; the other is to find ways to bring others who reject the conception to share it in due course, or failing that, to act in accordance with it, prompted if need be by penalties enforced by state power. As long as the means of persuasion or enforcement can be found, the conception is viewed as stable; it is not utopian in the pejorative sense.

But as a liberal conception, justice as fairness is concerned with stability in a second, very different way. Finding a stable conception is not simply a matter of avoiding futility. Rather, what counts is the kind of stability and the nature of the forces that secure it. The idea is that, given certain assumptions specifying a reasonable human psychology[29] and the normal conditions of human life, those who grow up under basic institutions that are just—institutions that justice as fairness itself enjoins—acquire a reasoned and informed allegiance to those institutions sufficient to render the institutions stable. Put another way, the sense of justice of citizens, in view of their traits of character and interests as formed by living under a just basic structure, is strong enough to resist

---

[28] In this and the next several paragraphs I am indebted to a very helpful discussion with T.M. Scanlon.

[29] The assumptions of such a psychology are noted briefly in Overlapping Consensus, supra note 1, at 22-23. In Section VI of the same essay I also consider the way in which a political conception can gain an allegiance to itself that may to some degree shape comprehensive doctrines to conform to its requirements. Id. at 18-22. This is plainly an important aspect of stability and strengthens the second part of the answer as to how political liberalism is possible. See Part VI supra.

I wish to thank Francis Kamm for pointing out to me several significant complications in the relation between a political conception and the comprehensive doctrines it shapes to accord with it, and how far as a result the viability of political liberalism depends on the support of such doctrines. It seems best not to pursue these matters here but to postpone them until a more complete account of stability can be given.

the normal tendencies to injustice. Citizens act willingly so as to give one another justice over time. Stability is secured by sufficient motivation of the appropriate kind acquired under just institutions.[30]

The kind of stability required of justice as fairness is based, then, on its being a liberal political view, one that aims at being acceptable to citizens as reasonable and rational, as well as free and equal, and so addressed to their free public reason. Earlier we saw how this feature of liberalism connects with the feature of political power in a constitutional regime, namely, that it is the power of equal citizens as a collective body. It follows that if justice as fairness were not expressly designed to gain the reasoned support of citizens who affirm reasonable although conflicting comprehensive doctrines—the existence of such conflicting doctrines being a feature of the kind of public culture which that conception itself encourages—it would not be liberal.[31]

The point, then, is that, as a liberal conception, justice as fairness must not merely avoid futility; the explanation of why it is practicable must be of a special kind. The problem of stability is not the problem of bringing others who reject a conception to share it, or to act in accordance with it, by workable sanctions if necessary—as if the task were to find ways to impose that conception on others once we are ourselves convinced it is sound. Rather, as a liberal political conception, justice as fairness relies for its reasonableness in the first place upon generating its own support in a suitable way by addressing each citizen's reason, as explained within its own framework.[32]

Only in this manner is justice as fairness an account of political legitimacy. Only so does it escape being a mere account of how those who hold political power can satisfy themselves, in the light of their own convictions, whether political or fully comprehensive, that they are acting properly—satisfy themselves, that is, and not citizens generally.[33] A con-

---

[30] As stated in *Theory*, the question is whether the just and the good are congruent. Theory, supra note 1, at 395, 567-77. In section 86 of *Theory*, it is argued that a person who grows up in a society well-ordered by justice as fairness, and who has a rational plan of life, and who also knows, or reasonably believes, that everyone else has an effective sense of justice, has sufficient reason, founded on that person's good (and not on justice) to comply with just institutions. Id. at 567-77. These institutions are stable because the just and the good are congruent. That is, no reasonable and rational person in the well-ordered society of justice as fairness is moved by rational considerations of the good not to honor what justice requires.

[31] Recall that reasonable comprehensive doctrines are ones that recognize the burdens of reason and accept the fact of pluralism as a condition of human life under free democratic institutions, and hence accept freedom of thought and liberty of conscience. See Parts II and III supra.

[32] The force of the phrase "within its own framework" as used in the text emerges in the two parts of the argument from the original position in Theory, supra note 1. Both parts are carried out within the same framework and subject to the same conditions embedded in the original position as a device of representation.

[33] For this distinction, see Nagel, What Makes Political Theory Utopian? 5 (unpublished

ception of political legitimacy aims for a public basis of justification and appeals to free public reason, and hence to all citizens viewed as reasonable and rational.

VIII

COMPARISON WITH *A THEORY OF JUSTICE*

It may seem that the idea of an overlapping consensus and related topics are a significant departure from *Theory*. They are some departure certainly; but how much? *Theory* never discusses whether justice as fairness is meant as a comprehensive moral doctrine or as a political conception of justice. In one place it says that if justice as fairness succeeds reasonably well, a next step would be to study the more general view suggested by the name "rightness as fairness."[34]

But *Theory* holds that even this view would not be fully comprehensive: it would not cover, for example, our relations to other living things and to the natural order itself.[35] *Theory* emphasizes the limited scope of justice as fairness, and the limited scope of the kind of view it exemplifies; the book leaves open the question of how far its conclusions might need revision once these other matters are taken into account. There is, however, no mention of the distinction between a political conception of justice and a comprehensive doctrine. The reader might reasonably conclude, then, that justice as fairness is set out as part of a comprehensive view that may be developed later were success to invite.

This conclusion is supported by the discussion of the well-ordered society of justice as fairness in Part III of *Theory*.[36] There it is assumed that the members of any well-ordered society, whether it be a society of justice as fairness or of some other view, accept the same conception of justice and also, it seems, the same comprehensive doctrine of which that conception is a part, or from which it can be derived. Thus, for example, all the members of a well-ordered society associated with utilitarianism (classical or average), are assumed to affirm the utilitarian view, which is by its nature (unless expressly restricted) a comprehensive doctrine.

Although the term was introduced in another context,[37] the idea of an overlapping consensus was first introduced to think of the well-ordered society of justice as fairness in a different and more realistic way.[38] Given the free institutions which that conception itself enjoins,

---

paper, dated Apr. 1988, on file at New York University Law Review).

[34] Theory, supra note 1, at 17.

[35] Id. at 512.

[36] Id. at 453-62.

[37] Id. at 387-88.

[38] Justice as Fairness, supra note 1, at 248-51.

we can no longer assume that citizens generally, even if they accept justice as fairness, also accept the particular comprehensive view in which it might seem to be embedded in *Theory*. We now assume citizens hold two distinct views; or perhaps better, we assume their overall view has two parts. One part can be seen to be, or to coincide with, a political conception of justice; the other part is a (fully or partially) comprehensive doctrine to which the political conception is in some manner related.[39]

The political conception may be simply a part of, or an adjunct to, a partially comprehensive view; or it may be endorsed because it can be derived within a fully articulated comprehensive doctrine. It is left to citizens individually to decide for themselves in what way their shared political conception is related to their wider and more comprehensive views. A society is well-ordered by justice as fairness so long as, first, citizens who affirm reasonable comprehensive doctrines generally endorse justice as fairness as giving the content of their political judgments; and second, unreasonable comprehensive doctrines do not gain enough currency to compromise the essential justice of basic institutions.

This is a better and no longer utopian way of thinking of the well-ordered society of justice as fairness. It corrects the view in *Theory*, which fails to take into account the condition of pluralism to which its own principles lead.

Moreover, because justice as fairness is now seen as a free-standing political conception that articulates fundamental political and constitutional values, endorsing it involves far less than is contained in a comprehensive doctrine. Taking such a well-ordered society as the aim of reform and change does not seem altogether impracticable; under the reasonably favorable conditions that make a constitutional regime possible, that aim is a reasonable guide and may be in good part realized. By contrast, a free democratic society well-ordered by any comprehensive doctrine, religious or secular, is surely utopian in a pejorative sense. Achieving it would, in any case, require the oppressive use of state power. This is as true of the liberalism of rightness as fairness, as it is of the Christianity of Aquinas or Luther.

IX

IN WHAT SENSE POLITICAL?

To trace our steps, I put before you this brief summary.[40] I have

---

[39] For example, in the well-ordered society of justice as fairness, some may hold a form of utilitarianism as their comprehensive doctrine, provided they understand that doctrine, as I believe J.S. Mill did, so as to coincide in its requirements with justice as fairness, at least for the most part. See J.S. Mill, supra note 23, ch.3, ¶ 10.

[40] I am grateful to Erin Kelley for valuable discussion about how to put this summary.

suggested that once we recognize the five general facts[41] and the inevitable burdens of reason even under favorable conditions,[42] and once we reject the oppressive use of state power to impose a single comprehensive doctrine as the way to achieve social unity, then we are led to democratic principles and must accept the fact of pluralism as a permanent feature of political life. Hence, to achieve social unity for a well-ordered democratic regime, what I have called political liberalism introduces the idea of an overlapping consensus and along with it the further idea of the political as a special domain. Political liberalism does this not only because its content includes the basic rights and liberties the securing of which leads to pluralism, but also because of the liberal ideal of political legitimacy, namely, that social cooperation, at least as it concerns the constitutional essentials, is to be conducted so far as possible on terms both intelligible and acceptable to all citizens as reasonable and rational. Those terms are best stated by reference to the fundamental political and constitutional values (expressed by a political conception of justice) that, given the diversity of comprehensive doctrines, all citizens may still be reasonably expected to endorse.

We must, however, be careful that a political conception is not political in the wrong way. It should aim to formulate a coherent view of the very great (moral) values applying to the political relationship and to set out a public basis of justification for free institutions in a manner accessible to free public reason. It must not be political in the sense of merely specifying a workable compromise between known and existing interests, nor political in looking to the particular comprehensive doctrines known to exist in society and in then being tailored to gain their allegiance.

In this connection let us ensure that the assumptions about pluralism do not make justice as fairness political in the wrong way. Consider first the five general facts reviewed in Parts I and II. These we suppose are accepted from the point of view of you and me as we try to develop justice as fairness. When the original position is viewed as a device of representation, these facts are made available to the parties in that position as they decide which principles of justice to select. So if principles that require free democratic institutions are accepted in the first stage, then the account of the stability in the second stage must show how justice as fairness can be endorsed by an overlapping consensus. As we have seen, this follows because free institutions themselves lead to pluralism.

The crucial question, then, is whether the five general facts, along with other premises allowed by the constraints of the original position in the first stage, suffice to lead the parties to select the two principles of

---

[41] See Parts I & II supra.
[42] See Part II supra.

justice;[43] or whether certain further assumptions related to pluralism are also needed, assumptions that make justice as fairness political in the wrong way. I cannot settle this matter here; it would require a survey of the argument from the original position.

I believe we need only suppose in the first stage that the parties assume the fact of pluralism to obtain, that is, that a plurality of comprehensive doctrines exists in society.[44] The parties must then protect against the possibility that the person each party represents may be a member of a religious, ethnic, or other minority. This suffices for the argument for the equal basic liberties to get going. In the second stage, when stability is considered, the parties again assume that pluralism obtains. They confirm principles leading to a social world that allows free play to human nature and thus, we hope, encourages a diversity of reasonable rather than unreasonable comprehensive doctrines, given the burdens of reason.[45] This makes stability possible.

Now it is often said that the politician looks to the next election, the statesman to the next generation. To this we add that the student of philosophy looks to the standing conditions of human life, and how these affect the burdens of reason. Political philosophy must take into account the five general facts we noted, among them the fact that free institutions encourage a diversity of comprehensive doctrines. But in doing this we abstract from the particular content of these doctrines, whatever it may be, and from the many contingencies under which the doctrines exist. A political conception so arrived at is not political in the wrong way but suitably adapted to the public political culture that its own principles shape and sustain. And although such a conception may not apply to all societies at all times and places, this does not make it historicist, or relativist; rather, it is universal in virtue of its extending appropriately to specify a reasonable conception of justice among all nations.[46]

---

[43] These two principles are:
1. Each person has an equal right to a fully adequate scheme of equal basic rights and liberties, which scheme is compatible with a similar scheme for all.
2. Social and economic inequalities are to satisfy two conditions: first, they must be attached to offices and positions open to all under conditions of fair equality of opportunity; and second, they must be to the greatest benefit of the least advantaged members of society.

Justice as Fairness, supra note 1, at 227.

[44] I should like to thank David Chow for very helpful comments on this point.

[45] The reasons for thinking reasonable rather than unreasonable doctrines are encouraged are sketched briefly in Overlapping Consensus, supra note 1, at 18-23.

[46] Perhaps I should explain briefly that the political conception so arrived at may not apply to some societies because the general facts we have assumed may not appropriately obtain in their case. Nevertheless, those facts do obtain widely in the modern world, and hence the political conception applies. Its not applying in some cases, however, does not make that conception relativist or historicist so long as it provides grounds for judging the basic institutions of different societies and their social policies. Thus, the appropriate test of a conception's

X

CONCLUDING REMARKS

The foregoing shows, I think, that the freedoms discussed have a dual role. On the one hand, they are the result of the working out, at the most basic level (in what I called the first stage of justice as fairness), of the fundamental ideas of a democratic society as a fair system of cooperation between citizens as free and equal. On the other hand, in the second stage, we know on the basis of general facts and the historical condition

---

universality is whether it can be extended to, or developed into, a reasonable political conception of justice for an international society of nation-states. In Theory, supra note 1, at 377-79, I noted briefly how, after the principles of justice have been adopted for the basic structure of society (viewed as a closed scheme of cooperation), the idea of the original position can be used once more at the higher level. The parties are now seen as representatives of states. We start with (closed) societies and build up to the international society of states. Doing this locates us where we are and follows the historical tendencies of democratic societies. Others may want to begin with an original position in which the parties are seen as representatives of citizens of the world society. I supposed that in any case the outcome would be something like the familiar principles of international justice governing a society of states rather than a world state, for example, a principle of equality among peoples as organized into states, although states who recognize certain duties towards other states. For I think that Kant is right that a world state would likely be either highly oppressive if not autocratic, or else torn by civil strife as separate peoples and cultures tried to win their autonomy. I. Kant, Perpetual Peace: A Philosophical Sketch (1795; L. Beck trans. 1949). If so, the principles of international justice will include a principle of equality among peoples as organized into states; and there will also be, I think, principles for forming and regulating loose confederations of states, and standards of fairness for various cooperative arrangements between them, and so on. In such a confederation or arrangement, one role of the state, however arbitrary its boundaries may appear from a historical point of view, is to be the representative of a people as they take responsibility for their territory and the numbers they put on it, and especially for maintaining its environmental integrity and its capacity to sustain them in perpetuity.

Theory does not pursue these larger matters but only mentions the extension to the international system as background for discussing conscientious refusal in section 58. Theory, supra note 1, at 377-82. But given this extension, as briefly indicated, we can see that justice as fairness as a political conception is universal in at least two ways. First, its principles extend to the international society and bind all its members, the nation-states; and second, insofar as certain of a society's domestic institutions and policies are likely to lead to war or to expansionist aims, or to render a people unreliable and untrustworthy as partners in a confederation of states or in a cooperative arrangement, those institutions and policies are open to censure and sanctions of varying degrees of severity by the principles of international justice. Here violations of what are recognized as human rights may be particularly serious. Thus, the requirements of a just international society may reflect back and impose constraints downwards on the domestic institutions of states generally. But these constraints will already be met, I assume, by a just constitutional regime.

I cannot pursue these matters further here, and have appended this footnote only to indicate why I think the political conception of justice as fairness is in a suitable way universal, and not relativist or historicist, even though it may not apply to all societies at all times and places. Thomas Pogge's work forthcoming from Cornell University Press includes an account of international justice from within a conception much like justice as fairness, but very importantly revised and extended in a different way to the global sphere. His much fuller discussion will sustain, I believe, the same general point about the universality of such a conception, although his approach to international justice is very different.

of the age that a conception of political justice leading to free institutions must be acceptable to a plurality of opposing comprehensive doctrines. That conception must, therefore, present itself as independent of any particular comprehensive view and must firmly guarantee for all citizens the basic rights and liberties as a condition of their sense of security and their peaceful, mutual recognition.

As the first role is perhaps clearer than the second, I comment on the latter. We know from the burdens of reason that even in a well-ordered society, where the basic freedoms are secure, sharp political disagreement will persist on their more particular interpretation. For instance, where exactly should the line be drawn between church and state? Or, granting there is no such crime as seditious libel, who precisely belongs to the class of public persons in regard to whom the law of libel is relaxed? Or, what are the limits of protected speech? So the question arises: if disagreements on such constitutional essentials always remain, what is gained by a publicly recognized political conception? Isn't the aim—to underwrite the basic rights and liberties of citizens by achieving an overlapping consensus, thereby giving everyone the sense that their rights are indeed secure—still unresolved?

There are two replies to this. First, by securing the basic rights and liberties, and assigning them a due priority, the most divisive questions are taken off the political agenda. This means that they are publicly recognized as politically settled, once and for all, and so contrary views on those questions are emphatically rejected by all political parties.[47] Though disagreements remain, as they must, they occur in areas of less central significance, where reasonable citizens equally attached to the political conception may reasonably be expected to differ. If liberty of conscience is guaranteed and separation of church and state is enjoined, we still expect there to be differences about what more exactly these provisions mean. Differences in judgment on the details in matters of any complexity even among reasonable persons are a condition of human life. But with the most divisive questions off the political agenda, it should be possible to reach a peaceful settlement within the framework of democratic institutions.

A second reply, complementing the first, is that the political conception, when properly formulated, should guide reflective judgment both to an agreed enumeration of the basic rights and liberties and to an agreement about their central range of significance. This it can do by its fundamental intuitive idea of society as a fair system of cooperation between

---

[47] For example, it is not on the political agenda whether certain groups are to have the vote, or whether certain religious or philosophical views have the protections of liberty of conscience and freedom of thought.

citizens as free and equal persons, and by its idea of such persons as having the two moral powers, one a capacity for a sense of justice and the other a capacity for a conception of the good, that is, a conception of what is worthy of their devoted pursuit over a complete life.[48] Basic rights and liberties secure the conditions for the adequate development and exercise of those powers by citizens viewed as fully cooperating members of society. Citizens are thought to have and to want to exercise these powers whatever their more comprehensive religious, philosophical, or moral doctrine may be. Thus, the equal political liberties and freedom of speech and thought enable us to develop and exercise these powers by participating in society's political life and by assessing the justice and effectiveness of its laws and social policies; and liberty of conscience and freedom of association enable us to develop and exercise our moral powers in forming, revising, and rationally pursuing our conceptions of the good that belong to our comprehensive doctrines, and affirming them as such.[49]

But in view of the truism that no conception, whether in law, morals, or science, interprets and applies itself, we should expect various interpretations of even the constitutional essentials to gain currency. Does this jeopardize the rule of law? Not necessarily. The idea of the rule of law has numerous elements and it can be specified in a variety of ways. But however this is done, it cannot depend on the idea of a clear, unambiguous directive that informs citizens, or legislators, or judges what the constitution enjoins in all cases. There can be no such thing. The rule of law is not put in jeopardy by the circumstance that citizens, and even legislators and judges, may often hold conflicting views on questions of interpretation.

Rather, the rule of law means the regulative role of certain institutions and their associated legal and judicial practices. It may mean, among other things, that all officers of the government, including the executive, are under the law and that their acts are subject to judicial scrutiny, that the judiciary is suitably independent, and that civilian authority is supreme over the military. Moreover, it may mean that judges' decisions rest on interpreting existing law and relevant precedents, that judges must justify their verdicts by reference thereto and adhere to a consistent reading from case to case, or else find a reasonable basis for distinguishing them, and so on. Similar constraints do not bind legislators; while they may not defy basic law and can try politically to change

---

[48] This conception of the person, which characterizes citizens, is also a political conception. Justice as Fairness, supra note 1, at 239-44. I add that persons understand their own conceptions of the good against the background of their own comprehensive doctrines.

[49] For further discussion of the basic rights and liberties, see Rawls, Basic Liberties and Their Priority, in 3 Tanner Lectures on Human Values 1 (S. McMurrin ed. 1982).

it only in ways the constitution permits, they need not explain or justify their vote, though their constituents may call them to account. The rule of law exists so long as such legal institutions and their associated practices (variously specified) are conducted in a reasonable way in accordance with the political values that apply to them: impartiality and consistency, adherence to law and respect for precedent, all in the light of a coherent understanding of recognized constitutional norms viewed as controlling the conduct of all government officers.[50]

Two conditions underwrite the rule of law so understood: first, the recognition by politically engaged citizens of the dual role of the basic rights and liberties; and second, its being the case that the main interpretations of those constitutional essentials take the most divisive matters off the political agenda and specify the central range of significance of the basic liberties in roughly the same way. The ideas of the domain of the political and of an overlapping consensus indicate how these conditions strengthen the stability of a political conception.

It is important for the viability of a just democratic regime over time for politically active citizens to understand those ideas. For in the long run, the leading interpretations of constitutional essentials are settled politically. A persistent majority, or an enduring alliance of strong enough interests, can make of the Constitution what it wants.[51] This fact is simply a corollary to the third general fact—that an enduring democratic regime must be freely supported by a substantial majority of its politically active citizens. As a fact, we must live with it and see it as specifying further one of the conditions of achieving a well-ordered constitutional state.

---

[50] I owe thanks to T.M. Scanlon for helpful discussion of the rule of law as summarized in the last two paragraphs.

[51] On this point, see A. Bickel, The Least Dangerous Branch 244-72 (1962) (discussing politics of Dred Scott v. Sanford, 60 U.S. (19 Haw.) 393 (1857), and the school segregation cases, notably Brown v. Board of Educ., 347 U.S. 483 (1954)).

[12]

The University of Chicago Law Review

Volume 64	Summer 1997	Number 3

© 1997 by The University of Chicago

The Idea of Public Reason Revisited

John Rawls†

INTRODUCTION

The idea of public reason, as I understand it,[1] belongs to a conception of a well ordered constitutional democratic society. The form and content of this reason—the way it is understood by citizens and how it interprets their political relationship—is part of the idea of democracy itself. This is because a basic feature of democracy is the fact of reasonable pluralism—the fact that a

---

† Emeritus Professor of Philosophy, Harvard University. This essay is a revision of a lecture given at The University of Chicago Law School in November 1993. I should like to thank Joshua Cohen, Erin Kelly, Percy Lehning, Michael Perry, Margaret Rawls, and T.M. Scanlon for their great help and advice in writing this paper. Throughout they have given me numerous suggestions, which I have gladly accepted. Above all, to Burton Dreben I am especially indebted: as so often before, he has been generous beyond measure in his efforts; in every section he has helped me reorganize and reshape the text, giving it a clarity and simplicity it would not otherwise have had. Without their constant advice and encouragement, and that of others mentioned below, I never could have completed the revisions of my original lecture.

[1] See John Rawls, *Political Liberalism*, lecture VI, § 8.5 (Columbia paperback ed 1996). References to *Political Liberalism* are given by lecture and section; page numbers are also provided unless the reference refers to an entire lecture, section, or subsection. Note that the 1996 paperback edition of *Political Liberalism* contains a new second introduction which, among other things, tries to make clearer certain aspects of political liberalism. Section 5 of this introduction, id at l-lvii, discusses the idea of public reason and sketches several changes I now make in affirming this idea. These are all followed and elaborated in what is presented here and are important to a complete understanding of the argument. Note also that the pagination of the paperback edition is the same as the original.

plurality of conflicting reasonable comprehensive doctrines,[2] religious, philosophical, and moral, is the normal result of its culture of free institutions.[3] Citizens realize that they cannot reach agreement or even approach mutual understanding on the basis of their irreconcilable comprehensive doctrines. In view of this, they need to consider what kinds of reasons they may reasonably give one another when fundamental political questions are at stake. I propose that in public reason comprehensive doctrines of truth or right be replaced by an idea of the politically reasonable addressed to citizens as citizens.[4]

Central to the idea of public reason is that it neither criticizes nor attacks any comprehensive doctrine, religious or nonreligious, except insofar as that doctrine is incompatible with the essentials of public reason and a democratic polity. The basic requirement is that a reasonable doctrine accepts a constitutional democratic regime and its companion idea of legitimate law. While democratic societies will differ in the specific doctrines that are influential and active within them—as they differ in the western democracies of Europe and the United States, Israel, and India—finding a suitable idea of public reason is a concern that faces them all.

§ 1: THE IDEA OF PUBLIC REASON

1. The idea of public reason specifies at the deepest level the basic moral and political values that are to determine a constitutional democratic government's relation to its citizens and their relation to one another. In short, it concerns how the political relation is to be understood. Those who reject constitutional democracy with its criterion of reciprocity[5] will of course reject the very idea of public reason. For them the political relation may be that of friend or foe, to those of a particular religious or secular community or those who are not; or it may be a relentless struggle to win the world for the whole truth. Political liberalism does

---

[2] I shall use the term *doctrine* for comprehensive views of all kinds and the term *conception* for a political conception and its component parts, such as the conception of the person as citizen. The term *idea* is used as a general term and may refer to either as the context determines.

[3] Of course, every society also contains numerous unreasonable doctrines. Yet in this essay I am concerned with an ideal normative conception of democratic government, that is, with the conduct of its reasonable citizens and the principles they follow, assuming them to be dominant and controlling. How far unreasonable doctrines are active and tolerated is to be determined by the principles of justice and the kinds of actions they permit. See § 7.2.

[4] See § 6.2.

[5] See § 1.2.

not engage those who think this way. The zeal to embody the whole truth in politics is incompatible with an idea of public reason that belongs with democratic citizenship.

The idea of public reason has a definite structure, and if one or more of its aspects are ignored it can seem implausible, as it does when applied to the background culture.[6] It has five different aspects: (1) the fundamental political questions to which it applies; (2) the persons to whom it applies (government officials and candidates for public office); (3) its content as given by a family of reasonable political conceptions of justice; (4) the application of these conceptions in discussions of coercive norms to be enacted in the form of legitimate law for a democratic people; and (5) citizens' checking that the principles derived from their conceptions of justice satisfy the criterion of reciprocity.

Moreover, such reason is public in three ways: as the reason of free and equal citizens, it is the reason of the public; its subject is the public good concerning questions of fundamental political justice, which questions are of two kinds, constitutional essentials and matters of basic justice;[7] and its nature and content are public, being expressed in public reasoning by a family of reasonable conceptions of political justice reasonably thought to satisfy the criterion of reciprocity.

It is imperative to realize that the idea of public reason does not apply to all political discussions of fundamental questions, but only to discussions of those questions in what I refer to as the public political forum.[8] This forum may be divided into three parts: the discourse of judges in their decisions, and especially of the judges of a supreme court; the discourse of government officials, especially chief executives and legislators; and finally, the discourse of candidates for public office and their campaign managers, especially in their public oratory, party platforms, and political statements.[9] We need this three-part division because, as I note later, the idea of public reason does not apply in the same

---

[6] See text accompanying notes 12-15.

[7] These questions are described in Rawls, *Political Liberalism*, lecture VI, § 5 at 227-30 (cited in note 1). Constitutional essentials concern questions about what political rights and liberties, say, may reasonably be included in a written constitution, when assuming the constitution may be interpreted by a supreme court, or some similar body. Matters of basic justice relate to the basic structure of society and so would concern questions of basic economic and social justice and other things not covered by a constitution.

[8] There is no settled meaning of this term. The one I use is not I think peculiar.

[9] Here we face the question of where to draw the line between candidates and those who manage their campaigns and other politically engaged citizens generally. We settle this matter by making candidates and those who run their campaigns responsible for what is said and done on the candidates' behalf.

way in these three cases and elsewhere.[10] In discussing what I call the wide view of public political culture,[11] we shall see that the idea of public reason applies more strictly to judges than to others, but that the requirements of public justification for that reason are always the same.

Distinct and separate from this three-part public political forum is what I call the background culture.[12] This is the culture of civil society. In a democracy, this culture is not, of course, guided by any one central idea or principle, whether political or religious. Its many and diverse agencies and associations with their internal life reside within a framework of law that ensures the familiar liberties of thought and speech, and the right of free association.[13] The idea of public reason does not apply to the background culture with its many forms of nonpublic reason nor to media of any kind.[14] Sometimes those who appear to reject the idea of public reason actually mean to assert the need for full and open discussion in the background culture.[15] With this political liberalism fully agrees.

Finally, distinct from the idea of public reason, as set out by the five features above, is the *ideal* of public reason. This ideal is realized, or satisfied, whenever judges, legislators, chief execu-

---

[10] Often writers on this topic use terms that do not distinguish the parts of public discussion, for example, such terms as "the public square," "the public forum," and the like. I follow Kent Greenawalt in thinking a finer division is necessary. See Kent Greenawalt, *Religious Convictions and Political Choice* 226-27 (Oxford 1988) (describing, for example, the differences between a religious leader's preaching or promoting a pro-life organization and leading a major political movement or running for political office).

[11] See § 4.

[12] Rawls, *Political Liberalism*, lecture I, § 2.3 at 14 (cited in note 1).

[13] The background culture includes, then, the culture of churches and associations of all kinds, and institutions of learning at all levels, especially universities and professional schools, scientific and other societies. In addition, the nonpublic political culture mediates between the public political culture and the background culture. This comprises media—properly so named—of all kinds: newspapers, reviews and magazines, TV and radio, and much else. Compare these divisions with Habermas's account of the public sphere. See Rawls, *Political Liberalism*, lecture IX, § 1.3 at 382 n 13 (cited in note 1).

[14] See id, lecture VI, § 3 at 220-22.

[15] See David Hollenbach, S.J., *Civil Society: Beyond the Public-Private Dichotomy*, 5 The Responsive Community 15 (Winter 1994/95). For example, he says:

> Conversation and argument about the common good will not occur initially in the legislature or in the political sphere (narrowly conceived as the domain in which interests and power are adjudicated). Rather it will develop freely in those components of civil society that are the primary bearers of cultural meaning and value— universities, religious communities, the world of the arts, and serious journalism. It can occur wherever thoughtful men and women bring their beliefs on the meaning of the good life into intelligent and critical encounter with understandings of this good held by other peoples with other traditions. In short, it occurs wherever education about and serious inquiry into the meaning of the good life takes place.

Id at 22.

tives, and other government officials, as well as candidates for public office, act from and follow the idea of public reason and explain to other citizens their reasons for supporting fundamental political positions in terms of the political conception of justice they regard as the most reasonable. In this way they fulfill what I shall call their duty of civility to one another and to other citizens. Hence, whether judges, legislators, and chief executives act from and follow public reason is continually shown in their speech and conduct on a daily basis.

How though is the ideal of public reason realized by citizens who are not government officials? In a representative government citizens vote for representatives—chief executives, legislators, and the like—and not for particular laws (except at a state or local level when they may vote directly on referenda questions, which are rarely fundamental questions). To answer this question, we say that ideally citizens are to think of themselves *as if* they were legislators and ask themselves what statutes, supported by what reasons satisfying the criterion of reciprocity, they would think it most reasonable to enact.[16] When firm and widespread, the disposition of citizens to view themselves as ideal legislators, and to repudiate government officials and candidates for public office who violate public reason, is one of the political and social roots of democracy, and is vital to its enduring strength and vigor.[17] Thus citizens fulfill their duty of civility and support the idea of public reason by doing what they can to hold government officials to it. This duty, like other political rights and duties, is an intrinsically moral duty. I emphasize that it is not a legal duty, for in that case it would be incompatible with freedom of speech.

2. I now turn to a discussion of what I have labeled the third, fourth, and fifth aspects of public reason. The idea of public reason arises from a conception of democratic citizenship in a constitutional democracy. This fundamental political relation of citizenship has two special features: first, it is a relation of citizens within the basic structure of society, a structure we enter only by birth and exit only by death;[18] and second, it is a relation of free

---

[16] There is some resemblance between this criterion and Kant's principle of the original contract. See Immanuel Kant, *The Metaphysics of Morals: Metaphysical First Principles of the Doctrine of Right* §§ 47-49 at 92-95 (AK 6:315-18) (Cambridge 1996) (Mary Gregor, trans and ed); Immanuel Kant, *On the Common Saying: 'This May be True in Theory, but it does not Apply in Practice,'* Part II, in *Kant: Political Writings* 73-87 (AK 8: 289-306) (Cambridge 2d ed 1991) (Hans Reiss, ed, H.B. Nisbet, trans).

[17] See also § 4.2.

[18] Rawls, *Political Liberalism*, lecture I, § 2.1 at 12 (cited in note 1). For concerns about exiting only by death, see id, lecture IV, § 1.2 at 136 n 4.

and equal citizens who exercise ultimate political power as a collective body. These two features immediately give rise to the
question of how, when constitutional essentials and matters of
basic justice are at stake, citizens so related can be bound to
honor the structure of their constitutional democratic regime and
abide by the statutes and laws enacted under it. The fact of reasonable pluralism raises this question all the more sharply, since
it means that the differences between citizens arising from their
comprehensive doctrines, religious and nonreligious, may be irreconcilable. By what ideals and principles, then, are citizens
who share equally in ultimate political power to exercise that
power so that each can reasonably justify his or her political decisions to everyone?

To answer this question we say: Citizens are reasonable
when, viewing one another as free and equal in a system of social
cooperation over generations, they are prepared to offer one another fair terms of cooperation according to what they consider
the most reasonable conception of political justice; and when they
agree to act on those terms, even at the cost of their own interests in particular situations, provided that other citizens also accept those terms. The criterion of reciprocity requires that when
those terms are proposed as the most reasonable terms of fair cooperation, those proposing them must also think it at least reasonable for others to accept them, as free and equal citizens, and
not as dominated or manipulated, or under the pressure of an inferior political or social position.[19] Citizens will of course differ as
to which conceptions of political justice they think the most reasonable, but they will agree that all are reasonable, even if barely
so.

Thus when, on a constitutional essential or matter of basic
justice, all appropriate government officials act from and follow
public reason, and when all reasonable citizens think of themselves ideally as if they were legislators following public reason,
the legal enactment expressing the opinion of the majority is legitimate law. It may not be thought the most reasonable, or the
most appropriate, by each, but it is politically (morally) binding
on him or her as a citizen and is to be accepted as such. Each
thinks that all have spoken and voted at least reasonably, and

---

[19] The idea of reciprocity has an important place in Amy Gutmann and Dennis
Thompson, *Democracy and Disagreement* chs 1-2 and passim (Belknap 1996). However,
the meaning and setting of our views are not the same. Public reason in political liberalism is purely political, although political values are intrinsically moral, whereas Gutmann and Thompson's account is more general and seems to work from a comprehensive
doctrine.

therefore all have followed public reason and honored their duty of civility.

Hence the idea of political legitimacy based on the criterion of reciprocity says: Our exercise of political power is proper only when we sincerely believe that the reasons we would offer for our political actions—were we to state them as government officials—are sufficient, and we also reasonably think that other citizens might also reasonably accept those reasons. This criterion applies on two levels: one is to the constitutional structure itself, the other is to particular statutes and laws enacted in accordance with that structure. To be reasonable, political conceptions must justify only constitutions that satisfy this principle.

To make more explicit the role of the criterion of reciprocity as expressed in public reason, note that its role is to specify the nature of the political relation in a constitutional democratic regime as one of civic friendship. For this criterion, when government officers act from it in their public reasoning and other citizens support it, shapes the form of their fundamental institutions. For example—I cite an easy case—if we argue that the religious liberty of some citizens is to be denied, we must give them reasons they can not only understand—as Servetus could understand why Calvin wanted to burn him at the stake—but reasons we might reasonably expect that they, as free and equal citizens, might reasonably also accept. The criterion of reciprocity is normally violated whenever basic liberties are denied. For what reasons can both satisfy the criterion of reciprocity and justify denying to some persons religious liberty, holding others as slaves, imposing a property qualification on the right to vote, or denying the right of suffrage to women?

Since the idea of public reason specifies at the deepest level the basic political values and specifies how the political relation is to be understood, those who believe that fundamental political questions should be decided by what they regard as the best reasons according to their own idea of the whole truth—including their religious or secular comprehensive doctrine—and not by reasons that might be shared by all citizens as free and equal, will of course reject the idea of public reason. Political liberalism views this insistence on the whole truth in politics as incompatible with democratic citizenship and the idea of legitimate law.

3. Democracy has a long history, from its beginning in classical Greece down to the present day, and there are many different ideas of democracy.[20] Here I am concerned only with a well or-

---

[20] For a useful historical survey see David Held, *Models of Democracy* (Stanford 2d ed

dered constitutional democracy—a term I used at the outset—
understood also as a deliberative democracy. The definitive idea
for deliberative democracy is the idea of deliberation itself. When
citizens deliberate, they exchange views and debate their supporting reasons concerning public political questions. They suppose that their political opinions may be revised by discussion
with other citizens; and therefore these opinions are not simply a
fixed outcome of their existing private or nonpolitical interests. It
is at this point that public reason is crucial, for it characterizes
such citizens' reasoning concerning constitutional essentials and
matters of basic justice. While I cannot fully discuss the nature of
deliberative democracy here, I note a few key points to indicate
the wider place and role of public reason.

There are three essential elements of deliberative democracy. One is an idea of public reason,[21] although not all such
ideas are the same. A second is a framework of constitutional
democratic institutions that specifies the setting for deliberative
legislative bodies. The third is the knowledge and desire on the
part of citizens generally to follow public reason and to realize its
ideal in their political conduct. Immediate implications of these
essentials are the public financing of elections, and the providing
for public occasions of orderly and serious discussion of fundamental questions and issues of public policy. Public deliberation
must be made possible, recognized as a basic feature of democracy, and set free from the curse of money.[22] Otherwise politics is
dominated by corporate and other organized interests who

1997). Held's numerous models cover the period from the ancient polis to the present
time and he concludes by asking what democracy should mean today. In between he considers the several forms of classical republicanism and classical liberalism, as well as
Schumpeter's conception of competitive elite democracy. Some figures discussed include
Plato and Aristotle; Marsilius of Padua and Machiavelli; Hobbes and Madison; Bentham,
James Mill and J. S. Mill; Marx with socialism and communism. These are paired with
schematized models of the characteristic institutions and their roles.

[21] Deliberative democracy limits the reasons citizens may give in supporting their political opinions to reasons consistent with their seeing other citizens as equals. See
Joshua Cohen, *Deliberation and Democratic Legitimacy*, in Alan Hamlin and Philip Petit,
eds, *The Good Polity: Normative Analysis of the State* 17, 21, 24 (Basil Blackwell 1989);
Review Symposium on Democracy and Its Critics, 53 J Pol 215, 223-24 (1991) (comments
of Joshua Cohen); Joshua Cohen, *Democracy and Liberty* 13-17 (manuscript on file with U
Chi L Rev), in Jon Elster, ed, *Deliberative Democracy* (forthcoming 1997).

[22] Ronald Dworkin, *The Curse of American Politics*, NY Rev Books 19 (Oct 17, 1996)
(describing why "money is the biggest threat to the democratic process"). Dworkin also
argues forcefully against the grave error of the Supreme Court in *Buckley v Valeo*, 424
US 1 (1976). Dworkin, NY Rev Books at 21-24. See also Rawls, *Political Liberalism*, lecture VIII, § 12 at 359-63 (cited in note 1) (*Buckley* is "dismaying" and raises the risk of
"repeating the mistake of the Lochner era.").

through large contributions to campaigns distort if not preclude public discussion and deliberation.

Deliberative democracy also recognizes that without widespread education in the basic aspects of constitutional democratic government for all citizens, and without a public informed about pressing problems, crucial political and social decisions simply cannot be made. Even should farsighted political leaders wish to make sound changes and reforms, they cannot convince a misinformed and cynical public to accept and follow them. For example, there are sensible proposals for what should be done regarding the alleged coming crisis in Social Security: slow down the growth of benefits levels, gradually raise the retirement age, impose limits on expensive terminal medical care that prolongs life for only a few weeks or days, and finally, raise taxes now, rather than face large increases later.[23] But as things are, those who follow the "great game of politics" know that none of these sensible proposals will be accepted. The same story can be told about the importance of support for international institutions (such as the United Nations), foreign aid properly spent, and concern for human rights at home and abroad. In constant pursuit of money to finance campaigns, the political system is simply unable to function. Its deliberative powers are paralyzed.

§ 2: THE CONTENT OF PUBLIC REASON

1. A citizen engages in public reason, then, when he or she deliberates within a framework of what he or she sincerely regards as the most reasonable political conception of justice, a conception that expresses political values that others, as free and equal citizens might also reasonably be expected reasonably to endorse. Each of us must have principles and guidelines to which we appeal in such a way that this criterion is satisfied. I have proposed that one way to identify those political principles and guidelines is to show that they would be agreed to in what in *Political Liberalism* is called the original position.[24] Others will think that different ways to identify these principles are more reasonable.

Thus, the content of public reason is given by a family of political conceptions of justice, and not by a single one. There are

---

[23] Paul Krugman, *Demographics and Destiny*, NY Times Book Rev 12 (Oct 20, 1996), reviewing and describing proposals in Peter G. Peterson, *Will America Grow Up Before It Grows Old? How the Coming Social Security Crisis Threatens You, Your Family, and Your Country* (Random House 1996), and Charles R. Morris, *The AARP: America's Most Powerful Lobby and the Clash of Generations* (Times Books 1996).

[24] Rawls, *Political Liberalism*, lecture I, § 4 at 22-28 (cited in note 1).

many liberalisms and related views, and therefore many forms of public reason specified by a family of reasonable political conceptions. Of these, justice as fairness, whatever its merits, is but one. The limiting feature of these forms is the criterion of reciprocity, viewed as applied between free and equal citizens, themselves seen as reasonable and rational. Three main features characterize these conceptions:

First, a list of certain basic rights, liberties, and opportunities (such as those familiar from constitutional regimes);

Second, an assignment of special priority to those rights, liberties, and opportunities, especially with respect to the claims of the general good and perfectionist values; and

Third, measures ensuring for all citizens adequate all-purpose means to make effective use of their freedoms.[25]

Each of these liberalisms endorses the underlying ideas of citizens as free and equal persons and of society as a fair system of cooperation over time. Yet since these ideas can be interpreted in various ways, we get different formulations of the principles of justice and different contents of public reason. Political conceptions differ also in how they order, or balance, political principles and values even when they specify the same ones. I assume also that these liberalisms contain substantive principles of justice, and hence cover more than procedural justice. They are required to specify the religious liberties and freedoms of artistic expression of equal citizens, as well as substantive ideas of fairness involving fair opportunity and ensuring adequate all-purpose means, and much else.[26]

Political liberalism, then, does not try to fix public reason once and for all in the form of one favored political conception of justice.[27] That would not be a sensible approach. For instance, political liberalism also admits Habermas's discourse conception

---

[25] Here I follow the definition in Rawls, *Political Liberalism*, lecture I, § 1.2 at 6, lecture IV, § 5.3 at 156-57 (cited in note 1).

[26] Some may think the fact of reasonable pluralism means the only forms of fair adjudication between comprehensive doctrines must be only procedural and not substantive. This view is forcefully argued by Stuart Hampshire in *Innocence and Experience* (Harvard 1989). In the text above, however, I assume the several forms of liberalism are each substantive conceptions. For a thorough treatment of these issues, see the discussion in Joshua Cohen, *Pluralism and Proceduralism*, 69 Chi Kent L Rev 589 (1994).

[27] I do think that justice as fairness has a certain special place in the family of political conceptions, as I suggest in Rawls, *Political Liberalism*, lecture IV, § 7.4 (cited in note 1). But this opinion of mine is not basic to the ideas of political liberalism and public reason.

of legitimacy (sometimes said to be radically democratic rather than liberal),[28] as well as Catholic views of the common good and solidarity when they are expressed in terms of political values.[29] Even if relatively few conceptions come to dominate over time, and one conception even appears to have a special central place, the forms of permissible public reason are always several. Moreover, new variations may be proposed from time to time and older ones may cease to be represented. It is important that this be so; otherwise the claims of groups or interests arising from social change might be repressed and fail to gain their appropriate political voice.[30]

2. We must distinguish public reason from what is sometimes referred to as secular reason and secular values. These are not the same as public reason. For I define secular reason as reasoning in terms of comprehensive nonreligious doctrines. Such doctrines and values are much too broad to serve the purposes of public reason. Political values are not moral doctrines,[31] however available or accessible these may be to our reason and common sense reflection. Moral doctrines are on a level with religion and

---

[28] See Jürgen Habermas, *Between Facts and Norms: Contributions to a Discourse Theory of Law and Democracy* 107-09 (MIT 1996) (William Rehg, trans) (defining the discourse principle). Seyla Benhabib in her discussion of models of public space in *Situating the Self: Gender, Community and Postmodernism in Contemporary Ethics* (Routledge 1992), says that: "The discourse model is the only one which is compatible both with the general social trends of our societies and with the emancipatory aspirations of new social movements like the women's movement." Id at 113. She has previously considered Arendt's agonistic conception, as Benhabib calls it, and that of political liberalism. But I find it hard to distinguish her view from that of a form of political liberalism and public reason, since it turns out that she means by the public sphere what Habermas does, namely what *Political Liberalism* calls the background culture of civil society in which the ideal of public reason does not apply. Hence political liberalism is not limiting in the way she thinks. Also, Benhabib does not try to show, so far as I can see, that certain principles of right and justice belonging to the content of public reason could not be interpreted to deal with the problems raised by the women's movement. I doubt that this can be done. The same holds for Benhabib's earlier remarks in Seyla Benhabib, *Liberal Dialogue Versus a Critical Theory of Discursive Legitimation*, in Nancy L. Rosenblum, ed, *Liberalism and the Moral Life* 143, 154-56 (Harvard 1989), in which the problems of the women's movement were discussed in a similar way.

[29] Deriving from Aristotle and St. Thomas, the idea of the common good is essential to much of Catholic moral and political thought. See, for example, John Finnis, *Natural Law and Natural Rights* 153-56, 160 (Clarendon 1980); Jacques Maritain, *Man and the State* 108-14 (Chicago 1951). Finnis is especially clear, while Aquinas is occasionally ambiguous.

[30] Thus, Jeremy Waldron's criticism of political liberalism as not allowing new and changing conceptions of political justice is incorrect. See Jeremy Waldron, *Religious Contributions in Public Deliberation*, 30 San Diego L Rev 817, 837-38 (1993). See the reply to Waldron's criticisms in Lawrence B. Solum, *Novel Public Reasons*, 29 Loyola LA L Rev 1459, 1460 (1996) ("[G]eneral acceptance of a liberal ideal of public reason would permit the robust evolution of political discourse.").

[31] See note 2 for my definition of *doctrine*.

first philosophy. By contrast, liberal political principles and values, although intrinsically moral values, are specified by liberal political conceptions of justice and fall under the category of the political. These political conceptions have three features:

> First, their principles apply to basic political and social institutions (the basic structure of society);
>
> Second, they can be presented independently from comprehensive doctrines of any kind (although they may, of course, be supported by a reasonable overlapping consensus of such doctrines); and
>
> Finally, they can be worked out from fundamental ideas seen as implicit in the public political culture of a constitutional regime, such as the conceptions of citizens as free and equal persons, and of society as a fair system of cooperation.

Thus, the content of public reason is given by the principles and values of the family of liberal political conceptions of justice meeting these conditions. To engage in public reason is to appeal to one of these political conceptions—to their ideals and principles, standards and values—when debating fundamental political questions. This requirement still allows us to introduce into political discussion at any time our comprehensive doctrine, religious or nonreligious, provided that, in due course, we give properly public reasons to support the principles and policies our comprehensive doctrine is said to support. I refer to this requirement as *the proviso*, and consider it in detail below.[32]

A feature of public reasoning, then, is that it proceeds entirely within a political conception of justice. Examples of political values include those mentioned in the preamble to the United States Constitution: a more perfect union, justice, domestic tranquillity, the common defense, the general welfare, and the blessings of liberty for ourselves and our posterity. These include under them other values: so, for example, under justice we also have equal basic liberties, equality of opportunity, ideals concerning the distribution of income and taxation, and much else.

The political values of public reason are distinct from other values in that they are realized in and characterize political institutions. This does not mean that analogous values cannot characterize other social forms. The values of effectiveness and efficiency may characterize the social organization of teams and clubs, as well as the political institutions of the basic structure of

---

[32] See § 4.

society. But a value is properly political only when the social form is itself political: when it is realized, say, in parts of the basic structure and its political and social institutions. It follows that many political conceptions are nonliberal, including those of aristocracy and corporate oligarchy, and of autocracy and dictatorship. All of these fall within the category of the political.[33] We, however, are concerned only with those political conceptions that are reasonable for a constitutional democratic regime, and as the preceding paragraphs make clear, these are the ideals and principles expressed by reasonable liberal political conceptions.

3. Another essential feature of public reason is that its political conceptions should be complete. This means that each conception should express principles, standards, and ideals, along with guidelines of inquiry, such that the values specified by it can be suitably ordered or otherwise united so that those values alone give a reasonable answer to all, or to nearly all, questions involving constitutional essentials and matters of basic justice. Here the ordering of values is made in the light of their structure and features within the political conception itself, and not primarily from how they occur within citizens' comprehensive doctrines. Political values are not to be ordered by viewing them separately and detached from one another or from any definite context. They are not puppets manipulated from behind the scenes by comprehensive doctrines.[34] The ordering is not distorted by those doctrines provided that public reason sees the ordering as reasonable. And public reason can indeed see an ordering of political values as reasonable (or unreasonable), since institutional structures are open to view and mistakes and gaps within the political ordering will become exposed. Thus, we may be confident that the ordering of political values is not distorted by particular reasonable comprehensive doctrines. (I emphasize that the only criterion of distortion is that the ordering of political values be itself unreasonable.)

The significance of completeness lies in the fact that unless a political conception is complete, it is not an adequate framework of thought in the light of which the discussion of fundamental political questions can be carried out.[35] What we cannot do in

---

[33] Here see Rawls, *Political Liberalism*, lecture IX, § 1.1 at 374-75 (cited in note 1).

[34] This thought I owe to Peter de Marneffe.

[35] Note here that different political conceptions of justice will represent different interpretations of the constitutional essentials and matters of basic justice. There are also different interpretations of the same conception, since its concepts and values may be taken in different ways. There is not, then, a sharp line between where a political conception ends and its interpretation begins, nor need there be. All the same, a conception greatly limits its possible interpretations, otherwise discussion and argument could not

public reason is to proceed directly from our comprehensive doctrine, or a part thereof, to one or several political principles and
values, and the particular institutions they support. Instead, we
are required first to work to the basic ideas of a complete political
conception and from there to elaborate its principles and ideals,
and to use the arguments they provide. Otherwise public reason
allows arguments that are too immediate and fragmentary.

4. I now note several examples of political principles and
values to illustrate the more specific content of public reason,
and particularly the various ways in which the criterion of reciprocity is both applicable and subject to violation.

(a) As a first example, consider the value of autonomy. It
may take two forms: one is political autonomy, the legal independence and assured integrity of citizens and their sharing
equally with others in the exercise of political power; the other is
purely moral and characterizes a certain way of life and reflection, critically examining our deepest ends and ideals, as in Mill's
ideal of individuality.[36] Whatever we may think of autonomy as a
purely moral value, it fails to satisfy, given reasonable pluralism,
the constraint of reciprocity, as many citizens, for example, those
holding certain religious doctrines, may reject it. Thus moral
autonomy is not a political value, whereas political autonomy is.

(b) As a second example, consider the familiar story of the
Good Samaritan. Are the values appealed to properly political
values and not simply religious or philosophical values? While
the wide view of public political culture allows us, in making a
proposal, to introduce the Gospel story, public reason requires us
to justify our proposal in terms of proper political values.[37]

(c) As a third example, consider appeals to desert in discussing the fair distribution of income: people are wont to say

---

proceed. For example, a constitution declaring the freedom of religion, including the freedom to affirm no religion, along with the separation of church and state, may appear to
leave open the question whether church schools may receive public funds, and if so, in
what way. The difference here might be seen as how to interpret the same political conception, one interpretation allowing public funds, the other not; or alternatively, as the
difference between two political conceptions. In the absence of particulars, it does not
matter which we call it. The important point is that since the content of public reason is a
family of political conceptions, that content admits the interpretations we may need. It is
not as if we were stuck with a fixed conception, much less with one interpretation of it.
This is a comment on Kent Greenawalt, *Private Consciences and Public Reasons* 113-20
(Oxford 1995), where *Political Liberalism* is said to have difficulty dealing with the problem of determining the interpretation of political conceptions.

[36] John Stuart Mill, *On Liberty* ch 3 ¶¶ 1-9 (1859), in 18 *Collected Works of John Stuart Mill* 260-75 (Toronto 1977) (John M. Robson, ed).

[37] See § 4.1 on the proviso and the example of citing the Gospel story. For a detailed
consideration of the wide view of public political culture, see generally § 4.

that ideally distribution should be in accordance with desert. What sense of desert do they have in mind? Do they mean that persons in various offices should have the requisite qualifications—judges must be qualified to judge—and all should have a fair opportunity to qualify themselves for favored positions? That is indeed a political value. But distribution in accordance with moral desert, where this means the moral worth of character, all things considered, and including comprehensive doctrines, is not. It is not a feasible political and social aim.

(d) Finally, consider the state's interest in the family and human life. How should the political value invoked be specified correctly? Traditionally it has been specified very broadly. But in a democratic regime the government's legitimate interest is that public law and policy should support and regulate, in an ordered way, the institutions needed to reproduce political society over time. These include the family (in a form that is just), arrangements for rearing and educating children, and institutions of public health generally. This ordered support and regulation rests on political principles and values, since political society is regarded as existing in perpetuity and so as maintaining itself and its institutions and culture over generations. Given this interest, the government would appear to have no interest in the particular form of family life, or of relations among the sexes, except insofar as that form or those relations in some way affect the orderly reproduction of society over time. Thus, appeals to monogamy as such, or against same-sex marriages, as within the government's legitimate interest in the family, would reflect religious or comprehensive moral doctrines. Accordingly, that interest would appear improperly specified. Of course, there may be other political values in the light of which such a specification would pass muster: for example, if monogamy were necessary for the equality of women, or same-sex marriages destructive to the raising and educating of children.[38]

5. The four examples bring out a contrast to what I have above called secular reason.[39] A view often expressed is that while religious reasons and sectarian doctrines should not be invoked to justify legislation in a democratic society, sound secular arguments may be.[40] But what is a secular argument? Some

---

[38] Of course, I don't here attempt to decide the question, since we are concerned only with the kinds of reasons and considerations that public reasoning involves.

[39] See § 2.2.

[40] See Robert Audi, *The Place of Religious Argument in a Free and Democratic Society*, 30 San Diego L Rev 677 (1993). Here Audi defines a secular reason as follows: "A secular reason is roughly one whose normative force does not evidentially depend on the

Justice

think of any argument that is reflective and critical, publicly intelligible and rational, as a secular argument; and they discuss
various such arguments for considering, say, homosexual relations unworthy or degrading.[41] Of course, some of these arguments may be reflective and rational secular ones (as so defined).
Nevertheless, a central feature of political liberalism is that it
views all such arguments the same way it views religious ones,
and therefore these secular philosophical doctrines do not provide public reasons. Secular concepts and reasoning of this kind
belong to first philosophy and moral doctrine, and fall outside of
the domain of the political.

Thus, in considering whether to make homosexual relations
between citizens criminal offenses, the question is not whether
those relations are precluded by a worthy idea of full human good
as characterized by a sound philosophical and nonreligious view,
nor whether those of religious faith regard it as sin, but primarily whether legislative statutes forbidding those relations infringe the civil rights of free and equal democratic citizens.[42] This
question calls for a reasonable political conception of justice
specifying those civil rights, which are always a matter of constitutional essentials.

§ 3: RELIGION AND PUBLIC REASON IN DEMOCRACY

1. Before examining the idea of the wide view of public political culture, we ask: How is it possible for those holding religious doctrines, some based on religious authority, for example,
the Church or the Bible, to hold at the same time a reasonable
political conception that supports a reasonable constitutional
democratic regime? Can these doctrines still be compatible for
the right reasons with a liberal political conception? To attain
this compatibility, it is not sufficient that these doctrines accept
a democratic government merely as a *modus vivendi*. Referring
to citizens holding religious doctrines as citizens of faith we ask:

---

existence of God or on theological considerations, or on the pronouncements of a person or
institution qua religious authority." Id at 692. This definition is ambiguous between
secular reasons in the sense of a nonreligious comprehensive doctrine and in the sense of
a purely political conception within the content of public reason. Depending on which is
meant, Audi's view that secular reasons must also be given along with religious reasons
might have a role similar to what I call *the proviso* in § 4.1.

[41] See the discussion by Michael Perry of John Finnis's argument, which denies that
such relations are compatible with human good. *Religion in Politics: Constitutional and
Moral Perspectives* ch 3 at 85-86 (Oxford 1997).

[42] Here I follow T.M. Scanlon's view in *The Difficulty of Tolerance*, in David Heyd, ed,
Toleration: An Elusive Virtue 226 (Princeton 1996). While the whole is instructive, § 3 at
230-33 is especially relevant here.

How is it possible for citizens of faith to be wholehearted members of a democratic society who endorse society's intrinsic political ideals and values and do not simply acquiesce in the balance of political and social forces? Expressed more sharply: How is it possible—or is it—for those of faith, as well as the nonreligious (secular), to endorse a constitutional regime even when their comprehensive doctrines may not prosper under it, and indeed may decline? This last question brings out anew the significance of the idea of legitimacy and public reason's role in determining legitimate law.

To clarify the question, consider two examples. The first is that of Catholics and Protestants in the sixteenth and seventeenth centuries when the principle of toleration was honored only as a _modus vivendi_.[43] This meant that should either party fully gain its way it would impose its own religious doctrine as the sole admissible faith. A society in which many faiths all share this attitude and assume that for the indefinite future their relative numbers will stay roughly the same might well have a constitution resembling that of the United States, fully protecting the religious liberties of sharply divided religions more or less equal in political power. The constitution is, as it were, honored as a pact to maintain civil peace.[44] In this society political issues might be discussed in terms of political ideas and values so as not to open religious conflict and arouse sectarian hostility. The role of public reason here serves merely to quiet divisiveness and encourage social stability. However, in this case we do not have stability for the right reasons, that is, as secured by a firm allegiance to a democratic society's political (moral) ideals and values.

Nor again do we have stability for the right reasons in the second example—a democratic society where citizens accept as political (moral) principles the substantive constitutional clauses that ensure religious, political, and civil liberties, when their allegiance to these constitutional principles is so limited that none is willing to see his or her religious or nonreligious doctrine losing ground in influence and numbers, and such citizens are prepared to resist or to disobey laws that they think undermine their positions. And they do this even though the full range of religious and other liberties is always maintained and the doctrine

---

[43] See Rawls, _Political Liberalism_, lecture IV, § 3.4 at 148 (cited in note 1).

[44] See Kent Greenawalt's example of the society of Diverse Fervent Believers in Greenawalt, _Private Consciences and Public Reasons_ at 16-18, 21-22 (cited in note 35).

in question is completely secure. Here again democracy is accepted conditionally and not for the right reasons.

What these examples have in common is that society is divided into separate groups, each of which has its own fundamental interest distinct from and opposed to the interests of the other groups and for which it is prepared to resist or to violate legitimate democratic law. In the first example, it is the interest of a religion in establishing its hegemony, while in the second, it is the doctrine's fundamental interest in maintaining a certain degree of success and influence for its own view, either religious or nonreligious. While a constitutional regime can fully ensure rights and liberties for all permissible doctrines, and therefore protect our freedom and security, a democracy necessarily requires that, as one equal citizen among others, each of us accept the obligations of legitimate law.[45] While no one is expected to put his or her religious or nonreligious doctrine in danger, we must each give up forever the hope of changing the constitution so as to establish our religion's hegemony, or of qualifying our obligations so as to ensure its influence and success. To retain such hopes and aims would be inconsistent with the idea of equal basic liberties for all free and equal citizens.

2. To expand on what we asked earlier: How is it possible— or is it—for those of faith, as well as the nonreligious (secular), to endorse a constitutional regime even when their comprehensive doctrines may not prosper under it, and indeed may decline? Here the answer lies in the religious or nonreligious doctrine's understanding and accepting that, except by endorsing a reasonable constitutional democracy, there is no other way fairly to ensure the liberty of its adherents consistent with the equal liberties of other reasonable free and equal citizens. In endorsing a constitutional democratic regime, a religious doctrine may say that such are the limits God sets to our liberty; a nonreligious doctrine will express itself otherwise.[46] But in either case, these

---

[45] See Rawls, *Political Liberalism*, lecture V, § 6 at 195-200 (cited in note 1).

[46] An example of how a religion may do this is the following. Abdullahi Ahmed An-Na'im, in his book *Toward an Islamic Reformation: Civil Liberties, Human Rights, and International Law* 52-57 (Syracuse 1990), introduces the idea of reconsidering the traditional interpretation of Shari'a, which for Muslims is divine law. For his interpretation to be accepted by Muslims, it must be presented as the correct and superior interpretation of Shari'a. The basic idea of An-Na'im's interpretation, following the late Sudanese author *Ustadh* Mahmoud Mohamed Taha, is that the traditional understanding of Shari'a has been based on the teachings of the later Medina period of Muhammad, whereas the teachings of the earlier Mecca period of Muhammad are the eternal and fundamental message of Islam. An-Na'im claims that the superior Mecca teachings and principles were rejected in favor of the more realistic and practical (in a seventh-century historical context) Medina teachings because society was not yet ready for their implementation. Now

doctrines formulate in different ways how liberty of conscience and the principle of toleration can cohere with equal justice for all citizens in a reasonable democratic society. Thus, the principles of toleration and liberty of conscience must have an essential place in any constitutional democratic conception. They lay down the fundamental basis to be accepted by all citizens as fair and regulative of the rivalry between doctrines.

Observe here that there are two ideas of toleration. One is purely political, being expressed in terms of the rights and duties protecting religious liberty in accordance with a reasonable political conception of justice. The other is not purely political but expressed from within a religious or a nonreligious doctrine, as when, for example, it was said above that such are the limits God sets on our liberty. Saying this offers an example of what I call reasoning from conjecture.[47] In this case we reason from what we believe, or conjecture, may be other people's basic doctrines, religious or philosophical, and seek to show them that, despite what they might think, they can still endorse a reasonable political conception of justice. We are not ourselves asserting that ground of toleration but offering it as one they could assert consistent with their comprehensive doctrines.

§ 4: THE WIDE VIEW OF PUBLIC POLITICAL CULTURE

1. Now we consider what I call the wide view of public political culture and discuss two aspects of it. The first is that reasonable comprehensive doctrines, religious or nonreligious, may be

---

that historical conditions have changed, An-Na'im believes that Muslims should follow the earlier Mecca period in interpreting Shari'a. So interpreted, he says that Shari'a supports constitutional democracy. Id at 69-100.

In particular, the earlier Mecca interpretation of Shari'a supports equality of men and women, and complete freedom of choice in matters of faith and religion, both of which are in accordance with the constitutional principle of equality before the law. An-Na'im writes:

> The Qur'an does not mention constitutionalism, but human rational thinking and experience have shown that constitutionalism is necessary for realizing the just and good society prescribed by the Qur'an.

> An Islamic justification and support for constitutionalism is important and relevant for Muslims. Non-Muslims may have their own secular or other justifications. As long as all are agreed on the principle and specific rules of constitutionalism, including complete equality and non-discrimination on grounds of gender or religion, each may have his or her own reasons for coming to that agreement.

Id at 100. (This is a perfect example of overlapping consensus.) I thank Akeel Bilgrami for informing me of An-Na'im's work. I also owe thanks to Roy Mottahedeh for valuable discussion.

[47] See § 4.3.

introduced in public political discussion at any time, provided
that in due course proper political reasons—and not reasons
given solely by comprehensive doctrines—are presented that are
sufficient to support whatever the comprehensive doctrines introduced are said to support. This injunction to present proper
political reasons I refer to as *the proviso,* and it specifies public
political culture as distinct from the background culture.[48] The
second aspect I consider is that there may be positive reasons for
introducing comprehensive doctrines into public political discussion. I take up these two aspects in turn.

Obviously, many questions may be raised about how to satisfy the proviso.[49] One is: when does it need to be satisfied? On
the same day or some later day? Also, on whom does the obligation to honor it fall? It is important that it be clear and established that the proviso is to be appropriately satisfied in good
faith. Yet the details about how to satisfy this proviso must be
worked out in practice and cannot feasibly be governed by a clear
family of rules given in advance. How they work out is determined by the nature of the public political culture and calls for
good sense and understanding. It is important also to observe
that the introduction into public political culture of religious and
secular doctrines, provided the proviso is met, does not change
the nature and content of justification in public reason itself.
This justification is still given in terms of a family of reasonable
political conceptions of justice. However, there are no restrictions
or requirements on how religious or secular doctrines are themselves to be expressed; these doctrines need not, for example, be
by some standards logically correct, or open to rational appraisal,
or evidentially supportable.[50] Whether they are or not is a matter
to be decided by those presenting them, and how they want what
they say to be taken. They will normally have practical reasons
for wanting to make their views acceptable to a broader audience.

2. Citizens' mutual knowledge of one another's religious and
nonreligious doctrines expressed in the wide view of public political culture[51] recognizes that the roots of democratic citizens' allegiance to their political conceptions lie in their respective com-

---

[48] Rawls, *Political Liberalism,* lecture I, § 2.3 at 13-14 (cited in note 1) (contrasting
public political culture with background culture).

[49] I am indebted here to valuable discussion with Dennis Thompson.

[50] Greenawalt discusses Franklin Gamwell and Michael Perry, who do evidently impose such constraints on how religion is to be presented. See Greenawalt, *Private Consciences and Public Reasons* at 85-95 (cited in note 35).

[51] Again, as always, in distinction from the background culture, where I emphasize
there are no restrictions.

prehensive doctrines, both religious and nonreligious. In this way citizens' allegiance to the democratic ideal of public reason is strengthened for the right reasons. We may think of the reasonable comprehensive doctrines that support society's reasonable political conceptions as those conceptions' vital social basis, giving them enduring strength and vigor. When these doctrines accept the proviso and only then come into political debate, the commitment to constitutional democracy is publicly manifested.[52] Made aware of this commitment, government officials and citizens are more willing to honor the duty of civility, and their following the ideal of public reason helps foster the kind of society that ideal exemplifies. These benefits of the mutual knowledge of citizens' recognizing one another's reasonable comprehensive doctrines bring out a positive ground for introducing such doctrines, which is not merely a defensive ground, as if their intrusion into public discussion were inevitable in any case.

Consider, for example, a highly contested political issue—the issue of public support for church schools.[53] Those on different sides are likely to come to doubt one another's allegiance to basic constitutional and political values. It is wise, then, for all sides to introduce their comprehensive doctrines, whether religious or secular, so as to open the way for them to explain to one another how their views do indeed support those basic political values. Consider also the Abolitionists and those in the Civil Rights Movement.[54] The proviso was fulfilled in their cases, however

---

[52] Political liberalism is sometimes criticized for not itself developing accounts of these social roots of democracy and setting out the formation of its religious and other supports. Yet political liberalism does recognize these social roots and stresses their importance. Obviously the political conceptions of toleration and freedom of religion would be impossible in a society in which religious freedom were not honored and cherished. Thus, political liberalism agrees with David Hollenbach, S.J., when he writes:

> Not the least important of [the transformations brought about by Aquinas] was his insistence that the political life of a people is not the highest realization of the good of which they are capable—an insight that lies at the root of constitutional theories of limited government. And though the Church resisted the liberal discovery of modern freedoms through much of the modern period, liberalism has been transforming Catholicism once again through the last half of our own century. The memory of these events in social and intellectual history as well as the experience of the Catholic Church since the Second Vatican Council leads me to hope that communities holding different visions of the good life can get somewhere if they are willing to risk conversation and argument about these visions.

David Hollenbach, S.J., *Contexts of the Political Role of Religion: Civil Society and Culture*, 30 San Diego L Rev 877, 891 (1993). While a conception of public reason must recognize the significance of these social roots of constitutional democracy and note how they strengthen its vital institutions, it need not itself undertake a study of these matters. For the need to consider this point I am indebted to Paul Weithman.

[53] See Rawls, *Political Liberalism*, lecture VI, § 8.2 at 248-49 (cited in note 1).

[54] See id, lecture VI, § 8.3 at 249-51. I do not know whether the Abolitionists and King

much they emphasized the religious roots of their doctrines, because these doctrines supported basic constitutional values—as they themselves asserted—and so supported reasonable conceptions of political justice.

3. Public reasoning aims for public justification. We appeal to political conceptions of justice, and to ascertainable evidence and facts open to public view, in order to reach conclusions about what we think are the most reasonable political institutions and policies. Public justification is not simply valid reasoning, but argument addressed to others: it proceeds correctly from premises we accept and think others could reasonably accept to conclusions we think they could also reasonably accept. This meets the duty of civility, since in due course the proviso is satisfied.

There are two other forms of discourse that may also be mentioned, though neither expresses a form of public reasoning. One is declaration: here we each declare our own comprehensive doctrine, religious or nonreligious. This we do not expect others to share. Rather, each of us shows how, from our own doctrines, we can and do endorse a reasonable public political conception of justice with its principles and ideals. The aim of doing this is to declare to others who affirm different comprehensive doctrines that we also each endorse a reasonable political conception belonging to the family of reasonable such conceptions. On the wide view, citizens of faith who cite the Gospel parable of the Good Samaritan do not stop there, but go on to give a public justification for this parable's conclusions in terms of political values.[55] In this way citizens who hold different doctrines are reassured, and this strengthens the ties of civic friendship.[56]

The second form is conjecture, defined thus: we argue from what we believe, or conjecture, are other people's basic doctrines, religious or secular, and try to show them that, despite what they might think, they can still endorse a reasonable political conception that can provide a basis for public reasons. The ideal of pub-

---

thought of themselves as fulfilling the purpose of the proviso. But whether they did or not, they could have. And had they known and accepted the idea of public reason, they would have. I thank Paul Weithman for this point.

[55] Luke 10:29-37. It is easy to see how the Gospel story could be used to support the imperfect moral duty of mutual aid, as found, say, in Kant's fourth example in the *Grundlegung*. See Immanuel Kant, *Groundwork for the Metaphysics of Morals* AK 4:423, in Mary Gregor, trans, *Practical Philosophy* (Cambridge 1996). To formulate a suitable example in terms of political values only, consider a variant of the difference principle or of some other analogous idea. The principle could be seen as giving a special concern for the poor, as in the Catholic social doctrine. See John Rawls, *A Theory of Justice* § 13 (Belknap 1971) (defining the difference principle).

[56] For the relevance of this form of discourse I am indebted to discussion with Charles Larmore.

lic reason is thereby strengthened. However, it is important that conjecture be sincere and not manipulative. We must openly explain our intentions and state that we do not assert the premises from which we argue, but that we proceed as we do to clear up what we take to be a misunderstanding on others' part, and perhaps equally on ours.[57]

§ 5: ON THE FAMILY AS PART OF THE BASIC STRUCTURE

1. To illustrate further the use and scope of public reason, I shall now consider a range of questions about a single institution, the family.[58] I do this by using a particular political conception of justice and looking at the role that it assigns to the family in the basic structure of society. Since the content of public reason is determined by all the reasonable political conceptions that satisfy the criterion of reciprocity, the range of questions about the family covered by this political conception will indicate the ample space for debate and argument comprehended by public reason as a whole.

---

[57] I will mention another form of discourse that I call witnessing: it typically occurs in an ideal, politically well ordered, and fully just society in which all votes are the result of citizens' voting in accordance with their most reasonable conception of political justice. Nevertheless, it may happen that some citizens feel they must express their principled dissent from existing institutions, policies, or enacted legislation. I assume that Quakers accept constitutional democracy and abide by its legitimate law, yet at the same time may reasonably express the religious basis of their pacifism. (The parallel case of Catholic opposition to abortion is mentioned in § 6.1.) Yet witnessing differs from civil disobedience in that it does not appeal to principles and values of a (liberal) political conception of justice. While on the whole these citizens endorse reasonable political conceptions of justice supporting a constitutional democratic society, in this case they nevertheless feel they must not only let other citizens know the deep basis of their strong opposition but must also bear witness to their faith by doing so. At the same time, those bearing witness accept the idea of public reason. While they may think the outcome of a vote on which all reasonable citizens have conscientiously followed public reason to be incorrect or not true, they nevertheless recognize it as legitimate law and accept the obligation not to violate it. In such a society there is strictly speaking no case for civil disobedience and conscientious refusal. The latter requires what I have called a nearly just, but not fully just, society. See Rawls, *A Theory of Justice* § 55 (cited in note 55).

[58] I have thought that J.S. Mill's landmark *The Subjection of Women* (1869), in 21 *Collected Works of John Stuart Mill* 259 (cited in note 36), made clear that a decent liberal conception of justice (including what I called justice as fairness) implied equal justice for women as well as men. Admittedly, *A Theory of Justice* should have been more explicit about this, but that was a fault of mine and not of political liberalism itself. I have been encouraged to think that a liberal account of equal justice for women is viable by Susan Moller Okin, *Justice, Gender, and the Family* (Basic Books 1989); Linda C. McClain, *"Atomistic Man" Revisited: Liberalism, Connection, and Feminist Jurisprudence*, 65 S Cal L Rev 1171 (1992); Martha Nussbaum, *Sex and Social Justice* (Oxford forthcoming 1998) (a collection of her essays from 1990 to 1996, including *The Feminist Critique of Liberalism*, her Oxford Amnesty Lecture for 1996); and Sharon A. Lloyd, *Situating a Feminist Criticism of John Rawls's* Political Liberalism, 28 Loyola LA L Rev 1319 (1995). I have gained greatly from their writings.

The family is part of the basic structure, since one of its main roles is to be the basis of the orderly production and reproduction of society and its culture from one generation to the next. Political society is always regarded as a scheme of social cooperation over time indefinitely; the idea of a future time when its affairs are to be concluded and society disbanded is foreign to the conception of political society. Thus, reproductive labor is socially necessary labor. Accepting this, a central role of the family is to arrange in a reasonable and effective way the raising of and caring for children, ensuring their moral development and education into the wider culture.[59] Citizens must have a sense of justice and the political virtues that support political and social institutions. The family must ensure the nurturing and development of such citizens in appropriate numbers to maintain an enduring society.[60]

These requirements limit all arrangements of the basic structure, including efforts to achieve equality of opportunity. The family imposes constraints on ways in which this goal can be achieved, and the principles of justice are stated to try to take these constraints into account. I cannot pursue these complexities here, but assume that as children we grow up in a small intimate group in which elders (normally parents) have a certain moral and social authority.

2. In order for public reason to apply to the family, it must be seen, in part at least, as a matter for political justice. It may be thought that this is not so, that the principles of justice do not apply to the family and hence those principles do not secure equal justice for women and their children.[61] This is a misconception. It may arise as follows: the primary subject of political justice is the basic structure of society understood as the arrangement of society's main institutions into a unified system of social cooperation over time. The principles of political justice are to apply directly to this structure, but are not to apply directly to the internal life of the many associations within it, the family among them. Thus, some may think that if those principles do

---

[59] Rawls, *A Theory of Justice* §§ 70-76 (cited in note 55) (discussing the stages of moral development and their relevance to justice as fairness).

[60] However, no particular form of the family (monogamous, heterosexual, or otherwise) is required by a political conception of justice so long as the family is arranged to fulfill these tasks effectively and doesn't run afoul of other political values. Note that this observation sets the way in which justice as fairness deals with the question of gay and lesbian rights and duties, and how they affect the family. If these rights and duties are consistent with orderly family life and the education of children, they are, *ceteris paribus*, fully admissible.

[61] See Okin, *Justice, Gender, and the Family* at 90-93 (cited in note 58).

not apply directly to the internal life of families, they cannot ensure equal justice for wives along with their husbands.

Much the same question arises in regard to all associations, whether they be churches or universities, professional or scientific associations, business firms or labor unions. The family is not peculiar in this respect. To illustrate: it is clear that liberal principles of political justice do not require ecclesiastical governance to be democratic. Bishops and cardinals need not be elected; nor need the benefits attached to a church's hierarchy of offices satisfy a specified distributive principle, certainly not the difference principle.[62] This shows how the principles of political justice do not apply to the internal life of a church, nor is it desirable, or consistent with liberty of conscience or freedom of association, that they should.

On the other hand, the principles of political justice do impose certain essential constraints that bear on ecclesiastical governance. Churches cannot practice effective intolerance, since, as the principles of justice require, public law does not recognize heresy and apostasy as crimes, and members of churches are always at liberty to leave their faith. Thus, although the principles of justice do not apply directly to the internal life of churches, they do protect the rights and liberties of their members by the constraints to which all churches and associations are subject. This is not to deny that there are appropriate conceptions of justice that do apply directly to most if not all associations and groups, as well as to various kinds of relationships among individuals. Yet these conceptions of justice are not political conceptions. In each case, what is the appropriate conception is a separate and additional question, to be considered anew in each particular instance, given the nature and role of the relevant association, group, or relation.

Now consider the family. Here the idea is the same: political principles do not apply directly to its internal life, but they do impose essential constraints on the family as an institution and so guarantee the basic rights and liberties, and the freedom and opportunities, of all its members. This they do, as I have said, by specifying the basic rights of equal citizens who are the members of families. The family as part of the basic structure cannot violate these freedoms. Since wives are equally citizens with their husbands, they have all the same basic rights, liberties, and opportunities as their husbands; and this, together with the correct

---

[62] The difference principle is defined in Rawls, *A Theory of Justice* § 13 (cited in note 55).

790   *The University of Chicago Law Review*   [64:765

application of the other principles of justice, suffices to secure their equality and independence.

To put the case another way, we distinguish between the point of view of people as citizens and their point of view as members of families and of other associations.[63] As citizens we have reasons to impose the constraints specified by the political principles of justice on associations; while as members of associations we have reasons for limiting those constraints so that they leave room for a free and flourishing internal life appropriate to the association in question. Here again we see the need for the division of labor between different kinds of principles. We wouldn't want political principles of justice—including principles of distributive justice—to apply directly to the internal life of the family.

These principles do not inform us how to raise our children, and we are not required to treat our children in accordance with political principles. Here those principles are out of place. Surely parents must follow some conception of justice (or fairness) and due respect with regard to their children, but, within certain limits, this is not for political principles to prescribe. Clearly the prohibition of abuse and neglect of children, and much else, will, as constraints, be a vital part of family law. But at some point society has to rely on the natural affection and goodwill of the mature family members.[64]

Just as the principles of justice require that wives have all the rights of citizens, the principles of justice impose constraints on the family on behalf of children who as society's future citizens have basic rights as such. A long and historic injustice to women is that they have borne, and continue to bear, an unjust share of the task of raising, nurturing, and caring for their children. When they are even further disadvantaged by the laws regulating divorce, this burden makes them highly vulnerable. These injustices bear harshly not only on women but also on their children; and they tend to undermine children's capacity to acquire the political virtues required of future citizens in a viable democratic society. Mill held that the family in his day was a school for male despotism: it inculcated habits of thought and ways of feeling and conduct incompatible with democracy.[65] If so,

---

[63] I borrow this thought from Joshua Cohen, *Okin on Justice, Gender, and Family*, 22 Can J Phil 263, 278 (1992).

[64] Michael Sandel supposes the two principles of justice as fairness to hold generally for associations, including families. See Michael J. Sandel, *Liberalism and the Limits of Justice* 30-34 (Cambridge 1982).

[65] Mill, *Subjection of Women* ch 2 at 283-98 (cited in note 58).

the principles of justice enjoining a reasonable constitutional democratic society can plainly be invoked to reform the family.

3. More generally, when political liberalism distinguishes between political justice that applies to the basic structure and other conceptions of justice that apply to the various associations within that structure, it does not regard the political and the nonpolitical domains as two separate, disconnected spaces, each governed solely by its own distinct principles. Even if the basic structure alone is the primary subject of justice, the principles of justice still put essential restrictions on the family and all other associations. The adult members of families and other associations are equal citizens first: that is their basic position. No institution or association in which they are involved can violate their rights as citizens.

A domain so-called, or a sphere of life, is not, then, something already given apart from political conceptions of justice. A domain is not a kind of space, or place, but rather is simply the result, or upshot, of how the principles of political justice are applied, directly to the basic structure and indirectly to the associations within it. The principles defining the equal basic liberties and opportunities of citizens always hold in and through all so-called domains. The equal rights of women and the basic rights of their children as future citizens are inalienable and protect them wherever they are. Gender distinctions limiting those rights and liberties are excluded.[66] So the spheres of the political and the public, of the nonpublic and the private, fall out from the content and application of the conception of justice and its principles. If the so-called private sphere is alleged to be a space exempt from justice, then there is no such thing.

The basic structure is a single social system, each part of which may influence the rest. Its basic principles of political justice specify all its main parts and its basic rights reach throughout. The family is only one part (though a major part) of the system that produces a social division of labor based on gender over time. Some have argued that discrimination against women in the marketplace is the key to the historical gendered division of labor in the family. The resulting wage differences between the genders make it economically sensible that mothers spend more time with their children than fathers do. On the other hand, some believe that the family itself is the linchpin[67] of gender in-

---

[66] Rawls, *A Theory of Justice* § 16 at 99 (cited in note 55).

[67] This is Okin's term. See Okin, *Justice, Gender, and the Family* at 6, 14, 170 (cited in note 58).

justice. However, a liberal conception of justice may have to allow for some traditional gendered division of labor within families—assume, say, that this division is based on religion—provided it is fully voluntary and does not result from or lead to injustice. To say that this division of labor is in this case fully voluntary means that it is adopted by people on the basis of their religion, which from a political point of view is voluntary,[68] and not because various other forms of discrimination elsewhere in the social system make it rational and less costly for husband and wife to follow a gendered division of labor in the family.

Some want a society in which division of labor by gender is reduced to a minimum. But for political liberalism, this cannot mean that such division is forbidden. One cannot propose that equal division of labor in the family be simply mandated, or its absence in some way penalized at law for those who do not adopt it. This is ruled out because the division of labor in question is connected with basic liberties, including the freedom of religion. Thus, to try to minimize gendered division of labor means, in political liberalism, to try to reach a social condition in which the remaining division of labor is voluntary. This allows in principle that considerable gendered division of labor may persist. It is only involuntary division of labor that is to be reduced to zero.

Hence the family is a crucial case for seeing whether the single system—the basic structure—affords equal justice to both men and women. If the gendered division of labor in the family is indeed fully voluntary, then there is reason to think that the single system realizes fair equality of opportunity for both genders.

4. Since a democracy aims for full equality for all its citizens, and so of women, it must include arrangements to achieve it. If a basic, if not the main, cause of women's inequality is their greater share in the bearing, nurturing, and caring for children in the traditional division of labor within the family, steps need to be taken either to equalize their share, or to compensate them

---

[68] On this point, see Rawls, *Political Liberalism*, lecture VI, § 3.2 at 221-22 (cited in note 1). Whether it is properly voluntary, and if so, under what conditions, is a disputed question. Briefly, the question involves the distinction between the reasonable and the rational explained thus: an action is voluntary in one sense, but it may not be voluntary in another. It may be voluntary in the sense of rational: doing the rational thing in the circumstances even when these involve unfair conditions; or an action may be voluntary in the sense of reasonable: doing the rational thing when all the surrounding conditions are also fair. Clearly the text interprets "voluntary" in the second sense: affirming one's religion is voluntary when all of the surrounding conditions are reasonable, or fair. In these remarks I have assumed that the subjective conditions of voluntariness (whatever they may be) are present and have only noted the objective ones. A full discussion would lead us far afield.

for it.[69] How best to do this in particular historical conditions is not for political philosophy to decide. But a now common proposal is that as a norm or guideline, the law should count a wife's work in raising children (when she bears that burden as is still common) as entitling her to an equal share in the income that her husband earns during their marriage. Should there be a divorce, she should have an equal share in the increased value of the family's assets during that time.

Any departure from this norm would require a special and clear justification. It seems intolerably unjust that a husband may depart the family taking his earning power with him and leaving his wife and children far less advantaged than before. Forced to fend for themselves, their economic position is often precarious. A society that permits this does not care about women, much less about their equality, or even about their children, who are its future.

The crucial question may be what precisely is covered by gender-structured institutions. How are their lines drawn? If we say the gender system includes whatever social arrangements adversely affect the equal basic liberties and opportunities of women, as well as those of their children as future citizens, then surely that system is subject to critique by the principles of justice. The question then becomes whether the fulfillment of these principles suffices to remedy the gender system's faults. The remedy depends in part on social theory and human psychology, and much else. It cannot be settled by a conception of justice alone.

In concluding these remarks on the family, I should say that I have not tried to argue fully for particular conclusions. Rather, to repeat, I have simply wanted to illustrate how a political conception of justice and its ordering of political values apply to a single institution of the basic structure and can cover many (if not all) of its various aspects. As I have said, these values are given an order within the particular political conception to which they are attached.[70] Among these values are the freedom and equality of women, the equality of children as future citizens, the freedom of religion, and finally, the value of the family in securing the orderly production and reproduction of society and of its culture from one generation to the next. These values provide

---

[69] See Victor R. Fuchs, *Women's Quest for Economic Equality* (Harvard 1988). Chapters 3 and 4 summarize the evidence for saying the main cause is not, as it is often said, employer discrimination, while chapters 7 and 8 propose what is to be done.

[70] See § 2.3.

public reasons for all citizens. So much is claimed not only for justice as fairness but for any reasonable political conception.

§ 6: QUESTIONS ABOUT PUBLIC REASON

I now turn to various questions and doubts about the idea of public reason and try to allay them.

1. First, it may be objected that the idea of public reason would unreasonably limit the topics and considerations available for political argument and debate, and that we should adopt instead what we may call the open view with no constraints. I now discuss two examples to rebut this objection.

(a) One reason for thinking public reason is too restrictive is to suppose that it mistakenly tries to settle political questions in advance. To explain this objection, let's consider the question of school prayer. It might be thought that a liberal position on this question would deny its admissibility in public schools. But why so? We have to consider all the political values that can be invoked to settle this question and on which side the decisive reasons fall. The famous debate in 1784-1785 between Patrick Henry and James Madison over the establishment of the Anglican Church in Virginia and involving religion in the schools was argued almost entirely by reference to political values alone. Henry's argument for establishment was based on the view that:

> Christian knowledge hath a natural tendency to correct the morals of men, restrain their vices, and preserve the peace of society, which cannot be effected without a competent provision for learned teachers . . . .[71]

Henry did not seem to argue for Christian knowledge as good in itself but rather as an effective way to achieve basic political values, namely, the good and peaceable conduct of citizens. Thus, I take him to mean by "vices," at least in part, those actions contrary to the political virtues found in political liberalism,[72] and expressed by other conceptions of democracy.

Leaving aside the obvious difficulty of whether prayers can be composed that satisfy all the needed restrictions of political

---

[71] See Thomas J. Curry, *The First Freedoms: Church and State in America to the Passage of the First Amendment* 139-48 (Oxford 1986). The quoted language, which appears in id at 140, is from the preamble to the proposed "Bill Establishing a Provision for Teachers of the Christian Religion" (1784). Note that the popular Patrick Henry also provided the most serious opposition to Jefferson's "Bill for Establishing Religious Freedom" (1779), which won out when reintroduced in the Virginia Assembly in 1786. Curry, *The First Freedoms* at 146.

[72] For a discussion of these virtues, see Rawls, *Political Liberalism*, lecture V, § 5.4 at 194-95 (cited in note 1).

justice, Madison's objections to Henry's bill turned largely on whether religious establishment was necessary to support orderly civil society. He concluded it was not. Madison's objections depended also on the historical effects of establishment both on society and on the integrity of religion itself. He was acquainted with the prosperity of colonies that had no establishment, notably Pennsylvania; he cited the strength of early Christianity in opposition to the hostile Roman Empire, and the corruption of past establishments.[73] With some care, many if not all of these arguments can be expressed in terms of the political values of public reason.

Of special interest in the example of school prayer is that it brings out that the idea of public reason is not a view about specific political institutions or policies. Rather, it is a view about the kind of reasons on which citizens are to rest their political cases in making their political justifications to one another when they support laws and policies that invoke the coercive powers of government concerning fundamental political questions. Also of special interest in this example is that it serves to emphasize that the principles that support the separation of church and state should be such that they can be affirmed by all free and equal citizens, given the fact of reasonable pluralism.

The reasons for the separation of church and state are these, among others: It protects religion from the state and the state from religion; it protects citizens from their churches[74] and citizens from one another. It is a mistake to say that political liberalism is an individualist political conception, since its aim is the protection of the various interests in liberty, both associational and individual. And it is also a grave error to think that the separation of church and state is primarily for the protection of secular culture; of course it does protect that culture, but no more so than it protects all religions. The vitality and wide acceptance

---

[73] See James Madison, *Memorial and Remonstrance* (1785), in *The Mind of the Founder* 8-16 (Bobbs-Merrill 1973) (Marvin Meyers, ed). Paragraph 6 refers to the vigor of early Christianity in opposition to the empire, while paragraphs 7 and 11 refer to the mutually corrupting influence of past establishments on both state and religion. In the correspondence between Madison and William Bradford of Pennsylvania, whom he met at Princeton (College of New Jersey), the freedom and prosperity of Pennsylvania without an establishment is praised and celebrated. See 1 *The Papers of James Madison* (Chicago 1962) (William T. Hutchinson and William M.E. Rachal, eds). See especially Madison's letters of 1 December 1773, id at 100-01; 24 January 1774, id at 104-06; and 1 April 1774, id at 111-13. A letter of Bradford's to Madison, 4 March 1774, refers to liberty as the genius of Pennsylvania. Id at 109. Madison's arguments were similar to those of Tocqueville I mention below. See also Curry, *The First Freedoms* at 142-48 (cited in note 71).

[74] It does this by protecting the freedom to change one's faith. Heresy and apostasy are not crimes.

of religion in America is often commented upon, as if it were a sign of the peculiar virtue of the American people. Perhaps so, but it may also be connected with the fact that in this country the various religions have been protected by the First Amendment from the state, and none has been able to dominate and suppress the other religions by the capture and use of state power.[75] While some have no doubt entertained that aim since the early days of the Republic, it has not been seriously tried. Indeed, Tocqueville thought that among the main causes of the strength of democracy in this country was the separation of church and state.[76] Po-

---

[75] What I refer to here is the fact that from the early days of the Emperor Constantine in the fourth century Christianity punished heresy and tried to stamp out by persecution and religious wars what it regarded as false doctrine (for example, the crusade against the Albigenses led by Innocent III in the 13th century). To do this required the coercive powers of the state. Instituted by Pope Gregory IX, the Inquisition was active throughout the Wars of Religion in the 16th and 17th centuries. While most of the American Colonies had known establishments of some kind (Congregationalist in New England, Episcopalian in the South), the United States, thanks to the plurality of its religious sects and the First Amendment which they endorsed, never did. A persecuting zeal has been the great curse of the Christian religion. It was shared by Luther and Calvin and the Protestant Reformers, and it was not radically changed in the Catholic Church until Vatican II. In the Council's Declaration on Religious Freedom—*Dignitatis Humanae*—the Catholic Church committed itself to the principle of religious freedom as found in a constitutional democratic regime. It declared the ethical doctrine of religious freedom resting on the dignity of the human person; a political doctrine with respect to the limits of government in religious matters; a theological doctrine of the freedom of the Church in its relations to the political and social world. All persons, whatever their faith, have the right of religious liberty on the same terms. *Declaration on Religious Freedom (Dignitatis Humanae): On the Right of the Person and of Communities to Social and Civil Freedom in Matters Religious* (1965), in Walter Abbott, S.J., ed, *The Documents of Vatican II* 675, 692-96 (Geoffrey Chapman 1966). As John Courtney Murray, S.J., said: "A long-standing ambiguity had finally been cleared up. The Church does not deal with the secular order in terms of a double standard—freedom for the Church when Catholics are in the minority, privilege for the Church and intolerance for others when Catholics are a majority." John Courtney Murray, S.J., *Religious Freedom*, in Abbott, ed, *Documents of Vatican II* at 672, 673. See also the instructive discussion by Paul E. Sigmund, *Catholicism and Liberal Democracy*, in R. Bruce Douglas and David Hollenbach, S.J., eds, *Catholicism and Liberalism: Contributions to American Public Philosophy* (Cambridge 1994). See especially id at 233-39.

[76] Alexis de Tocqueville, 1 *Democracy in America* 294-301 (Perennial Library 1988) (J.P. Mayer, ed, George Lawrence, trans). In discussing "The Main Causes That Make Religion Powerful in America," Tocqueville says the Catholic priests "all thought that the main reason for the quiet sway of religion over their country was the complete separation of church and state. I have no hesitation in stating that throughout my stay in America I met nobody, lay or cleric, who did not agree about that." Id at 295. He continues:

> There have been religions intimately linked to earthly governments, dominating men's souls both by terror and by faith; but when a religion makes such an alliance, I am not afraid to say that it makes the same mistake as any man might; it sacrifices the future for the present, and by gaining a power to which it has no claim, it risks its legitimate authority. . . .

> Hence religion cannot share the material strength of the rulers without being burdened with some of the animosity roused against them.

Id at 297. He remarks that these observations apply all the more to a democratic country,

litical liberalism agrees with many other liberal views in accepting this proposition.[77] Some citizens of faith have felt that this separation is hostile to religion and have sought to change it. In doing this I believe they fail to grasp a main cause of the strength of religion in this country and, as Tocqueville says, seem ready to jeopardize it for temporary gains in political power.

(b) Others may think that public reason is too restrictive because it may lead to a stand-off[78] and fail to bring about decisions on disputed issues. A stand-off in some sense may indeed happen, not only in moral and political reasoning but in all forms of reasoning, including science and common sense. Nevertheless, this is irrelevant. The relevant comparison is to those situations in which legislators enacting laws and judges deciding cases must make decisions. Here some political rule of action must be laid down and all must be able reasonably to endorse the process by which a decision is reached. Recall that public reason sees the office of citizen with its duty of civility as analogous to that of judge with its duty of deciding cases. Just as judges are to decide cases by legal grounds of precedent, recognized canons of statutory interpretation, and other relevant grounds, so citizens are to reason by public reason and to be guided by the criterion of reciprocity, whenever constitutional essentials and matters of basic justice are at stake.

Thus, when there seems to be a stand-off, that is, when legal arguments seem evenly balanced on both sides, judges cannot resolve the case simply by appealing to their own political views. To do that is for judges to violate their duty. The same holds with public reason: if, when stand-offs occur, citizens simply invoke grounding reasons of their comprehensive views,[79] the principle of reciprocity is violated. From the point of view of public reason, citizens must vote for the ordering of political values they sincerely think the most reasonable. Otherwise they fail to exercise political power in ways that satisfy the criterion of reciprocity.

---

for in that case when religion seeks political power it will attach itself to a particular party and be burdened by hostility to it. Id at 298. Referring to the cause of the decline of religion in Europe, he concludes, "I am profoundly convinced that this accidental and particular cause is the close union of politics and religion. . . . European Christianity has allowed itself to be intimately united with the powers of this world." Id at 300-01. Political liberalism accepts Tocqueville's view and sees it as explaining, so far as possible, the basis of peace among comprehensive doctrines both religious and secular.

[77] In this it agrees with Locke, Montesquieu, and Constant; Kant, Hegel, and Mill.

[78] I take the term from Philip Quinn. The idea appears in Rawls, *Political Liberalism*, lecture VI, § 7.1-2 at 240-41 (cited in note 1).

[79] I use the term "grounding reasons" since many who might appeal to these reasons view them as the proper grounds, or the true basis—religious, philosophical, or moral—of the ideals and principles of public reasons and political conceptions of justice.

In particular, when hotly disputed questions, such as that of abortion, arise which may lead to a stand-off between different political conceptions, citizens must vote on the question according to their complete ordering of political values.[80] Indeed, this is a normal case: unanimity of views is not to be expected. Reasonable political conceptions of justice do not always lead to the same conclusion;[81] nor do citizens holding the same conception always agree on particular issues. Yet the outcome of the vote, as I said before, is to be seen as legitimate provided all government officials, supported by other reasonable citizens, of a reasonably just constitutional regime sincerely vote in accordance with the idea of public reason. This doesn't mean the outcome is true or correct, but that it is reasonable and legitimate law, binding on citizens by the majority principle.

Some may, of course, reject a legitimate decision, as Roman Catholics may reject a decision to grant a right to abortion. They may present an argument in public reason for denying it and fail to win a majority.[82] But they need not themselves exercise the

---

[80] Some have quite naturally read the footnote in Rawls, *Political Liberalism*, lecture VI, § 7.2 at 243-44 (cited in note 1), as an argument for the right to abortion in the first trimester. I do not intend it to be one. (It does express my opinion, but my opinion is not an argument.) I was in error in leaving it in doubt whether the aim of the footnote was only to illustrate and confirm the following statement in the text to which the footnote is attached: "The only comprehensive doctrines that run afoul of public reason are those that cannot support a reasonable balance [or ordering] of political values [on the issue]." To try to explain what I meant, I used three political values (of course, there are more) for the troubled issue of the right to abortion to which it might seem improbable that political values could apply at all. I believe a more detailed interpretation of those values may, when properly developed in public reason, yield a reasonable argument. I don't say the most reasonable or decisive argument; I don't know what that would be, or even if it exists. (For an example of such a more detailed interpretation, see Judith Jarvis Thomson, *Abortion*, 20 Boston Rev 11 (Summer 1995), though I would want to add several addenda to it.) Suppose now, for purposes of illustration, that there is a reasonable argument in public reason for the right to abortion but there is no equally reasonable balance, or ordering, of the political values in public reason that argues for the denial of that right. Then in this kind of case, but only in this kind of case, does a comprehensive doctrine denying the right to abortion run afoul of public reason. However, if it can satisfy the proviso of the wide public reason better, or at least as well as other views, it has made its case in public reason. Of course, a comprehensive doctrine can be unreasonable on one or several issues without being simply unreasonable.

[81] Rawls, *Political Liberalism*, lecture VI, § 7.1 at 240-41 (cited in note 1).

[82] For such an argument, see Cardinal Joseph Bernardin, *The Consistent Ethic: What Sort of Framework?*, 16 Origins 345, 347-50 (Oct 30, 1986). The idea of public order the Cardinal presents includes these three political values: public peace, essential protections of human rights, and the commonly accepted standards of moral behavior in a community of law. Further, he grants that not all moral imperatives are to be translated into prohibitive civil statutes and thinks it essential to the political and social order to protect human life and basic human rights. The denial of the right to abortion he hopes to justify on the basis of those three values. I don't of course assess his argument here, except to say it is clearly cast in some form of public reason. Whether it is itself reasonable or not, or more

right to abortion. They can recognize the right as belonging to legitimate law enacted in accordance with legitimate political institutions and public reason, and therefore not resist it with force. Forceful resistance is unreasonable: it would mean attempting to impose by force their own comprehensive doctrine that a majority of other citizens who follow public reason, not unreasonably, do not accept. Certainly Catholics may, in line with public reason, continue to argue against the right to abortion. Reasoning is not closed once and for all in public reason any more than it is closed in any form of reasoning. Moreover, that the Catholic Church's nonpublic reason requires its members to follow its doctrine is perfectly consistent with their also honoring public reason.[83]

I do not discuss the question of abortion in itself since my concern is not with that question but rather to stress that political liberalism does not hold that the ideal of public reason should always lead to a general agreement of views, nor is it a fault that it does not. Citizens learn and profit from debate and argument, and when their arguments follow public reason, they instruct society's political culture and deepen their understanding of one another even when agreement cannot be reached.

2. Some of the considerations underlying the stand-off objection lead to a more general objection to public reason, namely, that the content of the family of reasonable political conceptions of justice on which it is based is itself much too narrow. This objection insists that we should always present what we think are true or grounding reasons for our views. That is, the objection insists, we are bound to express the true, or the right, as seen from our comprehensive doctrines.

However, as I said in the Introduction, in public reason ideas of truth or right based on comprehensive doctrines are replaced by an idea of the politically reasonable addressed to citizens as citizens. This step is necessary to establish a basis of political reasoning that all can share as free and equal citizens. Since we are seeking public justifications for political and social institutions—for the basic structure of a political and social world—we

---

reasonable than the arguments on the other side, is another matter. As with any form of reasoning in public reason, the reasoning may be fallacious or mistaken.

[83] As far as I can see, this view is similar to Father John Courtney Murray's position about the stand the Church should take in regard to contraception in *We Hold These Truths: Catholic Reflections on the American Proposition* 157-58 (Sheed and Ward 1960). See also Mario Cuomo's lecture on abortion in his Notre Dame Lecture of 1984, in *More Than Words: The Speeches of Mario Cuomo* 32-51 (St Martin's 1993). I am indebted to Leslie Griffin and Paul Weithman for discussion and clarification about points involved in this and the preceding footnote and for acquainting me with Father Murray's view.

think of persons as citizens. This assigns to each person the same basic political position. In giving reasons to all citizens we don't view persons as socially situated or otherwise rooted, that is, as being in this or that social class, or in this or that property and income group, or as having this or that comprehensive doctrine. Nor are we appealing to each person's or each group's interests, though at some point we must take these interests into account. Rather, we think of persons as reasonable and rational, as free and equal citizens, with the two moral powers[84] and having, at any given moment, a determinate conception of the good, which may change over time. These features of citizens are implicit in their taking part in a fair system of social cooperation and seeking and presenting public justifications for their judgments on fundamental political questions.

I emphasize that this idea of public reason is fully compatible with the many forms of nonpublic reason.[85] These belong to the internal life of the many associations in civil society and they are not of course all the same; different nonpublic reasons of different religious associations shared by their members are not those of scientific societies. Since we seek a shareable public basis of justification for all citizens in society, giving justifications to particular persons and groups here and there until all are covered fails to do this. To speak of all persons in society is still too broad, unless we suppose that they are in their nature basically the same. In political philosophy one role of ideas about our nature has been to think of people in a standard, or canonical, fashion so that they might all accept the same kind of reasons.[86] In political liberalism, however, we try to avoid natural or psychological views of this kind, as well as theological or secular doctrines. Accounts of human nature we put aside and rely on a political conception of persons as citizens instead.

3. As I have stressed throughout, it is central to political liberalism that free and equal citizens affirm both a comprehensive doctrine and a political conception. However, the relation be-

---

[84] These two powers, the capacity for a conception of justice and the capacity for a conception of the good, are discussed in Rawls, *Political Liberalism* (cited in note 1). See especially id, lecture I, § 3.2 at 19, lecture II, § 7.1 at 81, lecture III, § 3.3 at 103-04, lecture III, § 4.1 at 108.

[85] Id, lecture VI, § 4 at 223-27.

[86] Sometimes the term "normalize" is used in this connection. For example, persons have certain fundamental interests of a religious or philosophical kind; or else certain basic needs of a natural kind. Again, they may have a certain typical pattern of self-realization. A Thomist will say that we always desire above all else, even if unknown to ourselves, the *Visio Dei*; a Platonist will say we strive for a vision of the good; a Marxist will say we aim for self-realization as species-beings.

tween a comprehensive doctrine and its accompanying political conception is easily misunderstood.

When political liberalism speaks of a reasonable overlapping consensus of comprehensive doctrines,[87] it means that all of these doctrines, both religious and nonreligious, support a political conception of justice underwriting a constitutional democratic society whose principles, ideals, and standards satisfy the criterion of reciprocity. Thus, all reasonable doctrines affirm such a society with its corresponding political institutions: equal basic rights and liberties for all citizens, including liberty of conscience and the freedom of religion.[88] On the other hand, comprehensive doctrines that cannot support such a democratic society are not reasonable. Their principles and ideals do not satisfy the criterion of reciprocity, and in various ways they fail to establish the equal basic liberties. As examples, consider the many fundamentalist religious doctrines, the doctrine of the divine right of monarchs and the various forms of aristocracy, and, not to be overlooked, the many instances of autocracy and dictatorship.

Moreover, a true judgment in a reasonable comprehensive doctrine never conflicts with a reasonable judgment in its related political conception. A reasonable judgment of the political conception must still be confirmed as true, or right, by the comprehensive doctrine. It is, of course, up to citizens themselves to affirm, revise, or change their comprehensive doctrines. Their doctrines may override or count for naught the political values of a constitutional democratic society. But then the citizens cannot claim that such doctrines are reasonable. Since the criterion of reciprocity is an essential ingredient specifying public reason and its content, political liberalism rejects as unreasonable all such doctrines.

In a reasonable comprehensive doctrine, in particular a religious one, the ranking of values may not be what we might expect. Thus, suppose we call *transcendent* such values as salvation and eternal life—the *Visio Dei*. This value, let's say, is higher, or superior to, the reasonable political values of a constitutional democratic society. These are worldly values and therefore on a different, and as it were lower, plane than those transcendent values. It doesn't follow, however, that these lower yet reasonable values are overridden by the transcendent values of the religious doctrine. In fact, a *reasonable* comprehensive doctrine is

---

[87] The idea of such a consensus is discussed at various places in Rawls, *Political Liberalism* (cited in note 1). See especially id, lecture IV, and consult the index.

[88] See id at xviii (paperback edition).

one in which they are not overridden; it is the unreasonable doctrines in which reasonable political values are overridden. This is
a consequence of the idea of the politically reasonable as set out
in political liberalism. Recall that it was said: In endorsing a constitutional democratic regime, a religious doctrine may say that
such are the limits God sets to our liberty.[89]

A further misunderstanding alleges that an argument in
public reason could not side with Lincoln against Douglas in
their debates of 1858.[90] But why not? Certainly they were debating fundamental political principles about the rights and wrongs
of slavery. Since the rejection of slavery is a clear case of securing
the constitutional essential of the equal basic liberties, surely
Lincoln's view was reasonable (even if not the most reasonable),
while Douglas's was not. Therefore, Lincoln's view is supported
by any reasonable comprehensive doctrine. It is no surprise,
then, that his view is in line with the religious doctrines of the
Abolitionists and the Civil Rights Movement. What could be a
better example to illustrate the force of public reason in political
life?[91]

4. A third general objection is that the idea of public reason
is unnecessary and serves no purpose in a well established constitutional democracy. Its limits and constraints are useful primarily when a society is sharply divided and contains many hostile religious associations and secular groups, each striving to become the controlling political force. In the political societies of the
European democracies and the United States these worries, so
the objection goes, are idle.

---

[89] See § 3.2. It is sometimes asked why political liberalism puts such a high value on
political values, as if one could only do that by assessing those values in comparison with
transcendent values. But this comparison political liberalism does not make, nor does it
need to make, as is observed in the text.

[90] On this, see Michael J. Sandel, *Review of* Political Liberalism, 107 Harv L Rev
1765, 1778-82 (1994), and more recently Michael J. Sandel, *Democracy's Discontent:
America in Search of a Public Philosophy* 21-23 (Belknap 1996).

[91] Perhaps some think that a political conception is not a matter of (moral) right and
wrong. If so, that is a mistake and is simply false. Political conceptions of justice are
themselves intrinsically moral ideas, as I have stressed from the outset. As such they are
a kind of normative value. On the other hand, some may think that the relevant political
conceptions are determined by how a people actually establish their existing institutions—the political given, as it were, by politics. Viewed in this light, the prevalence of
slavery in 1858 implies that Lincoln's criticisms of it were moral, a matter of right and
wrong, and certainly not a matter of politics. To say that the political is determined by a
people's politics may be a possible use of the term *political*. But then it ceases to be a
normative idea and it is no longer part of public reason. We must hold fast to the idea of
the political as a fundamental category and covering political conceptions of justice as intrinsic moral values.

However, this objection is incorrect and sociologically faulty. For without citizens' allegiance to public reason and their honoring the duty of civility, divisions and hostilities between doctrines are bound in time to assert themselves, should they not already exist. Harmony and concord among doctrines and a people's affirming public reason are unhappily not a permanent condition of social life. Rather, harmony and concord depend on the vitality of the public political culture and on citizens' being devoted to and realizing the ideal of public reason. Citizens could easily fall into bitterness and resentment, once they no longer see the point of affirming an ideal of public reason and come to ignore it.

To return to where we began in this Section: I do not know how to prove that public reason is not too restrictive, or whether its forms are properly described. I suspect it cannot be done. Yet this is not a serious problem if, as I believe, the large majority of cases fit the framework of public reason, and the cases that do not fit all have special features that both enable us to understand why they should cause difficulty and show us how to cope with them as they arise. This prompts the general questions of whether there are examples of important cases of constitutional essentials and basic justice that do not fit the framework of public reason, and if so, why they cause difficulty. In this paper I do not pursue these questions.

§ 7: Conclusion

1. Throughout, I have been concerned with a torturing question in the contemporary world, namely: Can democracy and comprehensive doctrines, religious or nonreligious, be compatible? And if so, how? At the moment a number of conflicts between religion and democracy raise this question. To answer it political liberalism makes the distinction between a self-standing political conception of justice and a comprehensive doctrine. A religious doctrine resting on the authority of the Church or the Bible is not, of course, a liberal comprehensive doctrine: its leading religious and moral values are not those, say, of Kant or Mill. Nevertheless, it may endorse a constitutional democratic society and recognize its public reason. Here it is basic that public reason is a political idea and belongs to the category of the political. Its content is given by the family of (liberal) political conceptions of justice satisfying the criterion of reciprocity. It does not trespass upon religious beliefs and injunctions insofar as these are consistent with the essential constitutional liberties, including the freedom of religion and liberty of conscience. There

is, or need be, no war between religion and democracy. In this respect political liberalism is sharply different from and rejects Enlightenment Liberalism, which historically attacked orthodox Christianity.

The conflicts between democracy and reasonable religious doctrines and among reasonable religious doctrines themselves are greatly mitigated and contained within the bounds of reasonable principles of justice in a constitutional democratic society. This mitigation is due to the idea of toleration, and I have distinguished between two such ideas.[92] One is purely political, being expressed in terms of the rights and duties protecting religious liberty in accordance with a reasonable political conception of justice.[93] The other is not purely political but expressed from within a religious or a nonreligious doctrine. However, a reasonable judgment of the political conception must still be confirmed as true, or right, by a reasonable comprehensive doctrine.[94] I assume, then, that a reasonable comprehensive doctrine accepts some form of the political argument for toleration. Of course, citizens may think that the grounding reasons for toleration and for the other elements of a constitutional democratic society are not political but rather are to be found in their religious or nonreligious doctrines. And these reasons, they may well say, are the true or the right reasons; and they may see the political reasons as superficial, the grounding ones as deep. Yet there is no conflict here, but simply concordant judgments made within political conceptions of justice on the one hand, and within comprehensive doctrines on the other.

There are limits, however, to reconciliation by public reason. Three main kinds of conflicts set citizens at odds: those deriving from irreconcilable comprehensive doctrines; those deriving from differences in status, class position, or occupation, or from differences in ethnicity, gender, or race; and finally, those deriving

---

[92] See § 3.2.

[93] See Rawls, *Political Liberalism*, lecture II, § 3.2-4 at 60-62 (cited in note 1). The main points can be set out in summary fashion as follows: (1) Reasonable persons do not all affirm the same comprehensive doctrine. This is said to be a consequence of the burdens of judgment. See note 95. (2) Many reasonable doctrines are affirmed, not all of which can be true or right (as judged from within a comprehensive doctrine). (3) It is not unreasonable to affirm any one of the reasonable comprehensive doctrines. (4) Others who affirm reasonable doctrines different from ours are, we grant, reasonable also, and certainly not for that reason unreasonable. (5) In going beyond recognizing the reasonableness of a doctrine and affirming our belief in it, we are not being unreasonable. (6) Reasonable persons think it unreasonable to use political power, should they possess it, to repress other doctrines that are reasonable yet different from their own.

[94] See § 6.3.

from the burdens of judgment.[95] Political liberalism concerns primarily the first kind of conflict. It holds that even though our comprehensive doctrines are irreconcilable and cannot be compromised, nevertheless citizens who affirm reasonable doctrines may share reasons of another kind, namely, public reasons given in terms of political conceptions of justice. I also believe that such a society can resolve the second kind of conflict, which deals with conflicts between citizens' fundamental interests—political, economic, and social. For once we accept reasonable principles of justice and recognize them to be reasonable (even if not the most reasonable), and know, or reasonably believe, that our political and social institutions satisfy them, the second kind of conflict need not arise, or arise so forcefully. Political liberalism does not explicitly consider these conflicts but leaves them to be considered by justice as fairness, or by some other reasonable conception of political justice. Finally, conflicts arising from the burdens of judgment always exist and limit the extent of possible agreement.

2. Reasonable comprehensive doctrines do not reject the essentials of a constitutional democratic polity.[96] Moreover, reasonable persons are characterized in two ways: First, they stand ready to offer fair terms of social cooperation between equals, and they abide by these terms if others do also, even should it be to their advantage not to;[97] second, reasonable persons recognize and accept the consequences of the burdens of judgment, which leads to the idea of reasonable toleration in a democratic society.[98] Finally we come to the idea of legitimate law, which reasonable citizens understand to apply to the general structure of political authority.[99] They know that in political life unanimity can rarely if ever be expected, so a reasonable democratic constitution must include majority or other plurality voting procedures in order to reach decisions.[100]

The idea of the politically reasonable is sufficient unto itself for the purposes of public reason when basic political questions are at stake. Of course, fundamentalist religious doctrines and

---

[95] These burdens are discussed in Rawls, *Political Liberalism*, lecture II, § 2 (cited in note 1). Roughly, they are sources or causes of reasonable disagreement between reasonable and rational persons. They involve balancing the weight of different kinds of evidence and kinds of values, and the like, and they affect both theoretical and practical judgments.

[96] Id at xviii.

[97] Id, lecture II, § 1.1 at 49-50.

[98] Id, lecture II, §§ 2-3.4 at 54-62.

[99] Id, lecture IV, § 1.2-3 at 135-37.

[100] Id, lecture IX, § 2.1 at 393.

autocratic and dictatorial rulers will reject the ideas of public reason and deliberative democracy. They will say that democracy leads to a culture contrary to their religion, or denies the values that only autocratic or dictatorial rule can secure.[101] They assert that the religiously true, or the philosophically true, overrides the politically reasonable. We simply say that such a doctrine is politically unreasonable. Within political liberalism nothing more need be said.

I noted in the beginning[102] the fact that every actual society, however dominant and controlling its reasonable citizens may be, will normally contain numerous unreasonable doctrines that are not compatible with a democratic society—either certain religious doctrines, such as fundamentalist religions, or certain non-religious (secular) doctrines, such as those of autocracy and dictatorship, of which our century offers hideous examples. How far unreasonable doctrines may be active and are to be tolerated in a constitutional democratic regime does not present a new and different question, despite the fact that in this account of public reason we have focused on the idea of the reasonable and the role of reasonable citizens. There is not one account of toleration for reasonable doctrines and another for unreasonable ones. Both cases are settled by the appropriate political principles of justice and the conduct those principles permit.[103] Unreasonable doctrines are a threat to democratic institutions, since it is impossible for them to abide by a constitutional regime except as a *modus vivendi*. Their existence sets a limit to the aim of fully realizing a reasonable democratic society with its ideal of public reason and the idea of legitimate law. This fact is not a defect or failure of the idea of public reason, but rather it indicates that there are limits to what public reason can accomplish. It does not diminish the great value and importance of attempting to realize that ideal to the fullest extent possible.

3. I end by pointing out the fundamental difference between *A Theory of Justice* and *Political Liberalism*. The first explicitly attempts to develop from the idea of the social contract, represented by Locke, Rousseau, and Kant, a theory of justice that is no longer open to objections often thought fatal to it, and that proves superior to the long dominant tradition of utilitarianism. *A Theory of Justice* hopes to present the structural features of

---

[101] Observe that neither the religious objection to democracy nor the autocratic one could be made by public reasoning.

[102] See note 3.

[103] See Rawls, *A Theory of Justice* § 35 (cited in note 55) (on toleration of the intolerant); Rawls, *Political Liberalism*, lecture V, § 6.2 at 197-99 (cited in note 1).

such a theory so as to make it the best approximation to our considered judgments of justice and hence to give the most appropriate moral basis for a democratic society. Furthermore, justice as fairness is presented there as a comprehensive liberal doctrine (although the term "comprehensive doctrine" is not used in the book) in which all the members of its well ordered society affirm that same doctrine. This kind of well ordered society contradicts the fact of reasonable pluralism and hence *Political Liberalism* regards that society as impossible.

Thus, *Political Liberalism* considers a different question, namely: How is it possible for those affirming a comprehensive doctrine, religious or nonreligious, and in particular doctrines based on religious authority, such as the Church or the Bible, also to hold a reasonable political conception of justice that supports a constitutional democratic society? The political conceptions are seen as both liberal and self-standing and not as comprehensive, whereas the religious doctrines may be comprehensive but not liberal. The two books are asymmetrical, though both have an idea of public reason. In the first, public reason is given by a comprehensive liberal doctrine, while in the second, public reason is a way of reasoning about political values shared by free and equal citizens that does not trespass on citizens' comprehensive doctrines so long as those doctrines are consistent with a democratic polity. Thus, the well ordered constitutional democratic society of *Political Liberalism* is one in which the dominant and controlling citizens affirm and act from irreconcilable yet reasonable comprehensive doctrines. These doctrines in turn support reasonable political conceptions—although not necessarily the most reasonable—which specify the basic rights, liberties, and opportunities of citizens in society's basic structure.

[13]

Pluralism and Social Unity

William A. Galston

In the nearly two decades since the publication of *A Theory of Justice*, John Rawls has not significantly altered the content of the principles the denizens of the original position are said to embrace. But many other aspects of his theory have changed. Four shifts strike me as being of particular importance. First, Rawls has placed an expanded notion of "moral personality" at the center of his argument and has revised several aspects of his theory (in particular, the accounts of primary goods and of individual rationality) accordingly. Second, he has fleshed out his views on the good and on the role that a conception of the good can play within the priority of the right. Third, he now characterizes the overall theory as "political"—that is, as drawn in part from basic political facts that constitute practical constraints and as detached from broader philosophical or metaphysical considerations. Finally, he has come to view his theory of justice not as developed *sub specie aeternitatis* but, rather, as drawn from (and addressed to) the public culture of democratic societies.

Underlying these shifts, I believe, is a core concern that has become increasingly prominent in Rawls's thought. Modern liberal-democratic societies are characterized by an irreversible pluralism, that is, by conflicting and incommensurable conceptions of the human good (and, Rawls now stresses, of metaphysical and religious conceptions as well). The grounds of social unity are not hard to specify in homogeneous communities. But where are they to be found in societies whose members disagree so fundamentally? The answer, Rawls believes, lies in the lessons liberal-democratic societies have slowly learned in the modern era. Alongside the "fact of pluralism" is a kind of rough agreement on certain basics: the treatment of all individuals as free and equal; the understanding of society as a system of uncoerced cooperation; the right of each individual to claim a fair share of the fruits of that cooperation; and the duty of all citizens to support and uphold institutions that embody a shared conception of fair principles. Once we devise a strategy for excluding from public discourse the matters on which we fundamentally disagree and for reflecting collectively on the beliefs we share, we can be led to workable agreements on the content of just principles and institutions.

I believe that in focusing his recent thought on the problem of forging unity amid diversity, Rawls has posed exactly the right question.

Ethics 99 (July 1989): 711–726

712   *Ethics*   *July 1989*

I am less sure that he has arrived at the right answer. In addressing the fact of pluralism, I would argue, Rawls goes both too far and not far enough: too far, because in trying to avoid all deep differences of metaphysics and religion and to set questions of truth to one side, he deprives social philosophy (including his own) of resources essential to its success; not far enough, because the grounds of agreement he professes to find latent in our public culture would be rejected by many individuals and groups who form important elements of that culture. The alternative, I would suggest, is to recognize that social philosophy, liberalism included, cannot wholly rest its case on social agreement and must ultimately advert to truth-claims that are bound to prove controversial. This is a problem for liberalism only if the concept of individual freedom central to liberalism is construed so broadly as to trump the force of such truth-claims. But there are no sufficient reasons to understand liberal freedom so expansively, and many compelling reasons not to.[1]

I

Let me begin with Rawls's revised notion of moral personality. Moral persons are, Rawls tells us, "characterized by two moral powers and by two corresponding highest-order interests in realizing and exercising these powers. The first power is the capacity for an effective sense of justice, that is, the capacity to understand, to apply and to act from (and not merely in accordance with) the principles of justice. The second moral power is the capacity to form, to revise, and rationally to pursue a conception of the good."[2]

   As members of a democratic society, we agree not only on the content of this conception but also on the capacity of all (normal) members of our society to fulfill it. Rawls's account of moral personality thus lays the foundation for what might be called a democratic teleology. Individuals choosing principles of justice will seek, first and foremost, to create circumstances in which they can realize and express their moral powers. In addition, we as observers will appraise social institutions in light of their propensity to promote the realization and facilitate the expression of these powers. From the standpoint of both participants and observers, moreover, these goals will take priority over other concerns—in particular, over the realization of the specific conceptions of the good that individuals may embrace. (That is what it means to identify the moral powers as our "highest-order" interests.)

   1. In defending these contentions I have drawn on three of my previously published articles: "Liberalism and Public Morality," in *Liberals on Liberalism*, ed. Alphonso J. Damico (Totowa, N.J.: Rowman & Littlefield, 1986), "Moral Personality and Liberal Theory: John Rawls's 'Dewey Lectures,'" *Political Theory* 10 (1982): 492–519, and "Defending Liberalism," *American Political Science Review* 76 (1982): 621–29.
   2. John Rawls, "Kantian Constructivism in Moral Theory: The Dewey Lectures 1980," *Journal of Philosophy* 77 (1980): 525 (hereafter cited as "Dewey Lectures").

This expanded conception of moral personality places, if not a "thick" theory, at least a greater than thin theory, of the good at the very foundation of Rawls's conception of justice. An indication—and consequence—of this shift is a dramatically revised account of primary goods. In *A Theory of Justice*, these goods were defined relative to the undefined objectives of rational calculators. They were, Rawls specified, a class of goods "that are normally wanted as parts of rational plans of life which may include the most varied sorts of ends," and the specification of these goods depends on psychological premises.[3] In the wake of the new account of moral personality, by contrast, "primary goods are singled out by asking which things are generally necessary as social conditions and all-purpose means to enable human beings to realize and exercise their moral powers ... the conception of moral persons as having certain specified highest-order interests selects what is to count as primary goods. ... Thus these goods are not to be understood as general means essential for achieving whatever final ends a comprehensive empirical or historical survey might show people usually or normally have in common under all social conditions."[4]

I have discussed elsewhere, at length, the implications of Rawls's expanded conception of moral personality. Let me raise just two problems here.

First, Rawls asserts that for an ideal conception of personality to be acceptable, "it must be possible for people to honor it sufficiently closely." Hence, "the feasible ideals of the person are limited by the capacities of human nature."[5] In his view, nothing we now know, or are likely to learn, about human nature suggests that his own conception is beyond our capacities.[6] But that view is at least controversial. One may wonder, for example, whether the men who drafted the U.S. Constitution would have embraced it. There is much evidence to suggest that they did not, that in their view the dominance of both passion and interest was such as to make an effective sense of justice the exception rather than the rule. While they did not wholly denigrate the social role of individual virtue, they felt compelled to rely heavily on what they called "auxiliary precautions"—that is, on institutions whose workings did not depend on the just motives of officeholders or of ordinary citizens. At the very least, I would suggest, the question of the feasibility of Rawls's ideal deserves much more than the cursory, almost dismissive, treatment he provides.

Second, while Rawls's conception of moral personality may strike some as unattainable, it may strike others as unacceptable. Rawls says that he hopes to "invoke a conception of the person implicitly affirmed in [our] culture, or else one that would prove acceptable to citizens once

3. John Rawls, *A Theory of Justice* (Cambridge, Mass.: Harvard University Press, 1971), p. 260.
4. Rawls, "Dewey Lectures," pp. 526–27.
5. Ibid., p. 534.
6. Ibid., p. 566.

it was properly presented and explained."[7] But I wonder whether, for example, religious fundamentalists would regard the capacity to form and revise a conception of the good as a good at all, let alone a highest-order interest of human beings. They might well declare that the best human life requires the capacity to receive an external good (God's truth) rather than to form a conception of the good for oneself, and to hold fast to that truth once received rather than to revise it. Rawls's Kantian conception would strike them as a sophisticated, and therefore dangerous, brand of secular humanism. Nor would they be impressed with the suggestion that whatever may be true of their nonpublic identity, their public personality should be understood in Rawls's fashion. From their perspective, the disjunction between the public and nonpublic realms represents an injunction to set aside God's word, the only source of salvation, in determining the principles of our public order. I would argue, in short, that Rawls's conception of moral personality will appeal only to those individuals who have accepted a particular understanding of the liberal political community and that our public culture is at present characterized not by consensus but, rather, by acute conflict over the adequacy of that understanding.

II

The expanded account of moral personality is a part, but by no means the totality, of the second major shift in Rawls's position—the expanded account of the good and its enhanced role in the overall theory.

In 1982 I published an article in which I argued that every contemporary liberal theory relies, explicitly or tacitly, on the same triadic theory of the good, which asserts the worth of human existence, the value of the fulfillment of human purposes, and the commitment to rationality as the chief guide to both individual purposiveness and collective undertakings. This is, to be sure, a restricted theory of the good, but it is by no means a trivial one, for it is possible to identify approaches to social morality that deny one or more of its elements.[8]

In a recent paper, in part an explicit rejoinder to my argument, Rawls acknowledges the presence of these elements of the good in his theory. He writes that any workable conception of justice "must count human life and the fulfillment of basic human needs and purposes as in general good, and endorse rationality as a basic principle of political and social organization. A political doctrine for a democratic society may safely assume, then, that all participants in political discussions of right and justice accept these values, when understood in a suitably general way. Indeed, if the members of society did not do so, the problems of political justice, in the form with which we are familiar with them, would seem not to arise."[9]

7. Ibid., p. 518.
8. Galston, "Defending Liberalism," pp. 625–26.
9. John Rawls, "The Priority of Right and Ideas of the Good," *Philosophy and Public Affairs* 17 (1988): 254 (hereafter cited as "Priority of Right").

Nor is this the totality of the liberal theory of the good as Rawls now understands it. In another recent paper, he develops the notion of a workable political conception of justice for a modern democratic society as resting on the fact of pluralism, that is, on the existence of diverse and irreconcilable conceptions of the good. This "fact" does not, however, have the status of an unchangeable law of nature but is relative to specific institutions and policies. Rawls acknowledges that a public agreement on a single conception of the good can indeed be established and maintained, but "only by the oppressive use of state power."[10] The empirical fact of pluralism, then, rests on the normative commitment to noncoercion and to the achievement of "free and willing agreement."[11]

This commitment to noncoercion goes very deep. It might be thought, for example, that pluralism makes sense only if no conception of the good can be known to be rationally preferable to any other. Rawls denies this: "The view that philosophy in the classical sense as the search for truth about a prior and independent moral order cannot provide the shared basis for a political conception of justice . . . does not presuppose the controversial metaphysical claim that there is no such order."[12] Even if there were such an order and it could be rationally specified, it could not properly serve as the basis for a political order unless it happened to be generally accepted by the citizenry, which would be highly unlikely in the absence of a coercive or at least tutelary state. In short, the claims of noncoercion—of individual freedom—trump even claims based on comprehensive philosophical truths. The freedom to choose one's own conception of the good is among the highest-order goods

Finally, Rawls's expanded conception of the human good offers an account of justice itself as a key element of that good. Citizens of a just society "share one very basic political end, and one that has high priority: namely, the end of supporting just institutions and of giving one another justice accordingly." This is the case in large measure because "the exercise of the two moral powers [the basic elements of moral personality] is experienced as good."[13] Not only, then, is justice a highest-order moral power and interest, but also there is an intrinsic impulse to develop and employ it in society.

Yet Rawls hesitates to embrace this argument in its full rigor. In the very article in which he most decisively links justice to moral personality as an end in itself, he also asserts that justice must be compatible with the comprehensive conceptions of the good held by individuals: "Just institutions and the political virtues expected of citizens would serve no purpose—would have no point—unless those institutions and virtues not only permitted but also sustained ways of life that citizens can affirm

---

10. John Rawls, "The Idea of an Overlapping Consensus," *Oxford Journal of Legal Studies* 7 (1987): 4 (hereafter cited as "Overlapping Consensus").

11. Ibid., p. 5.

12. Ibid., p. 13n.

13. Rawls, "Priority of Right," pp. 269–70.

716   *Ethics   July 1989*

as worthy of their full allegiance. A conception of political justice must contain within itself sufficient space, as it were, for ways of life that can gain devoted support. In a phrase: justice draws the limit, the good shows the point."[14]

This assertion raises two very different kinds of issues. The first is conceptual: if doing justice is truly one of the two highest-order interests of moral personality, an end in itself, then why does it need a "point" outside itself? If individuals genuinely accept that justice is "supremely regulative as well as effective"[15] and that citizens' desires to pursue ends that transgress the limits of justice "have no weight,"[16] then, to be sure, adequate space for conceptions of the good lends added support for just institutions but it cannot be vital to their acceptability. Conversely, if space for ways of life is indeed critical, then a purportedly just regime that is systematically biased against certain kinds of lives cannot expect wholehearted support from individuals who cherish those lives.

This brings me to the second issue raised by Rawls's revised account of the relation between just institutions and individual ways of life. In his earlier account, Rawls had already conceded that certain ways of life were systematically likely to lose out in liberal society. But that did not imply (so he then argued) that this bias in any sense represented a morally relevant loss: "A well-ordered society defines a fair background within which ways of life have a reasonable opportunity to establish themselves. If a conception of the good is unable to endure and gain adherents under institutions of equal freedom and mutual toleration, one must question whether it is a viable conception of the good, and whether its passing is to be regretted."[17] The bias of liberalism, then, poses no special difficulty because the sorts of lives it tends to screen out are in themselves questionable from the standpoint of justice.

In Rawls's more recent account, however, the bias of liberalism becomes much more problematic. He now repudiates the view that only unworthy ways of life lose out in a just constitutional regime. "That optimistic view," he states flatly, "is mistaken." In its place, he endorses the view of Isaiah Berlin that "there is no social world without loss—that is, no social world that does not exclude some ways of life that realize in special ways certain fundamental values."[18] In particular, a society constructed in accordance with the conception of justice as fairness will ask certain individuals and groups to give up for themselves their ways of life or to surrender any real chance of passing their most cherished values on to children. Moreover, what Rawls calls "the facts of common-sense political sociology" tell us which ways of life are most likely to lose out—to wit, those that

14. Ibid., pp. 251–52.
15. Rawls, "Dewey Lectures," p. 525.
16. Rawls, "Priority of Right," p. 251.
17. John Rawls, "Fairness to Goodness," *Philosophical Review* 84 (1975): 549.
18. Rawls, "Priority of Right," p. 265.

presuppose more control over the immediate cultural environment than is feasible within liberal societies.

This new position, it seems to me. poses a deep difficulty for justice as fairness. If I know that the principles adopted in the original position may impair my ability to exercise, or even require me altogether to surrender, the values that give my life its core meaning and purpose, then how can I agree in advance to accept those principles as binding—any more than I could subscribe to a procedure that might result in my enslavement as the outcome of a utilitarian calculus? Freedom is a great good, but is one's moral identity a lesser good? If it is unimaginable to risk losing the former, how can it make sense to embrace a decision procedure that risks losing the latter?

Rawls's answer is that there is no alternative, once justice is cast as a fair system of cooperation among free and equal persons within the fact of pluralism: if the oppressive use of state power is ruled out, justice as fairness—with its characteristic bias—is the necessary outcome. It is not, however, adequate to depict adherents of endangered ways of life as facing a choice between becoming victims or oppressors. There is a third alternative—retreat or exit from pluralistic societies into communities marked by a greater degree of moral, religious, or cultural homogeneity. And this is likely to be the preferred option for groups that see themselves as the probable victims of liberal bias.

This line of argument amounts to the proposition that, for some, the costs of treating pluralism as a "fact" are prohibitive, for it is a pluralism that excludes them. We reach a similar conclusion, starting with the observation that Rawls takes for granted the existence of a demarcated society whose members already accept the necessity of living together under common rules. From his perspective, the question is not whether I will seek grounds of cooperation with the other members of my society but, rather, what form that cooperation will take. But it is perfectly possible to treat as problematic precisely what Rawls takes for granted. The costs of cooperation under common rules with individuals who differ radically from me may appear prohibitive, especially if those rules are to be drafted under procedures that require free and willing consent. It might well be rational for me to prefer a multiplicity of separate homogeneous communities, one of which is my natural home, to a single pluralistic community in which I fear I may have no real place.

A similar difficulty may be reached via another line of argument. In his recent work, Rawls has focused increasingly on the possibility of conflict between individual conceptions of the good on the one hand and the demands of social cooperation on the other. He has sought to reduce the probability—and severity—of this conflict in two ways: by emphasizing the respects in which justice as fairness both promotes its own political vision of the good and allows for the pursuit of many (though not all) individual conceptions of the good; and by indicating how justice as fairness can be seen as the focus of an "overlapping consensus" among differing religious and comprehensive philosophical views.

718 *Ethics* *July 1989*

As the role of the political good in Rawls's theory has expanded, the theory has become noticeably more teleological. Not only have existence, purposiveness, and social rationality received explicit recognition as intrinsic goods, but also the account of moral personality has provided the foundation for the recognition of freedom and justice as ends in themselves—that is, as essential aspects of our human good. In the process, justice as fairness has verged on a kind of democratic perfectionism.

We may then ask: if the teleological component of Rawls's theory is so enhanced, then what of the much-discussed priority of the right over the good? The answer, I think, is that the priority of the right is subtly reinterpreted as the priority of the public over the nonpublic. That is, permissible conceptions of the good are delimited by the determination to give priority to social cooperation. Over and over again in his recent writings, Rawls repeats his hope that, taking as his point of departure the core concept of a fair system of cooperation, he can arrive at an expression of political values that "normally outweigh whatever other values may oppose them."[19]

Yet matters are not so simple. Rawls never really addresses the charge, leveled by Bernard Williams, among others, that the public understanding of moral personality comports poorly with our nonpublic aims and attachments and that no basis for the unification of these two dimensions of our character is offered in the revised account of justice as fairness. The possibility therefore looms that giving priority to the requirements of social cooperation will compel individuals to make sacrifices of their core commitments and of aspects of their character they regard as basic to their identity and integrity.[20]

In the end, Rawls recognizes this. He concedes that the priority of the public is always provisional, always threatened: "Political good, no matter how important, can never in general outweigh the transcendent values—certain religious, philosophical, and moral values—that may possibly come into conflict with it."[21] And because a liberal society cannot be equally hospitable to all conceptions of the good, the social basis for such conflict is always likely to exist. From the standpoint of social stability, the best that can be hoped for is that the overwhelming majority of individuals and groups will find sufficient space within liberal society for the expression of their distinctive conceptions of the good. But for those who are left out, it is hard to see how liberalism can be experienced as anything other than an assault. Resistance is therefore to be expected, and it is far from clear on what basis it is to be condemned.

19. Rawls, "Overlapping Consensus," pp. 9, 17, 21–22. See also his "Priority of Right," pp. 252–53, 274–75, and "Dewey Lectures," pp. 552–53.

20. Bernard Williams, "Persons, Character, and Morality," in *The Identities of Persons*, ed. Amelie Oksenberg Rorty (Berkeley: University of California Press, 1976), pp. 210, 215.

21. Rawls, "Priority of Right," p. 275.

III

Of all the distinctive claims of Rawls's more recent work, the one he presses most forcefully and develops most fully is the assertion that justice as fairness is a *political* conception. In Rawls's hand, this adjective takes on manifold meanings. A political conception of justice is directed toward the basic structure of society rather than toward the full range of moral conduct, and it is therefore prepared to accept sharp differences between public and nonpublic principles. It is nevertheless a moral notion in the sense that it rests on the possibility of conscientious public action from, and not merely in accordance with, principles of public right; that is, it rejects as inadequate the pure "Hobbesian" appeal to rational self-interest. A political conception is based on the facts of political history and sociology. It is constrained by the requirements of practicality; indeed, these requirements are said to enter into the construction of first principles and not merely their application. It must meet the criterion of publicity; no principles that depend on secrecy or misrepresentation can be deemed acceptable. A political conception is both drawn from and addressed to a specific public culture, and its justification lies in its fidelity to the shared understandings of that culture rather than its correspondence to some universe of moral facts. Finally, it is (so far as possible) detached from, independent of, and neutral with respect to broader and inherently controversial philosophical, metaphysical, and religious commitments.

I have discussed many of these theses elsewhere, and the final section of this article will examine the notion of political philosophy as cultural interpretation. In this section, I want to focus on what I take to be Rawls's key—and highly controversial—contention that principles of justice can be independent of broader commitments.

Contemporary communitarians offer a searching critique of what they take to be the metaphysical conception of individuality peculiar—and necessary—to Rawlsian liberalism: a conception of the self as freely chosen and self-created; as separable from its aims and attachments; as detached from, critical of, unencumbered by, its history and circumstances. This critique is most closely identified with Michael Sandel, and I cannot improve on his summary:

> Can we view ourselves as independent selves, independent in the sense that our identity is never attached to our aims and attachments? I do not think we can, at least not without cost to those loyalties and convictions whose moral force consists partly in the fact that living by them is inseparable from understanding ourselves as the particular persons we are—as members of this family or community or nation or people, as bearers of that history, as citizens of this republic. . . . To imagine a person incapable of constitutive attachments such as these is not to conceive an ideally free and rational agent, but to imagine a person wholly without character, without moral depth. For to have character is to know that I move in a

720 *Ethics* *July 1989*

history I neither summon nor command, which carries consequences nonetheless for my choices and conduct.[22]

Any sensible response to this argument must begin by accepting one of its essential premises. There are aims and allegiances that are not in the first instance chosen, that arise out of our history and circumstances, and that to some considerable extent constitute our individual identities. No one chooses to be the child of these particular parents, a relationship that nonetheless creates not only special duties to those parents but also the special identity of that child. Analogous relationships exist between citizens and the communities into which they are born. To reject these facts would not only impoverish individual identity but also deny the obvious.

Once this point is granted, defenders of liberalism must choose between two strategies. The first, espoused most directly by Rawls, is to draw a sharp line between these constitutive relations and the conception of the person required by the political conception of liberal justice—that is, to deny that liberalism rests on any specific conception of individuality. Properly understood, liberalism is "political not metaphysical." The original position within which the various alternative principles of social cooperation are to be examined is simply a "device of representation." That is, it embodies the distinction between considerations that are held to be relevant in choosing principles of justice and those thought not to be relevant. The veil of ignorance, therefore, has "no metaphysical implications concerning the nature of the self; it does not imply that the self is on-tologically prior to the facts about persons that the parties are excluded from knowing." We enter the original position not by denying our unique selfhood but, rather, by screening out, for purposes of moral justification, knowledge of social position and other individual contingencies held to be morally arbitrary.[23]

Rawls's argument is exposed to several objections. To begin, as Amy Gutmann has argued, it is one thing to say that liberalism does not presuppose a single metaphysical view of the individual, but quite another to say that liberalism is compatible with all such views. Rawls depends on the latter—stronger—claim, which cannot be sustained. There are some conceptions of the individual (understood, e.g., as "radically situated") that liberalism simply cannot accommodate.[24]

The second objection to Rawls's argument is that conflict within liberal societies may force metaphysical issues onto the public agenda. Consider abortion. Many individuals who share an understanding of

22. Michael Sandel, "The Procedural Republic and the Unencumbered Self," *Political Theory* 12 (1984): 90–91.

23. John Rawls, "Justice as Fairness: Political not Metaphysical," *Philosophy and Public Affairs* 14 (1985): 237–39 (hereafter cited as "Political not Metaphysical").

24. Amy Gutmann, "Communitarian Critics of Liberalism," *Philosophy and Public Affairs* 14 (1985): 319. See also Rawls's own qualifications in "Political not Metaphysical," p. 240n.

moral personality disagree fundamentally on who is to be considered a moral person, so understood Opponents of abortion insist that fetuses must be taken to be persons; proponents of unrestricted abortion must at a minimum deny this proposition. Each position raises deep metaphysical issues, and the fact that the contending parties must live together under common rules means that—tacitly if not in its declaratory doctrine—the state must incline toward one or the other metaphysical view.

At this juncture, some liberals may retort that to the extent that the state neither commands nor prohibits, but merely permits, abortion, it is not inclining toward one or the other view but rather is refraining from offering an authoritative judgment. Yet this claim too is bound to be controversial. No one denies that the state should prohibit murder. To permit abortion is therefore to determine (at least implicitly) that abortion is not murder. But this is precisely the point at issue.

From the opponents' perspective, abortion is like slavery—an issue that raises the question of who is to be treated as an equal member of the moral community, an issue that deeply divides the public culture but about which one side is right and the other wrong. The thesis underlying state permissiveness on abortion is thus parallel to the position that Judge Douglas upheld in his debates with Abraham Lincoln—and just as mistaken. We violate no one's rights by using public authority to defend equal rights for all moral persons. Yes, doing this in circumstances of deep moral disagreement risks discord and even violence. But how many Americans believe that the Civil War was too high a price to pay for the abolition of slavery?

Rawls eventually acknowledges the force of this objection. In affirming a political conception of justice, he concedes, "We may eventually have to assert at least certain aspects of our own comprehensive . . . religious or philosophical doctrine. This happens whenever someone insists, for example, that certain questions are so fundamental that to ensure their being rightly settled justifies civil strife. . . . At this point we may have no alternative but to deny this, and to assert the kind of thing we had hoped to avoid."[25] I should note that while Rawls speaks only of rejecting the necessity of strife, the example of slavery suggests that we may sometimes be compelled to accept it.

There is yet a third objection to the sharp separation between the political conception of justice and broader commitments. It is that Rawls's argument manifestly depends on a specific affirmative conception of individuality. Persons must be emotionally, intellectually, and ontologically capable of drawing an effective line between their public and nonpublic identities and of setting aside their particular commitments, at least to the extent needed to enter the original position and to reason in a manner consistent with its constraints.

---

25. Rawls, "Overlapping Consensus," p. 14.

722   *Ethics   July 1989*

In reflecting on this fact and on the course of the preceding arguments, I am led to the conclusion that liberalism does indeed presuppose a conception of individuality. Liberalism, I suggest, rests not on the unencumbered self (which Sandel rightly criticizes) but rather on the *divided* self. On the one side stands the individual's personal and social history, with all the aims and attachments it may imply. On the other side stands the possibility of critical reflection on—even revolt against—these very commitments. Crucial to the liberal self is the potentiality for such critical distance from one's inheritance and the possibility that the exercise of critical faculties may in important respects modify that inheritance.

At the heart of the liberal vision is the conviction that individuality is not only shaped but also threatened by the community, that concentrations of social and political power can serve as vehicles for repressing as well as expressing individual identity. Liberalism endeavors to give due weight to both sides of this complex equation. On the theoretical level, this understanding requires that individuals be endowed both with the capacity for critical reflection on the institutions and presuppositions of their society and with the capacity for noncoerced choice essential to moral action. Properly understood, liberalism's Archimedean point is neither Cartesian nor Kantian but, rather, Socratic. To have the capacity to become aware of the inner contradictions of one's own society is precisely the kind of reflective distance required by the liberal conception of individuality. Rawls must, I think, concede no less; liberal theory needs no more; and the communitarian critics of liberalism cannot in the last analysis deny its possibility.

IV

I turn, finally, to Rawls's new conception of political philosophy as both drawn from and addressed to a specific public culture.

Liberalism in its classic form saw itself as the product of a decisive break with opinion, tradition, and myth. It claimed for its key premises the status of universal knowledge, independent of time and place, and it maintained that these premises could be used to judge all existing regimes.

In this self-understanding, at least, liberalism was simply a continuation of the tradition of political philosophy pioneered by Plato and Aristotle and taken over by medieval thinkers of different faiths. The highest task of political philosophy, so understood, was the comparative evaluation of regimes. To this end, philosophers developed idealized accounts of desirable political orders, in the form either of discursive principles or of concrete utopias. On this account, it should be noted, the discovery of truth is an activity quite distinct from argument within a public consensus. The former is the task of political philosophy, while the latter is the province of rhetoric.

The "death" of political philosophy proclaimed a generation ago was the loss of confidence in the possibility of transcultural, truth-based political evaluation. *A Theory of Justice* was greeted with excitement in part because it was seen as restoring the legitimacy of political evaluation so conceived. Rawls's "ideal theory," abstracted from the empirical contingencies that differentiate existing political orders, was designed to judge and (when possible) to improve them. And, he contended, his theory was neither produced by specific historical and social circumstances nor intended to defend any existing order. The theory was rather "impartial," for it was constructed *sub specie aeternitatis,* regarding the human situation "not only from all social but also from all temporal points of view."[26]

In the Dewey lectures and subsequently, however, Rawls abandons this effort. Political philosophy, he now contends, is always addressed to a specific "public culture." It either appeals to the principles latent in the common sense of that culture or proposes principles "congenial to its most essential convictions and historical traditions." In particular, justice as fairness addresses the public culture of a democratic society. It tries "to draw solely upon basic intuitive ideas that are embedded in the political institutions of constitutional democratic regimes and the public traditions of their interpretation." Justice as fairness "starts from within a certain political tradition" and (we may add) it remains there.[27] The question of truth or falsity is thus irrelevant. Justice as fairness presents itself "not as a conception of justice that is true, but one that can serve as a basis of informed and willing political agreement. . . . Philosophy as the search for truth about an independent metaphysical and moral order cannot, I believe, provide a workable and shared basis for a political conception of justice in a democratic society."[28] As a consequence, the classic distinction between political philosophy and rhetoric collapses: "On this view, justification is not regarded simply as valid argument from listed premises, even should these premises be true. Rather justification is addressed to others who disagree with us, and therefore it must always proceed from some consensus, that is, from premises that we and others publicly recognize as true; or better, publicly recognize as acceptable to us for the purpose of establishing a working agreement on the fundamental questions of political justice."[29]

In the Dewey lectures and subsequently, Rawls sets aside the central concern of traditional political philosophy and puts in its place a new set of questions, to which justice as fairness purports to provide the answer. How are "we"—reflective citizens of a liberal democracy—to understand freedom and equality, the ideals to which we are (or so we say) individually and collectively committed? How are we to resolve the recurrent conflict between these ideals? Which principles of justice are most consistent

26. Rawls, *A Theory of Justice,* p. 587.
27. Rawls, "Dewey Lectures," p. 518, and "Political not Metaphysical," p. 225.
28. Rawls, "Political not Metaphysical," p. 230.
29. Ibid., p. 229.

with them, and how are we to transform these principles into workable institutions?

These questions are well worth asking. But they raise three difficulties that Rawls does not appear to me to have adequately addressed.

To begin with, it is unlikely (to say the least) that the interpretation of a public culture will be less controversial than the interpretation of a literary creation. Thus, for example, Rawls's core notion of free and equal moral personality, allegedly derived from an inspection of our traditions, excludes knowledge of differing conceptions of the good from the original position and rules out individual desert as a core element of our collective self-understanding that should help structure the principles of justice we adopt. I and others have argued that this account of moral personality does violence not only to a reasonable account of the "moral point of view" but also to the most plausible description of the shared understanding of our public culture. Now is not the occasion to join this issue or other comparable controversies. The point is rather that cultural interpretation is far more likely to recapitulate than (as Rawls supposes) to resolve the deep disputes that now divide our political order.

The second difficulty with Rawls's account of political philosophy is that it leaves no basis for the comparative assessment of regimes. When we are faced with evils like Hitlerism, Stalinism, and apartheid, it is not enough to say that these practices violate our shared understandings. The point is that we insist on the right to apply our principles to communities that reject them. Indeed, these evils challenge the very validity of these principles, which therefore require a defense that transcends interpretation.

If principles of political right do not apply across the boundaries of public cultures, then many practices we take for granted would have to be abandoned. No American president could go to Moscow and criticize Soviet restraints on freedom of speech and expression—restraints that more nearly reflect than repudiate the tradition of Russia's public culture. Organizations such as Amnesty International could not rightly apply a common standard of decency to all nations. And forceful, even coercive, efforts to foster liberal democracy would be ruled out. In the wake of World War II, for example, the United States undertook to reconstruct not just the political institutions but also the public culture of its defeated enemies. Authoritarian social and economic groupings were dismantled; textbooks were purged; democratic doctrines were aggressively purveyed to bolster the viability of the democratic practices we had imposed. In virtually every respect, we overrode the preferred self-understandings of our adversaries. It was a perfect example of what political theory understood solely as cultural interpretation would preclude. But it was not wrong.

Now it is open to Rawls to reply (as indeed he does) that he does not wish to deny the possibility that certain normative principles may apply across cultural boundaries. Rather, he begins from the special case of the closed, self-sufficient community. The extent to which conclusions reached within this domain may be extended farther "cannot be foreseen in advance." Moreover, methods of moral argument, such as the appeal to independent and preexisting moral facts, ruled out in the construction principles of justice for a single society, may conceivably be used for the elucidation of principles governing relations among societies.[30]

Indeed, it may be argued that Rawls's entire argument tacitly proceeds in two steps. The first is the premise—supported perhaps by moral philosophy—that liberal democracy in its broad outlines is clearly superior to alternative forms of political organization, while the second step is the effort—to which Rawls devotes nearly all his attention—to arrive at the most plausible interpretation of what the core commitments of liberal democracy entail. The former step employs strategies of moral validation that cannot be reduced to (deep) consensus, while the latter can only appeal to what we believe, or can be led to believe, on due reflection.[31]

This reply raises, in turn, the following question: if there can be public principles whose validity rests on truth rather than agreement, then why can't such principles apply within liberal democratic communities? Rawls's answer is that, within such communities, the freedom of moral persons is not to be violated, not even in the name of truth. But is the absolute priority of freedom over truth really the polestar of liberal-democratic public culture? And how is that alleged priority to be squared with a public culture that begins by declaring, "We hold these truths to be self-evident"?

This question leads me to the third and final objection to Rawls's account of political philosophy: by asking us to separate general truth-claims from the elucidation of our shared understandings, it distorts the deepest meaning of those understandings. When Americans say that all human beings are created equal and endowed with certain unalienable rights, we intend this not as a description of our local convictions but, rather, as universal truths, valid everywhere and binding on all. Indeed, that claim is at the heart of their normative force. If our principles are valid for us only because we (happen to) believe them, then they are not binding even for us.

The reason is straightforward. If someone argues that we ought to do something because it corresponds to the best interpretation of the shared understandings that constitute our culture, it is always open to me to ask why I should consider myself bound by those understandings. That simple question launches the philosophic quest for grounds of action and belief beyond the sheer facticity of culture—a quest that cannot be set aside without doing violence to the profoundest of all human longings. There may in the end be no viable grounds of transcul-

---

30. Rawls, "Dewey Lectures," pp. 524, 561–62.
31. I am indebted to Richard Arneson for this suggestion.

tural justification, in which case we will be faced after all with Nietzsche's choice between life-denying openness and life-affirming horizons. But to set aside in advance the quest for truth, to insist as Rawls does that the principle of religious toleration must for political purposes be extended to philosophy itself, is to demand something that no self-respecting individual or public culture can reasonably grant.

[14]
Justice and the Aims of Political Philosophy*

Kurt Baier

I

In his two most recent publications, Rawls lays great stress on the relatively parochial nature of the proper aims of political philosophy and the suitable method for attaining them.[1] In general, "the aims of political philosophy depend on the society it addresses" (p. 1); in constitutional democracies one of the important long-term ends is attaining (or maintaining) stable social unity (p. 24). Perhaps the greatest obstacle to achieving this aim is our disagreement about how certain familiar values, such as freedom, equality, and efficiency, are to be understood, mutually accommodated, and realized in such a constitutional democracy; or more specifically, in the United States at this time.[2] Rawls's own "justice as fairness" may be a solution to this problem provided it also satisfies a certain "practical" condition which he now considers essential for Western political philosophers to meet because "political philosophy must be concerned, as moral philosophy need not be, with practical political possibilities" (p. 24). Rawls now argues that the best way for political philosophers to attain stable social unity is to aim for a certain sort of agreement among citizens, which he calls "an overlapping consensus" and which is the minimum sufficient for stable social unity. Under such a consensus, a given conception of justice is "affirmed by the opposing religious, philosophical, and moral doctrines likely to thrive over generations in a more or less just constitutional

* Some points in Sec. II of this article are adapted from my comments on Rawls's presentation of his "The Idea of an Overlapping Consensus" at the Chapel Hill, North Carolina, colloquium in October 1986. In Sec. VII, I borrow some ideas from the first of my three Perspectives Lectures given at Notre Dame in 1977 under the title "The Varieties of Justice." I am indebted to John Rawls and to some participants on these two occasions for some critical and clarifying remarks.

1. John Rawls, "Justice as Fairness: Political not Metaphysical," *Philosophy and Public Affairs* 14 (1985): 223–51, and "The Idea of an Overlapping Consensus," *Oxford Journal of Legal Studies* 7 (1987): 1–25, with which I shall mainly be concerned; unless otherwise specified, parenthetical references in the text refer to this latter article.

2. John Rawls, "Kantian Constructivism in Moral Theory: The Dewey Lectures 1980" (which Rawls would now retitle "Kantian Constructivism in Political Theory"), *Journal of Philosophy* 77 (1980): 515–72, 517–18.

Ethics 99 (July 1989): 771–790

772   *Ethics   July 1989*

democracy, where the criterion of justice is that conception itself." Rawls now believes that a nonutopian (p. 22) conception of justice, one that has some hope of gaining the support of such a consensus (p. 1), must satisfy four conditions: (*a*) it must be capable of bypassing philosophy's long-standing controversies (pp. 12–13); (*b*) to be thus capable, it must be "political"; (*c*) it also must be liberal; (*d*) and it must steer a course between two extreme strands of liberalism.

a) To be capable of by-passing philosophy's long-standing controversies, this conception of justice must be capable of being supported by "the method of avoidance," by which we neither "assert nor . . . deny any religious, philosophical or moral views, or their associated philosophical accounts of truth and the status of values. Since we assume each citizen to affirm some such view or other, we hope to make it possible for all to accept the political conception as true, or as reasonable, from the standpoint of their own comprehensive view, whatever it may be" (pp. 12–13).

b) To be "political," in Rawls's sense, it must—as I shall say—be narrow in scope and have a local political base.

It is narrow in scope if it is particular rather than "general (or universal)" and limited rather than "comprehensive" (p. 3, n. 4; p. 14, n. 23). It is particular if it is intended, at least in the first instance, for the appraisal solely of the basic structure of society rather than for the appraisal of many (or all) subjects to which justice applies (p. 3, nn. 3, 4). Thus a conception of justice that is particular could not be used, at least in the first instance, in the appraisal of international relations or of terrorism. A conception of justice is limited if for its appraisals it relies not on ideals, principles, and standards intended for much or all of our conduct (as is, I suppose, benevolence, courage, charity, or prudence), but on ideals, etc., intended for only a limited area of our life (such as, I suppose, individual political conduct; p. 3, n. 2).

A conception of justice has a local political base if it is worked up "from the fundamental intuitive ideas latent in the public political culture of a democratic society" (pp. 6–7) rather than from within a comprehensive religious, philosophical, or moral conception, such as utilitarianism or the theory of natural law or even philosophical (as opposed to political) liberalism, such as that of Kant or Mill, which "applies to the political order as if this order was but another subject, another kind of case, falling under that conception" (p. 3).

Rawls believes that only a political conception (in this sense of "political") has any hope of achieving an overlapping consensus because only such a conception can appeal to ideals already held and can bypass the disagreements arising from the inescapable diversity and mutual incompatibility of general and comprehensive religious and philosophical, including moral, doctrines likely to flourish there. A conception that is wide in scope would require a corresponding "enveloping" consensus, as we might call it, a consensus on the various competing comprehensive doctrines. But such a consensus cannot be hoped for and would not even be desirable in a constitutional democracy which is inevitably pluralistic (p. 4, n. 7). For a "public and workable agreement on a single general and comprehensive conception could be maintained only by the oppressive use of state power" (p. 4).

c) Rawls does not appear to think that only justice as fairness has hope of an overlapping consensus in our society, for he thinks that it is "also likely that more than one political conception may be worked up from the fund of shared political ideas; indeed this is desirable, as these rival conceptions will then compete for citizens' allegiance and be gradually modified and deepened by the contest between them" (p. 7).

However, he does think that "a workable conception of political justice for a democratic regime must be in an appropriate sense a liberal one" (p. 5). A liberal conception, as Rawls defines it, has three elements: (i) it specifies certain basic rights, liberties, and opportunities; (ii) it assigns a special priority to these rights etc.; (iii) it assures "to all citizens adequate all-purpose means to make effective use of their basic liberties and opportunities" (p. 18).[3]

d) A conception of justice steers the required middle course only if it can gain a stronger support than is provided by a Hobbesian "*modus vivendi* secured by a convergence of self- and group interests even when coordinated and balanced by a well-designed constitutional arrangement" (p. 23). Such a modus vivendi admittedly can secure agreement but not one that is "stable with respect to the distribution of power" (p. 12). At the same time, a conception of justice should not have to count on the support of "a comprehensive moral doctrine such as that of Kant or Mill . . . which cannot gain sufficient agreement" (p. 18). Thus, the Hobbesian balance of conflicting interests secures, at best, unstable agreement, and philosophical (as opposed to political) liberalism (p. 23) expects more agreement than is attainable or even desirable in a constitutional democracy.

This concludes my—necessarily impoverished—summary of Rawls's claims in his most recent papers, especially "The Idea of an Overlapping Consensus." In Sections II–VI of this article I examine these claims and some of their implications. In Section VII I offer some speculative remarks about various conceptions of justice and of the concept of justice and examine their bearing on Rawls's claims about the relation between moral and political philosophy.

II

Rawls clearly thinks that we do not now have a consensus on a conception of justice. He sketches a scenario of the progress of a society from a

3. Rawls also offers a "fuller idea of a liberal conception of justice" in n. 27 on the same page. We need not compare the two but should note that both contain requirement iii which would seem to be in conflict with libertarian conceptions of justice. Compare Rawls's discussion of Nozick in his "The Basic Structure as Subject," in *Values and Morals*, ed. A. I. Goldman and J. Kim (Dordrecht: Reidel, 1978), sec. 3.

774 *Ethics* *July 1989*

Hobbesian modus vivendi (pp. 9–12) to an overlapping consensus on such a conception (pp. 18–21). Under the former, toleration of different religious, metaphysical, and moral doctrines is grudgingly accepted as a faute de mieux. Under it, all or most citizens consider it the government's duty to uphold the true doctrine and repress false ones. The government is expected to return to intolerance as soon as there is a favorable change in the distribution of power. The people acquiesce in the practice of tolerance only because they lack the power to suppress opposing views and prefer toleration as a lesser evil to prolonged inconclusive war. Such an acquiescence depends on a fortuitous conjunction of contingencies (p. 1) and is therefore doomed to instability when the distribution of power changes.

In a genuine consensus on a political conception of justice in an essentially pluralistic society, tolerance, readiness to meet others halfway, reasonableness, and the sense of fairness are regarded as very great virtues, and when they are widespread and sustain the public conception of justice, they are regarded as constituting "a very great public good, part of a society's political capital" (p. 17). Rawls concludes that when there is such a consensus, then the values that conflict with it "may be normally outweighed" (p. 17). Hence such a situation will be stable even if the distribution of power changes and conflicting values become more widespread. Of course, this is so only to the extent that the values enshrined in the conception of justice for the basic structure of a constitutional democracy are placed by the bulk of at least the politically active members above the values enshrined in the conflicting religious, metaphysical, or moral doctrines.

Where are we now in this scenario sketched by Rawls? Obviously, Rawls must believe, we are no longer at the stage of a Hobbesian modus vivendi, for we have agreement on the workings of the legal process which we allow to adjudicate those of our disagreements on which we cannot simply agree to differ. This is not a mere Hobbesian modus vivendi, for the currently dominant group does not attempt or even want to use its power to impose its conception of justice on the whole community by an oppressive use of the state power, say, by suitable indoctrination of the young through compulsory public education or by censorship of and punishment for the expression of opposing views. Of course, the current majority probably hopes that its conception will remain the dominant one, and it uses whatever means it has within the limits permitted by the political process to ensure that its conception is given effect, but it recognizes the possibility or even probability that there will be a shift in the distribution of power and with it the dominance of another conception of justice. But they believe, and believe that most others believe, that the methods defined by the legitimate political process will continue to be generally accepted, whatever the adjudications resulting from the use of these methods in particular cases. They do not treat the limitations imposed by the legitimate political process as a necessary evil, but recognize and appreciate the great value to all of stable general adherence to that process.

Have we then reached a consensus on the principles of justice? I think the answer must be no, for there still are many different and conflicting conceptions of justice, for instance, the perfectionist, the utilitarian, the libertarian, the socialist, and now Rawls's justice as fairness, not all of them even liberal. But although there seems to be no consensus on a conception of justice, there is a consensus on something else, namely, on the procedures for making and interpreting law and, where that agreement is insufficiently deep to end disagreement, on the selection of persons whose adjudication is accepted as authoritative.[4] It is not the case that this agreement "is contingent on circumstances remaining such as not to upset the fortunate convergence of interests" (p. 11). On the contrary, such an agreement on the process of adjudication when interests conflict—call it a "constitutional consensus"—is valued for its own sake and for much the same reasons as a consensus on a principle of justice would be valued: it maintains stability over a wide range of distributions of power, and it fosters the virtues of tolerance, respect, and reciprocity (p. 12).

It would seem, then, that the practical aim of political philosophy— stable political unity—can be achieved in the absence of a consensus, whether overlapping or enveloping, on a narrowly political conception of justice.

An objector may perhaps concede that a constitutional consensus can achieve stability but insist that it cannot achieve adequate social unity. For, he may say, under such a consensus people would disagree not only on the good but also on the just and the right. Their agreement would be confined to a procedure, not for settling disagreements, but merely for what is to be done in the face of unsettleable disagreements about what is the just or right thing to do. And this would be too "thin" a consensus to constitute social unity. If we cannot have genuine political community under political liberalism because we cannot have agreement on the good, at least we must have agreement on the principles of justice, if we are to have anything deserving the name of social unity.

But would a consensus on justice as fairness, which ultimately is only pure procedural justice,[5] be significantly "thicker" in terms of social unity than a constitutional consensus? Suppose you and I disagree on the validity of the claims we both advance to the ownership of a particular horse and that we finally agree to toss a coin to settle the issue one way or the other rather than let the dispute drag on forever. This would not

4. For a helpful account of authority, see Joseph Raz, *The Authority of Law* (Oxford: Clarendon, 1979), esp. chap. 1, and "Authority, Law and Morality," *Monist* 68 (1985): 295–324, esp. 296–305; also my "The Justification of Governmental Authority," *Journal of Philosophy* 69 (1972): 700–716.

5. John Rawls, *A Theory of Justice* (Cambridge, Mass.: Harvard University Press, 1971), pp. 120, 136; henceforth *TJ*.

776   *Ethics   July 1989*

be regarded by us as pure procedural justice since we both believe that there is a substantive issue on which we cannot agree. We therefore abandon the quest for a just solution and let our conflict be settled by a mutually acceptable procedure.

Our current constitutional consensus is somewhat like this: a consensus that is neither on substantive nor on procedural justice. The former is not available, and the latter is inappropriate. We prefer to abide by the established legal procedures, which embody at least some (though perhaps confused or inconsistent) principles of substantive justice because we consider this solution superior to settling the issue by force, or to leaving it unsettled until we can come to agree on justice, or to settling it by pure procedural justice, such as tossing a fair coin, which last would settle it as if neither of us had any claim of substantive justice.

A constitutional consensus is a special case of imperfect (impure) procedural justice. We believe that our method does not always yield a solution in conformity with the requirements of justice. We believe this not because experience has taught us over the long run that the use of this method usually though not always yields substantively just solutions but, rather, because we have no way, convincing to all of us even in the long run, of telling whether the contentious solutions produced by our method were just or unjust.

It seems to me, then, that if social unity cannot be achieved in a democratic society, as Rawls argues it cannot be, by the establishment of a consensus on "the meaning, value and purpose of human life" (pp. 2–3), then the best we can hope for is indeed an agreement on justice to adjudicate between different and conflicting conceptions of the good. But even that is, on Rawls's own showing, at bottom, only an agreement on pure procedural justice, and it is not clear that the kind or degree of social unity achieved by an overlapping consensus on principles of pure procedural justice is significantly greater than that achieved by a constitutional consensus.

III

Let us, however, assume that a constitutional consensus, because it apparently lacks agreement on a conception of justice, is insufficient for stable social unity and that, therefore, contemporary Western political philosophers must present a conception of justice "such that there is some hope of gaining the support of [at least] an overlapping consensus" (p. 1) on it. A crucial question must therefore be exactly what conditions must be satisfied for such a consensus to exist. There would seem to be three dimensions in each of which a certain point would have to be reached if there is to be an "adequate" consensus: (i) the "level" of the consensus, depending on the degree of specificity with which that conception is formulated; (ii) the "extent" of the consensus, depending on the extent of support among the population; (iii) the "intensity"—as I shall call it—of the consensus, depending on the intensity of the agreement by those who agree. The three would seem to be interrelated. The greater the degree of specificity, the smaller the extent and the intensity required for adequacy, and so on, that are likely to be achieved. It may well be that for some low degree of specificity we already have a consensus of adequate extent and intensity. I shall discuss dimension i in this section and return to the other two dimensions in Section VI.

Although there seems to be an important connection between the concept of justice and various conceptions of it, as Rawls distinguishes the two,[6] I shall here assume that we do in fact agree on the concept of justice, that we have the same conception of the concept. (I shall say more about this in Sec. VII.) For the moment I shall consider only the level of the consensus depending on the degree of specificity with which the principle of justice is formulated: the higher that degree, the higher the level of consensus achieved, given the same magnitude of the other two dimensions, extent and intensity.

A fairly low level of consensus would be achieved if there were consensus on the following: "Institutions are just when no *arbitrary distinctions* are made between persons in the assigning of basic rights and duties and when the rules determine *a proper balance* between competing claims to the advantages of social life."[7] A much higher level would be

---

6. Ibid., pp. 4 ff. Thus, even if you and I agree on the principle of giving everyone his due, this need not be an agreement on the principle of justice if we disagreed on the concept of justice: not, for instance, if you thought the function of this principle was to distribute to people what the actually accepted rules of the institutions spelling out what is due from whom to whom award to them, whereas I think that their function is to distribute to them what is really due to them, i.e., what is awarded them by such institutions as long as they conform to some further principle, say, Rawls's justice as fairness. For further clarification, see nn. 7 and 19 below.

7. Rawls, *TJ*, p. 5; my emphasis. Rawls offers this formulation as an account of having the concept of justice because we "can agree to this description of just institutions since the notions of an arbitrary distinction and of a proper balance, which are included in the concept of justice, are left open for each to interpret according to the principles [i.e., the conception] of justice that he accepts" (*TJ*, p. 5). But note: (i) On the same page, Rawls says, "it seems natural to think of the concept of justice as distinct from the various conceptions of justice and as being specified by the role which these different sets of principles, these different conceptions have in common." On this account, having the concept of justice need not carry any implications of what are the empirical criteria by which we must appraise actual institutions as just or unjust. As Rawls suggests, this is one reason why it is more likely that we can agree on the concept of justice than on conceptions of justice. (ii) By contrast, Rawls's formulation in the first sentence of this note does carry such normative implications. Thus, the reason why we can agree on this conception of the concept is not that it is normatively noncommittal, but that it is so highly nonspecific that its normative implications will hardly ever come down on one side or the other of a disagreement about the justice or injustice of an institution. (iii) It is not the case that plainly we agree on the concept of justice. The history of ethics shows that there are many different conceptions of the concept. In Sec. VII I shall examine what I take to be five different conceptions of the concept of justice.

778   *Ethics   July 1989*

reached by agreement on Rawls's first formulation of the principles,[8] and a higher level still through his final formulation.[9]

It would seem, then, that we cannot say without prior clarification of the required specificity whether we already have an adequate consensus on a conception of justice, or only a constitutional consensus. For whether we have one or the other is likely to depend on how specific is our formulation of the principle(s) of justice. Suppose the level of specificity required is no higher than this: principles of justice (in the sense of principles with the appropriate function of "assigning basic rights and duties and [of] determining what people should take to be the appropriate distribution of benefits and burdens of social cooperation")[10] are principles of justice (in the sense of principles providing empirical criteria for correctly distinguishing the just from the unjust) "when no arbitrary distinctions are made between persons in the assigning of rights and duties and when the rules determine a proper balance between competing claims to the advantages of social life."[11] If we think of principles of justice on this high level of abstraction then, probably, we already have a consensus on the principles of justice. But if they must be formulated at the very high level of specificity of Rawls's final formulation in *A Theory of Justice*,[12] then we almost certainly do not have an adequate consensus.

IV

The question, therefore, arises what level of consensus is adequate. In *A Theory of Justice,* Rawls claims that, despite the diversity and incompatibility of our different conceptions of justice, we each have one or other such conception and therefore understand the need for, and are prepared to affirm, "a characteristic set of principles for assigning basic rights and duties for determining what [we] take to be the appropriate distribution of the benefits and burdens of social cooperation."[13] This suggests to me the view that, since we understand the need for agreement on principles of justice at the level of specificity at which we now have disagreement, the political philosopher should present principles of justice with a high degree of specificity, perhaps as high as Rawls's final formulation.[14]

However, Rawls also says things that suggest something rather different. "We suppose that these [implicitly shared fundamental] ideas and principles can be elaborated into a political conception of justice, which we hope can gain the support of an overlapping consensus. Of course, whether this can be done can be verified only by actually elaborating a

8. Ibid., p. 60.
9. Ibid., pp. 302–3.
10. Ibid., p. 4.
11. Ibid., p. 5.
12. Ibid., pp. 302–3.
13. Ibid., p. 4.
14. Ibid., pp. 302 ff.

political conception of justice and exhibiting the way in which it could be thus supported. It is also likely that, as we have seen, more than one political conception may be worked up from the fund of shared political ideas; *indeed this is desirable,* as these rival conceptions will then compete for citizens' allegiance and will be gradually modified and deepened by the contrast between them" (pp. 6–7; my emphasis). And in a long and important footnote he adds, "a comprehensive doctrine, whenever widely, if not universally shared in society, tends to become oppressive and stifling" (p. 4, n. 7, sec. 5).

It is not clear to me why a widely and freely adopted comprehensive doctrine, such as "the philosophical liberalism" of Mill or Kant, should be stifling whereas a widely shared narrowly political doctrine, such as "political liberalism," is not. It is, therefore, unclear to me whether development in the direction of an overlapping consensus on a political conception of justice with the degree of specificity of the final version (or some other higher or lower degree) is really desirable. If a constitutional consensus, such as we appear to have now, provides stable social union and if the competition of rival conceptions "worked up from the fund of shared political ideas" is desirable and if there is a danger that wide agreement on a very specific principle of justice, even if political, would tend to become "oppressive and stifling," should political philosophers hope or press for a higher-level consensus than we already have? Can we even define that level of specificity so that we know exactly what to aim at, or what to maintain when we have reached it? Is there any reason for going beyond the level of consensus we have now, supposing that what we now have gives us stable social unity?

V

Let us, however, set aside these difficult questions and grant, at least for argument's sake, that contemporary Western political philosophers should regard it as their aim to formulate a conception of justice, whatever may be the appropriate degree of specificity, that has "some hope" of commanding an adequate consensus rather than be satisfied with the present constitutional consensus. There remains the question why, as political philosophers, they must advance only (liberal) conceptions that are (narrowly) political (rather than philosophical) and why they must not widen these conceptions except where and to the extent that this is necessary to refute a comprehensive religious, metaphysical, or moral conception that conflicts with the political conception advanced by the philosopher.

Here, the three main points in question are (i) whether in order to produce or maintain stable social unity it is necessary or helpful to achieve a high-level consensus on a conception of justice for the basic structure; (ii) whether the characteristics of a constitutional democracy, such as pluralism in religion, metaphysics, and morality make it impossible or highly unlikely or even undesirable to achieve anything wider than an overlapping consensus; and (iii) whether the presentation of a political

780   *Ethics   July 1989*

conception of justice is always the only or the best way to bring about or maintain such a consensus.

We have already seen what distinctions and qualifications are necessary when considering i. As far as ii is concerned, Rawls himself concedes that, when people regard certain questions as so important that they advocate the use of force to ensure a correct settlement, we may have no alternative but to deny this and to assert something concerning which we had hoped as it turns out, vainly, to use the method of avoidance (p. 14). Rawls himself, even in a recent paper, defends the thesis of the priority of the right over the good, which would seem to be one of those long-standing philosophical controversies on which one might have wished to employ the method of avoidance.[15]

Thus clearly Rawls thinks that in certain circumstances it is both possible and desirable to achieve a wider than an overlapping consensus, or at any rate, that in these circumstances political philosophers must risk the attempt. However, he regards any widening of the conception of justice beyond the political as something they should engage in only when it is forced on them by the existence of comprehensive doctrines in conflict with the presented political conception of justice.

This brings us to iii. Should political philosophers venture beyond a political conception only when there already exist "dangerous" comprehensive doctrines in conflict with the liberal conception of justice they favor? It seems to me that political philosophers need not wait until such "dangerous" doctrines have begun to spread. If our presentation of a wider conception can have any effect once these passions of intolerance have arisen and their propagation is organized by believers (and perhaps others who expect to reap personal gains from the spread of hatred and mistrust), might it not also help to prevent these views from gaining adherents in the first place? Insofar as such hostile movements are based on comprehensive conceptions in conflict with liberal conceptions of justice, political philosophers concerned to reach or maintain an adequate consensus on such a conception or even on a constitutional consensus might do well to refute such comprehensive conceptions before they become popular.[16]

15. John Rawls, "The Priority of Right and Ideas of the Good," *Philosophy and Public Affairs* 17 (1988): 251–76.

16. In his illustration, Rawls says, "we do not state more of our comprehensive view than we think would advance the quest for consensus. The reason for this restraint is to respect, as far as we can, the limits of free public reason" (p. 14). The second of these two sentences is somewhat puzzling for it suggests that any widening of the conception advanced amounts to a failure to respect the limits of free public reason. But why should that be so? Under a constitutional consensus, we could offer, for instance, a doctrine of philosophical (rather than political) liberalism, such as that of Kant or Mill (pp. 5–6, 23–24) without, surely, infringing these limits. We would infringe them only if we pushed these doctrines in illegitimate ways, say, by indoctrination and suppression of contrary views. Thus, the only valid reason for political philosophers not to advance a doctrine more comprehensive than a narrowly political one would seem to be that it would not have a chance of achieving

Of course, this does not mean they should present fully comprehensive doctrines. For major parts of these would be simply irrelevant. It would be a waste of time for political philosophers to argue about transubstantiation or the role of memory in personal identity or the merits of virtue ethics versus duty ethics, or even "the status of values as expressed by realism and subjectivism" (p. 13). But it would not be irrelevant to include all those aspects of a moral doctrine that have been developed for a broader subject than the basic structure. For if they are convincing, that might help in converting those who are attracted by comprehensive religious or metaphysical doctrines that are in real conflict with a (narrowly) political conception of justice.

Our main problem does not seem to be that as political philosophers we take on unnecessary quarrels with rival comprehensive conceptions that are compatible with our narrowly political (liberal) conception of justice. It is, rather, that there are, and that we must attempt to refute, rival comprehensive conceptions that are in conflict not only with our liberal political conception of justice but even with the existing constitutional consensus. I share Rawls's aim to make political philosophy independent of the interminable controversies in religion and metaphysics, but I do not see political philosophy as similarly isolable from ethics. It seems to me that social justice is a branch of justice and justice a branch of morality. I think a consensus on a conception of justice might be easier to reach or maintain if political philosophers did not detach themselves from the relevant parts of moral philosophy. I return to this topic in Section VII.

VI

Let us now ask in precisely what sense the aims of political philosophy, unlike those of moral philosophy, are or should be practical. According to Rawls, the relevant difference between the politician and the political philosopher would seem to be a matter of the scope of the practical political concern: "The politician, we say, looks to the next election, the statesman to the next generation, and philosophy to the indefinite future" (p. 24). For this reason, Rawls thinks, political philosophy is compelled "to consider fundamental institutional questions and the assumptions of a reasonable moral psychology" (p. 24). For this reason also "the political conception [of justice presented by the political philosopher] needs to be such that there is some hope of its gaining the support of an overlapping consensus" (p. 1). Thus the relevant difference between the three would seem to be only the time frame of their practical aim. And this in turn suggests that the political philosopher must eliminate or at least rank lower those "utopian" (p. 22) conceptions with regard to which there is little or no hope that they will "gradually over generations become the

---

consensus. But if that is so, it will also be hopeless to "deny" such conflicting comprehensive views once they have become widespread. And respecting the limits of free public reason seems irrelevant. For further remarks on this topic see Sec. VI below.

782   *Ethics*   *July 1989*

focus of an overlapping consensus" (p. 24), just as the politician must eliminate or rank lower those political platforms that would jeopardize his election.

To clarify the question, we can distinguish two dimensions of practicality and its opposite. One ranges from the "stronger" realizability to the "weaker" foreseeability and their opposites, the other from the stronger empirical confirmability to the weaker imaginative envisageability and their opposites. This creates four senses. In order of strength, they are: the empirically realizable, the empirically foreseeable, the imaginatively realizable, and the imaginatively foreseeable. I begin by examining the stronger interpretation in each dimension.

On the first dimension, Rawls appears to favor the stronger interpretation. The political philosopher (unlike, presumably, the political scientist) is not merely trying to foresee which, if any, conception will gain consensus but tries, by a suitable presentation of one of the conceptions that have a hope of achieving a consensus, to make a difference to which conception will be accepted.

Three comments. First, this will pose a difficult (but perhaps unavoidable) choice for the political philosopher. He may have to play two potentially conflicting criteria against each other. Suppose among the conceptions that appear to have some hope of gaining consensus are justice as fairness, the libertarian, the socialist, and the utilitarian conceptions. And suppose also that, in his view, justice as fairness is the one that is best supported by those political values embedded in our culture that the philosopher most favors but that the utilitarian and the libertarian conceptions are more likely to gain consensus. Which conception should he present? If he presents justice as fairness, is he unacceptably utopian; is he failing to work for his proper end as a political philosopher?

Second, as far as practicality is concerned, I cannot see a significant difference between the aim of the political and the moral philosopher. Both present (among other things) conceptions of justice. Both will want to achieve adequate consensus on them. Both will attempt to work these up from values embedded in the culture. Both will be faced by the same choice between two potentially conflicting criteria: likelihood of gaining consensus and their own ranking of merit.

Third, there is a possible (though perhaps only partial) explanation of why someone might think that political philosophers have a practical aim while moral philosophers do not. The explanation is a failure to note an important difference between a politician and a statesman, on the one hand, and a political philosopher, on the other. The former, by their specifically political role, have various forms of power by whose exercise they shape the legally enforceable rules that determine the distribution of the benefits and burdens of cooperation. In their selection of principles to be presented they are often strongly motivated by the aim of retaining or extending this power. For them the choice of a principle to present will often be a means to achieving consensus, not on a principle they judge the morally best but, through its sufficiently wide acceptance *as* the best (even if they themselves do not share this appraisal), on a means to gaining or retaining the desired political power. In this respect, then, they are more "practical" than the moral, but also than the political, philosopher but in a different sense of "practical": their primary aim is power, not stable social unity or consensus.

Concerning the second dimension, empiricalness, the main problem is this. If a political philosopher is serious about rebutting the charge of utopianism and ignoring practical aims, he is likely to want to clarify how the existence of a consensus on a conception of justice can be empirically ascertained, what would constitute a consensus sufficient for stable social unity, and what features of a conception of justice increase or decrease the likelihood of such an adequate consensus. He would want to determine empirically under what conditions the presentation of a political conception is the best way to gain a consensus sufficient for stable unity.

It is unclear to me whether Rawls expects the political philosopher to be thus empirical. If not, if he is satisfied with a merely imaginatively realizable or foreseeable consensus on a principle of justice, is he not open to the charge of utopianism or failing to be practical in the sense explained? Are scenarios, such as those sketched by Rawls, of the transition from a Hobbesian modus vivendi to an overlapping consensus, more than armchair sociology or political science?

However, Rawls does not seem to want anything stronger than this. In the concluding sentences of "The Idea of an Overlapping Consensus," he says, "Political philosophy assumes the role Kant gave to philosophy generally: the defense of reasonable faith. In our case this becomes the defense of reasonable faith in the real possibility of a just constitutional regime" (p. 25).

If that is the extent of the practical aim of political philosophy, is moral philosophy even less practical than this? Does the moral philosopher not have to take consensus into account at all? Is morality a purely individual matter? Can we simply agree to differ? Do we not, in cases of moral disagreement, say, on abortion, need something like our constitutional consensus, quite as much as when we disagree on justice?

We have already noted the possible correlation between consensus and degree of specificity of the presented formulation of a conception of justice. Now we must attend to the two other dimensions, the extent and the intensity of the consensus.

What I call "extent" covers the number of the relevant people consenting. Rawls speaks of "the bulk of the politically active citizens." To settle the questions empirically, we would have to settle who exactly the politically active citizens are (the voters, the party members, the organizers, the readers/writers of political tracts, the marchers?) and what proportion of them is sufficient to amount to "the bulk."

What I call "intensity" spans the range of attitudes from reluctant to indifferent acquiescence, active support, explicit (self-conscious, rea-

784   *Ethics*   *July 1989*

soned) intellectual agreement, implicit agreement, that is, agreement that would become explicit under the appropriate conditions.

But perhaps all this is misguided, like asking how many hairs a person must have on his head if he is not to be regarded as bald. Perhaps we need a further theory which would allow us to determine "adequate" consensus by some "indicator"; thus, recidivism is often thought to be such an indicator of the deterring or rehabilitating efficacy of a type of punishment. But what would be a plausible indicator of consensus and its extent or intensity?[17]

It is unclear, then, what exactly Rawls wishes to emphasize about the aims of the political philosopher and how they must modify his writings to serve these aims when he stresses the practical aspect of his task, and why he thinks this is different from that of the moral philosopher.

VII

I now want briefly to formulate, explore, and contrast several of the conceptions of the concept of justice[18] which have been most widely advanced in the philosophical literature, and to draw attention to another which, though not to my knowledge previously advocated, is yet, at any rate by my lights, one that more accurately represents our intuitive understanding of justice than do the others. If I am right in this, then, since

17. In any case, Rawls does not seem to favor this approach, for he says (p. 5, n. 8), "Free and willing agreement is agreement endorsed by our considered convictions on due reflection, or in what I have called 'reflective equilibrium' " (see *TJ*, pp. 19 ff., 48 ff.).

18. I distinguish between (i) a conception of the concept of justice and (ii) (following Rawls) a conception (or principle or criterion) of justice. (i) A conception of the concept A I take to be a view of what it is for a linguistic community to have the concept A. Often there is no question but that a certain linguistic community has a certain concept, e.g., that the contemporary Anglo-American linguistic community has the concept of happiness, whereas it is not clear that the ancient Greeks had exactly the same concept. Where there is no such doubt, adherents of different conceptions of the concept normally disagree about what is the correct conception of the concept. Ryle took it that Descartes's linguistic community had the same concept of mind as Ryle's, but he thought that Descartes's conception of the concept was a misconception; he did not think it was a correct conception of a different superior or inferior concept. In other cases, as with Rawls's primary goods or reflective equilibrium, the conception advanced is a proposal for the introduction of a new concept. In the former case, the existence of the concept (the practice) precedes the conception, in the latter the conception precedes the existence of the concept (the practice). I assume that our linguistic community has a single (reasonably coherent) concept of justice, that different thinkers, especially philosophers, form different conceptions of that concept, and that some of these are misconceptions. One could but I do not here raise the difficult question of whether there are or were other concepts comparable to our concept of justice that are superior to ours, say, the Greek concept of *dikaiosyne*. (ii) The concept of justice is a normative moral concept. It determines how to distinguish the just from the unjust, and it morally requires those who can be either just or unjust to be just rather than unjust. In contradistinction to a conception of the concept of justice, a conception of justice is a view of how to tell what would satisfy this moral requirement. A correct conception of the concept of justice must enable us to tell what is a correct, what an incorrect, conception of justice.

this conception of the concept also involves a particular principle, or conception, of justice, albeit a highly nonspecific one, we already have a consensus on a conception of justice, though we may not be aware of this, since we may not yet realize that this is a correct conception of our concept of justice.

First, then, a brief delineation of five conceptions of the concept of justice. The first of these is probably the oldest and most widely held. Plato attributes it to Simonides, it was embraced by Cicero and Justinian, and philosophers have defended it more or less continuously since then.[19] On this view, justice consists in giving everyone his due, where something is due to someone if he has a right to it or if he deserves it. It is due to him from another if she has a duty or if, though she has no duty, she morally ought to secure it for him.

I think this is not a conception that captures all our important commonsense intuitions about the concept. If I have undertaken to get you to the church on time, then that is what is due to you from me and if I get you there on time, I have given you that due. But I have not exhibited the virtue of justice, I have not been just to you or done you justice. I have done my duty by you, I have lived up to my commitments, I have done what was morally required of me. Nor of course have I been unjust to you. Indeed, I would not have been unjust to you if I had not got you there on time either, though I would have failed in my duty, and so on. This is simply not a case in which either justice or injustice is applicable, as we commonly conceive of it.

The second conception is a slight modification of the first. It takes justice to be that part of morality which has to do with what is morally required of one, what others have a right to against one, and what can justifiably be exacted. This conception (developed by J. S. Mill as an account of duty) finds (misguided) support in Kant's division of morality into the domain of the *Rechts-* and *Tugendpflichten*, by the frequent (but misleading) translation of the former as *juridical duties* or *duties of justice*. Unlike the first conception, it includes duties, such as driving on the right, which are not due to anyone in particular, and it excludes what another deserves but has no right to. This does indeed delineate an important part of morality, namely, that which contrasts with what goes beyond the call of duty; but, like the first conception and for much the same reason, it does not seem to me to pick out our concept of justice.

These first two conceptions of the concept construe justice as an excellence of any individual moral agent who behaves in ways that conform to certain high-level principles. They identify the principles of justice with the principles enjoining the doing of one's duty, and the respecting of other people's rights and deserts.

19. See, e.g., the important and illuminating paper by Joel Feinberg, "Noncomparative Justice," *Philosophical Review* 83 (1974): 298.

The third is what Rawls calls "formal justice."[20] It is the impartial and conscientious administration of the institutions composing the basic structure of a society, that is, those institutions that determine people's rights and duties in a particular society. On this interpretation, justice is the conscientiousness of a judge or of those playing analogous adjudicative roles—for example, parent, teacher, administrator—rather than that of any moral agent irrespective of what institutional role he plays or whether he plays any such role. This seems to me to capture one important element of the concept. Those who think of justice as treating equals equally and unequals unequally[21] may have in mind such conscientious and impartial administration of institutions with adjudicating roles. However, as Rawls says, following Sidgwick, "law and institutions may be equally executed and yet be unjust."[22]

The fourth conception identifies justice with a certain excellence of institutions, namely, conformance with a certain principle, which we could call the principle of equitability. On this fourth conception, justice (or justness) is the characteristic excellence of the conventional devices determining what is due from whom to whom. These devices include those institutions which make this determination possible by assigning certain rights, duties, and normative powers[23] (such as authority) to certain roles, for instance, those of legislator and citizen, parent and child, employer and employee. But they also include noninstitutional devices such as publicly recognized precepts, rules, and principles that hold for classes of people not defined as institutional role players, for example, females, children, and persons in a good position to rescue someone in distress. We can call equitable or inequitable also those states of affairs that conform to these judgments and principles. Hence on this fourth conception they too could be called just or unjust. Thus, if the legal principles that led to *Plessy v. Ferguson* (U.S. Supreme Court 163, US 537 [1896], upholding racial segregation in public transport and education) violate the principle of equitability, then the state of affairs created by the correct enforcement of that ruling is also inequitable and therefore on this conception unjust.[24]

20. Rawls, *TJ*, pp. 58–59.

21. For example, William K. Frankena, *Some Beliefs about Justice*, Lindley Lecture (Lawrence: University of Kansas Press, 1966).

22. Rawls, *TJ*, p. 59.

23. In the sense explicated by Joseph Raz, "Voluntary Obligations and Normative Powers," *Proceedings of the Aristotelian Society* 46, suppl. (1972): 79–102. An example is the power of assuming obligations by promising or of imposing duties on others by legislating.

24. Thus, the provisions of a certain peace can be equitable and so just on this conception, if the peace treaty requires each party to provide to the other what has become due to or deserved by the other from it as a result of what happened in the preceding war. Similarly, a declaration of war can be equitable and so just, on this conception, if a country is due or deserves certain things from another which it can attain only by making war on the other. It is less plausible, on this conception, to speak of a just war since if the declaration of war by one party is just, engaging in war by the other party will not be just—unless the other party engages in war for unrelated reasons.

Thus, the principle of equitability applies to a good deal more than Rawls's basic structure and therefore might well have to be formulated in a less specific way than Rawls's two principles if it is to fit the many different contexts to which it must be applicable.

What is the content of this important moral principle? Perhaps the least controversial approach to this difficult question would seem to be this. Since this principle imposes a significant constraint on the content of a very wide range of social devices that determine the distribution of the benefits and burdens of social interaction regulated by them, its content must be such that all those whose interaction is regulated by it have at least adequate if not compelling reason to accept it (or at least welcome its social adoption). For then they will comply voluntarily insofar as they are reason-guided, with the requirements of social devices that conform to this principle.[25] Being "to everyone's advantage" or "for the good of everyone alike" would seem to be intended as more or less equivalent formulations of this principle.

The fifth conception combines the first, third, and fourth.[26] It ties justice to certain special institutions but subjects these to the principle of equitability. At the same time, it makes justice applicable not only to actions, persons, and institutions but also to judgments, states of affairs, and the world.[27] On this view of the concept, what can be just or unjust are only those persons (as well as their acts and the consequences of these acts) who play roles analogous to those of judges—those that dispense or mete out (what they purport to be) justice, those whose judgments of what is due from whom to whom constitute "declaratory justice," whether first-order (when people were not required to know what was due) or corrective (when they knew, or ought to have known but failed to act accordingly).

Thus on this conception anyone can receive justice and suffer injustice, but the only persons who can be just or unjust are those "dispensing justice." They are just if they follow the rules of equitable devices determining what is due from whom to whom. They are unjust if they fail to follow the rules of such an equitable device.[28]

25. Rawls's difference principle can be seen as the application, whether defensible or not, of the principle of equitability to the design of a market economy under certain conditions, i.e., "chain connection" (*TJ*, pp. 81 ff.). What Rawls calls the "General Conception" of justice (*TJ*, p. 302) can be seen as its application under somewhat different conditions to the distribution of all types of primary goods. What generates the different formulations of the principle seems largely or entirely due to the different contexts and circumstances of application.

26. Rawls's conception of the concept of justice can perhaps be construed as a combination of the second and fourth.

27. In "Noncomparative Justice," Feinberg examines the notion of cosmic justice/injustice but lists only two senses, the justice/injustice done by or to the cosmos. But this makes sense only if one thinks of the cosmos as something analogous to a person. More commonly, cosmic justice/injustice is the justice/injustice done or received in the cosmos.

28. This account leaves unclear whether such dispensers of justice are just or unjust if they follow the rules of an inequitable device, and whether the persons subject to such an inequitable device suffer an injustice. If such dispensers are unjust, then they can be

788   *Ethics   July 1989*

On this conception, justice is that part of morality which deals with the authoritative interpretation of the principle of equitability and its application to the rules of institutions authoritatively laying down what is due from whom to whom and the application of these rules by authoritative judges to particular cases brought before them. On this conception, a world in which each person is concerned to, and does, give to all what is due to them from her, but which lacks an agency with the task of determining authoritatively what is thus due, and of suitably nudging those who are or might be reluctant to provide what is due, would be a morally admirable one, but not one that is just; not of course because it would be an unjust one, but because such a world has no need and no work for justice so conceived. The moral excellence of the people in this wonderful world can be characterized without reference to justice: they never wrong anybody; they always discharge their duties and obligations to others; and they honor one another's rights and deserts. But no one in this world is just or has justice dispensed to him or receives injustice. Concern for justice and about injustice arises only when as is, alas, usually and perhaps necessarily the case in our sort of world (as Hobbes and Locke noted), people do not always agree on what is due from whom to whom and do not always give to others what they know or believe is due from them to others. In this wonderful world (where a stricter version of Rawls's ideal, or strict, compliance holds),[29] institutions of justice would wither away.[30]

On this version, certain role players can be not only just or unjust, but just or unjust to others. Since what is due from one person to another will normally be either a benefit or a burden, a judge's adjudication will be just if he either allocates no smaller a benefit or no greater a burden than is due to the person. If a judge is just, he will also be just to the persons between whom he adjudicates. If he grants one of them a greater benefit or imposes a lesser burden than is his due, he is unjust, but not to him: he is unjust to the other person from or to whom he judged that benefit to be due.

---

so unintentionally and unknowingly. In this case, if their victims suffer an injustice, then they do so without the dispensers' being iniquitous. It seems plausible to say that, as long as they do not believe that the rules they apply are inequitable, such dispensers are meting out justice, but that they are not just, even though they believe they are. There may then be cases in which they mete out justice without being either just or unjust.

29. Rawls, *TJ*, p. 8. Stricter because compliance occurs (as in an ideal state of nature) without the need for institutions of declarative justice.

30. As is well known, Marx thought that in a classless society, in the so-called realm of freedom, where everybody gets what he needs, there is no call for such an authoritative determination of what is due from whom to whom, let alone for institutions' enforcing such determinations. In this even more wonderful world, each will willingly give according to his ability, and this will produce and will be known to produce enough, perhaps more than enough, for each to be given according to his need (or is it his desire?). In this world of abundance, Marx thought, it will be unnecessary or pointless to determine how much or how little is due from whom to whom.

An interesting special case is that of judging character, a practice we all can and tend to engage in. The function of judgments of character is to acquaint members of the moral community with how well given individuals have, in the opinion of their peers, performed as moral agents. Such information is important for the formation of trust and distrust, without which morality could not work. Since every member of the moral community to a considerable extent depends, for the good life, on the reputation he has with others, the expression of such judgments constitutes powerful pressure in the direction of moral conformity. A good reputation is obviously an important asset, a bad reputation a liability. At the same time, a deservedly bad reputation serves to protect others against unwarranted trust. Thus, everyone has a legitimate claim to other people's making judgments no less favorable than is warranted by the facts. And his neighbors have a right to judgments no more favorable than is warranted by the facts.

This imposes a role-duty of conscientiousness and veracity on character judges. Since a bad reputation is a burden and a good reputation a good, it is clear that a person who judges another less favorably or more unfavorably than is warranted by the facts is wronging him, by being unjust to him. In the first case the injustice takes the form of failing to do him justice, in the second case of doing him an injustice. By contrast, if he judges him more favorably or less unfavorably than is warranted by the facts, he is not unjust to him, nor is he doing him or others an injustice nor failing to do him or them justice. The reason for this is, of course, that in this case the judgment of declaratory justice does not merely say or imply what is due to a person from another or from her to him. The judgment itself is the deliberate giving or not giving to the person judged of something which the judge knows or ought to know is due to that person or to others from the judge. What is due to her is that she not be judged less favorably or more unfavorably, what is due to others, that she not be judged more favorably or less unfavorably than is warranted by the facts. Hence judging her more favorably or less unfavorably than is warranted by the facts is an injustice not to her but to others, yet it is not the sort of injustice to them which is a failing to do them justice or doing to them an injustice.

On this fifth conception of the concept of justice, judgment of character is the main case in which the just or unjust behavior is both a judgment (though merely implicit) of what is due to someone from the judge himself and the giving or not giving her of what is her due. Perhaps it is attention to this special case that has misled some into thinking that the first conception offers the best account of our concept of justice.

On this fifth conception of the concept of justice and its implied conception of justice (the highly abstract principle of equitability) we may well already have an adequate consensus on this conception of justice. It is, of course, not clear that Rawls's two principles can be derived from this more abstract principle, and it is fairly clear that, even if there already is a consensus on it, there is no consensus on Rawls's two principles.

790   *Ethics   July 1989*

VIII

If I am right about the main points I made, then the following would seem to be reasonable conclusions.

1. Our existing constitutional consensus would seem to be sufficient for stable social unity, even though it does not amount to a consensus on a highly specific principle (or set of principles) of justice for the whole basic structure.

2. It is not clear that an overlapping consensus on a conception of justice would produce greater stability and social unity than our existing constitutional consensus or that, if it did, this would be desirable.

3. On one interpretation of the concept of justice, we may already have an adequate consensus on a principle of justice for the whole basic structure, namely, the principle of equitability.

4. Political philosophers need not necessarily present a (narrowly) political conception of (social) justice, but may, while avoiding unnecessary because irrelevant entanglements with the long-standing controversies in religion and metaphysics, present a political conception that can be seen as the application of the general moral principle of equitability to the special context of the basic structure. For this would add the backing of morality to the political conception presented.

5. There is no significant difference between the aims of political and moral philosophy, as far as practicality is concerned. Both must draw on the values embedded in our culture. Both must present conceptions that have a hope of commanding an adequate consensus. Neither is practical in the sense that its practitioners' theories and judgments are exercises of normative powers or of political power, nor attempts to gain or retain or increase such power. In this respect, political philosophers differ significantly from politicians and statesmen, but not from moral philosophers.

[15]

POLITICAL LIBERALISM

POLITICAL LIBERALISM. By John Rawls.[1] New York: Columbia University Press. 1993. Pp. xxxiv, 401. $29.95.

Reviewed by Michael J. Sandel[2]

Rare is the work of political philosophy that provokes sustained debate. It is a measure of its greatness that John Rawls's *A Theory of Justice*[3] inspired not one debate, but three.

The first, by now a starting point for students of moral and political philosophy, is the argument between utilitarians and rights-oriented liberals. Should justice be founded on utility, as Jeremy Bentham and John Stuart Mill argue, or does respect for individual rights require a basis for justice independent of utilitarian considerations, as Kant and Rawls maintain? Before Rawls wrote, utilitarianism was the dominant view within Anglo-American moral and political philosophy. Since *A Theory of Justice*, rights-oriented liberalism has come to predominate.[4]

The second debate inspired by Rawls's work is an argument within rights-oriented liberalism. If certain individual rights are so important that even considerations of the general welfare cannot override them, it remains to ask which rights these are. Libertarian liberals, like Robert Nozick and Friedrich Hayek, argue that government should respect basic civil and political liberties, and also the right to the fruits of our labor as conferred by the market economy; redistributive policies that tax the rich to help the poor thus violate our rights.[5] Egalitarian liberals like Rawls disagree. They argue that we cannot meaningfully exercise our civil and political liberties without the provision of basic social and economic needs; government should therefore assure each person, as a matter of right, a decent level of such goods as education, income, housing, health care, and the like. The debate between the libertarian and egalitarian versions of rights-oriented liberalism, which flourished in the academy in the 1970s, corresponds roughly to the debate in American politics, familiar since the New

---

[1] James Bryant Conant University Professor, Emeritus, Harvard University.

[2] Professor of Government, Harvard University. The author is grateful to Yochai Benkler, Joshua Cohen, Stephen Macedo, and J. Russell Muirhead for helpful comments and criticisms.

[3] JOHN RAWLS, A THEORY OF JUSTICE (1971).

[4] *See, e.g.,* H.L.A. Hart, *Between Utility and Rights, in* THE IDEA OF FREEDOM 77, 77 (Alan Ryan ed., 1979).

[5] *See* FRIEDRICH A. HAYEK, THE CONSTITUTION OF LIBERTY (1960); ROBERT NOZICK, ANARCHY, STATE, AND UTOPIA (1974).

Deal, between defenders of the market economy and advocates of the welfare state.

The third debate prompted by Rawls's work centers on an assumption shared by libertarian and egalitarian liberals alike. This is the idea that government should be neutral among competing conceptions of the good life. Despite their various accounts of what rights we have, rights-oriented liberals agree that the principles of justice that specify our rights should not depend for their justification on any particular conception of the good life.[6] This idea, central to the liberalism of Kant, Rawls, and many contemporary liberals, is summed up in the claim that the right is prior to the good.[7]

I. Contesting the Priority of the Right over the Good

For Rawls, as for Kant, the right is prior to the good in two respects, and it is important to distinguish them. First, the right is prior to the good in the sense that certain individual rights "trump," or outweigh, considerations of the common good. Second, the right is prior to the good in that the principles of justice that specify our rights do not depend for their justification on any particular conception of the good life. It is this second claim for the priority of the right that prompted the most recent wave of debate about Rawlsian liberalism, an argument that has flourished in the last decade under the somewhat misleading label of the "liberal-communitarian debate."

A number of political philosophers writing in the 1980s took issue with the notion that justice can be detached from considerations of the good. Challenges to contemporary rights-oriented liberalism found in the writings of Alasdair MacIntyre,[8] Charles Taylor,[9] Michael Wal-

---

[6] *See* Bruce A. Ackerman, Social Justice in the Liberal State 349–78 (1980); Ronald Dworkin, Taking Rights Seriously 90–100, 168–77 (1977); Charles Fried, Right and Wrong 114–19 (1978); Charles E. Larmore, Patterns of Moral Complexity 42–68 (1987); Nozick, *supra* note 5, at 33; Rawls, *supra* note 3, at 30–32, 446–51, 560; Ronald Dworkin, *Liberalism, in* Public and Private Morality 113, 127–36 (Stuart Hampshire ed., 1978); Thomas Nagel, *Moral Conflict and Political Legitimacy*, 16 Phil. & Pub. Aff. 215, 227–37 (1987).

[7] *See* Immanuel Kant, Critique of Pure Reason (Norman K. Smith trans., St. Martin's Press 1965) (1788); Immanuel Kant, Groundwork of the Metaphysic of Morals (H.J. Paton trans., Harper & Row 3d ed. 1964) (1785); Immanuel Kant, *On the Common Saying: "This May Be True in Theory, but It Does Not Apply in Practice," in* Kant's Political Writings 61, 73–74 (Hans Reiss ed. & H.B. Nisbet trans., 1970); Rawls, *supra* note 3, at 30–32, 446–51, 560.

[8] *See* Alasdair MacIntyre, After Virtue (2d ed. 1984) [hereinafter MacIntyre, After Virtue]; Alasdair MacIntyre, Is Patriotism a Virtue?: The Lindley Lecture (1984) [hereinafter MacIntyre, Is Patriotism a Virtue?]; Alasdair MacIntyre, Whose Justice? Which Rationality? (1988).

[9] *See* Charles Taylor, *The Nature and Scope of Distributive Justice, in* Philosophy and the Human Sciences, 2 Philosophical Papers 289 (1985); Charles Taylor, Sources of

zer,[10] and also in my own work,[11] are sometimes described as the "communitarian" critique of liberalism. The term "communitarian" is misleading, however, insofar as it implies that rights should rest on the values or preferences that prevail in any given community at any given time. Few, if any, of those who have challenged the priority of the right are communitarians in this sense.[12] The question is not whether rights should be respected, but whether rights can be identified and justified in a way that does not presuppose any particular conception of the good. At issue in the third wave of debate about Rawls's liberalism is not the relative weight of individual and communal claims, but the terms of relation between the right and the good.[13] Those who dispute the priority of the right argue that justice

---

THE SELF: THE MAKING OF THE MODERN IDENTITY (1989) [hereinafter TAYLOR, SOURCES OF THE SELF].

[10] *See* MICHAEL WALZER, SPHERES OF JUSTICE: A DEFENSE OF PLURALISM AND EQUALITY (1983).

[11] *See* MICHAEL J. SANDEL, LIBERALISM AND THE LIMITS OF JUSTICE (1982); Michael J. Sandel, *The Procedural Republic and the Unencumbered Self*, 12 POL. THEORY 81 (1984).

[12] Michael Walzer comes close to this view when he writes: "Justice is relative to social meanings. . . . A given society is just if its substantive life is lived . . . in a way faithful to the shared understandings of the members." WALZER, *supra* note 10, at 312–13. Walzer allows, however, that prevailing practices of rights can be criticized from the standpoint of alternative interpretations of a society's shared understandings. *See id.* at 84–91.

[13] Much of the debate about liberal political philosophy in the last decade has focused on the "communitarian" critique of liberalism, or, more broadly, on the challenge to the priority of the right over the good. The best overall account of this debate is STEPHEN MULHALL & ADAM SWIFT, LIBERALS AND COMMUNITARIANS (1992). Edited volumes on the subject include COMMUNITARIANISM AND INDIVIDUALISM (Shlomo Avineri & Avner de-Shalit eds., 1992); LIBERALISM AND ITS CRITICS (Michael J. Sandel ed., 1984); LIBERALISM AND THE GOOD (R. Bruce Douglass, Gerald M. Mara & Henry S. Richardson eds., 1990); LIBERALISM AND THE MORAL LIFE (Nancy L. Rosenblum ed., 1989); and UNIVERSALISM VS. COMMUNITARIANISM (David Rasmussen ed., 1990). Notable book-length works include DANIEL BELL, COMMUNITARIANISM AND ITS CRITICS (1993); WILL KYMLICKA, LIBERALISM, COMMUNITY AND CULTURE (1989); CHARLES E. LARMORE, PATTERNS OF MORAL COMPLEXITY (1987); and STEPHEN MACEDO, LIBERAL VIRTUES: CITIZENSHIP, VIRTUE, AND COMMUNITY IN LIBERAL CONSTITUTIONALISM (1990). The vast literature on the subject includes, among others: JEREMY WALDRON, *Particular Values and Critical Morality*, in LIBERAL RIGHTS 168 (1993); C. Edwin Baker, *Sandel on Rawls*, 133 U. PA. L. REV. 895 (1985); Sheyla Benhabib, *Autonomy, Modernity and Community: Communitarianism and Critical Social Theory in Dialogue*, in ZWISCHENBETRACHTUNGEN IM PROZESS DER AUFKLAERUNG 373 (Axel Honneth, Thomas McCarthy, Claus Offe & Albrecht Welmer eds., 1989); Allen E. Buchanan, *Assessing the Communitarian Critique of Liberalism*, 99 ETHICS 852 (1989); Gerald Doppelt, *Is Rawls's Kantian Liberalism Coherent and Defensible?*, 99 ETHICS 815 (1989); Stephen A. Gardbaum, *Law, Politics, and the Claims of Community*, 90 MICH. L. REV. 685 (1992); Emily R. Gill, *Goods, Virtues, and the Constitution of the Self*, in LIBERALS ON LIBERALISM 111 (Alfonso J. Damico ed., 1986); Amy Gutmann, *Communitarian Critics of Liberalism*, 14 PHIL. & PUB. AFF. 308 (1985); H.N. Hirsch, *The Threnody of Liberalism*, 14 POL. THEORY 423 (1986); Will Kymlicka, *Liberalism and Communitarianism*, 18 CAN. J. PHIL. 181 (1988); Will Kymlicka, *Rawls on Teleology and Deontology*, 17 PHIL. & PUB. AFF. 173 (1988); Christopher Lasch, *The Communitarian Critique of Liberalism*, 69 SOUNDINGS 60 (1986); David Miller, *In What Sense Must Socialism Be Communitarian?*, 6 SOC. PHIL. & POL. 57

is relative to the good, not independent of it. As a philosophical matter, our reflections about justice cannot reasonably be detached from our reflections about the nature of the good life and the highest human ends. As a political matter, our deliberations about justice and rights cannot proceed without reference to the conceptions of the good that find expression in the many cultures and traditions within which those deliberations take place.

Much of the debate about the priority of the right has focused on competing conceptions of the person and of how we should understand our relation to our ends. Are we, as moral agents, bound only by the ends and roles we choose for ourselves, or can we sometimes be obligated to fulfill certain ends we have not chosen — ends given by nature or God, for example, or by our identities as members of families, peoples, cultures, or traditions? In various ways, those who have criticized the priority of right have resisted the notion that we can make sense of our moral and political obligations in wholly voluntarist or contractual terms.

In *A Theory of Justice*, Rawls linked the priority of the right to a voluntarist, or broadly Kantian, conception of the person. According to this conception, we are not simply defined as the sum of our desires, as utilitarians assume, nor are we beings whose perfection consists in realizing certain purposes or ends given by nature, as Aristotle held. Rather, we are free and independent selves, unbound by antecedent moral ties, capable of choosing our ends for ourselves. This is the conception of the person that finds expression in the ideal of the state

---

(1989); Chantal Mouffe, *American Liberalism and Its Critics: Rawls, Taylor, Sandel and Walzer*, 8 PRAXIS INT'L 193 (1988); Patrick Neal, *A Liberal Theory of the Good?*, 17 CAN. J. PHIL. 567 (1987); Jeffrey Paul & Fred D. Miller Jr., *Communitarian and Liberal Theories of the Good*, 43 REV. METAPHYSICS 803 (1990); Milton C. Regan, Jr., *Community and Justice in Constitutional Theory*, 1985 WIS. L. REV. 1073; Richard Rorty, *The Priority of Democracy to Philosophy*, in THE VIRGINIA STATUTE OF RELIGIOUS FREEDOM 257, 257–82 (Merrill D. Peterson & Robert C. Vaughan eds., 1988); George Sher, *Three Grades of Social Involvement*, 18 PHIL. & PUB. AFF. 133 (1989); Tom Sorell, *Self, Society, and Kantian Impersonality*, 74 MONIST 30 (1991); Symposium, *Law, Community, and Moral Reasoning*, 77 CAL. L. REV. 475 (1989); Charles Taylor, *Cross-Purposes: The Liberal-Communitarian Debate*, in LIBERALISM AND THE MORAL LIFE, *supra*; Robert B. Thigpen & Lyle A. Downing, *Liberalism and the Communitarian Critique*, 31 AM. J. POL. SCI. 637 (1987); John Tomasi, *Individual Rights and Community Virtues*, 101 ETHICS 521 (1991); John R. Wallach, *Liberals, Communitarians, and the Tasks of Political Theory*, 15 POL. THEORY 581 (1987); Michael Walzer, *The Communitarian Critique of Liberalism*, 18 POL. THEORY 6 (1990); Iris M. Young, *The Ideal of Community and the Politics of Difference*, 12 SOC. THEORY & PRAC. 1 (1986); and Joel Feinberg, *Liberalism, Community and Tradition*, TIKKUN, May-June 1988, at 38. Prior to *Political Liberalism*, Rawls addressed these issues in a number of essays, including *The Idea of an Overlapping Consensus*, 7 OXFORD J. LEGAL STUD. 1 (1987); *Justice as Fairness: Political Not Metaphysical*, 14 PHIL. & PUB. AFF. 223 (1985); and *The Priority of Right and Ideas of the Good*, 17 PHIL. & PUB. AFF. 251 (1987). In *Political Liberalism*, however, he states: "The changes in the later essays are sometimes said to be replies to criticisms raised by communitarians and others. I don't believe there is a basis for saying this" (p. xvii).

as a neutral framework. It is precisely because we are free and independent selves, capable of choosing our own ends, that we need a framework of rights that is neutral among ends. To base rights on some conception of the good would impose on some the values of others and so fail to respect each person's capacity to choose his or her own ends.

This conception of the person, and its link to the case for the priority of the right, are expressed throughout *A Theory of Justice*. Its most explicit statement comes toward the end of the book, in Rawls's account of "the good of justice." There Rawls argues, following Kant, that teleological doctrines are "radically misconceived" because they relate the right and the good in the wrong way:

> We should not attempt to give form to our life by first looking to the good independently defined. It is not our aims that primarily reveal our nature but rather the principles that we would acknowledge to govern the background conditions under which these aims are to be formed and the manner in which they are to be pursued. For the self is prior to the ends which are affirmed by it; even a dominant end must be chosen from among numerous possibilities. . . . We should therefore reverse the relation between the right and the good proposed by teleological doctrines and view the right as prior.[14]

In *A Theory of Justice*, the priority of the self to its ends supports the priority of the right to the good. "[A] moral person is a subject with ends he has chosen, and his fundamental preference is for conditions that enable him to frame a mode of life that expresses his nature as a free and equal rational being as fully as circumstances permit."[15] The notion that we are free and independent selves, unclaimed by prior moral ties, assures that considerations of justice will always outweigh other, more particular aims. In an eloquent expression of Kantian liberalism, Rawls explains the moral importance of the priority of the right in the following terms:

> [T]he desire to express our nature as a free and equal rational being can be fulfilled only by acting on the principles of right and justice as having first priority. . . . It is acting from this precedence that expresses our freedom from contingency and happenstance. Therefore in order to realize our nature we have no alternative but to plan to preserve our sense of justice as governing our other aims. This sentiment cannot be fulfilled if it is compromised and balanced against other ends as but one desire among the rest. . . . [H]ow far we succeed in expressing our nature depends upon how consistently we act from our sense of justice as finally regulative. What we cannot do is express our nature by following a plan that views the sense of justice as but

---

[14] RAWLS, *supra* note 3, at 560.
[15] *Id.* at 561.

one desire to be weighed against others. For this sentiment reveals what the person is, and to compromise it is not to achieve for the self free reign but to give way to the contingencies and accidents of the world.[16]

In different ways, those who disputed the priority of the right took issue with Rawls's conception of the person as a free and independent self, unencumbered by prior moral ties.[17] They argued that a conception of the self given prior to its aims and attachments could not make sense of certain important aspects of our moral and political experience. Certain moral and political obligations that we commonly recognize — such as obligations of solidarity, for example, or religious duties — may claim us for reasons unrelated to a choice. Such obligations are difficult to dismiss as merely confused, and yet difficult to account for if we understand ourselves as free and independent selves, unbound by moral ties we have not chosen.[18]

II. DEFENDING THE PRIORITY OF THE RIGHT OVER THE GOOD

In *Political Liberalism*, Rawls defends the priority of the right over the good. He sets aside, for the most part, issues raised in the first two waves of debate, about utility versus rights and libertarian versus egalitarian notions of distributive justice. *Political Liberalism* focuses instead on issues posed by the third wave of debate, about the priority of the right.

Given the controversy over the Kantian conception of the person that supports the priority of the right, at least two lines of reply are possible. One is to defend liberalism by defending the Kantian conception of the person; the other is to defend liberalism by detaching it from the Kantian conception. In *Political Liberalism*, Rawls adopts the second course. Rather than defend the Kantian conception of the person as a moral ideal, he argues that liberalism as he conceives it does not depend on that conception of the person after all. The priority of the right over the good does not presuppose any particular conception of the person, not even the one advanced in Part III of *A Theory of Justice*.

---

[16] *Id.* at 574–75.

[17] The objection to the conception of the person presented in *A Theory of Justice* does not depend on failing to see the original position as a device of representation. It can be stated wholly in terms of the conception of the person presented in Part III of *A Theory of Justice*, which Rawls now recasts as a political conception. Not only critics, but also defenders of Rawls's liberalism interpreted *A Theory of Justice* as affirming a Kantian conception of the person. *See, e.g.*, LARMORE, *supra* note 6, at 118–30.

[18] *See* MACINTYRE, AFTER VIRTUE, *supra* note 8, at 190–209; MACINTYRE, IS PATRIOTISM A VIRTUE?, *supra* note 8, *passim*; SANDEL, *supra* note 11, at 175–83; TAYLOR, SOURCES OF THE SELF, *supra* note 9, at 508.

A. *Political Versus Comprehensive Liberalism*

The case for liberalism, Rawls now argues, is political, not philosophical or metaphysical, and so does not depend on controversial claims about the nature of the self (pp. 29–35). The priority of the right over the good is not the application to politics of Kantian moral philosophy, but a practical response to the familiar fact that people in modern democratic societies typically disagree about the good. Because people's moral and religious convictions are unlikely to converge, it is more reasonable to seek agreement on principles of justice that are neutral with respect to those controversies (pp. xvi–xvii).

Central to Rawls's revised view is the distinction between political liberalism and liberalism as part of a comprehensive moral doctrine (pp. 154–58). Comprehensive liberalism affirms liberal political arrangements in the name of certain moral ideals, such as autonomy or individuality or self-reliance. Examples of liberalism as a comprehensive moral doctrine include the liberal visions of Kant and John Stuart Mill.[19] As Rawls acknowledges, the version of liberalism presented in *A Theory of Justice* is also an instance of comprehensive liberalism. "An essential feature of a well-ordered society associated with justice as fairness is that all its citizens endorse this conception on the basis of what I now call a comprehensive philosophical doctrine" (p. xvi). It is this feature that Rawls now revises, by recasting his theory as a "political conception of justice" (p. xvi).

Unlike comprehensive liberalism, political liberalism refuses to take sides in the moral and religious controversies that arise from comprehensive doctrines, including controversies about conceptions of the self. "Which moral judgments are true, all things considered, is not a matter for political liberalism" (p. xx). "To maintain impartiality between comprehensive doctrines, it does not specifically address the moral topics on which those doctrines divide" (p. xxviii). Given the difficulty of securing agreement on any comprehensive conception, it is unreasonable to expect that, even in a well-ordered society, all people will support liberal institutions for the same reason — as expressing the priority of the self to its ends, for example. Political liberalism abandons this hope as unrealistic and contrary to the aim of basing justice on principles that adherents of various moral and religious conceptions can accept. Rather than seek a philosophical foundation for principles of justice, political liberalism seeks the support of an "overlapping consensus" (p. 134). This means that different

---

[19] For contemporary examples of comprehensive liberalism, see GEORGE KATEB, THE INNER OCEAN: INDIVIDUALISM AND DEMOCRATIC CULTURE (1992); and JOSEPH RAZ, THE MORALITY OF FREEDOM (1986). Ronald Dworkin describes his view as a version of comprehensive liberalism in *Foundations of Liberal Equality, in* 11 THE TANNER LECTURES ON HUMAN VALUES 1 (Grethe B. Peterson ed., 1990).

people can be persuaded to endorse liberal political arrangements, such as equal basic liberties, for different reasons, reflecting the various comprehensive moral and religious conceptions they espouse. Because political liberalism does not depend for its justification on any one of those moral or religious conceptions, it is presented as a "freestanding" view; it "applies the principle of toleration to philosophy itself" (p. 10).

Although political liberalism renounces reliance on the Kantian conception of the person, it does not do without a conception of the person altogether. As Rawls acknowledges, some such conception is necessary to the idea of the original position, the hypothetical social contract that gives rise to the principles of justice. The way to think about justice, Rawls argued in *A Theory of Justice*, is to ask which principles would be agreed to by persons who found themselves gathered in an initial situation of equality, each in temporary ignorance of his or her race and class, religion and gender, aims and attachments.[20] But in order for this way of thinking about justice to carry weight, the design of the original position must reflect something about the sort of persons we actually are, or would be in a just society.

One way of justifying the design of the original position would be to appeal to the Kantian conception of the person that Rawls advanced in Part III of *A Theory of Justice*. If our capacity to choose our ends is more fundamental to our nature as moral persons than are the particular ends we choose, if "[i]t is not our aims that primarily reveal our nature but rather the principles that we would acknowledge to govern the background conditions under which these aims are to be formed,"[21] if "the self is prior to the ends which are affirmed by it,"[22] then it makes sense to think about justice from the standpoint of persons deliberating prior to any knowledge of the ends they will pursue. If "a moral person is a subject with ends he has chosen, and his fundamental preference is for conditions that enable him to frame a mode of life that expresses his nature as a free and equal rational being as fully as circumstances permit,"[23] then the original position can be justified as an expression of our moral personality and the "fundamental preference" that flows from it.

Once Rawls disavows reliance on the Kantian conception of the person, however, this way of justifying the original position is no longer available. But this raises a difficult question: what reason remains for insisting that our reflections about justice should proceed without reference to our purposes and ends? Why must we "bracket," or set aside, our moral and religious convictions, our conceptions of

---

[20] *See* RAWLS, *supra* note 3, at 11–12.

[21] *Id.* at 560.

[22] *Id.*

[23] *Id.* at 561.

the good life? Why should we not base the principles of justice that govern the basic structure of society on our best understanding of the highest human ends?

B. The Political Conception of the Person

Political liberalism replies as follows: the reason we should think about justice from the standpoint of persons who abstract from their ends is not that this procedure expresses our nature as free and independent selves given prior to our ends. Rather, this way of thinking about justice is warranted by the fact that, for *political* purposes, though not necessarily for all moral purposes, we should think of ourselves as free and independent citizens, unclaimed by prior duties or obligations (pp. 29–35). For political liberalism, what justifies the design of the original position is a "political conception of the person" (p. 29). The political conception of the person embodied in the original position closely parallels the Kantian conception of the person, with the important difference that its scope is limited to our public identity, our identity as citizens. Thus, for example, our freedom as citizens means that our public identity is not claimed or defined by the ends we espouse at any given time. As free persons, citizens view themselves "as independent from and not identified with any particular such conception with its scheme of final ends" (p. 30). Our public identity is not affected by changes over time in our conceptions of the good.

In our personal or nonpublic identity, Rawls allows, we may regard our "ends and attachments very differently from the way the political conception supposes" (p. 31). There, persons may find themselves claimed by loyalties and commitments "they believe they would not, indeed could and should not, stand apart from and evaluate objectively. They may regard it as simply unthinkable to view themselves apart from certain religious, philosophical, and moral convictions, or from certain enduring attachments and loyalties" (p. 31). But however encumbered we may be in our personal identities, however claimed by moral or religious convictions, we must bracket our encumbrances in public, and regard ourselves, *qua* public selves, as independent of any particular loyalties or attachments or conceptions of the good (p. 31).

A related feature of the political conception of the person is that we are "self-authenticating sources of valid claims" (p. 32). The claims we make as citizens carry weight, whatever they are, simply by virtue of our making them (provided they are not unjust). That some claims may reflect high moral or religious ideals, or notions of patriotism and the common good, while others express mere interests or preferences, is not relevant from the standpoint of political liberalism. From a political point of view, claims founded on duties and obligations of citizenship or solidarity or religious faith are just things people want — nothing more, nothing less. Their validity as political claims has nothing to do with the moral importance of the goods they affirm, but consists solely in the fact that someone asserts them. Even divine commandments and imperatives of conscience count as "self-authenticating" claims, politically speaking.[24] This ensures that even those who regard themselves as claimed by moral or religious or communal obligations are nonetheless, for political purposes, unencumbered selves.

This political conception of the person explains why, according to political liberalism, we should reflect about justice as the original position invites us to do, in abstraction from our ends. But this raises a further question: why should we adopt the standpoint of the political conception of the person in the first place? Why should our political identities not express the moral and religious and communal convictions we affirm in our personal lives? Why insist on the separation between our identity as citizens and our identity as moral persons more broadly conceived? Why, in deliberating about justice, should we set aside the moral judgments that inform the rest of our lives?

Rawls's answer is that this separation or "dualism" between our identity as citizens and our identity as persons "originates in the special nature of democratic political culture" (p. xxi). In traditional societies, people sought to shape political life in the image of their comprehensive moral and religious ideals. But in a modern democratic society like our own, marked as it is by a plurality of moral and religious views, we typically distinguish between our public and personal identities. Confident though I may be of the truth of the moral and religious ideals I espouse, I do not insist that these ideals be reflected in the basic structure of society. Like other aspects of political liberalism, the political conception of the person as a free and independent self is "implicit in the public political culture of a democratic society" (p. 13).

But suppose Rawls is right, and the liberal self-image he attributes to us is implicit in our political culture. Would this provide sufficient grounds for affirming it, and for adopting the conception of justice it supports? Some have read Rawls's recent writings as suggesting that justice as fairness, being a political conception of justice, requires no moral or philosophical justification apart from an appeal to the shared understandings implicit in our political culture. Rawls seemed to

---

[24] The notion that we should regard our moral and religious duties as "self-authenticating from a political point of view" (p. 33) accords with Rawls's statement, in *A Theory of Justice*, that "from the standpoint of justice as fairness, these [moral and religious] obligations are self-imposed." RAWLS, *supra* note 3, at 206. But it is not clear what the justification can be on such a view for according religious beliefs or claims of conscience a special respect not accorded other preferences that people may hold with equal or greater intensity. *See id.* at 205–11.

invite this interpretation when he wrote, in an article published after *A Theory of Justice* but before *Political Liberalism*, as follows:

> What justifies a conception of justice is not its being true to an order antecedent to and given to us, but its congruence with our deeper understanding of ourselves and our aspirations, and our realization that, given our history and the traditions embedded in our public life, it is the most reasonable doctrine for us.[25]

Richard Rorty, in an insightful article, interprets (and welcomes) Rawls's revised view as "thoroughly historicist and antiuniversalist."[26] Although *A Theory of Justice* seemed to base justice on a Kantian conception of the person, Rorty writes, Rawls's liberalism "no longer seems committed to a philosophical account of the human self, but only to a historico-sociological description of the way we live now."[27] On this view, Rawls is not "supplying philosophical foundations for democratic institutions, but simply trying to systematize the principles and intuitions typical of American liberals."[28] Rorty endorses what he takes to be Rawls's pragmatic turn, a turn away from the notion that liberal political arrangements require a philosophical justification, or "extrapolitical grounding" in a theory of the human subject. "[I]nsofar as justice becomes the first virtue of a society," Rorty writes, "the need for such legitimation may gradually cease to be felt. Such a society will become accustomed to the thought that social policy needs no more authority than successful accommodation among individuals, individuals who find themselves heir to the same historical traditions and faced with the same problems."[29]

In *Political Liberalism*, Rawls pulls back from this purely pragmatic account. Although justice as fairness begins "by looking to the public culture itself as the shared fund of implicitly recognized basic ideas and principles" (p. 8), it does not affirm these principles simply on the grounds that they are widely shared. Though Rawls argues that his principles of justice could gain the support of an overlapping consensus, the overlapping consensus he seeks "is not a mere modus vivendi" (p. 147), or compromise among conflicting views. Adherents of different moral and religious conceptions begin by endorsing the principles of justice for reasons drawn from within their own conceptions. But, if all goes well, they come to support those principles as expressing important political values. As people learn to live in a pluralist society governed by liberal institutions, they acquire virtues that strengthen their commitment to liberal principles.

---

[25] John Rawls, *Kantian Constructivism in Moral Theory: Rational and Full Autonomy*, 77 J. PHIL. 515, 519 (1980).

[26] Rorty, *supra* note 13, at 257, 262.

[27] *Id.* at 265.

[28] *Id.* at 268.

[29] *Id.* at 264.

> The virtues of political cooperation that make a constitutional regime possible are . . . very great virtues. I mean, for example, the virtues of tolerance and being ready to meet others halfway, and the virtue of reasonableness and the sense of fairness. When these virtues are widespread in society and sustain its political conception of justice, they constitute a very great public good . . . (p. 157).

Rawls emphasizes that affirming liberal virtues as a great public good and encouraging their cultivation is not the same as endorsing a perfectionist state based on a comprehensive moral conception. It does not contradict the priority of the right over the good. The reason is that political liberalism affirms liberal virtues for political purposes only — for their role in supporting a constitutional regime that protects people's rights. Whether and to what extent these virtues should figure in people's moral lives generally is a question that political liberalism does not claim to answer (pp. 194–95).

III. Assessing Political Liberalism

If *Political Liberalism* defends the priority of right by detaching it from the Kantian conception of the person, how convincing is its defense? As I shall try to argue, *Political Liberalism* rescues the priority of the right from controversies about the nature of the self only at the cost of rendering it vulnerable on other grounds. Specifically, I shall try to show that liberalism conceived as a political conception of justice is open to three objections.

First, notwithstanding the importance of the "political values" to which Rawls appeals, it is not always reasonable to bracket, or set aside for political purposes, claims arising from within comprehensive moral and religious doctrines. Where grave moral questions are concerned, whether it is reasonable to bracket moral and religious controversies for the sake of political agreement partly depends on which of the contending moral or religious doctrines is true.

Second, for political liberalism, the case for the priority of the right over the good depends on the claim that modern democratic societies are characterized by a "fact of reasonable pluralism" about the good (p. xvii). Though it is certainly true that people in modern democratic societies hold a variety of conflicting moral and religious views, it cannot be said that there is a "fact of reasonable pluralism" about morality and religion that does not also apply to questions of justice.

Third, according to the ideal of public reason advanced by political liberalism, citizens may not legitimately discuss fundamental political and constitutional questions with reference to their moral and religious ideals. But this is an unduly severe restriction that would impoverish political discourse and rule out important dimensions of public deliberation.

A. Bracketing Grave Moral Questions

Political liberalism insists on bracketing our comprehensive moral and religious ideals for political purposes, and on separating our political from our personal identities. The reason is this: in modern democratic societies like ours, where people typically disagree about the good life, bracketing our moral and religious convictions is necessary if we are to secure social cooperation on the basis of mutual respect. But this raises a question that political liberalism cannot answer within its own terms. Even granting the importance of securing social cooperation on the basis of mutual respect, what is to guarantee that this interest is always so important as to outweigh any competing interest that could arise from within a comprehensive moral or religious view?

One way of assuring the priority of the political conception of justice (and hence the priority of the right) is to deny that any of the moral or religious conceptions it brackets could be true.[30] But this would implicate political liberalism in precisely the sort of philosophical claim it seeks to avoid. Time and again Rawls emphasizes that political liberalism does not depend on skepticism about the claims of comprehensive moral and religious doctrines. If political liberalism therefore allows that some such doctrines might be true, then what is to assure that none can generate values sufficiently compelling to burst the brackets, so to speak, and morally outweigh the political values of toleration, fairness, and social cooperation based on mutual respect?

One might reply that political values and values arising from within comprehensive moral and religious doctrines address different subjects. Political values, one might say, apply to the basic structure of society and to constitutional essentials, whereas moral and religious values apply to the conduct of personal life and voluntary associations. But if it were simply a difference of subject matter, no conflict between political values and moral and religious values could ever arise, and there would be no need to assert, as Rawls repeatedly does, that in a constitutional democracy governed by political liberalism, "political values normally outweigh whatever nonpolitical values conflict with them" (p. 146).

The difficulty of asserting the priority of "political values" without reference to the claims of morality and religion can be seen by considering two political controversies that bear on grave moral and religious questions. One is the contemporary debate about abortion rights. The other is the famous debate between Abraham Lincoln and Stephen Douglas over popular sovereignty and slavery.

---

[30] Thomas Hobbes, who can be interpreted as advancing a political conception of justice, ensured the priority of his political conception with respect to claims arising from contending moral and religious conceptions by denying the truth of those conceptions. *See* THOMAS HOBBES, LEVIATHAN 168–83 (C.B. Macpherson ed., Penguin Books 1985) (1651).

Given the intense disagreement over the moral permissibility of abortion, the case for seeking a political solution that brackets the contending moral and religious issues — that is neutral with respect to them — would seem especially strong. But whether it is reasonable to bracket, for political purposes, the comprehensive moral and religious doctrines at stake largely depends on which of those doctrines is true. If the doctrine of the Catholic Church is true, if human life in the relevant moral sense does begin at conception, then bracketing the moral-theological question when human life begins is far less reasonable than it would be on rival moral and religious assumptions. The more confident we are that fetuses are, in the relevant moral sense, different from babies, the more confident we can be in affirming a political conception of justice that sets aside the controversy about the moral status of fetuses.

The political liberal might reply that the political values of toleration and equal citizenship for women are sufficient grounds for concluding that women should be free to choose for themselves whether to have an abortion; government should not take sides on the moral and religious controversy over when human life begins.[31] But if the Catholic Church is right about the moral status of the fetus, if abortion is morally tantamount to murder, then it is not clear why the political values of toleration and women's equality, important though they are, should prevail. If the Catholic doctrine is true, the political liberal's case for the priority of political values must become an instance of just-war theory; he or she would have to show why these values should prevail even at the cost of some 1.5 million civilian deaths each year.

Of course, to suggest the impossibility of bracketing the moral-theological question of when human life begins is not to argue against a right to abortion. It is simply to show that the case for abortion rights cannot be neutral with respect to that moral and religious controversy. It must engage rather than avoid the comprehensive moral and religious doctrines at stake. Liberals often resist this engagement because it violates the priority of the right over the good. But the abortion debate shows that this priority cannot be sustained. The case for respecting a woman's right to decide for herself whether to have an abortion depends on showing — as I believe can be shown — that there is a relevant moral difference between aborting a fetus at a relatively early stage of development and killing a child.

A second illustration of the difficulty with a political conception of justice that tries to bracket controversial moral questions is offered by the 1858 debates between Abraham Lincoln and Stephen Douglas.

---

[31] Rawls seems to take this view in a footnote on abortion. But he does not explain why political values should prevail even if the Catholic doctrine were true (p. 243 n.32).

Douglas's argument for the doctrine of popular sovereignty is perhaps the most famous case in American history for bracketing a controversial moral question for the sake of political agreement. Because people were bound to disagree about the morality of slavery, Douglas argued, national policy should be neutral on that question. The doctrine of popular sovereignty he defended did not judge slavery right or wrong, but left the people of each territory free to make their own judgments. "[T]o throw the weight of federal power into the scale, either in favor of the free or the slave states," would violate the fundamental principles of the Constitution and run the risk of civil war. The only hope of holding the country together, he argued, was to agree to disagree, to bracket the moral controversy over slavery and respect "the right of each state and each territory to decide these questions for themselves."[32]

Lincoln argued against Douglas's case for a political conception of justice. Policy should express rather than avoid a substantive moral judgment about slavery. Though Lincoln was not an abolitionist, he believed government should treat slavery as the moral wrong that it was, and prohibit its extension to the territories. "The real issue in this controversy — the one pressing upon every mind — is the sentiment on the part of one class that looks upon the institution of slavery *as a wrong*, and of another class that *does not* look upon it as a wrong."[33] Lincoln and the Republican party viewed slavery as a wrong and insisted that it "*be treated* as a wrong, and one of the methods of treating it as a wrong is to *make provision that it shall grow no larger*."[34]

Whatever his personal moral views, Douglas claimed that, for political purposes at least, he was agnostic on the question of slavery; he did not care whether slavery was "voted up or voted down."[35] Lincoln replied that it was reasonable to bracket the question of the morality of slavery only on the assumption that it was not the moral evil he regarded it to be. Any man can advocate political neutrality

> who does not see anything wrong in slavery, but no man can logically say it who does see a wrong in it; because no man can logically say he don't care whether a wrong is voted up or voted down. He may say he don't care whether an indifferent thing is voted up or down, but he must logically have a choice between a right thing and a wrong thing. He contends that whatever community wants slaves has a right to have them. So they have if it is not a wrong. But if it is a wrong, he cannot say people have a right to do wrong.[36]

---

[32] CREATED EQUAL?: THE COMPLETE LINCOLN-DOUGLAS DEBATES OF 1858, at 369, 374 (Paul M. Angle ed., 1958) [hereinafter CREATED EQUAL?].

[33] *Id.* at 390.

[34] *Id.*

[35] *Id.* at 392.

[36] *Id.*

The debate between Lincoln and Douglas was not primarily about the morality of slavery, but about whether to bracket a moral controversy for the sake of political agreement. In this respect, their debate over popular sovereignty is analogous to the contemporary debate over abortion rights. As some contemporary liberals argue that government should not take a stand one way or the other on the morality of abortion, but let each woman decide the question for herself, so Douglas argued that national policy should not take a stand one way or the other on the morality of slavery, but let each territory decide the question for itself. There is of course the difference that in the case of abortion rights, those who would bracket the substantive moral question typically leave the choice to the individual, while in the case of slavery, Douglas's way of bracketing was to leave the choice to the territories.

But Lincoln's argument against Douglas was an argument against bracketing as such, at least where grave moral questions are at stake. Lincoln's point was that the political conception of justice defended by Douglas depended for its plausibility on a particular answer to the substantive moral question it claimed to bracket. This point applies with equal force to those arguments for abortion rights that claim to take no side in the controversy over the moral status of the fetus. Even in the face of so dire a threat to social cooperation as the prospect of civil war, Lincoln argued that it made neither moral nor political sense to bracket the most divisive moral controversy of the day.

> I say, where is the philosophy or the statesmanship based on the assumption that we are to quit talking about it . . . and that the public mind is all at once to cease being agitated by it? Yet this is the policy . . . that Douglas is advocating — that we are to care nothing about it! I ask you if it is not a false philosophy? Is it not a false statesmanship that undertakes to build up a system of policy upon the basis of caring nothing about *the very thing that every body does care the most about?*[37]

Present-day liberals will surely resist the company of Douglas and want national policy to oppose slavery, presumably on the grounds that slavery violates people's rights. The question is whether liberalism conceived as a political conception of justice can make this claim consistent with its own strictures against appeals to comprehensive moral ideals. For example, a Kantian liberal can oppose slavery as a failure to treat persons as ends in themselves, worthy of respect. But this argument, resting as it does on a Kantian conception of the person, is unavailable to political liberalism. Other historically important arguments against slavery are unavailable to political liber-

---

[37] *Id.* at 388–89.

alism for similar reasons. American abolitionists of the 1830s and 1840s, for example, typically cast their arguments in religious terms, arguments that political liberalism cannot invoke.

How, then, can political liberalism escape the company of Douglas and oppose slavery without presupposing some comprehensive moral view? It might be replied that Douglas was wrong to seek social peace at any price; not just any political agreement will do. Even conceived as a political conception, justice as fairness is not merely a modus vivendi. Given the principles and self-understandings implicit in our political culture, only an agreement on terms that treat persons fairly, as free and equal citizens, can provide a reasonable basis for social cooperation. For us twentieth-century Americans, at least, the rejection of slavery is a settled matter. The historical demise of Douglas's position is by now a fact of our political tradition that any political agreement must take as given.

This appeal to the conception of citizenship implicit in our political culture might explain how political liberalism can oppose slavery today; our present political culture was importantly shaped, after all, by the Civil War, Reconstruction, the adoption of the Thirteenth, Fourteenth, and Fifteenth Amendments, *Brown v. Board of Education*,[38] the civil rights movement, the Voting Rights Act,[39] and so on. These experiences, and the shared understanding of racial equality and equal citizenship they formed, provide ample grounds for holding that slavery is at odds with American political and constitutional practice as it has developed over the past century.

But this does not explain how political liberalism could oppose slavery in 1858. The notions of equal citizenship implicit in American political culture of the mid-nineteenth century were arguably hospitable to the institution of slavery. The Declaration of Independence proclaimed that all men are created equal, endowed by their Creator with certain unalienable rights, but Douglas argued, not implausibly, that the signers of the Declaration were asserting the right of the colonists to be free of British rule, not the right of their Negro slaves to equal citizenship.[40] The Constitution itself did not prohibit slavery, but to the contrary accommodated it by allowing states to count three-fifths of their slave population for apportionment purposes,[41] providing that Congress could not prohibit the slave trade until 1808,[42] and requiring the return of fugitive slaves.[43] And in the notorious *Dred*

---

[38] 347 U.S. 483 (1954).

[39] Voting Rights Act of 1965, 42 U.S.C. §§ 1971, 1973 (1988).

[40] *See* CREATED EQUAL?, *supra* note 32, at 374.

[41] *See* U.S. CONST. art. I, § 2, cl. 3.

[42] *See id.* art. I, § 9, cl. 1.

[43] *See id.* art. IV, § 2, cl. 3.

Scott case,[44] the Supreme Court upheld the property rights of slave-holders in their slaves and ruled that African-Americans were not citizens of the United States.[45] To the extent that political liberalism refuses to invoke comprehensive moral ideals and relies instead on notions of citizenship implicit in the political culture, it would have a hard time explaining, in 1858, why Lincoln was right and Douglas was wrong.

B. The Fact of Reasonable Pluralism

The abortion debate today and the Lincoln-Douglas debate of 1858 illustrate the way a political conception of justice must presuppose some answer to the moral questions it purports to bracket, at least where grave moral questions are concerned. In cases such as these, the priority of the right over the good cannot be sustained. A further difficulty with political liberalism concerns the reason it gives for asserting the priority of the right over the good in the first place. For Kantian liberalism, the asymmetry between the right and the good arises from a certain conception of the person. Because we must think of ourselves as moral subjects given prior to our aims and attachments, we must regard the right as regulative with respect to the particular ends we affirm; the right is prior to the good because the self is prior to its ends.

For political liberalism, the asymmetry between the right and the good is not based on a Kantian conception of the person but instead on a certain feature of modern democratic societies. Rawls describes this feature as "the fact of reasonable pluralism" (p. xvii). "A modern democratic society is characterized not simply by a pluralism of comprehensive religious, philosophical, and moral doctrines but by a pluralism of incompatible yet reasonable comprehensive doctrines. No one of these doctrines is affirmed by citizens generally" (p. xvi). Nor is it likely that sometime in the foreseeable future this pluralism will cease to hold. Disagreement about moral and religious questions is not a temporary condition but "the normal result of the exercise of human reason" under free institutions (p. xvi).

Given the "fact of reasonable pluralism," the problem is to find principles of justice that free and equal citizens can affirm despite their moral, philosophical, and religious differences. "This is a problem of political justice, not a problem about the highest good" (p. xxv). Whatever principles it generates, the solution to this problem must be one that upholds the priority of the right over the good. Otherwise, it will fail to provide a basis for social cooperation among adherents of incompatible but reasonable moral and religious convictions.

---

[44] Scott v. Sandford, 60 U.S. (19 How.) 393 (1857).
[45] *See id.* at 404–05.

But here there arises a difficulty. For even if the fact of reasonable pluralism is true, the asymmetry between the right and the good depends on a further assumption. This is the assumption that, despite our disagreements about morality and religion, we do not have, or on due reflection would not have, similar disagreements about justice. Political liberalism must assume not only that the exercise of human reason under conditions of freedom will produce disagreements about the good life, but also that the exercise of human reason under conditions of freedom will *not* produce disagreements about justice. The "fact of reasonable pluralism" about morality and religion only creates an asymmetry between the right and the good when coupled with the further assumption that there is no comparable "fact of reasonable pluralism" about justice.

It is not clear, however, that this further assumption is justified. We need only look around us to see that modern democratic societies are teeming with disagreements about justice. Consider, for example, contemporary debates about affirmative action, income distribution and tax fairness, health care, immigration, gay rights, free speech versus hate speech, and capital punishment, to name just a few. Or consider the divided votes and conflicting opinions of Supreme Court Justices in cases involving religious liberty, freedom of speech, privacy rights, voting rights, the rights of the accused, and so on. Do not these debates display a "fact of reasonable pluralism" about justice? If so, how does the pluralism about justice that prevails in modern democratic societies differ from the pluralism about morality and religion? Is there reason to think that, sometime in the foreseeable future, our disagreements about justice will dissolve even as our disagreements about morality and religion persist?

The political liberal might reply by distinguishing two different kinds of disagreement about justice. There are disagreements about what the principles of justice should be and disagreements about how these principles should be applied. Many of our disagreements about justice, it might be argued, are of the second kind. Although we generally agree, for example, that freedom of speech is among the basic rights and liberties, we disagree about whether the right to free speech should protect racial epithets, or violent pornographic depictions, or commercial advertising, or unlimited contributions to political campaigns. These disagreements, vigorous and even intractable though they may be, are consistent with our agreeing at the level of principle that a just society includes a basic right to free speech.

Our disagreements about morality and religion, by contrast, might be seen as more fundamental. They reflect incompatible conceptions of the good life, it might be argued, not disagreements about how to put into practice a conception of the good life that commands, or on reflection would command, widespread agreement. If our controversies about justice concern the application of principles we share or would share on due reflection, while our controversies about morality and religion run deeper, then the asymmetry between the right and the good advanced by political liberalism would be vindicated.

But with what confidence can this contrast be asserted? Do all of our disagreements about justice concern the application of principles we share or would share on due reflection, rather than the principles themselves? What of our debates about distributive justice? Here it would seem that our disagreements are at the level of principle, not application. Some maintain, consistent with Rawls's difference principle, that only those social and economic inequalities that improve the condition of the least-advantaged members of society are just. They argue, for example, that government must ensure the provision of certain basic needs, such as income, education, health care, housing, and the like, so that all citizens will be able meaningfully to exercise their basic liberties. Others reject the difference principle. Libertarians argue, for example, that it may be a good thing for people to help those less fortunate than themselves, but that this should be a matter of charity, not entitlement. Government should not use its coercive power to redistribute income and wealth, but should respect people's rights to exercise their talents as they choose, and to reap their rewards as defined by the market economy.[46]

The debate between liberal egalitarians like Rawls and libertarians like Robert Nozick and Milton Friedman is a prominent feature of political argument in modern democratic societies. This debate reflects disagreement about what the correct principle of distributive justice is, not disagreement about how to apply the difference principle. But this would suggest that there exists in democratic societies a "fact of reasonable pluralism" about justice as well as about morality and religion. And if this is the case, the asymmetry between the right and the good does not hold.

Political liberalism is not without a reply to this objection, but the reply it must make departs from the spirit of toleration it otherwise evokes. Rawls's reply must be that, although there is a fact of pluralism about distributive justice, there is no fact of *reasonable* pluralism.[47] Unlike disagreements about morality and religion, disagreements about the validity of the difference principle are not reasonable; libertarian theories of distributive justice would not be sustained on

---

[46] *See* MILTON FRIEDMAN, CAPITALISM AND FREEDOM 200 (1962); MILTON FRIEDMAN & ROSE FRIEDMAN, FREE TO CHOOSE 134–36 (1980); HAYEK, *supra* note 5, at 85–86, 99–100; NOZICK, *supra* note 5, at 149, 167–74.

[47] Although Rawls does not state this view explicitly, it is necessary in order to make sense of the "fact of reasonable pluralism" and the role it plays in supporting the priority of the right. He notes that reasonable disagreements may arise over what policies fulfill the difference principle, but adds, "[t]his is not a difference about what are the correct principles but simply a difference in the difficulty of seeing whether the principles are achieved" (p. 230).

due reflection. Our differences about distributive justice, unlike our differences of morality and religion, are not the natural outcome of the exercise of human reason under conditions of freedom.

At first glance, the claim that disagreements about distributive justice are not reasonable may seem arbitrary, even harsh, at odds with political liberalism's promise to apply "the principle of toleration to philosophy itself" (p. 10). It contrasts sharply with Rawls's apparent generosity toward differences of morality and religion. These differences, Rawls repeatedly writes, are a normal, indeed desirable feature of modern life, an expression of human diversity that only the oppressive use of state power can overcome (pp. 303–04). Where comprehensive moralities are concerned, "it is not to be expected that conscientious persons with full powers of reason, even after free discussion, will all arrive at the same conclusion" (p. 58). Since the exercise of human reason produces a plurality of reasonable moral and religious doctrines, "it is unreasonable or worse to want to use the sanctions of state power to correct, or to punish, those who disagree with us" (p. 138). But this spirit of toleration does not extend to our disagreements about justice. Because disagreements between, say, libertarians and advocates of the difference principle do not reflect a reasonable pluralism, there is no objection to using state power to implement the difference principle.

Intolerant though it may seem at first glance, the notion that theories of distributive justice at odds with the difference principle are not reasonable, or that libertarian theories of justice would not survive due reflection, is no arbitrary claim. To the contrary, in *A Theory of Justice* Rawls offers a rich array of compelling arguments on behalf of the difference principle and against libertarian conceptions: the distribution of talents and assets that enables some to earn more and others less in the market economy is arbitrary from a moral point of view; so is the fact that the market happens to prize and reward, at any given moment, the talents you or I may have in abundance; libertarians would agree that distributive shares should not be based on social status or accident of birth (as in aristocratic or caste societies), but the distribution of talents given by nature is no less arbitrary; the notion of freedom that libertarians invoke can be meaningfully exercised only if persons' basic social and economic needs are met; if people deliberated about distributive justice without reference to their own interests, or without prior knowledge of their talents and the value of those talents in the market economy, they would agree that the natural distribution of talents should not be the basis of distributive shares; and so on.[48]

My point is not to rehearse Rawls's argument for the difference principle, but only to recall the kind of reasons he offers. Viewing

[48] *See* RAWLS, *supra* note 3, at 72–75, 100–07, 136–42, 310–15.

justification as a process of mutual adjustment between principles and considered judgments that aims at a "reflective equilibrium,"[49] Rawls tries to show that the difference principle is more reasonable than the alternative offered by libertarians. To the extent that his arguments are convincing — as I believe they are — and to the extent they can be convincing to citizens of a democratic society, the principles they support are properly embodied in public policy and law. Disagreement will doubtless remain. Libertarians will not fall silent or disappear. But their disagreement need not be regarded as a "fact of reasonable pluralism" in the face of which government must be neutral.

But this leads to a question that goes to the heart of political liberalism's claim for the priority of the right over the good: if moral argument or reflection of the kind Rawls deploys enables us to conclude, despite the persistence of conflicting views, that some principles of justice are more reasonable than others, what guarantees that reflection of a similar kind is not possible in the case of moral and religious controversy? If we can reason about controversial principles of distributive justice by seeking a reflective equilibrium, why can we not reason in the same way about conceptions of the good? If it can be shown that some conceptions of the good are more reasonable than others, then the persistence of disagreement would not necessarily amount to a "fact of reasonable pluralism" that requires government to be neutral.

Consider, for example, the controversy in our public culture about the moral status of homosexuality, a controversy based in comprehensive moral and religious doctrines. Some maintain that homosexuality is sinful, or at least morally impermissible; others argue that homosexuality is morally permissible, and in some cases gives expression to important human goods. Political liberalism insists that neither of these views about the morality of homosexuality should play a role in public debates about justice or rights. Government must be neutral with respect to them. This means that those who abhor homosexuality may not seek to embody their view in law; it also means that proponents of gay rights may not base their arguments on the notion that homosexuality is morally defensible. From the standpoint of political liberalism, each of these approaches would wrongly base the right on some conception of the good; each would fail to respect the "fact of reasonable pluralism" about comprehensive moralities.

But does the disagreement in our society about the moral status of homosexuality constitute a "fact of reasonable pluralism" any more than does the disagreement about distributive justice? According to political liberalism, the libertarian's objection to the difference prin-

---

[49] *See id.* at 20–21, 48–51, 120, 577–87.

ciple does not constitute a "fact of reasonable pluralism" that requires government neutrality, because there are good reasons to conclude, on due reflection, that the arguments for the difference principle are more convincing than the ones that support libertarianism. But isn't it possible to conclude, with equal or greater confidence, that on due reflection, the arguments for the moral permissibility of homosexuality are more convincing than the arguments against it? Consistent with the search for a reflective equilibrium among principles and considered judgments, such reflection might proceed by assessing the reasons advanced by those who assert the moral inferiority of homosexual to heterosexual relations.

Those who consider homosexuality immoral often argue, for example, that homosexuality cannot fulfill the highest end of human sexuality, the good of procreation.[50] To this it might be replied that many heterosexual relations also do not fulfill this end, such as contracepted sex, or sex among sterile couples, or sex among partners beyond the age of reproduction. This might suggest that the good of procreation, important though it is, is not necessary to the moral worth of human sexual relations; the moral worth of sexuality might also consist in the love and responsibility it expresses, and these goods are possible in homosexual as well as heterosexual relations. Opponents might reply that homosexuals are often promiscuous, and hence less likely to realize the goods of love and responsibility. The reply to this claim might consist in an empirical showing to the contrary, or in the observation that the existence of promiscuity does not argue against the moral worth of homosexuality as such, only against certain instances of it.[51] Heterosexuals also engage in promiscuity and other practices at odds with the goods that confer on sexuality its moral worth, but this fact does not lead us to abhor heterosexuality as such. And so on.

My point is not to offer a full argument for the moral permissibility of homosexuality, only to suggest the way such an argument might proceed. Like Rawls's argument for the difference principle, it would proceed by seeking a reflective equilibrium between our principles and considered judgments, adjusting each in the light of the other. That the argument for the morality of homosexuality, unlike the argument

---

[50] In this paragraph, I draw on some of the arguments for and against the morality of homosexuality that appear in John Finnis & Martha Nussbaum, *Is Homosexual Conduct Wrong?: A Philosophical Exchange*, NEW REPUBLIC, Nov. 15, 1993, at 12–13; Stephen Macedo, *The New Natural Lawyers*, HARV. CRIMSON, Oct. 29, 1993, at 2; and Harvey C. Mansfield, *Saving Liberalism From Liberals*, HARV. CRIMSON, Nov. 8, 1993, at 2.

[51] An alternative line of reply might undertake to defend promiscuity and to deny that the goods of love and responsibility are necessary to the moral worth of sexuality. From this point of view, the line of argument I suggest mistakenly seeks to defend the moral legitimacy of homosexuality by way of an analogy with heterosexuality. *See* BONNIE HONIG, POLITICAL THEORY AND THE DISPLACEMENT OF POLITICS 186–95 (1993).

for the difference principle, explicitly addresses claims about human ends and conceptions of the good does not mean that the same method of moral reasoning cannot proceed. It is unlikely, of course, that such moral reasoning would produce conclusive or irrefutable answers to moral and religious controversies. But as Rawls acknowledges, such reasoning does not produce irrefutable answers to questions of justice either; a more modest notion of justification is appropriate. "[I]n philosophy questions at the most fundamental level are not usually settled by conclusive argument," writes Rawls, referring to arguments about justice. "What is obvious to some persons and accepted as a basic idea is unintelligible to others. The way to resolve the matter is to consider after due reflection which view, when fully worked out, offers the most coherent and convincing account" (p. 53). The same could be said of arguments about comprehensive moralities.

If it is possible to reason about the good as well as the right, then political liberalism's claim for the asymmetry between the right and good is undermined. For political liberalism, this asymmetry rests on the assumption that our moral and religious disagreements reflect a "fact of reasonable pluralism" that our disagreements about justice do not. What enables Rawls to maintain that our disagreements about distributive justice do not amount to a "fact of reasonable pluralism" is the strength of the arguments he advances on behalf of the difference principle and against libertarianism. But the same could be said of other controversies, including, conceivably, some moral and religious controversies. The public culture of democratic societies includes controversies about justice and comprehensive moralities alike. If government can affirm the justice of redistributive policies even in the face of disagreement by libertarians, why cannot government affirm in law, say, the moral legitimacy of homosexuality, even in the face of disagreement by those who regard homosexuality as sin?[52] Is Milton Friedman's objection to redistributive policies a less "reasonable pluralism" than Pat Robertson's objection to gay rights?

With morality as with justice, the mere fact of disagreement is no evidence of the "reasonable pluralism" that gives rise to the demand that government must be neutral. There is no reason in principle why in any given case, we might not conclude that, on due reflection, some moral or religious doctrines are more plausible than others. In such cases, we would not expect all disagreement to disappear, nor would we rule out the possibility that further deliberation might one day lead us to revise our view. But neither would we have grounds

---

[52] It is possible to argue for certain gay rights on grounds that neither affirm nor deny the morality of homosexuality. The question here is whether government is justified in supporting laws or policies (such as gay marriage, for example) on grounds that affirm the moral legitimacy of homosexuality.

to insist that our deliberations about justice and rights may make no reference to moral or religious ideals.

C. The Limits of Liberal Public Reason

Whether it is possible to reason our way to agreement on any given moral or political controversy is not something we can know until we try. This is why it cannot be said in advance that controversies about comprehensive moralities reflect a "fact of reasonable pluralism" that controversies about justice do not. Whether a moral or political controversy reflects reasonable but incompatible conceptions of the good, or whether it can be resolved by due reflection and deliberation, can only be determined by reflecting and deliberating. But this raises a further difficulty with political liberalism. For the political life it describes leaves little room for the kind of public deliberation necessary to test the plausibility of contending comprehensive moralities — to persuade others of the merits of our moral ideals, to be persuaded by others of the merits of theirs.

Although political liberalism upholds the right to freedom of speech, it severely limits the kinds of arguments that are legitimate contributions to political debate, especially debate about constitutional essentials and basic justice.[53] This limitation reflects the priority of the right over the good. Not only may government not endorse one or another conception of the good, but citizens may not even introduce into political discourse their comprehensive moral or religious convictions, at least when debating matters of justice and rights (pp. 15–16).[54] Rawls maintains that this limitation is required by the "ideal of public reason" (p. 218). According to this ideal, political discourse should be conducted solely in terms of "political values" that all citizens can reasonably be expected to accept. Because citizens of democratic societies do not share comprehensive moral and religious conceptions, public reason should not refer to such conceptions (pp. 216–20).

The limits of public reason do not apply, Rawls allows, to our personal deliberations about political questions, or to the discussions we may have as members of associations such as churches and universities, where "religious, philosophical, and moral considerations" (p. 215) may properly play a role.

> But the ideal of public reason does hold for citizens when they engage in political advocacy in the public forum, and thus for members of

---

[53] Rawls states that the limits of public reason apply to all discussions involving constitutional essentials and basic justice. As for other political questions, he writes that "it is usually highly desirable to settle political questions by invoking the values of public reason. Yet this may not always be so" (pp. 214–15).

[54] This idea is repeated at several other points (pp. 215, 224, 254).

political parties and for candidates in their campaigns and for other groups who support them. It holds equally for how citizens are to vote in elections when constitutional essentials and matters of basic justice are at stake. Thus, the ideal of public reason not only governs the public discourse of elections insofar as the issues involve those fundamental questions, but also how citizens are to cast their vote on these questions (p. 215).

How can we know whether our political arguments meet the requirements of public reason, suitably shorn of any reliance on moral or religious convictions? Rawls offers a novel test. "To check whether we are following public reason we might ask: how would our argument strike us presented in the form of a supreme court opinion?" (p. 254). For citizens of a democracy to allow their political discourse about fundamental questions to be informed by moral and religious ideals is no more legitimate, Rawls suggests, than for a judge to read his or her moral and religious beliefs into the Constitution.

The restrictive character of this notion of public reason can be seen by considering the sorts of political arguments it would rule out. In the debate about abortion rights, those who believe that the fetus is a person from the moment of conception and that abortion is therefore murder could not seek to persuade their fellow citizens of this view in open political debate. Nor could they vote for a law that would restrict abortion on the basis of this moral or religious conviction. Although adherents of the Catholic teaching on abortion could discuss the issue of abortion rights in religious terms within their church, they could not do so in a political campaign, or on the floor of the state legislature, or in the halls of Congress. Nor for that matter could opponents of the Catholic teaching on abortion argue their case in the political arena. Relevant though it clearly is to the question of abortion rights, Catholic moral doctrine cannot be debated in the political arena that political liberalism defines.

The restrictive character of liberal public reason can also be seen in the debate about gay rights. At first glance, these restrictions might seem a service to toleration. Those who consider homosexuality immoral and therefore unworthy of the privacy rights accorded heterosexual intimacy could not legitimately voice their views in public debate. Nor could they act on their belief by voting against laws that would protect gay men and lesbians from discrimination. These beliefs reflect comprehensive moral and religious convictions and so may not play a part in political discourse about matters of justice.

But the demands of public reason also limit the arguments that can be advanced in support of gay rights, and so restrict the range of reasons that can be invoked on behalf of toleration. Those who oppose anti-sodomy laws of the kind at issue in *Bowers v. Hardwick*[55]

---

[55] 478 U.S. 186 (1986).

cannot argue that the moral judgments embodied in those laws are wrong, only that the law is wrong to embody any moral judgments at all.[56] Advocates of gay rights cannot contest the substantive moral judgment lying behind anti-sodomy laws or seek, through open political debate, to persuade their fellow citizens that homosexuality is morally permissible, for any such argument would violate the canons of liberal public reason.

The restrictive character of liberal public reason is also illustrated by the arguments offered by American abolitionists of the 1830s and 1840s. Rooted in evangelical Protestantism, the abolitionist movement argued for the immediate emancipation of the slaves on the grounds that slavery is a heinous sin.[57] Like the argument of some present-day Catholics against abortion rights, the abolitionist case against slavery was explicitly based on a comprehensive moral and religious doctrine.

In a puzzling passage, Rawls tries to argue that the abolitionist case against slavery, religious though it was, did not violate the ideal of liberal public reason. If a society is not well-ordered, he explains, it may be necessary to resort to comprehensive moralities in order to bring about a society in which public discussion is conducted solely in terms of "political values" (p. 251 n.41). The religious arguments of the abolitionists can be justified as hastening the day when religious arguments would no longer play a legitimate role in public discourse. The abolitionists "did not go against the ideal of public reason," Rawls concludes, "provided they thought, or on reflection would have thought (as they certainly could have thought), that the comprehensive reasons they appealed to were required to give sufficient strength to the political conception to be subsequently realized" (p. 251).

It is difficult to know what to make of this argument. There is little reason to suppose, and I do not think Rawls means to suggest, that the abolitionists opposed slavery on secular political grounds and simply used religious arguments to win popular support. Nor is there reason to think that the abolitionists sought by their agitation to make a world safe for secular political discourse. Nor can it be assumed that, even in retrospect, the abolitionists would take pride in having contributed, by their religious arguments against slavery, to the emergence of a society inhospitable to religious argument in political debate. If anything the opposite is more likely the case, that by advancing religious arguments against so conspicuous an injustice as slavery, the evangelicals who inspired the abolitionist movement were

---

[56] *See* Michael J. Sandel, *Moral Argument and Liberal Toleration: Abortion and Homosexuality*, 77 CAL. L. REV. 521, 534–38 (1989).

[57] *See* ERIC FONER, POLITICS AND IDEOLOGY IN THE AGE OF THE CIVIL WAR 72 (1980); AILEEN S. KRADITOR, MEANS AND ENDS IN AMERICAN ABOLITIONISM 78, 91–92 (1967); JAMES M. MCPHERSON, BATTLE CRY OF FREEDOM: THE CIVIL WAR ERA 7–8 (1988).

hoping to encourage Americans to view other political questions in moral and religious terms as well. In any case, it is reasonable to suppose that the abolitionists meant what they said, that slavery is wrong because it is contrary to God's law, a heinous sin, and that this is the reason it should be ended. Absent some extraordinary assumptions, it is difficult to interpret their argument as consistent with the priority of the right over the good, or with the ideal of public reason advanced by political liberalism.

The cases of abortion, gay rights, and abolitionism illustrate the severe restrictions liberal public reason would impose on political debate. Rawls argues that these restrictions are justified as essential to the maintenance of a just society, in which citizens are governed by principles they may reasonably be expected to endorse, even in the light of their conflicting comprehensive moralities. Although public reason requires that citizens decide fundamental political questions without reference "to the whole truth as they see it" (p. 216), this restriction is justified by the political values, such as civility and mutual respect, that it makes possible. "[T]he political values realized by a well-ordered constitutional regime are very great values and not easily overridden and the ideals they express are not to be lightly abandoned" (p. 218). Rawls compares his case for restrictive public reason with the case for restrictive rules of evidence in criminal trials. There too we agree to decide without reference to the whole truth as we know it — through illegally obtained evidence, for example — in order to advance other goods (pp. 218–19).

The analogy between liberal public reason and restrictive rules of evidence is instructive. Setting aside the whole truth as we know it carries moral and political costs, for criminal trials and for public reason alike. Whether those costs are worth incurring depends on how significant they are compared to the goods they make possible, and whether those goods can be secured in some other way. To assess restrictive rules of evidence, for example, we need to know how many criminals go free as a result and whether less restrictive rules would unduly burden innocent persons suspected of a crime, lead to undesirable law enforcement practices, violate important ideals such as respect for privacy (exclusionary rule) and spousal intimacy (spousal privilege), and so on. We arrive at rules of evidence by weighing the importance of deciding in the light of the whole truth against the importance of the ideals that would be sacrificed if all evidence were admissible.

Similarly, to assess restrictive rules of public reason, we need to weigh their moral and political costs against the political values they are said to make possible; we must also ask whether these political values — of toleration, civility, and mutual respect — could be achieved under less-restrictive rules of public reason. Although political liberalism refuses to weigh the political values it affirms against competing values that may arise from within comprehensive moralities, the case for restrictive rules of public reason must presuppose some such comparison.

The costs of liberal public reason are of two kinds. The strictly moral costs depend on the validity and importance of the moral and religious doctrines liberal public reason requires us to set aside when deciding questions of justice. These costs will necessarily vary from case to case. They will be at their highest when a political conception of justice sanctions toleration of a grave moral wrong, such as slavery in the case of Douglas's argument for popular sovereignty. In the case of abortion, the moral cost of bracketing is high if the Catholic doctrine is correct, otherwise much lower. This suggests that, even given the moral and political importance of toleration, the argument for tolerating a given practice must take some account of the moral status of the practice, as well as the good of avoiding social conflict, letting people decide for themselves, and so on.

This way of thinking about the moral cost of liberal public reason is admittedly at odds with political liberalism itself. Although Rawls repeatedly states that a political conception of justice expresses values that normally outweigh whatever other values conflict with them (pp. 138, 146, 156, 218), he also insists that this involves no substantive comparison of the political values to the moral and religious values they override.

> We need not consider the claims of political justice against the claims of this or that comprehensive view; nor need we say that political values are intrinsically more important than other values and that is why the latter are overridden. Having to say that is just what we hope to avoid . . . (p. 157).

But because political liberalism allows that comprehensive moral and religious doctrines can be true, such comparisons cannot reasonably be avoided.

Beyond the moral costs of liberal public reason are certain political costs. These costs are becoming increasingly apparent in the politics of those countries, notably the United States, whose public discourse most closely approximates the ideal of public reason advanced by political liberalism. With a few notable exceptions, such as the civil rights movement, American political discourse in recent decades has come to reflect the liberal resolve that government be neutral on moral and religious questions, that fundamental questions of public policy be debated and decided without reference to any particular conception of the good.[58] But democratic politics cannot long abide a public life as abstract and decorous, as detached from moral purposes, as Su-

---

[58] I cannot elaborate this claim here, but will try to do so in a forthcoming book, provisionally entitled *Liberal Democracy in America: In Search of a Public Philosophy.*

preme Court opinions are supposed to be. A politics that brackets morality and religion too completely soon generates its own disenchantment. Where political discourse lacks moral resonance, the yearning for a public life of larger meanings finds undesirable expressions. Groups like the Moral Majority seek to clothe the naked public square with narrow, intolerant moralisms. Fundamentalists rush in where liberals fear to tread. The disenchantment also assumes more secular forms. Absent a political agenda that addresses the moral dimension of public questions, public attention becomes riveted on the private vices of public officials. Public discourse becomes increasingly preoccupied with the scandalous, the sensational, and the confessional as purveyed by tabloids, talk shows, and eventually the mainstream media as well.

It cannot be said that the public philosophy of political liberalism is wholly responsible for these tendencies. But its vision of public reason is too spare to contain the moral energies of a vital democratic life. It thus creates a moral void that opens the way for the intolerant and the trivial and other misguided moralisms.

If liberal public reason is too restrictive, it remains to ask whether a more spacious public reason would sacrifice the ideals that political liberalism seeks to promote, notably mutual respect among citizens who hold conflicting moral and religious views. Here it is necessary to distinguish two conceptions of mutual respect. On the liberal conception, we respect our fellow citizens' moral and religious convictions by ignoring them (for political purposes), by leaving them undisturbed, or by carrying on political debate without reference to them. To admit moral and religious ideals into political debate about justice would undermine mutual respect in this sense.

But this is not the only, or perhaps even the most plausible way of understanding the mutual respect on which democratic citizenship depends. On a different conception of respect — call it the deliberative conception — we respect our fellow citizen's moral and religious convictions by engaging, or attending to them — sometimes by challenging and contesting them, sometimes by listening and learning from them — especially if those convictions bear on important political questions. There is no guarantee that a deliberative mode of respect will lead in any given case to agreement or even to appreciation for the moral and religious convictions of others. It is always possible that learning more about a moral or religious doctrine will lead us to like it less. But the respect of deliberation and engagement affords a more spacious public reason than liberalism allows. It is also a more suitable ideal for a pluralist society. To the extent that our moral and religious disagreements reflect the ultimate plurality of human goods, a deliberative mode of respect will better enable us to appreciate the distinctive goods our different lives express.

Part IV
Feminist Critiques of Liberal Justice

[16]

Political Liberalism, Justice, and Gender*

Susan Moller Okin

In 1977, Jane English pointed out that "by making the parties in the original position heads of families rather than individuals, Rawls makes the family opaque to claims of justice." Since then, a number of feminists have written on issues having to do with gender and the family in Rawls's *A Theory of Justice*.[1] I argued in two earlier articles, and then in *Justice, Gender, and the Family*, that the absence of a discussion of justice in families and justice and gender was a significant problem, for reasons both internal and external to the theory.[2] I also argued, however, that Rawls's theory of justice had very great potential to address these issues. And I have tried to make some suggestions as to what a feminist extension of Rawls's ideas might include. I shall turn to these later in this article.

In the introduction to *Political Liberalism*, Rawls mentions, as one of a number of "major matters" omitted from *Theory*, "the justice of and in the family." He reminds us that he did, however, "assume that in some form the family is just."[3] It is not at all clear that, in *Political Liberalism*, he still holds to this assumption, or even to the requirement that families ought to be thought of in terms of justice. In publications

* I gratefully acknowledge the helpful comments of Gerald Dworkin, David Glidden, Elisabeth Hansot, Jeffrie Murphy, John Rawls, Deborah Rhode, David Strauss, and Cass Sunstein on an earlier version of this article.

1. John Rawls, *A Theory of Justice* (Cambridge, Mass.: Harvard University Press, 1971), hereafter referred to as *Theory*; Jane English, "Justice between Generations," *Philosophical Studies* 31 (1977): 91–104, p. 95; Karen Green, "Rawls, Women and the Priority of Liberty," *Australian Journal of Philosophy*, 64, suppl. (1986): 26–36; Deborah Kearns, "A Theory of Justice and Love—Rawls on the Family," *Politics* 18 (1983): 36–42. Most recently, see John Exdell's excellent article, "Feminism, Fundamentalism and Liberal Legitimacy," *Canadian Journal of Philosophy*, vol. 24 (1994), which includes a substantial discussion of *Political Liberalism* as well as some of the earlier works.

2. Susan Moller Okin, "Justice and Gender," *Philosophy and Public Affairs* 16 (1987): 42–72, "Reason and Feeling in Thinking about Justice," *Ethics* 99 (1989): 229–49, and *Justice, Gender, and the Family* (New York: Basic, 1989), esp. chap. 5.

3. John Rawls, *Political Liberalism* (New York: Columbia University Press, 1993), p. xxix (hereafter cited in the text).

Ethics 105 (October 1994): 23–43

24   *Ethics*   *October 1994*

between *Theory* and *Political Liberalism,* there had been signs going in both directions. On the one hand, Rawls has for some time now indicated clearly that his theory is intended to include women, by abandoning the "heads of families" assumption and by adopting consistently gender neutral language, instead of interspersing references to "men" with those to "persons."[4] Also, in a 1975 article, he explicitly added a person's sex to the list of morally irrelevant contingencies that are not to be known in the original position.[5] On the other hand, in the 1977 essay "The Basic Structure as Subject," the family is no longer mentioned—though it explicitly had been in *Theory*—as part of the basic structure of society, to which the principles of justice are to apply. But in the 1978 version of the essay—now included in *Political Liberalism*—this omission is rectified.[6]

   Political Liberalism continues to give us mixed signals about Rawls's views on the application of his principles of justice to issues of gender. He says that, in contemporary society, "among our most basic problems are those of race, ethnicity, and gender" (p. xxviii) and that his focus on toleration may therefore seem dated. From a political point of view, it does seem strange to find religious and philosophical toleration at the forefront of Rawls's more recent thinking. Race, ethnicity, and gender *have* been high on the political agenda, in the United States as well as many other countries, during the two decades since *Theory* was published. In this country, growing disparities in income and wealth, the deterioration of much public education, and rapid changes in family forms have also taken place. By contrast, issues of religious and philosophical toleration have hardly been at the top of the political agenda, except insofar as abortion is perceived as such an issue. Rawls's increased focus on toleration is more readily understood from a philosophical point of view, however: the primary purpose of the new book is to resolve what Rawls now sees as the unrealistic, because unstable, nature of the well-ordered society he argued for in *Theory*.

---

4. In *Theory*, Rawls argues that any different assignments of basic rights on the grounds of sex (as of race, culture, or caste) would have to be justified by the difference principle—that is to say, by being to the advantage of the less favored—which they "seldom, if ever," are (p. 99). This indicates that Rawls did not intend to omit women as subjects of his theory of justice. However, he then claims that, because distinctions on the grounds of sex (or race, culture, or caste) in the assignment of basic rights are most unlikely to be justified, the "relevant positions" (of women, blacks, and so on) need not ordinarily be taken into account when the two principles of justice are being applied to the basic structure of society. But this does not follow: whether or not the basic rights of such groups are equal to those of white men, they are still likely to have importantly different perspectives, bearing on questions of justice. For example, women are less likely to neglect justice in the family.

5. John Rawls, "Fairness to Goodness," *Philosophical Review* 84 (1975): 536–54.

6. John Rawls, "The Basic Structure as Subject," *American Philosophical Quarterly* 14 (1977): 159–65, p. 159; cf. Lecture 7 of *Political Liberalism*, p. 258.

Rawls first suggests that the problems of race, ethnicity, and gender "may seem of an altogether different character calling for different principles of justice, which *Theory* does not discuss" (p. xxviii). The suggestion that his principles of justice may be inadequate for addressing these pressing issues seems unwarranted, and Rawls himself soon concludes that, once we get the conceptions and principles right for the basic historical questions, they "should be widely applicable to our own problems also" (p. xxix). Referring to the criticism that *Theory* has received for not dealing with problems of gender and the family, he says he thinks his conceptions and principles can be applied to them. Unfortunately, though, he does not apply them in the new book, beyond a suggestive but rather open-ended statement in the introduction. He states: "The same equality of the Declaration of Independence which Lincoln invoked to condemn slavery can be invoked to condemn the inequality and oppression of women" (p. xxix). Later, I shall offer two interpretations of this proposal. First, however, I shall argue that central aspects of *Political Liberalism* render the problem of applying the principles of justice to the family and the gender structure of society more intractable than they were in *Theory*.

THE FAMILY AS PART OF THE BASIC STRUCTURE

In *Political Liberalism,* Rawls develops further his "political conception of justice"—one that is for "the main institutions of political and social life, not for the whole of life" (p. 175). This is not a wholly new departure, as even in *Theory* Rawls had made it clear that this theory of justice was not intended to be comprehensive in scope. What Rawls calls "the basic structure of society" is still the first or primary subject of justice.[7] In *Theory,* Rawls included "the monogamous family" as part of the basic structure.[8] And in *Political Liberalism,* "the nature of the family" is explicitly mentioned as belonging to the basic structure, along with "the political constitution, the legally recognized forms of property, and the organization of the economy" (p. 258). This is surely as it should be for, as Rawls explains in *Theory* and in *Political Liberalism,* all these institutions "have deep and long-term social effects and in fundamental ways shape citizens' character and aims, the kinds of persons they are and aspire to be" (p. 68).[9] Clearly, both different

---

7. Limitations on the application of the principles of justice are raised in *Theory,* pp. 7–8, where Rawls says: "I shall not consider the justice of institutions and social practices generally. . . . There is no reason to suppose ahead of time that the principles satisfactory for the basic structure hold for all cases. These principles may not work for the rules and practices of private associations or for those of less comprehensive social groups." Compare *Political Liberalism,* pp. 11–12 and Lecture 7.

8. *Theory,* p. 7.

9. Compare ibid.

family types and different allocations of responsibilities and privileges within families have a great impact on the characters, self-conceptions and lives of citizens. Not only is this so, but typical current family structure and division of responsibilities constrain considerably more the self-conceptions, life opportunities, and access to political power of women than those of men.[10]

But this means, of course, that families should be regulated by the principles of justice or fairness. Indeed, from a political point of view, it seems particularly urgent now that justice in families and between the sexes be attended to because, while our constitution, forms of property ownership, and organization of the economy have changed only incrementally in the last few decades, family forms have changed enormously. As is well-known, about half of all marriages in the United States now end in divorce, about one-quarter of all children live in single parent households (in 90 percent of cases, with a single mother), a still small but increasing proportion of children are being raised by same-sex couples, and the majority of women with children under the age of three are in the labor force. In *Political Liberalism*, however, families get even less attention than in *Theory*, where they appeared in part 3, playing a major role in early moral education. Instead, Rawls now insists more strongly on the public and political nature of the institutions of the basic structure and suggests—in contrast to his acknowledgment that the nature of the family is within the purview of the basic structure—that families, because they are based in affection, do not need to be regulated by principles of justice. In a clear statement that the family is nonpolitical, he says: "The political is distinct . . . from the personal and the familial, which are affectional, . . . in ways the political" is not (p. 137).[11]

There seems to be a clear inconsistency here. How can families be both part of the basic structure and not political? Are they to have the standards of justice or fairness applied to them, or are they exempt, because based in affection? Why is it not the case that, in *this* institution, which certainly meets Rawls's criteria for inclusion in the basic struc-

10. See Okin, *Justice, Gender, and the Family*, p. 93 and chap. 7, passim.

11. Rawls says earlier: "Political liberalism . . . aims for a political conception of justice as a freestanding view. . . . As an account of political values, a freestanding political conception does not deny there being other values that apply, say, to the personal, the familial, and the associational; nor does it say that political values are separate from, or discontinuous with, other values" (*Political Liberalism*, p. 10). See also pp. 13 and 78–80 for emphasis on the political culture as public. Further into the text, Rawls distinguishes the political virtues from "the virtues that characterize ways of life belonging to comprehensive religious and philosophical doctrines, as well as from the virtues falling under various associational ideals (the ideals of churches and universities, occupations and vocations, clubs and teams) and of those appropriate to roles in family life and to the relations between individuals" (ibid., p. 195).

ture, and is at times explicitly included there, the value of justice does not, as elsewhere, outweigh other values (p. 139)?[12] Might he perhaps agree that families need to be regulated by the principles of justice as a baseline, even though they should also be characterized by affection, a higher virtue than justice? If so, he does not say so.

The problem we face is that the family is a social institution that defies the political/nonpolitical dichotomy that Rawls has increasingly emphasized in recent years. For families do clearly fall within the basic structure, as defined, yet they are for the most part comparatively private relationships, where things both good and bad are frequently hidden from public view. Families *are* often characterized by affection—but sometimes by naked power and vulnerability. They are undeniably political, by usual definitions of the word[13]—though less so according to Rawls's recent definition, which I shall discuss below. Rawls's own ambivalence on the subject of families is apparent in the text: having said that they are "affectional," and therefore not political, he later acknowledges that "the individual members of families [need protection] from other family members (wives from their husbands, children from their parents)" (p. 221, n. 8). Let us try to understand Rawls's reluctance to apply consistently his standards of justice to families.

The main reason is, as I have mentioned, Rawls's emphasis on his theory as a political, not a comprehensive moral, conception of justice. The reason for this change from *Theory* is that he has become convinced that to hope for agreement on a more general conception is "unrealistic." Given "the fact of reasonable pluralism"—that in a democratic regime there will be many different reasonable yet incompatible comprehensive doctrines—he now sees the stability of a just society as a serious problem unless one confines one's aims to achieving a political conception of justice (pp. xvi–xvii). The distinction Rawls draws between the political and the nonpolitical coincides with his distinction between the public and the nonpublic. Both, it seems, have to do with the difference between what is commonly shared and what is not; the former, in each case, consists of a "more limited point of

12. Here Rawls explicitly lists those "great values ... [that] are expressed by the principles of justice for the basic structure: among them, the values of equal political and civil liberty; fair equality of opportunity; the values of economic reciprocity; the social bases of mutual respect between citizens." Since the family is part of the basic structure, all these values should surely apply within them. As I have argued in *Justice, Gender, and the Family* (pp. 28–33), requiring that families be just is in no way inconsistent with hoping and expecting them normally to function in accordance with more elevated moral qualities, such as generosity and love.

13. See Okin, *Justice, Gender, and the Family*, pp. 124–33, for an argument to this effect.

view" and deals with a narrower range of subjects.[14] The overlapping consensus on which the political conception of justice is focused is, Rawls says, neither wide nor deep. He also specifies that "a political conception [of justice] tries to elaborate a reasonable conception for the basic structure alone and involves, so far as possible, no wider commitment to any other doctrine" (p. 13).[15]

Rawls mentions that the public political culture of a society may be deeply and enduringly divided about important issues. One example he gives is "the most appropriate understanding of liberty and equality" (p. 9). In the pre–Civil War period, slavery was the crucial divisive issue. Now, one such issue is gender—meaning all the ways in which sexual differences are socially institutionalized. That this is a prominent example of public disagreement may be another reason Rawls is reluctant to apply his conception of justice to gender and the family. As we shall see, his emphasis on toleration of a wide range of comprehensive philosophical, religious, and moral doctrines comes into conflict with some important means by which greater equality between the sexes might be promoted.

Now I wish to turn to two problems, internal to the theory, that result from the confusion about whether the family really is part of the basic structure, needing to be regulated by the principles of justice. Both the problems I shall address are quite serious ones for the stability of a well-ordered society—the very issue that *Political Liberalism* is intended to solve. The first has to do with congruence; the second is the apparent loss to the theory of families as potential "schools of justice."

CONGRUENCE IN A WELL-ORDERED SOCIETY

Rawls notes the desirability of congruence—or at least the absence of conflict—between the values held by citizens in the other, nonpolitical, parts of their lives, and the values inherent in their political conception of justice (p. 11). However, he does not really follow through on this. On the one hand, the full autonomy of citizens "presupposes that the fundamental ideas of justice as fairness are present in the public culture, or at least implicit in the history of its main institutions and the traditions of their interpretation" (p. 78; also p. 15). But by contrast Rawls also strongly implies that in the nonpolitical aspects of their

---

14. See *Political Liberalism*, pp. xx, 8, 11–15, 175–76. For example: "The public culture" is "the shared fund of implicitly recognized basic ideas and principles" (p. 8).

15. The distinctions between the basic structure and the rest of social and personal life, on the one hand, and the political and the nonpolitical, on the other, have repercussions far broader than can be discussed here. For a brief though more general discussion, see my review of *Political Liberalism* in *American Political Science Review* 87 (1993): 1010–11.

lives—personal morality or religion, for example—they may hold views such as that there is a fixed natural order or a "hierarchy justified by religious or aristocratic values" (p. 15). These two notions are difficult to reconcile. Even if, as Rawls says, these other views are not to be introduced into the discussion of political essentials, how can a belief in natural hierarchy among persons be consistent with the requirements of the political conception of justice, which views them as free and equal citizens?[16] Are persons in the just society to be regarded as "split" into public and nonpublic, political and nonpolitical selves? This is reminiscent of those aspects of liberal theory that Marx critiqued for splitting persons into "abstract citizens" and "human beings," in his essay "On the Jewish Question."[17]

To see why this division of people's lives and beliefs into the political and the nonpolitical cannot work, let us think specifically about gender. Take as an example a girl and a boy raised in a traditionalist (fundamentalist or orthodox) religious household and educated entirely at religious schools and within the church, temple, or mosque. Suppose that all of these "nonpolitical" settings inculcate and reinforce in them the belief that there is a natural, God-given hierarchy of the sexes, each with its own proper sphere—the female's being narrow, circumscribed, and without authority, and the male's the opposite. How is such a socialization consistent with both children's becoming, in any sense, "free and equal citizens"—who, as Rawls says, must "regard themselves as self-authenticating sources of valid claims" (p. 32)? He mentions slavery as an "extreme case" of the absence of such self-regard, constituting "social death." But surely women within such religions present a not much less extreme case, which raises the question whether such forms of indoctrination should be allowed in a well-ordered society. Indeed, we must ask whether such views, while not uncommon in contemporary liberal societies, can be regarded as "rea-

16. Noncongruence of this type seems to be a bigger problem than that of some other types. For example, it seems possible (though hard) to hold, privately, the view that those who do not believe as one does will be damned, and yet (because of one's appreciation of values such as peace and stability) to be unwilling to insist that one's religion should be enforced by the state. But it is exceedingly difficult to see how one could both hold and practice (in one's personal, familial, and associational life) the belief that women or blacks, say, are naturally inferior, without its seriously affecting one's capacity to relate (politically) to such people as citizens "free and equal" with oneself. A suggestion made by Cass Sunstein in personal correspondence (May 26, 1993) made me think harder about this issue.

17. Karl Marx, "On the Jewish Question," in *The Marx-Engels Reader*, ed. Robert C. Tucker, 2d ed. (New York: Norton, 1978), pp. 26–52, esp. pp. 42–46. There are definite suggestions of this splitting in *Political Liberalism*. Rawls says, e.g., that citizens who have converted from one religious faith to another "do not cease to be, *for questions of political justice*, the same persons they were before" (p. 30; emphasis added). Why not say that they do not cease to be the same persons they were before?

sonable" by Rawls's definition of the term, which is very close to "fair." He says, for example: "Reasonable persons . . . desire for its own sake a social world in which they, as free and equal, can cooperate with others on terms all can accept. They insist that reciprocity should hold within that world so that each benefits along with others" (p. 50).

I turn now to what Rawls says about *un*reasonable comprehensive doctrines, and the extent to which they should be tolerated in a basically well-ordered society. This subject is raised quite frequently. Sometimes he writes of the need to "contain unreasonable and irrational, and even mad, comprehensive doctrines . . . so that they do not undermine the unity and justice of society," which goes along with the assumption that unreasonable comprehensive doctrines "always exist" (pp. xvi–xviii, 39). I regard this as the weaker of two positions Rawls takes regarding unreasonable doctrines and ways of life.

The stronger position is best summed up as follows: the principles of any reasonable political conception must impose restrictions on permissible comprehensive views, and the basic institutions those principles require inevitably encourage some ways of life and discourage others, or even exclude them altogether. His examples include "doctrines and . . . associated ways of life . . . in direct conflict with the principles of justice . . . [such as those] requiring the repression or degradation of certain persons on, say, racial, or ethnic, or perfectionist grounds" (pp. 195–96). Some comprehensive doctrines, he tells us, are "off the political agenda," and some conceptions of the good cannot be "allowed" or "permitted," since they do not respect the principles of justice and "involve the violation of basic rights and liberties" (pp. 151, 193, 187).[18] For example, those who demand that their religious truth requires enforcement by the state, or who assert the right to a mode of life involving serfdom or slavery, have no claims within a just society, because what they demand violates, respectively, equal liberty of conscience and equal political and civil liberties (pp. 151–52). Later, Rawls sums up this stronger position by saying that, in a well-ordered society, permissible comprehensive doctrines are subject to "the constraint of their being reasonable" (p. 210; see also p. 81).[19]

18. This is confirmed by the statement that "the priority of right . . . in its general form, . . . means that admissible ideas of the good must respect the limits of, and serve a role within, the political conception of justice" (p. 176). This conception, of course, includes the requirement that citizens be regarded as free and equal. Rawls explains that to take a matter "off the political agenda" means that it is no longer subject to majority decision: "The equal basic liberties in the constitution that cover these matters are reasonably taken as fixed, as correctly settled once and for all" (ibid., p. 151, n. 16).

19. This is still not quite unequivocal for, in closing the paragraph from which the quotation is drawn, Rawls seems again to qualify his position by saying: "The constraints do not refer to, although they limit, the substantive content of comprehensive doctrines of the good (ibid., p. 211). See n. 24 below for the near equation of "reasonableness" with fairness and reciprocity.

Okin   Political Liberalism, *Justice, and Gender*   31

If slavery and serfdom are impermissible and off the agenda, we need to ask again: What are the justifiable limits of toleration of religious and philosophical conceptions regarding gender? Rawls's inclination is to find religions reasonable. He says that he supposes, "perhaps too optimistically—that, except for certain kinds of fundamentalism, all the main historical religions [since they admit of an account of free faith] . . . may thus be seen as reasonable comprehensive doctrines" (p. 170). I think he is too optimistic, by far. For one thing, unless I totally misunderstand what is meant by "an account of free faith," it is difficult to see what is free about the faith allowed Roman Catholics, among other orthodox (but not necessarily fundamentalist) religions. Also, as we have seen, Rawls is very clear that free faith is not the only issue determining the reasonableness of a doctrine. Its accordance with the principles of justice is also a major factor. Surely the circumscription of women's roles in life, their segregation in religious life, and their exclusion from important religious functions and positions of leadership—doctrines and practices that are still common to many varieties of religion—render them unreasonable by Rawls's own criteria. There is a serious conflict between freedom of religion and the equality of women.

It seems, however, that Rawls does not apply the same strict criteria of reasonableness to comprehensive doctrines that involve considerable gender inequality that he does to those that treat people differently on racial or ethnic grounds. One indication of this is that he discusses sects that "oppose the culture of the modern world" and wish to educate their children for such a life, apparently finding the practices of such sects and their preferred socialization of their children permissible within political liberalism (pp. 199–200). But one aspect of modernity that these sects often reject is the trend toward sex equality; typically highly patriarchal, they advocate and practice the dependency and submissiveness of women. In this important respect, they clearly violate the anticaste principle that Rawls otherwise—in cases of race and ethnicity, for example—regards as reasonably established by the principles of justice.[20] Rawls does, however, argue that children raised within such sects must also be taught their constitutional and civic rights (especially freedom of conscience), that they understand the political conception of justice, and that they be

20. Such a principle is definitely implied by some of the passages referred to above, at n. 18. For a discussion of gender as caste, see Okin, *Justice, Gender, and the Family*, pp. 65–68. On the anticaste principle in U.S. constitutional law and its implications when taken seriously, see Cass Sunstein, *The Partial Constitution* (Cambridge, Mass.: Harvard University Press, 1993), pp. 338–45 and chap. 9, passim. This way of thinking about gender is discussed more in the final section of the article. For a fuller discussion of the conflict between fundamentalism and feminism, see Exdell.

encouraged to pursue the political virtues. These "reasonable requirements for children's education" may, he acknowledges, lead them to
reject the religion in which they were raised, to adopt a liberal conception of the good. Nevertheless, if political liberalism is to be sustained,
such requirements are necessary.

Because of the just society's concern for the education of its future
citizens, then, Rawls is prepared to reduce religious liberties in one
important respect. His requirement that all children receive the kind of
civic education just described clearly implies at least some compulsory
public schooling for all. This could be helpful in partially resolving
the conflict between religious toleration and gender equality. For it
could to some extent counteract the isolation some religious groups
now succeed in maintaining for their children. Its teaching of the
principles of justice, in particular, could act as a counterforce against
certain elements of comprehensive doctrines, such as gender inequality. It would, at least to some extent, counteract the noncongruence
between such doctrines and political liberalism. Whether it would suffice, however, to enable children whose primary environment taught
them basic inequalities to question these inequalities deeply and successfully seems highly dubious.

Rawls also says that, unlike a well-ordered society itself, associations within it can offer "different terms" to their members, depending
on the associations' ends and the members' potential contributions to
them. He says that they may do this, however, only when and because
their members are already guaranteed the status of free and equal
citizens and have other alternatives open to them (p. 42). But this is
not at all obviously the case with the boy and girl I mentioned earlier,
for whom the combined powers of family and religion conspire to
reinforce inequality between the sexes, any more than it would be if
such combined powers instilled in children the naturalness of slavery
or racial inferiority. Even if such religions were otherwise to pass
Rawls's test of reasonableness, the degree and extent of sex discrimination that they both preach and practice should make them impermissible in a just society. For good reason, political liberalism seems unable
to be as widely tolerant of different religious conceptions of the good
as Rawls would like it to be.

THE FAMILY AS A POTENTIAL SCHOOL OF JUSTICE

The second problem of the new version of Rawls's theory that I shall
address here has to do with the development of what he calls "the
political virtues." In *Theory,* as I mentioned earlier, Rawls regarded
the family—which he then assumed "in some form" to be a just institution—as playing an important first role in the formation of citizens'
sense of justice. He argued that healthy moral development in early
life depends upon parent-child love, trust, affection, example, and

guidance. And at a later stage in moral development, called "the moral-ity of association," he portrayed the family, though he described it in gendered and hierarchical terms, as the first of many associations in which, by moving through a sequence of roles and positions, we are able to see things from the perspectives of others and, thus, to increase our moral understanding.[21]

There is much that is valuable in this account. My only disagree-ments with it have been that it seems to assume a gendered family and also to depend upon the unwarranted assumption that families are just. As I argue in *Justice, Gender, and the Family* (and as John Stuart Mill argued long ago in *The Subjection of Women*), it is difficult to see how families that are not themselves regulated by principles of justice and fairness could play a positive role in the moral education of the citizens of a just society.[22]

Let us now look at the account of moral psychology presented in *Political Liberalism*. Rawls emphasizes a number of times that we are born into and grow up in society and "are not seen as joining [it] at the age of reason" (p. 41).[23] He speaks of the "prior and fundamental role of [society's] basic institutions in establishing a social world within which alone we can develop with care, nurture, and education, and no little good fortune, into free and equal citizens" (p. 43). He also pays considerable attention to the political virtues that are necessary in citizens if a just or well-ordered society is to be sustained and stable. These, it seems, supplement or substitute for what was more often in *Theory* called the "sense of justice." These "very great virtues" are, as specified in various places: reasonableness and a sense of fairness (which, as I have suggested, appear to be very close in meaning),[24] a

21. *Theory*, pp. 462–72. I have discussed these important stages of Rawls's theory of moral development more fully in "Reason and Feeling in Thinking about Justice," pp. 235–36.

22. Okin, *Justice, Gender, and the Family*, pp. 17–24, 195–96; J. S. Mill, *The Subjection of Women* (1869), in *Collected Works*, ed. J. M. Robson (Toronto: University of Toronto Press, 1984), vol. 24, pp. 293–95, 324–25.

23. This gives the impression that he considers early moral socialization important, as in *Theory*, where he says: "I assume that the sense of justice is acquired gradually by the younger members of society as they grow up" (p. 463). However, at another point in *Political Liberalism*, writing of the political relationship of persons within the basic structure, which "we enter only by birth and exit only by death," he adds: "To us it seems that we have simply materialized, as it were, from nowhere at this position in this social world, with all its advantages and disadvantages, according to our good or bad fortune" (p. 136). This, of course, gives much less of a sense of growing up within the basic structure, in particular within families.

24. In what is probably his fullest explanation of reasonableness in *Political Liberal-ism*, Rawls writes: "Persons are reasonable in one basic respect when, among equal say, they are ready to propose principles and standards as fair terms of cooperation and to abide by them willingly, given the assurance that others will likewise do so. . . . The

spirit of compromise and a readiness to meet others halfway, toleration and mutual respect, and a sense of civility (pp. 123, 157, 163). Rawls stresses frequently how important it is that citizens of a well-ordered society develop these virtues (pp. 35, 51, 77, 107). However, his brief account of how this happens is more Kantian—more autonomous and intellectualized, less relational and concerned with moral feelings—in *Political Liberalism* than is the much fuller account of moral development in *Theory*.[25] The new account is less satisfactory and plausible. It says nothing specifically about early childhood and the importance of trust and love at that stage of life. Indeed, it says very little about how people are to acquire the political virtues, except generally by living under just "basic institutions." Rawls aims to show that "those who grow up under just basic institutions acquire a sense of justice and a reasoned allegiance to those institutions sufficient to render them stable . . . [a sense of justice] strong enough to resist the normal tendencies to injustice" (p. 147; also p. 86). But even their basic trust, which in *Theory* was derived from the care of their parents, is now, it seems, to grow out of their experiences in political life.

I think Rawls was completely right in *Theory* to stress the significance of the family as the first "school of justice" (to use Mill's term), and I regret the absence of this emphasis in *Political Liberalism*. There are two important ambiguities here. First, as I have mentioned, Rawls now asserts that the family is part of the basic structure of society, but also indicates numerous times that it is not—that the political, to which the principles of justice are to apply, is to be distinguished from the personal, associational, and familial. Second, it is not clear from the text of *Political Liberalism* whether readers are supposed to assume as "carried over" from *Theory* sections on topics, such as the account of childhood moral development, that are not explicitly addressed in the new book.[26] If we are not, the new account of moral psychology is

---

reasonable is an element of the idea of society as a system of fair co-operation and that its fair terms be reasonable for all to accept is part of its idea of reciprocity. . . . Reasonable persons . . . desire for its own sake a social world in which they, as free and equal, can cooperate with others on terms all can accept" (pp. 49–50). Soon after, we learn that "situated reasonably" means "[situated] fairly or symmetrically, with no one having superior bargaining advantages over the rest" (pp. 52–53).

25. See, e.g., p. 100 in *Political Liberalism*, where Rawls accepts Kant's notions that "the principles of practical reason originate, if we insist on saying they originate anywhere, in our moral consciousness as informed by practical reason. They derive from nowhere else" and that "reason, both theoretical and practical, is self-originating and self-authenticating."

26. In the introduction, Rawls says: "The account of the stability of a well-ordered society in part III [of *Theory*] is . . . unrealistic and must be recast." Otherwise, he says, the new lectures "take the structure and content of *Theory* to remain substantially the same" (ibid., pp. xv–xvii). But the "account of stability" occupies most of chaps. 8 and 9 of *Theory*, including the entire account of the development of a sense of justice. It is

truncated and unconvincing. For Rawls himself acknowledges that it is the "background culture"—what he regards as "the social, not . . . the political"—that is "the culture of daily life" (p. 14). How, then, can the development of the virtues so crucial to the stability of a just society take place only within the sphere of the political culture, which people encounter mainly as adults and, in many cases, indirectly and sporadically even then?

If Rawls does intend us to bring to our reading of *Political Liberalism* the much fuller and more convincing account of the development of a sense of justice that is included in *Theory,* then we face the problem of trying to reconcile the old, clear yet undiscussed, assumption of *Theory* that families need to be just if such healthy development is to occur, with the distinction of the political from the nonpolitical that is central to *Political Liberalism.* This seems impossible. Thus while this distinction may solve some problems, it causes others at least as serious.

TYPICAL CONTEMPORARY FAMILIES AS POOR SCHOOLS OF JUSTICE

I now want to move from these two problems internal to Rawls's theory in its new form, to look outside of the theory, and to discuss justice, gender, and moral development in contemporary society. In *Justice, Gender, and the Family,* I argue at some length from sociological evidence that, typically, heterosexual couple–based families in our society are unjust in their distributions between women and men of work, power, opportunity, leisure, access to resources, and other important goods.[27] Many families are not even basically safe environments, as Rawls acknowledges in mentioning the protection sometimes needed by less powerful family members. These facts in themselves signify that attention should be paid to justice or fairness within families and to the ways in which it might be promoted by public policies. I shall discuss some of these at the end of the article. Now, I wish to look briefly at what we have begun to learn about the effects on children of growing up in families that are unjust in one or more ways. I shall refer to two recent pieces of research in order to address this issue—one on the division of labor between adolescents of both sexes in different kinds of families, the other on women's and girls' perceptions of their own lack of power in very traditional families.

First, how do unjust divisions of labor between the adults in a household affect children? A recent study shows that unequal divisions

---

not clear whether these chapters are to be regarded as wholly or partly "recast" by what is said in *Political Liberalism.* Where the latter work is silent, as on the importance of just families and associations in moral development, it is not clear what the reader is to assume.

27. Okin, *Justice, Gender, and the Family,* chap. 7, passim.

36   *Ethics   October 1994*

of work between mothers and fathers are reflected—even magnified—
in unequal divisions of work assumed by adolescent children of different sexes.[28] In traditional households, where fathers are wage workers
and mothers are housewives, Mary Benin and Debra Edwards found
that the girls and boys they studied do approximately the same amount
of household work, though what they do is divided up along traditional
gendered lines. By contrast, in "drudge wife" households, where mothers and fathers both work full-time for pay, but mothers do twice as
much unpaid family work as fathers, the amount of work done by
adolescents varies widely by sex. Girls do, on average, 25 percent more
than the girls in traditional households, whereas the boys do only one-
third as much as the traditional-household boys. This means that the
girls in these households are doing almost four times as much household work as their brothers. Since it is difficult to imagine that the
extra work on the part of the girls is purely voluntary, it seems that
the boys are learning the pattern of family injustice established by
their own fathers and, like them, getting away with as little as possible.
And the daughters are falling, at a young age, into an even more
exaggerated version of the "drudge-wife" model established by their
mothers. Unfortunately, those doing the study did not interview the
adolescents (or their parents) about their perceptions of the fairness
or unfairness of this situation. But we need to ask: Is such a family
environment a good place to learn to be just and to treat each other
as equals, to acquire what Rawls terms the political virtues—such as
fairness and a readiness to meet others halfway? Or is it a place where
people absorb the message that they have different entitlements and
responsibilities, based on a morally irrelevant contingency—their
sex?

Second, a recent study done in Israel investigated women's and
girls' perceptions of sex inequality in hierarchical traditional families.[29]
The families studied were Druze Arabs, but the results seem applicable
to highly patriarchal religious households more generally. Cecilia Wainryb and Elliot Turiel found that the wives and daughters in the religious households accepted as inevitable the power of the male family
head over many of their activities and decisions, such as whether they
could get a job, or even a driver's license, or spend time with their
friends. However, at the same time, they did not regard this as fair.
They could not resist the male power, because of the sanctions—including being thrown out of the house, beaten, or divorced—that

28. Mary Holland Benin and Debra A. Edwards, "Adolescents' Chores: The Difference between Dual- and Single-Earner Families," *Journal of Marriage and the Family* 52
(1990): 361–73.

29. Cecilia Wainryb and Elliot Turiel, "Dominance, Subordinance, and Personal
Entitlements in Cultural Contexts," *Child Development*, vol. 65 (1994), in press.

disobedience was likely to invoke. This acceptance of the inevitability of male dominance resulted in the curious combinations of answers they gave. While almost 80 percent of the women and girls judged that it was unfair for a husband to dictate his wife's choices, at the same time 93 percent of them said that the wife should acquiesce. What we are seeing, it seems, is the learned acceptance of injustice, enforced by male power. The women were quite prepared to acknowledge that this situation in which they had no choice but to live was unjust. Surely such hierarchical early learning environments are not suitable training grounds for just citizens of either sex.

TWO PROBLEMS OF STABILITY

With the issue of family injustice in mind, I shall now turn back to Rawls's *Political Liberalism* to address directly the issue of stability. Rawls states that "the problem of stability is fundamental to political philosophy" (p. xvii). Thus the stability problem that he now thinks exists in *Theory*—that no comprehensive conception of justice can be shared, given the fact of reasonable pluralism—has to be fixed. He addresses it by restricting his conception of justice to the political and by developing the idea of an overlapping consensus that enables different and conflicting comprehensive (religious or philosophical) doctrines to coexist with each other and with the shared political conception of justice.

However, as Rawls reminds us, "stability involves two questions: the first is whether people who grow up under just institutions (as the political conception defines them) acquire a normally sufficient sense of justice so that they generally comply with those institutions" (p. 141; also p. 142). This question, he says, is answered by his setting out the moral psychology by which citizens in a well-ordered society acquire an adequate sense of justice. But, as I have argued, given the absence of families from *Political Liberalism,* and the ambiguity about whether they are required to be just, this account of moral psychology has very uncertain foundations.

Perhaps I could be said to be exaggerating. After all, the family is but one of many social institutions, associations, and subcommunities to which citizens belong. Thus, it might be argued, citizens have many other opportunities to develop the political virtues, including a sense of justice. There are two problems with this suggestion. First, while Rawls concludes in *Political Liberalism* that a just society ought not permit associations and subcommunities that violate fundamental political liberties, he does not require such subgroups to be regulated by all the principles of justice. (In *Theory,* associations were required, and recognized, to be just.)[30] Thus they may be so structured as to inculcate

30. *Theory,* pp. 471, 490.

in their members the values of hierarchy and inequality rather than, for example, the type of egalitarianism represented by the difference principle. Such associations' potential for playing a major role in inculcating the political virtues seems severely limited.

Second, omitting justice in families would leave a large hole in the account of moral psychology even if other "nonpolitical" social institutions were required to be just, because of the important influences of early childhood. Since Aristotle at least, most acute and interested observers have noted that a very large part of moral development takes place in early childhood and, thus, mostly within families. Contemporary moral development research confirms this. In a fairly recent book, *The Moral Child,* William Damon says that it is now widely agreed that the potential for moral-emotional reactions, displayed by signs of empathy and recognition of the emotional states of others, can be observed even in infants. "There is by now ample evidence of consistency and regularity in children's moral behavior," Damon continues, "and . . . many indications that enduring aspects of character are indeed formed early." "By the age of four or five, children can be interviewed about their views on moral standards like sharing and fairness."[31]

Up to the age of four or five, however, most children spend a very large part of their waking lives at home with their families. Now, in many cases, this is combined with time in the care of others, whether a day care center, nursery school, or more frequently, in family day care. Only a comparatively small proportion of children spend most of their waking time up to this age in any setting other than a family. If these families are, as I have argued, frequently *not* environments in which justice is normally practiced, work equally shared, and people treated with equal dignity and respect—if they are often instead places where injustice ranges from moderate unfairness to outright abuse, then how are children to develop the sense of justice that they need if the well-ordered society is to be stable?[32]

Thus Rawls's resolution of one of the problems of stability renders the other problem of stability more intractable. By separating out the sphere of the political, to which justice is to apply, from the personal, associational, and familial, within which there is to be great tolerance for

31. William Damon, *The Moral Child: Nurturing Children's Natural Moral Growth* (New York: Free Press, 1988), pp. 7, 13–16, 35.
32. It has been suggested to me by several people, including Mary Shanley (1989) and Cecilia Wainryb (1993), that the claim that persons need to be raised in just families in order to develop a strong sense of justice is empirically dubious. At least some of us who have much concern with justice—and with justice between the sexes in particular—have come to that concern in part through having grown up in unjust families. This is an important point, which is causing me to think anew about these issues. Perhaps some are more inclined to absorb and accept the injustice, and some to resist and question it. The question would undoubtedly be helped by some good research.

many different beliefs and modes of life, he seems to close off the possibility of ensuring that families (and associations) are just. He thereby leaves it unclear how the necessary sense of justice and the other political virtues are to develop, even at the most formative time of a child's life.

WHAT DOES JUSTICE FOR WOMEN REQUIRE?

As I mentioned earlier, Rawls suggests in the introduction to *Political Liberalism* that the inequality and oppression of women can be thought about, within the framework of his theory, by appeal to the same principle of equality that Lincoln invoked in order to condemn slavery. He does not elaborate further on this intriguing suggestion. I shall conclude by exploring two possible interpretations of it, explaining why I think one interpretation is far more likely to be fruitful in terms of rendering justice to women than the other and summarizing some of the social changes that would be needed in order to implement this solution. The key issue is whether we read the legacy of Lincoln as entailing purely formal equality between black and white Americans or whether we read it as requiring various measures aimed at considerably more substantive equality.[33]

The Reconstruction or Civil War amendments have been and still are frequently interpreted as mandating the formal legal equality of the former slaves. Even measured by this standard, of course, Reconstruction failed. The foremost historian of the period, Eric Foner, says: "That [the failure of Reconstruction] was a catastrophe for blacks in America is clear."[34] In many respects, formal legal equality was not achieved until about a century later. But, more important, it has proved vastly insufficient for the achievement of anything like "fair equality of opportunity" for black Americans. There are more young black men in prison than in college, and only 55 percent are in the labor force; half of black children are growing up in poverty and more than half are living in single parent (almost all single-mother) households.[35] No one, surely, would want to claim that race relations

33. For my purpose in exploring the possible meanings of Rawls's suggestion, it is perhaps less crucial to focus in detail on exactly what Lincoln said and did than to understand the two interpretations of what can be called "the legacy of Lincoln." However, LaWanda Cox has argued persuasively that Lincoln himself aimed at far more than formal equality for the freed slaves—though as a good politician who needed first to win a war, he proceeded pragmatically (*Lincoln and Black Freedom: A Study in Presidential Leadership* [Columbia: University of South Carolina Press, 1981]).

34. Eric Foner, "Slavery, the Civil War, and Reconstruction," in *The New American History*, ed. Eric Foner (Philadelphia: Temple University Press, 1990), p. 89.

35. See, e.g., Andrew Hacker, *Two Nations: Black and White, Separate, Hostile, Unequal* (New York: MacMillan, 1992); Jonathan Kozol, *Savage Inequalities: Children in America's Schools* (New York: Harper, 1991); William Julius Wilson, *The Truly Disadvantaged* (Chicago: University of Chicago Press, 1990).

in the United States are in any way a model of justice. If it could be predicted that women would be where black Americans are today after a hundred and thirty years of "solution" of their inequality, we would undoubtedly be better off without one.

There is, however, a quite plausible alternative reading of the Civil War amendments and other aspects of Reconstruction and of Lincoln's policy intentions regarding the former slaves. This reading interprets them as aimed at formal equality in some respects, such as suffrage, equal treatment by the courts, and so on. But it interprets them as also asserting a considerably more substantive anticaste principle. Cass Sunstein provides an extremely lucid account of this: "Differences that are irrevelant from the moral point of view ought not without good reason to be turned, by social and legal structures, into social disadvantages." This is especially so when they are turned into "systemic disadvantages," which apply in realms such as "education, freedom from public and private violence, wealth, political representation, and political influence," "realms that relate to basic participation as a citizen in a democracy." Sunstein regards sex, race, and disability as clear examples of castelike disadvantage in our society, and the Civil War amendments as "an effort to counteract this sort of systemic disadvantage."[36] The anticaste principle does not require that members of different groups always be treated the same. Rather, differential treatment—such as affirmative action of various kinds—is sometimes not only permitted but actually needed to remedy the effects of past or present caste status.

It is of course impossible to know how far Lincoln would have been willing and able to go in moving toward greater substantive equality for the freed slaves if he had lived. However, he had already acted to provide at least some of them with land and educational opportunities, as well as political rights.[37] When, after his assassination, Congress continued to try to sustain and expand such race-conscious social welfare programs—aimed to remedy to some extent the fact that for so long the ex-slaves had been deprived of their labor, of education, and of any opportunity at all for advancement—most such attempts were thwarted by President Andrew Johnson's vetoes and by opposition from racist forces, especially in the South.[38] But it is quite

36. Sunstein, p. 339. See pp. 338–46 for Sunstein's full account of the anticaste principle, and chap. 9 for his very thoughtful and convincing application of it to the issues of pornography, abortion, and surrogacy. He makes it clear that he is not saying that current American "castelike practices" are exactly the same, in nature or extent, as those of real caste societies (p. 338).

37. Lincoln's most substantial achievement of this type was the Freedmen's Bureau Bill, signed in March 1865 (Cox, pp. 27–28).

38. Eric Schnapper, "Affirmative Action and the Legislative History of the Fourteenth Amendment," *Virginia Law Review* 71 (1985): 753, pp. 768–87. In this illuminating article, Schnapper argues for the constitutionality of contemporary affirmative

likely that the continuation of these substantive aspects of Reconstruction, by enabling blacks in practice to reappropriate their own long-alienated labor and potential, would have led to an entirely different outcome for black Americans and for race relations in the United States. Thus understood, the legacy of Lincoln goes far beyond formal equality.

How does this understanding of Lincoln's appeal to equality—as an anticaste principle—apply to women? Catharine MacKinnon and Deborah Rhode have been among the most influential feminists arguing from this perspective, though rather than using the language of caste, MacKinnon refers to "dominance" and Rhode to "disadvantage." I too have written of gender as a castelike system.[39] Though our approaches are by no means identical, we argue that society ought to be so organized as to restore to women what has historically been fully or partly expropriated from them and used to disadvantage rather than to empower them—their sexuality, reproductive capacities, and domestic labor. MacKinnon, Rhode, and Sunstein have written extensively from an anticaste perspective on issues of sexuality and the prebirth part of reproduction.[40] Thus I shall focus here more on how the principle applies to domestic labor and the child-rearing aspect of reproduction.

Social justice for women has not been achieved, and is unlikely to be achieved, by formal legal equality, because so much of the way that society is structured is a result of a history in which women were legally subordinated and in which it was assumed that it was their natural role to exchange sexual and domestic services, including the crucial social task of child care, for economic security in the form of dependence on men. The hours and location of paid work and political activity, the location and type of housing, the hours and vacations of schools and the lack of public child care, all depended on this legal

action on the grounds that explicitly race-conscious laws designed to aid the freed slaves were passed in the 1860s by the same Congress that, at the same time and with most of the same supporters, passed the Fourteenth Amendment.

39. Catharine A. MacKinnon, *Sexual Harassment of Working Women: A Case of Sex Discrimination* (New Haven, Conn.: Yale University Press, 1979), esp. chap. 5, *Feminism Unmodified: Discourses on Life and Law* (Cambridge, Mass.: Harvard University Press, 1986), esp. chap. 2, and *Toward a Feminist Theory of the State* (Cambridge, Mass.: Harvard University Press, 1989), esp. chap. 12; Deborah L. Rhode, *Justice and Gender* (Cambridge, Mass.: Harvard University Press, 1989), introduction, esp. pp. 3, 4, and passim; Okin, *Justice, Gender, and the Family*, esp. pp. 63–67.

40. MacKinnon, *Feminism Unmodified*, pt. 2 on sex and violence, abortion, and sexual harassment, and pt. 3 on pornography; Rhode, chap. 9 on reproductive freedom and chap. 10 on sex and violence; Sunstein, chap. 9 on pornography, abortion, and surrogacy. Rhode has also written extensively about workplace sex discrimination and conflicts for women between family expectations and wage work (see, e.g., chaps. 7, 8).

subordination of women and related assumptions about their natural role. Now the legal subordination has largely been overturned, and the assumptions are being questioned by many people, but the social structures based on them have remained. No matter how formally equal women are, so long as the social structures that depend upon a gendered division of labor are still in place, so long as women continue to bear disproportionate responsibility for domestic work, raising children, and caring for the sick and elderly, and so long as this work is privatized, undervalued, and unpaid or underpaid, the anticaste principle will continue to be violated and women will remain systematically disadvantaged.

I have argued, in *Justice, Gender, and the Family,* that Rawls's *Theory,* while it does not discuss such injustices of gender, has great potential for doing so.[41] In particular, I claim that thinking about gender and families from an original position in which the parties do not know their sex can yield important insights. Moreover, many of the changes that might follow from such insights about justice between the sexes and within families clearly follow from anticaste rather than formal principles of equality. This is partly because, in spite of many differences between racist and sexist exploitation, there are also many parallels.[42] Some of what women need, beyond formal equality, in order to overcome a castelike history, has parallels in what the freed slaves needed (but did not get, except sporadically and temporarily) after abolition. For example, just as they needed the material provision of land if they were not to be forced from a barbaric form of exploitation—slavery—into a somewhat less barbaric one—unregulated wage

41. Okin, *Justice, Gender, and the Family,* pp. 101–9, chap. 8, esp. pp. 174–86.

42. It is a mistake to try to push the gender/race analogy too far, for several reasons. First, at least in recent history, most white women have not been exploited to anything like the same extent as blacks of both sexes have been, especially under slavery. Second, the situation of women is in (at least) three respects different from that of the freed slaves. First, there is no widely established or approved alternative for what is now mostly women's unpaid (or very badly paid) labor—domestic work, including child care and the care of other dependents—whereas there were at least the wage labor and the share-cropping alternatives in place for slave labor, though they were often badly paid and exploitative. This has to do with the fact that at least what the slaves did was recognized as work, unlike much of what women do. It is therefore of the utmost importance for women's equality that reproductive work be recognized as important, socially necessary *work.* Second, much of women's current vulnerability is less visible than that of that of the ex-slaves. Their physical, sexual, and psychological vulnerability is hidden much of the time within households; and economic vulnerability often does not become explicit until separation or divorce. Third, as John Stuart Mill pointed out long ago, the oppression of women is made infinitely more complicated by the fact that most women live intimately with a man and, partly as a consequence, the entire subject of sex equality—or indeed any significant change in relations between the sexes—raises the most intense personal feelings.

Okin   Political Liberalism, *Justice, and Gender*   43

labor under racist conditions—so do we now need the material provision of parental leave and subsidized child care so that women, like men, can work for pay without being exploited because they are parents.

By calling on the example of Lincoln and the principle of equality he invoked, what does Rawls mean to say about justice between the sexes? To which example does he turn: the eventual and largely ineffectual outcome of abolition, based on the belief that formal equality would suffice? Or, rather the intentions (frustrated though they were) of those who aimed at a more substantive equality between the races? Does Rawls consider that all that women need in order to be treated justly is equal basic rights with men and the formal freedom to choose a traditionally female or a less or nongendered life? Or does he advocate, in the spirit of Lincoln that was never fulfilled, an anticaste solution for women to undo the long centuries of injustice?

[17]

"The Disorder of Women": Women, Love, and the Sense of Justice*

Carole Pateman

In his essay on *Politics and the Arts* Rousseau proclaims that "never has a people perished from an excess of wine; all perish from the disorder of women." Rousseau states that drunkenness is usually the sole failing of otherwise upright, decent men; only the immoral fear the indiscretion that wine will promote. Drunkenness is not the worst of the vices since it makes men stupid rather than evil, and wine turns men away from the other vices so it poses no danger to the polity. In contrast, the "disorder of women" engenders all the vices and can bring the state to ruin.[1]

Rousseau is not the only social or political theorist to regard women as a permanently subversive force within the political order. Freud (to whose arguments I shall also refer) argues in chapter 4 of *Civilization and Its Discontents* that women are "hostile to" and "in opposition to" civilization. In a similar vein, Hegel writes that the community "creates its enemy for itself within its own gates" in "womankind in general." Women are "the everlasting irony in the life of the community," and when "women hold the helm of government, the state is at once in jeopardy."[2] These arguments are by no means of only historical interest. Although women have now been granted citizenship in the liberal democracies, it is still widely believed that they are unfitted for political life and that it would be dangerous if the state were in their hands. This belief is very complex. One of its central dimensions, which I shall begin to explore in this paper, is the conviction that women lack, and cannot develop, a sense of justice.

* I am grateful to Anna Yeatman for discussing the questions raised in this paper.

1. J.-J. Rousseau, *Politics and the Arts: A Letter to M. d'Alembert on the Theatre*, trans. A. Bloom (Ithaca, N.Y.: Cornell University Press, 1968), p. 109. Rousseau also notes that wine attracts old men because youth have other desires; beliefs about the subversiveness of youth are outside the scope of this paper.

2. G. W. F. Hegel, *The Phenomenology of Mind*, trans. J. B. Ballie (London: Allen & Unwin, 1949), p. 496; *Philosophy of Right*, trans. T. M. Knox (Oxford: Oxford University Press, 1952), addition to par. 166. N. O. Keohane ("Female Citizenship: 'The Monstrous Regiment of Women'" [paper presented at the annual meeting of the Conference for the Study of Political Thought, New York, April 6–8, 1979]) discusses various aspects of the belief that women should not enter the political sphere, with particular reference to ancient Greece and Bodin's theory.

Ethics 91 (October 1980): 20–34

The belief in the essential subversiveness of women[3] is of extremely ancient origin and is deeply embedded in our mythological and religious heritage. However, it is only in the modern world that "the disorder of women" constitutes a general social and political problem. More specifically, it is only with the development of liberal individualism and the arguments of its democratic and socialist critics that beliefs about women become an acute, though not always acknowledged, problem in social and political theory and practice. In premodern conceptions of the world, animal and human life were seen as part of a divinely or "naturally" ordered hierarchy of creation; individuals were conceived as born into a natural order of dominance and subordination. Nature and culture were part of a whole in which the hierarchy of social life was grounded in natural differences such as age, sex, and strength. Rulers were those whose "natural" characteristics fitted them for the task. From about the seventeenth century a new and revolutionary conception of social life developed within which the relationship between "nature" and "society," and between women and society, became inherently problematic.

Individuals began to be seen as rational beings, born free and equal to each other—or as naturally free and equal—and as individuals who create their social relationships and institutions for themselves. Political institutions, in particular, began to be seen as, properly, based on convention—on contract, consent, and agreement. The conception of a conventionally grounded sociopolitical order brought with it a complex of problems concerning its relation to nature that, three centuries later, is still unresolved. The nature of the individuals who create and take their place within conventional or "civil" associations is one of these problems. Do all individuals have the requisite nature or natural capacities? Or are there some who lack, or cannot develop, the capacities required for participation in civil life? If these individuals exist, their nature will appear as a threat to social life and there has been wide agreement that women are dangerous for this very reason. Women, by virtue of their natures, are a source of disorder in the state.

"Disorder" can be used in either of two basic senses: first, there is the sociopolitical sense of "civil disorder" as in a rowdy demonstration, a tumultuous assembly, a riot, a breakdown of law and order. Second, "disorder" is also used to refer to an internal malfunction of an individual, as when we speak of a disordered imagination or a disorder of the stomach or intestines. The term thus has application to the constitution of both the individual and the state. In addition, its moral

3. Women have also been perceived from ancient times as guardians of morality and order. This contradictory view is briefly discussed below, but it should be noted that the two conceptions of women are not straightforwardly opposed to each other. The "morality" and "order" represented by women is not the same as the "order" of the political sphere.

content can also be made explicit when it is used to describe a "disorderly house" in which decency and propriety are cast aside. Women, it is held, are a source of disorder because their being, or their nature, is such that it necessarily leads them to exert a disruptive influence in social and political life. Women have a disorder at their very centers—in their morality—which can bring about the destruction of the state. Women thus exemplify one of the ways in which nature and society stand opposed to each other. Moreover, the threat posed by women is exacerbated because of the place, or social sphere, for which they are fitted by their natures—the family. Another of the problems thrown up by the individualist, conventionalist conception of social life is whether *all* social relations are conventional in character. The family is seemingly the most natural of all human associations and thus specially suited to women who cannot transcend their natures in the manner demanded by civil forms of life. However, if the family is natural, then it is a form of association that stands in contrast to, and, perhaps, in conflict with (conventional) social and political life. These two aspects of the problem of the disorder of women are revealed in the writings of the social contract theorists and especially in Rousseau's theory.

The social contract theorists set out the individualist and conventionalist conception of social life with particular clarity. Their arguments depend on, and thus illustrate, all the ambiguities and complexities inherent in the antimony between nature and "convention." Popular contemporary beliefs about women, no less than seventeenth-century patriarchal arguments, rely on an appeal to nature and also on the fact that what is natural or "ordered according to nature" is widely believed to be good and desirable.[4] The contract theorists appealed both to conceptions of individuals' natures and to the state of nature which natural individuals inhabited—but exactly in what form they inhabited it, and what kind of relationships existed between them, is one of the key questions in the contract story.

Rousseau's version of contract theory highlights the problems in an acute form. He was the only contract theorist willing to pursue the revolutionary implications inherent in the doctrine, but he also believed

4. But compare Nietzsche: "You desire to *live* "according to Nature'? Oh, . . . what fraud of words! Imagine to yourselves a being like Nature, boundlessly extravagant, boundlessly indifferent, without purpose or consideration, without pity or justice, at once fruitful and barren and uncertain: imagine to yourselves *indifference* as a power—how *could* you live in accordance with such indifference?" (F. Nietzsche, *The Complete Works*, ed. O. Levy [London: Foulis, 1911], vol. 12, *Beyond Good and Evil*, trans. H. Zimmer, chap. 1, par. 9). The same ambiguities and contradictions inherent in our perception of women also surround "nature." Social life can, for example, be regarded as properly a reflection of the harmony in nature or the "order of nature"; alternatively, nature can be seen as the sphere of the uncontrolled, the arbitrary, the capricious, the indifferent that must be transcended in social life. (A discussion of various meanings attributed to "natural" in relation to women can be found in C. Pierce, "Natural Law Language and Women," in *Women in Sexist Society*, ed. V. Gornick and B. K. Moran [New York: Basic Books, 1971].)

that women posed a permanent threat to political order. Rousseau's theory contains some profound sociological insights precisely because he was concerned with the interrelations of different dimensions of social life and with transformations of human consciousness. In the *Discourse on Inequality* he attacks the abstract individualism of the liberal contract theorists who postulated a familiar yet natural condition original to humanity. Rousseau argues that, strictly, a natural state is asocial, inhabited only by animals of various kinds, one species of which has the potential to develop into human individuals. That is to say, Rousseau denies that one can draw political conclusions from assertions about the natural characteristics of isolated individuals or individuals seen severally not collectively. His basic premise is that human life is social life, or sociality is natural to humans. According to Rousseau, and here he agrees with Locke, the social state of nature is inhabited not by (isolated) individuals but by families. He writes that "the oldest of all societies, and the only natural one, is that of the family."[5] This is another way of saying that the family precedes, or can exist in the absence of, wider social institutions or "civil society"; it exists in the natural condition. The family is also grounded in the natural ties of love and affection (which are natural because they are within human capacities as, say, flying is not) and it has its origin in the biological process of procreation, in the natural difference between the sexes. Rousseau argues that the family provides us with a major example of a social institution that follows the order of nature because, in the family, age naturally takes precedence over youth and males are naturally in authority over females. For Rousseau, the family is necessarily patriarchal.

The state of nature stands in contrast to civil society, but the family is common to both forms of existence. The family spans the divide between a condition grounded in nature and the conventional bonds of civil life. Few social and political theorists, with the notable exception of Hobbes,[6] have been willing to present the family as a conventional association. Indeed, in the *Philosophy of Right*, Hegel claims that it is "shameful" to see marriage and the family as merely contractual associations. The family is widely regarded as the natural basis of civil life. Familial, or domestic relations, are based on the natural ties of biology and sentiment, and the family is constituted by the particularistic bonds of an organic unity. However, the status of the family as the foundation of civil society means that the contrast between the different forms of social life in 'the state of nature' and 'civil society' is carried over into civil life itself. The distinction between and separation of the private

---

5. J.-J. Rousseau, *The Social Contract*, trans. M. Cranston (Harmondsworth, Middlesex: Penguin Books, 1968), bk. 1, p. 50.

6. Hobbes's view of the family is discussed in T. Brennan and C. Pateman, "'Mere Auxiliaries to the Commonwealth': Women and the Origins of Liberalism," *Political Studies* 27 (1979): 183–200.

and public, or particularistic and universal, spheres of association is a fundamental structural principle of the modern, liberal conception of social life. The natural, particularistic family nestles at the center of the private sphere, and it throws into prominence and stands opposed to the impersonal, universal, "conventional" bonds of public life.

Rawls has recently stated that "justice is the first virtue of social institutions."[7] Similarly, Freud argues that "the first requisite of civiliza-tion, . . . is that of justice—that is, the assurance that a law once made will not be broken in favour of an individual."[8] But justice is not the virtue of *all* social institutions. As the preceding discussion suggests, and as Freud (and Hegel) tell us, it is love, not justice, that is the first virtue of the family. The family is a naturally social not a conventionally social institution, but justice is a public or conventional virtue. In the family, individuals appear as unique and unequal personalities and as members of a differentiated unity grounded in sentiment. In civil life individuals transcend, or leave behind, the particular and ascribed characteristics which distinguish them in the private sphere and appear as unrelated equals. They enter the sphere of individualism—which is also uni-versalism—as bearers of rights (liberties), as owners of property, and as citizens. In a civil association, individuals are bound together and their actions are regulated solely by general or universal rules and laws that apply impartially to all. The rules and laws protect the rights and property of all individuals—providing that all do their share to uphold the rules, that is to say, to maintain justice. Particular or private interests of individuals must be subordinated to the public interest, or to the virtue of justice.

Individuals will more readily uphold the rules of civil association if they develop a sense of justice or a morality of order. Individuals must "internalize" the universal rules of the sociopolitical order, understand that they ought to be observed, and wish to act accordingly. The sense of justice is fundamental to the maintenance of public order. However, if individuals exist who, like women according to Rousseau and Freud, naturally are incapable of developing a sense of justice, the basis of civil association is threatened; it contains within itself a permanent source of disorder. The threat is all the greater because the natural morality, or deficiency in moral capacity, of women fits them only for the "natural society" of domestic life. But the family itself is a threat to civil life. Love and justice are antagonistic virtues; the demands of love and of family bonds are particularistic and so in direct conflict with justice which demands that private interest is subordinated to the public (universal) good. The family is thus simultaneously the foundation of the state and antagonistic to it. Moreover, the presence within it of women who have

7. J. Rawls, *A Theory of Justice* (Oxford: Oxford University Press, 1971), p. 3.
8. S. Freud, "Civilization and Its Discontents," in *The Standard Edition of the Complete Psychological Works,* trans. J. Strachey (London: Hogarth Press, 1961), 21:95.

no sense of justice—and whose natures prevent them from leaving the domestic sphere—can only work against and weaken the sense of justice of their male kin who must uphold justice in civil life. "Womankind," Hegel states, "perverts the universal property of the state into a possession and ornament for the family."[9]

Rousseau and Freud offer a remarkably similar diagnosis of why women are incapable of developing a sense of justice. Both agree that, for women, anatomy is destiny. The biological (natural) differences between the sexes influence and are reflected in their respective moral characters. Rousseau argues that the source of the disorder of women lies in their boundless sexual passion. Women, he claims, foreshadowing Freud, are unable to subdue and sublimate their sexual desires in the same manner, or to the same extent, as men. Men are the active and aggressive sex and are "controlled by nature"; passive and defensive women have only the control of modesty. There must therefore be a double standard of sexual conduct. If both sexes gave equal rein to their passions "the men, . . . would at last become [the women's] victims, and would be dragged to their death without the least chance of escape."[10] Modesty is natural to women, but it provides a weak and uncertain control of their sexual desires. Moreover, as Rousseau argues in *Politics and the Arts*: "even if it could be denied that a special sentiment of chasteness was natural to women, would it be any the less true that in society . . . they ought to be raised in principles appropriate to it? If the timidity, chasteness, and modesty which are proper to them are social inventions, it is in society's interest that women acquire these qualities. . . ."[11] However, even an education specifically designed to foster modesty is not sufficient guarantee against the disorderliness of women. Rousseau spells out this lesson in graphic fashion in *La Nouvelle Héloise*. Julie desires nothing more than to be virtuous and lead an exemplary life as a wife and mother, but she is unable, despite all her efforts and apparent success in passing through the trials set for her by Wolmar, to overcome her passion for Saint Preux. If the good order of Clarens is not to be fatally disrupted, Julie must take the one course left to her; the only solution to the problem of the disorder of women is her "accidental" death.

Rousseau and Freud argue that this fundamental difference between the sexes has existed since the very beginning of social life and, indeed, has structured it. Both claim that the creation of civil society, or "civilization," is the work of men. For Rousseau the sexes are equal only when isolated from each other among the animals in the true (asocial) natural condition. Social life develops as family life, and while charting its emergence Rousseau suddenly announces that "the first difference was

9. Hegel, *The Phenomenology of Mind*, p. 496.
10. J.-J. Rousseau, *Emile*, trans. B. Foxley (London: Dent, 1911), p. 322.
11. Rousseau, *Politics and the Arts*, p. 87.

established in the way of life of the two sexes, . . . women . . . grew accustomed to tend the hut and the children."[12] His conjectural history of the development of civil society and the transformation of human nature then continues as a history of male activity and male nature. Freud also presents a conjectural history of the development of civil society (civilization) in *Civilization and Its Discontents*. He argues that once "the need for genital satisfaction no longer made its appearance like a guest who drops in suddenly,"[13] males had a reason for keeping females close at hand and the latter, in their turn, were obliged to comply in order to care for their helpless young. Once the family was established, the development of civilization was the work of men alone because it required the "instinctual sublimations of which women are little capable." Only men are capable of sublimating their passions and thus capable of the justice that civil life demands. Furthermore, men's involvement in public life, and their consequent dependence on other men, means that they have little energy left for their wives and families: "thus the woman finds herself forced into the background by the claims of civilization and she adopts a hostile attitude towards it."[14]

No explanation was available of why women are less able than men to sublimate their passions, or how the "special stamp to the character of females as social beings"[15] comes about until Freud formulated his psychoanalytic theory. Rousseau can only tell us that men and women differ in this respect—and he prescribes an education for girls that will reinforce their disorderly natures and indifference to justice. Women are "naturally" made to be "at the mercy of man's judgement" and "to endure even injustice at his hands."[16] (Hegel, it might be noted, was content to leave women in their natural state; women, he says with resignation, are "educated—who knows how?—as it were by breathing in ideas, by living. . . . ")[17] Freud argues that the explanation for women's lack of, or deficiency in, a sense of justice is the differential passage of the two sexes through the Oedipus complex and a consequent difference in the development of their super-egos. The super-ego is the "representa-

12. J.-J. Rousseau, "Discourse on the Origin and Foundations of Inequality," in *The First and Second Discourses*, trans. R. D. Masters (New York: St. Martin's Press, 1964), p. 147. The speculations of classic theorists about the "natural condition" and "the origin of society" should be compared with the speculations of scientists studying animal life. See the fascinating discussion by D. Haraway, "Animal Sociology and a Natural Economy of the Body Politic, Part II: The Past Is the Contested Zone: Human Nature and Theories of Production and Reproduction in Primate Behavior Studies," *Signs* 4 (1978): 37–60.

13. Freud, "Civilization and Its Discontents," p. 99.

14. Ibid., pp. 103–4.

15. S. Freud, "Female Sexuality," in *On Sexuality*, ed. A. Richards (Harmondsworth, Middlesex: Penguin Freud Library, 1977), 7:377.

16. Rousseau, *Emile*, pp. 328, 359.

17. Hegel, *Philosophy of Right*, addition to par. 166.

tive for us of every moral restriction"[18] and, especially, of the restrictions that justice demands.

Civilization is the work of men in the most profound sense, for it is men alone who possess a fully developed super-ego. The emergence of the super-ego is bound up with (the conjectural history of) the "original" momentous move from the family to wider communal life. Freud argues that "originally" the "first" sons killed the "first" father, whom they simultaneously loved and hated. Out of the awful act of hatred, remorse and guilt grew from their love, and their subsequent identification with their dead father led to the emergence of the super-ego. The brothers, Freud argues, imposed on each other the mutual restrictions necessary to prevent a repetition of their dreadful deed. Thus the public virtue of justice, or "the first 'right' or 'law'" necessary for civil life, was established—by men; women had no part in this development.[19] In our own time the different manner in which little boys and girls pass through the Oedipus complex harks back to the purely masculine "origin" of justice, political right, and the super-ego.

Little boys have a dramatic passage through the Oedipus complex. The threat of castration, the force of which is confirmed when the boy sees the "castrated" female genitals, impels him to identify with his father, and so the Oedipus complex is "literally smashed to pieces."[20] The super-ego, which is "heir" to the Oedipus complex, then begins its development. The little boy "assimilates" his father's ego to his own and thereby internalizes all the restraints embodied in the paternal agency. Thus the male infant becomes a moral individual, in due course a "man," since the creation of the super-ego initiates him into "all the processes that are designed to make the individual find a place in the cultural community."[21] For females, however, the process is quite different. Females are already "castrated" and when they make this terrible discovery by comparing themselves to little boys, their Oedipus complex is created, not destroyed. It is a long and difficult journey through which the little girl comes to take her father as her object—in fact, she may never surmount the Oedipus complex. The result is that women lack or, at best, have a much weaker super-ego than men. Freud writes that "for women the level of what is ethically normal is different from what it is in men. Their super-ego is never so inexorable, so impersonal, so independent of its emotional origins as we require it to be in men. . . . They show less sense of justice than men, . . . they are less ready to submit to the

---

18. S. Freud, "The Dissection of the Psychical Personality," in *New Introductory Lectures Lectures on Psychoanalysis*, ed. J. Strachey (Harmondsworth, Middlesex: Penguin Freud Library, 1973), 2:98.

19. Freud, "Civilization and Its Discontents," pp. 101, 131–32.

20. Freud, "Some Psychical Consequences of the Anatomical Distinction between the Sexes," in Richards, ed., 7: 341.

21. Freud, "Female Sexuality," p. 375.

great exigencies of life, . . . they are more often influenced in their judgements by feelings of affection or hostility. . . . "[22]

Freud argues that the creation and dissolution of the Oedipus complex is a universal feature of human existence. The difference in moral capacity between the sexes must, therefore, be accepted. In Rousseau's terms, it is a social reflection of the order of nature. Freud emphasizes the costs of creating civilization,[23] but he has no suggestions for containing the disorderliness of women. Rousseau, however, concludes that the only way in which the state can be protected from the impact of women is through strict segregation of the sexes in their activities, including, as at Clarens, in domestic life. Sexual separation is necessary because even modest (good) women are a corrupting influence on men. Their disorder leads them always to pull men away from civic virtue and to mock at justice. But segregation is only a preventive measure; it does nothing to cure the disorder of women.

This is shown when the separation of the sexes is taken to its logical limit—the seraglio. The seraglio appears to be a secure "asylum against the onslaughts of vice," and the one place where a woman can "be sure about [herself], where there are no dangers to fear."[24] Nevertheless, as Usbek discovers, disorder can break out even in the seraglio. In *La Nouvelle Héloïse*, the presence of Wolmar, who epitomizes the qualities of a wise man with a highly developed sense of justice, is not enough to protect Clarens. Julie states that Wolmar never violates "conjugal solemnity," and that even his passion for her is of a kind in which he "loves only as much as he wishes to and . . . he wishes to only as much as reason permits."[25] Yet Julie's passion triumphs over Wolmar's justice. Neither the seraglio nor Clarens can provide a true asylum or substitute for a weak super-ego and natural lack of capacity for sublimation. In any social context "the life of a good woman is a perpetual struggle against self."[26] Julie says everything when she writes on her death-bed that "I dare pride myself in the past, but who might have been able to answer for my future? One day more, perhaps, and I might be guilty!"[27]

---

22. Freud, "Some Psychical Consequences of the Anatomical Distinction between the Sexes," 7:342.

23. Cf.: "Society cannot be formed or maintained without our being required to make perpetual and costly sacrifices. Because society surpasses us, it obliges us to surpass ourselves, and to surpass itself, a being must, to some degree, depart from its nature . . ." (E. Durkheim, "The Dualism of Human Nature and Its Social Conditions" in *Essays on Sociology and Philosophy*, ed. K. H. Wolff [New York: Harper & Row, 1964], p. 338).

24. Montesquieu, *Persian Letters*, trans. C. J. Betts (Harmondsworth, Middlesex: Penguin Books, 1973), letter 20, p. 68; letter 26, p. 76.

25. J.-J. Rousseau, *La Nouvelle Héloïse*, trans. J. H. McDowell (University Park: Pennsylvania State University Press, 1968), pt. 2, letter 20, p. 260.

26. Rousseau, *Emile* (n. 10 above), p. 332.

27. Rousseau, *La Nouvelle Héloïse*, pt. 4, letter 12, p. 405.

Rousseau presents us with many insights into the problem of the disorder of women. However he is, very surprisingly, far less aware of the problem posed by the family. Rousseau's political theory highlights the conflict between the private interests of sectional associations and the general will (or principles of justice) that governs the political order. However, he fails to see that the family, too, is a sectional association that threatens justice. Rousseau pictures the family, the little commonwealth with the father at its head, as the foundation of the state: "Will the bonds of convention hold firm without some foundation in nature? Can devotion to the state exist apart from the love of those near and dear to us? Can patriotism thrive except in the soil of that miniature fatherland, the home? Is it not the good son, the good husband, the good father, who makes the good citizen?"[28] Perhaps—if the father's sense of justice is strong enough to override his love for his family, his desire to protect its interests, and the baleful influence of his wife. Freud argues that the conflict between love, whether sensual or "aim-inhibited," and public life cannot be avoided: "love comes into opposition to the interests of civilization; . . . civilization threatens love with substantial restrictions." The more closely that family members are attached to each other, the harder it is for them to enter into public life.[29] Freud might have added that the more diligently husbands and fathers work for the interests of their families, the more likely it is that they will put those interests before the requirements of justice. There can be no easy reconciliation of the virtues of love and justice.

Paradoxically, because the family is the "foundation" of social life in the sense that it is the point of "procreative origin"[30] of society and because it stands directly at the border with nature, women are seen as the guardians of order and morality as well as inherently subversive. It is women who reproduce and have the major responsibility for educating the next generation; it is the mother who turns asocial, bisexual babies into little "boys" and "girls." Rousseau glorifies women's task as mothers. He was one of the first writers to emphasize the moral implications of breast-feeding, and he is careful to stress, for example, that when Julie constructs her natural garden retreat she does not allow the work to interfere with her duties as a mother. (However, it should be noted that the mother's task is completed in the early years; a male tutor takes over from her.) Women's guardianship of order reaches beyond motherhood. Within the shelter of domestic life women impose an order, a

28. Rousseau, *Emile*, p. 326. I was first alerted to this point by the excellent discussion of Rousseau in S. Okin, *Women in Political Thought* (Princeton, N.J.: Princeton University Press, 1980).

29. Freud, "Civilization and Its Discontents," pp. 102–3.

30. I am indebted for the phrase to A. Yeatman's unpublished paper "Gender Ascription and the Conditions of Its Breakdown: The Rationalization of the 'Domestic Sphere' and the Nineteenth-Century 'Cult of Domesticity.'"

social pattern, and thus give meaning to the natural world of birth and death and other physical processes, of dirt and raw materials, that is integral to domestic life. Women are direct mediators between nature and society. However, because women face nature directly, and because, in giving birth and in their other bodily functions, they appear as part of nature, they exemplify the ambiguous status of the family as both natural and social.[31] Women impose order and foster morality; but they are also in daily contact with dirt and with natural processes only partly under our control. They cannot escape being tainted by this contact or completely transcend the naturalness of their own being. Hence they represent both order and disorder, both morality and boundless passion.

It is worth remarking here that one way in which women (and their male kin and keepers) attempt to hide this contact with nature, their own natural functions, and hence their potential for disorder, is through cleanliness—presented as purity. In the *Persian Letters* the chief eunuch stresses to Usbek that he has always been trained to keep the women in the seraglio "absolutely clean . . . and [to take] an infinite amount of care over it."[32] Rousseau proclaims that "nothing could be more revolting than a dirty woman, and a husband who tires of her is not to blame." Emile will never find this fault in Sophy: "things are never clean enough for her. . . . She has always disliked inspecting the kitchen-garden . . . the soil is dirty, . . . absolute cleanliness . . . has become a habit, till it absorbs one half of her time and controls the other; so that she thinks less of how to do a thing than of how to do it without getting dirty. . . . Sophy is more than clean, she is pure."[33]

The profound insights into the contradictions and antagonisms in the dialectic between individuals and their social relations, and between the family and civil society, to be found in the work of thinkers of the stature of Rousseau and Freud, are sadly neglected (or not even recognized) in most contemporary work on the subject of justice and in much feminist writing. In part, this reflects the consolidation of liberal theory over three centuries as the ideology of the liberal capitalist state, centered on the separation of the political and private spheres. The problems which appear explicitly at the origins of liberal theory in the arguments of the social contract theorists and their critics are now either ignored or regarded as unproblematic. In particular, the tension be-

---

31. On these points see M. Douglas, *Purity and Danger* (Harmondsworth, Middlesex: Penguin Books, 1970), S. B. Ortner, "Is Female to Male as Nature Is to Culture?" in *Women, Culture and Society*, ed. M. Rosaldo and L. Lamphere (Stanford, Calif.: Stanford University Press, 1974); and L. Davidoff, "The Rationalization of Housework," in *Dependence and Exploitation in Work and Marriage*, ed. D. L. Barker and S. Allen (London: Longmans, 1976). (On purity see also Ortner's suggestive sketch "The Virgin and the State," *Feminist Studies* 8 [1978]: 19–36.)

32. Montesquieu, letter 64, p. 131.

33. Rousseau, *Emile*, pp. 357–58.

tween nature and convention or love and justice is continually glossed over or suppressed.

Early liberal feminist writers such as Mary Wollstonecraft and John Stuart Mill, for example, who agree that women lack a sense of justice, offer a much more superficial diagnosis of the problem than Rousseau (though that is not to underestimate their achievement). They see it primarily as a matter of extending the liberal principles of freedom, equality, and rationality to women through a process of education. In the *Vindication*, Wollstonecraft appeals for the "rights of men and citizens" to be extended to both sexes; reason has no sex. It appears that the virtues are sexually differentiated because women have been turned into "artificial" creatures. Their education (or, more accurately, lack of it) enforces their dependence on men and makes them mean and selfish, narrowing the range of their concerns to exclude the wider community so that they cannot develop a sense of justice. Similarly in *The Subjection of Women*, Mill argues that we cannot say that women are "naturally" fit only for subordination because we know nothing of what they might become if the principles of freedom and equality, now governing the rest of our social institutions, were extended to sexual relations. Mill argues that individuals develop a sense of justice through participation in as wide a range of public institutions as possible; confined to the family—which the law allows to be a "school of despotism"—women can never learn to weigh the public interest against selfish inclination.

The obvious problem with Mill's and Wollstonecraft's arguments is that although they both advocate a proper education for women and a widening of opportunities to enable them to be economically independent of men, they also assume that the opportunities will be largely irrelevant for the majority of women. Most women will continue working within the home since child-rearing will remain their major responsibility. But this means that, despite legal and educational reforms, men's moral understanding will continue to be more highly developed than women's. Women will not obtain within the family the breadth of social experience and practical education that will develop their sense of justice and allow them, with safety, to participate in political life. The problem of the disorder of women, while mitigated by education, remains unresolved. These feminist arguments assume that the family can become the bedrock on which the liberal state is raised, but they also contain a hint that love and justice can conflict. Mill implies that education is the answer here too; educated persons of both sexes should be able to control and subdue their "lower" passions.[34] Wollstonecraft

34. Victorian arguments about women's lack of sexual feeling, while oppressive, could also be used to women's advantage. There is an excellent discussion of this area in N. F. Cott, "Passionlessness: An Interpretation of Victorian Sexual Ideology, 1790–1850" *Signs* 4 (1978): 219–36.

contrasts love, that is, sexual passion, with friendship and mutual respect between equals, and she argues that the latter is the only true basis for marriage and family life. Rousseau, also, thought it "an error" to see sexual passion as the basis of domestic life (he makes it clear that Saint Preux, Julie's lover, would not make a good husband). He claims that: "people do not marry in order to think exclusively of each other, but in order to fulfill the duties of civil society jointly, to govern the house prudently, to rear their children well. Lovers never see anyone but themselves, they incessantly attend only to themselves, and the only thing they are able to do is love each other."[35]

However, given Rousseau's conception of women's nature and his plan for their education, it is impossible that marriage could be placed on this footing—as he shows clearly enough in his story of Wolmar's virtue and Julie's love. To state that sexual attraction is not the proper foundation for marriage solves nothing if it is also believed that women are naturally creatures governed wholly by their sexual passions. More generally, the liberal feminists' recognition that the relationship between the sexes contradicts basic liberal principles and their proposals for social reforms fail to get to the heart of the problem of the disorder of women. Their argument is undercut by the acceptance of the separation of domestic from civil life, which is also a sexual separation; women and love are irrevocably set in opposition to justice. Liberal theory presupposes the opposition between nature and convention but the opposition can be neither admitted nor its implications pursued. The account of the development of the sense of justice in Rawls's extremely influential *A Theory of Justice* shows how liberal theorists consistently obscure one of the major problems in their arguments.

Rawls states that he has drawn on both Rousseau and Freud, but he gives no indication that he has appreciated the relevance of their insights into sexual relationships for the question of justice. Rawls presents an apparently sexually undifferentiated account, arguing that "our moral understanding increases as we move in the course of life through a sequence of positions."[36] The sense of justice develops in three stages; first, the child learns the "morality of order" from its parents. Then the "morality of association," a morality characterized by the cooperative virtues of justice and impartiality, is developed when the individual occupies a variety of roles in a range of institutions. Finally, we reach the stage of the "morality of principles" in which we understand the fundamental role of justice in the social order and we wish to uphold it; the sense of justice is attained. Now this account, of course, has the same obvious failing as the liberal feminist arguments—only if men *and* women can move "through a sequence of positions" will both sexes

35. Rousseau, *La Nouvelle Héloise*, pt. 3, letter 30, pp. 261–62.
36. Rawls (n. 7 above), p. 468. The discussion here draws generally on secs. 70–72.

develop the sense of justice. Rawls, not surprisingly, rejects cries to "abolish the family," but he has nothing to say about the sexual division of labor or the conviction that domestic life is the proper sphere for women. On the contrary, he remarks that if a publicly recognized concept of justice regulates social life it will "reconcile us to the dispositions of the natural order."[37] And what is more natural, or in accordance, with the order of nature, than the division of social life and its virtues between the sexes: conventional political life and justice belong to men; domestic life and love belong to women?

One reaction from the feminist movement to the problems sketched in this paper has been a call for the last vestiges of nature to be swept away. In the *Dialectics of Sex,* Firestone claims that the problem of women and nature can be solved through artificial reproduction which will allow all relationships, including those between adults and children, to be based on convention or to be freely chosen. However, this is to argue that the whole of social life could be fashioned in the image of a philosophically and sociologically incoherent abstract, possessive individualism. It is a "solution" based on a continuing opposition between nature and society rather than an attempt to recreate this relationship. Another feminist response to claims about the disorder of women has been to argue that, since "justice" is the work of men and an aspect of the domination of women, women should reject it totally and remake their lives on the basis of love, sentiment, and personal relations. But this no more solves the problem than a declaration of war on nature; neither position breaks with liberal conceptions or can take account of the dialectic between individual and social life, between the particular or personal and the universal or political. To attempt technologically to banish nature or to deny that justice has any relevance, is to try to wish away fundamental dimensions of human life. Rather, the extraordinarily difficult and complex task must be undertaken of developing a critique of the liberal and patriarchal conception of the relation between nature and convention that will also provide the foundation for a theory of a democratic, sexually egalitarian practice.

The insights and failings of the theorists discussed in this paper provide one starting point for such a critique. I have concentrated on "love," that is to say, sexual passion. However, one of the most urgent tasks is to provide an alternative to the liberal view of justice, that assumes that "a" sense of justice presently exists, developed through the smooth passage of all individuals through social institutions. This claim rests on the uncritical acceptance that the structure of liberal capitalist institutions allows both men and women, working class and middle class, to develop in the same fashion. It ignores the reality of institutions in which the subordination of women and the "despotic organization of

---

37. Ibid., p. 512.

production"[38] are seen as natural. Rousseau's critique of abstract individualism and the liberal theory of the state can assist in building a critical theory, just as his many insights into the relationship between sexual and political life, disentangled from his patriarchalism, are essential to a critical theory of the relation between love and justice. Similarly, Freud's psychoanalytic theory is indispensable, but used carefully as part of an account of the historical development of civil society—which includes a specific form of domestic association and "masculine" and "feminine" sexuality—and not, as Freud presents it, an abstract theory of the "individual" and "civilization."[39] This project may sound daunting, even completely overwhelming. Yet once the problem of the disorder of women begins to be seen as a question of social life, not as a fact that confronts us in nature, the reality of the structure of our personal and political lives is beginning to be revealed within the appearance presented in liberal and patriarchal ideology, and the task has already begun.

38. The phrase is taken from B. Clark and H. Gintis, "Rawlsian Justice and Economic Systems," *Philosophy and Public Affairs* 4 (1978): 302–25. This essay forms part of the "left" critique of Rawls which, so far, has largely ignored the sexual (in contrast to the class) dimension of subordination and its relevance for justice.

39. See M. Poster, *Critical Theory of the Family* (London: Pluto Press, 1978), chap. 1 (though women are relegated to a footnote); and "Freud's Concept of the Family," *Telos* 30 (1976): 93–115.

[18]

A Theory of Justice—and Love; Rawls on the Family

Deborah Kearns[1]

ABSTRACT

In *A Theory of Justice* John Rawls constructs an apparently universal moral theory. However among its most basic assumptions are ones which could justify a differential morality for women.

Rawls assumes love and the family unit to be so natural that he excludes them from the scope of the principles of justice to which all other institutions are subject in the just society. Having done so Rawls can retain a nuclear family structure with a sexual division of labour. Female and male children will have different experiences within this type of family. This institutionalised injustice is likely to prevent both sexes from developing the crucial sense of justice.

Rawls's whole theory is thus flawed from its very inception. An unjust family structure cannot produce just citizens.

It is over ten years since John Rawls published *A Theory of Justice* (1972). Rawls's achievement in presenting a detailed moral and political theory was rewarded with the publication of an enormous number of critical and evaluatory works. However, there is one aspect of Rawls's discussion which has been largely ignored. That concerns the relationship between justice and the family; between the public and private spheres of life.

My approach to the concept of the public-private dichotomy is quite specific. The tradition from which Rawls derives his basic arguments has always accepted that a line can be drawn between public and private activities. However, theorists were often ambiguous about where the dividing line lay. Often the private sphere was considered to be the family and such self-interested activity as economic affairs and personal undertakings. By defining the private sphere this way liberal theorists hoped to protect economic activities from government interference (Lukes 1973:62). Under these circumstances the public sphere was concerned only with the state and the activities of citizenship. Placing the family and economic activity together in the private sphere obscures the fact that the two are based on diffeent views of human nature and motivation. The more revealing distinction for my purposes is one which identifies only the family and close personal relations as private: economic and political activity both being public. Thus identified the two spheres are based on conflicting principles of association. Both economic and political activity assume individuals to be rational, self-interested and responsible. Individuals in this sphere can be considered in isolation from their private lives. Considered morally autonomous and morally equal they are free to order their lives by contract and obligation. In contrast there is little talk of contract within the private sphere.[1] It is based upon the natural ties of sentiment and love. Individuals are inherently unequal in the family due to their recognised differences. In many ways the familial bonds and the family unit are assumed to be more important than the interests of the individual members.

I find it quite surprising how little of the commentary on Rawls has addressed itself to the particular problem of how justice, which I argue is a public virtue, must not only exist in the private world of the family but must necessarily exist there if it is to exist in the broader public sphere. Most of the commentary on *A Theory of Justice* concentrates upon the theory and arguments of the first two sections of the book—'Theory' and 'Institutions'; there has been little analysis of the third section, 'Ends'. Yet I suggest this section has much to offer those of us interested from a feminist perspective. Careful analysis shows why a seemingly universal theory such as Rawls's remains, in effect, biased against women. The lack of attention focused on Rawls's arguments in his final section is revealing because much of Rawls's basic ground is undermined by turning a critical eye to his discussion of the family and the development of the sense of justice.

The discussion which follows is in four parts. Firstly, I shall argue that the family is not necessarily a just institution. Rawls recognises this and effectively removes the family from the scope of the principles of justice. Consequently, and this is the second point, Rawls is able to assume that the family can retain a nuclear family structure with a sexual division of labour. As the family is a vital institution for the development of the sense of justice, which is essential for social stability and coherence, this institutionalized injustice is likely to retard the development of the sense of justice.

[1]Deborah Kearns is employed as a Research Officer in the Public Service Board, Canberra.

This leads us to the fourth and crucial point—that the result is likely to be a sexually-differentiated morality. Rawls's theory, in fact, justifies the very differences in male-female behaviour that feminism is trying to overcome.

Sex and the Family in the Original Position

Individuals in the original position are to select principles by which to order their society from behind a 'veil of ignorance' regarding specific facts. Thus no agent would know her intelligence, class situation, appearance, height or even her conception of the good. But all parties would have access to general information about human society, economics and psychology. One of the functions of the original position is to guarantee that the same principles would always be chosen if the conditions of ignorance, rationality and self-interest were met. But what information is available behind the veil of ignorance: 'They understand political affairs and the principles of economic theory; they know the basis of social organisation and the laws of human psychology' (Rawls 1972: 137). I can hardly imagine four more debatable topics. Rawls recognises the diversity of theories on these topics but still implies that only one will be generally available (which economic theory? what laws of human psychology?). Besides diversity at any one time, historically the leading principles of economic theory and the dominant understanding of social organisation have changed. Consequently the veil of ignorance seems insufficient to produce the same result if applied at different times or in different cultures.

One of the only theories that can be identified in most cultures and periods is a theory of sexual difference. In modern western culture this has been a theory of sexual inequality and would permeate the information which Rawls makes available to the contracting parties.[2] Would this be one of the 'facts' about human society which the contracting parties would understand? Rawls specifies that agents would not know their race and so 'from the standpoint of persons similarly situated in an initial situation which is fair, the principles of explicit racist doctrine are not only unjust. They are irrational' (Rawls 1972: 149). But do individuals know their sex? If not then obvious principles of sexist doctrines would be unfair and irrational. But if they do know their sex and they also know the general facts of male-biased psychology and economic theory and that the basis of social organisation is the nuclear family (a dominant assumption in much sociology), will the initial situation really be fair? Rawls never comments on whether the contracting parties know their sex. He makes the usual misguided assumption that it will not matter.

The only instance where the veil of ignorance fails to secure the desired result according to Rawls is the difficult situation of ensuring savings so that justice will exist between, as well as within, generations (Rawls 1972:140). Self-interested individuals would have no rational reason to choose to preserve natural resources or to maintain capital accumulation in order to benefit posterity. Rawls tries to resolve this problem by introducing a motivational assumption: 'the parties are thought of as representing continuing lines of claims, as being, so to speak, deputies for a kind of everlasting moral agent or institution'. Rawls tends to use the formulation 'heads of families'. All that this requires is that each person in the original position should care about the well-being of some of those in the next generation. But Rawls claims that 'A conception of justice should not presuppose then, extensive ties of natural sentiment' (1972: 128-129). The savings principle does in effect exactly that.

Having assumed ties of natural sentiment between family members Rawls has established that the family is in itself 'natural'. It becomes very difficult to make this 'natural' institution subject to the principles of justice. For example, if the contracting parties represent the interests of a family and are presumed to be trying to defend those interests, perhaps against other families, then 'some undesirable principles might be chosen in the original position . . . For example, suppose that due to efficiency, all families gain significantly if the natural childbearers are universally appointed as child rearers' (English 1977: 94). This would be rational from the perspective of the family as a unit, but would it have been a principle chosen by self-interested, rational individuals? 'By making the parties in the original position heads of families rather than individuals, Rawls makes the family opaque to claims of justice' (English 1977: 94). Traditionally this has been the path of social contract and liberal theorists who explicitly excluded the family from the sphere of justice.[3]

I do not believe that Rawls intended the 'heads of families' reference to be construed as limiting the contracting parties to a representative from each family, or even to suggest that each agent would be primarily family-interested rather than self-interested. But the other interpretation, that the contracting parties are merely aware that they care for their descendents and so will select a saving principle, still creates problems. It assumes that the family (and this may well be true) is more 'natural' than other social institutions. By assuming that all individuals party to the contract are concerned about their descendents, but that their affection for friends and current associates is hidden by the veil of ignorance, the idea that the family is the place for affection and natural sentiment is institutionalised. Other relationships are presumed to be those of self-interest. And the affection assumed cannot be explained as merely prudential self-interest because what can one expect from one's descendants? It may be more realistic to assume parents are not disinterested in the welfare of their children, 'but the assumption of mutual disinterest is artificial and unrealistic in other cases too . . . ' (English 1977:93).

Besides suggesting the sentiment of the family to be something distinct from prudential self-interest Rawls's assumption somehow makes the family structure implicit in the original position. By this I mean that it would be difficult to imagine the parties, given that their biological family is meant to be important to them, and especially as the family corresponds to 'continuing lines of claims', deciding to abolish individual families and to institute a platonic style community of property and females. Yet this might be a more 'just' arrangement.

Thus even allowing all rational individuals to be parties to the contract does not overcome the problem (for Rawls's theory) that this places the family outside the original position and so not subject to the principles selected there. The idea that they are part of a family means more than just that they will care about a future generation. It implies that the family is not only about caring but perhaps primarily about caring and about 'continuing lines of claims'.[4] The family becomes one of the general facts about society. As I will try and demonstrate, there is also a definite assumption about the structure of this family. It becomes obvious that Rawls cannot imagine a more desirable (and 'natural') family structure than the nuclear family arrangement of western society. As his whole theory is to some extent a justification of the basic institutions of a liberal-democratic society and in support of the way they operate in a capitalist system this is not surprising.

The Nuclear Family and the Principles of Justice

It is significant that Rawls never defines what he means by 'family'. The second part of A Theory of Justice concerns 'Institutions': political and economic institutions are considered, the institution of the family is not. Rawls appears to have forgotten that he has already referred to 'the monogamous family' as a major social institution (1972:7). Rawls sees no need to discuss the various forms of family structure which can exist. He claims to make no assumptions about the economic institutions of society, preferring to derive the possible forms which would accord with the principles of justice. But he makes a very specific assumption about the nature and organisation of the family.

The assumption is that the family will be a biological grouping, which exists over time, in which affection is present and which is functional for the 'continuation of his line' (Rawls 1972:525). This effectively rules out a large number of possible sexual and child-rearing structures. As Rawls provides no information it is perhaps unfair to say that he speaks of a nuclear rather than extended family. But the interpretation seems justified. He refers to the family as 'characterised by a definite hierarchy, in which each member has certain rights and duties'

(1972:467). He never questions why this should be so. Family structure does not seem to be an issue.

Perhaps it isn't—it would not be unusual for a political theorist to exclude totally consideration of the family from a work on justice. But that is in itself a problem, for a well-ordered society would need a familial institution whose structure accorded with the principles of justice. But the family is not an institution of which justice is the first virtue (Pateman 1980; Schrag 1976: 197).

When we examine Rawls's two principles of justice we find that they are not compatible with a nuclear family structure. The principles are listed below: 2(a) will be referred to as the difference principle, 2(b) as the principle of fair or equal opportunity:

1. Each person is to have an equal right to the most extensive total system of equal basic liberties compatible with a similar system of liberty for all.
2. Social and economic inequalities are to be arranged so that they are both:
(a) to the greatest benefit of the least advantaged, consistent with the just savings principle, and
(b) attached to offices and positions open to all under conditions of fair equality of opportunity (Rawls 1972: 302).

Rawls claims that the difference principle corresponds to a meaning of fraternity and mutual concern. The family is a prime example of an area where this type of concern operates:[5]

Members of a family commonly do not wish to gain unless they can do so in ways that further the interests of the rest. Now wanting to act on the difference principle has precisely this consequence (1972:105).

Rawls is trying to integrate a principle of mutual benefit into his conception of justice. By using the family as an example he reminds us that natural sentiment, the capacity for affection, has already been assumed at the very foundations of this just society. But when we examine the principle of fair opportunity we find it to be one which cannot co-exist with the family partly because the family is an area of affection and partial behaviour.

The family cannot logically be made subject to the principle of fair opportunity because of its biological existence. Whoever heard of the position of father being opened to all family members under conditions of equal opportunity?[6] Such a statement would make sense only if the nuclear family were abolished and replaced with something I, for one, cannot imagine. The family remains an institution which is not subject to the primacy of justice.

Rawls faces this dilemma but cannot resolve it. He admits that 'the principle of fair opportunity can be only imperfectly carried out, at least as long as the institution of the family exists' (1972:74). He realises that the 'consistent application of the principle of fair opportunity requires us to view persons independently from the influences of their social position' (1972:511) and that this might require the family to be abolished (see Wolff 1976). But he rejects such a move: the conception of justice when effective, and the influence of the difference principle, will dispose us to dwell on our good fortune rather than our loss of opportunities and 'reconcile us to the dispositions of the natural order and the conditions of human life' (1972:512). The family apparently is part of the natural order, a condition of human life—and what could be more natural than the allocation of women to the family and the private sphere? For there is another aspect of the two principles of justice which is not immediately obvious and which Rawls does not recognise. The principles consider and can apply only to public life—that is to questions of state and citizenship, of business and of civic behaviour. Rawls sees their formulation as suggesting that the social structure can be divided into two parts. The first principle relates to 'those aspects of the social system that define and secure the equal liberties of citizenship . . . The second principle applies . . . to the distribution of income and wealth and to the design of organisations that make use of differences in authority and responsibility, or chains of command' (1972:61). Rawls refers to the latter areas as 'private' but this is because he uses the traditional liberal approach. The two principles are designed only to affect the public sphere. This is why contradictions arise when the family is also considered. Neither principle relates directly to the privatised nuclear family. Rawls cannot recognise this—he wishes to preserve private life and also argue that it can be just. However, neither of his principles offer guidance as to what would be just behaviour within a nuclear family.

The nuclear family is not inevitable. It is a very specific and historically located institution. The identification of women with the private sphere is also an historical product. Alternatives do exist. But the problem here cannot be overcome merely by changing the structure of private life so that the principles of justice can apply and equal opportunity be implemented. There is something very valuable in our private existence. The principles of justice must abstract people from the reality of their lives to treat them as free and equal, rational individuals. And though people may be equal in a moral or legal sense (or at least they should be), people are not all the same. Levels of 'rationality' vary for example. It is in the private sphere that individual differences and uniqueness exist. It may be Rawls feared to tamper with the family in case such tampering destroyed the private sphere and made subject to the principles of justice something very important and inherently unsuited to the claims of justice. This is a real problem for Rawls's theory as it cannot explain what would be a good family structure. The family, for all its problems, represents the sphere of love and caring, of emotional support and personal development. To lose these and retain only the public sphere would be tragic.

One of the most important functions of the family is to provide the framework in which the sense of justice can develop. To this we now turn.

The Sense of Justice: Who can Develop It?

The discussion of the development of the sense of justice is one of the most interesting, and yet neglected, in Rawls. He postulates that in a just society people will develop a sense of justice which will help bring stability to the society. He sketches 'the development of the sense of justice as it presumably would take place once just institutions are firmly established and recognised to be just . . .' (1972:453). But as we have seen he provides no evidence that the family will be just. As the family has a major role in socialisation and early development this results in a major problem: how can the sense of justice develop in an unjust institution? The problem is that Rawls is trying to develop the public virtue of justice, which is to uphold and regulate public institutions, within a private area not necessarily subject to the principles of justice.

I have no need to present the nuclear family in a particularly bad light. It may be a structure which can offer a great deal to members. But it is a structure based on a sexual division of labour whereby women assume greater responsibility for housework and childcare. It has a tendency to reinforce a value system which undervalues family and private activities. Due to the entrenched nature of the public-private split it is often not explicitly recognised that the public sphere is the area of life seen as most important. Rawls is a fine example. Though he is depending on the nuclear family to be there to provide the childhood experiences which will help the sense of justice develop he fails to consider how the family should be internally structured. All he says is that he will assume 'that the basic structure of a well-ordered society includes the family in some form, and therefore that children are at first subject to the legitimate authority of their parents' (1972: 462-463).

Rawls identifies three stages in his account of moral development: they are the moralities of authority, association and principles. I shall look briefly at each. The morality of authority depends upon the child coming to trust and love his parents due to their love and encouragement of him. (As Rawls uses the masculine, I will also). 'If he loves and trusts his parents, he will tend to accept their injunctions' (Rawls 1972: 464). Thus he will accept their standards and be likely to feel (authority) guilt if he transgresses. The morality to which the child is subject is imposed by those in authority but as such authority is justified and given that they care about him and exemplify the standards that they profess the morality they enjoin will help his moral development.

The child's morality of authority is primitive because for the most part it consists of a collection of precepts, and he cannot comprehend the larger scheme of right and justice within which the rules addressed to him are justified . . . The prized virtues are obedience, humility, and fidelity to authoritative persons; the leading vices are disobedience, self-will, and temerity (1972:466).

In contrast, the content of the morality of association 'is given by the moral standard appropriate to the individual's role in the various associations to which he belongs'. The family is explicitly considered to be a small association. Rawls speaks of the virtues of a good son, a good daughter, a good wife, a good husband, and then of a good friend and a good citizen. Realising the essentially co-operative nature of the association and the value of others' contributions, the desire to uphold the ideals of that group grows. Once these ties are established failure to do one's duty will lead to (association) guilt (1972: 467-70).

Rawls's account of the morality of association also depends upon the group in question being just. But as we must constantly recognise, not only has Rawls not brought the family under the principles of justice but the lack of impartial and equal opportunity makes the family inherently unjust. The determination of duties and obligations, the ordering of a hierarchy are not done according to principles of fairness, efficiency or rationality. Thus when Rawls speaks of the 'various conceptions of a good wife and husband' (1972:468) leading to the virtues of those positions he makes no mention that wife and husband are traditional, ascriptive roles. The duties and obligations of each are sex-specific, maintained by a so-called contract, the terms of which cannot be altered even by mutual agreement (Barker 1978; Pateman 1981b). There is nothing just about the division of these duties and they are thoroughly sexist; not only are different duties and rights accorded to the different sexes but there are different assumptions about character and personality which back up the different allocation of duties. Rawls just takes it for granted that it means something different to be a wife than a husband, to be a daughter than a son.

As a result males and females will have different experiences within a nuclear family structure. The virtues of a good daughter are different from those of a good son because the sexes are being socialised for different futures. They learn different things, their roles stress different goals: as a result they internalise a different morality. Within the family and other (unfortunately unjust) institutions such as schools, girls are encouraged to view themselves as primarily interested in the home and family and not to concentrate on their future in the public sphere. Rawls ignores this possible effect of a sexual division and consequently allows the moral development of males and females to proceed differently. In many ways the effect of a morality of association on girls would be to encourage them to accept their inferior status for the benefit of family

life and to be willing to submit to an extended morality of authority. By distancing themselves from the demands of public life girls become less likely to develop a sense of justice.

The morality of principles is the stage at which the principles of justice are valued for themselves. The desire to apply and act upon the principles of justice arises 'once we realise how social arrangements answering to them have promoted our good and that of those with whom we are affiliated' (Rawls 1972: 474). The morality of association has provided an important preliminary step by providing a knowledge of the standards of justice. But what if some individuals do not gain this knowledge of the public conception of justice because their major roles and the associations of which they have been members are mainly private and not subject to the principles of justice? And what if this lack is reinforced because even when the person operates within a public, just institution she is treated as a private individual who is unsuited to the public sphere? In general this is the situation of women due to the nature of the public-private split. If women are expected and encouraged to place their family commitments above everything how are they supposed to achieve a morality of principles which means that 'moral attitudes are no longer connected solely with the well-being and approval of particular individuals and groups, but are shaped by a conception of the right chosen irrespective of those contingencies' (Rawls 1972: 475)?

How many Just People does the Just Society Need?

It would appear that Rawls's willingness to retain the nuclear family threatens not only his principle of fair opportunity but the whole stability of his system. As an institution not subject to the principles of justice the family may thwart all children's moral development, socialising them to unjust roles and hindering the development of the morality of principles. This is likely to be especially damaging for women.

Rawls's conception of the sense of justice is very revealing. He argues that 'the sense of justice is continuous with the love of mankind . . . The difference between the sense of justice and the love of mankind is that the latter is supererogatory going beyond the moral requirements and invoking the exceptions which the principles of natural duty and obligation allow' (1972:436). As we noted earlier Rawls consistently uses a motivational assumption of natural sentiment to explain certain aspects of the principles of justice. Now we learn that the sense of justice is a form of love: a love for just institutions and a desire that all be treated fairly. Once again we must place Rawls' statement in the circumstances of a just society such as he foresees, one with a market economy. Rawls's basic psychological assumption about economic behaviour is self-interest but his main assumption for the psychological analysis of politics is co-operation and a desire to promote justice (Barry 1973:154). 'A peculiarity of the ideal market process, as distinct from the ideal political process . . ., is that the market achieves an efficient outcome even if everyone pursues his own advantage' (Rawls 1972: 359).

Now I am not sure what overall effect this dichotomy has on Rawls's theory but I know what it suggests to me about the possibility of people developing a sense of justice. Concentrating on men for the moment we must remember that economic activity, working for a living, consuming to live, is by far most people's major concern. Self-interest is not always incompatible with justice but I doubt its effectiveness in promoting a sense of justice which requires one to discount both self-interest and the attitude of others so that decisions can be made based on a conception of right derived from the principles of justice. Most men may thus fail to develop a sense of justice due to the dominance of self-interest in the economic sphere. And women will also lack a sense of justice and moral autonomy due to their confinement to the private sphere. The only persons who may be well placed to develop the sense of justice would be those involved in politics and the making of decisions (Rawls 1972: 473).

Interestingly, Rawls admits that his theory might be construed so as to give those few individuals involved in politics a greater say in the decision-making process (1972:228-234). At another point Rawls stresses that individuals are not absolutely free to form their moral convictions and that someone whose 'conscience is misguided' could have their actions limited. A misguided conscience is indicated by someone seeking to 'impose on us conditions that violate the principles to which we would each consent in that situation' (1972: 518-19). In other words the person lacks a sense of justice, a sense of what is fair. I would suggest that Rawls's system could in fact contain a significant amount of injustice, that a large number of people could fail to develop the sense of justice and it would be legitimate for certain others to limit their freedom, and perhaps their right, to participate in the system in order to preserve the stability of the system. Within this structure there would be nothing contradictory about women being subject to a differential morality. One which stressed the virtues of a morality of authority could support the idea that their major role was as a private wife or mother and that they should not be concerned with public life. In fact, it might be essential so to train them, for otherwise why would women agree to be private beings and raise children when the structure of the nuclear family so flagrantly infringes on the principles of justice?

Rawls himself provides good evidence for the suggestion that women might be necessarily subject to a morality of authority:

Now it is characteristic of the morality of authority when conceived as a morality for the social order as a whole to demand self-sacrifice for the sake of a higher good and to deprecate the worth of the individual and lesser associates. The emptiness of the self is to be overcome in the service of larger ends (1972:500).

In western society it is not too difficult to recognise that many women feel themselves subject to this morality: a 'morality of self-sacrifice'. Rawls has given us no indication that this will change. Strangely enough he also provides evidence for the idea that the differential morality to which women are subject, though insufficient as a moral principle, is perhaps more admirable than the morality of men. Rawls speaks of supererogation highly: it is a love of mankind which advances 'the common good in ways that go well beyond our natural duties and obligations'. It is not for 'ordinary persons' (1972: 478, 479). Ordinary people are apparently self-interested, for 'supererogatory actions are ones that would be duties were not certain exempting conditions fulfilled which make allowance for reasonable self-interest' (1972:439). However, are women ordinary persons in this sense? The philosophical tradition which Rawls uses simply does not accommodate the possibility of women having a self-interest in a self-conscious, expressible (through the market place) way; or, at least, their self-interest is not assumed to be sufficient to override the demands of the private sphere. The confusion becomes clearer when we list the virtues which attach to a morality of supererogation: 'benevolence, a heightened sensitivity to the feelings and wants of others, and a proper humility and unconcern with self' (Rawls 1972: 479). Surely these are also virtues of the private sphere, virtues of women? So women would most likely be the supererogators. They are, in the sense that they do sacrifice; but in a moral sense they cannot be truly supererogatory for they do not choose their sacrifice, it attaches to one of their positions in life. Their morality is incomplete for, like the morality of authority, it tends to be founded on precepts which are followed because they seem authoritative and not because they are right and just. It is a long way from Rawls's desired morality of principles.

Rawls's scheme is flawed by the ramifications of the public-private split. No-one wants to abolish private life, but can a totally just public structure be erected upon an unjust base? And how desirable is justice as fairness? Justice as it is usually understood requires that individuals are seen as free and equal, morally responsible rational beings who can thus be treated alike in similar circumstances. But 'Humans are "essentially" time bound, biologically conditioned, historically situated and culturally specific' (Pateman 1981a:21). A theory of justice which must ignore these aspects cannot provide a model of society which can overcome the problems of liberal theory. Rawls's theory is a 'comprehensive and systematic statement of a thoroughgoing liberal position' (Barry 1973:4) and, though apparently enlightened on issues of sexism and racism, is unable to surpass the limitations of a tradition which institutionalises a public-private split between the areas of ascription, status and functionalism and those of achievement, contract and individualism.

END NOTES

1. The fiction of the marriage contract is not an exception to this statement. The marriage contract is not a true contract in many ways. It acts to give a gloss of convention to the 'natural' roles of husband and wife. Certainly within the family unit, once it is established, even that gloss is lacking. On the marriage contract, see Barker 1978; Pateman 1981b.
2. Examples are numerous but consider the fact that economic theory prefers to deal with household units of income and so ignore the value of women's domestic labour. Also it is well documented that the estimation of a person's psychological health is affected by knowledge of that person's sex: a 'well' woman would be judged neurotic if a man.
3. Hegel is a clear example of this tradition. As Rawls claims to have drawn upon Hegel for his conception of the private sphere (1972: 521 note), it is a shame that he did not appreciate the complexity of Hegel's position.
4. The idea of continuing lines of claims is very much a masculine one; women have never had the privilege of being the head, or founder of a family which retains its identity through name and property. Rawls is obviously viewing the family from a male position and it makes it easy for him to minimise its role as the family has never been for 'liberal' man the main area of activity.
5. Of course whether family members actually do cooperate so as to benefit each equally is a matter of empirical dispute. More commonly they are likely to operate so as to improve the situation of the most favoured.
6. The example may seem facetious but it is important to realise that 'father' is a biological fact. The social connotations are specific to time periods and cultures.

To that extent it is possible to imagine the role of father being voluntary and even competitive. For example, recent custody cases involving foster children and biological parents are in some way a competition to be judged the best parent.

REFERENCES

Barker, D.L. 1978, 'The Regulation of Marriage: Repressive Benevolence' in (eds.) G. Littlejohn et. al., *Power and the State*, Croom Helm, London.

Barry, B. 1973, *The Liberal Theory of Justice*, Clarendon Press, Oxford.

Blum, L., Homiak, M., Housman, J., Scheman, N. 1976, 'Altruism and Women's Oppression' in C. Gould and M. Wartofsky (eds.) *Women and Philosophy*, Putnams, New York.

English, J. 1977, 'Justice between Generations', *Philosophical Studies*, 31: 91-104.

Hegel, G.W. 1896, *Philosophy of Right*, Trans. S.W. Dyde, George Bell and Sons, London.

Lukes, S. 1973, *Individualism*, Basil Blackwell, Oxford.

Parekh, B. 1972 'Liberalism and Morality', in Parekh and R.N. Berki (eds.) *The Morality of Politics*, George Allen and Unwin, London.

Pateman, C. 1980, '"The Disorder of Women": Women, Love and the Sense of Justice', *Ethics*, 91: 20-34.

———— 1981a 'Feminist Critiques of the Public-Private Dichotomy', Paper prepared for the project 'Conceptions of the Public and Private in Social Life': co-ordinators S. Benn and G. Gaus.

———— 1981b 'The Shame of the Marriage Contract', Distributed Paper.

Rawls, J. 1963 'The Sense of Justice', *Philosophical Review*, LXXII: 281-305.

———— 1972 *A Theory of Justice*, Clarendon Press, Oxford.

Schrag, F. 1976 'Justice and the Family', *Inquiry*, 19: 193-208.

Tormey, J.F. 1976 'Exploitation, Oppression and Self-Sacrifice' in C. Gould and M. Wartofsky (eds.) *Women and Philosophy*, Putnams, New York.

Urmson, J.O. 1969 'Saints and Heroes' in J. Feinberg (ed.) *Moral Concepts*, Oxford University Press, Oxford.

Wolff, R.P. 1976 'There's Nobody Here but us Persons', in C. Gould and M. Wartofsky (eds.) *Women and Philosophy*, Putnams, New York.

Name Index

DATE